TERRYTOONS

The Story of Paul Terry and His Classic Cartoon Factory

W. Gerald Hamonic, Ph.D.

Foreword by Jerry Beck

D1694095

British Library Cataloguing in Publication Data

Terrytoons
The Story of Paul Terry and His Classic Cartoon Factory

A catalogue entry for this book is available from the British Library

ISBN: 0 86196 729 2 (Paperback)

Published by
John Libbey Publishing Ltd, 205 Crescent Road, New Barnet, Herts EN4 8SB, United Kingdom   e-mail: john.libbey@orange.fr; web site: www.johnlibbey.com

Distributed Worldwide by
Indiana University Press, Herman B Wells Library—350, 1320 E. 10th St., Bloomington, IN 47405, USA. www.iupress.indiana.edu

© 2018 Copyright John Libbey Publishing Ltd. All rights reserved.
Unauthorised duplication contravenes applicable laws.

Printed and bound in the United States of America..

Contents

	Acknowledgements	vii
	Foreword by *Jerry Beck*	ix

PART ONE: CHRONICLE OF THE TERRY FAMILY

Chapter 1	From the Mayflower to Market Street: The Terry Family Saga, 1613–1864	1
Chapter 2	In Old San Francisco: The Terry Family Saga, 1864–1887	10

PART TWO: THE YOUNG LIFE AND EARLY ANIMATION CAREER OF PAUL TERRY

Chapter 3	Birth of an Animation Pioneer: The Childhood and Young Life of Paul Terry, 1887–1902	18
Chapter 4	Explorations in Photography: Paul Terry's Start in the San Francisco Newspaper Industry, 1902–1906	28
Chapter 5	The Tremor that Shook the World: The San Francisco Earthquake, April 18, 1906	38
Chapter 6	A Tour of the West: The *Anaconda Standard,* Portland *Oregonian, Evening Standard* and Return to the Bay City, 1906–1911	45
Chapter 7	The Move to Metropolis: Barron Collier, Park Row and the Winsor McCay Dinner, 1911–1914	58
Chapter 8	A Spark Ignites: *Little Herman* and the Beginnings of a New Career in Animation, 1914–1915	67
Chapter 9	Animated Antics: Cartoon Burlesques, Phrenology, and Paul Terry's Early Adventures in the Cartoon World, 1915–1917	77
Chapter 10	You're in the Army Now: George Washington University, the Spanish Influenza Epidemic, and Work for Paramount Pictures, 1917–1920	87
Chapter 11	A Barnyard of Animal Friends: Farmer Al Falfa and Fables Pictures Studios, Part One, 1921–1925	98
Chapter 12	A Decade of Drawing Mice: Fables Pictures Studio, Part Two, 1925–1929	114

PART THREE: TERRYTOONS: THE STORY OF A CLASSIC CARTOON STUDIO

Chapter 13	Sweat Equity is the Best Start-up Capital: The Founding and Early Development of the Terry-Toons Studio, 1929–1932	124
Chapter 14	Enduring Adversity: The Early Struggles at the Studio, 1932–1935	143
Chapter 15	A Rising Storm and a Studio in Distress: The Search to Improve the Entertainment Value of the Cartoon Product, 1935–1936	159
Chapter 16	Cartoons Go to Court: A House Divided, the Moser–Terry Trial, and Terry Takes Control, 1936–1938	173

Chapter 17	A Studio Transformed: Gandy Goose, Dinky Duck and New Directions for Terrytoons, 1938–1942	187
Chapter 18	Here I Come To Save The Day!: The Mouse that Saved a Cartoon Studio, 1942–1945	203
Chapter 19	Those Magnificent Mischievous Magpies: Heckle and Jeckle and the Terrytoons Labor Strike, 1946–1947	225
Chapter 20	Rounding Out the Cast: Little Roquefort, The Terry Bears and the Glory Years of Terrytoons, 1948–1951	242
Chapter 21	Relinquishing the Reins: The New Challenge of Television, the Sale of Terrytoons to CBS, and the Retirement of Paul Terry, 1952–1956	255
Chapter 22	Paul Terry's Cartoon Legacy: A Comparative Analysis of Golden Age Animation	267

PART FOUR: TERRYTOONS: LIFE AFTER THE RETIREMENT OF PAUL TERRY

Chapter 23	A Studio in Transition: The Gene Deitch Years and the Animation Renaissance, 1956–1958	278
Chapter 24	A New Cast of Characters: Hashimoto Mouse, Hector Heathcote, Deputy Dawg, Luno, and Astronut, 1959–1964	294
Chapter 25	L'Enfant Terrible and the Twilight of Terrytoons: Ralph Bakshi, the Adventures of Sad Cat, The Mighty Heroes, Possible Possum, and James Hound, and the Studio Closure, 1965–1968	308
Chapter 26	Cartoon End Credits: The Retirement and Death of Paul Terry, 1956–1971	321
Chapter 27	The Terrytoons Retrospective: A Meeting of Old Friends, 1982	328

PART FIVE: APPENDICES

Appendix 1	Terrytoons Who's Who: Biographies of the Key Players	333
Appendix 2	Paul Terry/Terrytoons: Theatrical Shorts Filmography	347
Appendix 3	Paul Terry/Terrytoons: Television Cartoon Series	363
	Image credits	375
	Index of Personalities	377
	Index of Animated Film Production Titles and Characters	386
	General Index	397

Acknowledgements

When I first began the journey to author a book on Terrytoons, a process which involved painstakingly researching and compiling information on Paul Terry and his studio, I had little appreciation as to the gargantuan effort that would be required to complete the project, a nearly two decade undertaking. However, this book would never had seen the light of day had it not been for Harvey Deneroff, a pioneer in animation research and a dedicated scholar whom I have never had the privilege to meet. In a series of interviews conducted in 1969 and 1970 Mr. Deneroff had the foresight to obtain seminal oral histories from Paul Terry and a few of his studio contemporaries, research sources that formed the backbone of the narrative of this book. Patricia Leahy, the daughter of Paul, not only graciously allowed me access to her family's archive of studio documentation, but meticulously transferred the documentation to a digital format for ready access. When a question arose in my research, she was always available to offer whatever assistance was required. Without her support, this book would have been a mere shadow of the final published work.

From 1996 to 1999 I conducted over 50 interviews of former studio artists and management executives. I consider myself very fortunate because many of these interviewees were not with us for very long after their interviews. Studio personalities such as Bill Weiss, Eli Bauer, and Howard Beckerman generously invited me into their homes or offices to share their stories with me, while others like Dayton Allen, who delivered enough one-liners to earn a job headlining a Las Vegas comedy club, spent hours with me over the telephone recalling with pleasure their time at Terrytoons. These individuals include (in alphabetical order) Nick Alberti, Dayton Allen, Alex Anderson, Cosmo Anzilotti, Cliff Augustson, Ralph Bakshi, Vinnie Bell, Charles Budney, George Budney, Bob Bushell, Jordan Caldwell, Mrs. Nicholas Chiovetta, Doug Crane, Hope Cummings, Joan Cunningham, Diana Dadone, Dan Danglo, George Davis, Jean Davis, Gene Deitch, Polly Donnelly, Ray Favata, Bill Focht, John Gentilella, Joe Gray, Muriel Gushue, Warren Hawkinson, Mike Hickie, Helen Komar, Bill Kresse, Michel Kuwahara, Arnold Levy, Jim Logan, Tina Martini, Mary McPherson, Bill Quigley, Sid Raymond, Irene Scagnelli, Paul Soccodato, Barbara Solomon, Al Stahl, Mary Taracka, Angelo Tarricone, Dave Ubinas, Sandy Vogel, Mary Zaffo, Tom Zaffo, John Zago, and Jack Zander.

Very special thanks must go to Conrad Rasinski, the son of Terrytoons cameraman Joseph Rasinski and the nephew of famed animator Connie Rasinski. Over the course of seven days in 2002 Conrad not only arranged my transfer to and from the Newark airport but gave me a personal guided tour of the Connecticut area where his father and uncle were raised and provided invaluable information on their life stories and contributions to the studio. Many librarians and archivists toiled behind the scenes for me gathering wonderful bits of secondary information that connected the narrative dots along the way. These individuals include Lucy Shelton Caswell at the Billy Ireland Cartoon Library & Museum (Columbus, Ohio), Pamela Thornton at the New Rochelle Public Library, Lyle Slovick at George Washington University, Dave Smith at the Walt Disney Archives, Helice Koffler at New York University, Charles Silver with the Department of Film at the Museum of Modern Art, and Colleen M. Ferguson, Assistant

TERRYTOONS: The Story of Paul Terry and His Classic Cartoon Factory

Fig. AC.1 – Original production background to the Mighty Mouse cartoon *Loves Labor Won* (1948).

Director at Hearst Free Library (Anaconda, MT).

Film starlet Claire Trevor responded to my request for information on her role with persuading Bill Tytla to leave California and work at Terrytoons. Bill Janocha at the National Cartoonists Society provided dozens of samples of artwork from the studio. Rev. Gregory I. Carlson with the Jesuit Community offered information on Ray Kelley. J. Michael Barrier contributed some of his interview materials on early Terrytoons artists. R.O. Blechman penned feedback on his masterpiece *The Juggler of Our Lady* (1958). Roy Halee Jr. supplied information on his late father, the singing voice of Mighty Mouse.

Last, but certainly not least, credit must go to cartoon historian Jerry Beck who helped me make my first connections to former Terrytoons artists and executives. Not only did he inspire me to undertake the project which otherwise may never have occurred, but he also provided me with copies of about 650 Terrytoons cartoons for my critical analysis and viewing pleasure. Now that the journey has ended I can look back and better appreciate the friendships made and the work these friends have so charitably undertaken as they followed me along in this endeavor. Now having reached the destination, I feel that we all have arrived together, whether in body or in spirit, and have accomplished the collective objective of chronicling a significant and much overlooked chapter in the history of American animation.

Foreword

Jerry Beck

Hundreds of mice running off into the distance. Once upon a time that sentence might have summed up all you ever had to know of Terrytoons – but clearly there is more to it than that. Much more.

At a time when Walt Disney was taking the medium to new heights, when Max Fleischer was inventing innovative ways to create animated depth, and a fella named Tex Avery was breaking a fourth wall in cartoon humor – Paul Terry was puttering away in an east coast suburb, making sure his annual contract for 26 cartoons to 20th Century-Fox was adequately fulfilled.

To be sure, Paul Terry was one of the pioneers of the American animated cartoon. But he was also an artist (a good one) who turned into a businessman – a shrewd businessman, who kept up with technological developments and artistic innovations, yet he knew his limitations and was perfectly happy to quietly maintain his place in the motion picture industry. Not unlike a farmer (Farmer Al Falfa?) who is content to simply tend his field, grow his crops and sell them at the market.

Not much more to it than that – or is there? As you will learn in this book, there is much more to Paul Terry and his Terrytoons.

Terry was oft-quoted as stating his operation was the "Woolworth" to Disney's "Tiffany" studio, and his Terrytoons were likewise treated as such in Hollywood – with little respect. Moviegoers as well, for over two decades, patiently tolerated the on-screen antics of his various mangy cats, heroic mice, top-hatted mustachioed villains and assorted damsels in distress.

Terry was indeed a fine artist, a funny cartoonist and a true animation pioneer. Walt Disney himself admired Terry's *Aesop's Fables* shorts in the silent era. Terrytoons gave a first job to many of the most significant names in the field – from Art Babbitt and Bill Tytla, to Joe Barbera and Ralph Bakshi.

As a child, I was enthralled by the Terrytoons I saw on TV. The studio "splash" sound effect was oft imitated in my house. That funny-jittery animation (which I now know is the work of Jim Tyer) seemed to be a trademark of their house style. The monotone narrations, and cheery chorus singers in the background, were inviting. Speaking of backgrounds, the gorgeous artwork used for settings were quite lavish and long remembered.

His studio may have churned out film for a price, but his product had charm, personality and – yeah – provided a few good laughs. Even more, his team created several famous name cartoon superstars, most notably Mighty Mouse, Heckle and Jeckle, Farmer Al Falfa and Gandy Goose. It wasn't only luck, nor only the skills of the staff, for such a studio to last so long – and endure.

Clearly there was more to know about this remarkable man and his company. And yet, few were interested in taking a closer look.

Enter W. Gerald Hamonic. Wynn has spent decades researching the Terry studio, its pioneer founder, the artists and crew, and the films they produced. I know this because he contacted me almost 25 years ago in his quest for further research materials.

I tried to warn him. The subject was so vast, so deep, so unknown – and becoming more obscure as the years rolled on. But he

TERRYTOONS: The Story of Paul Terry and His Classic Cartoon Factory

Fig. F.1 – Production cel and key master background setup to the Super Mouse cartoon *Pandora's Box* (1943).

persisted in tracking down animators, their heirs, the films, press clippings and other hard info – and after a generation of work I'm happy to report his work has been compiled here in a concise and very entertaining way.
Like Mighty Mouse flying down and singing "Here I come to save the day!" this book comes out at a time when we need it most. Animation has never been more popular or commercially successful – and historical scholarship of the medium must now look beyond Disney. Wynn's book permits us to view a larger picture of the animation scene during its 'golden age', filling a gap long missing in its story.
"Hundreds of mice running off into the distance". Thanks to Wynn Hamonic, now we know why, who and how – and where they ran off to. And animation history will never be the same. ✌

Chapter 1

From the Mayflower to Market Street: The Terry Family Saga, 1613–1864

In 1914, Paul Terry, a 27-year-old New York City newspaper cartoonist, embarked on his career in animation and created his first animated cartoon *Little Herman*, a short approximately 3 minutes and 20 seconds in length.[1] The short took approximately four months to create and was released theatrically by the Thanhouser Film Corporation on June 19, 1915.[2] Terry's pioneering efforts in animation predated Walt Disney's first animated cartoon, *Little Red Riding Hood*, a *Laugh-O-Grams* fairytale short produced in Kansas City in 1922, by seven years.[3] Terry's early trailblazing efforts in animation were bold, ambitious, and risky for a financially struggling artist, but plunging headfirst into an uncertain future filled with economic uncertainty was not uncommon to Terry's forefathers.

Terry could proudly lay claim to being a descendant of John Alden (1599 [1598]–1687), one of the 30 to 40 crew members working aboard the *Mayflower*, and Priscilla Mullins (1602–1688), one of the 102 passengers also crowded on the seafaring vessel. After about a month's delay in England, the ship left from Plymouth, England on September 6 [16], 1620 and arrived in Cape Cod Hook, later called Provincetown Harbor, Massachusetts, on November 9 [19], 1620. In 1621, John and Priscilla were married. The couple would have 10 children, with a possible eleventh dying in infancy.[4]

Paul Terry's maternal great grandmother, Susanna [Susannah] Proctor (b. December 23, 1781, Fairhaven, Massachusetts; d. September 15, 1865, Fairhaven, Massachusetts), is a descendant of John and Priscilla Alden through her mother Susanna Alden (1745–1824). The legendary *Mayflower* voyagers Alden and Mullins were Susanna's great-great grandparents. Susanna Proctor married Levi Jenney on October 2, 1800 in New Bedford, Bristol, Massachusetts. Levi and Susanna would have two children, William Proctor Jenney (1802–1881) and Caroline Coleman Jenney (1812–1851).[5] Caroline Coleman Jenney is Paul Terry's paternal grandmother.[6]

The surname Terry is distinct in origin from the forename Terry. Contemporary scholarship ascribes the surname from the Germanic Theodoric. In comparison, the forename Terry derives from the Latin Terentius or Terence. As a family name, Terry, which is rated English and Irish, had a lengthy and circuitous development. The source Theodoric[7] (literal meaning: people-rule) was picked up by the French, turned into Thierry and passed along to the British in the 11th century. In Britain it underwent the customary changes. In 1086 it was Tedric, in 1200 Tericus, in the 1400s Terrick and in the 1600s Tcrye. By the 18th century it had settled

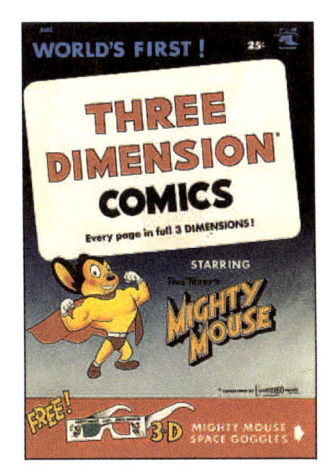

Fig. 1.1 – *Three Dimension Comics* starring Mighty Mouse with 3D glasses.

TERRYTOONS: The Story of Paul Terry and His Classic Cartoon Factory

Fig. 1.2 – Terrytoons theatrical stock lobby cards.

Chapter 1 • From the Mayflower to Market Street

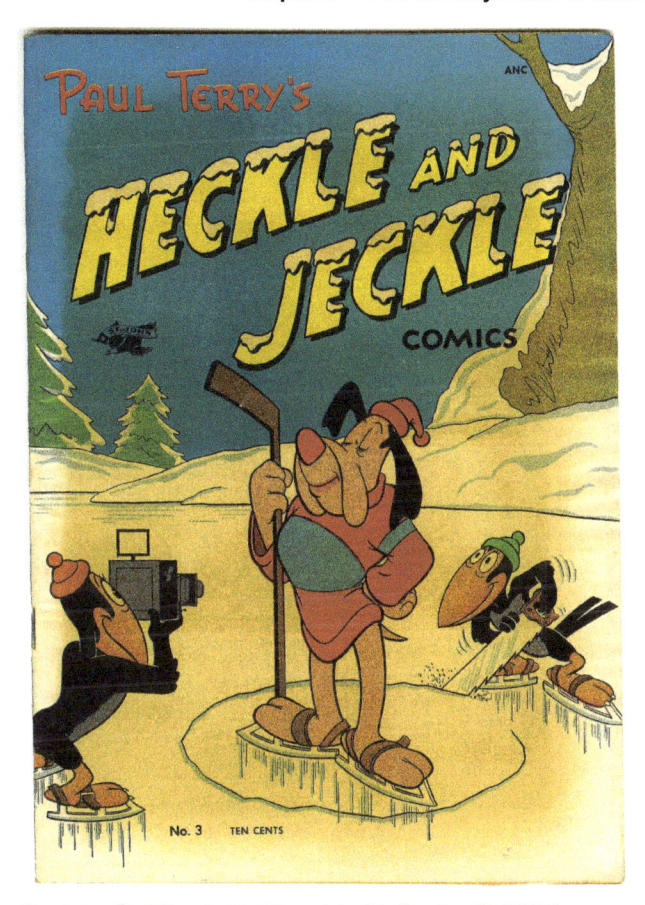

Fig. 1.3 – Paul Terry's *Heckle and Jeckle Comics* #3 (1951).

on Terr(e)y. For the last several centuries it has been spelled Terry.[8]

Paul Terry could trace his Terry family lineage back to Sir Thomas Terry (b. November 9, 1606, Throwley, County Kent, England [Barnet, Wiltshire, England]; d. June 5, 1672 in Southold, Suffolk, New York), a Hampshire clergyman.[9] Sir Thomas Terry married Maria (Marie) Bigge (b. December 13, 1612, Biddenden, Kent, England; d. January 14, 1659 in Southold, Suffolk, New York) in 1640 [1636] in Brookhaven, Suffolk, New York. Paul Terry is the 8th generation Terry descended from Sir Thomas Terry. The Terry family first established themselves as residents of the state of Massachusetts in 1663 when Sir Thomas Terry's second son, Lieutenant Thomas Terry (b. 1640, England; d. October 1691 in Freetown, Bristol County, Massachusetts), settled at Braintree, Massachusetts. He later moved to "Block Island" where he was made freeman in 1664. In 1665, he was appointed Deputy of the Court. In 1672, he was influential in obtaining a town charter for "Block Island".[10]

Lieutenant Terry relocated to Freetown, Massachusetts (Fall River), and on January 16, 1683, he bought the land of John Bryant of Taunton at Bryant's Neck. Lieutenant Terry soon became a leading figure in Freetown. As a sign of their confidence in his bravery and military prowess he was honored on June 4, 1686 with the rank and commission of a Lieutenant, empowered to command all the militia of the town. He was elected on June 2, 1685 as a member of the First Freetown Board of Selectmen. He was re-elected in 1688 and served until 1690. He was appointed Deputy of the General Court in Plymouth in 1689 and 1690. He was appointed to the Council of War in 1690. He was rated as one of the largest taxpayers in Freetown during this period. Lt. Terry married Anna (Hannah) Rogers (b. 1644, Duxbury, Plymouth, Massachusetts; d. aft. July 1710, Taunton, Bristol, Massachusetts [died about 1704]) in Weymouth, Suffolk, Massachusetts in 1677. By his wife, he had three sons: Thomas (b. 1674), John (b. 1676), and Benjamin (b. 1685). The descent to Paul Terry is from the third son, Benjamin Terry.[11]

Benjamin Terry (b. 1685, Freetown, Bristol, Massachusetts; died before March 1773) married Margaret Holloway (b. 1689, Middleboro, Massachusetts) in 1710. Benjamin Terry (II) (born 1710/1715 in Freetown, Bristol, Massachusetts and died October 6, 1797) was one of at least 14

3

Fig. 1.4 – Theatrical Poster for *In Dutch* (1925), an Aesop's Fables cartoon.

Fairhaven, Bristol, Massachusetts), a sea captain, married Elizabeth Stevens (1776–1867) of Fairhaven, Massachusetts on September 23, 1797. To them were born two sons: Phenius Terry and Isaiah Franklin Terry. The line of descent is through Isaiah Terry.

Isaiah Franklin Terry, Paul Terry's paternal grandfather, was born in the town of Fairhaven, December 15, 1805, and died at the Terry homestead on Middle Street, Fairhaven, December 20 [28], 1896, the immediate cause of his death, pneumonia. During his 91 years, he was a man of enterprise and progress. He was educated in the public schools and Hawes Academy. The death of his father Elias while he was yet a young man of 23 years threw the burden of his own support upon his youthful shoulders, and so he traveled to New York City where he spent several years in the employ of the shipping firm of Hicks, Jenkins & Company.[13]

Isaiah Terry returned to Fairhaven having acquired substantial business skills, thoroughly experienced, and capable of managing the large business enterprises in which he later became engaged. In Fairhaven he entered the employ of Ezekiel R. Sawin, who was engaged in the ship chandlery business, operated a saw mill and involved commercially in coal. Sawin's place of business was located at Union Wharf, Fairhaven.[14] After several years spent with Mr. Sawin, he engaged in business for himself as ship agent and fire insurance adjuster, a business he

children born to Benjamin Terry with the first born being Robert Terry (b. 1708) and the last born being Dinah Terry (b. 1734). Benjamin Terry (II) married Joanna Pope (b. February 20, 1715, Dartmouth, Massachusetts) on September 27, 1741 in Rochester, Plymouth, Massachusetts. Benjamin Terry (III) was the fifth child of eight children born to Benjamin Terry (II) with the first born being Sarah Terry (b. November 17, 1742) and the last born being Seth Terry (b. January 22, 1764).[12]

Benjamin Terry (III) (born March 12, 1750, Dartmouth, Massachusetts; d. April 29, 1817) married Mary Eldridge (b. 1754, Dartmouth, Massachusetts) on September 25, 1773 in Dartmouth, Massachusetts. By their marriage was born Elias (Elisha) P. Terry. Elias P. Terry (b. 1773 in Fairhaven, Bristol, Massachusetts; d. October 1829,

Chapter 1 • From the Mayflower to Market Street

conducted successfully for several years.

Later Isaiah Terry formed a partnership with his brother-in-law, Francis H. Stoddard, and as Terry & Stoddard engaged in the oil business and for many years they were successfully identified with that industry, one with which Fairhaven and New Bedford were long famous, the capture, marketing, and sale of whale products.[15] The buildings used by Terry & Stoddard in their business were later purchased by the New Bedford & Fairhaven Street Railway Company, and used for storing railcars.

During the gold fever of 1849, Mr. Terry fitted out one of his ships, loaded it with freight and dispatched it around Cape Horn with a large list of passengers also on board. By the 1870s, Mr. Terry had retired from active participation in commercial affairs. Thereafter he pursued the recreations of the home he loved, and to the positions he still retained in the banking institutions of Fairhaven. Mr. Terry was one of the incorporators of the Fairhaven National Bank, was elected a member of the first board of directors, and held that position for 18 years. He held the same functions with the Fairhaven Savings Bank in 1832, and from incorporation in that year until 1879, he was a member of the bank board of trustees, and during those 47 years he accomplished much to the prosperity of the bank. He was a member of the first board of directors of the Fairhaven Branch Railroad Company, and until the railroad

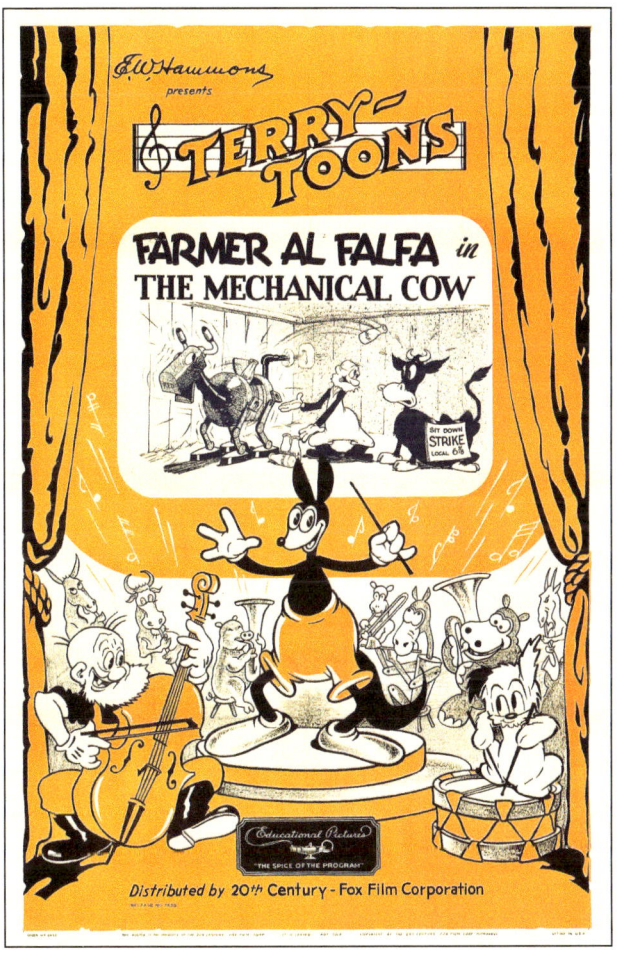

Fig. 1.5 – Theatrical Poster for *The Mechanical Cow* (1937), a Farmer Al Falfa cartoon.

was sold he retained his place on the board.[16]

Although banking and the railroad were his principal interests, there were few enterprises started in Fairhaven during his professional career in which he did not have a part, either advisory or official. Isaiah Terry was honored as a good citizen, a loyal friend and neighbor, and a man deeply devoted to his family. He was well respected in the community, and, during his senior years, the interest displayed in him and his welfare by fellow citizens was remarkable. Mr. Terry married Caroline Coleman Jenney on February 29, 1832 in Fairhaven.[17] Caroline Jenney was born on May 25, 1812 in Fairhaven, Massachusetts, died February 6, 1851, and is buried with her husband in Riverside Cemetery, Fairhaven. Mr. Terry married again (his second wife) on March 31, 1853, Phebe Hussey Bryant, daughter of Gamaliel and Mary (Potter) Bryant, who is also buried in Riverside Cemetery.

During their 18 year marriage, Isaiah and Caroline Coleman Terry had eight children, two daughters and six sons, the first being born in 1833 and the last in 1847.[18] Joseph Tripp Terry was the sixth child and the fourth son born to Isaiah and Caroline. The oldest, Loretta, died as an infant, about 14 months old. A similar fate unfortunately occurred to the Terry family's third oldest, Atkin, who died at age three years and three months.

Joseph Tripp Terry was raised in Fairhaven, Massachusetts and attended the local schools. Fairhaven is located on the south coast of Massachusetts where the Acushnet River flows into Buzzards Bay, an arm of the Atlantic Ocean. The town shares a harbor with the city of New Bedford, a place well known for its whaling and fishing heritage. Like New Bedford, Fairhaven was also a whaling port; in fact, in the year 1838, Fairhaven was the second-largest whaling port in the United States, with 24 vessels sailing for the whaling grounds. Fairhaven's history, economy, and culture are closely associated with those of its larger neighbor across the bay. Prior to the second half of the 19th century, whale oil was the primary source of fuel for lighting in the United States. The whaling industry was an economic mainstay for many New England coastal communities for over two hundred years and both Fairhaven and New Bedford profited heavily from the American thirst for whale oil and other Cetacean products.[19]

With the boom in the whaling industry during the early 1800s, both New Bedford and Fairhaven's population swelled. The population of the once tiny Fairhaven in 1840 was 3,951 and by 1850 had reached 4,304. During the early to mid-1800s, Fairhaven became a popular location for ship-owners and ship-captains to build their homes and raise their children. However with the decline of the whaling industry in the mid-1850s, by 1860, the population had dropped over 27 percent to 3,118 from the previous decade. Conversely, New Bedford during the same 1840 to 1860 period had experienced a population growth of over 84 percent (12,087 to 22,300).[20] The reason for the differences in population growth can be found in commercial sectors of both towns. Once New Bedford's predominance in the whaling industry became apparent, Fairhaven's economy evolved into one that supplemented the New Bedford economy rather than competing directly with it. Fairhaven became a town of shipwrights, ship chandlers, rope makers, coopers, and sail makers.

By 1850, Joseph Terry's father was earning a substantial income from his business and commercial activities in the banking and whaling industries and could afford the services of a domestic servant. At the time of the 1850 U.S. Census, Mary Rock, a 25-year-old Irish-born domestic servant, was also residing in the Terry home where she attended to the many household chores while assisting with the upbringing of the six Terry children. By 1860, Ms. Rock had left the household and 19-year-old Catherine Dugan, another Irish-born domestic servant, was residing with the Terry family.

Joseph's early years in Fairhaven were uneventful by the most part. He enjoyed the comforts of an upper middle class existence. Unlike the other boys his age, he had no interest in pursuing a career in the whaling industry. During his childhood, he became good friends with Henry Huddleston Rogers (1840–1909), three years older than Terry. Rogers is best known as the industrialist and financier who made his fortune in the oil refinery business, becoming a leader at Standard Oil alongside John D. Rockefeller.[21] Like Terry, Rogers was brought up in Fairhaven, Massachusetts. As a boy Rogers carried newspapers and delivered groceries for his father's grocery business, later working three to four years as a railroad brakeman and expressman for the Fairhaven Branch Railroad while carefully saving his money.

By 1855, the whaling business in Fairhaven was already in the decline. By the mid-1850s gas lighting was used in many public venues in North America. In the late 1850s, the clean burning kerosene lamp was introduced. The first oil well drilled was in the middle of quiet farm country in northwestern Pennsylvania in 1859. The emergence of petroleum and later natural gas as a replacement fuel for lighting in the second half of the 19th century caused a significant

Chapter 1 • From the Mayflower to Market Street

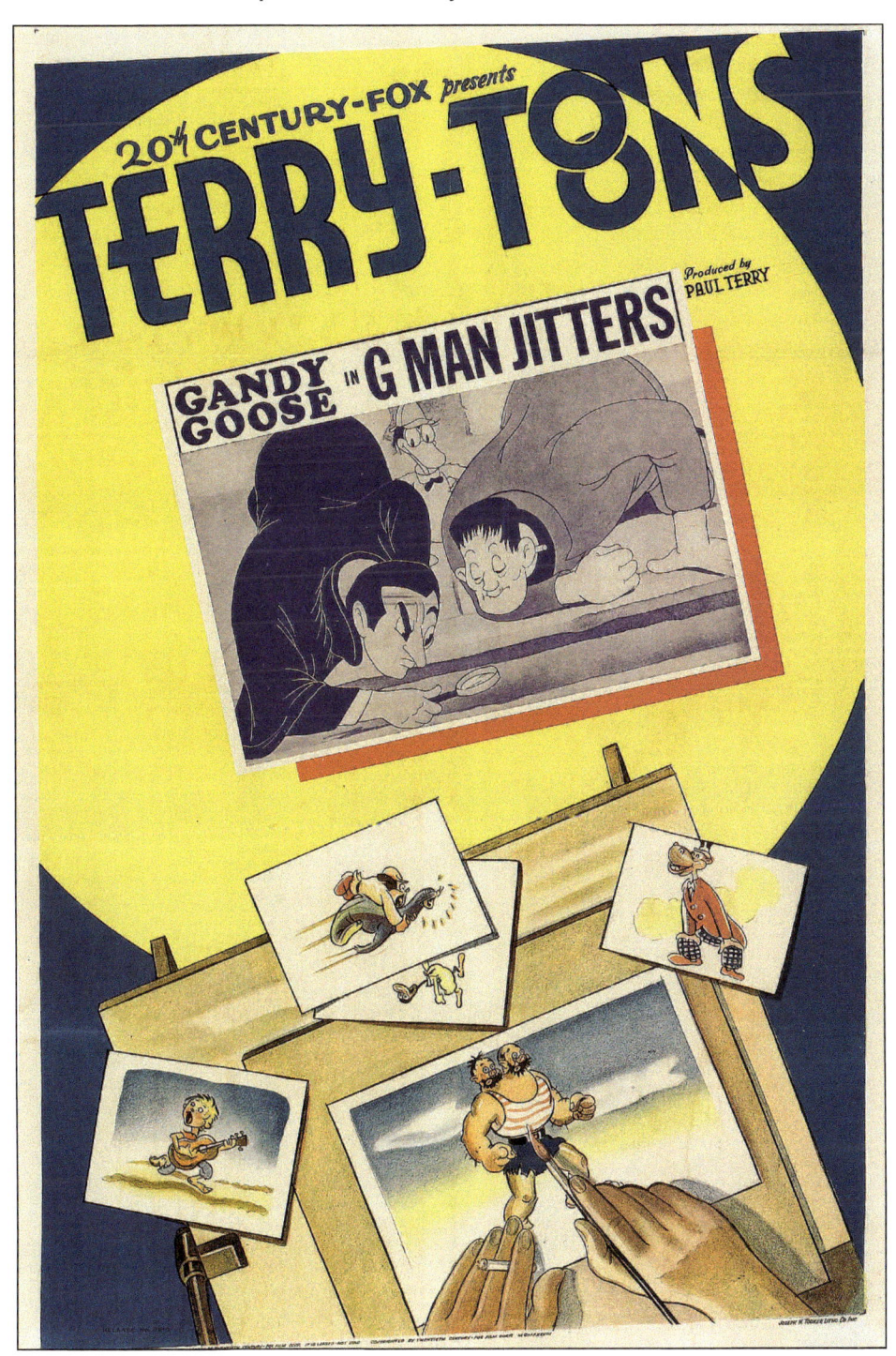

Fig. 1.6 – Poster for *G Man Jitters* (1939), a Gandy Goose cartoon.

economic depression to the New England whaling industry and their families. When Rogers was 21 years of age, he decided to leave Fairhaven and traveled with a friend, Charles P. Ellis, to Pennsylvania where oil had been recently discovered. Both Rogers and Ellis each carried with them about $600 in savings. Soon they had built an oil refinery. Rogers would eventually devise the machinery by which naphtha was first successfully separated from crude oil and by 1874 Rogers had joined forces with Rockefeller to build Standard Oil.

By the mid-1860s whales were no longer considered as a primary source of oil. With the whaling industry in New England in continued decline as the need for whale oil waned, Joseph believed Fairhaven had little to offer his career. Like his childhood friend Henry Rogers, at the same age of twenty-one Joseph Tripp decided to leave New England and seek his fortune elsewhere. While Rogers pursued his dream of becoming an oil baron, Joseph sought to make his fortune in gold and chose to try his luck in San Francisco. ❧

Notes

1.   While some sources have *Little Herman* (1915) running anywhere from five to six minutes, Terry stated that the cartoon was about 300 feet in length (Paul Terry, interview by Harvey Deneroff, New Rochelle, New York, 20 December 1969. John Canemaker Animation Collection, Fales Library, Elmer Holmes Bobst Library, New York University, New York City, 21). Animated films run at 24 frames per second (fps). 24fps multiplied by 60 (seconds in a minute) = 1,440 frames per minute. 1,440 (frames per minute) divided by 16 (frames per foot) = 90 feet per minute. Based on 90 feet per minute, the animated short would have been approximately 3 minutes and 20 seconds in length.

2.   Release date as listed in: Graham Webb, *The Animated Film Encyclopedia. A Complete Guide to American Shorts, Features, and Sequences, 1900–1979* (Jefferson, NC: McFarland & Company, Inc., 2000). The four month period to create the film is recorded in: Nancy Barr Mavity, "Romance Born in Studio with Terry's 'Fables' Cat", *Oakland Tribune*, 16 January 1928, p. 2.

3.   See Timothy S. Susanin, *Walt Before Mickey: Disney's Early Years, 1919–1928* (Jackson: University Press of Mississippi, 2011); Brian Burnes, Robert W. Butler, and Dan Viets, *Walt Disney's Missouri: The Roots of a Creative Genius*, edited by Donna Martin (Kansas City, MO: Kansas City Star Books, 2002).

4.   For further biographical information on John Alden, Priscilla Mullins and their fellow pilgrims see Caleb H. Johnson, *The Mayflower and Her Passengers* (Philadelphia, Pa.: Xlibris, 2006).

5.   A detailed history of Fairhaven, Massachusetts can be found in: Ebenezer Weaver Peirce, *Brief Sketches of Freetown, Fall River, and Fairhaven* (Boston, Mass.: Printed for the author by Dean Dudley, 1872); Duane Hamilton Hurd, *History of Bristol County, Massachusetts* (Philadelphia, J. W. Lewis & Co., 1883); Daniel Ricketson, *The History of the New Bedford, Bristol County, Massachusetts: Including a History of the Old Township of Dartmouth and the Present Townships of Westport, Dartmouth, and Fairhaven, From Their Settlement to the Present Time* (New Bedford: The author, 1858); James L. Gillingham, Cyrus D. Hunt, Lewis S. Judd, Jr., and George H. Tripp, *Brief History of the Town of Fairhaven* (New Bedford, Mass.: Standard Print, 1903). The Massachusetts Archives at Columbia Point has holdings dating from the beginning of the Massachusetts Bay Colony in 1628 and document the settlement of lands in Maine and Massachusetts, the arrival of immigrants, and the development of state government.

6.   Caroline Coleman Jenney's father Levi was a descendant of John Jenney, of Norwich, England, who early went to Holland, there married Sarah Carey, an English girl, and moved to Rotterdam. John and Sarah Jenney came with their three children to New England in 1623 in the ship *James*, a small vessel of 44 tons. John Jenney became an important man in the Plymouth Colony. Levi Jenney was a sergeant in Captain Manasseh Kempton's Company and with Colonel Carpenter's Regiment for services at Rhode Island in alarm. He enlisted July 26, 1777 and was discharged August 29, 1777. Reference: Virginia Terry Simon to the National Society of the Daughters of the American Revolution, "Application for Membership to the National Society of the Daughters of the American Revolution", 18 September 1957, Paul Terry Papers, Fayetteville, North Carolina.

7.   The first known bearer of the name was Theodoric I, son of Alaric I, king of the Visigoths (d. 451). The Gothic form of the name would have been Þiudareiks, which was Latinized as Theodericus. The notability of the name is due to Theodoric the Great, son of Theodemir, king of the Ostrogoths (454–526), who became a legendary figure of the Germanic Heroic Age as Dietrich von Bern.

8.   Henry Kingsbury Terry, ed., *The English Founders of the Terry Family* (London, H.K. Terry & co. [18–]); Stephen Terry, *Notes of Terry Families, in the United States of America* (Hartford, Connecticut: Published by the Compiler, 1887); David Sanders Clark, *Notes on the Terry Family and Related Families* (Washington, 1957).

9.   The Terry family genealogy relied upon was researched and compiled by Joseph T. Terry, Paul Terry's brother (Joseph T. Terry, *Genealogy of Our Family*, Los Angeles, California, February 5, 1948). For more on the Terry genealogy in Massachusetts refer to: James Savage, *A Genealogical Dictionary of the First Settlers of New England, Showing Three Generations of Those Who Came Before May, 1692*,

Chapter 1 • From the Mayflower to Market Street

on the Basis of Farmer's Register (Boston, Little, Brown and Company, 1860–62); Charles Henry Pope, *The Pioneers of Massachusetts* (Baltimore: Genealogical Publishing Company, 1965).

10. Block Island is part of the U.S. state of Rhode Island. It is located in the Atlantic Ocean about 13 miles (21 km) south of the coast of Rhode Island, 14 miles (23 km) east of Montauk Point on Long Island, and is separated from the Rhode Island mainland by Block Island Sound.

11. The history of Thomas Terry and his adventures in Rhode Island can be found in Samuel Truesdale Livermore, *History of Block Island From its Discovery, in 1514, to the Present Time, 1876* (Hartford, Conn., The Case, Lockwood & Brainard Co., 1877).

12. The first three generations of the Terry family can be referenced in William Richard Cutter, *New England Families, Genealogical and Memorial: A Record of the Achievements of Her People in the Making of Commonwealths and the Founding of a Nation* (Baltimore, Md.: Clearfield Co., 1994).

13. The story of Isaiah Terry and a history of New Bedford, Massachusetts can be referenced in: Zephaniah Walter Pease, *History of New Bedford* (New York, The Lewis Historical Publishing Company, 1918); Leonard Bolles Ellis, *History of New Bedford and its Vicinity, 1602–1892* (Syracuse, N.Y.: D. Mason & Co., 1892).

14. Ezekiel Sawin was also senator for Bristol County in 1857 and had also been a member of the Legislature at other times. In 1862 he resigned the presidency of the Fairhaven Bank which he held for 31 years (Thomas E. Sawin, *Sawin: Summary Notes Concerning John Sawin and His Posterity* (Athol Deport, Massachusetts: Rufus Putnam, 1867)).

15. For a detailed early account of the whale fishery in Fairhaven, Massachusetts refer to: Alexander Starbuck, *History of the American Whale Fishery From its Earliest Inception to the Year 1876* (Waltham, Mass.: The author, 1878).

16. Pease, *History of New Bedford*, 485–488.

17. Other noted 19th century Jenneys descended from John and Sarah Jenney include physician and educator James Nathaniel Jenne [Jenney] (1859–1937), and architect and inventor William Le Baron Jenney (1832–1907) who is known for building the first skyscraper in 1884 and became known as the "Father of the American skyscraper".

18. Loretta Hitchcock Terry (b. November 13, 1833; d. January 25, 1835, [Fairhaven, Massachusetts]), Franklin Terry (b. November 12 [6], 1835; d. November 3, 1920, District of Columbia), Atkin Adams Terry (b. May 31, 1838; d. September, 1841, Fairhaven, Massachusetts), Susan Burt Terry (b. July 31, 1840; d. October 21 [May 16], 1923, Fairhaven, Massachusetts), Bernard Jenny Terry (b. March 25, 1842 [1847], Fairhaven, Massachusetts; d. March 12, 1862, Lost at sea), Joseph Tripp Terry (b. January 24, 1843, Fairhaven, Massachusetts; d. October 21, 1921, Berkeley, California), John Coleman Terry (b. September 5, 1847 [February 17, 1850], Massachusetts; d. February 11, 1908, San Francisco, California), and Horatio Proctor Terry (b. September 5, 1848 [1847], Massachusetts; d. January 3, 1912 [October 1911], San Francisco, California). The birth dates were retrieved from Terry, *Genealogy of Our Family*, 2. The death dates for the eight children were found using the Ancestry and FamilySearch databases.

19. Federal Writers' Project of the Works Progress Administration of Massachusetts, *Fairhaven, Massachusetts* (Fairhaven, Massachusetts: Federal Writers' Project of the Works Progress Administration of Massachusetts, 1939); Marsha McCabe, ed., *A Picture History of Fairhaven* (New Bedford, Mass.: Spinner Publications, 1986).

20. U.S. Department of State, "Massachusetts", *Compendium of the Enumeration and Inhabitants and Statistics of the United States* (Sixth Census) (Washington: Thomas Allen, 1841), 8; U.S. Department of the Interior, Census Office, *Populations of Such Cities, Towns, Townships, Hundreds, &c.* (Seventh Census) (Washington: Beverley Tucker, Senate Printer, 1854), 338–393; U.S. Department of the Interior, Census Office, "State of Massachusetts Table no. 3. Populations of Cities, Towns, &c.", *Population of the United States in 1860; Comp. from the Original Returns of the Eighth Census* (Washington: Government Printing Office, 1864), 220–226.

21. Biographical entries on H.H. Rogers can be referenced in: *The National Cyclopaedia of American Biography*, volume 19 (New York: James T. White & Co., 1926); John A. Garraty and Mark C. Carnes, ed., *American National Biography*, 24 volumes (New York: Oxford University Press, 1999). For a full-length biography see: Earl J. Dias, *Henry Huttleston Rogers: Portrait of a "capitalist"* (Fairhaven, Mass.: Millicent Library, 1974).

Chapter 2

In Old San Francisco: The Terry Family Saga, 1864–1887

In 1864, travelers from the east coast of the United States intending to journey to San Francisco did so primarily by ocean travel via the Isthmus of Panama. The earliest opportunity for rail passengers to travel coast to coast did not occur until the First Transcontinental Railroad (known originally as the "Pacific Railroad" and later as the "Overland Route") was opened for through traffic on May 10, 1869, with the driving of the "Last Spike" with a silver hammer at Promontory Summit.[1] In early 1864, Joseph Terry traveled to New York City to begin his voyage west and boarded the *Ocean Queen*, a side-paddled wooden ship originally named *Queen of the Pacific* built in 1857 by Stephen G. Bogert, of the Westervelt & Co. Shipyard of New York City and powered by engines built by the Morgan Iron Works, also in New York.

Unfortunately, by the time of the *Queen of the Pacific*'s completion and inaugural voyage, the California Gold Rush (1848–1855) had ended and as a result there was a decreased demand for traffic. In 1859, the ship was sold to Cornelius Vanderbilt's European Line, altered and renamed the *Ocean Queen*. The marine vessel made five Atlantic crossings on the New York – Southampton – Le Havre route.[2] During the United States Civil War (April 12, 1861 – May 10, 1865), the ship was

Fig. 2.1 – Paul Terry's father, Joseph Tripp Terry (c. 1870).

Chapter 2 • In Old San Francisco

chartered to the United States War Department. After the Civil War, the vessel once again sailed between New York and Panama, carrying passengers destined for California, who then had to take a train across the Isthmus and find passage on the Pacific side.[3]

Although the Civil War had not ended and the *Ocean Queen* was under military control, Joseph Terry was able to find passage on the vessel from New York City to Ancon, Panama, a suburb of Panama City. From there he boarded a Panama Canal Railroad train[4] and railed across the Isthmus of Panama, a 47.6 mile (75 km) trip. From the west coast of Panama he then sailed on the steamer *Orizaba*, a 1,450 ton, wooden hull, side paddle wheel, two-masted steamship with accommodation for 1,028 passengers,[5] arriving in San Francisco on April 27, 1864. The transit time from New York City to San Francisco was about 30 days.[6]

When Joseph Terry stepped off the passenger steamer, the population of the Bay City was about 100,000.[7] For the 16 years leading up to Terry's arrival, San Francisco had transformed from a small port to a thriving metropolis. The population boom was sparked when on January 24, 1848 the first gold was found at Sutter's Fort, in the California foothills. Within months, San Francisco (renamed from Yerba Buena on January 30, 1847[8]) became the central port and depot of the frenzied Gold Rush. Between January 1848 and December 1849, the population of San Francisco increased from approximately 1,000 to 25,000. The city was incorporated on April 15, 1850 and over the next two decades experienced extraordinary growth.[9]

With the greed for gold and the lack of police authority in the early years of San Francisco, the city was lawless and wild, its Barbary Coast district full of prostitution and gambling.[10] In 1849, bands of hoodlums such as the Sydney Ducks[11] roamed the city, committing crimes that ranged from petty theft to murder, knowing that their victims had recourse to neither police nor courts.[12] To add further drama and misery, six major fires broke out between 1848 and 1851. All caused heavy damages, rendered many homeless, and created acute shortages of food and other essentials. The first of the series broke out on Christmas Eve of 1848. It consumed all buildings on both sides of Kearny Street between Washington and Clay Streets and caused a loss estimated at one million dollars.[13]

A larger and more destructive fire, on May 4, 1849, leveled the two

Fig. 2.2 – Paul Terry's mother, Minnie (née Perrin) Terry.

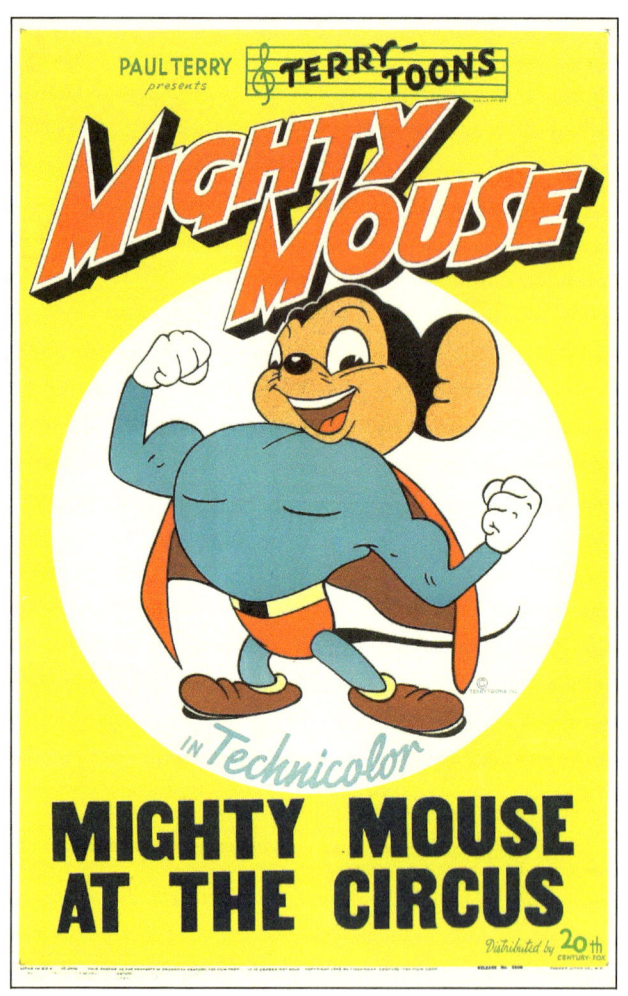

TERRYTOONS: The Story of Paul Terry and His Classic Cartoon Factory

Fig. 2.3 – Theatrical lobby poster for *At The Circus* (1944), a Mighty Mouse cartoon.

Mark Hopkins (1813–1878), Collis P. Huntington (1821–1900) and Leland Stanford (1824–1893) – drew thousands of laborers from China. Although many were later forced to leave by exclusionary U.S. policies, San Francisco's thriving Chinatown quickly became the largest Chinese settlement outside of Asia.

For most settlers arriving in San Francisco, finding employment in the rapidly growing city was not a daunting task. Not long after his arrival, Joseph Terry was able to secure a position as a clerk with William T. Coleman and Co. Wholesale Grocery and Ship Outfitters.[17] William Tell Coleman (1824–1893) is famous for having the secondary mineral Colemanite named after him,[18] and for manufacturing borax, a mineral and salt of boric acid. During the 1880s Coleman was owner of the Harmony Borax Works in Death Valley, operating 20 mule teams to carry the product from 1883 to 1889.

Coleman led a remarkable life and much has been written on him.[19] He established a line of clipper ships that traveled regularly from New York to San Francisco, and is probably most famous for his efforts to bring criminal justice to San Francisco. He was president of the vigilance committees of 1852 [1851] and 1856 to help maintain law and order and chase many criminals out of the city. One of his most publicized acts was as president of the executive committee that hung four criminals. During the labor troubles and anti-Chinese riots of 1877 he organized the Committee of Safety and raised and equipped

blocks bounded by Kearny, Clay, Washington, and Montgomery Streets to the east of Portsmouth Square, and facing the Square to the north, a block bounded by Kearny, Washington, Dupont, and Jackson. On May 3, 1851, San Francisco's fifth and most disastrous fire destroyed 20 blocks, causing $12 million loss.[14] The cause of these fires was likely wood stoves and kerosene or whale-oil lamps, the usual

sources of heart or light, although gangs such as the Sydney Ducks may have played a part in their efforts to loot.[15]

Just as the Gold boom busted, the Comstock Lode[16] was discovered in 1858 and the silver boom again filled the city's docks and lined its pockets. Construction of the Central Pacific Railroad – funded by the "Big Four" businessmen Charles Crocker (1822–1888),

Chapter 2 • In Old San Francisco

Fig. 2.4 – Animation background for *Mighty Mouse Meets Jeckyll and Hyde Cat* (1944).

a force of 5,000 persons to patrol the streets and protect property.[20]

In 1849, Coleman had traveled with the tide of gold-seekers to California settling in Sacramento to open a building construction establishment on a small scale. He also began to deal in cattle and real estate. In 1850, he moved to San Francisco and set up as a shipping and commission merchant.[21] Coleman's San Francisco business operations expanded rapidly and he opened a branch in New York (1852–1855), and in 1856 started a line of ships between that port and San Francisco.[22] From 1857 to 1864, Coleman resided in New York City before returning to San Francisco.[23]

During his tenure with Coleman, Joseph Terry enjoyed secure employment in a rapidly expanding business that prospered from the steady flow of passengers and cargo into the busy port. Coleman's grocery business expanded to the point where his firm controlled the fruit canning industry of California. Coleman is also remembered for developing an extension to the town of San Rafael, with 34 miles of streets, and planting 275,000 trees in the California settlement.

While employed at William T. Coleman & Co., Joseph Terry lost his temper and in a fit of rage resigned his appointment with the company, a decision he regretted the rest of his life as the position he occupied had security and promise for advancement.[24] By late 1865 he had found similar work as a clerk with Henry B. Williams at an office located at 305 Front Street. Williams was a shipping and commission merchant and agent for Rollinson's California Line Clipper Ships.[25] Terry was with Henry Williams for about a year when he decided by 1866 to become self-employed as a tea merchant. Terry left Williams and partnered with James E. Dixon selling teas and groceries under the firm name Dixon & Terry. At the time, Terry was residing at 131 3rd Avenue.[26] Over the next 25 years, the residential address of the Terry family would change frequently, partly due to shifting economic issues arising from Joseph's self-employment, but more importantly the result of increasing spatial needs of a growing family.

By 1868, Joseph Terry had left the tea and grocery business and began a long career as an auction and commission merchant partnering with William H. Cummings under the firm name Cummings and Terry at an office

Fig. 2.5 – Mighty Mouse after the redesign from Super Mouse.

13

located at the southeast corner of Pine and Montgomery.[27] Terry's residence was located at 611 [1611] Mason Street removing to 400 Geary Street by 1869.[28] In 1871, Terry resided at the Russ House, San Francisco's first grand hotel.[29]

On July 10, 1872 in San Francisco, California, Joseph Terry married Minnie Bernice Perrin. The marriage was officiated by Rev. Dr. Scott.[30] She was born on January 1, 1854, in Coldwater, Michigan.[31] She was an attractive and artistically-gifted individual with a talent for sculpting. After their marriage she created a number of fine works of sculpture that decorated the Terry family home. Joseph and Minnie had met in San Francisco, California and began their courtship in the city. By 1872, Terry had parted company with Cummings and formed his own company, J. T. Terry & Co. auction and commission merchants, partnering with Mark Ezekiels with offices at 309 and 311 Pine Street.[32]

Joseph and Minnie's first child, Horatio Proctor Terry, was born on July 24, 1873, in San Francisco, California. Tragically, he died as an infant on April 3, 1877, in San Francisco, California.[33] By 1875, along with his auctioneering work, Joseph Terry began working as a fruit importer in an attempt to bolster his income. He developed friendships with important men in the community, including lawyer Samuel Shortridge who would later became a member of the U.S. Senate, 1921–1933.[34] The family residence was at 419 Hyde Street.[35] On May 21, 1876, the second Terry child was born in San Francisco, California, Caroline Dell Terry.[36] By 1876, while raising his family Terry added real estate agent and broker to his work as auctioneer with the office located at 238 Montgomery Street,[37] and by 1877 relocated to 6 Montgomery Street. In 1877, the Terry residence was located at 1706 Polk Street.[38]

On August 17, 1878, Joseph Tripp Terry Jr., the third eldest Terry child was born to Joseph and Minnie in San Francisco, California.[39] By that time Terry was partnered with Robert W. Taylor as auctioneers under the firm name Joseph T. Terry & Co. located at 1124 Market Street and 19 Turk Street. The Terry residence was at 1553 ½ Market Street.[40] In 1879, he partnered with Julius M. Pearlman under the same firm name with an office at 747 Market Street.[41]

By 1880, after failing in partnerships with various business associates, Terry decided to

Fig. 2.6 – Theatrical lobby poster for *Mopping Up* (1943), a Gandy Goose cartoon.

partner with his younger brother John C. Terry in the auctioneering firm. The Terry brothers would also engage in work as furniture dealers. Joseph's brother Horatio was employed as a salesman for the firm. The Terry residence was then briefly located at 207 Hyde Street. His partnership with his brother John would be his most stable.

On May 25, 1880, the fourth Terry child, John Coleman Terry, was born in San Francisco California.[42] By that time, the Terry residence was relocated to 610 Ellis Street to make room for the growing family.[43] Residing in the home was his wife and two children (Carrie and Joseph), his brother-in-law Maurice Perrin (a 30-year-old expressman born in New York), and niece Bessie Shute (17 years old, born in New York).

Joseph Terry's place of business would remain at its address for a number of years while in 1882 the family residence was again relocated, this time to 631 Harrison Street.[44] On May 28, 1882, the fifth Terry child, Olga Bernice Terry, was born in San Francisco, California.[45] By 1884, the Terry family residence was at 559 Seventh Avenue.[46] In 1885, the Terry family moved out to farm property in San Mateo, California, about 19 miles (31 km) south of San Francisco, while Joseph's brother and business partner John remained in San Francisco to oversee more directly the ongoing operations. Joseph's brother Horatio continued his position as a salesman for the company.[47] The move to San Mateo was a decision based on Joseph Terry's belief that the air was cleaner outside of the city.[48] For the next four to five years, the Terry family would call San Mateo home. ❧

Fig. 2.7 – San Francisco downtown, c. 1865 at the time of Joseph Terry's arrival, view of the Occidental Hotel at Montgomery Street.

Fig. 2.8 – San Francisco from Russian Hill, looking down Vallejo Street, c. 1865 about the time of Joseph Terry's arrival.

Notes

1. The railroad was a 1,907-mile (3,069 km) contiguous railroad line constructed between 1863 and 1869 across the western United States to connect the Pacific coast at San Francisco Bay with the existing Eastern U.S. rail network at Council Bluffs, Iowa, on the Missouri River. See: Enid Johnson, *Rails Across the Continent; The Story of the First Transcontinental Railroad* (New York: J. Messner, 1965); Dee Alexander Brown, *Lonesome Whistle: The Story of the First Transcontinental Railroad* (New York: Holt, Rinehart, and Winston, 1980).

2. Statistics and history on the *Ocean Queen* can be referenced in: N. R. P. Bonsor, *North Atlantic Seaway: An Illustrated History of the Passenger Services Linking the Old World with the New in Four Volumes* (Newton Abbot [Eng.]: David & Charles, 1975–1980).

3. This was a 2,801 gross ton ship, with a length of 327 feet and a beam measuring 42 feet. It had a straight stem, two funnels and two masts. The ship was of wooden construction, with side-paddle propulsion and a speed of 12 knots. There was accommodation for 350 1st- and 2nd-class passengers. The ship was scrapped in 1875 in Wilmington, Delaware.

4. The railroad became one of the most profitable in the world, charging up to $25 per passenger to travel over 47 miles (76 km) of hard laid track. Upon completion, the railway was proclaimed an engineering marvel of the era. Until the opening of the Panama Canal, it carried the heaviest volume of freight per unit length of any railroad in the world. For a detailed history of its construction and subsequent history, see: Julius Grigore, *The Influence of the United States Navy Upon the Beginnings of the Panama Railroad: The Greatest Engineering Feat Since the Construction of the Great Wall of China* (Balboa, Republic of Panama: Balboa Press, 1987). See also: Fessenden Nott Otis, *Illustrated History of the Panama Railroad; Together with a Traveler's Guide and Business Man's Hand-book for the Panama Railroad and its Connections with Europe, the United States, the North and South Atlantic and Pacific Coasts, China, Australia, and Japan, by Sail and Steam*, 2nd ed. (New York: Harper, 1862).

5. The ship was launched on January 14, 1854 by Jacob A. Westervelt & Co., New York for Morgan & Harris for the New York – New Orleans – Vera Cruz service. She made two New York – San Juan de Nicaragua sailings in April–May 1856 and was then sent to San Francisco, arriving October 30th. She operated for Vanderbilt's Nicaragua Steamship Company until February 1857 and after April 1858 sailed from San Francisco to Panama for the New York & California Steamship Company. Purchased by Pacific Mail Steamship Company in 1860 and sailed the San Francisco to Panama City route between June 1, 1861 and April 1864. She was sold to the California Steam Navigation Company in April 1865 and used on their San Francisco – Portland – Victoria service until 1867 when she was sold to Holladay & Brenham. She was purchased again by Pacific Mail Steamship Company in 1872 and by Goodall, Nelson & Perkins in 1875. She remained in coastal services throughout all these changes of ownership and was scrapped in 1887. See: Robert J. Chandler and Stephen J. Potash, *Gold, Silk, Pioneers and Mail: The Story of the Pacific Mail Steamship Company* (San Francisco, CA: Friends of the San Francisco Maritime Museum Library, 2010); Bonsor, *North Atlantic Seaway*.

6. Society of Mayflower Descendants in the State of California, *Register of the Society of Mayflower Descendants in the State of California; A Record of Descent from Passengers on the Good Ship "Mayflower"*, A. D. 1620; with an appendix (San Francisco, Cal.: Society of Mayflower Descendants in the State of California, 1917).

7. The population is a rough estimate based on an interpolation between the 1860 (56,802) and 1870 (149,473) U.S. Census populations of the city.

8. Oscar Lewis, *San Francisco: Mission to Metropolis* (Berkeley, Calif.: Howell-North Books, 1966), 43.

9. Writers' Program of the Work Projects Administration in Northern California, *San Francisco, the Bay and its Cities* (New York: Hastings House, 1940), 498–499. Other sources consulted: Tom Moulin and Don DeNevi, *San Francisco, Creation of a City* (Millbrae, Calif.: Celestial Arts, 1978); Lewis Francis Byington, *The History of San Francisco* (Chicago, San Francisco: The S. J. Clarke Publishing Company, 1931).

10. By the mid-1850s, gambling was so firmly entrenched and wielded so much influence in official circles, that attempts to outlaw or to regulate their activities had uniformly failed (Lewis, *San Francisco: Mission to Metropolis*, 71).

11. A gang of criminal immigrants from Australia.

12. Lewis, *San Francisco: Mission to Metropolis*, 58–59.

13. In 1848 dollars.

14. Writers' Program, California, *San Francisco, the Bay and its Cities*, 497.

15. Lewis, *San Francisco: Mission to Metropolis*, 64–65.

16. The Comstock Lode is a lode of silver ore located under the eastern slope of Mount Davidson, a peak in the Virginia Range in Nevada (then western Utah Territory). It was the first major discovery of silver ore in the United States.

17. Other sources list his company as William Tell Coleman & Co. Wholesale Dealers and Commission Merchants.

18. Colemanite ($CaB_3O_4(OH)_3 \cdot H_2O$) is a borate mineral found in evaporite deposits of alkaline lacustrine environments. Colemanite is a secondary mineral that forms by alteration of borax and ulexite. It was first described in 1884 for an occurrence near Furnace Creek in Death Valley and was named after Coleman the owner of the mine Harmony Borax Works where it was first found.

19. Eugene B. Block, *The Immortal San Franciscans for Whom the Streets Were Named* (San Francisco: Chronicle Books, 1971), 113–116; Mary Floyd Williams, *History of the San Francisco Committee of Vigilance of 1851; A Study of Social Control on the California Frontier in the Days of the Gold Rush* (New York: Da Capo Press, 1969 [c1921]); James A. B. Scherer, *"The lion of the vigilantes" William T.*

Chapter 2 • In Old San Francisco

Coleman and the Life of Old San Francisco (Indianapolis, New York: The Bobbs-Merrill Company, 1939).

20. "William Tell Coleman", *The National Cyclopaedia of American Biography* (New York: James T. White & Company, 1924; Ann Arbor, Michigan: University Microfilms, 1967), 336.

21. A commission merchant is one to whom goods are sent for sale, and who charges a certain percent on the price of the goods sold for his service, which is called a commission.

22. "Coleman, William Tell", *Who Was Who in America. Historical Volume, 1607–1896* (Chicago: Marquis Who's Who, 1963).

23. It is not known whether Joseph Terry was acquainted with Coleman before he arrived in San Francisco in 1864, although both men traveled from New York to San Francisco the same year.

24. *Genealogy of Our Family*, 2–3.

25. Henry G. Langley, *The San Francisco Directory, For the Year Commencing December, 1865* (San Francisco: Henry G. Langley; Excelsior Steam Presses: Towne and Bacon, Book and Job Printers, 1865), 426.

26. Henry G. Langley, *The San Francisco Directory, For the Year Commencing September, 1867* (San Francisco: Towne and Bacon, Excelsior Steam Presses, 1867), 467.

27. Henry G. Langley, *The San Francisco Directory, For the Year Commencing October 1868* (San Francisco: Henry G. Langley; Bacon & Company, Excelsior Steam Presses, 1868), 536.

28. Henry G. Langley, *The San Francisco Directory, For the Year Commencing December 1st, 1869* (San Francisco: Henry G. Langley; Bacon & Co., Excelsior Steam Presses, 1869), 597.

29. Henry G. Langley, *The San Francisco Directory, For the Year Commencing April, 1871* (San Francisco: Henry G. Langley; Bacon & Co., Excelsior Steam Presses, 1871), 630.

30. "Married", *Daily Alta California*, 11 July 1872, 4.

31. *Genealogy of Our Family*, 3.

32. Henry G. Langley, *The San Francisco Directory, For the Year Commencing March, 1872* (San Francisco: Henry G. Langley; Bacon & Co., Excelsior Steam Presses, 1872), 635.

33. "Deaths", *Daily Alta California*, 4 April 1877, 4.

34. "Shortridge, Samuel Morgan", *Who Was Who in America*, volume III, 1951–1960 (Chicago: A.N. Marquis Co., 1943), 783.

35. Henry G. Langley, *The San Francisco Directory, For the Year Commencing March, 1875* (San Francisco: Henry G. Langley; Francis & Valentine, Commercial Steam Presses, 1875), 707; D. M. Bishop & Co., *New City Annual Directory of San Francisco* (San Francisco: D. M. Bishop & Co., 1875), 988.

36. She was married on October 19, 1895 and died on December 29, 1959, in Berkeley, California (*Genealogy of Our Family*, 3).

37. Henry G. Langley, *The San Francisco Directory, For the Year Commencing April, 1876* (San Francisco: Henry G. Langley; Francis & Valentine, Commercial Steam Presses, 1876), 784.

38. Henry G. Langley, *The San Francisco Directory, For the Year Commencing March, 1877* (San Francisco: Henry G. Langley; Francis & Valentine, Commercial Steam Presses, 1877), 837; *Supplement to the Annual Directory of the City of San Francisco For 1877* (San Francisco: B.C. Vandall, 1877), 1136.

39. He was married on December 29, 1914, in Highwood, Minnesota, and died on July 31, 1959, in Los Angeles, California (*Genealogy of Our Family*, 3).

40. Henry G. Langley, *The San Francisco Directory, For the Year Commencing February, 1878* (San Francisco: Henry G. Langley; Francis & Valentine, Commercial Steam Presses, 1878), 823; *Bishop's Directory of the City and County of San Francisco, 1878* (San Francisco: B.C. Vandall, 1878), 830.

41. Henry G. Langley, *The San Francisco Directory, For the Year Commencing April, 1879* (San Francisco: Francis, Valentine & Co., 1879), 847.

42. He married Bessie Spratt Terry (b. October 5, 1881, Alpens, Michigan), and died on February 28, 1934, in Coral Gables, Florida (*Genealogy of Our Family*, 3).

43. The Directory Publishing Co., *The San Francisco Directory, For the Year Commencing April, 1880* (San Francisco: Francis, Valentine & Co., 1880), 879; *Genealogy of Our Family*, 3.

44. The Directory Publishing Co., *Langley's San Francisco Directory, For the Year Commencing April, 1882* (San Francisco: Francis, Valentine & Co., 1882), 918.

45. She was married to Alexander Hume Anderson (b. Nairn, Scotland, May 17, 1867) on July 3, 1918 in San Francisco, California, and died on December 23, 1956, in Alameda, California (*Genealogy of Our Family*, 4).

46. The Directory Publishing Co., *Langley's San Francisco Directory, For the Year Commencing April, 1884* (San Francisco: Francis, Valentine & Co., 1884), 1053.

47. W. H. L. Corran, *Langley's San Francisco Directory, For the Year Commencing April, 1885* (San Francisco: Francis, Valentine & Co., 1885), 1110.

48. Paul Terry, interview, 20 December 1969, 8.

Chapter 3

Birth of an Animation Pioneer: The Childhood and Young Life of Paul Terry, 1887–1902

The year 1887 was filled with a broad spectrum of newsworthy historical events including artistic achievements, ceremonial festivities, natural disasters, and Victorian-era scientific discoveries: the French Riviera was struck by a large earthquake, killing around 2,000 people along the coast of the Mediterranean Sea (February 23), Anne Sullivan began teaching the blind and deaf Helen Keller (March 3), the Catholic University of America was founded (April 10), and the British Empire celebrated Queen Victoria's Golden Jubilee, marking the 50th year of her reign (June 21). During the latter half of 1887, the start of the Yellow River flood in China occurred, tragically killing 900,000 to 2 million people (September 28), Emile Berliner was granted a patent for his Gramophone (November 8), and Arthur Conan Doyle's detective character Sherlock Holmes made his first appearance, in the novel *A Study in Scarlet* published in *Beeton's Christmas Annual* (late November).[1]

The headline on the front page of the Saturday, February 19, 1887 edition of the *New York Times* read: "War Clouds Still Black". At the time, the Russian government was becoming increasingly convinced that war between France and Germany over Bulgaria and the Balkan States was inevitable.[2] In Milan, Giuseppe Verdi (1813–1901) was achieving success with what many were considering his finest tragic opera, *Otello*, a work based on William Shakespeare's play, with a libretto written by the younger composer of *Mefistofele*, Arrigo Boito.[3] On the same day in the United States, lightning destroyed a large cotton warehouse on Staten Island,[4] a test occurred for a new way to heat railway cars by hot water in New York City,[5] charges were being made of the feeding of unhealthy meat to patients in the South Carolina Lunatic Asylum,[6] and a branch post office was being considered for Yale University in New Haven.[7]

The biggest news that year in San Francisco was the arrival on January 9 of Penny-farthing bicycler Thomas Stevens completing his nearly three-year trek around the world after leaving San Francisco at 8 a.m. on April 22, 1884. Along the way, Stevens sent a series of letters to *Harper's* magazine detailing his experiences and later collected those experiences into a two-volume book of 1,000 pages, *Around the World on a Bicycle*.[8] The news making the headlines on February 19, 1887 in San Francisco included the death of Frank M. Green, a well known Nevada man, who was buried alive beneath a slide of ore tailings on which he was at work for with the Tombstone, A.T., Mill and Mining Company, and in the Tehachapi Mountains an immense mass of rock falling on the Southern Pacific track fell between two sections of a passenger train and as a result a horrible tragedy was averted by a fraction of a second. The track was cleared and the train reached San Francisco on the night of February 18, 1887.[9]

For the Terry family, February 19, 1887 was a very special date for this was the day their sixth and last child was born. The weather in San Francisco and area that day

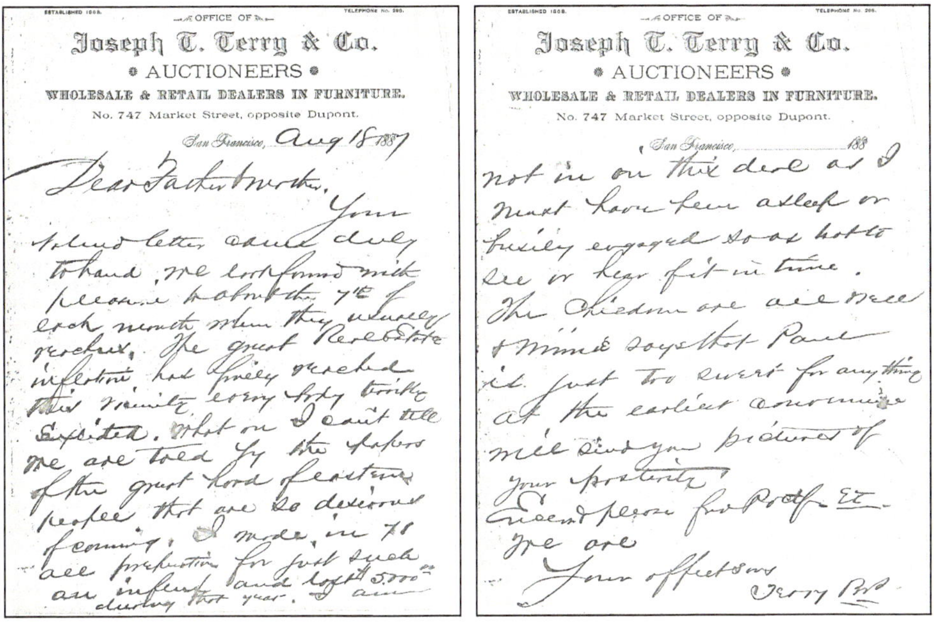

Chapter 3 • Birth of an Animation Pioneer

Fig. 3.1 – Letter from Paul Terry's father to his parents announcing the birth of Paul Terry.

was a mild 50°F (10°C), clear, with winds out of the northeast.[10] Rains wouldn't fall on San Mateo and area until the 21st.[11] He would be named Paul Houlton Terry.[12] He was named Paul after St. Paul from the New Testament. In fact, his brothers John and Joseph were also named after Biblical figures.[13] He was given the middle name Houlton after a sheep rancher by the same name who was a very good friend of his father and lived near the Terry family farm in San Mateo.[14] By the time their newest member of the family was born, Joseph, Minnie and their four children had been residing on the family farm in San Mateo for about two years.

The birth of their son was reported in the San Francisco *Morning Call* published on March 6, 1887.[15] About five months after Paul's birth, on August 18, 1887, Joseph Terry wrote his parents proudly informing them that his family is well and that his wife says that "Paul is too sweet for anything". He closes his letter with a promise to send a photograph of his new son.[16] For Joseph Terry, a family farm in San Mateo was an ideal environment to raise a large family with plenty of acreage to allow the curious Terry children to play and explore. The region experiences mild weather sheltered by hills from ocean, wind, and fog that so commonly plague San Francisco.

The area, like the most of California, has a history rooted in Spanish exploration. In 1776, a Spanish exploring party named a creek at the site, San Mateo, after St. Matthew. In 1793, a Spanish mission hospice was established along the creek, and in the 1850s an American village grew up there surrounded by farms.[17] The county, carved out of San Francisco County, was created and named on April 19, 1856.[18] The modern city was laid out by C. B. Polhemus in 1863 when the San Francisco-San Jose Railroad was built. The first train reached the station on October 18, 1863.[19]

After the locality was connected by railroad with San Francisco, men with fortunes made during the gold rush settled there to establish their country "estates". Improvements continued and stimulated San Mateo's progress toward becoming a prosperous community. Clean water for the residents was realized a year after Paul's birth in 1888 when the Crystal Springs dam was built on San Mateo Creek. The establishment of a newspaper, *The Leader*, shortly thereafter brought current events to the residents, and the paper's founders, Richard H. Jury and Charles N. Kirkbride, pushed for

19

Fig. 3.2 – The infant Paul Terry (c. 1888).

Fig. 3.3 – Paul Terry and his father, Joseph Terry (c. 1892).

the town's incorporation. Under this initiative, San Mateo officially became a town on September 3, 1894, with a majority vote of its citizens.[20]

By 1890, the Terry family had moved back to reside in San Francisco where it was more convenient for Joseph to conduct his business as a furniture auctioneer.[21] In those days Market Street was paved with cobblestones and streetcars were drawn by horses. At the time, Joseph Terry had one of the largest furniture stores west of Chicago, Illinois taking up the 747 to 749 Market Street addresses. The Terry residence was located at 1016 Fillmore Street northeast of what is now Alamo Square where it would remain until 1895.[22] While the family would live in the city during the winter months, in the summers, when school was not in session, they would reside back on their farm in San Mateo.[23]

Paul was the youngest by five years and all his older siblings were artistically inclined to some extent. His eldest sister Caroline was a talented sculptress and his brother John was a gifted cartoonist.[24] His siblings likely inherited their talents from their mother, Minnie.[25] Paul's mother was a very gifted sculptress. After her marriage, she used her artistic talents to create various sculptures of all shapes and sizes and then decorated the family home with these art objects. She even sculpted a model of Paul as an infant. She also carved a large cornucopia and fruit rolling out of this horn of plenty along with a life-sized figure holding sheaves of wheat.[26] His older brother Joseph Tripp was interested in geology and the Terry home was decorated with all kinds of quartz, agates, crystals and other types of rock formations.[27]

The first few years of Paul's infancy were peaceful and prosperous times for the Terry family as Joseph's furniture and auctioneering business prospered with the growth of the city. In the evenings his mother liked to do sculpture for relaxation. She was a very warm and affectionate individual who was proud of her children. Tragically, Minnie died on November 16 [17], 1890 in San Francisco. Her funeral records list the cause of her death as typhoid fever.[28] Her physician, Joseph

Chapter 3 • Birth of an Animation Pioneer

Fig. 3.4 – Paul Terry and family (c. 1895) (left to right): Joseph Tripp Terry, Jr., Olga Bernice Terry, Joseph Tripp Terry, Caroline Dell Terry, Paul Houlton Terry, John Coleman Terry.

Anton Prosek (1846–1917), a skilled and experienced physician who was a graduate of the Cooper Medical College, San Francisco, and Medical College of the Pacific, 1876, was unable to save her from the deadly disease.[29]

At the time of her death, Paul was three years old, and as a result, by the time he had reached adulthood he had no memories of her.[30] When the will of Minnie Terry was filed for probate on November 27, 1890, the deceased bequeathed her estate, valued at $3,200, to her husband.[31] After his mother's death, his father took on the role of both parents and as a result became that much more of an important parental figure to his children. He eventually hired a domestic servant to provide homemaker and child care services while he was busy with his daily work at the furniture store and auction house.

Although Paul's father followed a demanding schedule as an auctioneer in a growing business, he always found time in the evenings and on weekends to spend with his children. Joseph was nicknamed "Honest Judge Terry". He enjoyed wearing grey trousers, a stovepipe hat made of silk, cutaway coat, white piqué necktie, white piqué vest, and white high collar both at work and home.[32] He was a talented showman who could move a crowd to laughter or make them cry and was also a lively raconteur. When he was standing on the auction stand he always endeavored to provide some historical background or story to the items that were being auctioned. He was constantly acquiring historical information connected with the items he auctioned.[33] Joseph thought it important to offer some fact or piece of trivia that moved the item

beyond the intrinsic value of the object and provided some sense of dignity or notable distinction to the item. For example, he might note that the object was given as a gift from an important person to his wife, or was used at a newsworthy ceremony.[34]

Paul was allowed to accompany his father on the auction stand while the public sale was being held. Paul's first duty as a young auctioneer in training was assisting his father by ringing the bell causing the auction to come to order while telling everyone that "Honest Judge Terry's" auction was about to commence.[35] Despite his love to tell stories, Joseph was also very honest and sincere, a man who took pride in describing each item truthfully while accurately estimating its value to his audience.[36] Joseph was a believer in following faith-based religious values. After he was married the

Terry family attended the Episcopalian Church, but after the death of his wife, he would take his children to Jewish synagogues, or Presbyterian or Baptist churches. Joseph was not concerned with the religious faith or Christian denomination of the church he attended as long as his children received a sermon that edified them and offered wholesome values.[37]

Paul's father believed that it took at least 10 days for the incubation of any germ in your system, so he had a motto: "An empty house is better than a bad tenant". Every Saturday night the children would line up with a glass of home brewed cascara tea in hand. They would clink their glasses and say "Here's to your health" and the down the liquid. The following morning Terry and his siblings would make a mad rush to the bathroom with 100 percent attendance guaranteed. No germ lasted in the Terry household for very long and Paul could never bring to memory a time when a doctor visited their home. Baths were on Saturday night and children were made to bathe two or three at a time to conserve hot water and fuel as water was heated in dish pans and kettles on the stove.[38] Before retiring for the night, Paul and his family would go out in front of their house and exercise, taking deep breaths, inhaling and exhaling, which Joseph believed was responsible for no respiratory ailments in the family.[39]

Joseph Terry was also an educator at heart. In the Terry home, he decorated two walls of the living room with blackboards from floor to ceiling, an interior design that never would have been accepted if his wife was still alive. After he returned from work, Joseph would invite the neighborhood children to come into his home where he would teach them lessons they never received in the regular grade school curriculum. The children had a great affection for him and he delighted in teaching them. On the blackboard he would illustrate pieces of information to the children as they sat and watched. These teachings involved short pieces of poetry, verses from the Bible, theatrical lines and sonnets of Shakespeare, and other writings from famous and historical personalities.[40] Paul believed his father conducted these classes to help the children create better lives for themselves by using their imagination.[41]

For his ability to move children to follow him into his home, Paul Terry humorously labeled his father "The Pied Piper of Hamelin". A common occurrence for Paul and his friends was after a long day at work Joseph would board the cable car heading west along Geary Boulevard and Point Lobus Avenue which would then bank right heading south towards Golden Gate Park. As he exited the trolley car the children, many of whom had been playing in the rain, mud and dirt, would be waiting for him, including his son Paul, who would then follow him home for some more lessons sketched out on the blackboards. By the time these events occurred Paul was at least eight years old, because it was not until late 1895 or early 1896 that the Terry family residence had moved west from near city center to 335 11th Avenue in the eastern portion of the Richmond District of San Francisco.[42]

Between 1870 and 1900, America experienced rapid economic growth and expansion, especially in the North and West, a period of time which has been termed "the Gilded Age", a term coined by writers Mark Twain and Charles Dudley Warner in *The Gilded Age: A Tale of Today* (1873).[43] In their work, the two authors satirized what they believed to be an era of serious social problems disguised by thin gold gilding. The expansion during the Gilded Age was interrupted by the "Panic of 1893", an economic depression that had a profound effect on Terry family fortunes.

One of the problems with the rapid expansion during the Gilded Age was that it eventually became driven by railroad speculation. Railroads were over-built, incurring expenses that surpassed revenues. To add further economic problems, new mines flooded the market with silver, causing its price to plummet. In addition, farmers – particularly in wheat and cotton areas of the country – struggled under a decline in prices for agricultural commodities.[44] One of the first real indicators of financial trouble occurred on February 23, 1893, when the Philadelphia and Reading Railroad, which had greatly overextended itself 10 days before Grover Cleveland's second inauguration, declared bankruptcy. In addition, a failure in the Argentine wheat crop and a coup in Buenos Aires ended further investments. This

Chapter 3 • Birth of an Animation Pioneer

Fig. 3.5 – Paul Terry on the family farm (c. 1897).

shock started a run on gold in the U.S. Treasury, as investors were cashing in their investments.[45]

Upon becoming President, Grover Cleveland immediately began dealing directly with the Treasury crisis, and successfully convinced Congress to repeal the *Sherman Silver Purchase Act*, which he felt was mainly responsible for the economic crisis. As concern for the state of the economy worsened, people hurried to withdraw their money from banks in an escalating series of bank runs.[46] The credit crunch rippled through the economy. At the same time, a financial panic in the United Kingdom and a drop in trade in Europe caused foreign investors to sell American stocks to obtain American funds backed by gold.[47] A series of bank failures followed, and three giant railroad concerns, the Northern Pacific Railway, the Union Pacific Railroad and the Atchison, Topeka & Santa Fe Railroad, failed. These railroad bankruptcies were followed by the bankruptcy of many other companies.[48]

The causes of the Panic of 1893 and depression have been traced by historians to a number of reasons including the deflation since the Civil War, under-consumption (i.e. production of goods and services at a rate higher than could be consumed, resulting at some point in too large an inventory holding, so producers cut back on production and employment), government over spending and extravagance, or government purchases of a commodity – silver – for which it had no use. During the Panic of 1893 over 15,000 companies and 500 banks, many of them in the west, failed. According to high estimates, about 17 to 19 percent of the United States workforce was unemployed at the Panic's peak. The unemployment rate in Pennsylvania reached 25 percent, in New York 35 percent, and in Michigan 43 percent.[49]

The huge spike in unemployment, combined with the loss of life savings kept in failed banks, meant that a once-secure middle-class could not meet their mortgage obligations. Many walked away from recently built homes as a result. Soup kitchens were opened in order to help feed the destitute and starving. Facing starvation, people chopped wood, broke rocks, and sewed in exchange for food. In some cases, women resorted to prostitution to feed their families.[50]

The Panic of 1893 and the resulting depression caused major economic havoc in San Francisco as bankruptcies soared and the unemployed queued up in bread lines.[51] The economic blight of the mid-1890s was preceded by a stifling of the city's economic prosperity and growth through excessive freight rates charged by the monopoly of the Southern Pacific Railroad and the Pacific Mail Steamship Company. As a result, commercial groups brought about the entrance of the rival Atchison, Topeka and Santa Fe Railway into the Bay area, as well as gave impetus for the development of a new terminal city of Richmond in Contra Costa, California.[52]

As the result of the financial pressures put on the Terry family, it was necessary for Paul to earn his own pocket money. His first job as a young boy was at a nearby amusement park where his particular chores were that of hitching up goat carts, burros, and other equipment for children's rides at the park. In this way he had ample opportunity to observe the animals and their daily activities which would come in handy later when he was in the animation business drawing from his experiences with farm animals to produce the Farmer Al Falfa series of cartoon shorts.[53]

23

One of the first principles of wealth acquisition Terry acquired as a child was to focus on marketing goods which impelled the purchaser to return to the salesman to purchase additional goods after acquiring the original product. When he was a young teen, Paul developed a little business which consisted of trapping linnets (songbirds similar to the household finch) and selling them to people for pets.[54] Terry discovered that if he could sell a bird, he would make big profits from sales of bird food, bird cages and other aviary equipment. Then, once the bird died, Terry knew the owner would come back to him to buy another bird to put in the cage rather than have an empty cage sitting around the house and the cycle would repeat itself. In 1901, when Terry was 14 years of age, King Camp Gillette (1855–1932) and William Emery Nickerson invented the disposable safety razor, a razor with a disposable blade, making a fortune in the process. Whether Terry acquired this way of doing business from Gillette and Nickerson's success is unclear but later in life he heralded the development of the disposable safety razor as another example of this principle at work.[55]

With the economic depression already causing financial strains on the Terry family, a lawsuit brought against Joseph Terry added to the family's financial problems. In January 1896 the Supreme Court of California reversed the ruling of the Superior Court in the case of Grace Lewis against Joseph Terry. The lawsuit brought by Ms. Lewis was for damages for injuries she sustained as a result of the collapse of a folding-bed purchased from Joseph. The folding-bed was purchased from Terry by a third party, from whom the plaintiff Lewis had rented a room containing the aforesaid folding-bed. During her stay, the bed closed down on her arm one evening and broke it, and she sued Terry, the one who sold the bed, for damages.

Terry's lawyer argued in his demurrer that there was no contract of sale between the plaintiff Lewis and the defendant Terry and therefore no privity of contract.[56] The Supreme Court disagreed recognizing an implied contract on the part of the salesman for Terry's furniture store to sell folding-beds that were safe. The demurrer was therefore overruled and Terry was forced to pay damages to the plaintiff Lewis.[57]

The Panic of 1893 and resulting depression over the next five years resulted in economic ruin for the Terry family.[58] Joseph Terry's once prosperous furniture dealer and auctioneering business closed its doors in 1897. As a result, Joseph moved into the insurance business, a profession he would follow until his retirement, at an office at the corner of California and Sansome Streets in a region which is now the city's financial district.[59] That same year, the Terry family residence moved addresses south to 426 11th Avenue.[60] The U.S. economy began to recover in 1897. After the election of Republican McKinley, confidence was restored with the Klondike Gold Rush and the economy began 10 years of rapid growth.[61]

Joseph Terry loved children and certainly had his children's best interests at heart. If they showed any inclination, in any direction, whether it be music, drawing, or other passion, Joseph would smother them in it.[62] Paul Terry exhibited an early interest in drawing and at the same time tested his father's patience. As a very young child he would draw sketches on the wallpaper, and pilloried unpopular neighbors on chalk on the front steps.[63] His father's efforts in restraining Paul from continuing in these artistic activities met with failure. When Paul came across an animation flip book, a book with a series of pictures that vary gradually from one page to the next, so that when the pages are turned rapidly, the pictures appear to animate by simulating motion or some other change, he was not content with simply flipping the pages but went out and created his own flip book. This was Terry's first experience with animation.[64]

Paul Terry was educated at local schools in San Francisco. As a school child he applied himself to drawing to the detriment of the other school curricula. Paul considered himself "rather a dull kid"[65] and did not receive school grades that he would be proud to show his father. Rather than apply himself to mathematics or writing, Paul liked to draw, daydream and develop new ideas.[66] These same interests and ambitions would carry over into his work on stories for the animated cartoons he worked on and produced.

Throughout his life, Paul struggled with a speech disorder, stuttering. While his stuttering was

Chapter 3 • Birth of an Animation Pioneer

Fig. 3.6 – Terry Family (c. 1898) (left to right) Bottom row: Carrie Terry, Joseph Tripp Terry, Paul Terry. Top row: John C. Terry, Daniel Webster Donnelly (Carrie's husband), Alex Anderson (Olga Terry's husband), Olga Terry.

considered on the milder side, he experienced the usual flow of speech disrupted by involuntary repetitions and prolongations of sounds, syllables, words or phrases as well as involuntary silent pauses or blocks in which he was unable to produce sounds. As a result of his speech impediment, Terry experienced the usual teasing and insults common to school children with the disorder. Paul was also afflicted with poor eyesight necessitating the use of corrective lenses at an early age. As is typical with myopia and similar eye diseases, the condition would worsen as he got older and Paul would wear eye glasses for the rest of his life.[67]

One of his childhood dreams was to attend The World's Columbian Exposition (also known as The Chicago World's Fair) which was held in Chicago in 1893 to celebrate the 400th anniversary of Christopher Columbus' arrival in the New World in 1492.[68] Paul became inspired to draw caricatures that would enable him to earn an income and go to the Exposition. Over the two or three years leading up to the Fair, he became quite skilled at drawing caricatures. Although he never attended the Fair, he learned a valuable lesson that he just needed to apply himself to be successful, a new understanding far more important than going to the Fair.[69]

By 1900, the three youngest Terry children were still residing at home with their father. Paul's brother John was employed as a newspaper artist while Olga and Paul were continuing their studies at school.[70] Around this time period, when Paul was 13 years old, Olga became the primary caregiver around the house when their father was at work.[71] His father, although still advertising himself as an auctioneer, had established a thriving insurance practice, specializing in fire and accident indemnification, at an office at 325 California Street[72] and by 1901 at 214 Sansome Street. By 1902, Joseph had expanded his practice into loans for real estate purposes, as well as selling real estate and fire insurance. He represented a number of prominent real estate and insurance concerns including the Continental Building and Loan Association of San Francisco, the Phoenix Fire Insurance Company (of Hartford), London Guarantee and Accident Company, and the German American Fire Insurance Company.[73] While history may remember Joseph Terry as a lively raconteur and the owner and operator of one of California's largest furniture stores and auction houses during the last two decades of the 19th century, it was his later career in the insurance industry that provided the financial stability required to properly care for Paul and his siblings.

Notes

1. Events as recorded in: *The World Almanac Dictionary of Dates* (New York: Longman, 1982).

2. "War Clouds Still Black", *New York Times*, 19 February 1887, p. 1.

3. "Verdi's Success in Milan", *New York Times*, 20 February 1887, p. 11, col. 1.

TERRYTOONS: The Story of Paul Terry and His Classic Cartoon Factory

4. "Electric Bolts in Winter", *New York Times*, 19 February 1887, p. 1, col. 5.

5. "Testing a Heater: An Invention Designed to Solve the Car-Warming Problem", *New York Times*, 19 February 1887, p. 8.

6. "Unhealthy Meat Fed to Lunatics", *Chicago Tribune*, 19 February 1887, p. 1.

7. "A Post Office for Yale", *Hartford Courant* (CT), 19 February 1887, p. 4.

8. Thomas Stevens, *Around the World on a Bicycle* (Mechanicsburg, PA: Stackpole Books, 2001).

9. "Pacific Coast Items", *The Evening Bulletin* (San Francisco), 19 February 1887, p. 1.

10. "Pacific Coast Weather For The Week", *Pacific Rural Press*, 28 February 1887, p. 185.

11. San Francisco would receive .37 inches of rain on the 21st while San Mateo would receive .12 inches. "Pacific Coast Weather For The Week", p. 185; "The Rainfall", *Evening Bulletin* (San Francisco), 22 February 1887.

12. Sometimes incorrectly cited in the literature as Paul "Houghton" Terry.

13. Paul Terry, interview by Harvey Deneroff, New Rochelle, New York, 13 June 1970, John Canemaker Animation Collection, Fales Library, Elmer Holmes Bobst Library, New York University, New York City, 91.

14. Terry, interview, 20 December 1969, 6–7.

15. The birth notice simply reads: "TERRY – In San Mateo, February 19, to the wife of J. T. Terry, a son. "Born", *Morning Call* (San Francisco), 6 March 1887, p. 6, col. 7.

16. Joseph T. Terry to Isaiah Terry, 18 August 1887, Paul Terry Papers, Fayetteville, North Carolina.

17. Mitchell Postel, *San Mateo County: A Sesquicentennial History* (Belmont, CA: Star Pub. Co., 2007).

18. Erwin Gustave Gudde, *California Place Names: The Origin and Etymology of Current Geographical Names*, 3rd ed. (Berkeley, California: University of California Press, 1969).

19. For a history of San Mateo and San Mateo County see: Frank Merriman Stanger, *History of San Mateo County* (San Mateo, Calif., The San Mateo Times, 1938); Philip W. Alexander, *History of San Mateo County From the Earliest Times: With a Description of its Resources and Advantages: And the Biographies of its Representative Men* (Burlingame, Calif.: Press of Burlingame Publishing Co., 1916); *The Illustrated History of San Mateo County: The Reduced Facsimile of a Volume Entitled the Illustrated History of San Mateo County, published in 1878 by Moore and DePue*, 1st ed. (Woodside, Calif.: G. Richards Publications, [1974]); Roy Walter Cloud, *History of San Mateo County, California* (Chicago, S. J. Clarke Pub. Co., 1928); Frank Merriman Stanger, *South from San Francisco; San Mateo County, California, its History and Heritage* (San Mateo: San Mateo County Historical Association, 1963).

20. The establishment of *The Leader* and biographies of its founders is chronicled in Cloud, *History of San Mateo County, California.*

21. Terry, interview, 20 December 1969, 3.

22. Painter & Co., *Langley's San Francisco Directory, For the Year 1895* (San Francisco: J. B. Painter Co., 1885), 1445.

23. Terry, interview, 20 December 1969, 7.

24. Ibid., 2.

25. Paul noted in his interview that she had journeyed from Connecticut to take up residence in San Francisco. Terry, interview, 20 December 1969, 6.

26. In his 1969 interview Paul referred to the cornucopia and the figure holding the sheaves as being pieces from the Great Seal of California. Terry, interview, 20 December 1969, 7. Although the cornucopia figured prominently as a motif in California municipal and state government instruments it does not form part of the Great Seal.

27. Terry, interview, 20 December 1969, 4.

28. *Genealogy of Our Family*, 3; "Minnie Terry", Kremple & Halsted Funeral Records, San Francisco, San Francisco, California, Record Book vol. 1, 1883–1897, 16 Nov 1890, Public Library, History and Archive Center, Salt Lake City, Utah.

29. Arthur W. Hafner, ed., *Directory of Deceased American Physicians, 1804–1929: A Genealogical Guide to Over 149,000 Medical Practitioners Providing Brief Biographical Sketches Drawn from the American Medical Association's Deceased Physician Masterfile* (Chicago: American Medical Association, 1993).

30. In his 1969 interview, Paul guessed he was about a year old when she died but as to his memories of her: "It's just a blank". Terry, interview, 20 December 1969, 3–4.

31. "Probate Proceedings", *Daily Alta California*, 27 November 1890, p. 6. $3,200 adjusted for inflation is about $95,000 at the time of the publication of this book.

32. Terry, interview, 20 December 1969, 5.

33. "Lunch With Paul Terry", *The Cartoonist*, February 1967, p. 18.

34. Terry, interview, 20 December 1969, 3.

35. Ibid.; "Paul Terry, Creator of Terrytoons", *San Francisco Examiner*, undated (circa 1950).

36. Ibid.

37. Terry, interview, 13 June 1970, 89.

38. Paul Terry, "As Twigs are Bent Bows Will Grow", undated, Paul Terry Papers, Fayetteville, North Carolina, p. 1.

39. Ibid., 2.

40. Terry, interview, 20 December 1969, 5.

41. Terry, "As Twigs Are Bent Bows Will Grow", 2.

42. Paul mentions that when he was a child the Terry family home was out near the Cliff House in the Richmond District of San Francisco (Terry, interview, 20 December 1969, 5). However, searches of city directories during the period of 1887 to 1910 found that the Terry residences were all located no further west than 11th Avenue in the eastern area of the Richmond District. "The Richmond" is bounded roughly by Fulton Street to the south, Arguello Boulevard and Laurel Heights to the east, The Presidio National Park and

Chapter 3 • Birth of an Animation Pioneer

Lincoln Park to the north, and Ocean Beach and the Pacific Ocean to the west. Terry claimed that his house around the time he was five (1882–1883) was not far from the Pacific Ocean and that there was nothing between their house and the ocean except sand dunes. All night long the fog horns would blow and he could hear the booming of the surf. Terry, "As Twigs Are Bent Bows Will Grow", 1–2.

43. Full citation: Mark Twain and Charles Dudley Warner, *The Gilded Age: A Tale of To-day* (Hartford: American Pub. Co., 1873). For more on the Gilded Age, see Judith Freeman Clark, *America's Gilded Age: An Eyewitness History* (New York: Facts on File, 1992).

44. Brandon R. Dupont, "Panic in the Plains: Agricultural Markets and the Panic of 1893", *Cliometrica* 3(1) (January 2009): 27–54.

45. Sources referred to: William Jett Lauck, *The Causes of the Panic of 1893* (Boston, New York: Houghton, Mifflin and Company, 1907); Frank P. Weberg, *The Background of the Panic of 1893* (Washington, D.C.: The Catholic University of America, 1929); Frank Brown Latham, *The Panic of 1893; A Time of Strikes, Riots, Hobo Camps, Coxey's "army", Starvation, Withering Droughts, and Fears of "Revolution"* (New York, F. Watts, 1971).

46. Alexander D. Noyes, "The Banks and the Panic of 1893", *Political Science Quarterly* 9 (1) (March 1894): 12–30.

47. Douglas W. Steeples and David O. Whitten, *Democracy in Desperation: The Depression of 1893* (Westport, Conn.: Greenwood Press, 1998), 74.

48. E. G. Campbell, *The Reorganization of the American Railroad System, 1893–1900: A Study of the Effects of the Panic of 1893, the Ensuing Depression, and the First Years of Recovery on Railroad Organization and Financing* (New York: AMS Press, 1968).

49. Charles Hoffman, *The Depression of the Nineties: An Economic History* (Westport, CT: Greenwood Publishing, 1970), 109.

50. Samuel Reznick, "Unemployment, Unrest, and Relief in the United States During the Depression of 1893–97", *Journal of Political Economy* 61(4) (August 1953): 324–345.

51. Western U.S. banks fared well through the 1893–1897 depression as they lacked connections to the eastern banks which closed their doors.

52. Mel Scott, *The San Francisco Bay Area: A Metropolis in Perspective*, 2nd ed. (Berkeley: University of California Press, 1985), 87.

53. "Lunch With Paul Terry", 19.

54. Ibid.

55. Patricia Leahy and Caron Lazar, interview with author, August 11, 1999, Marriott Marquis Hotel, Atlanta, Georgia, p. 2.

56. The doctrine of privity in the common law of contract provides that a contract cannot confer rights or impose obligations arising under it on any person or agent except the parties to the contract. The premise is that only parties to contracts should be able to sue to enforce their rights or claim damages as such. However, the doctrine has proven problematic due to its implications upon contracts made for the benefit of third parties who are unable to enforce the obligations of the contracting parties.

57. "The Folding-Bed Closed", *San Francisco Call*, 22 January 1896, p. 7.

58. Terry, interview, 20 December 1969, 3; Terry, interview, 13 June 1970, 104.

59. H. S. Crocker Company, *Crocker-Langley San Francisco Directory 1897* (San Francisco: H. S. Crocker Company, 1897), 1665.

60. Crocker, *Crocker-Langley San Francisco Directory 1897*, 1665.

61. The rapid growth after 1897 was once again halted by another panic, this time by the Panic of 1907.

62. Terry, interview, 20 December 1969, 3.

63. Nancy Barr Mavity, "Romance Born in Studio With Terry's "Fables" Cat", *The Oakland Tribune*, 16 January 1928, p. D2.

64. Ibid.

65. Terry, interview, 20 December 1969, 10.

66. Ibid., 10–11.

67. "Lunch With Paul Terry", 19.

68. The exposition covered more than 600 acres (2.4 square km) (about 685 acres in total), featuring nearly 200 new (but purposely temporary) buildings of predominantly neoclassical architecture, canals and lagoons, and people and cultures from 46 countries. More than 27.5 million people attended the exposition during its six-month run. Its scale and grandeur far exceeded the other world fairs, and it became a symbol of the emerging American Exceptionalism. The Fair enjoyed a profit of $807,000. See: Norman Bolotin and Christine Laing, *The World's Columbian Exposition: the Chicago World's Fair of 1893* (Washington, D.C.: Preservation Press, 1992); John Allwood, *The Great Exhibitions* (London: Macmillan Publishers, 1977).

69. Terry, interview, 20 December 1969, 11.

70. United States of America, Bureau of the Census, *Twelfth Census of the United States, 1900*, "Schedule no. 1. – Population", Census Place: San Francisco, San Francisco, California, Roll: 105, Page: 10A, Enumeration District: 0221", Washington, D.C.: National Archives and Records Administration, 1900.

71. Terry, "As Twigs are Bent Bows Will Grow", p. 1.

72. H. S. Crocker Company, *Crocker-Langley San Francisco Directory 1901* (San Francisco: H. S. Crocker Company, 1901), 1684.

73. H. S. Crocker Company, *Crocker-Langley San Francisco Directory 1902* (San Francisco: H. S. Crocker Company, 1902), 1744.

Chapter 4

Explorations in Photography: Paul Terry's Start in the San Francisco Newspaper Industry, 1902–1906

In 1901,[1] Paul Terry began his high school studies at Polytechnic High School located at the corner of Bush and Stockton Streets in San Francisco.[2] He would spend three years at the educational institution, about 3.7 miles away from his residence located at 426 11th Avenue.[3] Polytechnic High School was originally called the Commercial School, was founded in 1884, and located on Powell Street between Clay Street and Sacramento Street. In 1890 academic subjects were added to the curriculum and in 1894 art and shop were introduced. In the fall of 1894 the school moved to the corner of Bush Street and Stockton Street. The school was officially named Polytechnic High School.[4] By the time of Paul's arrival, the institution was considered one of the leading schools in the city.[5]

Paul's time at Polytechnic was not much different from his earlier years in the public school system. His grades were far from impressive and he devoted most of his time to his art classes under the tutelage of Miss Maria Van Vleck and Miss Rosa Murdoch. Paul enjoyed their instruction and found these teachers warm and understanding, each having their own "way of inspiring their students to seek a place in the sun".[6] At Polytechnic, Paul belonged to the Poly Glee Club and was assigned to singing counterpoint to the main melody. His vocal abilities left a sour impression with the audience causing one spectator to gaze upon him with a "sort of fish eye". It wasn't long before he was tossed out of the group.[7]

While in high school, to earn some extra money Paul found work as an usher at a vaudeville theater.[8] These early experiences in vaudeville would provide him with the inspiration to later develop his own vaudeville act with his brother John. Around this period of time, Paul began developing ambitions to become a naval architect.[9] He soon found work as an illustrator for S. N. Wood & Co., tailors and a retailer of men and boy's clothing representing Columbian Woolen Mills. S. N. Wood & Co. was operated by four partners, including most notably author and manufacturer Benjamin Wood (b. 1865, Monitor, California). Wood was the author of *The Successful Man of Business* (1900), which outlines the general principles upon which successful businesses are founded, written in prose, and *Bugle Calls* (1901), a book promoting the labor movement.[10] Other principals were Samuel N. Wood, Meyer Wood, and Abraham Peyser. In 1902, the company had stores located at 718–722 Market Street and the NW corner of Powell Street and Eddy Street.[11] In November 1907, in an effort to rebuild after the 1906 quake, the company would open up a large store in San Francisco, the largest concrete building in the world at the time.[12]

During his employment at S. N. Wood & Co., Terry worked alongside painter Randal William Borough[13] and both were responsible for stipple drawings, an ink drawing technique where the artist applies tone and texture in small dots. By varying the density and distribution of the dots, the illustrator can adjust the depth of tone and the roughness of texture. Both Terry and Borough were responsible for creating advertising art for the company's clothing products. A photographer would first take pictures of models for clothing. Terry and Borough would then make stipple drawings from the photographs and take the wrinkles out of the clothing or put folds in wherever they were necessary polishing them up in pen and ink.[14]

Eager to showcase his artistic skills, while continuing his studies at Polytechnic Paul Terry found work providing illustrations for *The Stanford Chaparral*, the official humor magazine of Stanford University.[15] The serial first began publication by students of Stanford University in October 1899. Legendary Walt Disney animators Frank Thomas and Ollie Johnston, and Disney writer/director/producer James Algar, would later contribute to the periodical. Randal Borough was also a member of the artistic staff of the *Chaparral*.[16] Terry would continue to contribute to the magazine after he had left high school with the hopes of one day attending Stanford University.[17] The *Chaparral* has always had a dedication to the production of quality humor and the illustrations completed by Terry and submitted to the serial were well rendered and very comical.

Paul adored his brother and considered him his "idol". As far as Paul was concerned, "Everything he (John) did was right, no matter what he did".[18] Paul wanted to follow in the footsteps of his brother. Terry later admitted that like a dog following a little kid, "I'd wag my tail and I'd follow him".[19] In 1904, Paul decided to follow his brother John into the newspaper business. John Terry, nearly seven years older than Paul, studied at local public schools and attended the Mark Hopkins Art Institute in San Francisco, California throughout 1899 and the early part of 1900.[20]

John began his artistic career as a newspaper cartoonist on the San Francisco *Call* around June 1900 drawing illustrations for Sunday feature articles. At this time, most of the other illustrators and cartoonists in the *Call* bullpen were Hopkins alumni as well including cartoonist, Gustavo A. Bronstrup. During this time, John produced mostly wrap-around art for the *Call*'s book review page, sometimes in collaboration with illustrators Henry Ivens Hawxhurst (1877–1962) and George Edward Parmenter (1875–1946), who had been Terry's classmates at the Hopkins Institute.[21]

In 1901, the three artists left the *Call* and formed "Parmenter, Terry & Hawxhurst", a short lived art studio. John Terry moved to Anaconda, Montana in 1901 [1902] to work as a cartoonist for the *Anaconda Standard*. As part of his duties, he was the Sunday editorial cartoonist for the *Standard*, penning cartoons that reflected the politics and topics of the day. His early work for the *Standard* is rough, unsophisticated and restricted in style highlighting a lack of understanding of the finer elements of cartooning. However, by 1903 John developed an appealing cartooning style that he would personalize and further refine later in his career. Within only a few years, John Terry's skills as an artist enabled him to become head of the *Standard*'s art department.

With his brother achieving considerable success as a newspaper cartoonist in Montana, Paul began looking for a job in the tabloid industry in San Francisco. During the first decade of the 20th century there were dozens of presses for Paul to choose from in San Francisco. Based on circulation figures, the four largest papers were the San Francisco *Examiner*, *Chronicle*, *Bulletin*, and *Call*. The largest circulating newspaper in San Francisco in 1903 was the *Examiner* with circulation of 144,260[22] in a city having a population base of approximately 365,000.[23] In the spring of 1904, Paul was offered a job as an office boy for the *Bulletin*, an offer he quickly accepted.

The newspaper was first published as the *Daily Evening Bulletin* on October 8, 1855. The paper was founded by James King of William, who was also editor of the newspaper. King was shot dead by James P. Casey of the rival *Weekly Sunday Times* in 1856. His shooting death resulted in the establishment of the second San Francisco Vigilance Committee and changed the politics of the city. King was among the first newspapermen to be honored by the California Journalism Hall of Fame. Casey was subsequently hanged by local vigilantes. At King's death, James W. Simonton obtained a half-interest. Thomas King, brother of James, took over the *Bulletin* with C. O. Gerberding as

Fig. 4.1 – Newspaper row, San Francisco, California (c. 1904). Left to right: Chronicle Building, Examiner Building, Call Building.

part-owner. Gerberding sold his portion to George K. Fitch (Deacon Fitch). Fitch bought the holdings of his partners, James Nesbitt, F. Tuthill, and Leland Bartlett, but sold a portion to New Hampshire-born Loring Pickering.[24]

By 1860, Simonton, formerly a successful *New York Times* journalist, was in editorial control of the newspaper.[25] Pickering had made his fortune in the newspaper business in St. Louis, Missouri and had become an elected member of the state legislature and a director of the Bank of Missouri. He headed west during the California gold rush in 1848 where he purchased the *Placer Times* and combined it with the Sacramento *Transcript* to form the *Times-Transcript* then moved the merged newspaper to San Francisco. He sold that newspaper to purchase the *Alta California* in 1855. He would then sell the *Alta California* to find the capital to purchase an interest in the *Bulletin* teaming up with Simonton.[26]

In 1869, Fitch, Pickering, and Simonton owned the San Francisco *Call* and San Francisco *Bulletin*, Pickering managing the *Call* and Fitch the *Bulletin*. Simonton went east to become president of the Associated Press and his partners ran the San Francisco paper. Fitch's *Bulletin* vigorously protested against municipal extravagance, bond issues, the stock exchange, and tried to hold the tax rate at $1. Pickering's *Call* developed news, and published spicy scandals. The *Bulletin*'s circulation fell below 10,000, the *Call* paying its losses.[27]

After the death of Pickering in 1892, the newspaper was put up at an auction sale in 1895 and purchased by Robert Crothers, Rose Crothers Pickering, widow of Loring, and her minor son, Loring.[28] Crothers was born in Clarenceville, Québec, Canada, graduated from McGill University in 1876 and received a law degree there two years later. He came to San Francisco in 1891 and became business manager of the *Bulletin* and the *Call*. After purchasing the *Bulletin* he then in 1897 persuaded Fremont Older to leave his post as city editor of the *Morning Call* to become managing editor of the *Bulletin*.[29] Older came from an impoverished Wisconsin family whose male members of the family had been decimated during the American Civil War. Older was an imposing figure at six-foot-two with an athletic physique. Along with his attractive and intelligent wife, the couple made news nearly every

Fig. 4.2 – San Francisco Chronicle Building (c. 1904).

Chapter 4 • Explorations in Photography

Fig. 4.3 – Gandy Goose and Sourpuss, animation cel for the Terryscopes machine.

time they stepped out into the public spotlight.

At the time of the Older's hiring, the *Bulletin* was struggling and losing $3,000 a month.[30] Older's ambition was to stimulate circulation by developing stories that would catch the interest of the readers by publishing articles that mixed sensationalism with moral zeal while continuing the *Bulletin*'s long history of fighting lawlessness and political corruption in the city. He also introduced novelties to the newspaper including factual serials. Donald Lowrie's *My Life in Prison*, *The Healing of Sam Leake*, and Alice Smith's *Voice from the Underworld*, skyrocketed sales.[31] To Older, the character of the stories did not matter even if the articles made people suffer, or would outright wound someone. Older would become best known for his campaigns against civic corruption and support of Tom Mooney and Warren Billings, wrongly convicted of the Preparedness Day bombing of 1916. Older was a lifelong opponent of capital punishment

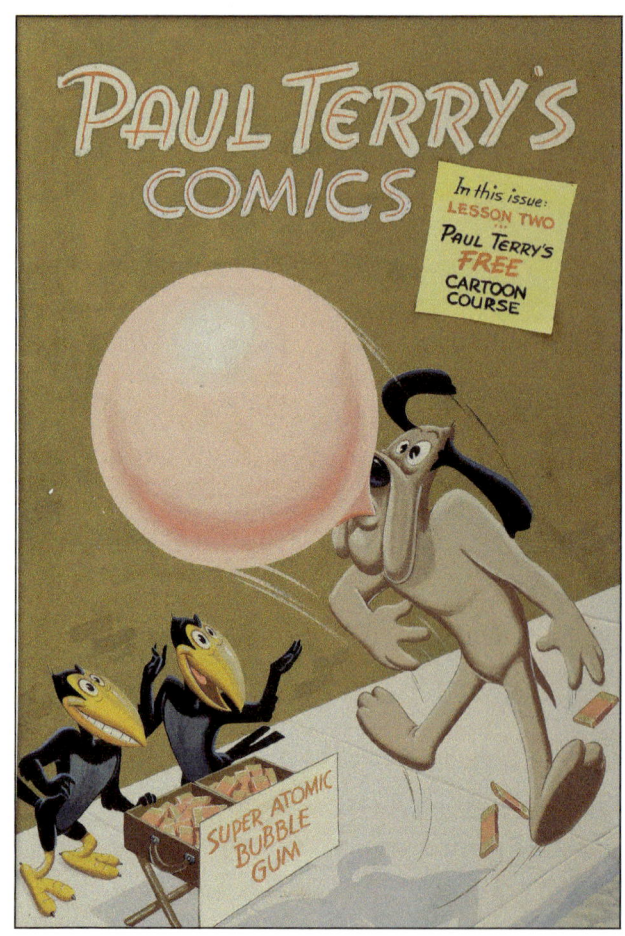

TERRYTOONS: The Story of Paul Terry and His Classic Cartoon Factory

Fig. 4.4 – *Paul Terry's Comics* cover.

Bulletin in 1891 at the age of 14 working for $5 a week.[34] Like Terry, Polytechnic High School art teachers Rosa Murdoch and Maria Van Vleck recognized and encouraged Tad's talent as an artist.[35] He created his first comic strip, *Johnny Wise*, for the *San Francisco Chronicle* in 1902.

By 1905 Dorgan was working in New York City at the *New York Journal* as a sports writer and cartoonist. He is best known for his cartoon panel *Indoor Sports* and the many words and expressions he added to the language including "dumb-bell", "cake-eater", and "drug-store cowboy". Four years earlier, the *Bulletin* hired Haig Patigian as member of their art staff. Haig would later establish himself as one of America's premier sculptors. His statuary works include the McKinley statue in Arcata, California (1906), the General John Pershing, San Francisco, California (1921), Abraham Lincoln, San Francisco, California (1928), and Thomas Starr King, National Statuary Hall Collection, The Capitol, Washington D.C.[36]

and he took active moves designed to abolish the death penalty in California.[32] He later wrote *My Own Story*, a book which focused on the San Francisco newspaper and political scene 1895–1917, rather than on Older's biography.[33]

Older had a unique gift for attracting talent. The *Bulletin* became the testing ground for writers and artists who afterward achieved national fame: Sinclair Lewis; playwright Maxwell Anderson; Rose Wilder Lane of the *Saturday Evening Post*; and dramatist Bayard Veiller. Among others on the paper were Judge Sylvester McAtee, Congressman Franck Havenner, and John Coghlan, later vice-president of the Pacific Gas and Electric Company. At the time of Terry's hire, the *Bulletin* could already boast of having employed a number of very notable newspaper cartoonists, the most noteworthy being Thomas Aloysius Dorgan ("Tad"). Dorgan began his career in the art department of the

Upon being hired, Paul Terry diligently applied himself at the San Francisco *Bulletin*. Unfortunately for Terry, there was little opportunity at the newspaper for the aspiring artist to break into the cartooning business. During Paul's approximate one-year tenure at the *Bulletin*, the cartoon bullpen at the newspaper included such talented artists as Ralph Oswald Yardley and Russell Westover. By 1904 Yardley was an experienced cartoonist having spent time as a quick sketch artist

Chapter 4 • Explorations in Photography

with the San Francisco *Examiner* (1897–1898) and *San Francisco Chronicle* (1899–1901), and as a cartoonist with the *Honolulu Advertiser* (1901–1902) before joining the *Bulletin* that year.[37] Russell Channing Westover, although only 18 years old and just a year older than Terry (born on March 8, 1886, Los Angeles, California), was a highly promising artist when he joined the *Bulletin* as a sports cartoonist in 1904. He is best known for his long-running comic strip *Tillie the Toiler* after he sold the strip to King Features Syndicate in 1921.[38]

Herb Roth, the son of a Hungarian sculptor, also began his career in 1904 as an office boy on the *Bulletin* earning $5 a week. Like Terry he attended Polytechnic High School and was a pupil of Maria Van Vleck and Rosa Murdoch. Terry and Roth were high school pals and would remain lifelong friends until Roth's death in 1953. They would later meet in New York City where both became employed as cartoonists. Roth would quit his job at the *Bulletin* and went to Europe where he studied art in Munich. He later studied boxing and became a champion heavyweight boxer in Bavaria. He returned to the United States and became an illustrator for the *New York World* in 1910. He is most noted for his 30-year collaboration with panel cartoonist H. T. Webster. Webster is known for the cartoons *The Timid Soul*, *Bridge*, and *Life's Darkest Moments*. Roth also illustrated magazine articles for Robert Benchley and Irvin S. Cobb and about a dozen children's books for Peter Pauper Press in Mount Vernon, New York.[39]

In 1905, Terry was joined at the *Bulletin* by Reuben Lucius Goldberg and shared the office with him. Goldberg was also classmate of Terry's at Polytechnic High School.[40] In grammar school, Goldberg went to school with Terry's brother John.[41] Goldberg is best known for a series of popular cartoons depicting complicated gadgets that perform simple tasks in indirect, drawn-out ways. Goldberg received numerous honors in his lifetime, including a Pulitzer Prize for his political cartooning in 1948 and the Banshees' Silver Lady Award in 1959. Goldberg was a founding member and the first president of the National Cartoonists Society, and he is the namesake of the Reuben Award, which the organization awards to the Cartoonist of the Year. He is the inspiration for multiple international competitions, known as Rube Goldberg Machine Contests, which test participants to create a complicated machine to perform a very simple task.

Earlier, Goldberg went to work for the *Chronicle* as a sports cartoonist after graduation in 1904 and remained there until 1905 when he went to work for the *Bulletin*, where he remained until he moved to New York City in 1907. Goldberg produced several comic strip or cartoon panel series simultaneously, including *Mike and Ike (They Look Alike)*, *Boob McNutt*, *Foolish Questions*, *"Lala Palooza"* and *The Weekly Meeting of the Tuesday Women's Club*. The cartoons that brought him lasting fame involved a character named Professor Lucifer Gorgonzola Butts. In that series, Goldberg drew labeled schematics of the comical "inventions" that would later bear his name.[42]

By the spring of 1905, Paul Terry decided to move from the *Bulletin* and began seeking opportunities elsewhere. He found work at the Norman Pierce Company, a printing, engraving and designing firm located at 36 Geary Street.[43] Paul was eventually given some interest by the *Chronicle*, but if he wanted a job as their office boy he had to learn how to use a camera. Paul decided to ask the clothing photographer at S. N. Wood & Co. whether he could give him a speedy lesson in how to take a good photograph. Over the weekend the eager Terry was given the basics on how to operate a camera and take a photograph. The newly trained photographer then went back to the *Chronicle* office where they sent him out to take a photograph of a streetcar coming up Market Street. Terry was fortunate enough to take a great photograph of a cable car and was offered a job as an office boy and photographer with the paper.[44] As part of his work as a photographer he was required to go around the city and shoot the photograph the editor wanted, even under the most trying circumstances. As a result, Terry acquired some aggressiveness which helped him tremendously when he moved into the nascent world of animation in the mid-1910s.[45]

Unlike the *Bulletin*, the *Chronicle* belonged to one family, the de

33

Fig. 4.5 – Animation background for *The Witch's Cat* (1948).

Youngs. The newspaper was founded by Meichel Harry de Young and his brother Charles. Meichel was born in St. Louis, Missouri on October 1, 1848. He was taken to California in 1854 and settled in San Francisco where on January 16, 1865, he began to publish with his brother Charles, a small advertising sheet called the *Dramatic Chronicle* distributed free in stores, hotels, and places of amusement. Their capital was $20, but within a short time the net receipts of the paper aggregated about $1,000 a month, and by the end of the year $2,000 a month.[46] On September 1, 1868, the *Morning Chronicle* appeared proclaiming to support "no party, no clique, no faction ...We shall be independent in all things, neutral in nothing".[47] Charles de Young managed the editorials while Meichel had charge of the business.

After shooting and wounding Isaac C. Kalloch, a Baptist minister running for mayor, Charles de Young was shot dead by Kalloch's son on April 27, 1880. Kalloch pleaded self-defense and was acquitted while a witness to shooting, Clemshaw, was sent to prison for perjury. As a result of his brother's death, Meichel became editorial and financial manager. He remained in that position until his death on February 15, 1925 in San Francisco, California. In 1890, he erected the Chronicle building, a 10 story structure. His other notable achievements included owner of the Alcazar theater in San Francisco, representation as state delegate to the Republican national conventions in 1888 and 1892, president of the International League of Press Clubs, and director of the Associated Press (1882).[48]

His most notable achievements were as president and director-general of the California Mid-Winter International Exposition of 1894, commonly referred to as the "Midwinter Exposition" or the "Midwinter Fair", a World's Fair that operated from January 27 to July 5[1] in San Francisco's Golden Gate Park. In 1892, U.S. President Benjamin Harrison appointed de Young as a national commissioner to the 1893 World's Columbian Exposition held in Chicago. The San Francisco fair was the idea of de Young. The fair encompassed 200 acres centered on the park's current Music Concourse. More than 100 buildings were erected for the exposition, and more than two million people visited. The most enduring legacies are the Palace of Fine Arts, which became the M. H. de Young Memorial Museum (and has been rebuilt in a much different design); and the park's famed Japanese Tea Garden.[49]

If Terry found it difficult trying to break into the cartoon bullpen at the *Bulletin*, he would find it no easier at the *Chronicle*. At the time, the newspaper had arguably one of the most talented and creative newspaper cartoonists in the country, Bud Fisher (1885–1954).[50] Fisher had joined the *Chronicle* as a layout man. While with the *Chronicle*, he conceived the idea for a daily comic strip, *Augustus Mutt*, which eventually became the world-famous *Mutt and Jeff*. At the height of his fame, he made $4,600 a week from his syndicated comic strip, and had frequent vaudeville engagements, royalties from books, animated cartoon films, and stage shows.[51]

For Terry, the move to the *Chronicle* was a step up in responsibility. No longer was he confined to the office and assigned an assortment of

Chapter 4 • Explorations in Photography

rudimentary tasks handed down by the editor and his senior crew. Rather, as part of his new position he now could tour the city and photograph the people, places, and events that would hopefully make the front page of the newspaper. At the time, the editor of the newspaper was John Philip Young who began his career at the age of 20 in 1869 when he assisted in the establishment of the *Daily Union* of San Diego, California later taking over the city editorship of the *San Francisco Chronicle*. He joined the *Chronicle*'s editorial staff in 1877, and in 1878 became managing editor.[52]

Young was a historian, writer, and pedant. He enjoyed systematically collecting data on a great variety of economic and historical subjects. He wrote articles for the *Chronicle*, writings which include *Bimetallism or Monometallism* (1896), *Protection and Progress* (1900) and *Modern Trusts* (1902)

before they were published in other collections. His *Journalism in California*, published in 1915, provided a scholarly and exhaustive treatment of the history of journalism and the newspaper industry in California during the 19th and early 20th centuries.[53] He would remain with the newspaper until his death in 1921.[54]

While employed at the *Chronicle*, Paul began studying Latin at Grauman's Institute, a night school based in San Francisco.[55] Since Paul had not graduated from high school he was making up some coursework in an attempt to be admitted to Stanford University. At the same time he was also continuing to draw cartoons for Stanford's *The Chaparral*. Paul was a busy young man but was he determined to earn an income while acquiring the educational credits required for admittance to Stanford University.

The university was founded in 1885 by Leland Stanford and his wife Jane Lathrop Stanford who from 1885 to 1905 donated over $40 million in assets (over 1 billion dollars adjusted for inflation) to the university. Despite her good intentions Jane's actions were sometimes eccentric. She forbade students from sketching nude models in life-drawing class, banned automobiles from campus, and did not allow a hospital to be constructed so that people would not form an impression that Stanford was unhealthy. In 1906, all the students attending the university were self-supporting, many living in poverty, as the institution was financially in trouble despite the Stanford's generous gifts.[56] While Paul's earnest intention was to attend the university, his path in life would be forever changed on April 18, 1906. ❧

Notes

1. All records housed at Polytechnic High School were burnt in the fire that followed the April 18, 1906 quake. Therefore, exact dates of his admittance to Polytechnic are not known. Paul mentioned he worked for the San Francisco Bulletin beginning in 1904 and then was with the *San Francisco Chronicle* for about a year before the quake hit the city. If he was a student at Polytechnic for three years as he states in his 1969 interview (p. 9) before quitting and joining the *Bulletin* staff, he was likely admitted as a student at Polytechnic in 1901 or 1902.

2. H. S. Crocker Company, *Crocker-Langley San Francisco Directory 1905* (San Francisco: H. S. Crocker Company, 1905), 57.

3. H. S. Crocker Company, *Crocker-Langley San Francisco Direc-

tory 1904* (San Francisco: H. S. Crocker Company, 1904), 1803.

4. *San Francisco Chronicle*, 20 July 1894; *San Francisco Chronicle*, 24 November 1894; *San Francisco Chronicle*, 26 November 1985; *San Francisco Chronicle*, 10 December 1987; *San Francisco Examiner*, 19 April 1972.

5. By 1900, 950 students were attending classes. Shortly thereafter, the commercial classes separated from Poly and created Commerce High School. Only 120 students remained at Poly.

6. "Paul Terry Remembers 'Hot Time in The Old Town'", *Polytechnic Parrot* (San Francisco), 25 April 1957.

7. "Paul Terry Remembers."

8. "Lunch With Paul Terry", 19.

9. Leahy and Lazar, interview, 4.

10. "Wood, Benjamin", *Who Was Who in America*, volume IV (1961–1968) (Chicago, Illinois: Marquis Who's Who Inc., 1968), 1029.

11. H. S. Crocker Company, *Crocker-Langley San Francisco Directory 1902* (San Francisco: H. S. Crocker Company, 1902), 1900.

12. "S. N. Wood & Co.'s New Clothing Store Open For Business To-Morrow", *San Francisco Call*, 14 April 1905, p. 4; "S. N. Wood & Co. Open Big Store in Market", *San Francisco Call*, 24 November 1907, p. 32.

13. Randal Borough (b. 1878, Memphis, Tennessee; d. 1951, Sarasota, Florida) was a portrait painter, advertising artist, and art director. He later in 1913 joined the advertising agency of Lord, Thomas & Logan, where he eventually became the vice president

35

and art director. "Randal Borough", *New York Times*, 6 February 1951, p. 27:5; Peter Hastings Falk, ed., *Who Was Who in American Art, 1564–1975: 400 Years of Artists in America* (Madison, CT: Sound View Press, 1999), 386.

14. Terry, interview, 20 December 1969, 12.

15. Ibid, 9.

16. "Junior Class Annual Quickly Disposed of", *San Francisco Call*, 14 May 1903, p. 16; Didier Ghez, ed., *Walt's People: Talking Disney With the Artists Who Knew Him*, volume 9 (Bloomington, IN: Xlibris Corporation, 2010), 99.

17. Terry, interview, 20 December 1969, 9.

18. Terry, interview, 13 June 1970, 91.

19. Ibid., 92.

20. General biographical information on John Terry can be referenced in: Doris Ostrander Dawdy, *Artists of the American West: A Biographical Dictionary* (Chicago: Sage Books, 1974–1985); *Who's Who in American Art*, 1st edition (New Providence, NJ: Marquis Who's Who, 1936); Edan Milton Hughes, *Artists in California, 1786–1940*, 3rd ed. (Sacramento, CA: Crocker Art Museum, 2002); Donald Crafton, *Before Mickey: The Animated Film, 1898–1928* (Cambridge, Mass.: MIT Press, 1982). His obituary is found in: "John C. Terry", *Variety*, 6 March 1934, 71.

21. "Press Club Show Today", *The San Francisco Call*, 18 April 1913, p. 2; "Local Artist's Work Will Be Displayed", *The Oakland Tribune*, 27 June 1915, p. 20; "San Francisco", *Moving Picture World*, volume 22, no. 4, 24 October 1914, 517.

22. Winifred Gregory, ed., *American Newspapers 1821–1936: A Union List of Files Available In The United States and Canada* (New York: Kraus Reprint Corp., 1967), 50–51; Ian Gordon, *Comic Strips and Consumer Culture, 1890–1945* (Washington: Smithsonian Institute Press, 1998), 161; *N.W. Ayer & Son's American Newspaper Annual* (Philadelphia: N.W. Ayer and Son, 1880–1909).

23. An estimate based on the San Francisco U.S. Census city populations of 1900 (342,782) and 1910 (416,912).

24. Cora Older, *San Francisco: Magic City* (New York: Longmans, Green & Co., 1961), 61.

25. The obituary of James Simonton (1822–1882) can be found at: "James W. Simonton", *Sacramento Daily Union*, 4 November 1882, p. 8.

26. "Pickering, Loring", *The National Cyclopaedia of American Biography*, vol. 25 (New York: James T. White & Co., 1936), 107.

27. Older, *San Francisco*, 61.

28. Ibid., 61–62; John C. Ralston, *Fremont Older & the 1916 San Francisco Bombing: A Tireless Crusade for Justice* (Charleston, South Carolina: The History Press, 2013), 12.

29. "Robert Crothers, Retired Publisher", *New York Times*, 8 February 1945, p. 19:3.

30. Older, *San Francisco*, 62.

31. Ibid.

32. "Fremont Older, 78, Dies in California", *New York Times*, 4 March 1935, p. 17:3.

33. Fremont Older, *My Own Story* (Oakland: The Post-Enquirer Publishing Co., 1925).

34. "'Tad,' Cartoonist, Dies In His Sleep", *New York Times*, 3 May 1929, p. 25:3.

35. Amy McCrory, "Sport Cartoons in Context: TAD Dorgan and Multi-Genre Cartooning in Early Twentieth-Century Newspapers", *American Periodicals: A Journal of History, Criticism, and Bibliography* 18(1) (2008): 45–68.

36. Haig Patigian was born on January 22, 1876 in the city of Van, Armenia and died on September 19, 1950 in San Francisco, California. His parents were teachers at the American Mission School in Armenia. He was largely self-taught as a sculptor. Patigian spent most of his career in San Francisco, California and most of his works are located in California. The Oakland Museum in Oakland, California, includes a large number of his works in its collection. For further biographical information on Patigian see: James D. Hart, *A Companion to California* (New York: Oxford University Press, 1978); *The National Cyclopaedia of American Biography*, volume 18 (New York: James T. White & Co.,

1922); *Who Was Who in America. A Component of Who's Who in American History*, volume III, 1951–1960 (Chicago: Marquis Who's Who, 1966); Falk, *Who Was Who in American Art* (1999); Glenn B. Opitz, *Mantle Fielding's Dictionary of American Painters, Sculptors & Engravers* (Poughkeepsie NY: Apollo Book, 1986).

37. Yardley spent the years 1905–1907 in New York City in the art department of the *Globe*. He would move back to California to work as manager of the art department for the San Francisco *Call* (1908–1910). For more than three years he did freelance magazine cover work in New York for *Harper's*, *Leslie's* and other national periodicals. In 1919 Yardley opened a commercial studio in San Francisco and supplied the *Bulletin* a cartoon daily for its editorial page until 1922 when he left to join the *Stockton Record* in the city of his birth on September 2, 1878. He retired in 1952 and died on December 6, 1961, in San Joaquin, California. "Yardley, Ralph O.", in *Who's Who on the Pacific Coast* (Chicago: A. N. Marquis Company, Chicago, Illinois, 1951); 770; Falk, *Who Was Who in American Art*, 1999.

38. Westover was 80 when he died on May 3, 1966 in San Rafael, California. His work is archived at the Huntington Library in San Marino, California. Maurice Horn, ed., *The World Encyclopedia of Comics*, two volumes (New York: Chelsea House Publishers, 1976); *Who Was Who in America*, volume VII, 1977–1981 (Chicago: Marquis Who's Who, 1981); Falk, *Who Was Who in American Art*.

39. Falk, *Who Was Who in American Art*; Fridolf Johnson, ed., *Treasury of American Pen-and-Ink Illustration, 1881 to 1938: 236 Drawings by 103 Artists* (New York: Dover Publications, 1982). Newspaper articles on Herb Roth can be found in the *Larchmont Times* and New Rochelle *Standard-Star* ("Herb Roth, Illustrator, Takes Great Part in Larchmont Community Affairs", 18 December 1931). His obituaries include: "Herb Roth, Continued Webster Cartoons", *New York Times*, 28 October 1953, p. 29:2; "'Herb' Roth, Cartoonist, Dies; Lived in Larchmont Since '20s", [*The Standard-Star*], 28 October 1953.

40. Stephen Becker, *Comic Art in*

Chapter 4 • Explorations in Photography

America (New York: Simon and Schuster, 1959), p. 98.

41. Terry, interview, 13 June 1970, 115.

42. *ASCAP Biographical Dictionary*, fourth edition, compiled for the American Society of Composers, Authors and Publishers by Jaques Cattell Press (New York: R.R. Bowker, 1980); *Contemporary Authors, New Revision Series. A Bio-Bibliographical Guide to Current Writers in Fiction, General Nonfiction, Poetry, Journalism, Drama, Motion Pictures, Television, and Other Fields*, volume 9 (Detroit: Gale Research, 1983); Donald Paneth, *The Encyclopedia of American Journalism* (New York: Facts on File, 1983); *Who Was Who in America*, volume VII, 1977–1981; W.J. Burke and Will D. Howe, *American Authors and Books. 1640 to the Present Day*, third revised edition, revised by Irving Weiss and Anne Weiss (New York: Crown Publishers, 1972); *Contemporary Authors. A Bio-Bibliographical Guide to Current Writers in Fiction, General Nonfiction, Poetry, Journalism, Drama, Motion Pictures, Television, and Other Fields*, volumes 5–8, 1st revision (Detroit: Gale Research, 1969); *Dictionary of American Biography*, supplement 8 (London: Collier Macmillan Publishers, [1988]); *Who Was Who in America*, volume VI, 1974–1976 (Chicago: Marquis Who's Who, 1976); *Who Was Who Among North American Authors, 1921–1939*, compiled from *Who's Who among North American Authors*, volumes 1–7, 1921–1939, two volumes (Detroit: Gale Research, 1976); Elizabeth A. Brennan and Elizabeth C. Clarage, *Who's Who of Pulitzer Prize Winners* (Phoenix, AZ: Oryx Press, 1999); Horn, *The World Encyclopedia of Comics*. Obituary: Alden Whitman, "Rube Goldberg, Cartoonist, Dies at 87", *New York Times*, 8 December 1970, p. 1:4, 51:1; "Rube Goldberg Honored at Rites", *New York Times*, 11 December 1970, p. 50:3.

43. H. S. Crocker Company, *Crocker-Langley San Francisco Directory 1905* (San Francisco: H. S. Crocker Company, 1905), 1805.

44. Terry, interview, 20 December 1969, 12.

45. "Lunch With Paul Terry", 19.

46. Rossiter Johnson, ed., *The Twentieth Century Biographical Dictionary of Notable Americans*, volume III (Boston: Biographical Society, 1904).

47. Older, *San Francisco*, 71.

48. *Who Was Who in America. A Component Volume of Who's Who in American History*, volume I, 1897–1942 (Chicago: A.N. Marquis Co., 1943), p. 320; *National Cyclopaedia of American Biography*, volume I (New York: James T. White & Co., 1898), 269. Obituary: "Low Mass for De Young: Publisher of San Francisco Chronicle Buried With Simplest Rites", *New York Times*, 19 February 1925, p. 19.

49. *Official Guide to the California Midwinter Exposition in Golden Gate Park, San Francisco*, 1st ed. (San Francisco, G. Spaulding & Co., 1894); Arthur Chandler & Marvin Nathan, *The Fantastic Fair: The Story of the California Midwinter International Exposition, Golden Gate Park, San Francisco, 1894* (St. Paul, Minnesota: Pogo Press, 1993); *The Official History of the California Midwinter International Exposition. A Descriptive Record of the Origin, Development and Success of the Great Industrial Expositional Enterprise, Held in San Francisco from January to July, 1894*, compiled from the Official Records of the Exposition and Published by Authority of the Executive Committee (San Francisco, H.S. Crocker Co., 1894).

50. Paul Terry confirms that Bud Fisher was at the *Chronicle* when he was there: Terry, interview, 20 December 1969, 12. They would end up sharing offices together: Becker, *Comic Art in America*, 98.

51. Charles Van Doren, ed., *Webster's American Biographies* (Springfield, MA: G. & C. Merriam Co., 1979); *Who Was Who in Journalism, 1925–1928. A Consolidation of all Material Appearing in the 1928 Edition of Who's Who in Journalism, With Unduplicated Biographical Entries from the 1925 Edition of Who's Who in Journalism, Originally Compiled by M.N. Ask (1925 and 1928 editions) and S. Gershanek (1925 edition)* (Detroit: Gale Research, 1978); Burke and Howe, *American Authors and Books. 1640 to the Present Day; Dictionary of American Biography*, supplement 5 (New York: Charles Scribner's Sons, 1977); Ron Goulart, ed., *The Encyclopedia of American Comics* (New York: Facts on File, 1990); *Who Was Who in America*, volume III; Falk, *Who Was Who in American Art* (1999); *The National Cyclopaedia of American Biography*, volume 43 (New York: James T. White & Co., 1961); Horn, *The World Encyclopedia of Comics*; Jerry Robinson, *The Comics: An Illustrated History of Comic Strip Art* (New York: G.P. Putnam's Sons, 1974), 45. Obituary: "Harry C. (Bud) Fisher, Creator Of 'Mutt and Jeff', Is Dead at 69", *New York Times*, 8 September 1954, p. 31:3.

52. Oscar Fay Adams, *A Dictionary of American Authors*, fifth edition, revised and enlarged (New York: Houghton Mifflin Co., 1904); W. Stewart Wallace, *A Dictionary of North American Authors Deceased Before 1950* (Toronto: Ryerson Press, 1951); *The National Cyclopaedia of American Biography*, volume 17 (New York: James T. White & Co., 1921), 449; *Who Was Who in America. A Component Volume of Who's Who in American History*, volume I, 1897–1942 (Chicago: A.N. Marquis Co., 1943), 1392.

53. John P. Young, *Journalism in California, Pacific Coast and Exposition Biographies* (San Francisco, Calif.: Chronicle Publishing Company, 1915).

54. Older, *San Francisco*, 72.

55. Terry, interview, 20 December 1969, 9–10. The author completed exhaustive research in an attempt to uncover information on the educational institution without success. Quite possibly with advanced age Terry was mistaken with respect to the name of the school, or maybe the interviewer transcribed the wrong name.

56. Orrin Leslie Elliott, *Stanford University: The First Twenty-five Years* (New York: Arno Press, 1977, 1937); Edith Ronald Mirrielees, *Stanford, The Story of a University* (New York, Putnam, 1960, [1959]); Richard Joncas, David J. Neuman, and Paul V. Turner, *Stanford University*, 2nd ed. (New York: Princeton Architectural Press, 2006).

Chapter 5

The Tremor that Shook the World: The San Francisco Earthquake, April 18, 1906

In 1905, Joseph Terry and family were residing at 426 – 11th Avenue, an address they had occupied since 1897. According to Paul, by April 1906 the family had moved to a new residential address on Steiner Street, about 2 miles east of 11th Avenue.[1] San Francisco at the time was the ninth largest city in the United States. On the unseasonably warm evening of Tuesday April 17, 1906, the city was the proud host to a grand visitor. The great Enrico Caruso was appearing in the Conried Metropolitan Opera's opening performance of *Carmen* at the Grand Opera House. The leading citizens of the city went to bed that night with the voice of the great tenor fresh in their memories. Mozart's *The Marriage of Figaro* starring Giuseppe Campanari (1855–1927) in the title role was scheduled for 2 p.m. on the 18th while Wagner's *Lohengrin* with Alois Burgstaller (1872–1945) in the titular part was scheduled for the 8 p.m. performance later that evening.[2] These performances would never take place.

At almost precisely 5:12 a.m., local time, a foreshock occurred with enough force to be felt widely throughout the San Francisco Bay area. The great earthquake erupted some 20 to 25 seconds later, with an epicenter near San Francisco. Violent shocks punctuated the strong shaking which lasted some 45 to 60 seconds. The earthquake was felt from southern Oregon to south of Los Angeles and inland as far as central Nevada, an area of about 375,000 square miles, approximately half of which was in the Pacific Ocean. Many sleepers were hurled from their beds. Floors and walls undulated and shook, then cracked like eggshells. Buildings collapsed. Clouds of dust ascended, and shards of glass and chunks of brick rained down on the streets.[3] Entire blocks of downtown buildings were leveled, including San Francisco's "earthquake-proof" City Hall which was completed in 1899 after 27 years of planning and construction. The roof of the Grand Opera House collapsed. Later, Caruso would be found crumpled on the ground and weeping in fear among a crowd of shocked survivors in a downtown square. He vowed never to come back to San Francisco – and he never did.[4]

At the time of eruption, Paul was asleep in his bed. The chimney next door, a story higher than the Terry home, had collapsed and fallen through the roof of the Terry residence and into Paul's bedroom where he was hit on the head with one of the falling bricks. While the brick did not render Terry unconscious, the top of his head received a tiny laceration resulting in a small scar.[5] The earthquake was the result of the rupturing of the northernmost 296 miles of the 800-mile San Andreas fault. The epicenter of the 1906 quake has moved around in the past 100 years, as advances in seismology have been made. It was first thought to have been in Marin County, then northwest of the Golden Gate, and most recently, in the Pacific Ocean about two miles west of San Francisco.[6] The 1906 earthquake was assigned a Richter rating of 8.3, but on the newer moment

Chapter 5 • The Tremor that Shook the World

Fig. 5.1 – Fire from Nob Hill, April 18, 1906.

magnitude scale it has been demoted to one measuring 7.8 or 7.9.[7]

Residing in the Terry house at the time of the earthquake were Paul, his father, and his sister Olga Bernice. After the initial quake had subsided, Paul and Olga began tidying up their home as pictures on the wall were turned around and dishes were knocked off the shelves and had shattered on the floor.[8] Unbeknownst to both, 10 minutes after the earthquake fires had broken out across the city. After tending to the housekeeping, the two siblings decided to walk up to Nob Hill, centered on the intersection of California Street and Powell Street and home to the rich and famous, to take a look at the extent of damage caused by the quake across the city.[9] The rocky elevation is one of San Francisco's 44 hills, and one of its original "Seven Hills".[10]

As Terry and his sister were making their way to Nob Hill, Paul could not help but be amused by the fronts of the buildings having collapsed allowing him to peer right into bedrooms like one would look into a miniature dollhouse. Beside each house was a small pile of bricks where the chimney once stood. The air was filled with dust and at times breathing was a little difficult but there was no panic. On Mission Street lay a dozen steers, in a neat row stretching across the street, just as they had been struck down by the flying ruins of the earthquake. When the fire later passed through, the animals that were left to rot would all be roasted.[11]

When Paul and his sister had arrived at the top of Nob Hill they could get a clear view of the city in all directions. Both Paul and Olga could see small fires burning in various sections of the city. They had no idea that the fires would continue to spread and eventually engulf most of the city in flames.[12] Horse drawn engines found themselves helpless. San Francisco was without water. Pipes throughout the city had been fractured by the convulsions, making the fire-fighting system useless. Gas mains were broken and pockets of gas fed the fires. By this time, city officials began appraising the full potential of the disaster. By noon, the many small fires had merged and were out of control.[13]

In Market Street, the main downtown core street in the city, buildings had also collapsed and

39

clouds of dust drifted everywhere. A huge crowd of half-clothed people, some clasping children, others bits of their personal belongings, were shouting and screaming as they blindly surged towards the lower end of the street, which led to the ferry buildings and the sea. The five-story Valencia Hotel collapsed as the earthquake struck, 40 [100][14] people were buried in the ruins. Those who had rooms on the fourth floor simply stepped out onto the street. When a large aftershock occurred at 8:14 a.m. [the third large aftershock], a street split open and a horse and cart disappeared into the yawning crevice, to be followed by dozens of screaming people, who were pushed forward to their death by crowds that followed at their heels. Many were doomed to be roasted alive. One man trapped beyond hope of release pleaded with a policeman to shoot him before the rapidly approaching flames got to him. The policeman took his name and then put a bullet through his head.[15]

At Nob Hill, Paul left his sister Olga who went back to the Terry home. The Terry residence would survive the earthquake and fire relatively intact.[16] Paul then decided to walk down to the newspaper office, the 10-story Chronicle Building located at 690 Market Street, about a mile away.[17] On the way Paul noticed people pushing trunks along the sidewalk with nothing in them and talking to themselves. While he never saw anyone injured from the quake, he did notice a number of people in shock and acting "deranged".[18]

Upon arriving at the Chronicle Building, Paul noticed that the marble walls had all broken up and the elevators were out of order. He started to walk up the cracked and broken steps which stairway circled around the elevator. At the time he did not imagine that if another large aftershock had occurred the entire building may have come down. He arrived at the top floor and proceeded to the roof where there was a "penthouse" darkroom. He loaded up all the plate holders and brought them with him along with a couple of cameras.

When he reached the bottom floor, the City Editor, 40-year-old Ernest S. Simpson, was milling about and inspecting the damage.[19] Simpson would later become managing editor of the San Francisco *Call* and then become head of public relations for International Harvester from 1916 to 1938.[20] Simpson was on duty with his editorial staff since 6 a.m. urged to work by M. H. De Young. Simpson had composed himself enough to write an editorial minimizing the extent of the disaster. An edition was prepared, and the printers were cajoled into standing by the presses waiting for the signal to begin printing.[21]

Simpson suggested to Terry that they go around the city and take photographs of the devastation caused by the earthquake and fire, so away they went in his automobile, a white Stanley Steamer, and began taking photographs. Meanwhile, looting, violence and disorder had started in the city. Brigadier-General Frederick Funston, acting commander of the Pacific Division, took command of law enforcement. He immediately ordered the mobilization of troops surrounding military installations. He ordered the Presidio troops into San Francisco. The 10th, 29th, 38th, 66th, 67th, 70th and 105th Companies of Coast Artillery, Troops I and K of the 14th Cavalry and the First, Ninth and 24th Batteries of Field Artillery arrived to take up patrol in the downtown core.[22]

Funston also took control of establishing communications, sanitation, medical facilities, and housing and re-establishing general order to a destroyed city.

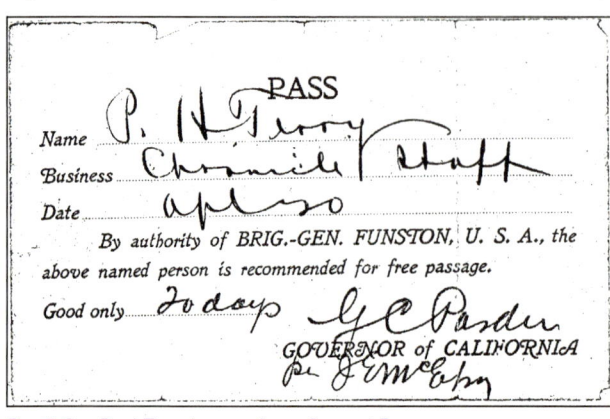

Fig. 5.2 – Paul Terry's pass from General Funston.

Chapter 5 • The Tremor that Shook the World

City mayor Eugene Schmitz gave orders to send for dynamite and Funston was placed in charge of blowing up buildings to create firebreaks. As dynamiting to form firebreaks was undertaken by volunteers, very few men were experienced in explosives. An army officer was blown up and killed when checking a short fuse. The decision to blow up a chemical factory only created pyrotechnics and added fuel to the fire.[23] In the end, the firebreaks never succeeded in containing the fires. The inexperienced men bungled the job repeatedly, and the flames simply leapt across Funston's too narrow fire line and continued unimpeded.[24]

Schmitz also formed an emergency committee of 50 leading citizens.[25] With looting becoming rampant, the mayor did not have the authority to give a shoot-to-kill order for anyone found pillaging. Rather, he left the lawmaking decisions with Funston and the police.[26] Amid the chaos, thousands of residents, dressed in layers upon layers of their best clothes, began making their way on foot to the ferryboats to evacuate across San Francisco Bay to Oakland or to tent camps scattered throughout the city. Many neighborhoods that survived the quake were now slowly being consumed by fire. The disaster would leave 3,000 dead, perhaps more. And in a city of 400,000, about 300,000 were left homeless.[27] The damages were estimated at about $400 million in 1906 dollars, which would translate to about $10 billion in current dollars.

After Terry and Simpson had finished touring the city taking photographs, Paul asked Ernest whether he could take some of the negatives with him in lieu of salary and Simpson agreed.[28] Postal telegraph operators transmitted their last message to the outside world as army troops ordered them from the building at 534 Market Street, opposite Second Street, at 2:20 p.m. because of the approaching fire. Paul thought of going back to the Chronicle Building to develop the negatives but the wind had shifted and the Chronicle Building was soon to be the victim of the fire.[29]

The fires south of Market Street had swept swiftly toward the newspaper buildings on Market Street. The Call Building was the first to go up in flames. The temperatures rose to an estimated 2,000 degrees Fahrenheit, and the firemen watched helplessly as the windows blew out. The Examiner Building was the next to burn, but did so less dramatically. At the Chronicle Building, the edition was finally ready to go. The word came out that the water supply had been cut off and it would be impossible to start the presses so the printers abandoned their posts. Shortly after the Examiner Building had caught fire the Chronicle Building caught fire from the top. In a short time tons of zinc, used by the printers to make press castings, poured down onto

Fig. 5.3 – Paul Terry (right) in San Francisco just prior to the 1906 earthquake and fire.

Fig. 5.4 – Ruins after the San Francisco Earthquake.

the Linotype machines. The accumulated mass crashed through the building carrying everything with it.[30] As all three presses were located on Market Street in San Francisco and suffered the same fiery fate, each would need to find another newspaper press in order to meet their next publication deadline.

Now unemployed and without any bank account or savings to draw from, Paul was financially destitute. He quickly developed the photo negatives in San Francisco and then traveled with his bounty in a little ferry boat across the bay to Alameda and from there to Oakland.[31] He was given a pass to allow movement in the city and although newspaper headlines later declared the city was under martial law, the city was never put under military control.[32] After docking, Paul headed to the offices of the *Oakland Tribune* located at 413–417 8th Street in Oakland where the *Call*, *Chronicle* and *Examiner* printed a combined newspaper on the presses of the *Oakland Tribune* for the April 19, 1906 edition.[33] For Friday's edition, Hearst's *Examiner* gained exclusive control of the *Oakland Tribune*'s printing offices and as a result the *Chronicle* and *Call* went elsewhere in Alameda County to continue publishing.[34]

By the time Paul had arrived at the *Tribune* office, he had become reacquainted with his newspaper cartoonist friend Bud Fisher. On the evening of the 18th both exhausted men slept on piles of newspapers in rolls while the paper was being printed that night. The *Tribune*'s printer had a room where he would take a rest. Paul and Bud found that room, went inside, and slept comfortably on the bed's mattress. Around three o'clock in the morning, the printer found them in his bed and chased both of them out of his room.[35]

Bulletin cartoonist Reuben Goldberg's home at 1288 McAllister Street, like Terry's family residence, escaped the devastation.[36] On the evening before the holocaust, Goldberg was across town from the Mission Street Opera House at a colossal masked roller-skating carnival with a $1,000 prize for the winner, an event promoted by sports promoter Jimmy Coffroth. Goldberg likely then went to a saloon with Coffroth before heading home to bed. On the morning of the disaster, Goldberg walked the streets, and every few blocks was drafted into service to help clear the streets of debris or load dynamite into wagons in support of Funston's men.

When his hands were free, he sketched continuously, making an attempt to find jokes in near-death experiences. Later, having worked as a city engineer in charge of water mains he designed, he comically blamed himself for the disaster in that he designed things so that "water would run around instead of through pipes", making it impossible to extinguish the flames. The water that did make it to the hydrants by that time had got dizzy flowing through Goldberg's spaghetti-like maze and, "as anyone knows, dizzy water is incapable of performing any useful function".[37]

Paul remained in the Oakland area for about a week sleeping on newspapers and living off the generosity of others.[38] He had no reason to head back home having no job in San Francisco to return to. He wasn't worried about his predicament. The weather was warm and the city had soup kitchens along the street. He took comfort in knowing that the world had responded to their need with much needed clothing, blankets,

Chapter 5 • The Tremor that Shook the World

food supplies, and other necessities of life.

During those chaotic days following the great quake Paul began to accept the fact that his dream of studying at Stanford had to be put on hold. Paul later stated: "The earthquake changed the pattern of my life and I stayed in the newspaper field".[39] He decided to head north to Anaconda, Montana to visit his brother John who was by then the head of the *Anaconda Standard* art department.[40] Possibly, there were doors his brother could open for him with the Montana publisher. He didn't feel the need to send his brother notice of his impending arrival as his family was always very close, "you didn't have to be announced, you just walked in".[41]

Fig. 5.5 – Chinatown as the fire approaches.

Notes

1. Terry, interview, 13 June 1970, 95. The author was unable to locate documents to confirm at which address the Terrys resided on Steiner Street. City directories for residential listings were not printed in 1906 due to the earthquake and fire.

2. Blanche Partington, "Caruso Makes Don Jose the Leading Role", *The San Francisco Call*, 18 April 1908, p. 5.

3. William E. Maloney, *The Great Disasters* (New York: Grosset & Dunlap, 1976), 96.

4. Enrico Caruso, Jr. & Andrew Farkas, *Enrico Caruso: My Father and My Family* (Portland, Ore.: Amadeus Press, 1997), 96–99; Dorothy Caruso, *Enrico Caruso, His Life and Death* (Westport, Conn.: Greenwood Press, 1987, c1945).

5. Terry, interview, 13 June 1970, 94. Terry's nephew, Alex Anderson, claimed that the night before the earthquake Terry had banged his head which produced the scar and that Paul did not suffer any physical injuries as a result of the 1906 earthquake. Claiming the quake caused the scar seemed much more dramatic to Paul (Alexander Anderson, interview by author (transcript), Kelowna, B.C., Canada, 9 November 1997, Paul Terry Papers, Victoria, B.C., 2).

6. David J. Wald, Hiroo Kanamori, Donald V. Helmberger and Thomas H. Heaton, "Source Study of the 1906 San Francisco Earthquake", *Bulletin of the Seismological Society of America*, vol. 83, no. 4 (August 1993): 981–1019; Anthony Lomax, "Location of the Focus and Tectonics of the Focal Region of the California Earthquake of 18 April 1906", *Bulletin of the Seismological Society of America*, vol. 98, no. 2 (April 2008): 846–860.

7. Seok Goo Song, Gregory C. Beroza, and Paul Segall, "A Unified Source Model for the 1906 San Francisco Earthquake", *Bulletin of the Seismological Society of America*, vol. 98, no. 2 (April 2008): 823–831.

8. Terry, interview, 13 June 1970, 94.

9. Paul estimated the distance of travel to be three miles which would have made their residence considerably north or south of California Street.

10. Katherine Powell Cohen, *San

TERRYTOONS: The Story of Paul Terry and His Classic Cartoon Factory

Francisco's Nob Hill (Charleston, South Carolina: Arcadia Publishing, 2010).

11. Woody Gelman and Barbara Jackson, *Disaster Illustrated: Two Hundred Years of American Misfortune* (New York: Harmony Books, 1976), 19.

12. Terry, interview, 13 June 1970, 95. The author Jack London would visit Nob Hill at 5:15 a.m. the next day and by that time the flames were rapidly approaching the district. By the time the flames were brought under control a few days later, the neighborhood was completely destroyed, except for the granite walls surrounding the Stanford, Crocker, Huntington and Hopkins mansions (Gelman and Jackson, *Disaster Illustrated*, 19).

13. Maloney, *Great Disasters*, 96.

14. Different accounts on the death toll range from 40–100 guests and staff who died in the collapse of the Valencia.

15. Michael Prideaux, "The City That Died of Shock", in *World Disasters* (Secaucus, New Jersey: Chartwell Books, Inc., 1976), 95–98.

16. Terry, interview, 13 June 1970, 94.

17. In 1888, M. H. de Young, owner of the *San Francisco Chronicle*, commissioned Burnham and Root to design a signature building to house his newspaper. Finished in 1890, the Chronicle Building stood ten stories, with a clock tower reaching 218 feet (66 m) in height, becoming San Francisco's first skyscraper and the tallest building on the West Coast. *The San Francisco Chronicle and its History. The Story of its Foundation, the Struggles of its Early Life, its Well-Earned Successes. The New Chronicle Building, the Edifice and Machinery Described, Comments of the Press* (San Francisco, Cal., 1879).

18. Terry, interview, 13 June 1970, 94.

19. Ibid., 96.

20. "Ernest S. Simpson", *New York Times*, 14 August 1941, p. 17.

21. Gordon Thomas and Max Morgan Witts, *The San Francisco Earthquake* (New York: Stein and Day, 1971), 107.

22. Recommended texts on the 1906 earthquake and fire include: Charles Morris, ed., *The San Francisco Calamity by Earthquake and Fire: A Complete and Accurate Account of the Fearful Disaster Which Visited the Great City and the Pacific Coast, The Reign of Panic and Lawlessness, The Plight of 300,000 Homeless People and The World-Wide Rush to the Rescue/ Told by Eye Witnesses* (Secaucus, N.J.: Citadel Press, 1986, c1906); Frank W. Aitken and Edward Hilton, *A History of the Earthquake and Fire in San Francisco; An Account of the Disaster of April 18, 1906 and its Immediate Results* (San Francisco: The E. Hilton Co., 1906); John Castillo Kennedy, *The Great Earthquake and Fire, San Francisco, 1906* (New York: Morrow, 1963); Eric Saul and Don DeNevi. *The Great San Francisco Earthquake and Fire, 1906* (Millbrae, Calif.: Celestial Arts, 1981); Dan Kurzman, *Disaster!: The Great San Francisco Earthquake and Fire of 1906*, 1st ed. (New York : W. Morrow, 2001); H. Paul Jeffers, *Disaster by the Bay: The Great San Francisco Earthquake and Fire of 1906* (Guilford, Conn.: Lyons Press, 2003); Dorothy H. Fowler, *A Most Dreadful Earthquake: A First-hand Account of the 1906 San Francisco Earthquake and Fire, With Glimpses Into the Lives of the Phillips-Jones Letter Writers* (Oakland, Calif.: California Genealogical Society, 2006).

23. Prideaux, *World Disasters*, 97.

24. Peter C. Marzio, *Rube Goldberg: His Life and Work* (New York: Harper & Row, 1973), 33.

25. Ibid., 96.

26. Some 500 looters were shot and wounded by the police and military.

27. Prideaux, *World Disasters*, 96.

28. Terry, interview, 13 June 1970, 93.

29. Ibid., 96.

30. Thomas and Witts, *The San Francisco Earthquake*, 107.

31. Terry, interview, 13 June 1970, 96.

32. "Martial Law Is Placed Over the City", *San Jose Mercury and Herald*, 19 April 1906. Paul was under the belief that the city was under martial law (Terry, interview, 13 June 1970, 96). However, neither Mayor Schmitz nor General Funston advocated martial law, but without an organized center of control, the various groups issued and followed contrasting orders.

33. Philip L. Fradkin, *The Great Earthquake and Firestorms of 1906: How San Francisco Nearly Destroyed Itself* (Berkeley: University of California Press, 2005), 89.

34. Ibid.

35. Terry, interview, 13 June 1970, 96.

36. Marzio, *Rube Goldberg*, 34.

37. Ibid., 35.

38. In his June 1970 interview, Paul stated that he remained in San Francisco for about a week before leaving for Portland. If true, his claim that he had the first photographs to be published in the *Oregonian* is false. On April 22, photographs of the quake stricken California city on fire first appeared in the newspaper.

39. Terry, interview, 20 December 1969, 9.

40. According to a 1930 newspaper article on John Terry, it was John who photographed the disaster as he was spending a vacation near San Francisco. After the earthquake struck, he rushed to the city and took photographs of the disaster. Then by a "devious route" managed to get them on a train to Anaconda, Montana where they were published, the first photographs seen in the region. "Noted Artist Draws New Strip of Flying Adventures", *Monitor-Index and Democrat* (Moberly, Missouri), 26 July 1930, p. 10.

41. Terry, interview, 13 June 1970, 92. Paul's daughter Patricia remembers her father stating a number of times that he was not in San Francisco at the time of the earthquake but residing south of the city (Leahy and Lazar, interview, 6). If this is true then it would better explain Paul being issued a pass by Funston to move about the city. Paul may have been staying with his brother John south of the city which would also better explain Paul reconnecting with his sibling in Montana later that month rather than travelling up to Montana and arriving at his brother's residence unannounced.

Chapter 6

A Tour of the West: The *Anaconda Standard*, Portland *Oregonian*, *Evening Standard* and Return to the Bay City, 1906–1911

Before arriving in Anaconda, Paul traveled first to Portland, Oregon where he hoped to process and sell some photographs of the disaster. Portland was a distance of 635 miles from San Francisco and about 16 to 18 hours overnight by train taking into account all stops along the way. With very little money, he approached the Salvation Army who funded his trip to the Oregon city. Although Terry had regularly taken the train for a short distance between San Francisco to the family farm in San Mateo, this was the first time he had taken a long trip on the rails. He would have to stand for the entire journey in the crowded rail coach.[1]

The young photographer arrived in Portland sleepy and hungry but his brother John had a friend in the city, Portland *Oregonian* cartoonist Benjamin Clarence Bubb,[2] who Paul hoped would offer shelter and assist him in developing some photographs of the earthquake devastated city. John Terry and Bubb likely met in San Francisco before John moved north to Montana. Bubb was born in Mountain View, California and attended Stanford, class of 1904. After leaving school, Bubb became a commercial artist working for various newspapers in the northwest United States, eventually retiring after working 24 years in the San Francisco newspaper business, most notably for the *San Francisco News*.[3]

After arriving at the *Oregonian* office, Bubb introduced Terry to the other newspaper staff as if he was a famous celebrity, one who experienced the San Francisco earthquake and fire first-hand, taken some photographs of the disaster, and lived to tell the tale. Terry bargained with the newspaper editor offering to trade some of his very valuable negatives for use of their darkroom and some photographic paper. The editor agreed and Paul made some prints of the earthquake and fire ravaged city which were subsequently published in the *Oregonian*. Terry later claimed that these were the first photographs published in the Portland newspaper.[4]

Terry had to remain in Portland to sell some of his photographs in order to earn his train fare to Montana. He began selling pictures to proprietors of cigar stores and other businesses in Portland where the merchants hung them up in order to draw crowds to their establishments. He also sent some photographs to the *Anaconda Standard* where they were published in the newspaper in advance of his arrival. Using the *Anaconda Standard* newspaper office as his address he mailed some photographs to *Collier's* magazine and various other national publications speculating that they would publish them and compensate him for his pictures. His efforts were rewarded as he would later receive cheques from many of these magazines over the next few years whenever they used them in their publications.[5]

Once again Paul approached the Salvation Army for financial assistance to travel, this time to

45

Fig. 6.1 – Bird's-Eye View of Anaconda, MT about the time Terry arrived.

Montana, and he received half his fare from Portland to Butte, a distance of about 666 miles. At the time, Butte had a population of about 35,000, and was one of the largest and most notorious copper boomtowns in the American West, home to hundreds of saloons and a famous red-light district.[6] When Terry arrived at Butte by train, he went up the street and at the top of the hill saw a big crowd that was looking at the photographs that he had sent the *Standard*. Terry proudly proclaimed that he was the one who mailed the photographs to the Montana newspaper.[7] The first photographs of the disaster ("Views of San Francisco During the Early Hours of the Fire") were published on the front page in the April 23, 1906 edition. Along with the photographs was a short narrative by his brother John titled "Stirring Incidents of Shock and Fire" describing the devastation wrought by the earthquake and fire, and a comic panel drawn by John titled "The Rush for the Ferry" illustrating several San Francisco citizens, including a policeman clutching an exhausted woman, fleeing the fire.[8]

The city of Anaconda, the former county seat of Deer Lodge County, is about 24 miles northwest of Butte. The area was laid out in 1883 as Copperopolis by "Copper King" Marcus Daly, founder of Montana's copper industry. The settlement grew rapidly after 1884 when Daly built a copper smelter on nearby Warm Springs Creek. The plant became one of the world's largest non-ferrous and reduction works with a 585-foot (178-meter) smokestack. The city was incorporated in 1888 and was renamed Anaconda after the Anaconda Mine at Butte owned by Daly. Michael Hickey, owner of the mine, chose this peculiarly odd name from a remark attributed to Horace Greeley to the effect that McClellan's army would surround Lee's like a giant anaconda.[9]

Daly had hoped to make the settlement the state capital and built the Hotel Marcus Daly, then one of the most ornate hotels in the United States, to attract tourists. Born in Ireland in 1842, he emigrated to the United States and by way of Panama traveled to San Francisco where he arrived in 1855. After briefly working in the potato farming industry he found work in the mining sector in Nevada. Through industrious work he was promoted and eventually became foreman of the Comstock Mine. Daly was then put in charge by the syndicate of the Alice Mine in Butte. He wisely heavily invested his capital in Montana mining stocks, then bought the Anaconda Mine and subsequently hit a large cooper vein, the largest bed of copper ever discovered, making him a multi-millionaire.[10]

Both Daly and banker-mine owner William Andrews Clark had political aspirations and fought for control of the Democratic Party. This rivalry dominated the mining and political history of Montana during the 1880s and 1890s. In 1888, Andrews was nominated as a delegate for Congress but lost by about 5,000 votes and where Daly's influence was strong his defeat was overwhelming. When the state was admitted into the Union in 1889, Clark was endorsed by the Democrats for United States senator. The legislative vote was close but the United States Senate however seated the Republicans. In 1893 Clark was again a candidate for the Senate and now Daly was openly fighting him. Both sides spent money lavishly in attempt to further their political agendas.[11]

The dispute between Daly and Andrews gave birth to the *Anaconda Standard*. On September 4, 1889, on the eve of Montana statehood, Daly founded the *Standard*, Montana's best financed and most prestigious newspaper.[12] To run the *Standard*, Daly sought out John

Chapter 6 • A Tour of the West

Hurst Durston, a former professor of philology from New York University with a Ph.D. in philology from the University of Heidelberg, and an editor of the *Syracuse Standard*. In 1888 Durston, a Yale graduate, had brought his family west to operate a failing gold mine east of Butte, but in 1889 he signed on with Daly to bring the newspaper to life.[13] Daly's initial investment of $30,000 provided for a state-of-the-art printing press, luxurious editorial offices, and the money to hire experienced editors, reporters, and graphic designers. The *Anaconda Standard* was to be the rival of newspapers in Minneapolis and the Pacific Northwest. By the early 1900s the *Standard* appeared regularly on the newsstands of 14 cities outside Montana, including New York, Chicago, and all major cities on the west coast of the United States.[14]

During the 1890s, the *Anaconda Standard* became known for its political attacks against Daly's bitter rival. The scathing attacks began with Clark's bid for Congress and later for the U.S. Senate, followed by the battle over the location of Montana's capital. While Daly promoted Anaconda as the state capital, Clark poured his financial resources and editorial venom in support of Helena, through his newspaper, the *Butte Miner*. Prior to Daly's death in 1900, both men purchased a number of newspapers, but by 1910, the Amalgamated Copper Company (heir to the Daly mining empire) acquired a number of the state's largest dailies, and its offspring,

Fig. 6.2 – Bird's-Eye View of Anaconda, MT about the time Terry arrived (west view).

the Anaconda Company, came to dominate Montana politics through the press. That dominance persisted up to 1959, when the Anaconda media empire was sold to Lee Enterprises, a Midwestern newspaper chain.

A late arrival in the war of the copper kings was Fritz Augustus Heinze. In 1889, Heinze went to Butte as a mining engineer. In 1894, with an inheritance from his father, Heinze's Montana Ore Purchasing Company opened a sophisticated new smelter, allowing Heinze to offer inexpensive smelting to small mining companies. Initially, Heinze had to lease mines and obtain ore from independent companies in order to keep operating. Heinze succeeded in locating rich ore bodies and the Rarus Mine, purchased in 1895, turned out to be one of Butte's premier mining properties.

Heinze had arrived in Butte well after the "Copper Kings" Clark and Daly were well established. In order to become their equal, Heinze's strategies included reducing the working day for his miners from 10 to eight hours.

After this change the miners considered Heinze a hero. In 1898 he founded the Butte *Reveille*. Heinze's venomous editor, P. A. O'Farrell, specialized in attacking Standard Oil and the Amalgamated Copper Company. In 1902, Heinze combined his various mining interests into a company called United Copper, valued at $80 million with capacity to produce 40 million pounds of copper a year, compared to 143 million a year produced by Daly's Amalgamated. In 1906, after a decade of the mining war, Heinze sold his Butte interests to Amalgamated for a reported $12 million, and in 1907 moved to New York City.[15]

In late April 1906, when Terry arrived in Anaconda, the population of the city was just under 10,000.[16] At the time, his brother John and family were residing at 418 West 4th Street. To Terry's surprise his brother wasn't there when he arrived although his wife and young son were home and offered him accommodation. John had traveled to Los Angeles, California and was in that city the morning

47

of the earthquake. On the way home, concerned with his family's welfare, John visited his father and sister in San Francisco before making his way back to Anaconda.[17]

After John returned home, he helped Paul locate work as a photographer at the *Standard*. At the time, the newspaper had a circulation of about 14,000.[18] Paul would establish his residence at his brother's address.[19] Although Paul had aspirations of becoming a cartoonist and did some sketches when called upon, his lack of training and experience as a newspaper cartoonist prevented him from securing a position with the *Standard* art department.[20] If Terry was to earn a spot in the *Standard*'s cartoon bullpen, he would need to acquire the necessary skills to compete with the staff's artists, most of whom were paid some of the highest salaries in the country as newspaper cartoonists.

Daly was never shy about spending money on his newspaper. In 1894, Daly's newspaper installed Mergenthaler Linotype machines, bolstering the *Standard*'s claim to having the industry's most up-to-date technology. A sophisticated engraving process run by Charles Knox allowed a cadre of *Standard* cartoonists to print a large number of political cartoons daily. Assisting Durston in his editorial duties were two associates from the *Syracuse Standard*, Charles Hayden Eggleston and Warren W. Wallsworth. Eggleston had impressive credentials. He was the son of a professor of languages in the Falley Seminary at Fulton,

New York, and a graduate of Syracuse University before becoming city editor of the *Syracuse Standard*.[21] Another Syracuse refugee was Edwin B. Catlin coming to the *Standard* in 1889 after many years in the Weedsport, Syracuse and Auburn printing business to assume the position of the mechanical and business management of the *Standard* newspaper.[22]

When colored comics made their debut in New York City with *The Yellow Kid*, Daly wanted the same for his newspaper. He ordered color decks and photoengraving equipment and published a four-page colored comic section on Sundays.[23] Daly also ensured his cartoon bullpen featured some of the nation's brightest cartoonists. John William Trowbridge was chief of the art department of the *Anaconda Standard* after it was first created in September 1899.[24] He was employed for the *New York World* and *New York Herald* before he headed west to work for a number of newspapers, eventually the *Standard*. He headed back to New York City in 1900 for an operation on his stomach where he died later that year.[25] William H. Loomis, cartoonist and illustrator, was on the *Standard* art staff from 1902 to 1903, although his work appeared in the newspaper as late as 1905. Loomis is most famous for the *Widow Wise* series which he drew for the Sunday colored supplement of the *New York Herald*.[26]

Rudolph Leppert (1872–1949), cartoonist, illustrator, and portrait painter, spent four years in Anaconda, Montana as art editor

of the *Standard* from 1900 to 1904. He is most noted for being the art director of *The Literary Digest* during its last 25 years of its existence. He was also associated with *The Brooklyn Eagle*, *The Press* (Binghamton N.Y.), and illustrated many reference books including the *New Standard Dictionary*. He had painted the portraits of every President of the United States up to the time of his death.[27] Another noted cartoonist employed for the *Standard* art department was Willis H. Thorndike. He was born on February 8, 1872 in Stockton, California. Thorndike studied art in San Francisco (Art Institute), Paris (Académie Julian with J. P. Laurens and Constant) and New York City. He began his career with the *San Francisco Chronicle* in 1890 and worked at the *Standard* from 1901 to 1904. He then was employed for the *New York Herald* and *Baltimore Sun* until 1915 when he returned to California. He was best known as a political cartoonist, and was active in Los Angeles from 1928 until his death there on March 18, 1940.[28]

Having been raised in the Bay area, working in the rough northern wilds of Montana was a unique experience for Terry. Anaconda was still a frontier town with plenty of dirt roads and little automobiles.[29] Although having spent time as a child on a family farm, Terry wasn't familiar with riding horses nor had he any particular inclination to do so. Rather he preferred to walk wherever he wanted to go, which usually wasn't far as the distance between his residence and the

Chapter 6 • A Tour of the West

ALADDIN AND HIS WONDERFUL LAMP

Fig. 6.3 – John Terry's artwork.

Anaconda Standard office at the corner of Main and 3rd Street (northeast corner) was only a few city blocks. However, one night Terry was out late a few miles from town and decided to return to Anaconda requiring a walk through a forest.

As he was walking among the trees, he observed that much of the vegetation was sick or dying from the environmental damage caused by the nearby copper smelting operations. At the same time, he began to sense a presence following him. He turned his head and could see a wolf in the distance slowly closing in on him. The hair began to rise on the back of his neck. With each step the lights of Anaconda were getting closer and his hope of reaching them rose with every stride. He decided to make a run to the nearest building and started to race towards the town. The wolf began to chase him. Never an athlete, Terry was no match for the animal as the wolf was gaining ground. Paul dashed out of the forest and onto the street with the wolf just a few meters behind him. He ran into the nearest lit establishment, a saloon, hoping to elude the creature. The wolf followed him into the tavern. Once inside Terry ran to take cover only to discover the animal was not a ferocious beast after all but the pet of the bartender.[30]

The winter of 1906–1907 in Anaconda, Montana was not much different from other years. The first weeks of January 1907 were particularly cold and snowy, with temperatures reaching 23 to 32 degrees below zero.[31] Since becoming a cartoonist at the *Standard* was not likely to occur in the very near future, Paul began to realize that he might have better luck back in Oregon where he had made such a great impression with his photographs. He had been a house guest of his brother John for many months and had tested his good hospitality long enough. Oregon also offered more temperate surroundings and so he traveled back to Portland to look for work with the Portland *Oregonian*.

The *Oregonian* was established in 1850, one year prior to the incorporation of the tiny town of Portland, Oregon with a population of about 700, by Col. W. W. Chapman and prominent local businessman Henry W. Corbett. Chapman and Corbett had traveled to San Francisco, the largest city on the West Coast of the United States at the time, in search of an editor interested in and capable of producing a weekly newspaper in Portland. The two men chose Thomas J. Dryer, a transplanted New Yorker who was a dynamic writer with previous experience in the

49

production of a small circulation community newspaper in his native Ulster County, New York. Dryer also had printing equipment which was transported to Portland and on December 4, 1850 the first issue of *The Weekly Oregonian* was published. The newspaper paid little attention to current news events, with the bulk of the paper's content devoted to political themes, primarily supporting the Whig Party, and biographical commentary.

Henry Pittock (1835–1919), the *Oregonian* manager, became the owner in 1861 as compensation for unpaid wages, and he began publishing the paper daily, except Sundays. Pittock would later make his fortune in the pulp and paper industry as well as holding significant assets in the railroad business.[32] Pittock's goal was to focus more on news. From 1866 [1865] to 1872 Harvey Winfield Scott (1838–1910)[33] was the editor. Henry W. Corbett bought the paper from a cash-poor Pittock in October 1872 and placed William Lair Hill as editor. Scott, fired by Corbett for supporting Ben Holladay's candidates, became editor of Holladay's rival *Bulletin* newspaper.

The paper went bankrupt around 1874, Holladay having lost $200,000 during the period. Corbett sold *The Oregonian* back to Pittock in 1877. Scott also became part-owner and returned as editor in 1877, a position he held until shortly before his death in 1910. Scott was noted for avoiding rhetorical art or indirection of language and writing with an incisive directness to his subject matter. His writings commanded attention through the clearness and vigor of his statement, the fairness of his arguments and the thorough and careful investigation of his subject.[34] In December 1881, the first *Sunday Oregonian* was published. In 1894 the *Oregonian* installed Linotypes, 10 years after Mergenthaler invented the machine. The daily moved into its new building in 1892 and again a new press went in. By 1900, in a city with a population of 90,000, the circulation of the newspaper reached 15,000.[35]

On the strength of his photographic work covering the 1906 earthquake and fire, Terry was offered a position as a newspaper photographer with the *Oregonian*. While his ultimate goal was to find work in the art department, similar to the problem he encountered at the *Standard* he had not yet achieved a level of artistry that would allow him to compete with the artists the *Oregonian* was hiring. In 1907, the art department at the *Oregonian* featured several capable cartoonists, the most prolific being Harry Daniels Murphy whose work for the *Oregonian* frequently appeared on the front pages of the newspaper. Murphy was born in Eureka, California on October 9, 1880. He was a self-taught artist who worked as a political and sports cartoonist for the Hearst papers from 1898 to 1940. He worked for the *Seattle Post-Intelligencer* until joining the staff of the Portland *Oregonian* in 1901 and remained with the paper for 10 years. He then joined the staff of the San Francisco *Call* until 1913. After working in Denver for the *Rocky Mountain News* and a St Louis newspaper, he returned to California. He settled in La Jolla, California in 1929 and remained there until his death on May 9, 1973.[36]

At the time of Terry's hire, the *Oregonian* sports cartoonist on staff was Joseph Archie Hollingworth who was born on April 12, 1880 in Nebraska. He was employed both for the *Oregonian* and for many years as a vocal teacher at a local fine arts school. He died in Portland, Oregon in 1943. Probably one of the more multi-talented artists on staff was fine arts painter, commercial artist, and newspaper cartoonist, Francis Marion Keane. He was born in San Francisco, California on June 6, 1876 [1866]. Keane studied art in his native city at the School of Design. A resident of San Francisco at the turn of the century, he moved to Portland to work for the Chapman Advertising Company before becoming employed as an artist with the *Oregonian*. By 1940 he had retired to Coral Gables, Florida and died in Dade County in 1941.[37] Another gifted artist in the cartoon bullpen was Milton Waters Werschkul (1883–1955) who was with the *Oregonian* art department for 16 years before leaving to work in a similar capacity for the Portland *Evening Telegram* in 1917 where he remained until at least 1922. By 1930 he had returned to the *Oregonian* to become the head of the art and photography

Chapter 6 • A Tour of the West

department at the newspaper until his retirement in 1952.[38]

Terry wasn't at the *Oregonian* for very long before he found similar work for the Portland *Evening Journal*. The *Evening Journal* was purchased by Charles Samuel Jackson in 1902. At that time the newspaper was a political campaign newspaper which had been established four months previously and was on the verge of failure. Jackson changed the name to the *Oregon Journal* and as its publisher gradually extended its circulation, size and influence until it became one of the leading newspapers on the Pacific coast. When he assumed charge of the *Journal* it had less than 5,000 subscribers. At the time of his death in 1924, the circulation was nearly 100,000. Through the *Journal*, Jackson secured the adoption of a $100 million highway improvement program and the passage of industrial welfare and workmen's compensation laws. He waged a successful pure milk campaign, helped secure the initiative, referendum and recall laws for Oregon, and won a campaign for the creation of a state railroad commission.[39] The *Oregon Journal* was the home of noted cartoonist James Edward Murphy, Jr. (1891–1965) during the early 1910s. Murphy is best known for his long-run family comic strip, *Toots and Casper* for the *New York American* running from 1919 to 1951.[40]

By the spring of 1907, Terry had decided that it was best to return home to San Francisco where he would try and break into the newspaper business as a cartoonist. Upon arriving in the Bay City Paul went back to reside with his father at the residential address of 3006 ½ Sacramento Street.[41] He continued to develop his skills as an artist and searched for work at the local newspapers. He would over the course of the next four years work for three different newspapers: the San Francisco *Examiner*, the San Francisco *Call*, and the *San Francisco Chronicle*.[42] Shortly after arriving back home, he was hired by the *Examiner*, a Hearst newspaper, as a photographer and sketch artist.

The *Examiner* was founded in 1863 as the *Democratic Press*, a pro-Confederacy, pro-slavery paper opposed to Abraham Lincoln, but after his assassination in 1865 the paper's offices were destroyed by a mob, and starting on June 12, 1865 it was called the *Daily Examiner*. The *Examiner*'s management was taken over in 1867 by William Randolph Hearst, who was only 23 at the time. Hearst's father, George Hearst, accepted control of the paper as payment of an outstanding poker debt. William Randolph Hearst's name and notoriety made the paper's circulation enlarge, as did some of the writers he brought on to craft stories, including literary giants Mark Twain and Jack London.[43] Yellow Journalism came into style during the time Hearst ruled over the paper, and the *Examiner* quickly adhered to Yellow Journalism's formula of gossip, scandal, and vicious satire. The paper's sales increased, and the *Examiner* became known as a somewhat trashier, less stuffy counterpart to its more serious-minded competition, the *Chronicle*.[44] By 1910, the newspaper had a circulation of 103,663, the largest distribution figures in the city.[45]

Since the *Examiner* had a habit of publishing stories that other newspapers would not touch, articles which were sensational in nature and sometimes gruesome and titillating, Terry's first artistic assignments at the *Examiner* were not easy. One stormy Saturday evening, Terry was asked by the editor of the *Examiner* to attend to the morgue and draw a portrait of the corpse of a woman that was brutally murdered. Up to that point in time, Terry had been assigned primarily photographic work so he was glad to have been given the opportunity to display his talents as an illustrator. Terry hoped that the project could lead to better illustration assignments and eventually a job as a full-time cartoonist for the newspaper. He attended the morgue with the wind howling, thunder booming overhead, and lightning forks touching down in the distance. As he entered the morgue Terry became increasingly uneasy about his task but the job needed to get done.

Deep in the bowels of the morgue, he sat alone in front of the lifeless corpse with pencil in hand carefully drawing the facial features of the victim. Suddenly the fingers of the corpse twitched, and the body started to move and slump down the slab. Between the noises outside, the gas lights casting shadows on the inside walls and a slowly moving corpse, Terry grabbed his pencil and pad

51

Fig. 6.4 – Paul Terry in Anaconda, Montana (winter 1906–1907).

and dashed out the door, leaving the crumpled body where it fell. Gasping for breath, he ran down the hill to the reassuring lights of town. What Terry didn't understand at the time was that what he had witnessed was not a body coming back to life and re-animating but rather natural post-mortem movements related to bodily decomposition.[46]

In another *Examiner* assignment, Terry was asked to sit in on a trial of a suspect charged with a serious criminal offence [murder]. Hearst wanted a photograph of the suspect even though photographs were strictly forbidden inside the courtroom. Only drawings were allowed to be made of the courtroom proceedings. Feeling he had no other choice, Terry decided to take a photograph and quickly leave the room before he was apprehended. Unfortunately, the courtroom was packed with members of the public and media.

With the suspect on the stand, Terry aimed his camera at the accused. Unlike the cameras of today, the camera Terry was operating did not use roll film. Rather, there was a treated glass plate in a light-proof container at the back of the camera that was fairly easy to slide into place and remove. When the camera went off, Terry caused a commotion by the firing of the black powder flash. He quickly removed the container and threw it out the window to a waiting reporter then made his way through the crowd to the exit door. Unfortunately for Terry he never made it to the street and was apprehended and hauled off to jail while Hearst got his photograph.[47] In another assignment, Terry took a flash photograph of an African-American woman and startled by the experience she ended up chasing after him down the street for a few blocks.[48]

After leaving the *Examiner*, by 1909 Paul had decided to capitalize on his growing experience as a newspaper photographer by establishing the Paul Terry Co., a photography business headquartered at the Pacific Building in San Francisco at the corner of 4th and Market Streets. By this time the Terry family home was relocated from Sacramento Street to 2026 Broderick Street.[49] Paul was continuing to reside with his father and sister Olga. Unfortunately, Paul's photography business wasn't generating the income he had expected necessitating his return to work in the newspaper industry. Paul also found artistic work with drama critic Walter Cavanaugh, most likely making caricatures of theatrical personalities.[50]

Chapter 6 • A Tour of the West

Paul's brother John returned to San Francisco in late spring 1909 to work for the San Francisco *Call* as a cartoonist.[51] Paul joined his brother in the art department of the *Call* where he was reunited with Ernest Simpson who had moved from the *Chronicle* to become managing editor at the *Call*. Charles W. Hornick, later a director of the Panama-Pacific Exposition, the World's Fair held in 1915, was the general manager.[52] John was the daily political cartoonist while Paul provided illustrations and a comic strip called *Alonzo* for the paper's weekend editions. *Alonzo* was Paul's first regular assignment on a comic strip. Some of John Terry's daily cartoons from this period caricaturing Theodore Roosevelt were reprinted in *T.R. in Cartoon* (1910), edited by Raymond Gros.[53]

The *Call* was founded by Canadian journalist, politician, and author, David William Higgins in 1856. Higgins did not have the paper for long and sold the *Call* in 1858.[54] Between December 1856 and March 1895 the *San Francisco Call* was named *The Morning Call*, but its name was changed when it was purchased by John D. Spreckels in 1895. In 1880, with $2 million in capital, he organized J. D. Spreckels and Brothers, a company to establish a trade between the mainland United States and the Hawaiian Islands. The company began with one sailing vessel, the *Rosario*, and later controlled two large fleets of sail and steam ships. The firm also engaged extensively in sugar refining, and became agents for leading sugar plantations in Hawaii. Through his corporate operations Spreckels became the wealthiest man in San Diego.[55]

In the period from 1863 to 1864 Mark Twain worked as one of the paper's writers. On the staff were world class writers Frederick Hastings Dewey[56] who became the commercial and financial editor of the newspaper, and John Davenport Bromfield, reporter and sports writer.[57] In the cartoon bullpen at the *Call* was another familiar face to Paul, Ralph Yardley, who was formerly a cartoonist at the *Bulletin* when Terry was employed there five years earlier. Another *Call* cartoonist on staff at the time was Donald McKee. Over the next decade McKee and Terry would become very good friends. McKee would later become an integral member of the Fables Studios, Inc. stable of artists in the 1920s producing Farmer Al Falfa animated cartoons working under Terry. McKee would then join the Terrytoons studio in the 1930s and eventually became a valued member of the story department.[58]

While in Montana, as early as 1906 John Terry had developed a "lightning sketch" act, sketches drawn very quickly by an artist on stage or in a vaudeville act, sometimes involving trick drawing. His act was performed alongside Alan Lester [Lister] Lovey, a cartoonist based in Butte, Montana and employed for the *Butte Inter Mountain* newspaper.[59] Lovey (1877–1907) who died at age 30 from pneumonia, had worked earlier in the decade for the *Herald* in Salt Lake City, Utah. In early 1907, John Terry made a foray to New York City to work on the *New York World*, befriending *World* sports cartoonist Jesse "Vet" Anderson, who would later animate cartoons for Paul Terry at the Fables Studios, Inc. John returned to Montana [on April 18, 1907] and resumed work on the *Standard*.[60]

Upon returning to San Francisco in 1909, John Terry continued to develop his lightning sketch act, this time with his brother Paul as his partner. By January 1910, the brothers were performing an exceedingly clever 20-minute act, appearing as clowns in pantomime and drawing cartoons fast enough to dazzle the audience. The two Terrys used a drop curtain of their own, designed and painted by the brothers, representing all the chief characters in current comic art, such as the Katzenjammers, Buster Brown, Muggsy and others.[61]

The Terrys auditioned before the manager of the Orpheum theater (San Francisco), others involved in the Orpheum circuit, and a few newspaper men. The act would prove highly popular to their audience. One of John Terry's lightning sketches consisted of drawing the figures "1912" and in them, without erasing the smallest portion, filling in around them so that within a few seconds the face of Teddy Roosevelt appears. In the sketch, the first figure "1" is elongated and turns into the cord to the eyeglasses. A few clever turns convert the "9" into an eye and an ear. The second "1" of "1912" grows into a nose, and the "2" develops into the other eye and ear.[62]

After close to a year drawing

TERRYTOONS: The Story of Paul Terry and His Classic Cartoon Factory

Alonzo, from after June 12, 1909 until his last strip published on May 7, 1910, a strip originally created by Ralph Yardley and titled *Have You Seen Alonzo?* Paul Terry was replaced by John Terry as the artist of the strip starting May 14, 1910. John Terry drew the strip for only about two months, leaving the paper in early July to join his brother Paul at the *San Francisco Chronicle.* All together, seven different artists drew the *Alonzo* strip at various times between 1908 and 1912 including Mike Randall and Jim Navoni.[63]

At the *Chronicle,* Paul worked alongside several artists who would make significant contributions to popular media including Thomas McNamara, Harry Hershfield, and Robert Ripley. Thomas J. McNamara was born in San Francisco on May 7, 1886. He studied at the Mark Hopkins Art Institute and began his career as an illustrator for the *Chronicle* in the early 1900s. He later gained fame in New York as the creator of *Us Boys* comic strip. From 1921 to 1954 he spent time in Hollywood as a writer and director on live action features and shorts including the *Our Gang* series. He was an assistant director on the Mary Pickford film *Little Annie Rooney* (1925). Nearly blind, McNamara spent his last 10 years in San Francisco at the Laguna Honda Hospital. He died there on May 19, 1964.[64]

Cartoonist, humor writer and radio personality Harry Hershfield studied in Chicago at the Frank Holmes School of Illustration and the Chicago Art Institute, and his career began at age 14, drawing sports cartoons and his comic strip about a dog, *Homeless Hector,* for the *Chicago Daily News* in 1899. He headed to California drawing for the *San Francisco Chronicle* by 1907. He later moved to New York City to draw comic strips for the New York *Evening Journal,* New York *Graphic,* and New York *Herald Tribune* creating the popular strips *Desperate Desmond, Dauntless Durham of the U.S.A.,* and *Abie the Agent.*[65]

While at the *Chronicle* Terry also developed a friendship with LeRoy Ripley, American cartoonist, entrepreneur and amateur anthropologist, later known as Robert LeRoy Ripley, most noted for creating the *Ripley's Believe It or Not!* newspaper panel series, radio show, and television show which feature odd facts from around the world. At age 14, he sold his first cartoon to *Life* Magazine for eight dollars. By age 15 [16], Ripley was working at the San Francisco *Bulletin* as a sports cartoonist for $8 a week and soon moved on to the *San Francisco Chronicle* where he was earning up to $20 a week.[66]

By 1911, at age 24, Paul decided it was time to leave the family home and establish his career as a newspaper cartoonist in another city. In Terry's words, "Well, you just thought it was time. It's like a bird leaving a nest: you get your feathers."[67] Taking his inspiration from cartoonists such as Tad Dorgan who left San Francisco in 1905 to find success as an artist and writer for the *New York Journal,* and Bud Fisher who left for New York City in 1909 to work on comics for the *New York American,* Terry decided his best chance of locating work as a cartoonist was New York City. Therefore he packed his belongings and traveled the 2,564 miles (4,126 kilometers) across the country with the goal of following in the footsteps of Dorgan and Fisher. What Terry could not imagine was that in three short years he would leave the newspaper business behind without regret for a completely new career in animated cartoons. ❧

Notes

1. Terry, interview, 13 June 1970, 97–98.

2. Bubb's name is transcribed incorrectly as "Budd" in Deneroff's June 1970 interview of Terry.

3. Bubb was born on March 30, 1881. He died on July 28, 1958 in San Francisco, San Francisco County, California. The Benjamin Bubb School in Mountain View is named after his father. The Bubb family settled on the Mountain View ranch in 1851. "Settlers' Son Rites Tomorrow", *Mountain View Register Leader* (Mountain View, Santa Clara Co., CA), 30 July 1958, p. 2:7.

4. Terry, interview, 13 June 1970, 93. Terry is likely mistaken that his photographs were the first published

Chapter 6 • A Tour of the West

by the *Oregonian* staff. He would had to have been in Portland before the 22nd as on that date a photograph taken of the Chronicle Annex and Claus Spreckels Building (home of the *Call*) prior to being on fire was published in the newspaper. The source of another photograph published in the newspaper is listed as the *Sacramento Union*. Photographs continued to be published in the newspaper many days later, some of which may have been photographs taken by Terry.

5. Ibid., 98.

6. Writers' Program, Montana, *Copper Camp; Stories of the World's Greatest Mining Town, Butte, Montana* (New York: Hastings House; New York: AMS Press, 1976); Pat Kearney, *Butte Voices: Mining, Neighborhoods, People* ([Butte, Mont.]: Skyhigh Communications, 1998).

7. Terry, interview, 13 June 1970, 98.

8. More photographs and another chronicle by John Terry followed on the 24th. John Terry attributed the photographs that were published in the *Anaconda Standard* as pictures he had sent to the paper. "Pictures of the Fire", *Anaconda Standard*, 24 April 1906, p. 1.

9. *The Montana Almanac 1957* (Missoula: Montana State University, 1957), 26.

10. For more on Daly (1842–1900): *Who Was Who in America*, volume I, 1897–1942, 292; *Dictionary of American Biography*, volumes 1–20 (New York: Charles Scribner's Sons, 1928–1936); John A. Garraty and Mark C. Carnes, ed., *American National Biography*, 24 volumes (New York: Oxford University Press, 1999). Obituary: "Death of Marcus Daly", *New York Times*, 13 November 1900, p. 2:3.

11. For more on William Andrews Clark (1839–1925): *Who Was Who in America*, volume I, 1897–1942, 225; Wheeler Preston, *American Biographies* (New York: Harper & Brothers Publishers, 1940); Garraty and Carnes, *American National Biography*; *The National Cyclopaedia of American Biography*, volume 25 [21], 301; Johnson and Malone, *Dictionary of American Biography*, vol. 4, 144–146.

12. Winifred Gregory, ed., *American Newspapers 1821–1936: A Union List of Files Available In The United States and Canada* (New York: Kraus Reprint Corp., 1967), 25.

13. Durston would remain as editor on the *Standard* until 1912. In 1913 he established the *Butte Daily Post* as the successor of the *Butte Inter Mountain*. For more on Durston (1848–1920) see: *Who Was Who in America*, volume I, 1897–1942, 350; Tom Stout, ed., *Montana: its Story and Biography. A History of Aboriginal and Territorial Montana and Three Decades of Statehood*, volume II (Chicago and New York: The American Historical Society, 1921), 471–472.

14. Michael P. Malone and Richard B. Roeder, *Montana: A History of Two Centuries* (Seattle: University of Washington Press, 1976), 280.

15. Isaac F. Marcosson, *Anaconda* (New York: Dodd, Mead & Co., 1957); Sarah McNelis, *Copper King at War; The Biography of F. Augustus Heinze* (Missoula: University of Montana Press, 1968); Michael P. Malone, *The Battle for Butte – Mining and Politics on the Northern Frontier, 1864–1906* (Seattle, Washington: University of Washington Press, 1981); Dennis L. Swibold, *Copper Chorus: Mining, Politics, and the Montana Press, 1889–1959* (Helena, Mont.: Montana Historical Society Press; Guilford, Conn.: Distributed by Globe Pequot Press, 2006).

16. *Montana Almanac*, 174.

17. Terry, interview, 13 June 1970, 98.

18. Circulation figures for 1903 and 1908 were 14,704 and 14,075 respectively. Ian Gordon, *Comic Strips and Consumer Culture, 1890–1945* (Washington: Smithsonian Institute Press, 1998), 161.

19. R. L. Polk & Co.'s *Anaconda, City Directory* (Helena, MT: R. L. Polk & Co., 1906).

20. Terry, interview, 13 June 1970, 98. Terry would claim he spent "a couple of years" in Anaconda but in fact spent less than a year.

21. Stout, *Montana: its Story and Biography*, 333–334.

22. Ibid., 415–416.

23. Patrick F. Morris, *Anaconda Montana: Copper Smelting Boom Town on the Western Frontier* (Bethseda, MD: Swann Publishing, 1997), 82; Matt J. Kelly, *Anaconda, Montana's Copper City* (Anaconda, MT: Soroptimist Club of Montana, 1983), 20.

24. He was born on August 18, 1870 and died on August 1, 1900 from liver cancer in Englewood, New Jersey.

25. "People We Read About", *The Red Lodge Picket* (Montana), 10 August 1900, 7; "By Way of Introduction", *Anaconda Standard*, 5 September 1899, p. 4; "John W. Trowbridge Dead", *The World* (New York), 4 August 1900, p. 5

26. "William H. Loomis", *New York Times*, 1 December 1917, p. 13.

27. "Rudolph E. Leppert", *New York Times*, 5 October 1949, p. 29:3.

28. "Willis H. Thorndike", *New York Times*, 20 March 1940, p. 34:8; Doris Ostrander Dawdy, *Artists of the American West: A Biographical Dictionary* (Chicago: Sage Books, 1974); Falk, *Who Was Who in American Art* (1999), 3294; Nancy Dustin Wall Moure, *Dictionary of Art and Artists in Southern California Before 1930* (Glendale, Calif.: Dustin Publications, 1975); Edan Milton Hughes, *Artists in California, 1786–1940*, 3rd ed. (Sacramento, CA: Crocker Art Museum, 2002); Bob Vine also makes mention of two other cartoonists ("Brinstey" and "Callahan") who were cartoonists at the *Standard* but the author could find no information on these artists. Bob Vine, "Going for the Gold", *Historic Review Quarterly* (Anaconda/Deer Lodge County Historical Society), vol. 7, no. 2 (Summer 1999): 12.

29. The first automobile dealership in Anaconda was established by Charles Branscombe in 1905. By 1906, there were only 120 automobiles on the road in Montana. Morris, *Anaconda Montana*, 234.

30. Patricia Leahy, *Paul Terry Stories*, Paul Terry Papers, Fayetteville, North Carolina, 1–2.

31. "Zero Weather on New Year's in Anaconda", *Anaconda Standard*, 1 January 1907, p. 3; "Bad Weather in North", *Anaconda Standard*, 9 January 1907, p. 13; "Cold weather and Snow Interfere With Traffic", *Anaconda Standard*, 15 January 1907, p. 11; "Zero Weather Again Prevails in

Butte", *Anaconda Standard*, 25 January 1907, p. 2.

32. Charles Henry Carey, "Henry Lewis Pittock", in *History of Oregon*, volume II (Portland, Oregon: The Pioneer Historical Publishing Company, 1922), 14–17; "Pittock, Henry Lewis", in *The National Cyclopaedia of American Biography*, volume XVI (Ann Arbor, Michigan: University Microfilms, 1967), 27; *Who Was Who in America*, volume I, 1897–1942, 976; Garraty and Carnes, *American National Biography; Dictionary of American Biography*.

33. Burke and Howe, *American Authors and Books. 1640 to the Present Day*; L.E. Dearborn, ed., *Appleton's Cyclopaedia of American Biography. A supplement*, six volumes (New York: Press Association Compilers, 1918–1931); Joseph P. McKerns, ed., *Biographical Dictionary of American Journalism* (New York: Greenwood Press, 1989); *Dictionary of American Biography*; "Scott, Harvey Whitefield", *The National Cyclopaedia of American Biography*, volume 16 (New York: James T. White & Co., 1918), 151; *Who Was Who in America*, volume I, 1897–1942. Obituaries: "H.W. Scott Dies After Operation", *The Oregonian*, 8 August 1910, p. 1, 4; "Mr. Scott Became Editor By Chance", *The Oregonian*, 9 August 1910, p. 11.

34. Carey, "Harvey Whitefield Scott", *History of Oregon*, 5–7.

35. Sidney Kobre, *The Yellow Press and Gilded Age Journalism* ([Tallahassee:] Florida State University, [1964]), 274–275.

36. "Murphy, Harry (Daniels)", in *Who's Who in American Art*, ed. Dorothy B. Gilbert (New York: R.R. Bowker Co., 1959), 413; "Murphy, Harry D.", in *Who's Who in American Art*, ed. Alice Coe McGlauflin (Washington, DC: The American Federation of Arts, 1937), 378; "Murphy, Harry Daniels", in *Artists of the American West*, 206; Falk, *Who Was Who in American Art, 1564–1975* (1999).

37. Falk, *Who Was Who in American Art, 1564–1975* (1999).

38. The Milton W. Werschkul Collection which contains photocopy newspaper articles regarding the work, retirement and death of Milton Werschkul, as well as original art and photographs can be accessed at the Oregon Historical Society Research Library, Oregon Historical Society Davies Family Research Library, Portland, Oregon.

39. "Jackson, Charles Samuel", in *The National Cyclopaedia of American Biography*, volume XXXIII, 63; Joseph Gaston, *Portland Oregon: Its History and Builder*, volume II (Portland: The S.J. Clarke Publishing Company, 1911), 167–168; *Dictionary of American Biography*; "Jackson, Charles Samuel", in *Who Was Who in America. A Component Volume of Who's Who in American History*, volume I, 1897–1942 (Chicago: A.N. Marquis Co., 1943). Obituaries: "C. S. Jackson Succumbs", *The Oregonian*, 28 December 1924, p. 1; "Simple Rites Held For C. S. Jackson", *The Morning Oregonian*, 30 December 1924, p. 7.

40. Horn, *The World Encyclopedia of Comics*; Dawdy, *Artists of the American West*; *Who Was Who in America*, volume IX, 1985–1989 (Wilmette, IL: Marquis Who's Who, 1989).

41. H. S. Crocker Company, *Crocker-Langley San Francisco Directory 1907* (San Francisco: H. S. Crocker Company, 1907), 1563.

42. Terry, interview, 20 December 1969, 13.

43. Older, *San Francisco: Magic City*, 66–68.

44. William L. Rivers and David M. Rubin, *A Region's Press: Anatomy of Newspapers in the San Francisco Bay Area* (Berkeley, Institute of Governmental Studies, University of California, 1971). Marion Davies, *The Times We Had: Life with William Randolph Hearst*, edited by Pamela Pfau & Kenneth S. Marx (Indianapolis: Bobbs-Merrill, 1975); Mrs. Fremont Older, *William Randolph Hearst, American* (New York, London: D. Appleton-Century Company, Incorporated, 1936); Ben H. Procter, *William Randolph Hearst: The Early Years, 1863–1910* (New York: Oxford University Press, 1998).

45. *N.W. Ayer & Son's American Newspaper Annual and Directory, 1910* (Philadelphia: N.W. Ayer & Sons, 1910), 74.

46. Leahy, *Paul Terry Stories*, 1.

47. Ibid. The other version of this story has Terry simply being warned by the presiding judge (Carmel Marchionni, "Paul Terry, At 82, Still Calls the Toon", *Herald Statesman* (Yonkers, N.Y.), 19 March 1969, p. 28.

48. Marchionni, "Paul Terry, At 82, Still Calls the Toon", p. 28.

49. H. S. Crocker Company, *Crocker-Langley San Francisco Directory 1909* (San Francisco: H. S. Crocker Company, 1909), 1531.

50. "Paul H. Terry – Defendant – Direct", *Case on Appeal from Judgment*, Frank H. Moser v. Paul H. Terry, William M. Weiss, Earl W. Hammons, and Terrytoons, Inc., 254 A.D. 873 (New York Supreme Court, Appellate Division – Second Department), 20 September 1937, New York State Library, Albany, New York, 513–514.

51. "Butte Briefs", *The Anaconda Standard*, 12 September 1909, p. 7.

52. Ellis A. Davis, *Commercial Encyclopedia of the Pacific Southwest: California, Nevada, Utah, Arizona* (Berkeley, Cal., Seattle, Wash.: E. A. Davis, 1911), 58.

53. Raymond Gros, *T.R. in Cartoon. Four Hundred Illustrations by Leading Cartoonists of the Daily and Weekly Press All Over the World* (New York: Saalfield Pub. Co., 1910).

54. Higgins was born in Halifax, Nova Scotia on November 30, 1834 and died on November 30, 1917. In 1858, he settled in Victoria, British Columbia and was editor and proprietor of the *British Colonist*. He organized and was first president of the Victoria fire department and was a member of the Board of Education from 1866 to 1869. He was elected to the Legislative Assembly of British Columbia for the electoral district of Esquimalt in 1886. He was re-elected in 1890 and 1898. From 1890 to 1898, he was Speaker of the Legislative Assembly of British Columbia. He was defeated in 1900. He later wrote two books: *The Mystic Spring and Other Tales of Western Life* (Toronto, 1904) and *The Passing of a Race and More Tales of Western Life* (Toronto, 1905). "Higgins, Hon. David Williams", in *Biographical Dictionary of Well-Known British Columbians*, by J. B. Kerr (Vancouver, B.C.: Kerr & Begg, 1890), 192; "Higgins, Hon. David Williams", in *Canadian Men and Women of the Time: A Handbook of Canadian Biography of*

Chapter 6 • A Tour of the West

Living Characters, by Henry J. Morgan (Toronto: William Briggs, 1912), 532–533; *A Dictionary of North American Authors Deceased before 1950*, compiled by W. Stewart Wallace (Toronto: Ryerson Press, 1951); *The Macmillan Dictionary of Canadian Biography*, fourth edition, edited by W. Stewart Wallace (Toronto: Macmillan of Canada, 1978); Ramsay Cook, ed., *Dictionary of Canadian Biography*, volume XIV: 1911 to 1920 (Toronto: University of Toronto Press, 1998).

55. At various times he owned all of Coronado Island, the San Diego-Coronado Ferry System, the Union-Tribune Publishing Co., the San Diego Electric Railway, the San Diego & Arizona Railway, and Belmont Park in Mission Beach. He built several downtown buildings, including the Union Building in 1908, the Spreckels Theater Building in 1912, the Hotel San Diego, and the Golden West Hotel. He employed thousands of people and at one time he paid 10 percent of all the property taxes in San Diego County. James D. Hart, *A Companion to California* (New York: Oxford University Press, 1978); John N. Ingham, *Biographical Dictionary of American Business Leaders* (Westport, CT: Greenwood Press, 1983); *Dictionary of American Biography, Who Was Who in America*, volume I, 1897–1942.

56. Justice B. Detwiler, ed., *Who's Who in California: A Biographical Directory 1928–1929* (San Francisco: Who's Who Publishing Company, 1929), 425.

57. *Who's Who on the Pacific Coast: A Biographical Dictionary of Noteworthy Men and Women of the Pacific Coast and the Western States* (Chicago: The A.N. Marquis Co., 1949), 124.

58. Donald McKee was born on March 1, 1883 in Indianapolis, Marion [Richland, Wayne], Indiana. He became a cartoonist and illustrator for the *New Yorker*, *Life*, *Judge*, *Saturday Evening Post* and *Collier's* magazine. He was a newspaper cartoonist with the San Francisco *Call* and the San Francisco *Bulletin*. He was employed in the animation industry both at the Aesop's Fables Studio and later the Terrytoons studio. Donald McKee died in October 1945. Falk, *Who Was Who In American Art* (1985), 409.

59. "Juggling and Charcoal", *The Anaconda Standard*, 19 February 1906, p. 5.

60. "About the City", *The Anaconda Standard*, 19 April 1907, p. 5.

61. "Going into Vaudeville in a Lively Cartoon Act", *The Anaconda Standard*, 23 January 1910, p. 5.

62. Ibid.

63. The San Francisco *Call* newspaper archives, 1890–1913, are available online at the California Digital Newspaper collection.

64. Falk, *Who Was Who in American Art 1564–1975*, 2148; Hughes, *Artists in California, 1786–1940*; Ron Goulart, ed., *The Encyclopedia of American Comics* (New York: Facts on File, 1990); Obituary: San Francisco *Chronicle*, 20 May 1964.

65. In the 1930s, Hershfield was in demand as a banquet toastmaster, averaging some 200 banquets and dinners annually. During his lifetime, he was toastmaster or emcee at an estimated 16,000 events, including charity affairs, dinners and stage benefits. On March 11, 1938, he was signed to head the story department of MGM's cartoon studio. He then became a radio personality and a columnist for the New York *Daily Mirror*. He died on December 15, 1974 in New York City. Falk, *Who Was Who In American Art*; Goulart, *The Encyclopedia of American Comics*. Obituary: Michael T. Kaufman, "Harry Hershfield Dead; Humorist and Raconteur", *New York Times*, 16 December 1974, p. 36.

66. Ripley was born on December 25, 1890 in Santa Rosa, California. On December 19, 1918 his newspaper cartoon series on random sports facts *Champs and Chumps* was published in the *New York Globe*. On July 9, 1929, William Randolph Hearst's King Features Syndicate featured *Believe It or Not!* in 17 papers worldwide. In 1930 he began an 18-year run on radio and a 19-year association with show producer Doug Storer. Hearst funded Ripley's travels around the world, where Ripley recorded live radio shows from underwater, the sky, caves, snake pits and foreign countries. His odditoriums opened in San Diego (1935), Dallas (1936), Cleveland (1937), and San Francisco and New York (1940). On May 27, 1949, he died of a heart attack in New York City, New York. *Dictionary of American Biography*, supplement 4 (New York: Charles Scribner's Sons, 1974); Van Doren, *Webster's American Biographies*, 1979 edition; *The National Cyclopaedia of American Biography*, volume 41 (New York: James T. White & Co., 1956); Martin Sheridan, *Comics and their Creators: Life Stories of American Cartoonists* (Westport, CT: Hyperion Press, 1971), 243–246; Bob Considine, *Ripley, the Modern Marco Polo* (Garden City, N.Y.: Doubleday, 1961); Neal Thompson, *A Curious Man: The Strange & Brilliant Life of Robert "Believe It or Not" Ripley* (New York: Crown Archetype, 2013).

67. Terry, interview, 20 December 1969, 13.

Chapter 7

The Move to Metropolis: Barron Collier, Park Row and the Winsor McCay Dinner, 1911–1914

In 1911, the population of New York City, the largest city in the United States, was just over 4.76 million people, over twice the size of Chicago, the 2nd largest city in the United States.[1] Much of the population of New York City was in Manhattan, which reached its historical high of over 2.3 million. However, the other boroughs began to grow rapidly as the Interborough Rapid Transit system expanded. Soon after Paul arrived in New York City he began enquiring at various newspaper offices looking for employment opportunities as a newspaper artist but at the time none of the dailies were hiring.

Having little funds to draw upon, Paul did not have the luxury to wait until a cartoonist position came available. Rather, he found work with the Street Railways Advertising Company headed by capitalist Barron Gift Collier at an office located at 175 5th Avenue.[2] Terry formed part of the staff that created ideas for advertising car cards that were placed in subways and streetcars throughout the city.[3] Collier was born in Memphis, Tennessee in 1873 and in his late teens while in partnership with another youth obtained his first contract for placing advertising cards in street cars, this in Springfield, Missouri. He soon followed by his second in Chattanooga and his third in Memphis. In 1900 he moved to New York City, where he rapidly expanded his surface transportation advertising operations.[4]

In 1905–1906 he organized the Street Railways Advertising Company as a national sales organization. He then began to purchase the streetcar and bus advertising companies in New York, Boston, Chicago, Philadelphia and other cities. His final important purchase was that of Artemas Ward, Inc., which controlled the advertising and vending privileges in the Interborough subways in New York City.[5] By the time of his death in 1939, in New York City alone, transportation advertising cards accounted for $4 million in advertising billings a year (approximately $70 million adjusted for inflation).[6]

Paul was employed as an ad writer and idea man with Barron Collier for about a year, work involving sketching ideas for advertising cards marketing a wide variety of products and services. These advertising cards were placed in buses, streetcars, and other mass public transportation vehicles. In 1912, he found work as a cartoonist for the New York *Press*. The *Press* was owned by Frank Andrew Munsey. Munsey was born in 1854 in Mercer, Maine. After a brief career as a telegraph operator and later as a manager of the Augusta telegraph office, and after several months study at Poughkeepsie Business College, he moved to New York City to launch a children's magazine, the *Golden Argosy*, which later became the *Argosy*, a pulp magazine for adults specializing in adventure stories. It was selling about 500,000 copies per issue from the newsstands at its peak in 1910. He founded *Munsey's Weekly* in 1889 which was renamed *Munsey's Magazine* in 1891 which publication led the world in circulation in 1907. In 1901 he began to acquire newspapers extensively. During

Chapter 7 • The Move to Metropolis

Fig. 7.1 – Park Row (Newspaper Row), New York City (first decade of the 20th century).

the next 23 years he bought and then discontinued, sold or merged a large number of newspapers, including seven New York dailies.[7]

In 1912, Munsey bought the New York *Press* for a million dollars cash, expecting to make it the New York member of his chain. The newspaper was a successful daily founded in 1887 by Frank Hatton, former Postmaster General and Chicago publisher, and Robert P. Porter, economist and journalist, as the *Progressive Republican*.[8] As the title of the newspaper suggests, the publication was strongly Republican in politics and for most of its existence had a circulation of about 100,000. The paper had strong sports coverage and a somewhat sensational personality. By 1915, the newspaper had a circulation of 106,827.[9] Since the newspaper did not immediately prosper, in 1916 Munsey bought both the morning and evening editions of the *Sun* for $2.5 million, merged the larger and far older morning edition with the *Press* (which effectively disappeared in the process), and spent an additional $2 million over the next four years to establish the fattened *Sun* as a major factor in the morning field.[10]

The New York *Press* was located on Park Row, a street located in the Financial District of the New York City borough of Manhattan. The roadway was previously called Chatham Street and during the late 19th century it was nicknamed "Newspaper Row", as most of New York City's newspapers were located on the street to be close to the action at New York City Hall. By 1911, at the time of Terry's arrival in New York City, all but two of New York's 14 daily newspapers were still located in the Park Row area. The seven papers published in the morning were: *The World*, *The Times*, *The Tribune*, *The Herald*, *The Sun*, *The American*, and *The Press*. Evening papers were: the *Evening World*, *Evening Sun*, *Evening Journal*, *The Post*, *The Mail*, *The Telegram*, and *The Globe*.[11]

Terry was employed for the *Press* in an artistic capacity for about

59

two to three years, until 1915. Little is known as to what artistically he contributed to the newspaper although it appears he did occasional work on comic strips and retouching.[12] What is known is that working under Munsey was no easy task. His eccentricities were legion; he was known to disapprove of fat men and soon separated them from his employment. His distaste for smoking caused the habit to be outlawed from the premises of his properties, though the ban was rarely enforced among his heavily puffing employees except when he was at the office.[13] The editor-in-chief of the newspaper was Ervin Wardman, a Harvard graduate. He had been in that position since 1896, having previously been a managing editor from 1895 to 1896. Prior to his employment at the *Press*, Wardman was on the editorial staff with the New York *Tribune* from 1888 to 1895.[14]

As a writer, Waldman was both well-informed and aggressive. In the field of editorials, his expertise was in the area of economics and labor.[15] Wardman is most noted for being the first to publish the term "yellow journalism" to refer to the late 19th century circulation battles between Joseph Pulitzer's *New York World* and William Randolph Hearst's *New York Journal*. The battle peaked from 1895 to about 1898, and historical usage often refers specifically to this period. Both papers were accused by critics of sensationalizing the news in order to drive up circulation, although the newspapers did serious reporting as well. Wardman had also used the expression "yellow kid journalism" referring to the then-popular comic strip character, Yellow Kid, created and drawn by Richard F. Outcault in the comic strip *Hogan's Alley* that ran from 1895 to 1898 in Joseph Pulitzer's *New York World*, and later William Randolph Hearst's *New York Journal*. The strip was one of the first Sunday supplement comic strips in an American newspaper, although it's graphical layout had already been thoroughly established in political and other, purely-for-entertainment cartoons.[16]

In 1913, Terry's old friend from the *San Francisco Chronicle*, Robert Ripley, moved to New York City and both artists, as bachelors, shared a studio in the city for about 18 months.[17] Terry and Ripley's address in April 1913 was located at 65 West 50th Street in Manhattan.[18] At the time, Ripley had found work as a sports cartoonist for the New York *Globe*.[19] During this same period, Terry began working on a comic strip for a Hearst newspaper.[20] Another of Terry's friends from California, Herbert "Hype" Igoe, sports writer and cartoonist, had moved to New York City in 1907. Igoe, like Paul Terry, Rube Goldberg, Herb Roth, and Tad Dorgan, attended Polytechnic High School where he was taught art and now was employed as an artist in New York City. Igoe began employment with *The Evening Journal* before being employed with the New York *Sun*. Both were brief positions. He spent the majority of his career at the *New York World* where he became an expert on boxing and conducted a column *Pardon My Glove*, the title of which is said to have been suggested to him by Irving Berlin.[21]

By 1914, while Paul was continuing to labor under Wardman at the *Press*, a new film medium had been born, animation. The birth of this new film form can largely be traced to the work of two filmmakers, James Stuart Blackton (1895–1941) and Emile Cohl (1857–1938). James Stuart Blackton, a newspaper cartoonist/reporter and lightning sketch artist, moved into creating animated "trick-films" to attract audiences to Vitagraph's live-action features. In 1900 he produced and directed *The Enchanted Drawing* a silent film best known for containing the first animated sequences recorded on standard motion picture film. The film shows a man drawing a cartoon face on an easel. He draws a hat on the head and then a bottle of wine, a glass and a cigar. He then takes objects off the canvas and they go back into the image.

In 1907, Blackton undertook frame-by-frame animation of objects to produce the trick film *The Haunted Hotel*. The film concerns a tourist spending the night in a tavern run by invisible spirits. Most of the effects are live-action using wires and other stage equipment, but one scene of a dinner making itself was produced using stop-motion, and was presented in a tight close-up that allowed nascent animators to study it for technique. Blackton's *Humorous Phases of Funny Faces* (1906) is generally considered to

Chapter 7 • The Move to Metropolis

Fig. 7.2 – Animation drawing of Oil Can Harry dancing with Pearl Pureheart from *A Fight to the Finish* (1947).

be the first entirely animated film and used frame-by-frame animation of drawings. In the film, faces of a man and a woman drawn on a blackboard undergo progressive changes – the man flirts with the woman, she smiles, he blows smoke in her face, and so forth. The animation was accomplished by turning the camera crank once, erasing part of the artwork on the blackboard, redrawing the art in a new position, and then turning the crank again, and so on.[22]

Emile Cohl began his career as a film animator at age 50 after many years as a newspaper caricaturist and political satirist. After viewing and studying Blackton's *The Haunted Hotel*, Cohl discovered the techniques of animation. Cohl expanded the work of Blackton by moving out of drawn and object animation as a novelty in "trick film" so that an entire story could be told using animation. One of Cohl's first films *Fantasmagorie* (1908) ran only two minutes but was composed of 700 drawings narrating the surreal adventures of a little clown. The short, which uses a stream of consciousness style, is a direct tribute to *Les Arts Incohérents*, a short-lived art movement noted for its satirical irreverence. The short was the first animated film produced from traditional hand-drawn animation, a technique popularized later by Hollywood animation studios.

The rest of the films Cohl made for Gaumont involve strange transformations (*Les Joyeaux Microbes* [*The Joyous Microbes*, aka *The Merry Microbes* (UK)] (1909)), some outstanding matte effects (*Clair de lune espagnol* [*Spanish Moonlight*, aka *The Man in the Moon* (US), aka *The Moon-Struck Matador* (UK)] (1909)), and adorable puppet animation (*Le Tout Petit Faust* [*The Little Faust*, aka *The Beautiful Margaret* (US)] (1910)). Other films used jointed cut-outs or animated matches (the latter an especial favorite of Cohl). In his lifetime, Cohl's most famous film was *Le Peintre néo-impressionniste* [*The Neo-Impressionistic Painter*], made in 1910. The plot concerns an artist who sells blank colored canvases to a collector. As he gives their ridiculous titles, the collector imagines them being drawn on the canvas. For example, the red canvas is "a cardinal eating lobster with tomatoes by the banks of the Red Sea". Quite obviously, the artist is not a neo-Impressionist (the name taken from the latest vogue in Paris) – he's an Incoherent.[23]

The work of Blackton and Cohl would change the career path of cartoonist Winsor McCay (1867–1934). From 1889 to 1903 McCay spent his early career doing artwork on posters and pamphlets at the National Printing and Engraving Company,[24] designed posters and other advertisements for the Kohl & Middleton Dime Museum, Heck and Avery's Family Theater (1896), Avery's New Dime Museum (1898), and Will S. Heck's Wonder World and Theater (1899),[25] undertook illustrative work for the *Cincinnati Commercial Tribune*,[26] and then became head of the art department at *The Cincinnati Enquirer*.[27] From 1903 to 1911, McCay's body of work was in

61

TERRYTOONS: The Story of Paul Terry and His Classic Cartoon Factory

Fig. 7.3 – Original comic book story artwork to *Mighty Mouse* #6 (St. John, 1948).

newspaper comics. His most notable comic strip creations included *Little Sammy Sneeze* (published in the *New York Herald*, 1904–1906), *Dream of the Rarebit Fiend* (published in the *Evening Telegram*, 1904–1911), and *Little Nemo in Slumberland* (published in the *New York Herald*, 1905–1911). In addition, in 1906 he began performing on a vaudeville tour as a chalk-talk

Chapter 7 • The Move to Metropolis

sketch artist while completing his comic strip and illustration work on time, often working in hotel rooms or backstage.[28]

Inspired by flip books his son brought home and the Cohl animated films imported from Gaumont in France and released in the United States by distributor George B. Kleine, in 1909 McCay began to experiment in animation.[29] He completed 10 animated films between 1911 and 1921,[30] and three more were planned but never produced.[31] His first animated creation was the 11½ minute film *Little Nemo in Slumberland* (aka *Little Nemo*) based on characters from his comic strip. McCay borrowed from both Blackton and Cohl in creating this film. From Blackton he adapted the motif of a live artist drawing characters that come to life, while from Cohl he used the free-flowing abstract metamorphosis of pencil lines that become recognizable characters.[32]

In 1911, under the supervision of Blackton, both the drawings and live-action prologue and epilogue for *Little Nemo* (about McCay betting some gentlemen that he could complete 4,000 drawings that move in one month) were shot under the supervision of Blackton at the Vitagraph studio on Avenue M.[33] The film was released on April 8, and McCay used it in his vaudeville act beginning on April 12 at New York's Colonial Theater. The critical and commercial success of the film inspired McCay to hand-color each of the frames of the originally black-and-white animation[34] and then create his next animated short *How a*

Mosquito Operates (aka *The Story of a Mosquito*, 1912), based on a *Rarebit Fiend* episode from June 5, 1909,[35] a silent six-minute short about a giant mosquito who torments a sleeping man and drinks so much blood he ends up exploding. The short features a high technical quality of naturalistic animation, considered far ahead of its contemporaries. *How a Mosquito Operates* was enthusiastically received when McCay first unveiled it as part of his "chalk talk" vaudeville act, and in a theatrical release that soon followed.[36]

McCay's next animated film *Gertie the Dinosaur* debuted in February 1914 as part of McCay's vaudeville act.[37] McCay wanted Gertie to be his finest animated cartoon to date. He visited the museums of New York to conduct more research on dinosaurs.[38] Gertie was McCay's first piece of animation with detailed backgrounds traced by assistant John A. Fitzsimmons.[39] In his vaudeville act McCay introduced Gertie as "the only dinosaur in captivity", and commanded the animated beast with a bullwhip.[40] Gertie seemed to obey McCay. She emerged from behind some rocks, raised her foot, bowed to the audience, and ate a tree and a boulder, though she had a will of her own and sometimes rebelled by lunging forward and snapping at McCay with her huge jaws. When McCay admonished her, she cried, and this becomes the most endearing moment. McCay consoled her by tossing her an apple. In reality he pocketed the cardboard prop apple as a cartoon

apple simultaneously appeared on screen.[41]

Gertie later tosses a woolly mammoth unluckily wandering by, and then dances an absurd tango. She drinks a lake dry and the cliff on which Gertie stands gives way and crumbles under her increased weight. In the finale, McCay walked offstage, reappeared in animated form in the film, and had Gertie carry him away off-screen to immortality.[42] Producer William Fox's Box Office Attractions obtained distribution rights to a modified version of *Gertie* that could be played in regular movie theaters. This version was prefaced with a live-action sequence and replaced the interactive portions with intertitles.[43]

In late 1914, Robert Ripley alerted Paul to a dinner being given for newspaper cartoonists by Winsor McCay that was being held at Reisenweber's Restaurant located at 987 8th Avenue (8th Avenue and 58th Street) near Columbus Circle[44] where McCay would be performing his *Gertie the Dinosaur* vaudeville act.[45] The restaurant was founded by John Nicholas Reisenweber who established a small country tavern in the middle of farms on Bloomingdale Road, later 8th Avenue, in 1856. The tavern, which remained at its location until it closed during the prohibition era, grew into a large nationally famous restaurant with 12 dining rooms and about 1,000 employees. The restaurant became a symbol for the free-spending, amusement-seeking crowds of Broadway.

The restaurant was taken over by John Reisenweber, Jr.

63

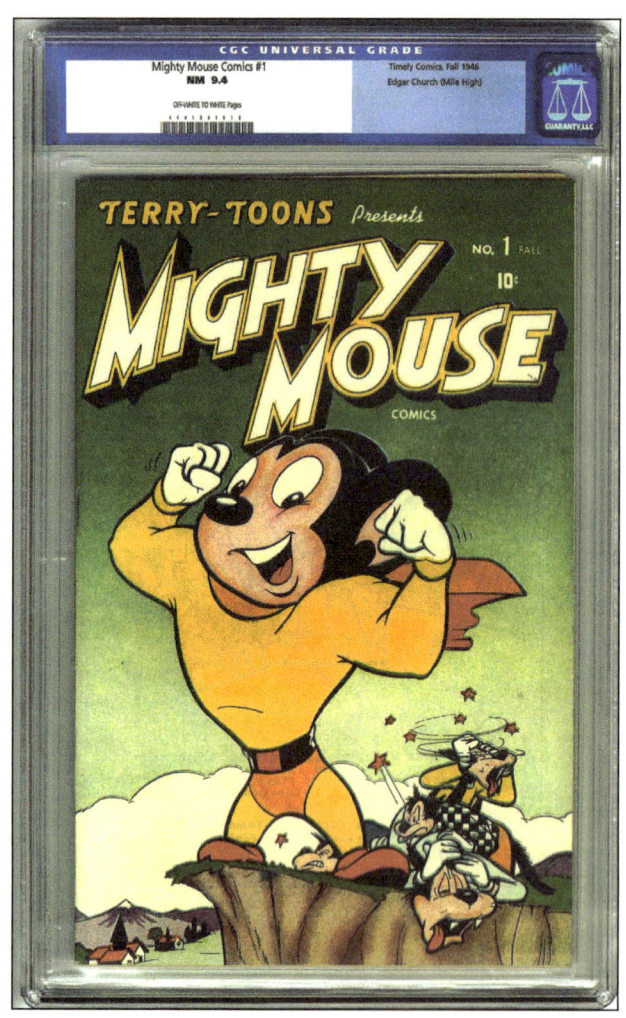

TERRYTOONS: The Story of Paul Terry and His Classic Cartoon Factory

Fig. 7.4 – *Mighty Mouse* #1 (Timely, 1946).

(1851–1931) while still a young man after the death of his father. The restaurant became a cabaret and was the first to offer a floor show with principals, chorus, and settings, and although other restaurants of the time had offered single acts, Reisenweber's was the first to offer a space for patrons to dance. Among the headliners were Gracie Fields, Sophie Tucker, and the Original Dixieland Jazz Band. In 1913, choreographer Ned Wayburn (1874–1942) staged a floor spectacle. Expenses were so heavy that management sought some way to meet the increased overhead. After much consideration, each patron was asked to pay a 25 cents "couvert charge". Diners protested vehemently against the charge, but the charge remained. Soon the charge gave the restaurant distinction and other restaurant proprietors followed the precedent of Reisenweber's.[46]

Present that night was some of New York's finest newspaper cartoonists including Rube Goldberg and Frank Moser.[47] Moser was born in Oketo, Kansas on May 27, 1886, was raised on a family farm, and received his preliminary education at public schools in Marysville, Kansas. He studied at the Albert T. Reid Art School in Topeka, Kansas, 1907–1908, and at the Cumming School of Art, Des Moines, Iowa, 1908–1910. He attended the Art Students League and the National Academy of Design, both in New York City. While attending school in Des Moines, he worked with Jay N. Darling, cartoonist for the *Register*, as part-time cartoonist and illustrator, doing general utility sketch assignments. In 1910, when Ding left the newspaper, Moser replaced him and drew a daily cartoon for two years. He moved to New York City in 1912 and while attending art school worked illustrating for the New York *Globe* a daily story "In Our School" which ran for four years.[48]

At the dinner, McCay screened *Gertie the Dinosaur* while performing his stage act to his enthralled audience of newspaper men. As soon as Terry glimpsed the first few frames of *Gertie* flickering on the screen he knew what he wanted to spend the rest of his career doing, it was the perfect marriage of photography and cartooning. As Terry explained in his 1969 interview:

> But after I came to New York, I went to a dinner one night, when I was on the New York

Chapter 7 • The Move to Metropolis

Press, and that's where Winsor McCay showed us his picture, *Gertie the Dinosaur*. And that gave me the...that's it! You see you've been floundering around; advertising agencies, and this and that, but all at once it consolidated, right there.[49]

Terry didn't have to ask McCay how he was able to make Gertie perform on film as he had been a photographer,[50] and may have been exposed to his brother John's earlier work experimenting with animation in California. McCay encouraged all those who attended the dinner to enter the field of animation and develop the craft. McCay told Terry and his fellow artists that the art of animation had tremendous possibilities although he was not in the position to further the film form as he was a very busy and well-paid newspaper cartoonist.[51]

As Terry left Reisenweber's that night he was already planning his first animated production. Anything seemed possible in the atmosphere of the early part of the 20th century. He was young, single, with no dependents and could support himself without yielding all his time and energies to his employer. If McCay could work outside of his newspaper work to create such a masterpiece of animation, so could he. To Terry, his future never seemed brighter. ❧

Notes

1. Department of Commerce, Bureau of the Census, "Table 50. Area and Population of Central City, Metropolitan District, and Adjacent Territory, For Cities of 200,000 Inhabitants or More: 1910 and 1900", Chapter I. Number and Distribution of Inhabitants, volume I. Population, Thirteenth Census of the United States Taken in the Year 1910 (Washington: Government Printing Office, 1913), 74.

2. *Trow Business Directory of the Boroughs of Manhattan and the Bronx City of New York 1913* (New York: Trow Directory, Printing & Bookbinding Co., 1913), 11.

3. Terry, interview, 20 December 1969, 14.

4. "Collier, Barron Gift", in *Dictionary of American Biography, Supplement 2*, ed. R.L. Schuyler (New York: Charles Scribner's Sons, 1958), 112–113.

5. He would invest heavily in Florida real estate and at one point owned 1,186,000 acres in that state. He had a county as well as a bridge over the Punta Gorda named after him. He established a chain of Florida hotels and extended his interests to include bus lines, banking, newspapers, a telephone company, a steamship line, and various farming operations. "Collier, Barron [Gift]", in *The National Cyclopaedia of American Biography*, vol. XXXIX, 49–50; *Who Was Who in America*, volume I, 1897–1942, p. 244. Obituaries: "Barron Collier Dies Suddenly, 65", *New York Times*, 14 March 1939, p. 21:1–2.

6. "Advertising News and Notes", *New York Times*, 15 March 1939, p. 39:2.

7. "Munsey, Frank Andrew", in *Webster's American Biographies*, 753–754; "Munsey, Frank Andrew", *Encyclopedia of American Biography*, ed. John A. Garraty (New York: Harper & Row, 1974), 796–797; "Munsey, Frank Andrew", in *The National Cyclopedia of American Biography*, volume XX, 47–49. Obituary: "Frank Munsey", *Variety*, 23 December 1925, 42.

8. Frank Luther Mott, *American Journalism: A History of Newspapers in the United States Through 250 Years, 1690 to 1940* (New York: The Macmillan Company, 1941), 637–638.

9. *N.W. Ayer & Son's American Newspaper Annual and Directory 1915* (Philadelphia: N. W. Ayer & Son, 1915), 670.

10. "Munsey", *The National Cyclopedia of American Biography*, 48; Richard Kluger, *The Paper: The Life and Death of the New York Herald Tribune* (New York: Alfred A, Knopf, 1986), 209; John Tebbel, *The Compact History of the American Newspaper* (New York: Hawthorn Books, Inc., 1969), 219.

11. Allen Churchill, *Park Row* (New York: Rinehart & Company, 1973), 290.

12. *Lunch with Paul Terry*, 19.

13. Kluger, *The Paper*, 209.

14. "Wardman, Ervin", *Who Was Who in America*, volume I, 1897–1942, 1299.

15. "Ervin Waldman, Publisher, Dies", *New York Times*, 14 January 1923, Sec. I, Pt. 2, p. 6:3.

16. Churchill, *Park Row*, 82.

17. Paul Terry, interview by Harvey Deneroff, New Rochelle, New York, 14 July 1970, John Canemaker Animation Collection, Fales Library, Elmer Holmes Bobst Library, New York University, New York City, 133.

18. "Paul Houlton Terry", Passport Applications, January 2, 1906 – March 31, 1925, Collection Number: ARC Identifier 583830 / MLR Number A1 534, NARA Series: M1490, Roll #: 182, National Archives and Records Administration (NARA), Washington D.C. Terry confirms that he and Ripley shared the studio at 50th Street (Marchionni, "Paul Terry, At 82, Still Calls The Toon", 28).

19. Sheridan, *Comics and their Creators*, 244.

20. In his 1969 interview, Terry mentioned that after working for the New York *Press* in 1912 he drew a comic strip *Alonzo* which was syndicated by King Features in 1912. In fact he drew *Alonzo* for the San Francisco *Call* (1909–1910) three years earlier in San Francisco and King Features did not syndicate any comic strips in 1912 as the syndicate was not formed until 1914 (Terry, interview, 20 December

65

1969, 14); Becker, *Comic Art in America*, 98.

21. Obituary: "Hype Igoe, Writer, Boxing Expert, 67", *New York Times*, 12 February 1945, p. 19:2.

22. The most comprehensive and authoritative source on Blackton is: Marian Blackton Trimble, *J. Stuart Blackton: A Personal Biography by His Daughter* (Metuchen, N.J.: Scarecrow Press, 1985). Biographical entries can also be found in: Maurice Horn, ed., *The World Encyclopedia of Cartoons* (New York : Chelsea House Publishers,1980), 123 (2nd ed. (Philadelphia: Chelsea House, 1999)); Garraty and Carnes, *American National Biography*; *Dictionary of American Biography*, supplement 3; *Who Was Who in America*, volume I, 1897–1942; Falk, *Who Was Who in American Art*; *Current Biography Yearbook*, 1941 edition (New York: H.W. Wilson Co., 1941); Maurice Horn, ed., *Contemporary Graphic Artists. A Biographical, Bibliographical, and Critical Guide to Current Illustrators, Animators, Cartoonists, Designers, and Other Graphic Artists*, volume 3 (Detroit: Gale Research, 1988); Christopher Lyon, ed., *The International Dictionary of Films and Filmmakers*, first edition, volume 2: Directors/Filmmakers (Detroit: St. James Press, 1984); Nicholas Thomas, ed., *The International Dictionary of Films and Filmmakers*, second edition, volume 2: Directors (Chicago: St. James Press, 1991); Laurie Collier Hillstrom, ed., *The International Dictionary of Films and Filmmakers*, third edition, volume 2: Directors (Detroit: St. James Press, 1997).

23. The two best sources on Cohl are: Donald Crafton, *Emile Cohl, Caricature, and Film* (Princeton, N.J.: Princeton University Press, 1990); Pascal Vimenet, *Émile Cohl* (Montreuil: Oeil; Annecy: Communauté de l'agglomération d'Annecy, 2008). Another source: Richard John Neupert, *French Animation History* (Malden, Me.: Wiley-Blackwell, 2011). Biographical references: Horn, *The World Encyclopedia of Cartoons*; Lyon, *The International Dictionary of Films and Filmmakers*, volume 2; Samantha Cook, ed., *The International Dictionary of Films and Filmmakers*, second edition, volume 4: Writers and Production Artists (Detroit: St. James Press, 1993); Grace Jeromski, ed., *The International Dictionary of Films and Filmmakers*, third edition, volume 4: Writers and Production Artists (Detroit: St. James Press, 1997); Tom Pendergast and Sara Pendergast, ed., *The International Dictionary of Films and Filmmakers*, fourth edition, volume 4: Writers and Production Artists (Detroit: St. James Press, 2000). Obituary: "Emile Cohl", *New York Times*, 22 January 1938, p. 15:3.

24. John Canemaker, *Winsor McCay: His Life and Art*, revised ed. (New York: Abrams Books, 2005), 38.

25. Canemaker, *Winsor McCay*, 38, 43.

26. Ibid., 47.

27. Ibid., 57.

28. Ibid., 131.

29. Ibid., 157.

30. Howard Beckerman, *Animation: The Whole Story* (New York: Allworth Press, 2003), 18–19.

31. Robert C. Harvey, *The Art of the Funnies: An Aesthetic History* (Jackson: University Press of Mississippi, 1994), 33.

32. Canemaker, *Winsor McCay*, 157–160.

33. Ibid., 160.

34. Ibid., 163.

35. Ibid., 167.

36. Ibid., 164–167.

37. Ibid., 175.

38. Ibid., 171.

39. Ibid., 169.

40. Ibid., 175.

41. Ibid., 176.

42. Ibid., 177.

43. Ibid., 182; "Gertie", *Variety*, 19 December 1914, 26. For more on Winsor McCay: Winsor McCay, *Winsor McCay: Early Works* (Miamisburg, OH: Checker Book Pub. Group, 2003); Katherine Roeder, *Wide Awake in Slumberland: Fantasy, Mass Culture, and Modernism in the Art of Winsor McCay* (Jackson: University Press of Mississippi, 2014). Other biographical sources: Falk, *Who Was Who in American Art*; Garraty and Carnes, *American National Biography*; *Contemporary Authors. A Bio-Bibliographical Guide to Current Writers in Fiction, General Nonfiction, Poetry, Journalism, Drama, Motion Pictures, Television, and Other Fields*, volume 169 (Detroit: Gale Group, 1999); Horn, *Contemporary Graphic Artists*, volume 1; Goulart, *The Encyclopedia of American Comics*; Lyon, *The International Dictionary of Films and Filmmakers*, volume 2; Cook, *The International Dictionary of Films and Filmmakers*, second edition, volume 4; Jeromski, *The International Dictionary of Films and Filmmakers*, third edition, volume 4; Pendergast and Pendergast, *The International Dictionary of Films and Filmmakers*, fourth edition, volume 4; *Something about the Author. Facts and Pictures About Authors and Illustrators of Books for Young People*, volumes 41 and 134 (Detroit: Gale Research, 1985 and 2003).

44. *Trow Business Directory of the Boroughs of Manhattan and the Bronx City of New York 1913*, volume LXVI (New York: Trow Directory, Printing and Bookbinding Company, 1913), 189.

45. Terry, interview, 14 July 1970, 133.

46. "John Reisenweber, Restaurateur, Dies", *New York Times*, 10 August 1931, p. 15:1; "Reisenweber Gravely Ill", *New York Times*, 9 August 1931, p. 3:4; "600 Attend Funeral of John Reisenweber", *New York Times*, 12 August 1931, p. 19:2.

47. Terry, interview, 13 June 1970, 133.

48. "Moser, Frank H.", in *National Cyclopedia of American Biography*, volume 52 (New York: James T. White and Co., 1970), 607; "Moser, Frank H." in *Who's Who in American Art*, ed. Dorothy B. Gilbert (New York: R.R. Bowker Company, 1953), 298; Falk, *Who Was Who in American Art* (1985), 433; Horn, *World Encyclopedia of Cartoons*, 401. Obituary: "Frank Moser", *Variety*, 21 October 1964, 79.

49. Terry, interview, 20 December 1969, 15–16.

50. Ibid., 16.

51. Ibid.

Chapter 8

A Spark Ignites: *Little Herman* and the Beginnings of a New Career in Animation, 1914–1915

When he created *Gertie the Dinosaur*, Winsor McCay drew each frame separately and completely. The process was very labor intensive and challenged even his remarkable drafting abilities. But producing such films in large numbers was impossible without dividing the work and automating the non-creative aspects. While J. Stuart Blackton and Winsor McCay demonstrated the potential of cartoon animation as a curiosity, it was John Randolph Bray, the "Henry Ford of Animation"[1] and Earl Hurd who made the medium economically feasible.

Bray, Like McCay, started his career in journalism. He began working for the Detroit *Evening News* as a reporter before moving to New York City to work for the *Brooklyn Daily Eagle* as a cartoonist in 1903.[2] He eventually created his own weekly full page comic strip, *Little Johnny and His Teddy Bears*, which capitalized on the 1903 fervor for the stuffed toy in the wake of Theodore Roosevelt's presidency and was published by *Judge* magazine from 1907 to 1910.[3] Bray also regularly contributed cartoons to *Harpers* and *Life*, as well as created the strip *Mr. O. U. Absentmind* for the McClure Newspaper Syndicate.

Around 1910 Bray began experimenting with the development of an original animated cartoon. He was apparently influenced by Edwin S. Porter's *The Teddy Bears*, released in 1907, which was created by using stop motion photography of real teddy bears to portray a satirical animated recreation of *Goldilocks and the Three Bears*.[4] But Bray, unfamiliar with the process involved in transferring the animated action to the screen, was unhappy with his own results and dropped the project. Bray concluded that the number of drawings required by the process was cost and time prohibitive.[5] Wishing to create an animated cartoon that was both entertaining and financially lucrative, he began to look for ways to eliminate the massive amount of detail necessary to produce an animated version of a comic.

By 1913, inspired by McCay's success with *Little Nemo*, Bray was willing to give animation another try. Bray produced *The Artist's Dream* (aka *The Dachshund and the Sausage*) a live-action/animation film in which Bray stars with a ravenous animated dachshund. When Bray signed a deal with Pathé to distribute *The Artist's Dream*, the company expressed an interest in distributing even more animated shorts.[6] Bray had to figure out a way to avoid drawing and redrawing each individual frame, a process that added up to hundreds upon hundreds of drawings. Bray realized that by delegating work to other artists – essentially dividing the production of each cartoon into several different units who could work concurrently on multiple shorts – he could greatly streamline production, saving time and money. About the same time as Bray was trying to design more efficient systems for animation, Frederick Winslow Taylor (1856–1915), American mechanical engineer, had died after completing his life's work on how to improve industrial

67

Fig. 8.1 – (Left to right): Olga Terry (Paul's sister), Alex Anderson (infant), Joseph Terry (Paul's father) (circa 1921).

Pathé, he assembled a team of artists and production personnel at his home in Highland Falls, New York.[8] Despite Bray's best efforts, it took his team six months to complete the first animated short *Colonel Heeza Liar's African Hunt* released on January 14, 1914.[9] Subsequent entries in the *Colonel Heeza Liar* series followed later that year. In July 1914 Bray took out a second patent (Patent 1,159,740) that covered the technique of applying gray shades to drawings in order to counteract the flicker caused by all-white backgrounds.[10] By the end of 1914, at about the time Paul was attending the McCay dinner, Bray had formed Bray Studios Incorporated with $10,000 in capital and an office on 26th Street in New York. Bray, both a businessman and animator, hired talented artists and ceased contributing artistically to his films. Instead, he focused on improving the technological processes and streamlining production.

Meanwhile, in 1914 Earl Hurd (1880–1940),[11] a cartoonist from Kansas City, Missouri who had been cartooning in the *Chicago Journal* since 1904,[12] applied for a patent in December 1914 (U.S. patent 1,143,542) where the key concept was the use of celluloid and the illusion of movement was to be produced "by drawing upon a series of transparent sheets".[13] Celluloid had been in use as a photographic base for years and Hurd correctly contended that he was the first to use it for this application. Drawn or painted figures could obscure the background, move across pictorial

efficiency. Bray would end up "Taylorizing" his animation production.

To eliminate the time-consuming task of completely redrawing the entire cartoon for each frame, Bray came up with the idea of using a printed background. Using zinc etching, hundreds of identical background scenes with the center left blank were printed on tracing paper. Bray then added the moving components of the cartoon to the blank center, thus drastically reducing the time and the number of skilled artists needed to complete an animated cartoon. The new technique was considered an improvement over fellow cartoon animator Winsor McCay's method of retracing all the lines in each frame, which often would appear to wiggle and wobble when cast on the film screen. Wishing to protect his new technique, Bray filed for his first U.S. patent, which was granted as No. 1,107,193.[7]

To meet the production requirements under contract with

Chapter 8 • A Spark Ignites

space, and repeat motions with relative simplicity. As celluloid sheets were transparent, only the actual moving parts of a drawing were required to be redrawn. Multiple layers of stacked cels were feasible making possible the illusion of depth to the images photographed. Hurd's registration differed from Bray's in specifying a large glass and metal frame to clamp the drawings in place. Hurd's patent was non-infringing and now he could compete with Bray.[14]

How Bray and Hurd began developing a business relationship is left to conjecture. Some of Hurd's cartoons for the *Journal* appeared periodically in the *New York Herald* where Bray may have seen them. Alternatively, the Brays may have viewed some of Hurd's independently made films.[15] In 1914, Bray and Hurd formed a mutually advantageous joint venture as opposed to litigation and a lengthy and expensive battle over rights The two formed the partnership, the Bray-Hurd Process Company, which concern lasted until the 1920s. Hurd's patent was much more important than Bray's, but after hiring Hurd in 1915 to produce animated shorts for his company,[16] Bray considered Hurd strictly as an employee[17] and never publicly acknowledged Hurd's contributions.[18]

Terry decided that the first step in the process of producing his own animated film was to purchase a motion picture camera. Terry chose a second-hand motion picture camera manufactured by the Prestwich Manufacturing Company, established in London, England in 1895 by engineer John Alfred Prestwich (1874–1952).[19] Terry found the camera to be "horrible" to use as it was a hand cranked camera with a claw movement that pulled the film down leaving a "little float" especially if you increased speed. The other more expensive cameras such as the Bell & Howell or Mitchell models picked the film up and set it on pins ensuring no film slippage or floatage.[20] Another problem that Terry had with the camera was with the shutter which required a little extra effort to properly control the exposures.[21] To register the drawings and ensure that the alignment was consistent from shot to shot, Terry slid the drawings up to a corner which provided his registration.[22]

Various animators had come up with different methods to keep their drawings lined up, but none of them worked very well. Raoul Barré (1874–1932), who was born in Montréal, Québec, and studied art at the École des Beaux-Arts in Paris, France, starting in 1891, and remained there for several years as a political cartoonist, is responsible for devising the peg system of registration still in use today. On returning to Canada in 1898, he gave birth to the French Canadian comic strip. Barré then moved to New York City in 1903. In 1912, Barré saw an animated film that inspired him to enter the industry. He picked Edison Studios to produce his cartoons and while visiting the studio, met Bill Nolan, a live-action shorts producer who became his business and artistic partner. The two worked together for a year putting out animated and live-action commercials for various companies. In 1915, Barré devised the solution to ensure consistent alignment of drawings – the peg system which involved punching two holes at the bottom of all of their sheets and passing them through two pegs glued to the animation table.[23]

The next step for Paul was to find a location to shoot the animated film. The studio site he chose was the top floor of a dilapidated building at 138 W. 42nd Street, later the location of the Cameo Theatre, where he set up his camera and equipment.[24] The subject for Terry's first cartoon was the famed magician Alexander Herrman (1843–1896),[25] better known as "Herrman the Great" whom he claimed to have seen perform as a high school student while an usher in a vaudeville house.[26] Herrman was noted for developing the now-familiar "devilish" magician's personality and for having a number of death defying acts in his routine including his marvelous bullet catching performance. In the Terry cartoon, Little Herman rolls out a little cannon and lights the fuse. He stands in front of the cannon as if he is going to catch the cannon ball. The cannon goes off and seemingly knocks his head off. The magician goes hunting for his head but then his real head pops out of his collar.

Herman then takes a sack and throws a dog and some scissors into the sack and bangs it on the floor a few times. As a result, a number of sausages come out of the sack and then the sausages change into a long dachshund dog.

69

Fig. 8.2 – Bill Tytla artwork for Hyde Cat from *Mighty Mouse Meets Jeckyll and Hyde Cat* (1944).

As the dog walks off the stage, his head pokes around the other side of the stage as though his body is able to stretch and go all the way around and behind the stage. On the end of his tail is the American flag which Terry hoped would receive applause for a patriotic theme.[27]

The cartoon was about 300 feet in length and 3 minutes and 20 seconds in running time.[28] He shot the film using the "double exposure" method. In 1915 Terry had patented his "double exposure" method which involved photographing the background first. Then he would reverse the film and shoot the film again exposing the film twice,[29] the second time with the character in a matte effect.[30] The short, consisting of about 4,800 drawings, took him four months to complete outside of his work for the New York *Press*. After completing the film in the spring of 1915, Terry began trying to find a film head interested in purchasing the short. Around this point in time Terry was determined to leave the newspaper business. An upcoming contract from the *Press* was much too restrictive and so he decided to focus all of his efforts in establishing a new career in animation.[31] After 10 years as a newspaper artist with no control over his work, Terry was looking forward to a career as an independent producer of animated cartoons.[32]

He went to see Lewis J. Selznick, Vice-President and General Manager of World Film Corporation located at 130 West 46th Street in New York City.[33] Selznick was a newcomer in the film business. Before moving into film production and distribution, Selznick made his fortune in the jewelry business operating a chain of stores in Cleveland, Ohio and Pittsburgh, Pennsylvania. During the "Panic of 1907" he closed his jewelry company and moved into patent promotion and wholesale electrical supplies. His Independent Electrical Supply Co. prospered and he continued to head this firm until 1912. In 1914, he obtained a position as assistant to Carl Laemmle, president of the Universal Film Corp., and after a few weeks was appointed its general manager.[34]

The World Special Films Corporation was announced in November 1913 and founded by E. Mandelbaum and Philip Gleichman. The name was changed when on February 16, 1914 the World Film Corporation was formed after Mandelbaum and Gleichman interested Wall Street bankers, W. A. Pratt, Van Horn Ely, and others in the enterprise.[35] World was also unique in that they sold stock openly to the public.[36] On June 10, 1914, World and the Shubert Theatrical Company, representing the interests of William A. Brady, Charles E. Blaney, and Owen Davis enterprises, formed a $3 million corporation to film the theatrical successes of the Shubert Company. The plan was for World to release and distribute one feature-length film a week produced by the Shubert Film Corporation. Mandelbaum sold his interest in World in mid-1914, the company became incorporated for $2 million, and Lewis J. Selznick became vice-president and general manager in July 1914. By this time World had 24 distributing offices across the United States. In May 1915, about the time Terry had visited Selznick, World had taken over completely the Shubert Film Corporation.[37]

Terry attended Selznick's office and after looking at the film the motion picture head offered him a dollar a foot for it, "the positive and a negative". Terry informed Selznick that the negative, the film he used "cost me more than a dollar to make the picture".

Chapter 8 • A Spark Ignites

Fig. 8.3 – Paul Terry at work (c. 1920) (the only known photograph of Terry with a moustache).

Selznick's response was, "Well, I could pay you more for it if you hadn't put those pictures on it".[38] In other words, if Terry had sold him the raw film stock, Selznick probably could have paid him more money. Fifty-four years later Terry was still unsure as to whether Selznick was kidding.[39] Based on the 1933 obituary of Selznick in the *New York Times*, frankness was one of Mr. Selznick's defining characteristics and, therefore, it was more likely that he was being candid and blunt with Terry rather than humorous or sarcastic at the time of their 1915 meeting.[40]

Undaunted, Terry traveled all over New York City trying to sell the film. After many weeks without any interest in his film he began to become discouraged and thought about resigning himself to a newspaper career. He then heard about a producer-exhibitor in New Rochelle named Thanhouser. He decided to travel to the office of the Thanhouser Film Corporation in New Rochelle, New York. The film corporation was established in 1909 by theatrical entrepreneur Edwin Thanhouser, with studios located at Grove and Warren Streets and Crescent Avenue in New Rochelle, New York.[41] Edwin Thanhouser (1865 – 1956) was born in Baltimore, Maryland and went on stage in the 1880s. By the turn of the century he was producing stock in Milwaukee, Wisconsin. Realizing theater would be supplanted by film, he moved into organizing his own film company.[42] Thanhouser's first motion picture was *The Actor's Children* (March 15, 1910) and featured Orilla Smith and Yale Boss and was directed by one of the studio's first contract directors, Barry O'Neil or Lloyd B. Carleton.[43] Thanhouser often featured children in its films, which may have attracted Terry to the possibility of selling his animated cartoon, tailored for children, to the studio head.[44]

Thanhouser child stars included Helen Badgley (The Thanhouser Kidlet), Marie Eline (The Thanhouser Kid), and Marion and Madeline Fairbanks (The Thanhouser Twins).[45] Other stars included Florence La Badie, Mignon Anderson, Marguerite Snow, James Cruze, and William Russell.[46] In 1912, Thanhouser

Fig. 8.4 – Original art (first page) for a Heckle and Jeckle comic book.

Chapter 8 • A Spark Ignites

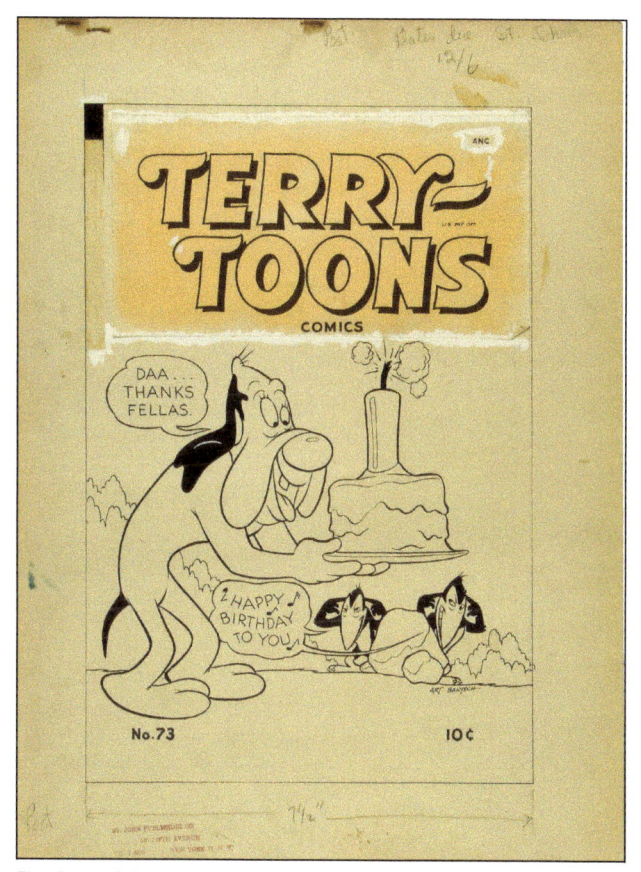

Fig. 8.5 – Original cover art for *Terrytoons Comics* No. 73.

opened a winter studio in Jacksonville, Florida, and that same year Charles J. Hite, on behalf of a syndicate, purchased the company while Edwin Thanhouser retired at the end of the year.[47] In 1913, Thanhouser's New Rochelle studio was destroyed by fire on January 13 while the company's first serial, *The Million Dollar Mystery*, was released to strong box office receipts grossing $1.6 million on production costs of $80,000.[48]

On August 22, 1914, Charles J. Hite died as a result of an automobile accident the previous day.[49] Despondent over the death of his friend, in December 1914, long-time writer and chief of the scenario department, Lloyd Lonergan, retired from his employ with Thanhouser thereby striking a creative blow to the company.[50] On February 22, 1915 Edwin Thanhouser returned as studio head.[51] The current major film in production at the time of Terry's arrival was the five-reel motion picture based on George Eliot's novel *The Mill on the Floss* released on December 16, 1915.[52]

In order to travel to the Thanhouser studio, he had to borrow the money for the train ride. Terry remembered the day to be a bright, sunny spring day.[53] When Terry arrived at the office of Thanhouser and approached him with his animated short, the studio head wasn't interested in looking at it. Terry tried to reason with Thanhouser explaining to him that he had come all the way from New York City with the hope that he could at least take a look at it. Puzzled by Terry's reply, the producer sat staring back at the young filmmaker. New York City is only a 40-minute commute by car to New Rochelle. Thanhouser then smiled gently, and probably with a little empathy for Terry offered to screen the short after lunch. Terry went off for a quick lunch and returned to the studio.[54]

Near the projection room in the front of the building there were some children playing on the sidewalk. Terry approached the kids and asked them whether they wanted to see a picture. Terry invited them into the projection room and sat them down front. Thanhouser returned from his lunch and ran the short with the children watching. Soon the children were laughing and squealing with delight over the humorous antics of the animated Herman.[55] Thanhouser and his crew laughed as well, although Paul was not sure whether they were laughing at the cartoon or because the children were laughing.[56] The infectious laughter of the children convinced Thanhouser to purchase the film,[57] and offered Terry $1.35 a foot, including the print, or about $405 (about $10,000 adjusted for inflation).[58] Thanhouser also

73

wanted to purchase another film from Terry which Paul agreed to produce.[59]

The reviews of the animated short in the trade literature were very positive. A 1915 review in *Moving Picture World* states:

> Little Herman, a queer-looking magician, juggles cannon balls, ducks lamps and a variety of other articles in a surprising and terrifying fashion. He even shot himself out of the mouth of a cannon, and then shoots himself in again. This stunt reminds us of the man who jumped into the bramble bush – but Little Herman is more wonderful even than he.[60]

Similarly, the film reviewer for the June 26, 1915 edition of *Moving Picture World* also provided a positive review:

> A half reel of animated drawings, picturing the adventures of Little Herman, the mustacheless magician. This is amusing and the drawings are good.[61]

Most likely Terry would have either read or been aware of these glowing reviews in *Moving Picture World* and have been encouraged to further his artistic ambitions in the field of animation.

The next film Paul produced for Thanhouser was *Down on the Phoney Farm* (1915) released on October 16.[62] The film is likely the first short featuring the animated antics of Farmer Al Falfa. Although all copies of the film were reportedly lost, a print has since resurfaced bearing that title. A 1915 review in *Moving Picture World* stated: "An excellent animated cartoon on the last reel of the above, showing what happened when a farmer took undue advantage of the thirst of his cow".[63] The extant print features Farmer Al Falfa who is able to grow such interesting cultivations as a pitcher of beer and an alcoholic cocktail. He feeds the cocktail to his thirsty cow, Clara. However, the drink makes her drunk and she goes a little wild. She starts to chase Al Falfa through his vast farm property. But since his acreage isn't really real, Al Falfa can employ some unusual methods to avoid the bovine.

For his second film, Terry used a method involving the same applications devised by Hurd, that of drawing the moving element on celluloid which were used as overlays on backgrounds which gave Terry the opportunity to put tone in the backgrounds.[64] In his 1969 interview, Terry contended he "invented the celluloid system".[65] Recent research has indicated that Terry likely produced the second film for Thanhouser at the Raoul Barré studio at the old Edison studio in the Bronx on the corner of Fordham Road and Webster Avenue.

During this period, Terry began to explore further opportunities in the animation business. Around mid-1915 Terry was interested in forming an organization of animators, Talent, Incorporated, which included Earl Hurd, Leighton Budd, Frank Moser, Jerry Shields, Terry and his brother John.[66] Hurd wasn't so sure he wanted to join the company and only agreed to do so if his uncle, a patent attorney in Washington, D.C., agreed that the venture was a good idea. Hurd would regularly take advice from his uncle. Paul and Earl traveled to Washington where over the course of the next few weeks or so he convinced Hurd's uncle that the venture was solid. However, since the group could not raise the seed capital the company was never formed.[67]

During this same period of time, Terry approached William Randolph Hearst with the proposition to start an animation studio to produce animated cartoons featuring the comic strip characters found in his newspapers but Hearst was not interested.[68] The persistent Terry then contacted Bud Fisher, the creator of Mutt and Jeff, if he was interested in collaborating on producing a series of Mutt and Jeff animated cartoons. Terry figured that by animating an established property that he would move ahead faster in his career. Terry had earlier made a Mutt and Jeff animated cartoon for Bud Fisher which Fisher used in his vaudeville act similar to what McCay was doing with *Gertie the Dinosaur*. Fisher thought about Terry's offer for about six months and then came back to Terry and agreed to the proposition, but by this time Paul had agreed to work for J. R. Bray to produce the Farmer Al Falfa animated cartoons.[69] ❧

Chapter 8 • A Spark Ignites

Notes

1. Much of the biographical information on Bray was retrieved from John Canemaker's unpublished manuscript of his interview with Bray conducted on March 25, 1974. For the published version, see "Profile of a Living Animation Legend: John Randolph Bray", *Filmmakers Newsletter* VIII, no. 3 (January 1975): 28–31. Other sources: *Encyclopedia of World Biography*, second edition supplement, volume 21 (Detroit: Gale Group, 2001); Horn, *The World Encyclopedia of Cartoons*; *International Motion Picture Almanac*, 1979 edition (New York: Quigley Publishing Co., 1979); *Who Was Who in America*, volume VII, 1977–1981; *Who's Who in America*, 39th edition, 1976–1977 (Wilmette, IL: Marquis Who's Who, 1976); Cook, *The International Dictionary of Films and Filmmakers*, second edition, volume 4: Writers and Production Artists; Jeromski, *The International Dictionary of Films and Filmmakers*, third edition, volume 4: Writers and Production Artists; Pendergast and Pendergast, ed., *The International Dictionary of Films and Filmmakers*, fourth edition, volume 4: Writers and Production Artists. Richard Eder, "Grandfather of the Film Cartoon Honored at 96", *The New York Times Biographical Service*, August 1975, 944–945.

2. Donald Crafton, *Before Mickey: The Animated Film, 1898–1928* (Chicago: The University of Chicago Press, 1993), 139.

3. Crafton, *Before Mickey*, 140.

4. Ibid., 142; John Randolph Bray, "Development of Animated Cartoons", *Moving Picture World*, 21 July 1917, p. 395–398.

5. Crafton, *Before Mickey*, 143.

6. Ibid., 144–145.

7. Ibid., 145.

8. Ibid., 147.

9. Ibid., 148.

10. Ibid., 149–150. In fact, Bray attempted to patent practically every aspect of the animation process, even techniques that his predecessors like McCay had utilized for years before Bray ever animated his first frame. He sued anyone he thought had violated his patents – including McCay – until the patents expired in 1932.

11. Hurd drew the comic strip *Trials of Elder Mouse* between 1911 and 1915, *Brick Bodkin's Pa* in 1912 and *Susie Sunshine* from 1927 to 1929. His obituary can be found in *Variety*, 2 October 1940, 62.

12. Crafton, *Before Mickey*, 150–151.

13. Earl Hurd, U.S. patent 1,143,542, granted June 15, 1915.

14. Crafton, *Before Mickey*, 153.

15. Ibid.

16. Hurd would work for Bray until 1918.

17. A 1915 article listed "Earl Herd" only as a staffer. Lynde Denig, "Cartoonist Bray with Paramount", *Moving Picture World*, 11 December 1915, 1990.

18. Crafton, *Before Mickey*, 153.

19. Stephen Herbert and Luke McKernan, ed., *Who's Who of Victorian Cinema: A Worldwide Survey* (London: BFI, 1996). There were a number of Prestwich camera models for 35mm film on the market in the early 1900s. Which model Terry used has not been ascertained at the time of writing.

20. Terry, interview, 20 December 1969, 17.

21. Ibid., 17–18.

22. Ibid., 18.

23. Maureen Furniss, *Maureen, Art in Motion: Animation Aesthetics* (London: John Libbey, 1998), 18–19; Crafton, *Before Mickey*, 194. For a detailed biography on Barré, see André Martin, *Barré l'introuvable (In Search of Raoul Barré)* [English translation by Martha and Ron Burnett, with the assistance of Mary Wilson and Liska Bridle] (Montreal: Cinémathèque Québécoise, 1976).

24. "Paul H. Terry – Defendant – Direct", *Case on Appeal from Judgment*, 513–514.

25. Frank Cullen, *Vaudeville, Old & New: An Encyclopedia of Variety Performers in America* (New York: Routledge, 2007), 507–508; Albert A. Hopkins, *Magic: Stage Illusions Special Effects and Trick Photography* (New York: Dover Publications, 1976), 21–22; Adam Woog, *Magicians and illusionists* (San Diego, CA: Lucent Books, 2000).

26. Terry would have had to have seen Herrman before the age of ten as the famed magician died in 1896.

27. Terry, interview, 20 December 1969, 21.

28. See Chapter 1, endnote 1. Other sources cite the length of the film as being 400 feet. Since there is no extant film negative, the author is referencing the length of the cartoon as being 300 feet based on Terry's 1969 interview as this transcription appears to be the most reliable primary source.

29. In what Terry termed as creating "a male and female of it". Terry, interview, 14 July 1970, 130.

30. The character was drawn on paper for the first cartoon which was superimposed upon the background previously shot.

31. *Lunch with Paul Terry*, 19.

32. Terry, interview, 14 July 1970, 147.

33. "World Film Corporation", *Variety*, 18 December 1914, 30.

34. "Selznick, Lewis Joseph", in *National Cyclopaedia of American Biography*, volume 41 (Ann Arbor, Michigan: University Microfilms, 1967), 419. Selznick lived one of the most ostentatious and outrageous lifestyles of any studio administrator. After losing his position at World, he started his own company, Lewis J. Selznick Productions, Inc. in 1916. He openly caroused with leading stars, but he also could not resist the parade of beautiful young hopefuls. His casting couch was well worn and legendary. The long corridor to his office was lined with uniformed guards. Selznick's penchant for outrageous publicity upset the sensibility of a young industry. The suicide of Ziegfeld showgirl Olive Thomas in 1920 along with losing starlet Clara Kimball Young to Zukor's Famous Players contributed to his company's demise. He was left to living in a three room apartment, surrounded by remnants of his former wealth. His son David would become a super producer, his most notable production being *Gone*

with the Wind (Selznick International Pictures, 1939). His other son Myron became a leading and powerful Hollywood agent.

35. "World Film Corporation", in *The American Film Industry: A Historical Dictionary*, by Anthony Slide (New York: Greenwood Press, 1986), 393–394.

36. Eileen Bowser, *History of the American Cinema*, volume 2, 1907–1915, ed. Charles Harpole (New York: Charles Scribner's Sons, 1990), 227.

37. "World Film Corporation", 394.

38. Terry, interview, 20 December 1969, 85–86.

39. Ibid., 86.

40. "L.J. Selznick Dies; A Film Pioneer", *New York Times*, 26 January 1933, p. 17:3.

41. Anthony Slide, "The Thanhouser Company", in *Aspects of American Film History Prior to 1920* (Metuchen, New Jersey: Scarecrow Press, 1978), 69.

42. "Edwin Thanhouser Dies", *New York Times*, 23 March 1956, p. 27:4; "Edwin Thanhouser", *Variety*, 28 March 1956, 75.

43. Slide, "The Thanhouser Company", 69.

44. For more on Thanhouser see: "A Day with Thanhouser", *The Moving Picture World*, 24 April 1915, 563; Robert C. Duncan, "Forty-Five Minutes from Broadway", *Picture Play*, January 1917, 90–96; Louis Reeves Harrison, "Studio Saunterings", *The Moving Picture World*, 13 July 1912, 123–126; *Photoplay Arts Portfolio of Thanhouser Moving-Picture Stars* (New York: Photoplay Arts, 1914).

45. Slide, "The Thanhouser Company", 71.

46. Ibid., 70.

47. Ibid., 71.

48. Ibid., 73; "Thanhouser Rewriting; "Zudora" Not Pleasing", *Variety*, 19 December 1914, 23.

49. "C.J. Hite Dies of Injuries", *New York Times*, 23 August 1914, p. 13:7;

"Obituary. Charles J. Hite", *Variety*, 28 August 1914, 15. Some sources (see June Schetterer, "New Rochelle was home for Terry's cartoon genius", *The Standard-Star* (New Rochelle, N.Y.), 7 February 1982, Section 3 (Local), p. 1) have Charles J. Hite exhibiting the film rather than Thanhouser but if this is fact, Terry would have had to have visited him before August 23, 1914.

50. "Lonergan Quits Thanhouser", *Variety*, 5 December 1914, 23.

51. In 1916, Pathé took over the distribution of its product. The studio had always released its films independently. Edwin Thanhouser retired in February 1918, and the studio was loaned out to Clara Kimball Young. In 1919, it was sold to Crawford Livingston and Wilbert Shallenberger, and later that year it was acquired as the site for B.A. Rolfe Productions. Slide, "The Thanhouser Company", 77–78. "Thanhouser Film Corporation", in *The American Film Industry: A Historical Dictionary*, 343; "Thanhouser Retiring", *Variety*, 21 September, 1917, 39.

52. Slide, "The Thanhouser Company", 75.

53. Paul Terry, "They All Laughed", *Parade*, 13 April 1952.

54. Terry, interview, 20 December 1969, 22.

55. Ibid., 22–23.

56. Dick Tracy, "Terrytoons' departure ends an era", *The Herald Statesman*, 4 January 1973, p. 28.

57. Terry tells a slightly different story nearly forty years earlier. In this retelling of the events leading up to his first film sale to Thanhouser, it was the New Rochelle studio owner that brought the children in off the street to view the film, and only after the film had already been viewed. Terry states: "With fear in my heart I took the long trek to the Westchester wilderness, and after waiting in the outer office for a number of hours, I was informed that Mr. Thanhouser would show the reel in the projection room. He called in several members of his staff who sat silently through the running of the reel. My little ray of hope died an instantaneous death. Mr. Thanhouser, however, asked me to come back after lunch, and when I returned, found he had picked up a number of kids from the street and packed them into the projection room. The reel was run off again, the youngsters howled with glee and the men who hadn't cracked a smile before, laughed loudly with them. And cartoon comedies were born". Phil M. Daly, "I Remember When.........." By Paul Terry as Told to Phil M. Daly of the The Film Daily Editorial Staff, *Film Daily*, 12 April 1933, p. 6.

58. Terry, interview, 20 December 1969, 21.

59. Ibid., 23.

60. "Mutual Film Corp. Little Herman", *Moving Picture World*, 19 June 1915, 2006.

61. "Mutual Film Corporation. Little Herman", *Moving Picture World*, 26 June 1915, 2096.

62. Denis Gifford, *American Animated Films: The Silent Era, 1897–1929* (Jefferson, NC: McFarland & Company, Inc, 1990), 33.

63. "Mutual Film Corporation Specials", *The Moving Picture World*, 16 October 1915, 441.

64. Terry was unsure whether he used his "double exposure" method for the second cartoon as well. After the second picture (*Down on Phoney Farm* (1915)) he realized that if he drew the background first and then made the drawings on a transparent material and colored them in, it would serve the same purpose. Terry claimed he made the first animated cartoons on celluloid. Terry, interview, 14 July 1970, 131.

65. Terry, interview, 20 December 1969, 19.

66. Terry, interview, 14 July 1970, 121.

67. Ibid., 135.

68. Crafton, *Before Mickey*, 148.

69. Terry, interview, 13 June 1970, 113.

Chapter 9

Animated Antics: Cartoon Burlesques, Phrenology, and Paul Terry's Early Adventures in the Cartoon World, 1915–1917

The employment arrangement between Terry and J. R. Bray was not entered into under the most happiest of circumstances. Margaret Till Bray,[1] John Bray's wife, happened to notice a newspaper advertisement for Terry's *Little Herman*. Margaret went to screen the cartoon and was impressed by the quality of the animation. She decided to go see Terry who was up on Broadway and told him that he had to purchase a license from her to produce his animated cartoons. Having already invented his own successful method to produce cartoons using characters painted on transparent celluloid, Paul was not pleased with her license demand. Cooler heads prevailed.[2]

Rather than become involved in expensive litigation, both parties agreed to work together. After having Pathé as his distributor since 1913, Bray had just signed a new contract with Paramount for distribution beginning in 1916 and was eager to have "experienced" animators like Terry on staff to expand his production output.[3] Many of the other cartoonists Bray was to hire would have to be trained in the relatively new art of animated filmmaking. Consequently, Terry was offered the opportunity to create cartoons starring his new character, Farmer Al Falfa, for Bray Productions, an invitation he gladly accepted.[4]

The Bray studio was founded in December 1914 and was one of the first studios entirely devoted to series animation at the time.[5] Its first series was Bray's *Colonel Heeza Liar*. In 1913, Bray had created the character based on a mixture of Baron Munchausen and Theodore Roosevelt and the general stereotype of the 19th and early 20th century former adventurer and lion hunter. The Colonel, a little man with a huge and bullying wife, told far-fetched tales of his brave adventures in far-off lands.[6] The Col. Heeza Liar series is one of utmost significance in animation history, as it was the first cartoon series to feature a recurring animated star – the title character.

From the beginning the studio brought in outsiders to direct the promising new series. During Terry's one year tenure at the Bray studio located at 23 East 26th Street in Manhattan he rubbed shoulders with some of the finest cartoonists, illustrators, fine art painters, designers and commercial artists in the United States, all of whom were tasked with directorial duties to bring to life their comic strip characters and other artistic creations in animated form. These artists included L. M. Glackens, Charles Allan Gilbert, Carl Thomas Anderson, Clarence Rigby, Earl Hurd, Frank Moser, A. D. Reed, Leighton Budd, and Harry C. Greening.[7] Earl Hurd was formally hired in 1915 and continued his Bobby Bumps series which cartoons first appeared in his Earl Hurd cartoons series released through Universal.[8] Inspired by R. F. Outcault's Buster Brown, Bobby Bumps was a little boy who, accompanied by his dog Fido, regularly found himself in and out of mischief.[9]

77

Other artists on staff included Harry Cornell Greening (1876–1949), newspaper cartoonist and toy inventor, and a frequent contributor to *Puck, Life, Harper's, Scribner's* and *Judge*. Greening's newspaper work was primarily completed for the *New York Herald*, and there he created such strips as *Percy, Fritz von Blitz*, and the classic *Prince Errant*, a masterpiece of whimsy and visual delights. He was the creator of features like *Si Swapper* (1902), *Uncle George Washington Bings* (1907), *The Woo Woo Bird* (1909) and *Percy – Brains He Has Nix* (1912–1913). For Bray he brought his Percy strip to animated cartoons. *Percy – Brains He Has Nix*, a Sunday only newspaper feature, follows the comical misadventures of a professor and his "mechanism man", Percy. Percy is a mechanical man that can perform any task by simply pushing a button on his back. Unfortunately for those who cross his path, Percy is not the most gentle of creatures. As Percy is inclined to take instructions quite literally, his creator often laments Percy's actions by explaining that when it comes to brains, Percy has nix.[10]

Louis M. Glackens (1866–1933) was the brother of Ashcan school painter and illustrator William Glackens. L. M. Glackens is most noted for his work on *Puck* magazine where by the late 1890s he was a staffer producing much of the interior art of the weekly. His artwork was understated, uncluttered and always attractively rendered. Glackens remained with *Puck* almost until it was sold to the Strauss dry-goods concern in 1914.[11] He joined Bray Productions in 1915 to work on the *Bray Cartoons* (*A Stone Age Adventure* (29 May 1915), *When Knights Were Bold* (19 June 1915)) and *Pathé News* (*Another Fallen Idol* (28 May 1915)) series. In the fall of 1916, Pathé-News formed a cartoon department to produce topical sketch films for their newsreel which were duly licensed by Bray (*Greenland's Icy Mountains*).[12]

Charles Allan Gilbert (1873–1929) was a prominent American illustrator and painter. He is especially remembered for a widely published drawing (a memento mori or vanitas) titled *All Is Vanity*. The drawing employs a double image (or visual pun) in which the scene of a woman admiring herself in a mirror, when viewed from a distance, appears to be a human skull, reminding her of her mortality. Gilbert patented new forms of motion pictures that combined living actors with animated drawings.[13] Bray was constantly looking to expand his studio. Bray and Gilbert teamed up in a short-lived Bray subsidiary: Bray-Gilbert Studios. For Bray, Gilbert worked on the production of a series of moving shadow plays, called *Silhouette Fantasies*. These Art Nouveau-styled films, which were made by combining filmed silhouettes with pen-and-ink components, were serious interpretations of Greek myths and tragedies.[14]

Production of these silhouette films was an enterprise quite unlike that of the traditional animated cartoons already being produced at the Bray studio. The Bray-Gilbert studio was located in Washington Mews, a private gated street in New York City between Fifth Avenue and University Place just north of Washington Square Park. Structure No. 44 had been modified to facilitate production of the silhouette films. The historic structure had been rebuilt to facilitate big arc lights, unusual stage properties, and elaborate early movie cameras inside the building. A stage had been added in the back of the lot; the ceiling removed from some of the rooms of the building; and the building's inner walls painted a glittery white. Powerful electric lights were installed to throw silhouettes into bold relief; background walls were painted diverse colors to create a shaded effect in the completed film. The camera was buried in a pit, making the actors' feet visible to the camera's eye but the floor not visible. These films were a combination of live action, filmed in silhouette, and penned artwork; animated cut-outs may also have been used. Transitions between live action and animation were seamless and unnoticeable to audiences at the time.[15]

Carl Thomas Anderson (1865–1948), best remembered for his Henry pantomime strip he created in 1932, was 51 years old and probably the oldest artist at the studio in 1916. His main duties at the production facility were to write, animate, and direct the *Police Dog* series starring Pinkerton Pup who always had a habit of getting human Officer Piffles in trouble.[16] Anderson left the studio in May 1916 and found work animating at Mutt and Jeff

Chapter 9 • Animated Antics

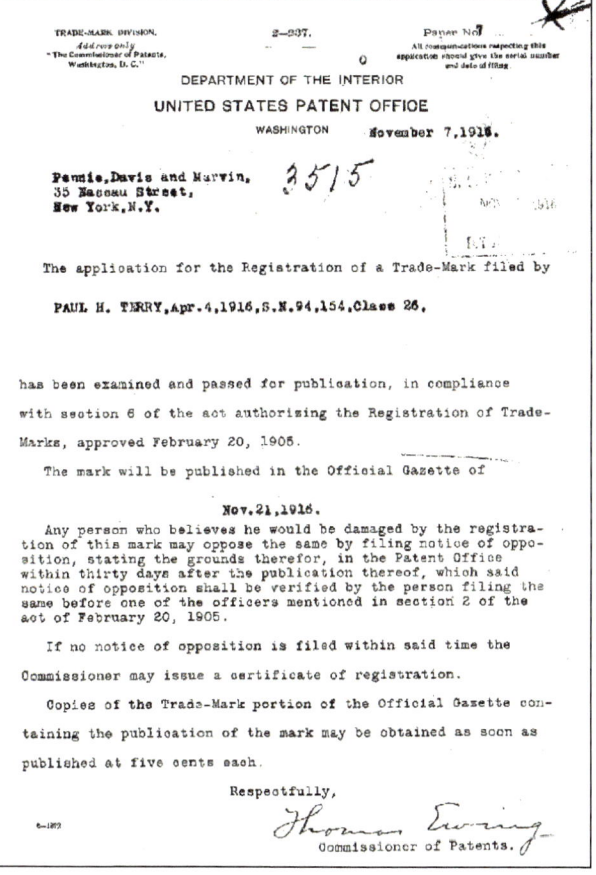

Fig. 9.1 – Terry's Trademark Registration for "Alfalfa".

Films, Inc.[17] Clarence Rigby (1864–1926) held positions as staff artist with the *New York Herald*, *New York World*, and *Brooklyn Eagle*. He had worked on comic strips such as *Toyland* (1900–1902), *The Story of the Wooden Babes in the Wonder Woods* (1902), *Bruno and Pietro* (1904–1906), and *Inquisitive Clarence* (1907–1908). One of his more notable strips was *Little Ah Sid, The Chinese Kid* (1904–1907). He also illustrated the strips *Adventures of a Pair of Jacks* (1910), *Professor Blackart* (1910) and George Herriman's *Major Ozone's Fresh Air Crusade* (1904/1906) and *Alexander the Cat* (1911). In 1916, Rigby was writing, animating, and directing the *Miss Nanny Goat* series of cartoon shorts for John R. Bray. He later continued the cartoon series for Bray's *Paramount-Bray Pictographs*. Rigby also helped to animate cartoons for the Mutt and Jeff Studio (aka Bud Fisher Film Corp.) under producer/director Raoul Barré.[18]

Leighton Budd was born Roy Leighton Budd in Ohio on December 12, 1872 [1873]. He was a popular illustrator and noted cartoonist for newspapers such as the *New York Herald*, 1900–1902, and magazines such as *Puck*, 1904. For the Boston *Herald* he created the humorous strip *Every Move a Picture*, *Yours Truly the Tumblebug Brothers*. The feature ran in the Boston *Herald* from May 6 to September 16, 1906. In 1914, he entered animation and worked as animator and director on his first animated film *Lunyland Pictures*, a 3-minute film made for John Randolph Bray in 1914 for Universal release. In 1916, he was working as an animator and director with John C. Terry, W. C. Morris, Vincent Colby, Flohri, Louis Glackens, and Jack Leventhal for Bray on the *Pathé News* series for the Pathé Exchange release (director credits: *The Courtship of Miss Vote* (Oct. 1916), *The Mexican Border* (Dec. 1916), *Uncle Sam's Christmas* (Dec. 1916)). For *Paramount-Bray Cartoons* he worked as a director on the animated short *In Lunyland* (July 1916). During his career, he was also a book illustrator, inventor, and comic book artist. He would reunite with Terry at the Fables Pictures studio in the early 1920s.[19]

In producing his Farmer Al Falfa animated shorts, Terry, like most of the other artists, acted as writer, animator, and director on his cartoons.[20] John R. Bray, having a studio to manage, was probably the sole exception to this rule. Bray animated and directed the Colonel Heeza Liar cartoons from the start until likely some point in 1915 or 1916. Animation for Heeza in 1916 and 1917 was likely done by others at the studio, such as Les Elton. Bray's objective

79

was to have four units working on four cartoons at any one time. On average, the production of one animated film took a month to complete.

Therefore, four units with staggered schedules produced one cartoon a week for inclusion in the "screen magazines" (a one-reel collection of live-action educational or informational pieces and travelogs in addition to the cartoon that was played before the feature film). Bray arranged his four production units so that one unit produced his *Colonel Heeza Liar* cartoon, one unit produced Hurd's *Bobby Bumps* short, and one unit produced non-series cartoons, usually topical commentaries on the news directed by Leighton Budd, J. D. Leventhal, and others. The fourth unit was the one that kept changing directors and was the one which produced Terry's Farmer Al Falfa cartoons in 1916.[21]

During his one year tenure at Bray Productions, Terry was able to develop the personality of the Farmer Al Falfa character that first appeared in *Down on the Phoney Farm* (1915). In 1916, Terry directed 11 Farmer Al Falfa animated shorts, about one a month; with the first being *Farmer Al Falfa's Catastrophe* (February 3) and the last being *Farmer Al Falfa's Blind Pig* (December 7). Farmer Al Falfa was a bald-headed, white-bearded, pot-bellied hayseed who lived on a farm with his animal friends including chickens, donkeys, cows, goats, and plenty of mice. Many of the plots of these cartoons involved the farmer having to deal with problems caused by his animals with his furry friends usually getting the better of him.

Terry's inspiration for Farmer Al Falfa came from his childhood days on the family farm in San Mateo. His father had the only barn in his section of town so as a result many of the children in the neighboring areas who could not keep their pets would drop their animals off with the Terry family. As a result, the family had guinea pigs, goats, chickens, a sheep, and even a 14-hand mule that had wandered away from the San Francisco Presidio.[22] By assisting his father with the care, breeding and feeding of the farm animals, Paul was able to better appreciate and more fully understand their different personalities and particular temperaments which he later applied in his cartoon shorts.

Terry chose animals as the central antagonists for Farmer Al Falfa because he believed that their ridicule, derision, crazy behaviors, and mistreatment by a disgruntled Al Falfa would not offend audiences.[23] Terry believed that humor generated from ethnicity, religion, or the color of one's skin is inappropriate and capable of offending people. In his 1969 interview, Terry drew an example to the once popular *Amos 'n' Andy* television program which over the course of a decade or so had to been removed from broadcasting due to public protest over the depiction of the racial stereotypes of African-Americans. Terry felt that the dignity of a man was "his most precious possession", but with animals, "nobody takes offense at that".[24] Terry felt you can solve any problem by using animals instead of humans as the players because to Terry animals represented a facet of human behavior rather than a nationality or racial heritage.[25]

The cel process, involving the drawing of characters on transparent celluloid sheets, which then were applied over painted background scenes, had a distinct advantage over other methods previously applied.[26] Because of the sheets' transparency, only the moving parts needed to be drawn without worrying about blending them into a printed background as in Bray's method. Terry designed the Farmer Al Falfa character in order to use the cel process to avoid labor. The arms, which were a different color than the body, were put on a separate cel so they could move without having to re-draw the entire character. Overalls (usually without pockets and of one color) was used as one-piece body attire and was less expensive to draw then more detailed multi-layered clothing such as a shirt, tie and pants.[27]

In late 1916, Terry decided to leave the Bray studio. After a year working under Bray he was tired of toiling for someone else and wanted to produce his own animated cartoons.[28] About March 1917, the A. Kay Company, headquartered at 729 7th Avenue in New York City, was organized with the purpose of distributing short length topical features.[29] The directors of the A. Kay Company were Lewis Epstein, Hannah C. Dennin, and Mary Gilbridge.[30] During 1917, the A. Kay Company released and

Chapter 9 • Animated Antics

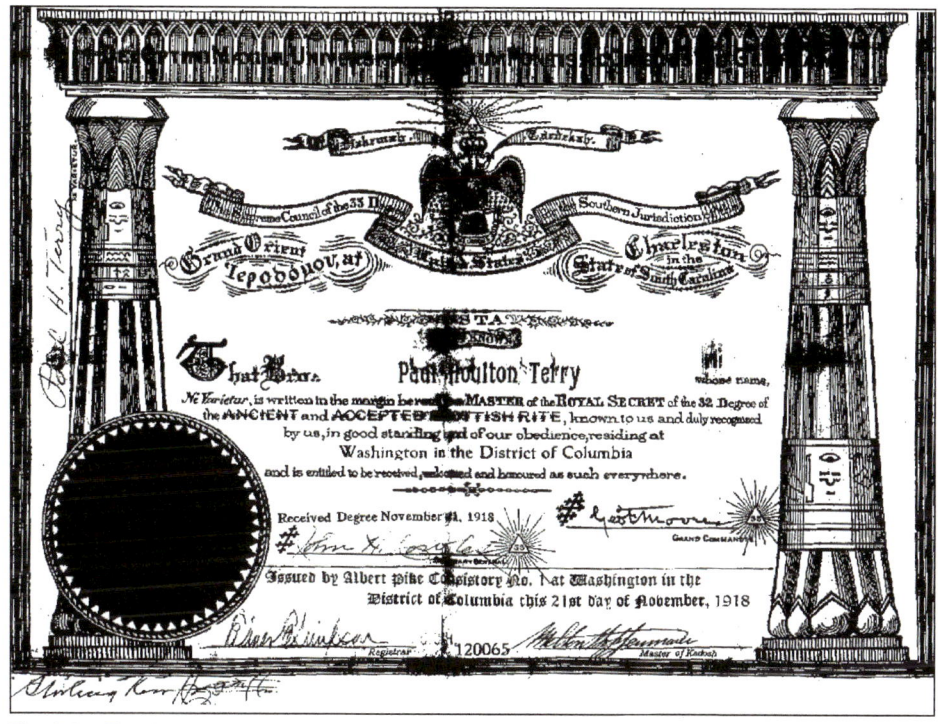

Fig. 9.2 – Terry's Masonic Degree.

distributed two Terry animated cartoon series, the *Terry Feature Burlesques*, a series of four animated cartoons which parodied the big features of the day, and *Terry Human Interest Reels*, a series of four animated cartoons that focused on phrenology, the science which studies the relationships between a person's character and the morphology of the skull.

The first from the *Terry Feature Burlesques* series was the 800-foot length *20,000 Feats Under the Sea*, an amusing burlesque of the Jules Verne novel, which was released on April 23. The short played alongside the feature film by the same name produced by the Williamson Submarine Film Corporation and starring Dan Hanlon and Edna Pendleton. The cartoon story follows an old sea pirate who lives in a barrel boat and follows the profession of sinking ships and eating raw fish. The short features inhabitants of the sea at play and intent on business. An octopus handles singlehanded a fish community kitchen, a sardine shoots the chutes on the back of an eel, and the mermaid goes walking with her dog fish. A weak fish hobbles by on crutches and the blue fish is blue because his friend, the weak fish, is on crutches.

According to the reviewer, the most amusing scene is the rambunctious daughter of the sea pirate living on an island and frolicking with her only playmates, elephants and lions. She goes for a swim, is attacked by a giant crab, and then rescued by her father who lassoes her and pulls her into his barrel boat. The reviewer found that the cartoon would delight children and be a valuable addition to any collection.[31]

As a result of the critical success of *20,000 Feats Under the Sea*,[32] the trade papers reported that a large number of booking agents across the United States had signed contracts for the distribution of Terry's *Burlesque* cartoons to theaters in their networks. L. J. Schlaifer purchased the series for the Seattle market,[33] while National Film Features [National Film Booking Service] (Pittsburgh

THE TERRY HUMAN INTEREST REEL

Do you know it is possible to tell what nature intended you to be by signs in your face and bumps on your head?

Every faculty is represented somewhere and the Terry Human Interest Reel Series will tell you where to look. It will aid you in picking competent help; it will show you whether you are on the right track; it will tell you more of yourself than you ever knew. This reel deals chiefly with the face showing the different types, taking men who have made their marks for examples.

All this knowledge is based upon the life studies of Jessie Allen Fowler, the eminent delineator of character.

Added to this reel are some intensly interesting views of Foreign Settlements in America.

Cartoons Produced by Paul H. Terry
Distributed by
The A. KAY COMPANY, NEW YORK

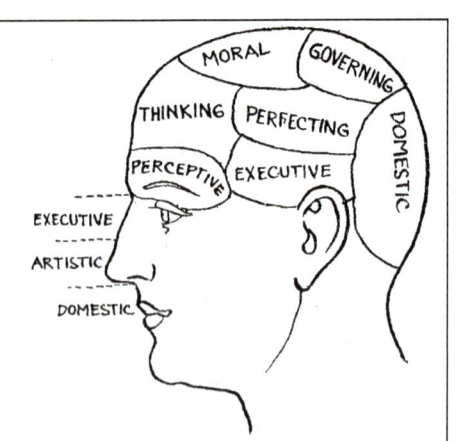

The Terry Human Interest Reel

No. 2 of a Series

How character is revealed in the face

and

A Trip to Little Italy
"Somewhere in New York"

Fig. 9.3 – Pamphlet cover promoting *Terry Human Interest Reel* No. 2.

office), was one of the first to sign a contract to arrange bookings of the Terry shorts in their regional theaters. These early successes in animation encouraged Terry to produce more animated cartoons from the series.[34]

The next *Terry Feature Burlesque* animated short released on April 30 was the 800-foot length *Golden Spoon Mary*, a burlesque on *The Poor Little Rich Girl* (1917) starring Mary Pickford. The cartoon follows the weird adventures, trials, and tribulations of a very rich, very poor little girl whose "sad" plight Terry is able to satirize and bring to ludicrous and comical ends. One reviewer found the cartoon short to be a "superlative work of comic burlesque art". Another reviewer found the animation to be good and the slapstick humor to be "quite funny".[35]

In July, two other *Terry Feature Burlesques* were released, *Some Barrier*, a parody on the critical and box office success *The Barrier* (1917) starring Mabel Julienne Scott and Russell Simpson and based on the novel by Rex Beach, and *His Trial* (July) a short which burlesqued the popular feature *On Trial* (1917) produced by the Essanay Film Manufacturing Company. The feature film was based on the popular novel of the day and starred Barbara Castleton, Sidney Ainsworth, and Mary McAllister. Terry's *His Trial*, starring Farmer Al Falfa as the central character, although not following the plot of the play or feature, was the recipient of favorable critical reviews.[36]

The success of the *Terry Feature Burlesques* series of shorts can be attributed to quality animation, interesting storylines, appealing characters, and an unsophisticated humor that appealed to audiences of all ages. These shorts were like warped fairy tales, and everyone loves a creative twist on an old tale. Terry used his gags in his cartoons with the appropriate emphasis, timing, silence, pauses, non-verbal

Chapter 9 • Animated Antics

reactions, and body gestures from his characters. His wisecracks were delivered with honesty and sincerity while never forcing the humor upon his audience.

Terry's other series distributed by the A. Kay Company, the *Terry Human Interest Reels*, were a set of four cartoons based on the work of phrenologist Jessie Allen Fowler (1856–1932). Fowler, born in New York City, studied medicine and anatomy in London, England and intended to follow her mother into medicine. When her mother died in 1879, Fowler became identified with her father's Phrenological Institute where she headed the examination department, 1879–1881. She was the editor of *Phrenological Magazine* in London (1889–1896), and taught phrenology by mail. She returned to the United States in 1896.

After her father's death in 1896, she headed his phrenological firm, Fowler & Wells Co., in New York. She was a graduate of the women's law class of New York University in 1900. As a writer Miss Fowler was associated with her father in the compilation of the *Phrenological Dictionary* (1895), and was the author of *Hand Book on Mental Science* (1896) which aimed to link phrenology with modern psychology as well as a number of other important books on phrenology including *Life of Francois J. Gall* (1896), *Brain Roofs and Porticoes* (1898) and *Brain and Skull* (1909).[37]

By 1916, Terry, who was residing at 138 West 42nd Street,[38] had become fascinated with phrenology and palmistry[39] and approached Fowler, who at the time was vice-president of the American Institute of Phrenology located at 1358 Broadway and had the head office of Fowler & Wells Company at 27 East 22nd Street, with the idea to produce a series of cartoons on the subject of phrenology.[40] Fowler agreed to assist Terry in the production of these cartoons. The cartoons claim to teach us how to read the capabilities of individuals by the shape and size of facial features. Considering Terry's belief in using animals as subjects for his cartoons to avoid offending his audience, it is remarkable to find him producing cartoons that categorize humans based on the measurements of the human skull.

The first in the series was titled *Character as Revealed by the Nose* released in June 1917. The short features various specimens of noses (Roman nose, Grecian nose, "commercial" nose, celestial nose, snub nose, and broad and thick nose) and tells the dominant characteristics of the owners of these particular noses. To back up statements made with regards to the qualities found behind the noses, pictures of men whose achievements are well-known and who possess these certain types of noses are shown, among them Napoleon Bonaparte, Marshal Joseph Jacques Césaire Joffre, President Woodrow Wilson, President Theodore Roosevelt, and Rubens the painter.[41] The first entry in the series was received favorably by movie audiences.

The *Terry Human Interest Reels* also attracted the attention of booking agents nationwide. The dominant distribution system in motion pictures at the time was States' Rights distribution. In order to distribute a film across the country, an independent producer would lease the rights in the film to independent exchanges in each territory of the United States, with the territory usually being a state. The exchanges had the exclusive rights to the film in their territory and then rented the film to exhibitors in the area and handled the physical chores of distribution, such as booking and cleaning prints, collecting rentals, and related duties.[42]

Harold Edel, manager of the Strand (New York), decided to run the entire series after reviewing the first entry in the series, as did David Mundstock of the Strand in Detroit. Similarly, the head of the film department with the Marcus Loew circuit of theaters booked the entire series for their chain of theaters. Kaufman Specials, of Memphis, Tennessee purchased the States Rights for Tennessee, Alabama, Louisiana, Mississippi, Georgia, Florida, and South Carolina.

The second entry in the series *Character as Revealed by the Eye* released in July 1917 followed the same format as the first entry. The cartoon short featured a series of pen sketches of various kinds of eyes (large, small, slant eyes, very full) and eye colors while comparing each to personality traits. The short then demonstrated the truth of these statements by examples of the eyes of famous figures including President Woodrow Wilson, William H. Taft, General Pershing, Abraham Lincoln and Billy Sunday. The other two entries in the series

83

TERRYTOONS: The Story of Paul Terry and His Classic Cartoon Factory

Fig. 9.4 – Terry's description of the origination of cel animation.

were *Character as Revealed by the Mouth* released in August and *Character as Revealed by the Ear* released in September, both followed the same format as the first two cartoons from the series and each received good reviews from the critics.[43]

The *Terry Human Interest Reels* were popular with studio audiences and critics because the cartoons capitalized upon a renewed interest in the pseudo-science during the early 20th century, an interest largely due to efforts by the Fowler family and academics such as London psychiatrist Bernard Hollander (1864–1934).[44] Further, the cartoons were smartly produced. Not only were they competently animated but by comparing phrenological concepts to the facial features of popular personalities and historical figures audiences easily recognized, Terry was able to bring some perceived credibility to the discipline.

Assisting Paul with animation on the *Terry Human Interest Reels* was his brother John. After Paul had left San Francisco to do advertising work for Barron Collier in New York City in 1911, John did work for the *San Francisco Chronicle*, the San Francisco *Examiner* and the St. Paul *Dispatch*, and also continued his lightning sketching act with San Francisco area cartoonist Russ Westover (1886–1966) (later of *Tillie the Toiler* fame).[45] He was with the San Francisco *Call* as late as April 1913. Around this period, John Terry also began to experiment with animation in collaboration with *Oakland Tribune* sports cartoonist Hugh M. "Jerry" Shields. Shields claimed that he and John Terry began experimenting with animation as early as 1911. John usually claimed it was in 1912. However, the date may actually have been closer to 1913, when John and Shields began working together in the *San Francisco Chronicle* bullpen.[46]

John and Shields left the paper late in 1914 (Terry after sixteen years as a newspaper cartoonist) to form the Movca Film Company. The company was incorporated at San Francisco with a capital stock of $150,000 by J. C. Terry, H. M. Shields, T. Healy, C. D. Longhurst, and T. E. J. Gardner. Terry and associates planned to make moving pictures for export to South and Central America and equipped a large studio in San Francisco for this purpose.[47] John and Shields set to work creating a series of unlicensed Charlie Chaplin cartoons, as well as an unknown number of one shot cartoons. About nine months later, in June 1915, the cartoons started to see release in local San Francisco theaters.[48]

In January 1916, the *Motion Picture News* announced that the sales of the "Comedy Cartoons" produced by Movca had been

84

taken over by the Herald Company, a New York City based distributor S. J. Sangretti. Movca's producer and east coast representative announced that the studio would soon have 20 subjects ready for release, and that distribution had already been secured on the Pacific Coast and Greater New York Territories on a States' Rights basis.[49] At least 11 known "Charlie" cartoons, usually starring caricatures of Charlie Chaplin, Mabel Normand, and Fatty Arbuckle, were released in 1916. It is likely that John did not have permission from Chaplin to produce the films. Mabel Normand, the Hollywood actress, called these Charlie cartoons the "greatest cartoons" she had ever seen.

In May, 1916 *Charlie in Carmen* was copyrighted plainly as *Carmen: a Moving Cartoon* by "Movca Film Service, inc., New York". A 1916 document issued by the state of California includes the Movca Film Service, located at 660 O'Farrell Street, on a list of corporations "forfeiting the right to do business in the state of California by reason of failing to Pay Corporation Taxes Levied by the State Board of Equalization", perhaps explaining Terry and Shields' abrupt relocation to New York City. In November 1916, John Terry's name was announced in conjunction with a new cartoon studio. Although it was incorporated as early as August, Terry's name was not mentioned until an article ran in the *NY Dramatic Mirror*, November 4, 1916.[50]

John Terry then worked on the *Pathé News* series (1916–1926) produced by Bray Productions for Pathé release.[51] These cartoons were produced by the Cartoon Film Service, Inc., a new corporation which featured some of the most experienced cartoonists in the country. The management team at Cartoon Film Service included Watson D. Robinson, president, John C. Terry, secretary, and Henry D. Bailey, treasurer of the new company. Between October 1916 and March 1917, Pathé released at least five animated political cartoons credited to John C. Terry and at least one credited to Hugh M. Shields within its newsreels. J. R. Bray may have been involved as a producer. By the fall of 1917, both John and Paul had established themselves firmly in the nascent animation industry as promising talents. Like what his brother John had accomplished with Movca Film Company, Paul was looking forward to establishing his own studio. His dream would have to be put on hold for a while as Uncle Sam was about to call. ☙

Notes

1. Bray's wife, Margaret Till Bray – a successful businesswoman in her own right who also managed her own real-estate company while working alongside her husband – was instrumental in helping Bray run the new studio. She was given the title of production manager, which meant that it was her responsibility to corral the animators on staff and ensure that they were meeting deadlines.

2. Crafton, 148–149. With a monopoly on the technological processes, Bray made a substantial fortune by selling licenses for the use of the patented techniques, until the patents ran out in 1932.

3. Bray remained with Paramount until 1919 when he signed on with Goldwyn Pictures.

4. Crafton, *Before Mickey*, 148–149.

5. Ibid., 148.

6. John Grant, *Masters of Animation* (New York: Watson-Guptil Publications, 2001), 48.

7. Gifford, *American Animated Films*, 44.

8. Crafton, 148; Bachman and Slater, *American Silent Film*, 99.

9. Michael S. Shull and David E. Wilt, *Doing Their Bit: Wartime American Animated Short Films, 1939–1945*, 2d ed. (Jefferson, N.C.: McFarland & Co., 2004), 21.

10. Horn, *World Encyclopedia of Cartoons*, 268; "Greening, Harry Cornell", in *Who Was Who in America*, volume V (1969–1973) (Chicago: Marquis Who's Who, 1973), 287; Falk, *Who Was Who in American Art*.

11. Horn, *World Encyclopedia of Cartoons* (1983), 260.

12. Gifford, *American Animated Films*, 10, 21, 38; Gregg Bachman and Thomas J. Slater, eds., *American Silent Film: Discovering Marginalized Voices* (Carbondale: South Illinois University, 2002), 261.

13. "Gilbert, Charles Allan", *Who Was Who In America*, volume I, 453; Falk, *Who Was Who in America*, 1985 edition, 231.

14. Crafton, *Before Mickey*, 265; Bachman and Slater, *American Silent Film*, 261–262.

15. "Motion Silhouette Pictures", *Moving Picture World*, 15 January 1916, 429.

16. Falk, *Who Was Who in American Art*, 1985 edition, 13; Maurice Horn, ed., *The World Encyclopedia of Comics*, two volumes (New York: Chelsea House Publishers, 1976); *Who Was Who in America. A Companion Bio-*

graphical *Reference Work to Who's Who in America*, volume II, 1943–1950 (Chicago: A.N. Marquis Co., 1963), 25; Burke and Howe, *American Authors and Books, 1640 to the Present Day*; Jay Rath, "Silents, Please! The Unspeakable Greatness of Carl Anderson's 'Henry'", *Nemo, the Classic Comics Library #26*, (September 1987): 42–52; Dave Strickler, *Syndicated Comic Strips and Artists, 1924–1995: The Complete Index* (Cambria, California: Comics Access, 1995).

17. Crafton, *Before Mickey*, 289; Bachman and Slater, *American Silent Film*, 261.

18. Falk, Peter Hastings, *Who Was Who in American Art*; "Press Art Head is Dean of Craft Here", *Pittsburgh Press*, 18 April 1927, New Press Plant Section, p. 13. Obituaries: "Noted Cartoonist Dies", *New York Times*, 27 May 1926, p. 25; "Comic Strip Artist Succumbs in Seattle", *Victoria Daily Colonist*, 26 May 1926, p. 12d; "Rigby Services To Be Held in Ohio", *Seattle Daily Times*, 26 May 1926, p. 5.

19. Bachman and Slater, *American Silent Film*, 261; Crafton, *Before Mickey*, 149, 165, 269.

20. Terry, interview, 14 July 1970, 134.

21. It then produced Max Fleischer's *Out of the Inkwell* until 1921, when Fleischer left, taking Koko the Clown with him. The influx of Hearst's International Film Service cartoon series at the same time broke up the four-unit system – in 1920 there were ten series going simultaneously, with Heeza Liar in hiatus from 1917.

22. Terry, interview, 20 December 1969, 42. The Presidio of San Francisco is a park and former military base on the northern tip of the San Francisco Peninsula, and part of the Golden Gate National Recreation Area.

23. Terry, interview, 20 December 1969, 43.

24. Ibid.

25. Ibid.

26. The transparent sheet was called "cel" in English, and "cellulo" in French (from celluloid).

27. Terry, interview, 20 December 1969, 42–43.

28. Terry, interview, 14 July 1970, 128.

29. "A. Kay Offers Short Reels", *Moving Picture World*, 7 April 1917, 126.

30. "Firm of Julius Kahn, Inc., Formed", *The Dramatic Mirror*, 1 September 1917, 29.

31. Margaret I. MacDonald, "20,000 Feats Under the Sea. A. Kay Company Presents Entertaining 800 Foot Animated Cartoon Burlesque By Paul Terry As Their First Release", *Moving Picture World*, 7 April 1917, 108; "Miscellaneous. 20,000 Feats Under the Sea (A. Kay)", *Moving Picture World*, 7 April 1917, 118.

32. In his 1969 interview Terry remembered the cartoon as *20,000 "Legs" Under the Sea* which would have been a more humorous pun than *20,000 Feats Under the Sea*.

33. "Seattle State Rights Men Active", *Moving Picture World*, 2 June 1917, 1468.

34. "In Pittsburgh", *Moving Picture World*, 28 April 1917, 657; "Business Notes from Pittsburgh", *Moving Picture World*, 23 June 1917, 1971.

35. "Gold Spoon Mary (A. Kay)", *Moving Picture World*, 12 May 1917, 987; "A-Kay Company. Golden Spoon Mary (Terry-Made)", *Moving Picture World*, 19 May 1917, 1144.

36. "New Terry Burlesque Entitled His Trail [sic]", *Moving Picture World*, 11 August 1917, 960.

37. Madeleine B. Stern, *Heads & Headlines: The Phrenological Fowlers* (Norman, Oklahoma: University of Oklahoma Press, 1971); John D. Davies, *Phrenology. Fad and Science: A 19th Century American Crusade* (New Haven, Yale University Press, 1955); "Fowler, Jessie Allen", *National Cyclopedia of American Biography*, volume 16 (Ann Arbor, Michigan: University Microfilms, 1967), 45; "Fowler, Jessie Allen", *Who Was Who in America*, volume I, 1897–1942, 419. Obituary: "Jessie A. Fowler, Phrenologist, Dies", *New York Times*, 16 October 1932, p. 38:3.

38. *R.L. Polk & Co.'s Trow General Directory of New York City, 1916* (New York: R.L. Polk & Co., 1916), 1656.

39. Terry, interview, 20 December 1969, 23.

40. *R.L. Polk & Co.'s Trow General Directory of New York City, 1916*, 634.

41. "Terry Human Interest Reel. A. Kay Company Distributing Series on Physiognomy Based on Studies of Jessie Allen Fowler", *Moving Picture World*, 9 June 1917, 1605; "Terry Human Interest Reel. A. Kay Company Presents Split-Reel Educational. Reading Character Through Characteristics of Nose Shown", *Moving Picture World*, 7 July 1917, 79.

42. "States Rights", *The American Film Industry*, 326.

43. "Terry Completes Fourth Human Interest Reel", *Moving Picture World*, 8 September 1917, 1549.

44. Hollander introduced a quantitative approach to the phrenological diagnosis, defining a method for measuring the skull, and comparing the measurements with statistical averages. Bernard Hollander, "A Contribution to a Scientific Phrenology", *The Journal of the Anthropological Institute of Great Britain and Ireland*, vol. 20 (1891): 227–234.

45. "Press Club Show Today", *The San Francisco Call*, 18 April 1913, p. 2

46. Biographical references can be found on John Terry in: Dawdy, *Artists of the American West*; *Who's Who in American Art*, 1st edition, New Providence, NJ: Marquis Who's Who, 1936; Hughes, *Artists in California, 1786–1940*, 3rd ed.

47. "San Francisco", *Moving Picture World*, volume 22, no. 4, 24 October 1914, 517;

48. Gifford, *American Animated Films*, 60–61; "Local Artist's Work Will be Displayed", *The Oakland Tribune*, 27 June 1915, p. 20;

49. "State Rights Buyers Attracted By Quality of Star Comedy Cartoons", *The Motion Picture News*, vol. 13, no. 5, 5 February 1916, 674.

50. "New Firm Makes Cartoons". *NY Dramatic Mirror*, 4 November 1916, p. 35.

51. Crafton, *Before Mickey*, 269; Gifford, *American Animated Films*, 29–30.

Chapter 10

You're in the Army Now: George Washington University, the Spanish Influenza Epidemic, and Work for Paramount Pictures, 1917–1920

On April 2, 1917, U.S. President Woodrow Wilson asked a special joint session of Congress to declare war on the German Empire. Wilson put to Congress a call for "a war to end all wars" that would "make the world safe for democracy". The United States' entry into World War I came after two-and-a-half years of struggles by Wilson to keep the United States neutral. During the course of the First World War, the U.S. public opinion on whether to enter the war began to change as they increasingly came to see the German Empire as the enemy. News of the "Rape of Belgium" in 1914, the sinking of the Cunard passenger liner RMS *Lusitania* in 1915 in contravention of international law, Germany's decision in 1917 to resume a determined submarine warfare on all commercial ships headed toward Britain, and the interception of the Zimmerman Telegram wherein Germany offered a military alliance to Mexico if they joined the war against the United States all helped to shape public opinion that the United States should enter the conflict. President Wilson got his declaration when on April 6, 1917 Congress voted to declare war on Germany.[1]

In 1917 Woodrow Wilson's administration decided to rely primarily on conscription, rather than voluntary enlistment, to raise military manpower for World War I. This decision was made after only 73,000 volunteers enlisted in the first six weeks of the war when the target set was one million.[2] The *Selective Service Act of 1917* was passed that authorized a selective draft of all those between 21 and 31 years of age (later from 18 to 45). Administration was entrusted to local boards composed of leading civilians in each community which issued draft calls in order of numbers drawn in a national lottery and determined exemptions.[3]

In 1917 10 million men were registered,[4] and among these males was Paul Houlton Terry. He registered on June 5, 1917 at the draft board office located at 60 West 13th Street, New York City. He listed his height as 5'7" with blue eyes, light hair and medium build. On his Registration Card, Paul claimed exemption from military service on the grounds that his work was primarily of an artistic nature and that he supported his family with nine people living off his efforts.[5] Since Paul was residing by himself with no wife or child dependents, it is curious who Terry considered these nine dependents to be.

His elderly father who was still residing in San Francisco may have been one dependent Terry was referring to, but the other eight people Paul claimed to support are left to conjecture. The thought of traveling overseas to participate in the bloody conflict probably terrified Paul who by his very nature and belief was a non-violent individual. Paul was of the opinion that wars are based on covetousness and greed. He believed that human and animal life is precious, and "everyone

87

Fig. 10.1 – George Washington University Hospital (center) with the medical school (far right) (c. 1912).

that's born has a right to live and has a right to have a spot on the earth".[6] He did not see armed aggression as a means to resolving disputes amongst the nations but rather believed that diplomacy and patience was required to settle issues.

Terry's opinion was that going to war to protect the world for democracy "is a lot of nothing" and engaging the enemy in combat because of irrational fears such as fear of communism is "a lot of malarky". He believed that these motives were excuses attempting to justify a bloody conflict. Terry did not believe in running from an aggressor as one should stand up to an assailant like an animal would to protect his rights, but you should never move in on another person's rights.[7] If Terry was under the impression that he might see frontline duty on the Western Front, then he had little to worry about as he would never have seen combat duty as a soldier due to his poor eyesight.

In 1917, Paul was asked to come to Washington, D.C. where the U.S. Army wanted to discuss with him the use of animation to assist in the production of educational and training filmstrips for medical purposes. In November 1917, Lt. Thomas L. W. Evans, head of a New York firm of commercial cinematographers and a man of experience in the then young motion picture industry, was put in charge of the new Instruction Laboratory. The operation of the Laboratory grew to include a section on still photography headed by Roy M. Reeve, a section of motion pictures headed first by Lt. Robert Ross, and when Ross went to France by Lt. Charles W. Wallach, an anatomical art service headed by Lt. William T. Schwarz then by Lt. Morris L. Bower, and a section on wax modelling headed by Captain James Frank Wallis.[8] Through these various graphic methods, the Army's Instruction Laboratory sought to reach and inform a threefold audience – troops in training, medical officers, and the civilian world, including especially civilian medical men.[9]

The Army had already established a number of units for the production of live action training films on subjects such as hand to hand combat, use of gas masks, cavalry training, and other related topics. However, despite Major Thomas L. W. Evans' best efforts to date, the Army was on the verge of abandoning the use of

Chapter 10 • You're in the Army Now

animation in training films.[10] Major Evans, who before entering the military had completed film laboratory work for Terry's animated cartoons, was now managing the Instruction Laboratory for the Army alongside producer Patrick Anthony Powers.[11] Both Evans and Powers had a key role in recruiting Terry to the university.

Powers started his career as a distributing representative of the Edison Phonograph Company and Victor Talking Machine Company in Buffalo, New York. In 1912, Powers and a partner formed Universal Pictures Corporation in New York from eight independent production companies.[12] Powers was always striving to be at the leading edge of new motion picture technology and there is little surprise the military had called upon him to assist in the film production. In April 1910 his company, the Powers Company,[13] came out with talking pictures which it made for the American Fotofone Company. He was president of Powers Film Products Company of Rochester, New York.[14] Later in 1928 he introduced sound animated cartoons; in particular Mickey Mouse and *Silly Symphonies* animated shorts, and developed the Powers Cinephone recording and reproducing equipment for talking pictures. Thereafter, in the 1930s he became president of Celebrity Productions, a studio which produced Flip the Frog and Willie Whopper animated cartoons.[15]

Major Evans explained to Paul that he wanted to record the medical history of the war and create instructional filmstrips for the Army medical staff of physicians and surgeons. The films would demonstrate surgical processes and explain internal body functions through a combination of live action film and animation. With bloody trench warfare raging on the Western Front, the U.S. Army expected there to be plenty of wounded soldiers for the medical staff to surgically treat. It was hoped that the training films along with many opportunities to treat the soldiers on the front lines would assist the doctors in improving their techniques and advance medical science.

In performing operations, because blood photographed black the viewer could not appreciate what the surgeon was doing with his instruments during the operation. To perform the operation bloodlessly required drawing and animating the procedures.[16] Further, there was no device or technology that allowed a filmmaker to transfer images of internal bodily functions onto film. In 1917, fluoroscopic technology was not advanced to the point where it was possible to capture these internal images and bodily functions on film. Evans asked Terry whether he would head a new department in charge of creating animation of these surgical processes, internal organs and bodily functions that would be combined, primarily as bridging sequences,[17] with live action sequences.[18] Terry jumped at the opportunity to assist in creating these very interesting instructional films through animation.

Terry was officially enlisted on April 1, 1918 in New York City[19] and sent to the medical school at George Washington University where he first began his military assignment by studying under Dr. King about anatomy from a surgeon's perspective.[20] The Dean of the School of Medicine and Health Sciences at The George Washington University at the time was William Cline Borden (1858–1934). Borden was the initiator, planner and effective mover for the creation, location, and first Congressional support of the Medical Center. For this reason, it is still referred to today as "Borden's Dream".[21]

At the time, the faculty at The George Washington University Medical School and Hospital boasted many of the nation's most prominent doctors: Major Walter Reed, who identified the mosquito as the carrier of yellow fever; his associate, Dr. James Carroll; Dr. Theobald Smith, whose pioneering research identifying germs as the cause of diseases thereby changing the course of medicine; Dr. Frederick Russell, who introduced typhoid vaccine into the Army; and Dr. A. F. A. King, whose *Manual of Obstetrics* was the standard at the time.[22] Terry's studio was situated right in the middle of the Army Medical Museum, near the U.S. Army Surgeon General Merritte Weber Ireland's (1867–1952) office,[23] and he worked alongside three different doctors.[24]

These doctors included Huron Willis Lawson (1873–1949) and Philemon Edwards Truesdale (1874–1945). Dr. Lawson graduated from Columbian University (later George Washington University) in 1904.

TERRYTOONS: The Story of Paul Terry and His Classic Cartoon Factory

Fig. 10.2 – Paul Terry, United States Army (frontal).

He was a surgeon to the Washington Police and Fire departments during the first 10 years of his practice. Thereafter, he became a leading physician and surgeon in the fields of obstetrics and gynecology. In 1904 he joined the faculty of medical school of George Washington University as an assistant demonstrator of anatomy. By 1915, he was professor of obstetrics at the university. During the First World War he served as medical director of the Students' Army Training Corps at George Washington University.[25]

During his career Dr. Truesdale, who graduated from Harvard with his M.D. in 1898, contributed extensively to the literature on the clinical manifestations and surgical treatment of cancer of the tongue, breast, lip, neck, stomach, intestine, gall bladder, pancreas and the female generative organs, and also on gall stones, appendicitis and tumors, as well as hernia of the diaphragm. During World War One, Truesdale served in France for 18 months as a captain and later as a major in the Yale Mobile Hospital Unit, acting as director of surgery with one mobile hospital and later as a commander of another. He erected the Truesdale Hospital in Fall River, Massachusetts in 1909 and was the founder of the New England Surgical Society.[26]

Terry entered his military career as first class private and was subsequently promoted to the rank of sergeant on May 27, 1918.[27] He was promoted to second lieutenant, the normal entry-level rank for most commissioned officers in the Army, because he was working alongside other officers.[28] His appointment to Second Lieutenant in the Sanitary Corps of the U.S. Army occurred on September 9, 1918.[29]

After receiving his education in the basics of anatomy at the university and assigned to his commission, Terry carefully gathered a team of artists to produce the animated shorts.[30] At first Terry hired girls to trace drawings or paint the animation cels. Eventually there were four animators working under Terry including Harry Leonard and an artist named "Lungard", and about six production assistants.[31] Jacob Leventhal was also affiliated with the unit. Leventhal was a pioneer researcher in animated cartoons and 3-D screen techniques. After the First World War, Mr. Leventhal produced the *Out of the Inkwell* animated series. As a member of the firm Ives-Leventhal he turned out the first 3-D movies in the United States in 1924. Called "Plastigrams", these movies were viewed through glasses with red and green filters. Along with John A. Norling he produced a series of shorts known as "Audioscopics" for Metro.[32]

During his time heading the animation department his unit produced filmstrips on

Chapter 10 • You're in the Army Now

orthopedics, straightening club feet, transplanting tendons, three reels on hernias (umbilical, femoral inguinal), venereal diseases, and the peristaltic motions of intestines.[33] While in the military, Terry became friends with artist Frank Godwin who was involved in illustrating posters and propaganda materials for the Army. Godwin is best known for the syndicated comic strip *Rusty Riley* which ran in 153 newspapers in the United States and Canada at the time of his death.[34] Terry also developed cordial relations with Hollywood photographer Lucien Andriot, and live-action directors Sidney and Chester Franklin all of whom were affiliated with the live action film unit.[35]

In late January and early February 1918 in Haskell County, Kansas, a county comprised of rural farming communities, an outbreak of influenza gripped the small region and citizens began to die. This outbreak is considered to be the first recorded occurrence of the 1918/1919 "Spanish Flu" in the United States and prompted local doctor Loring Miner to warn the U.S. Public Health Service's academic journal.[36] On March 11, 1918, at nearby Camp Funston (Fort Riley) Kansas, company cook Albert Gitchell reported sick. By noon on March 11, 1918, over 100 soldiers were in the hospital. Within days, 522 men at the camp had reported sick.[37]

There is no consensus as to where the flu originated. Many of the theories pinpoint Asia.[38] One recent research paper identifies northern France where the Etaples camp had the necessary mixture of factors for the emergence of pandemic influenza including overcrowding of soldiers, live pigs, and nearby live geese, duck and chicken markets, horses and an additional factor, 24 gases (some of them mutagenic) used in large 100 ton quantities to contaminate soldiers and the landscape.[39] Historian Mark Humphries argues that the mobilization of 96,000 Chinese laborers to work behind the British and French lines on World War I's Western Front, may have been the source of the pandemic. In the new report, Humphries finds archival evidence that a respiratory illness that struck northern China in November 1917 was identified a year later by Chinese health officials as identical to the Spanish flu.[40] Recent genetic sequencing reveals that the virus originated from avian sources.[41]

Fig. 10.3 – Paul Terry, United States Army (profile).

The global mortality rate from the 1918/1919 pandemic is not known, but an estimated 10 to 20 percent of those who were infected died. With about a third of the world population infected, this case-fatality ratio means 3 to 6 percent of the entire global population died.[42] Influenza may have killed as many as 25 million people in its first 25 weeks. Older estimates say the virus killed 40 to 50 million people,[43] while current estimates say 50 to 100 million people worldwide were killed.[44] This pandemic has been described as "the greatest medical

Fig. 10.4 – Paul Terry's Appointment as Second Lieutenant.

were both deadly.[47] By the end of September 1918, influenza cases were being reported at military bases near Washington, D.C. at Camp Devens (Mass.) and Camp Dix (N.J.). The first Washingtonian to die of the virus was reported in the *Washington Post* on September 22, 1918.[48] The *Washington Post* published on September 24 that 20,211 U.S. soldiers had influenza across the country.[49] On September 28, seven deaths in the District of Columbia were reported and the number continued to climb.[50]

By the first week of October the influenza had invaded Washington, D.C. On October 1, seven deaths were reported.[51] By October 3 Washington began to close down public schools. Mercantile stores and department stores and all stores that sold in direct competition with them were ordered closed. Many streetcar motormen and conductors were unable to report to work causing public transportation problems.[52]

holocaust in history".[45] It is said that this flu killed more people in 24 weeks than AIDS killed in 24 years, more in a year than the Black Death killed in a century.[46]

Globally, the first wave of the 1918 pandemic occurred during spring-summer 1918 (as recognized in the Northern Hemisphere) and was associated with high morbidity but low mortality. The two following waves, in summer/fall (late August) 1918 and winter (October/November) 1918–1919,

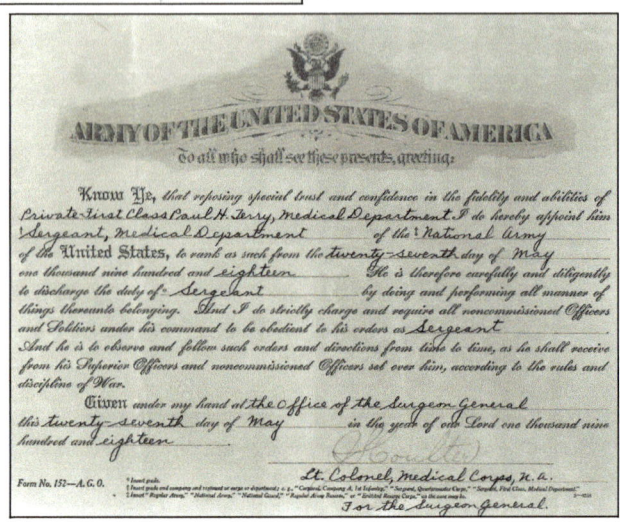

Fig. 10.5 – Paul Terry's Appointment as Sergeant, Medical Department.

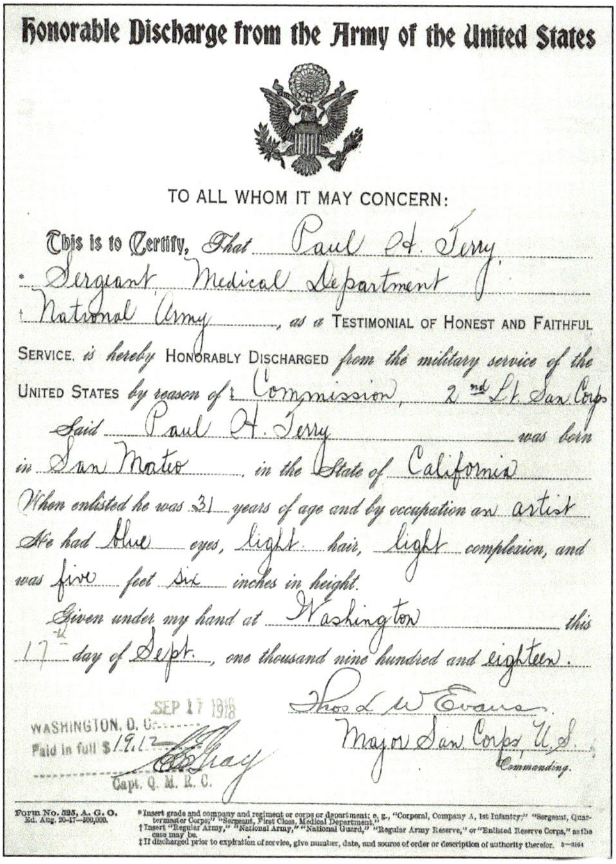

Chapter 10 • You're in the Army Now

Fig. 10.6 – Paul Terry's Honorable Discharge.

On October 5, churches were ordered closed and children were banned from playgrounds by district commissioners, while the deaths continued to mount; 17 lost their lives the previous day.[53] Thirty-seven deaths were reported on October 6,[54] while libraries closed and the city's public service sector began to close down.[55] The numbers continued to climb. Forty deaths were reported on October 8 by the *Washington Post*,[56] 72 deaths were reported on October 11,[57] 88 deaths on October 16,[58] 91 deaths published on October 18,[59] and 95 deaths listed in the newspaper on October 19.[60] By October 20, the epidemic had peaked in the city and the number of deaths recorded in the Washington daily began to decline.

At George Washington University, the difficulties in staffing were tragically increased by the lengthy flu epidemic. On October 9, 1918, the president of the university reported to the Board that all civilian activity in the University had been suspended by order of the Health Department. Four weeks of instruction would be lost and the academic year was extended to June 18, on which day the Commencement was held. The situation was especially critical at the University Hospital with the care and treatment of the public ill with the virus.[61]

Terry did his best to avoid the influenza but working around sick and dying soldiers was a dangerous and unavoidable part of his job and he was soon infected with the virus. He had watched many soldiers die from pneumonia caused by the virus, soldiers whom he later described "died like flies".[62] Modern research, using the virus taken from the bodies of frozen victims, has concluded that the virus kills through a cytokine storm (overreaction of the body's immune system). The strong immune reactions of young adults ravaged the body, whereas the weaker immune systems of children and middle-aged adults resulted in fewer deaths among those groups.[63] The hardest hit group was 20 to 40 year olds. At the time of his infection, Terry was 31 years of age.

Terry remained in bed for many days extremely ill and dehydrated. Early symptoms of the disease included a temperature in the range of 102 to 104 degrees. Along with this high temperature, patients also experienced a sore throat, exhaustion, headache, aching limbs, bloodshot eyes, a cough and occasionally a violent nosebleed. Some patients also suffered from digestive symptoms such as vomiting or diarrhea. Compared to other influenza strains, excess deaths above the expected background were caused by two overlapping clinical-pathologic syndromes: severe aggressive bronchopneumonia and severe acute respiratory distress-like

93

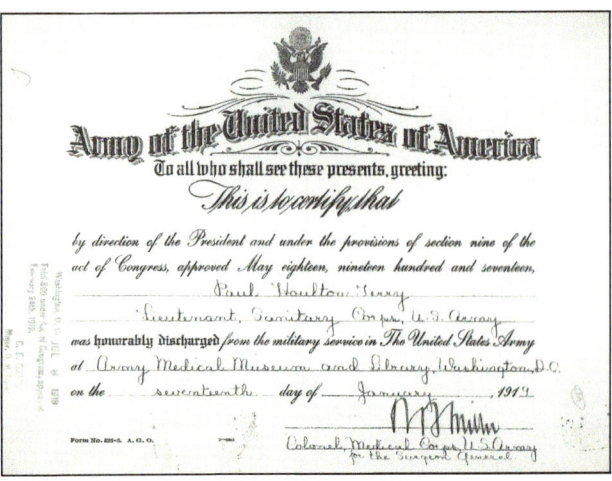

Fig. 10.7 – Paul Terry's Honorable Discharge – Certification.

syndrome.[64] Paul likely experienced many of the symptoms in what he referred to as a "horrible, horrible, horrible" virus.[65]

Terry did recover and when he got out of bed he had lost so much weight he felt as light as a feather.[66] At the time, he took the bout in stride, although years later he realized how lucky he had been and was grateful for another day on planet Earth.[67] With the hostilities in Europe and around the world officially ending on November 11, 1918, it was not long before Terry had been notified that his time in the military was coming to a close. Terry was officially discharged from the United States Army at the Army Medical Museum and Library in Washington, D.C. on January 17, 1919. He was awarded one silver service chevron during his service.[68]

On November 21, 1918, Paul became a "Master of the Royal Secret of the 32 Degree of the Ancient and Accepted Scottish Rite", a degree issued in Washington, D.C., Southern Jurisdiction.[69] Little is known about Terry's involvement with Freemasonry. Although he paid his dues and apparently attended a local lodge, the level of his involvement with the fraternal organization is unknown. He never publicly acknowledged his involvement with the group.

Meanwhile, Paul's brother John was continuing to be busy in animation. By the end of 1917, the Cartoon Film Service had folded and John Terry was on staff as a full time animator at William Randolph Hearst's International Film Service studio. At IFS Terry animated cartoons starring many of the same famous Hearst comic characters he had painted on his vaudeville curtain seven years earlier. In 1917, he directed one *Powers Cartoons* series short for producer Patrick A. Powers and Universal distribution (*When Noah's Ark Embarked* (May 1917)).[70] For the war effort during World War I, he helped animate *Your Flag and My Flag*, a patriotic poem set to animation, released by the Thomas A. Edison Co. for KESE (Kline, Edison, Selig & Essanay) release in July 1917.[71]

On July 6, 1918, the entire staff of Hearst's IFS animation studio was abruptly laid off when the Hearst corporation decided it was not a profitable venture. It is not known exactly how long the Hearst animators were laid off, but the fact that IFS stopped releasing weekly cartoons only between October 1918 and January 1919 indicates that it was likely a short interruption. According to Walter Lantz, who worked at all three incarnations of the studio between 1917 and 1921, John Terry was soon commissioned by Hearst to put together and manage a new studio to continue producing the films. The staff was rehired and set back to work, this time in a new studio space John Terry had located in Greenwich Village.[72]

In 1919, John was directing for International Film Service on the *Joys and Glooms* series (*Doctor Soakem* (1919)).[73] In August 1919, the Bray studio split with their previous distributor Paramount to sign up with MGM. IFS became a subsidiary of Bray, and for some reason John Terry was no longer the studio producer. After being discharged from the Army in early 1919 Paul Terry headed back to New York City almost right after his release. He first set up a studio on 8th Avenue and it took him a few months to get the electricians into the studio to do the wiring and get the cameras set up.[74] However, before he began production, Paramount Pictures

Chapter 10 • You're in the Army Now

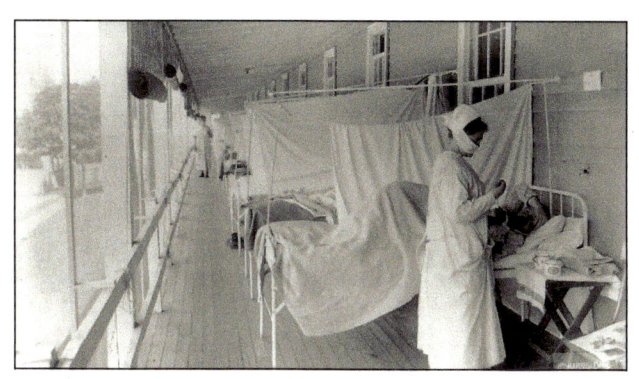

Fig. 10.8 – Influenza Ward, Walter Reed Hospital, Washington, D.C., 1918.

offered him and John the opportunity to establish an animation studio for them. Paramount wanted him to oversee the operations of a staff of animators and to produce his own Farmer Al Falfa cartoons for their screen magazine, *Paramount Magazine* which Paramount would distribute.[75] Earl Hurd, Frank Moser, Harry Leonard, Harry D. Bailey, and Jerry Shields were hired as animators. The first cartoon Terry produced for Paramount was *Bone of Contention* released on March 14, 1919 through *Paramount Magazine* [*Paramount Picture Magazine*].[76]

Paul had wisely registered the trademark "Alfalfa" for Motion-Picture Films of Animated Cartoons Issued Serially. The trademark "Alfalfa" was now Terry's property, and would be identified with Terry's animated cartoon shorts starring the farmer. The application for the Registration of the Trademark was filed by Terry on April 4, 1916 and was published in the *Official Gazette* of November 21, 1916.[77] By a letter dated January 4, 1917, Terry received a letter from the United States Patent Office that his Application for Registration of Trade-Mark for Motion-picture Films of Animated Cartoons Issued Serially had been examined and allowed.[78] On February 5, 1917, Terry received the certificate of registration of the trade-mark "Alfalfa", a certificate issued under date of January 30, 1917, No. 115, 250.[79]

Famous Players-Lasky Corporation announced in the June 28, 1919 issue of *Moving Picture World* that each week there would be a release of a comedy cartoon to include Bobby Bumps by Earl Hurd, Farmer Al Falfa by Paul Terry, and a new cartoon from a very funny series by Frank Moser.[80] The series Moser was directing was the *Bud and Susie* animated cartoons. Other animators and directors at the studio included Australian Pat Sullivan who was producing his popular Felix the Cat cartoons, and Henry D. Bailey who was animating his *Silly Hoots* cartoon series.[81] Paramount planned for John Terry, along with Bert Clark and Harry Leonard, to create a series of animated films on scientific drawings. The editors at *Popular Mechanics* were to edit the renderings of the scientific subjects and would give publicity in their publication that clearer and more detailed exposition of scientific subjects treated in the magazine would be found in *Paramount Magazine*.[82] These cartoons were produced at the Famous Players-Lasky studio on 40th Street.[83] Paul and John would be with Paramount for most of 1919. Paul's fortunes would begin to change when he was approached by a Hollywood actor, director, writer, and future Academy Award winner. ✥

Notes

1. Justus D. Doenecke, *Nothing Less Than War: A New History of America's Entry into World War One* (Lexington, Kentucky: The University of Kentucky Press, 2011); Sue Vander Hook, *The United States Enters World War I* (North Mankato, Minnesota: ABDO Publishing, 2010), 1–28.

2. Howard Zinn, *People's History of the United States* (Harper Collins, 2003), 134.

3. Christopher Cappozola, *Uncle Sam Wants You: World War I and the Making of the Modern American Citizen* (New York: Oxford University Press, 2008), 21–25; "Selective Service" in *The United States in the First World War: An Encyclopedia*, ed. Anne Cipriano Venzon (New York: Routledge, 1999), 540–541.

4. This figure was deemed to be inadequate, so age ranges were increased and exemptions reduced, and so by the end of 1918 this increased to 24 million men that were registered with nearly three million inducted into the military services.

95

5. "Paul Houlton Terry", Registration State: New York, Registration County: New York, Roll: 1786816, Draft Board: 154, United States, Selective Service System, *World War I Selective Service System Draft Registration Cards, 1917–1918*, M1509, 4,582 rolls (Washington, D.C.: National Archives and Records Administration).

6. Terry, interview, 20 December 1969, 30.

7. Ibid., 32.

8. Terry, interview, 13 June 1970, 99.

9. Henry, Robert Selph, *The Armed Forces Institute of Pathology, Its First Century, 1862–1962* (Washington: Office of the Surgeon General, Dept. of the Army, 1964), 171.

10. Terry, interview, 20 December 1969, 28.

11. Ibid., 37.

12. "Powers, Patrick Anthony", *The 1944–45 Motion Picture Almanac*, ed. Terry Ramsaye (New York: Quigley Publications, 1944), 355–356.

13. Slide, *American Film Industry*, 267–268.

14. "Patrick A. Powers, Film Official, Dead", *New York Times*, 1 August 1948, p. 57:2; "Pat Powers", *Variety*, 4 August 1948, 55.

15. "Patrick A. Powers, Film Official, Dead", 57.

16. Terry, interview, 20 December 1969, 28.

17. Ibid., 29.

18. Ibid., 37.

19. Army of the United States ,"Enlistment Record", Paul H. Terry, undated, Paul Terry Papers, Fayetteville, North Carolina.

20. Terry, interview, 20 December 1969, 28. Terry may be referring to Dr. Albert Freeman Africanus King who was for 42 years a professor in the medical faculty of George Washington University. He was the foremost authority on obstetrics in the United States, a medical speciality. Terry animated films that illustrated surgical techniques in the field of obstetrics. However, Dr. King had died three years earlier (1914) so Terry might be referring to either the writings of Dr. King or mentors of Dr. King's teaching at GWU. Alternatively, according to the university archivist, there was one other "Dr. King" in the teaching faculty at GWU in 1917 as listed in the *University Bulletin*, Dr. Ernest Frothingham King, clinical professor of genito-urinary surgery (Lyle Slovick, letter to author, 8 June 2000). For more on Dr. A. F. A. King, see: "King, Dr. A(lbert) F(reeman) A(fricanus)", *American Men of Science: A Biographical Dictionary*, ed. J. McKeen Cattell, 2nd ed. (New York: The Science Press, 1910), 258; "King, Albert Freeman Africanus", in *National Cyclopaedia of American Biography*, volume 24 (Ann Arbor, Michigan: University Microfilms, 1967), 94–95; "King, Albert Freeman Africanus", *Dictionary of American Biography*, ed. Dumas Malone (New York: Charles Scribner's Sons, 1933), 381–382. Obituary: "Dr. A. F. A. King Dead", *Washington Post*, 15 December 1914, p. 3.

21. Mary W. Standlee, *Borden's Dream* (Washington, DC : Borden Institute, 2009).

22. Elmer Louis Kayser, *A Medical Center; The Institutional Development of Medical Education in George Washington University* (Washington, George Washington University Press, 1973); Robert Williams Prichard, *Historical Sketch of the Medical School, 1825–1947* (Washington, D.C.: George Washington University, 1947); Elmer Louis Kayser, *Bricks Without Straw; The Evolution of George Washington University* (New York, Appleton-Century-Crofts, 1970).

23. Terry, interview, 13 June 1970, 90. For more on Ireland see: *Who Was Who in America*, volume III, 1951–1960, 1286. Obituary: "Gen Ireland Buried", *New York Times*, 10 July 1952, p. 31:5.

24. Terry, interview, 20 December 1969, 28.

25. Lawson, Huron Willis", in *The National Cyclopedia of American Biography*, volume XXXVII (Ann Arbor, Michigan, 1967), 167–168; *Who Was Who in America*, volume V. 1943–1950, 539.

26. "Truesdale, Philemon Edwards", in *The National Cyclopedia of American Biography*, volume XL (Ann Arbor, Michigan, 1967), 184–185; *Who Was Who in America*, volume II, 1943–1950, 539.

27. Army of the United States of America, Form no. 152 – A.G.O., Appointed to Sergeant, Paul Houlton Terry, 27 May 1918, Washington, DC.

28. Terry, interview, 20 December 1969, 37.

29. The President of the United States of America, Appointment to Second Lieutenant in the Sanitary Corps, Paul H. Terry, 20 November 1918, Washington, D.C.

30. Terry, interview, 20 December 1969, 37.

31. Terry, interview, 14 July 1970, 137. The identity of artist "Lungard" is unknown and the spelling may be incorrect due to a transcription error.

32. "Jacob F. Leventhal", *Variety*, 22 July 1953, 63; "Jacob Leventhal, Movie Researcher", *New York Times*, 20 July 1953, p. 17:3.

33. Terry, interview, 20 December 1969, 37; Terry, interview, 14 July 1970, 136.

34. "Frank Godwin, 69, Cartoonist, Dead", *New York Times*, 6 August 1959, p. 27:3; *Who Was Who in American Art* (1985), p. 235; Horn, *The World Encyclopedia of Comics*; Garraty and Carnes, *American National Biography*; Ron Goulart, ed., *The Encyclopedia of American Comics* (New York: Facts on File, 1990); Walt Reed and Roger Reed, *The Illustrator in America, 1880–1980. A Century of Illustration* (New York: Madison Square Press, 1984).

35. Terry, interview, 20 December 1969, 37–38, 61.

36. John M. Barry, *The Great Influenza; The Story of the Deadliest Pandemic in History* (New York: Penguin Books), 92–95; John Barry, "The Site of Origin of the 1918 Influenza Pandemic and its Public Health Implications", *Journal of Translational Medicine*, vol. 2 (2004): 3–4.

37. Barry, *The Great Influenza*, 95–97.

38. W.I.B. Beveridge, *Influenza: The Last Great Plague. An Unfinished Story of Discovery* (New York: Prodist, 1977), 40–41.

39. J.S. Oxford, R. Lambkin, A.

Chapter 10 • You're in the Army Now

Sefton, R. Daniels, A. Elliot, R. Brown, and D. Gill, "A Hypothesis: The Conjunction of Soldiers, Gas, Pigs, Ducks, Geese and Horses in Northern France During the Great War Provided the Conditions for the Emergence of the "Spanish" Influenza Pandemic of 1918–1919", *Vaccine* 23 (7) (4 January 2005): 940–945.

40. Mark Osborne Humphries, "Paths of Infection: The First World War and the Origins of the 1918 Influenza Pandemic", *War In History* 21(1) (January 2014): 55–81.

41. Robert B. Belshe, *The Origins of Pandemic Influenza – Lessons from the 1918 Virus*, The New England Journal of Medicine 353 (2005): 2209–2211.

42. Jeffery K. Taubenberger and David M. Morens, "1918 Influenza: The Mother of All Pandemics", *Emerging Infectious Diseases* 12 (2006): 15–22.

43. Richard Collier, *The Plague of the Spanish Lady. The Influenza Pandemic of 1918–1919* (London: MacMillan London, Limited, 1974), 305–306.

44. Niall P. A. S. Johnson and Juergen Mueller, "Updating the Accounts: Global Mortality of the 1918–1920 "Spanish" Influenza Pandemic", *Bulletin of the History of Medicine*, 76 (2002): 105–115

45. C. W. Potter, "A History of Influenza". *Journal of Applied Microbiology*, 91 (4) (October 2006): 572–579.

46. Barry, *The Great Influenza*, 5.

47. David M. Morens and Anthony S. Fauci, "The 1918 Influenza Pandemic: Insights for the 21st Century", *The Journal of Infectious Diseases* 195 (7) (2007): 1018–1028.

48. "Influenza Kills Here", *Washington Post*, 22 September 1918, p. 3.

49. "20,211 Soldiers Have Influenza", *Washington Post*, 24 September 1918, p. 3.

50. "Seven Die in Epidemic", *Washington Post*, 28 September 1918, p. 3.

51. "Seven Die of Epidemic", *Washington Post*, 1 October 1918, p. 4.

52. "Drastic Measures to Fight Epidemic", *Washington Post*, 3 October 1918, p. 1.

53. "Flu Still Spreads", *Washington Post*, 5 October 1918, p. 1.

54. "'Flu' Grows by 1,300", *Washington Post*, 6 October 1918, p. 1.

55. "Influenza Closes Library", *Washington Post*, 6 October 1918, p. 10.

56. ""Flu" Still Spreads", *Washington Post*, 8 October 1918, p. 1.

57. "72 Dead from 'Flu,' Day's Record in D.C.", *Washington Post*, 11 October 1918, p. 1.

58. "88 Deaths By "Flu", High Record in City", *Washington Post*, 16 October 1918, p. 1.

59. "91 More Die of 'Flu', D.C.'s High Record", *Washington Post*, 18 October 1918, p. 1.

60. ""Flu" Deaths Climb", *Washington Post*, 19 October 1918, p. 1.

61. Kayser, *Bricks Without Straw*, 230–231.

62. Terry, interview, 13 June 1970, 100.

63. Morens and Fauci, "The 1918 Influenza Pandemic: Insights for the 21st Century", 1022–1023.

64. Ibid., 1019–1020.

65. Terry, interview, 13 June 1970, 100.

66. Ibid.

67. Ibid.

68. Army of the United States of America, "Honorable Discharge from the Army of the United States", Paul Houlton Terry, Washington, DC, 8 July 1919.

69. A copy of Paul's Master of the Royal Secret of the 32 degree of the Ancient and Accepted Scottish Rite issued by Albert Pike Consistory no. 1 at Washington, D.C. on November 21, 1918 is on file with the Paul Terry Papers.

70. Gifford, *American Animated Films: The Silent Era, 1897–1929*, 23–27.

71. Webb, *The Animated Film Encyclopedia*, 541.

72. Joe Adamson, *The Walter Lantz Story* (New York: G.P. Putnam's Sons, 1985), 47; Leonard Maltin, *Of Mice and Magic: A History of American Animated Cartoons* (New York: New American Library, 1987), 17.

73. Gifford, *American Animated Films: The Silent Era, 1897–1929*, 48–49.

74. Terry, interview, 14 July 1970, 138.

75. Ibid., 128–129, 138. Terry, interview, 20 December 1969, 38.

76. Webb, *The Animated Film Encyclopedia*, 362.

77. Letter from Thomas Ewing, Commissioner of Patents, United States Patent Office to the law firm of Pennie, Davis and Marvin, 7 November 1916.

78. Letter from Thomas Ewing, Commissioner of Patents, United States Patent Office to Paul H. Terry, 4 January 1917.

79. Letter from William H. Davis to Paul H. Terry, 5 February 1917.

80. "One-Reel Subjects", *Moving Picture World*, 28 June 1919, no page number.

81. Terry also remembered Harry Leonard, Jerry Shields, and his brother John as being part of the studio. Terry, interview, 14 July 1970, 138.

82. "Paramount Magazine Production Plans Are Told By Nathan Friend. Epigrams from Smart Set Magazine and New York and Animated Drawing from Popular Mechanics Are Features", *Exhibitor's Herald and Motography*, volume IX, no. 5, 26 July 1919, 84.

83. Terry, interview, 14 July 1970, 128. Terry was most likely referring to the Famous Players-Lasky Corporation Studio located at 458, 5th Avenue between 40th and 42nd Streets near Bryant Park. *R.L. Polk & Co.'s Trow General Directory of New York City, 1917* (New York: R.L. Polk & Co., 1917), 727.

Chapter 11

A Barnyard of Animal Friends: Farmer Al Falfa and Fables Pictures Studios, Part One, 1921–1925

As Paul was in the process of leaving Paramount to form his own studio, he was presented with a two-year employment contract by the Universal Film Manufacturing Company to produce his Farmer Al Falfa cartoons for their distribution. The contract was dated to be signed on November 24, 1919. The terms of the contract were that employment would begin January 5, 1920 and end on January 5, 1922. For the first year, Terry was promised $250 a week for his services and during the second year $300 a week. Terry was to supervise, under the direction of the Head of the Industrial and Educational Departments of Universal, all cartoon work of said departments. The animation would be undertaken at Universal's New York studio at 1600 Broadway. At the time, Universal was producing the *The Whozit Weekly* and *Cinema Luke* cartoon series animated and directed by Leslie Elton, and the *Tad's Cat* animated series created by Tad Dorgan.[1]

For reasons unknown, Paul decided not to enter the employment contract with Universal and continued his work for Paramount while living with his brother at 204 – West 96th Street in Manhattan. The fact that Paul wanted to become an independent producer and establish his own cartoon studio at the time probably played a factor in his decision. In 1920, he was approached by stage and film actor and writer Howard Estabrook. Estabrook is best noted for winning the Academy Award in the category "Best Writing (Adapted Screenplay)" adapting Edna Ferber's novel *Cimarron* for the motion picture of the same name. Estabrook was born Howard Estabrook Bolles in Detroit, Michigan, in 1884. His appearances as a stage actor in Detroit's theatrical and stock company productions led to his first professional engagement under Charles Frohman's management in New York in 1904.

Estabrook dropped his surname in 1907. Estabrook's first play script was for *Mrs. Avery*, which premiered at Weber's Theatre, New York, in 1911. Estabrook continued acting on the stage and moved into stage direction in the 1910s. He made his film debut in George Kleine Productions' silent film comedy *Officer 666* (1914), and had the leading role as Captain Harry Faversham in *Four Feathers* (1915). He directed three films in 1917, one in New York and two in Los Angeles. He left the world of film and stage and returned to New York to enter the world of business.[2] Estabrook was serving as assistant sales manager at the Vacuum Oil Company and conducting related business interests at the time he met Paul.[3]

While it is unclear how Terry made his first acquaintance with Estabrook, the former actor and director called upon Terry and suggested to him that he make a series of animated cartoons involving Aesop's Fables.[4] Terry found the idea appealing because he appreciated the fact that Aesop's Fables had been around over 2,500 years, and present in the popular media, fables credited to Aesop, a slave and story-teller believed to have lived in ancient Greece between 620 and 560

98

Chapter 11 • A Barnyard of Animal Friends

Fig. 11.1 – Paul Terry (c. 1921). Studio publicity shot likely promoting the Fables short *The Rooster and the Eagle* (1921).

BCE.[5] Terry believed their popularity was due to the fact that the stories involved human weaknesses and frailties. His opinion was that audiences are interested in stories involving misfortune, disaster, and an individual's imperfections as opposed to perfection or normality.[6] While Terry mulled over leaving Paramount and would eventually do so by 1921, John Terry continued to produce cartoons for Paramount and subcontract cartoons for IFS between 1919 and 1921. He also may have been responsible for the mysterious "Roving Thomas" cartoons of the early 1920s.

Terry agreed to produce two animated cartoon shorts for Estabrook, *The Fox and the Crow* (1921) and *The Mice in Council* (1921). Terry produced both cartoons in 1920 which Estabrook purchased. After viewing the quality of the shorts and upon further discussions between the two parties Estabrook entered into a five-year contractual arrangement dated August 9, 1920 with Terry. Terry agreed to produce each week one animated *Aesop's Fables* cartoon featuring Terry's Farmer Al Falfa cartoon character within a certain range of footage (400 to 500 feet in length) up to the same standard as the first two cartoons produced.[7] Terry was to be paid $300 weekly for his services[8] while Estabrook would be responsible to sell, license or otherwise dispose of the cartoons.[9]

However, by the end of 1920 Estabrook was encountering difficulties in finding a distributor for the cartoon product. A contractual amendment was drafted in December 1920 wherein Terry's weekly salary was to be reduced by 1/3rd from $300 to $200 which carried the parties through to April 1, 1921.[10] Another amendment to carry the two parties under the same terms and conditions from June to August 1921 was also prepared but not entered into by both parties but an agreement through to October 1921 was signed by Terry.[11] Based on the extant documentation, with time passing and Estabrook unable to find a party to purchase, use or distribute the product, Terry and Estabrook were continually renegotiating terms of the contract with each subsequent agreement having terms less favorable for Paul.

In the spring of 1921, Estabrook found a party interested in purchasing the animated cartoon series, the Keith-Albee theater circuit. The Keith-Albee circuit was a theater chain of vaudeville theaters formed originally in 1885 by Benjamin Franklin Keith (1846–1914) and Edward Franklin Albee II (1857–1930).[12] As the circuit comprised theater owners throughout the United States and Canada, Terry was assured that the cartoons would be shown across both countries. In 1906,

99

TERRYTOONS: The Story of Paul Terry and His Classic Cartoon Factory

Fig. 11.2 – Paul Terry illustrating a mouse from a Fables cartoon.

Keith and Albee established the United Booking Office. Every act that sought employment at any of the member theaters had to work through this central office, which in turn charged a five percent commission per act. Thus Keith and Albee expanded their power base.[13] The Keith-Albee circuit was one of the two largest theater chains in the United States, the other being the Orpheum chain headed by Morris Meyerfeld Jr. and Martin Beck. The distributor of the cartoon product for Keith-Albee was Pathé.[14]

To manage and administer the production of the animated cartoons, Paul Terry and Amedee Van Beuren[15] founded Fables Pictures, Inc. with Van Beuren as President and Terry as an employee of the studio in charge of production. E. J. Lander was vice-president while J. Henry Walters was secretary treasurer. The studio was located in a small studio space at 1562 Broadway, 4th floor. Fables Pictures, Inc. was owned 90 percent by the Keith-Albee theater chain while Paul Terry would come to own 10 percent of the animated film production company.[16] This ownership structure would remain the same from inception in 1921 through to 1929.

Van Beuren was ideally suited for his role at Fables. He had years of experience in the entertainment industry and was seen as a leader in the New York film industry. In his early days, Van Beuren worked in the livery business, groceries, and then as a salesman. Van Beuren would make a fortune distributing mutoscopes and peep show machines (individual viewers for short, sometimes spicy, films) to penny arcades and amusement parks. His interests in the amusement line included the ownership and management of the Moorish Gardens and the Van Kelton Stadium Airdomes, the Notlek Tennis Courts, and ice skating rinks in New York City. For many years he was vice-president of the Van Beuren Billposting Company. By 1920, he was President of Timely Films, AyVeeBee Corporation and V.B.K. Corporation. The AyVeeBee Corporation produced the Paramount – Ernest Truex comedies. The V.B.K. Corporation produced the Paramount – Drew comedies.

The Keith-Albee management through Fables Pictures, Inc., agreed to assume by assignment the contractual responsibilities of Estabrook (the assignor) under the August 9, 1920 contract of employment between Terry and Estabrook. As a result, Fables Pictures, Inc. (the assignee) became responsible for all of the contractual responsibilities of the assignor under the employment contract. The agreement was formalized by way of a contract entered on June 23, 1921, between Fables Pictures, Inc., and Paul Terry, wherein the Terry and Estabrook agreement of August 9, 1920 was duly assigned to Fables Pictures, Inc., and Terry agreed to produce the animated shorts as per the Terry-Estabrook agreement for the agreed upon salary plus an additional five percent of the net profits as shown upon the books of Fables Pictures, Inc. The Keith-Albee theater chain would underwrite the studio's expenses and guarantee bookings.[17]

On June 19, 1921, Van Beuren announced that Terry's *Aesop's Fables* would appear every week and would be distributed by Pathé.[18] Estabrook would soon

Chapter 11 • A Barnyard of Animal Friends

Fig. 11.3 – Farmer Al Falfa and his cat Thomas illustrated by Paul Terry.

leave the arrangement to move back into live-action motion picture work as writer, director and producer. In order to produce the *Aesop's Fables* cartoons required a staff of artists with the talent and experience to create one animated cartoon a week for the remainder of the contractual term. As early as 1920 when Terry was producing the first two animated cartoons for Estabrook, he had been overseeing artists who would eventually comprise his production staff at Fables Pictures, Inc.[19]

To produce the animated shorts, Terry oversaw a production staff of 18 (and sometimes 19) artists, four of which were directors. There were always four and sometimes five animated cartoons in production at any one time with each animated cartoon taking about four weeks to produce thereby ensuring that the studio was meeting its contractual responsibilities. For the next nine years, beginning on June 19, 1921 with the release of *The Goose That Laid the Golden Egg*,

on schedule[20] without fail Terry would produce one Fables cartoon a week.[21] Terry would write the stories and spend most of his time in the story department even though he officially maintained a directorial role.[22]

On the production staff during the first years of the studio were animators Jerry Shields, Harry Bailey, Jesse "Vet" Anderson, Frank Moser, John Foster, Don McKee, Nathan Collier, and Leighton Budd. Hugh "Jerry" Shields (1884–1939) was considered the king of the "crude but funny" style among the first generation animators in New York City. He had a reputation as a fast worker and a talented cartoonist. Unfortunately he was a hard drinker and likely an alcoholic which may have played a factor in his death as a result of a fall on May 31, 1939 from his eleventh floor apartment at 305 West 72nd Street. During his career as an animator he formed the Movca Film Company in 1914 with Paul's brother John producing the *Charlie* series of cartoons. He animated

and directed *Aesop's Fables* shorts, 1921–1929, and then was employed as an animator for Paul Terry's Terrytoons, 1930–1939. He also animated for Bray Productions, Paramount (*Paramount Magazine*), Cartoon Film Service and Amedee Van Beuren.[23] At the Fables studio he would take a nip of his alcohol when Terry had his back turned and by three or four in the afternoon was "really singing".[24]

Henry Bailey (1892–1958) had been employed for Bray Studios as early as 1914 where he was the first camera operator. By 1917 he was with Bray Productions as manager of the art department overseeing the work of the female assistants. He was both an animator and director for *Paramount Magazine*, 1920–21, with the series continuing as *Paramount Cartoons* and both series produced by Patrick A. Powers for Paramount release. He was working as an animator for Paul Terry and the Fables Pictures studio, beginning as early as 1923. By 1927, he was directing

101

Fig. 11.4 – Aesop's Fables Studio, New York City (mid-1920s).

animated cartoons at the studio. Bailey was later employed for Amedee Van Beuren both animating and directing, 1929–1933 (*Aesop's Sound Fables*, 1929–1933; Cubby Bear, 1933; Tom and Jerry, 1933). He was later employed at the Terrytoons studio (1937). He finished his animation career in California.[25]

Jesse Sylvester "Vet" Anderson (1873–1966) worked as a cartoonist and comic strip artist for *Puck, Judge, Life*, the Detroit *Free Press*, the New York *Globe*, the New York *Herald Tribune* (abt.1902), and the *New York World* (abt. 1908) before entering animation. His first position was at Bray Studios where he worked as an animator on the *Police Dog* series. In 1917, Anderson joined Barré-Bowers Studio where he, together with Dick Huemer and Raoul Barré, animated the *Mutt and Jeff* series. After studying sculpture in Europe, Anderson moved to work under Paul Terry at Fables Pictures studio in New York through to about 1929. He would later complete a number of important sculptures, most notably in Golden Gate Park at the Horseshoe Courts.[26]

John Foster (1886–1959) began his career in 1915 with no art experience illustrating at Raoul Barré's cartoon unit at the Edison company studio on Fordham Road, Bronx, New York doing Mutt and Jeff animated cartoons. During 1917 and 1918, John Foster, Gregory La Cava and George Vernon Stallings were animating the *Katzenjammer Kids* series based on Rudolph Dirks comic strip for producer William Randolph Hearst's International Film Service. After the American entry into the First World War, he left International Film Service to serve in the United States Army. Upon his return to the United States in early 1919, he went back to animated cartoon work with Hearst International Features Service at Cosmopolitan Studios as an animator alongside Walter Lantz and George Stallings on the *Goldwyn-Bray Comic* series working on the Happy Hooligan, Shenanigan Kids, and Judge Rummy cartoons that were adapted from the comic strips.

In 1923, he joined Fables Pictures working with Paul Terry on Farmer Al Falfa and *Aesop's Fables* animated shorts.[27] At the Fables Pictures studio he worked as both an animator and the studio's key story man. In his latter days at the Fables studio, when Foster began directing the shorts, he had the habit of coming up with new gags and then changing scripts halfway through production resulting in studio production output getting behind schedule.[28] Not helping the situation was the frequent shenanigans that occurred after lunch. Hicks Lokey noted:

> Paul Terry would get in late after lunch. We were having a ball up there, and then somehow the guys could hear the elevator coming up and know it was Paul, so everything would stop.[29]

Foster would eventually become a very good friend of Terry and spend almost the rest of his career working under Paul at the Terrytoons studio in the 1930s and 1940s.

Before working at Fables Studios, Inc., Nathan Leo Collier (1883–1961) was a cartoonist and illustrator for a number of prominent New York and London magazines such as *Saturday Evening Post, Life, Judge, The Country Gentleman, Ladies' Home Journal, Bystander, Passing Show, London Opinion*, and

Chapter 11 • A Barnyard of Animal Friends

London Humorist. Collier also illustrated Will Rogers' *Illiterate Digest* (1927) and *Breaks* (1932) authored by W. W. Scott and Nate Collier. He was a sports, editorial, and humorist cartoonist for the *New York American* and other Hearst newspapers, 1906–1916, working as a freelance cartoonist thereafter. From 1909 to 1910, he was residing in Sandusky, Ohio working as a newspaper cartoonist for *The Star-Journal*. By November 1916, he had moved to Cleveland, Ohio to work as an animated cartoonist for a studio in that city. He moved back to Sandusky, Ohio and had a comic strip titled *Our Own Movies*, featuring local residents in the comic strip he drew for that city, 1919–1920. By 1920, he was living in Manhattan working as a comic artist for New York newspapers. He was an artist in early animated cartoon production working on the *Mutt and Jeff* cartoon series.[30]

The process of producing the *Aesop's Fables* cartoon shorts followed the traditional hand-drawn cel animation process found in animation studios during the Golden Age of American Animation and involved creating about 4,000 drawings a week[31] for the 400 to 500 foot animated cartoon.[32] While Terry was responsible for overseeing production and ensuring that one animated short of a minimum footage of 400 feet and a maximum footage of 500 feet was produced every week, only in rare instances would he assist in the animation, and if so, strictly on the key shorts.[33] Rather, he concentrated on writing the

Fig. 11.5 – Fables Studio (Frank Moser (extreme left)).

stories for the cartoon shorts and laying out the principal scenes. In Terry's words, "I was the story department".[34] Although he never ceased being a director, he would focus his efforts on the layouts for the stories and then pass them along to the directors to oversee the animation.[35]

Terry understood the most difficult task in animation was to write entertaining stories. Many of his staff could take a story and render (draw) it but they lacked the creative ability to write a story. Terry found that stories would lack in continuity, or an element of the story became so potent that it shifted the focus off the main character and line of action. A Fables cartoon story usually had the five basic story elements to keep the animated short running smoothly (characters, setting, plot, conflict, and resolution), but the focus was to get a laugh out of each scene. Many times scenes would shift abruptly from one setting to another for no reason at all except to obtain more laughs.[36]

Terry's secret to writing great stories while ensuring continuity was maintained and pace balanced was to work backwards always questioning what could happen before the last action took place. By starting at the end of the story Terry always knew what was going to happen thereby having more control on the various plot elements of each story as he worked backwards.[37] As the series progressed over the years Terry began to elicit more story ideas from the artists.

Story creation at the Fables studio followed a very loose process. The first step involved a conference of artists deciding upon the basic storyline, plot, and gags to be used in the cartoon. All suggestions were taken down at the conference, typed, and then left with Paul. At his desk Terry would run through the gags and story ideas and map out a scenario. The characters were chosen, scenes, actions, and titles were put into their proper and fitting order, and the animators were assigned scenes from the

103

Fig. 11.6 – Fables Studio artists (c. 1921) (Moser (extreme right)).

animated cartoon.[38] Other times, an animator or director would create his own story and bring it over to Terry. He would explain to Terry what he wanted to accomplish. Terry would use the ideas he thought were appealing from what was submitted and the staff worked together to refine the script.[39] In the latter years of the studio, Terry would share the story writing with others. For example, Terry and John Foster collaborated on the writing for *The June Bride* (January 23, 1926) and *Died in the Wool* (May 12, 1927)). He collaborated with Frank Moser on the script for *Little Brown Jug* (January 23, 1926), Jerry Shields on *Cutting a Melon* (July 22, 1927), and Harry Bailey on *The Big Reward* (May 12, 1927)). Sometimes a script was written by Terry but the film never produced.[40] It was not uncommon for Terry to change the title of a short and the moral during production. The short *The Ball Park* (May 4, 1929) with the moral "Don't invite trouble it always accepts" was originally titled *Socking the Apple* having the moral "A limburger sandwich is two pieces of bread travelling in bad company".

Most of the *Aesop's Fables* cartoons involved anywhere from 32 to 48 scenes and were created by about six to eight animators. *Amateur Night on the Ark*, released April 27, 1923, is a six-minute Fables cartoon about the animals on Noah's ark performing various amateur stage acts for an all-animal audience. Noah's act involves him wrestling a bear which causes the audience to cheer. When the bear skin comes apart and a dog and cat come out of the bear costume, the crowd yells "Fake!" and begins throwing objects at Noah. The animals eventually chase Noah off the ship and into the water where he swims away into the distance. For *Amateur Night on the Ark* there were 44 scenes, two intertitles and involved the work of eight animators (Frank Moser (assigned 11 scenes including 1 scene shared with John Foster), Nathan Collier (assigned 10 scenes), Harry Bailey (assigned 7 scenes), Vet Anderson (assigned 2 scenes), Don McKee (assigned 3 scenes), John Foster (8 scenes including one scene shared with Frank Moser), Jerry Shields (assigned 4 scenes)).

One of the secrets to the success of the series was the morals found at the end of every cartoon. At the end of the short, the moral appeared on the screen followed by *Aesop's Fables* slogan "Sugar coated pills of wisdom". Many of morals had nothing to do with the actual cartoon itself. The ambiguity of the moral was what made the short funny.[41] Animator Mannie Davis explained:

> But they had a moral on the end which always kept you alive. And it was very funny. Some of them really had good gags. And they were funnier than the whole picture itself. Sometimes, they were all that people remember is the moral. They don't remember the pictures.[42]

During the production of each cartoon, the moral was added by Terry after the animated short had been completed. Rather than take a moral and develop a cartoon story around the maxim, Terry would find a moral that was somewhat relevant to the storyline, and then add the maxim after the cartoon was in post-production.[43]

Paul would glean the morals from the weekly *Topics of the Day* produced by Timely Films, Topics of the Day Film Company headed by A. E. Siegel.[44] The *Topics of the Day* were 200 foot novelty films referred to as a "pictureless motion picture". Each release contained 15 bright, clever paragraphs culled by the *Literary Digest*. For example (referring to the then current diplomatic matters on the Eastern Front during World War One), "The Germans have put one over on Luther Burbank, for they have handed the Russians a perfectly good olive branch bearing full grown lemons".[45] If the moral used in these shorts received a big laugh from the audience, Terry would use them as morals in his *Aesop's Fables* cartoons.

The morals were humorous ("Girls may catch men with face powder but it takes baking powder to hold them" (*The Mail Pilot* (February 14, 1927)); "A stitch in time saves embarrassment" (*The One Man Dog* (May 12, 1927))), traditional non-comical ("Whatever is worth doing is worth doing well" (*The Musical Parrot* (December 31, 1926)); "One good turn deserves another" (*The Ugly Duckling* (August 28, 1925))), and inspiring ("Fortune favors the brave" (*The Walrus Hunters* (August 11, 1923)); "Never give up the chase" (*The Bad Bandit* (July 19, 1923))). Many times there was no moral at all but purely comical one-liners ("No one cares how bad your English is if your Scotch is good" (*High Stakes* (December 12, 1927))). Other shorts featured traditional morals but with a comical twist ("A rolling stone gathers no moss but it gets a great polish" (*Wine, Women and Song* (May 18, 1925))). Other times, Terry relied on puns ("Short skirts reveal a multitude of shins" (*A Battling Duet* (April 2, 1928)); "Ice is not what it is cracked up to be" (*On the Ice* (December 3, 1924) (this later moral was related to the plot))).

Terry would have some of his staff screen his cartoons when playing at a local theater such as the Cameo Theatre (138 W. 42nd Street), Rivoli Theatre (1620 Broadway) or Riverside Theatre (Broadway and 96th). For example, animator Bill Hicks screened the cartoon *Taking the Air* (March 4, 1927) at the Cameo and noted "Moral got a very big laugh". A percentage score was given to each moral depending on the approximate number of people who laughed at the moral. If a moral was very well-received by an audience, Terry would occasionally use the moral again. The moral "A rolling stone gathers no moss but it gets a great polish" was used both in *Wine, Women and Song* and 10 months later in *The Merry Blacksmith* (March 12, 1926). As previously noted, the moral "Don't invite trouble it always accepts" was used in *The Ball Park*, but it was also used in *The English Channel Swim* (December 17, 1925), a short produced over three years earlier.

The early critical reviews on the *Aesop's Fables* cartoons in the newspapers, journals and trade papers were extremely positive. The reviewer for *Wid's Daily* writes:

There is a good laugh in each reel of this series. Paul Terry is the cartoonist responsible for the clever animation and the amusing drawings. The action is quite brisk and the movement of the animals well studied. A good deal of imagination and sense of humor is shown. The first of the series is called "Mice in Council". The mice come out of their hole and fish the cheese out of the trap. Mr. Cat walks up and down policing the kitchen. The mice have a meeting and carry banners that read –"Down with the Cat", and "Freedom of the Cheese".[46]

The *Times-Union* (Albany, N.Y.) declared that the cartoon short *The Goose That Laid the Golden Egg* to be the "biggest screen novelty of the year".[47] The reviewer for the *Exhibitors' Herald* wrote: "The animation is good, the photography excellent, and he gets a laugh without striving for it in every scene".[48] Mae Tinée for the *Chicago Tribune* proclaimed: ""The Goose that Laid the Golden Egg" is the first of the series, and it is smart and snappy and funny as can be". The reviewer further states: "The artist, Mr. Paul, proves himself a man of humor. He doesn't appear to try to make you laugh, he just goes ahead and DOES make you laugh. That's art."[49] Anna Temeg for *The Billboard* announced: "We can only say that it was humorous and the actions of the rodents were so natural and comical in their dress that it is certain that every class of audience will find a measure of entertainment in this short reel material".[50]

The *Aesop's Fables* cartoons featured one of the main plot elements found in Terry's Terrytoons cartoons of the 1930s and 1940s namely an ongoing war

105

Fig. 11.7 – Paul Terry (left) and actor Charley Chase (right).

between cats and mice. Jeff Missinne notes that in a scene in *One Good Turn Deserves Another* (1924) that the concept of a strong mouse was first introduced, which Terry developed into his Mighty Mouse character.[51] While the cartoon does feature a mouse with the ability to perform tasks his fellow mice are unable to carry out, to draw a comparison to Mighty Mouse, a mouse having similar abilities as DC Comics' Superman, is a long stretch.

Terry can get credit for being the first to use mouse cartoon characters in an animated cartoon, which he did with the animated cartoon *Mice in Council* (1921). In 1931, the Van Beuren Corporation and Pathé Exchange, Incorporated were being sued by Walt Disney Productions in a suit alleging trademark infringement in the imitation of certain cartoon characters and unfair competition. In his affidavit, Van Beuren stated: "At this time [1920] Paul Terry had already made two or three cartoon subjects, among them being one entitled *Mice in Council*, which I believe were among the first instances of the use of mouse cartoon characters on film".[52]

There were a number of reasons for the success of the *Aesop's Fables* cartoons, some of which are previously mentioned in the reviews. First, *Aesop's Fables* cartoons were relatively fast-moving cartoons, filled with sometimes nasty mayhem, and sprinkled with enough surprises to keep one guessing from scene to scene.[53] Second, the animation was competently rendered and better than most produced by other studios during the 1920s from a staff of gifted artists. Walt Disney would later remark as late as 1930 that "my ambition was to be able to make cartoons as good as the *Aesop's Fables* series".[54] Third, the stories were filled with plenty of gentle, understated humor that was uncommon and fresh for the period where slapstick comedy ruled the box office, shtick practiced by film comedians such as Charlie Chaplin, Laurel and Hardy, the

Chapter 11 • A Barnyard of Animal Friends

Marx Brothers, the Keystone Cops, and the Three Stooges. Fourth, as previously mentioned, the cartoons ended with a clever "moral" or saying that usually left the audience laughing. As aforementioned, sometimes it was the only thing the audience would remember about the cartoon.

Joining the cast of talented artists at the studio in 1923 were Ferdinand Horvath and John R. McCrory. Ferdinand Horvath (1891–1973) was born in Budapest, Hungary and as a member of the Austro-Hungarian army during World War One was captured by the Russians and imprisoned. He spent two-and-a-half years as a prisoner in a number of Russian prison camps in the Ural Mountains and after learning Russian donned a Russian uniform and escaped to Finland later writing about his wartime adventures in *Captured!* (Dodd, Mead & Co., 1930). As a steerage passenger with $45 in his pocket and some ivory miniatures he had designed, Horvath immigrated to the United States on November 11, 1921. He was able to secure employment painting window frames on Avenue A and C hanging between the 11th floor and the sidewalk.

He thereafter graduated to caulking and painting boat hulls, including a coal barge, on the river Hudson. He then took about a dozen odd jobs until landing a position doing some stage design work including stage effects and stage lighting, part of which involved painting fat little cupids for revolving micadiscs. He was fired after two months of work and for several months thereafter painted doll heads. In 1923, he began his animation career as a layout artist, art director, and worked on model sheets for *Aesop's Fables* cartoons at Fables Pictures (averaging 100 to 150 drawings a day) where he stayed for six years and along the way became a naturalized citizen of the United States in October 1927.[55]

John Robert McCrory (1898–1984) was an artist and cameraman with the K.C. Motion Picture Company working with advertising films in the late 1910s. He was employed for two years with Bray Pictures Corporation and helped to animate such series as *Out of the Inkwell* and *Goldwyn-Bray Pictographs* (*If We Lived on the Moon* (1920)) and *Your 25th Anniversary*. He was a producer of animated "lightning" effects in motion pictures. John McCrory animated the *Aesop's Fables* cartoons at Fables Pictures until his departure in 1926.[56]

In 1924, Emanuel "Mannie" Davis (1894–1975), who would become an integral member of the Terrytoons studio from the 1930s until the 1960s, was hired by Terry. Davis was a graduate of Cooper Union Art School where he studied for two years and continued his art studies for another year at the Art Students League. He first went to work in the art department of the American Press Association syndicate with aspirations of becoming a comic strip artist but ended up staying for a number of years doing "dingbats" (decorative art) and small sketches for the stories. After the American Press Association folded up, he went up to the Edison studio in the Bronx working for Raoul Barré and Charles Bowers starting around 1916. While with the studio he animated for Barré-Bowers on the *Mutt and Jeff* series with Bud Fisher.

He then served in World War I as a cartographer and Corporal in the 472nd Engineers, Washington, D.C. and was animating medical and training films during this time until being discharged in 1918. He returned to Barré-Bowers on the *Mutt and Jeff* series to run the studio where Davis stayed until 1921. He is credited with being the first to combine live actors with animation on the screen. He also joined Pat Sullivan's "Felix the Cat" company for about a year working with Otto Messmer. In 1922, he worked as an animator for the Fleischer Studios on the *Out of the Inkwell* series (Koko the Clown and Betty Boop) before joining Terry.[57]

Adding to the talent base at Fables in 1924 were George Vernon Stallings, Burton Gillett and Robert Chambers. George Vernon Stallings (1891–1963) began his animation career animating the Rube Goldberg cartoon series, *The Boob Weekly*, a series based on Goldberg's comic strip on his crazy inventions, distributed by Pathé Exchange. Stallings also worked for the Raoul Barré-Charles Bowers studio on the *Mutt and Jeff* series, 1917. He worked for Hearst's International Film Service from 1916 to 1918 on a few series (*Joys and Glooms* (animating alongside Frank Moser); *Katzenjammer Kids*) then relocated to work for John R. Bray around 1919. While at Bray

107

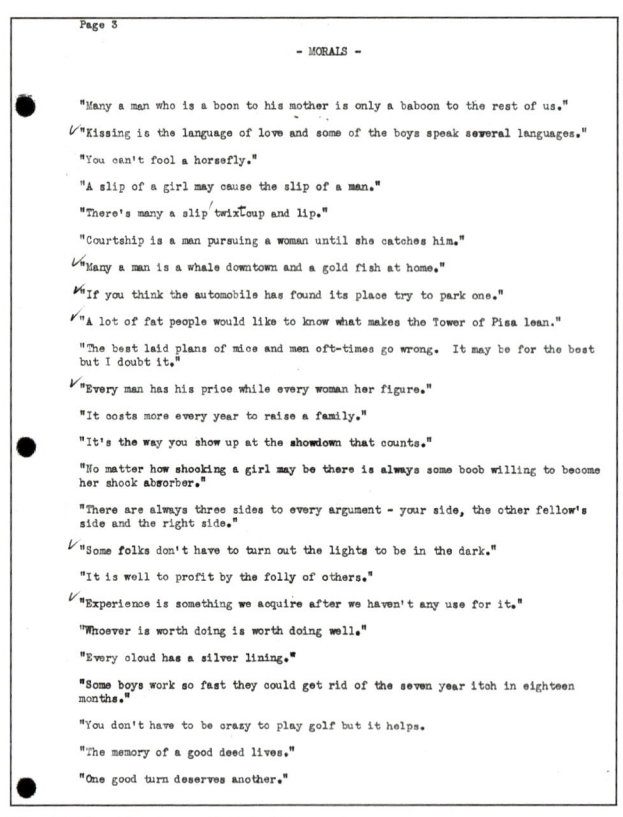

```
Page 3
              - MORALS -

"Many a man who is a boon to his mother is only a baboon to the rest of us."
✓"Kissing is the language of love and some of the boys speak several languages."
"You can't fool a horsefly."
"A slip of a girl may cause the slip of a man."
"There's many a slip twixt cup and lip."
"Courtship is a man pursuing a woman until she catches him."
✓"Many a man is a whale downtown and a gold fish at home."
✓"If you think the automobile has found its place try to park one."
✓"A lot of fat people would like to know what makes the Tower of Pisa lean."
"The best laid plans of mice and men oft-times go wrong. It may be for the best
but I doubt it."
✓"Every man has his price while every woman her figure."
"It costs more every year to raise a family."
"It's the way you show up at the showdown that counts."
"No matter how shocking a girl may be there is always some boob willing to become
her shock absorber."
"There are always three sides to every argument - your side, the other fellow's
side and the right side."
✓"Some folks don't have to turn out the lights to be in the dark."
"It is well to profit by the folly of others."
✓"Experience is something we acquire after we haven't any use for it."
"Whoever is worth doing is worth doing well."
"Every cloud has a silver lining."
"Some boys work so fast they could get rid of the seven year itch in eighteen
months."
"You don't have to be crazy to play golf but it helps."
"The memory of a good deed lives."
"One good turn deserves another."
```

Fig. 11.8 – Morals used in Fables cartoons.

he directed shorts from the *Goldwyn-Bray Pictographs* (and *Goldwyn-Bray Comic*, 1920) series. Later with Bray he supervised the direction and animation on the *Colonel Heeza Liar* series, 1922–1924. He moved to work for Fables Pictures studio, 1923–1926 (possibly through to 1929).[58]

Burton Gillett (1891–1971)[59] was a student at the Art Students League. By January 1911 Gillett was employed for *The Daily Courier* in Connellsville as a newspaper correspondent and an artist working on chalk plate cartoons. He then moved to work for a number of years as a cartoonist and reporter for the *Newburgh Daily News*. By 1918 Gillett had begun work in the animation business. Gillett worked with Charles Bowers in 1916 animating *The Katzenjammer Kids* for International Film Service. Gillett worked as an animator for Barré-Bowers from 1916 to 1918/19 running the studio alongside Mannie Davis on the *Mutt and Jeff* series.

Gillett was with Hearst's International Film Service from 1918/19 to 1920 on *Judge Rummy* and *The Shenanigan Kids* cartoons. In 1920, he was working for John R. Bray and Bray Productions on the *Lampoons* series. He moved to work with the Fleischers and the *Out of the Inkwell Films* series from 1921 to 1925. While with the Fleischers he worked as an animator on the *Fun from the Press* cartoons (3 "magazine films" featuring a series of animated sequences adapted from *Literary Digest* and released April to June 1923) and *Song Car-Tunes*, 1924–1925. In 1924, he was working for Paul Terry at the Fables Pictures studio in New York City on *Aesop's Fables* shorts.[60]

Robert Chambers (1905–1996), born in Wolfville, Nova Scotia, Canada, took a year of art instruction at Acadia University's Ladies' Seminary under Lewis E. Smith. He started freelancing as a cartoonist in Halifax in the early 1920s. On May 2, 1923, his first cartoon was published in the *Halifax Chronicle* (the subject was Nova Scotia seceding from the rest of Canada). He earned $2.50 for the cartoon. In 1924, at the age of 19, Chambers left for New York City where he drew cartoons by the day and attended night classes at the Art Students League. For two years he worked at the Fables Pictures studio with Paul Terry earning $18 a week animating *Aesop's Fables* cartoons. He later was employed by Paul Terry in the 1930s. He returned to Canada where he worked as a cartoonist for the *Herald* and its successor the Halifax *Chronicle-Herald* (the two papers merged in 1949) for nearly four decades ridiculing the likes of Canadian politicians John Diefenbaker, Pierre Trudeau and Bob Stanfield.[61]

Even Paul's brother joined the

Chapter 11 • A Barnyard of Animal Friends

ÆSOP'S FILM Fables

"MICE IN COUNCIL"

WE DIDN'T RAISE OUR BOYS FOR CAT MEAT!

The Mice agreed it would be well
Upon the Cat to hang a bell
So that when Tabby came around
The bell would give a warning sound.

An old mouse thereupon arose
And said, "The stunt that you propose
Is great—there's no denying that,
But—who is gonna bell the cat?"

Moral—Big talk's a total loss,
Unless with deeds you come across!
                             Æsop, Jr.

Fig. 11.9 – Promotional clipping for Fables cartoon *Mice in Council* (1921).

Fables crew for a brief period later in the 1920s. From 1922–1933, John was producer and director on a number of the *Hodge Podge* cartoon series for Pathé release. In early 1925, John acted as producer, director and animator for the Crossword Film Company on [*Judge* magazine's] the *Judge's Crossword Puzzles* ["Judge's Crossward Puzzles"] series distributed by Educational Pictures. The series featured a crossword clue allowing the viewer to guess the synonym before a hand crossed the screen and filled in the crossword grid. There were 10 shorts released weekly beginning with No. 1 (January 31, 1925) and ending with No. 10 (April 3, 1925).[62] Around this time he also returned to freelance newspaper cartooning, and even experimented with toy design. John Terry also sub-contracted Krazy Kat cartoons from his friend Bill Nolan between 1925 and 1927, and produced them with Bill Tytla and Larry Silverman as his assistants.

By 1925, Paul Terry could boast of overseeing one of the most talented groups of animation artists on the planet. However, despite the gifted crew of production artists Terry had gathered, the *Aesop's Fables* cartoons of the early 1920s had a few production concerns that plagued the aesthetics of the studio's animated product. First, the cartoons suffered from very sparse backgrounds with little detail and decoration reflective that the cartoons were produced on a budget. This flaw did not escape the comments of critics. The reviewer for *Wid's Daily*

109

plainly commented: "Many of the background drawings could have been improved".⁶³ Second, some of the cartoons reused drawings such as the animals chasing Noah around the deck of the ark and Noah diving overboard in *Amateur Night on the Ark* (April 27, 1923), some of the stork flying sequences in *Love in a Cottage* (September 1, 1923), and the fish bowl scenes in *The Window Washers* (July 20, 1925).

Third, although the backgrounds became more elaborate during the early to mid-1920s, an *Aesop's Fables* cartoon from 1921 looked very much like a *Fables* cartoon produced at the end of the decade. In comparison, some of the other production houses had made significant improvements in the quality of their cartoon products during the 1920s. While in 1923 Max Fleischer was producing two 20-minute educational features explaining Albert Einstein's Theory of Relativity (*The Einstein Theory of Relativity*) and Charles Darwin's Theory of Evolution, both features using a combination of animated special effects and live action, and was busy inventing the "follow the bouncing ball" technique for his *Song Car-Tunes* series of animated sing-along shorts beginning in May 1924, Paul Terry was content with grinding out one cartoon a week for Fables Pictures, Inc.

The relationship between Terry and the Keith-Albee Circuit group had become very profitable for both parties, but especially the latter one. In 1924 the Keith-Albee people wanted to ensure that this successful commercial venture continued into the distant future as the five-year contract between Estabrook and Terry was set to expire. Accordingly, on July 11, 1924 the agreement between the parties entered into in 1920 was extended a further seven years while Terry was to be paid $400 weekly during the seven year extension and retained his five-percent interest in Fables. The contract would carry the parties until August 1932.⁶⁴

On the family front, Terry's father passed away in Berkeley, California on October 21, 1921 sending Terry to California for the funeral. On September 29, 1923, Paul married Irma Heimlich in the Bronx, New York at a civil wedding performed by Deputy City Clerk Thomas J. McCabe and witnessed by Charles J. Hirliman. At the time of the wedding, Paul was residing at 19 West 50th Street in New York City and Irma at 810 Tinton Avenue.⁶⁵ In honor of the marriage, B.F. Keith Vaudeville Circuit executives tendered a banquet at the New York Athletic Club. Among those present were J. J. Murdock, E. G. Lauder, Major Thompson, Senator Henry Walters, Amedee J. Van Beuren, Frank Vincent, Pat Casey, and Herman Freedman. Terry received a large chest of silver as a wedding gift.⁶⁶ Irma Heimlich was the daughter of Gerson and Freda [Bertha] (née Nussbaum) (1873–1943) Heimlich. She was born on July 5, 1898 in New York City [Hungary]. Her father was a machinist and sewing machine salesman. He was founder of the Consolidated Sewing Machine Company of New York.⁶⁷

Paul first met Irma after the First World War when he opened up his studio. She attended Columbia University and was a fine art painter by background before entering animation. She started in animation working for the Mutt and Jeff cartoon studio. She then worked for International Film Service and William R. Hearst on his animated cartoons and during the war worked for Paul's brother John on his animated cartoons. Paul adored her and their marriage would last until her death in 1969. When Irma was employed for Paul at Fables Pictures, Inc., she would try to make all the staff feel valued and did her best to improve morale and employee satisfaction while keeping the organization on an even keel. She had that special quality that no matter who you were, she made you feel important. It was a natural and honest quality without pretence. She loved humanity no matter who you were.⁶⁸

Paul found her to be a wonderful critic and a large part of his success. "I always thought in terms of her, no matter what I put into a picture".⁶⁹ Before releasing a film short Paul would question "What would she think about this?"⁷⁰ If he thought she would not approve of the effort, Paul would either abandon the matter or change his approach. Irma was a very sensitive individual, decent and never wanting to offend another individual by the content found in an animated cartoon.⁷¹

After a European honeymoon vacation, the Terrys settled in the Bronx, New York. By 1927 Paul and Irma had moved to Larchmont, New York and established

Chapter 11 • A Barnyard of Animal Friends

themselves in a well-appointed family home at 61 Beach Avenue. They would remain there until the mid-1930s when they moved up the street to 115 Beach Avenue.[72] In 1941 the Terry family home had moved to 40 Ocean Avenue. In 1943, Terry moved to reside at the Westchester Country Club until 1946 then moving to 40 Vandenburgh Avenue until 1953. During their stay at the Vandenburgh Avenue address Terry kept his apartment at the Westchester Country Club and moved back there in 1953 where he and Irma remained until their deaths.[73] ❧

Notes

1. "Employment Contract between Universal Film Manufacturing Company and Paul H. Terry", 24 November 1919, unsigned, Paul Terry Papers, Fayetteville, North Carolina.

2. "Estabrook, Howard", *The 1944–45 Motion Picture Almanac*, 101; *Who Was Who in the Theatre: 1912–1976. A Biographical Dictionary of Actors, Actresses, Directors, Playwrights, and Producers of the English-speaking Theatre*, four volumes (Detroit: Gale Research, 1978); James Vinson, ed., *The International Dictionary of Films and Filmmakers*, first edition, volume 4: Writers and Production Artists (Chicago: St. James Press, 1987); Samantha Cook, ed., *The International Dictionary of Films and Filmmakers*, second edition, volume 4: Writers and Production Artists (Detroit: St. James Press, 1993). Obituary: "Howard Estabrook, Won Oscar For 'Cimarron' Screenplay, at 94", *New York Times*, 28 July 1978, II, p. 2:3.

3. The Howard Estabrook papers are archived at the Margaret Herrick library located in Beverly Hills at the Academy of Motion Picture Arts and Sciences' Fairbanks Center for Motion Picture Study.

4. Terry, interview, 20 December 1969, 47.

5. Ibid., 33.

6. Ibid., 33–34.

7. "Memorandum of Agreement between Paul H. Terry and Howard Estabrook", 9 August 1920, notarized by King County Clerk's no. 62, 27 August, 1920, Paul Terry Papers, Fayetteville, North Carolina.

8. "Memorandum of Agreement", 9 August 1920, 2.

9. Ibid., 4.

10. "Amendment to Contract of 9 August 1920 between Paul H. Terry and Howard Estabrook", unsigned, December 1920, Paul Terry Papers. While the document referenced for this book was unsigned, a similar agreement was signed by Terry carrying the parties through to April 1921.

11. The contractual amendments are all on file in the Paul Terry Papers.

12. For more on B.F. Keith: *Dictionary of American Biography*; *The National Cyclopaedia of American Biography*, volume 15 (New York: James T. White & Co., 1914), 297. For more on Edward Albee: *Dictionary of American Biography*, supplement 1 (New York: Charles Scribner's Sons, 1944); *The National Cyclopaedia of American Biography*, volume 22 (New York: James T. White & Co., 1932), 53.

13. The Keith/Albee Vaudeville Theater Collection, MsC 356, Collection Dates: 1890–1952, featuring manager's reports (1903–1923), clipping books, financial records, and subject files is accessible at the University of Iowa Libraries and Special Collections Archives.

14. Terry, interview, 20 December 1969, 40.

15. For further biographical information on producer Amedee Van Beuren (born 10 July 1880, New York City; died 12 November 1938, New York City) see I. Klein, "Cartooning Down Broadway", *Film Comment* XI, no. 1 (January – February 1975): 62–63; *Who Was Who in America*, volume 1, 1897–1942, 1267. Obituaries: "A.J. Van Beuren, 58, Film Official, Dies", *New York Times*, 13 November 1938, p. 45:3; "A. J. Van Beuren, 58, Dies; Had Retired", *Variety*, 16 November 1938, 4:5.

16. Terry, interview, 20 December 1969, 40.

17. "Memorandum of Agreement between Fables Pictures, Inc. and Paul H. Terry", 23 June 1921, Paul Terry Papers.

18. "Aesop's Fables Modernized", *Dramatic Mirror and Theatre* (N.Y.), 28 May 1921, 942; "Screening Aesop", *Variety*, 3 June 1921, 46.

19. Terry, interview, 20 December 1969, 50.

20. The order of release of the first five cartoons as listed in the trade papers were (release dates later reported in round "( )" brackets): *The Goose That Laid the Golden Egg* (June 19), *Mice in Council* (July 26), *The Rooster and the Eagle* (June 3), *Ants and the Grasshopper* (July 10), and *Cats at Law* (July 17). "Aesop's Fables Filmed", *Wid's Film Daily*, vol. XVI, no. 25, 25 May 1921, p. 1.

21. For the complete list of approximately 460 shorts produced and/or directed by Paul Terry at Fables Studios, Inc., refer to: Gifford, *American Animated Films* (full citation earlier) or see Appendix 2 of this book.

22. Terry, interview, 20 December 1969, 52.

23. Biographical sketches on Shields can be referenced in Crafton, *Before Mickey: The Animated Film, 1898–1928*; "Newspaper Artist Wedded to Pretty Society Girl", *Oakland Tribune*, 29 November 1909, p. 16; "Press Club Show Today", *The San Francisco Call*, 18 April 1913, p. 2; "Local Artist's Work Will be Displayed", *The Oakland Tribune*, 27 June 1915, p. 20; "San Francisco", *Moving Picture World*, volume 22, no. 4, 24 October 1914 , 517; "State Rights Buyers Attracted By Quality of Star Comedy Cartoons", *The Motion Picture News*, vol. 13, no. 5, 5 February 1916, 674; "New Firm Makes Cartoons", *NY Dramatic Mirror*, 4 November 1916, 35. Obituary: "Artist Plunges to Death", *New York Times*, 1 June 1939, p. 8.

24. Hicks Lokey, interview, 4 May 1990, J. Michael Barrier collection, 3.

25. Bray, "Development of Animated Cartoons", 395–398; Crafton, *Before Mickey*, 148, 165, 186, 192.

111

TERRYTOONS: The Story of Paul Terry and His Classic Cartoon Factory

Obituary: "Harry D. Bailey", *Los Angeles Times*, 5 April 1958, p. A7.

26. He later worked for the Fleischer brothers (1930–1931). He moved to California about 1931 and began working as an animator at Walter Lantz's studio, 1931–1933. He then worked for New York City based Ted Eshbaugh Productions around 1932 through to 1933. As a sculptor, Anderson made two concrete bas-relief sculptures, "Horse" and "Horseshoe Pitcher", for the WPA Horseshoe Courts in San Francisco's Golden Gate Park in 1937. William Young, ed., *Dictionary of American Artists, Sculptors and Engravers; From the Beginnings through the Turn of the Twentieth Century* (Cambridge, Massachusetts: William Young and Co., 1968); Falk, *Who Was Who in American Art* (1999); Hughes, *Artists in California, 1786–1940*, 3rd ed.; Chris Pollock, *San Francisco's Golden Gate Park: A Thousand and Seventeen Acres of Stories* (Portland, Oregon: WestWinds Press, 2001); Jean Bosquet, "The City of Forgotten Men", *Los Angeles Times*, 23 June 1935, p. H8; "Artists' Exhibit Postponed a Month", *The Telegram* (Syracuse, New York), 13 February 1904, p. 6; "Notables Who Were Sketched by Cartoonists in Senate Chambers", *The Sun* (New York), 27 October 1912, sec. 4, p. 10; "Cartoonist's Stepson is at Home with Mystery", *San Jose Mercury News*, 3 December 1990, p. 1B.

27. Information on Foster was also located in Fox's Dynamo (20th Century-Fox Film Corporation, "Terrytoon Creators: John Foster", *Dynamo* (Terrytoon Section), 15 April 1940, Chicago, Illinois, 5B. Obituaries: "John Foster", *The Standard-Star* (New Rochelle), 16 February 1959, p. 2; "John Foster" (Obituary News), *The Standard-Star* (New Rochelle), 18 February 1959, p. 2.

28. Lokey, interview, 3.

29. Ibid., 4.

30. *Who Was Who in American Art* (1999).

31. At 16 frames per foot, 7,200 frames of animation were photographed for a 450 foot animated cartoon. As Terry was creating about 4,000 drawings for each cartoon produced, his production staff were using labor saving methods such as creating sketches of the positions of the character's body which must move rather than the entire character in order to reduce the number of complete drawings being produced.

32. For a detailed description of the process used by the staff at Fables Studios, Inc.: "How Pathe's "Aesop's Film Fables" Are Made", *Moving Picture World*, 6 June 1925, 666; "Eighteen Artists and Four Thousand Sketches for an Eight Minute Laugh", *Newark Sunday Call* (Newark, N.J.), 10 June 1923, Part III (Magazine), p. 13.

33. "Eighteen Artists and Four Thousand Sketches for an Eight Minute Laugh", *Newark Sunday Call*.

34. Terry, interview, 14 July 1970, 141.

35. Terry, interview, 20 December 1969, 52.

36. Emanuel (Mannie) Davis, interview by Harvey Deneroff, New Rochelle, New York, 28 July 1970, John Canemaker Animation Collection, Fales Library, Elmer Holmes Bobst Library, New York University, New York City, 6e–7e.

37. Terry, interview, 20 December 1969, 51–52.

38. "Aesop on the Screen", *New York Times*, 3 June 1928, p. 3:2.

39. Davis, interview, 28 July 1970, 6e–7e.

40. Production scripts with scene descriptions and animators listed for each scene animated for most of the Aesop's Fables cartoons can be found in the Paul Terry Papers.

41. Terry, interview, 20 December 1969, 48–49.

42. Davis, interview, 28 July 1970, 14e.

43. Terry, interview, 20 December 1969, 48.

44. Ibid.

45. "Clever Punch Paragraphs in "Topics of the Day"", *Moving Picture World*, 27 July 1918, 577.

46. ""Aesop's Fables" – Fables Pictures, Pathe", Review of Aesop's Fables (Animated Cartoons), *Wid's Daily*, vol. XVI, no. 86, 26 June 1921, p. 19.

47. "The Leland", *Times-Union* (Albany, N.Y.), 5 July 1921.

48. "Aesop's Fables (Pathe)", Review of Aesop's Fables (Animated Cartoons), *Exhibitors' Herald* (Chicago), 9 July 1921.

49. Tinée, Mae. "Potpourri of Fable, Comedy, and Dempsey", Review of Aesop Fables (Animated Cartoons), *Chicago Tribune*, 24 June 1921, p. 14. Please note that Mae Tinée was a pseudonym for an unknown reviewer. Combined the first name with the surname and you have "Matinee".

50. Anna Temeg, "Aesop's Fables", Review of Aesop's Fables (Animated Cartoons), *The Billboard*, 25 June 1921, p. 107.

51. "Aesop's Fables Cartoons", *The World of Yesterday*, no. 8, October 1976, 5–10.

52. Craig Andrews, *Broken Toy: A Man's Dream, A Company's Mystery* (Miami, Florida: 1st Books Library, 2002), 187.

53. J. Michael Barrier, *Hollywood Cartoons: American Animation in its Golden Age* (New York: Oxford University Press, 1999), 35.

54. Walt Disney, "Growing Pains", *Journal of the Society of Motion Picture Engineers*, January 1941, 32.

55. He later became a magazine and book illustrator. In 1930, Horvath worked briefly for Terrytoons at the Audio-Cinema facilities in the Bronx. Horvath moved to California and on January 7, 1933, began working for Walt Disney on *Silly Symphonies* shorts and later Mickey Mouse shorts. Horvath was with Disney until October 30, 1937. He moved to Charles Mintz studios and left Mintz in 1938 to work at Columbia/Screen Gems to 1939 (Scrappy, Krazy Kat, Color Rhapsodies) cartoons). By 1940, he was a character sculptor for George Pal's Puppetoons. After the outbreak of the Second World War, he went to North American Aviation to complete design work and then later to Howard Hughes in a technical capacity to work on confidential designs. Further biographical information on Horvath can be found in: Dawdy, *Artists of the American West. A Biographical Dictionary*, volume II, 134; Bertha E. Mahony and Elinor Whitney, comp., *Contemporary Illustrators of Chil-*

Chapter 11 • A Barnyard of Animal Friends

dren's Books (Boston: Bookshop for Boys and Girls, 1930), 38–39; Bertha E. Mahony, Louise Payson Latimer, and Beulah Folmsbee, comp., *Illustrators of Children's Books, 1744–1945* (Boston: Horn Book, 1947), 321; Falk, *Who Was Who in American Art* (1985), 293; Dorothy Gilbert, ed., *Who's Who in American Art 1961* (New York: R.R. Bowker Co., 1962), 286.

56. From 1926–1927, he was producer and director for Sherwood Wadsworth Pictures. By 1930, he had his own studio, McCrory Studios, at 110 West 46th Street, New York City producing and directing the Buster Bear series, and by 1932 was producing and directing Krazy Kid Kartoons for the Harper Producing and Distributing Company. He was also the producer of the *Trader Korn's Laffalong* series (*Korn Plastered in Africa*) for Featurettes Production Company for a Screen Classics release. He is the author of *How to Draw for the Movies* (1918). For more information on McCrory see: *Motion Picture Studio Directory and Trade Annual*, 1921 (New York: Motion Picture News Inc., 1921).

57. Davis, interview, 28 July 1970; "Emanuel Davis", (Obituaries), *Variety*, 15 October 1975, 78; "Emanuel Davis", (Obituary), *The Standard-Star* (New Rochelle), 11 October 1975, p. A20; "Emanuel Davis, Cartoonist, Helped Create Terrytoons", *New York Times*, 11 October 1975, p. 34:4. 20th Century-Fox's special promotional magazine on Terrytoons features information on Davis (20th Century-Fox Film Corporation, "Experts Are Born: Emanuel Davis", Dynamo (Terrytoon Section), 15 April 1940, Chicago, Illinois, 5B). Information on Davis can be found in his National Cartoonists Society biography ("Mannie Davis", in *The National Cartoonists Society Album* 1996, Fiftieth Anniversary Edition, Bill Janocha, ed. (Buffalo, New York: National Cartoonists Society, 1996), 325).

58. He later worked for the Van Beuren studio, from 1929 to 1931 animating the Aesop's Fables series. He moved to Walt Disney Studios in 1935 and was a story man and occasionally a director on Disney animation until 1946. He was a syndicated comic strip writer (Uncle Remus) for Disney from 1946 to 1963. "George Stallings", *Variety*, 17 April 1963, 71.

59. Michael Barrier, *The Animated Man: A Life of Walt Disney* (University of California Press, 2007); Richard Koszarski, *Hollywood on the Hudson: Film and Television in New York from Griffith to Sarnoff* (New Brunswick, N.J.: Rutgers University Press, 2008); Tom Sito, *Drawing the Line: The Untold Story of the Animation Unions from Bosko to Bart Simpson* (Lexington, Kentucky: University Press of Kentucky, 2006). Obituary: "Burton Gillette [sic]", *Variety*, 12 January 1972, 78.

60. His other studio credits include Associated Animators (1925–1926), Charles Bowers (1926–1928/9), Walt Disney Studios (1928/9–1934, 1936–1939), Ub Iwerks (1934), Van Beuren Studios (1934–1936), Walter (1939–1940).

61. Syd Hoff, *Editorial and Political Cartooning: From Earliest Times to the Present with over 700 Examples from the Works of the World's Greatest Cartoonists* (New York: Stravon Educational Press, 1976). Obituaries: "Cartoonist R. Chambers dies in Halifax", *The Chronicle-Herald* (Halifax), 29 March 1996, p. B16; "Lives Lived: Bob Chambers", *Globe and Mail* (Toronto), 5 April 1996, p. A14; Don MacDonald, "Chambers Recalled as Cutting Not Cruel", *Chronicle-Herald* (Halifax), 29 March 1996, p. A1-A2; Ben Wicks, "King of Cartoons Finds His Heaven", *Toronto Star*, 9 August 1986, p. M2.

62. "Judge's Crossword Puzzle", *The Reel Journal*, 14 March 1925, 14; Gifford, *American Animated Films: The Silent Era, 1897–1925*, 151; Webb, *The Animated Film Encyclopedia*, 256.

63. ""Aesop's Fables" – Fables Pictures, Pathe", *Wid's Daily*, 26 June 1921.

64. "Memorandum of Agreement between Paul H. Terry and Fables Pictures, Inc.", 11 July 1924, Paul Terry Papers.

65. State of New York, Borough of the Bronx "Certificate and Record of Marriage of (Groom) Paul H. Terry and (Bride) Irma Heimlich", Certificate no. 4756, 29 September 1923, New York City Department of Records and Information Services Municipal Archives

66. Rutgers Neilson, "Keith Executives Dine Paul Terry", December 1923.

67. "Mrs. Gerson Heimlich", *New York Times*, 12 June 1943, p. 13.

68. Terry, interview, 13 June 1970, 111; "Mrs. Paul Terry", *New York Times*, 8 January 1969, p. 44:1, 47 (funeral notice); "Mrs. Paul H. Terry, Wife of Animator", *The Standard-Star* (New Rochelle, N.Y.), 8 January 1969, p. 2.

69. Terry, interview, 13 June 1970, 111.

70. Ibid.

71. Ibid.

72. Some sources have Terry moving to 115 Beach Avenue in 1925. See Marchionni, "Paul Terry, At 82, Still Calls The Toon", p. 28.

73. The residential addresses and dates are based on mortgage documents and correspondence directed to Paul Terry, documentation found in the Paul Terry Papers.

113

Chapter 12

A Decade of Drawing Mice: Fables Pictures Studio, Part Two, 1925–1929

Vladimir Peter William ("Bill") Tytla (1904–1968) has been described as the "Michelangelo of animators" by producer Chuck Jones and "the greatest animator of all time" by animation director and animator Art Babbitt. At the age of nine Tytla saw a presentation by Winsor McCay of the recently completed *Gertie the Dinosaur* (1914) and like Terry this production inspired him to be an animator. While at high school, he attended evening classes in art at the New York Evening School of Industrial Design and eventually quit high school in favor of a career in art. By 1920, he was working for Paramount lettering title cards and balloon captions for the studio's animated cartoons earning him the nickname "Tytla the Titler".[1]

John Terry had discovered the 16-year-old art student and given him the titling job, his first job in the animation business. Tytla did some animation work for Raoul Barré on the Mutt and Jeff shorts and for John Terry, who had a studio in Greenwich Village, on the *Joys and Glooms* [*Judge Rummy*, and *Happy Hooligan*] cartoons. For years afterward he regarded John Terry as a sort of mentor, and frequently asked him for his advice. Appreciating the early genius of the young artist, Paul Terry poached Tytla from his brother John's studio and had him work for him on the *Aesop's Fables* series of shorts beginning in March 1923.[2]

Tytla's early work at Fables can be seen in *The Hero Wins* (September 28, 1925) (along with Mannie Davis he animated the scene of the mouse trying to catch a bull fish, sticks the fish with a spear, and puts the hook on the fish), *Little Brown Jug* (January 23, 1926) (the "stove scene" involving the fish putting the farmer in a frying pan), *Spanish Love* (February 6, 1926) (Mouse announces matador. Matador sees girl. Matador gets rose. Matador announces bull. Matador bowing to crowd), *The Farm Hands* (April 20, 1926) (the farmer going to bed scene near the end of the short), *The Big-Hearted Fish* (April 20, 1926) (the mouse and bubble scenes), *Subway Sally* (June 20, 1927) (the scene where the policemen pounce upon Sally, a fight erupts, and Sally emerges from the skirmish dressed as a policeman), *The Big Reward* (May 12, 1927) (the scene of the farmer discovering the mule in his bed then chasing him out with a slat), and *Buck Fever* (October 26, 1926) (the close up of the manicure).[3]

Tytla was able to draw anything that was assigned to him and quickly proved his value turning out prodigious amounts of animation. Studio records indicate he was at the studio as early as 1923, and by 1925 Tytla had developed into a fine animator. He was animating extensively from 1926 to 1929. John Terry advised him to ask Paul for a "100 percent increase" in salary. To Tytla's surprise the raise was granted without argument. According to animator I. Klein, Paul Terry "said he would have given Bill even more money at that time if he had asked for it. William Tytla was a brilliant animator from the very start of his career."[4]

In order to look mature, he grew a moustache that filled out

Chapter 12 • A Decade of Drawing Mice

Fig. 12.1 – 1926 Fables Studio group (left to right) Front Row: James Tyer, Oscar Van Brunt, Norman Ferguson, Eddie Donnelly, Hicks Lokey. Middle Row: Jesse Sylvester "Vet" Anderson, Hugh "Jerry" Shields, Paul H. Terry, Frank Moser, Mannie Davis. Back Row: George Williams, Ted Waldeyer, Vladimir "Bill" Tytla, Bill Hicks, John Foster, John McManus, Harry Bailey, Frank Sherman, Ferdinand Horvath, (unknown).

luxuriously over the years. Beginning in November 1928, he attended evening classes at the Art Students League on West 57th Street. Some of Tytla's later work at the Fables Studio can be seen in *The Small Town Sheriff* (July 22, 1927) (Big Dipper scene. Cat comes out of Big Dipper rowing a boat, throws Farmer Al Falfa a life preserver, and exits), *Lindy's Cat* (September 2, 1927) (Three cats doing the sailor dance on the ark), *The Fox Hunt* (October 13, 1927) (Closing scene: foxes kissing in automobile), *The Ball Park* (May 4, 1929) (Pitcher knocking out the mouse catcher with his pitch to the Octopus sticking all arms out and catching ball with all gloves). Tytla was more interested in becoming a master painter and illustrator than working in animation. Although Tytla would leave the studio to study art in Paris, Terry would later hire Tytla on two different occasions to work for his Terrytoons studio.[5]

Adding to the studio talent pool in 1926 were Ving Fuller, Bill Hicks, Frank Sherman, Hicks Lokey and Norman Ferguson. Ving Fuller (1903–1965), began his career as a cartoonist. In the early 1920s Fuller completed work as writer and artist on gag cartoons for the *Daily Graphic*. In the mid-1920s (about 1925–1926), he was working for John Randolph Bray animating cartoons. By 1926, he was employed at the Fables Pictures studio working for Terry and Van Beuren. Between 1924 and 1948, Fuller did comic strip and gag freelance work for radio and motion pictures. He also did work on the syndicated comic strips *Laffs in News Dispatches*, 1928–1929, and *Elza Poppin*, 1939, for the King Features Syndicate but he is most noted for his syndicated comic strip *Doc Syke* first published in the New York *Evening Sun* in 1944 running through to 1948 [1960].[6]

Frank Sherman (b. June 1897, Long Branch, New Jersey) was a veteran of the Barré-Bowers studio animating on Mutt and Jeff cartoons. He also worked for Hearst International Features Service alongside artists John Foster, Burton Gillett, Bert Green, Frank Moser, Walter Lantz, Leon Searl, John C. Terry, Bill Nolan, Jack King, and Albert Hurter. Frank Sherman was employed for Paul Terry at Fables Pictures studio, 1925–1929, working on Farmer Al Falfa shorts.[7] Norm Ferguson (1902–1957) was

115

Fig. 12.2 – Film editing room, 1920s.

trained as an accountant but pursued an artistic career. He worked for a period at Pat Sullivan's studio. He then worked on *Aesop's Fables* shorts at Fables Pictures studio under Paul Terry beginning as early as 1923. At the Fables studio, he started as a bookkeeper and moved into animation production as a cameraman. One evening he stayed late to shoot a scene and discovered that some of the drawings were missing. Since no one else was around, he drew them himself-with such skill that he was offered a job as an animator and rapidly learned the animated craft. He left Terry in 1928 to work at Disney for nearly 25 years from late 1928 to 1953.[8]

Other studio notables included Theodore Waldeyer (1902–1987) and Warren Oscar Van Brunt (1900–1928). Van Brunt later worked as a commercial artist and an instructor at the New York School of Design until his death on December 9, 1928. After his death, the Warren O. Van Brunt scholarship at the American School of Design was established in his memory.[9] Hicks Lokey (1904–1990) started at the Fables studio in 1925. As a kid he went to military school. He had been to art school and had taken a correspondence course in animation. He had spent a year-and-a-half at Vanderbilt University where he had problems with math and dropped out. He got a job as a statistician for a truck company before joining Fables as an inker and painter. After six to eight months there he was assigned to the camera after Ferguson moved to the animation department. He shot film on the camera until it broke down and could not fix the camera. He was then moved to the animation department.[10] His wage was 18 dollars a week, enough for him to pay his rent and eat at the Automat.[11] Lokey left the studio in 1929 and would enjoy a long career in animation employed for Van Beuren Studios, Fleischer Studios, Walt Disney Studios, Paul Fennell's Cartoon Films, Inc., and Hanna-Barbera Productions.

At the Fables studios, Terry had been using the celluloid process patented by Bray and Hurd without recompense to Bray. For about five years various legal proceedings took place between Terry and Bray. Bray was attempting to force Terry to make payments for using the Bray-Hurd process but was not trying to exert a monopoly or drive artists out of business.[12] Eventually he and Terry were able to come to a friendly arrangement where Bray agreed to drop the lawsuit if Terry bought a license. On July 29, 1926, Terry signed an agreement as a licensee with the Bray-Hurd Process Company as licensor obtaining a license to use the cel process patented by Bray and Hurd for the full term of the patents. Pursuant to the agreement, Terry was restricted to producing no more than two shorts a week.[13] This restriction was suitable for Terry because he was only obliged under his contract with Fables to produce one short a week.

Despite the frantic production studio schedule, Terry was able to pursue other business interests and investments. While Terry was in Washington, D.C. working at George Washington University he had become acquainted with Charles Hirliman who was involved in various phases of film laboratory work, had owned a film lab, and was involved in sales work.[14] After Hirliman entered the army he was evidently involved with Terry in some aspect of film production for the United States military. A few years later after Terry had begun work at Fables, Hirliman approached Terry asking for a job. While Terry refused the request he mentioned to Hirliman

Chapter 12 • A Decade of Drawing Mice

that he would help him financially if he established a film laboratory.[15]

Not long thereafter, about March 1922, Hirliman returned to Terry informing him he and his brother George[16] had acquired a film laboratory in Fort Lee, New Jersey, the Hirlagraph Motion Picture Company.[17] The Hirlagraph company operated a plant and laboratory that developed and processed raw film stock. The process involved treating the films chemically and mechanically before their exhibition by taking the negatives from the producer, developing them, making prints from them and sending them to the exchanges designated by the distributors.[18] Terry agreed to loan Hirliman some money to help buy some film stock.

When Terry asked for his investment back and the Hirlimans could not return the amount as they had re-invested the money in more film stock, Terry asked for a note.[19] In April 1922 Terry received a promissory note from the Hirlimans granting him 1/3rd of the stock in the Hirliman brothers' interest for his $3,000 investment.[20] In January 1923 Terry was formally issued, by way of a transfer agreement, 71 shares of the total of 284 shares, or a 25 percent stake in the company.[21] The company became a very profitable concern over the next few years at one point processing 1.5 million feet of film each month.[22] In 1927, the company was sold to Consolidated Film Laboratories[23] headed by Herbert Yates.

Along with work with the

Fig. 12.3 – Jerry Shield's animation being inspected by fellow artists.

investment in the laboratory, Terry got involved with loaning or financing films for States' Rights producers. In the early 1920s releasing companies were non-existent. As aforementioned, the United States was split into territories where films were sold outright in each territory.[24] The person who bought the rights to a picture for a certain territory would pay on a per footage basis with the money then received by the producer used to finance the production of the films. Terry established a company called the Terry Trading Corporation to finance the States' Rights producers. The benefit for Terry was two-fold: the interest and financing charges on the loans to the producers and the fact that these producers used their (Hirlagraph) laboratory to process the films.[25] Terry would finance a number of producers including W. Ray Johnston, the Weiss brothers, Clarion Pictures, and Bud Barsky.

Bud Barsky would loan money from Terry to produce half-reelers at the Hirlagraph Laboratories to help provide product for a company for which he was film salesman.[26] Terry ran the Terry Trading Corporation for about four or five years and according to Terry "it worked out pretty well for a while".[27] Apparently, financing activities ceased when the laboratory was sold.[28] In January 1928, Paul Terry and his wife visited California, his first vacation in three years.[29] On December 12, 1928, Patricia Ann, the daughter and only child of Paul and Irma, was born in East Hampton, Long Island, New York.[30]

On the whole the critical reviews of the *Aesop's Fables* shorts in the trade magazines during the last half of the 1920s were positive, encouraging and sometimes quite flattering to Terry and his artists. *Variety* magazine reviewed the short *In the Rough* (released January 22, 1927) with the following critique:

> Another clever Aesop reel with a golf theme. Again the facile

117

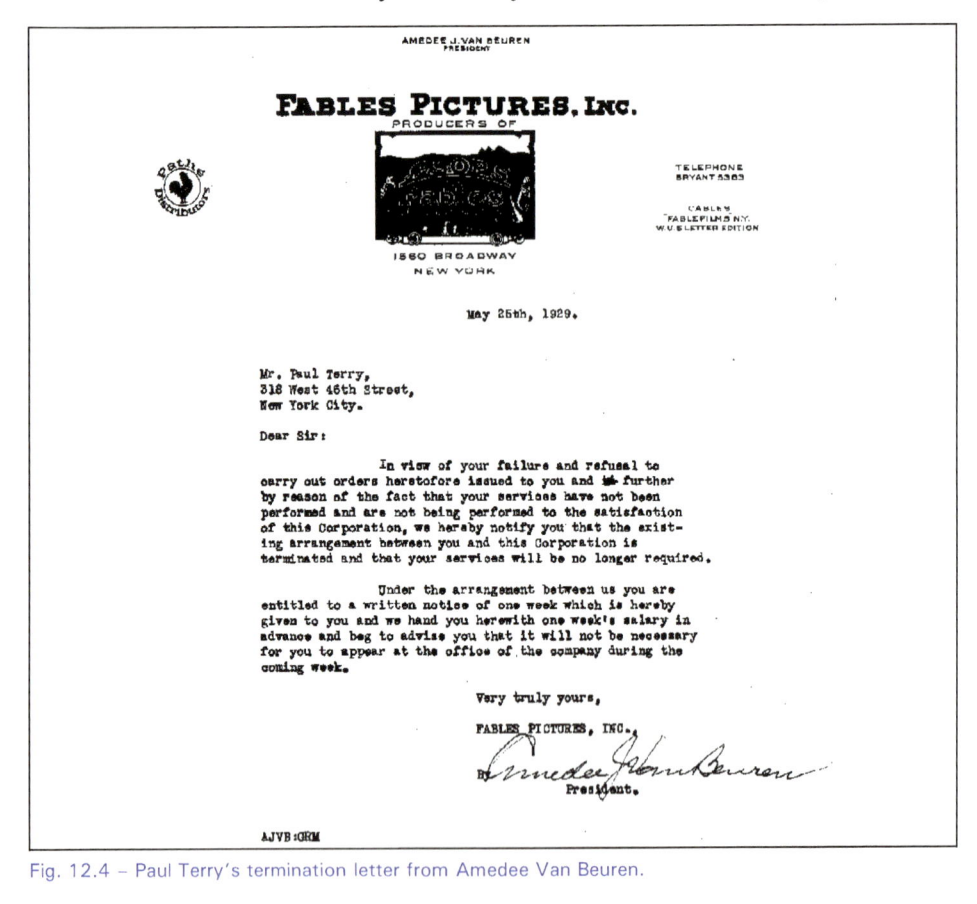

TERRYTOONS: The Story of Paul Terry and His Classic Cartoon Factory

```
AMEDEE J. VAN BEUREN
      PRESIDENT

FABLES PICTURES, INC.
       PRODUCERS OF

                                        TELEPHONE
                                        BRYANT 5303

                                        CABLES
                                        "FABLEFILMS N.Y."
                                        W.U. & LETTER EDITION
    1560 BROADWAY
       NEW YORK

                      May 25th, 1929.

Mr. Paul Terry,
318 West 46th Street,
New York City.

Dear Sir:
           In view of your failure and refusal to
carry out orders heretofore issued to you and in further
by reason of the fact that your services have not been
performed and are not being performed to the satisfaction
of this Corporation, we hereby notify you that the exist-
ing arrangement between you and this Corporation is
terminated and that your services will be no longer required.

           Under the arrangement between us you are
entitled to a written notice of one week which is hereby
given to you and we hand you herewith one week's salary in
advance and beg to advise you that it will not be necessary
for you to appear at the office of the company during the
coming week.

                      Very truly yours,

                      FABLES PICTURES, INC.

                      By [signature]
                                 President.

AJVB:ORM
```

Fig. 12.4 – Paul Terry's termination letter from Amedee Van Beuren.

Terry has a clever collaborator in a new "idea" man. Hugh Shields (assuming that Shields is the "story" contriver), and the development of the Scotch game's farcical sidelights leads up to the observation that one does not have to be crazy to play golf – but it helps.[31]

In reviewing *The War Bride* (April 20, 1928), the reviewer George J. Reddy comments:

The striking originality of the gags injected into this cartoon rates this Fables release way above the average. Cartoonist Terry takes the typical war-time theme of the sweetheart who goes away to battle, leaving his girl to the unwelcome advances of a villainous member of the cat family. It is while Milt Mouse is at the front amid cannon roar and bursting shells that the business of a big war is cleverly burlesqued. This short reel is ideal for any program.[32]

Reddy had similar positive reviews concerning *Grandma's House* (February 11, 1929), "a clever pen takeoff on the 'Little Red Riding Hood' yarn".[33] Other reviews in 1929 included "The best cartoons on the market" and "These Fables have certainly improved since five or six years ago".[34]

Although Terry was unable to keep pace with some of the technological innovations introduced by his New York City competitor Max Fleischer, by the end of the 1920s the Fables cartoon product had improved in terms of aesthetics. The visuals were enhanced evidenced by a finer attention to detail in the background design found in the cartoons produced in the latter part of the decade.[35] Character design had improved depth and personality and animation was more finely rendered. These

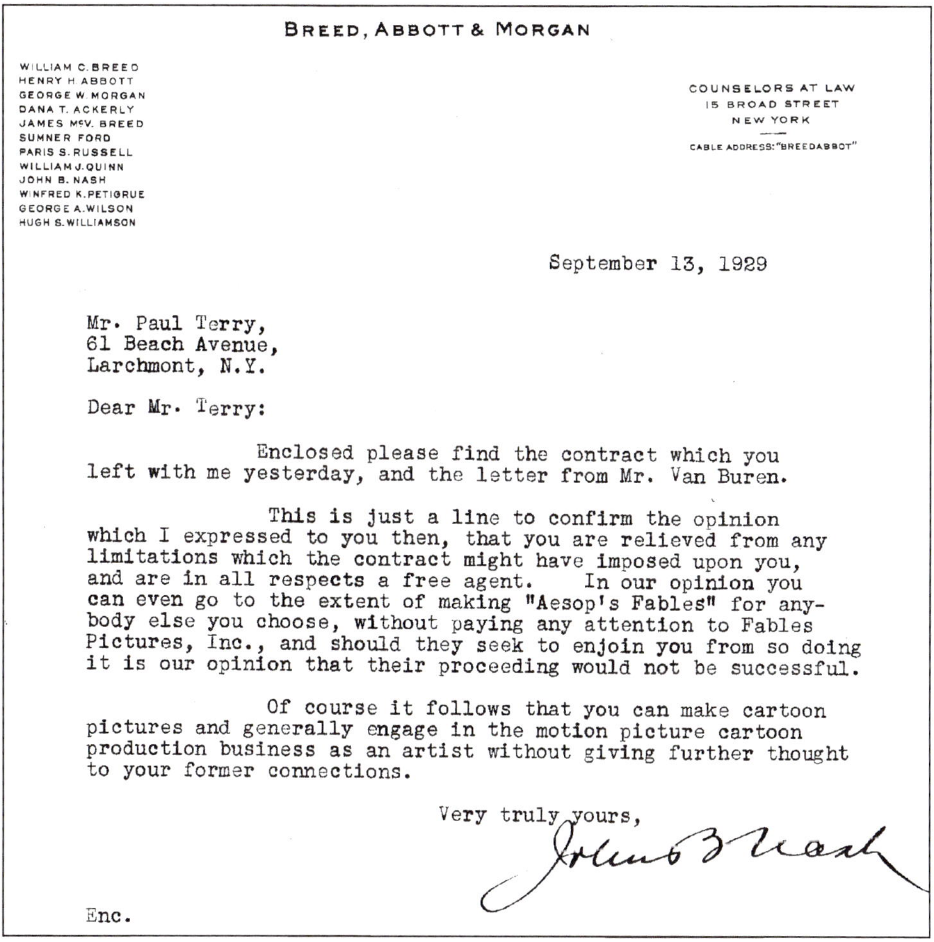

Chapter 12 • A Decade of Drawing Mice

BREED, ABBOTT & MORGAN

WILLIAM C. BREED
HENRY H. ABBOTT
GEORGE W. MORGAN
DANA T. ACKERLY
JAMES McV. BREED
SUMNER FORD
PARIS S. RUSSELL
WILLIAM J. QUINN
JOHN B. NASH
WINFRED K. PETIGRUE
GEORGE A. WILSON
HUGH S. WILLIAMSON

COUNSELORS AT LAW
15 BROAD STREET
NEW YORK

CABLE ADDRESS: "BREEDABBOT"

September 13, 1929

Mr. Paul Terry,
61 Beach Avenue,
Larchmont, N.Y.

Dear Mr. Terry:

    Enclosed please find the contract which you left with me yesterday, and the letter from Mr. Van Buren.

    This is just a line to confirm the opinion which I expressed to you then, that you are relieved from any limitations which the contract might have imposed upon you, and are in all respects a free agent. In our opinion you can even go to the extent of making "Aesop's Fables" for anybody else you choose, without paying any attention to Fables Pictures, Inc., and should they seek to enjoin you from so doing it is our opinion that their proceeding would not be successful.

    Of course it follows that you can make cartoon pictures and generally engage in the motion picture cartoon production business as an artist without giving further thought to your former connections.

Very truly yours,

John B Nash

Enc.

Fig. 12.5 – Letter from Terry's lawyer advising him he can make Aesop's Fables cartoons.

improvements can be traced to the animation talent base in the studio which had deepened over the course of the 1920s. Some of the veteran artists such as John Foster, Frank Moser, Jerry Shields, Mannie Davis, and Harry Bailey spent a good portion of the decade at the studio refining their skills. Reused drawings and recycled animation were kept to a minimum of no more than one or two scenes in any one cartoon, and used very sparingly across the entire series of cartoons. While Terry had final say on the script, as the series progressed he continually sought more input from all of his staff on the gags used in the cartoons. In effect, he had an 18-man story department always at his disposal.[36]

Around 1926 the studio's production system was reorganized so that Terry's five key animators would write and animate their cartoons almost entirely themselves. While Frank Moser, Jerry Shields, and Mannie Davis had no trouble animating an entire cartoon themselves on many occasions, John Foster and Harry Bailey tended to rely more heavily on several other animators in the "Fables" bullpen to fill out their cartoons. For example, Davis and Sherman shared the animation on *The Wind Jammers* (January 23, 1926). Davis animated *School Days* (December 31, 1926) almost entirely himself animating 31 of the 41 scenes (Tytla, Anderson and Ferguson animated the other 10). Moser animated 41 of the 45

119

Fig. 12.6 – Irma (née Heimlich) Terry, Paul Terry's spouse.

product, it is not surprising that Terry did not want to fix what was not broken. He argued that adding sound would only complicate the production process. Van Beuren was insistent that sound be added to keep pace with advances in technology and a series of verbal arguments ensued with the end result of Terry reluctantly agreeing to add sound (the series would now be renamed *Aesop's Sound Fables*). The cartoon short, *Dinner Time*, was announced on August 18, 1928 and premiered at the Mark Strand in New York on or before September 1.[37] *Dinner Time* is noted for being the first all-talking cartoon short with synchronized dialogue and sound preceding the production of Disney's *Steamboat Willie* (1928).

The roars, barks, and meows of elephants, dogs, and cats are soon to be part of theatre entertainment, it seems, for the Van Beuren Enterprises has announced that *Dinner Time*, one of the "Aesop's Film Fables" has been synchronized with the RCA Photophone. All the animals of the jungle as pen-and-inked in animation in Aesop's Fables will annunciate aloud in their more or less natural "voices", it is said. A background of orchestral music is offered throughout the reel.[38]

Walt Disney was treated to a sneak preview when he attempted to interest RCA in recording his own film. After viewing the short, Disney cried out:

MY GOSH – TERRIBLE – A lot of racket and nothing else. I was terribly disappointed. I

scenes in *Horses, Horses, Horses* (May 12, 1927) (Ferguson, Sherman, Hicks, and Horvath did the other four scenes), and all of the scenes in *The River of Doubt* (August 16, 1927).

By 1927, the talking motion picture had arrived with the release of *The Jazz Singer*, the first feature-length motion picture with synchronized dialogue sequences. Producer Amadee J. Van Beuren realized the potential of sound films and urged Terry to add innovation to his films. The Fleischers had already been releasing *Song Car-Tunes*, a series of short three minute animation films produced between May 1924 and September 1927, pioneering the use of the "Follow the Bouncing Ball" device used to lead audiences in theater sing-alongs. However, only the music and not the dialogue was synchronized. There were 36 titles in the *Song Car-Tune* series, with 19 using the Phonofilm sound-on-film process developed by Lee DeForest beginning with *Oh, Mabel*; *Mother, Pin a Rose on Me*; *Goodbye, My Lady Love*; and *Come Take a Trip on My Airship* (all May and June 1924). Another 17 titles were released silent, designed to be played with live music in theaters.

Terry was opposed to adding sound to the animated shorts. Considering the critical success of the Fables cartoons and that their distributor was happy with the

Chapter 12 • A Decade of Drawing Mice

really expected to see something half-way decent. BUT HONESTLY – it was nothing but one of the rottenest fables I believe that I ever saw, and I should know because I have seen almost all of them. It merely had an orchestra playing and adding some noises. The talking part does not mean a thing. It doesn't even match. We sure have nothing to worry about from these quarters.[39]

The film was soon overshadowed by the release of Disney's *Steamboat Willie* on November 18, 1928. That same month, Van Beuren had announced that he was converting to all sound production for *Aesop's Fables*.[40]

Terry would direct 14 *Aesop's Film Fables* series shorts with synchronized soundtracks with release dates from April 16, 1929 to August 15, 1929. The sound *Fables* shorts received very positive reviews from the critics with many reviewers impressed with the entertainment value that sound brought to the animated medium while commenting that the shorts delivered "rapid fun",[41] "quite a few chuckles",[42] and "all the laughs any fan would want".[43] A good portion of the credit should be placed at the feet of the two musical directors. The musical directors for these shorts were both brilliant composers of note: Carl Edouarde (credited on three of these shorts) and Josiah Zuro (credited on nine of the shorts). Carl Edouarde (1875–1932) is most noted in animation for helping to synchronize the sound for the Walt Disney Mickey Mouse cartoon *Steamboat Willie*. For the film, to make the synchronization easier for the orchestra, he filmed a bouncing ball in the unseen lower right hand corner of the screen to show where the beats (and accents) went and the synchronization worked perfectly.

Edouarde received his musical education at the Royal Conservatory in Leipzig, graduating in 1889. He became the first musical director of The Strand theater in New York City in the early 1910s. The Strand was the first movie theater to have a symphony orchestra and was opened on April 11, 1914 with a small orchestra. He left the Strand in 1927 to devote himself to motion picture sound production. As a result of his near death and injury due to a fire and the destruction of the Pathé Manhattan film studio, Edouarde retired from cartoon musical synchronization. He also composed the background music to the films *Kismet* (1920), *The Hunchback of Notre Dame* (1923) and *The Private Life of Helen Troy* (1927). He was also music arranger for *The Blonde Captive* (1931).[44]

Josiah Zuro (1887–1930) directed opera companies in New York and Boston. He was assistant conductor at the Manhattan Opera House in Oscar Hammerstein's company. He was musical director at several theaters and for Hammerstein's grand operas, later becoming the musical director for the Pathé motion picture studio in the late 1920s. In 1915, he directed grand opera at San Francisco while the World's Fair was being held there. Mr. Zuro also organized an opera company, the Zuro Opera Company, which gave performances for a number of years. In 1928, he went to Hollywood to work for a motion picture concern and became known in that field as the composer of the score for *Old San Francisco* (1927), *King of Kings* (1927) and *The Covered Wagon*. The most notable cartoon Zuro worked on was Paul Terry's *Dinner Time*.[45]

In 1928, Keith-Albee sold their interest in the renamed Fables Studio to Amedee J. Van Beuren.[46] Van Beuren negotiated a new agreement with Terry dated June 28, 1928 wherein Terry was to be paid $320 weekly to June 30, 1929 and $400 a week thereafter to August 9, 1932.[47] However, this contract would never be completed as a disagreement between Terry and Van Beuren erupted resulting in Terry's departure. The conventional story has the dispute centered on Van Beuren wanting to synchronize the sound tracks, and Terry being satisfied with adding simple sound tracks to his silent product. According to Moser, Van Beuren approached Paul and wanted him to produce in sound to keep pace with Disney. Terry told Van Beuren that he was not prepared to go into sound, and immediately thereafter Van Beuren fired him.[48] This story does not appear to be supported by the fact that Terry had acquiesced on adding sound to the film product months before his official departure from the studio.

Another explanation for Terry's exodus provided by Mannie Davis centers on a financial disagreement between Terry and

Radio-Keith-Orpheum (RKO) over the share of the profits due Terry. In 1928, the distributor of the cartoons, Pathé Exchange, had been bought out by RKO. RKO was generating more earnings than the production company expected. Therefore, to circumvent the strict terms of the 1924 agreement between Terry and the company, the company undertook some creative accounting to try and hide the profits.[49] Terry found out that RKO was generating more earnings than the production company expected. When the company refused to comply with Terry's demand for a rightful share of the profits, Terry left the studio.[50]

In a letter dated May 25, 1929, Van Beuren, president of the Fables Pictures, Inc., advised Terry that his services with the company were terminated.[51] Pursuant to the letter of dismissal, Terry was officially released for the failure and refusal to carry out orders issued to him and further by reason of the fact that his services had not been performed and were not being performed to the satisfaction of the Corporation.[52] He was given one week's salary in advance and advised not to attend the studio. Terry argued the severance pay was inadequate considering length of service. He eventually signed a release on June 13, 1929 releasing Fables Pictures, Inc. and The Van Beuren Corporation from all actions, suits and debts for a sum of $5,000.[53] Terry then sold his 10 percent interest in Fables Studios to RKO for $33,000. In a letter dated September 13, 1929, Terry's lawyer advised him that he is relieved from all contractual obligations with Van Beuren but can continue to pursue making "Aesop's Fables" for anybody else.[54] Amedee Van Beuren then changed the name of the company from Fables Pictures to Van Beuren Studios.

With Terry's departure, Van Beuren gave Terry's job and contract to John Foster. ◆

Notes

1. Much of the biographical information on Tytla in this chapter was retrieved from John Canemaker, *Vladimir Tytla: Master Animator*, Katonah Museum of Art, Catalogue essay for exhibition at The Katonah Museum of Art, Katonah, N.Y. September 25, 1994-January 1, 1995.

2. John Terry would also spend some time animating cartoons with his brother Paul at the Fables studio in the early 1920s. Gifford, *American Animated Films: The Silent Era, 1897–1929*, 117–130.

3. Scene descriptions from scripts found in the Paul Terry Papers collection.

4. Canemaker, *Vladimir Tytla: Master Animator*.

5. John Canemaker, "Vladimir William Tytla (1904–1968): Animation's Michelangelo", *Cinefantastique* (Winter 1976): 9–19; John Canemaker, "Vlad Tytla: Animation's Michelangelo", in *The American Animated Cartoon: A Critical Anthology*, ed. Danny Peary and Gerald Peary (New York: Dutton, 1980), 82–89; Frank Thomas and Ollie Johnston, *Disney Animation: The Illusion of Life* (New York: Abbeville Press, 1981); John Canemaker, *Vladimir Tytla: Master Animator*, Grant, *Masters of Animation*, 190–192. Obituaries: "Vladimir Tytla, Cartoonist, Dies; Creator of Dumbo for Disney", *New York Times*, 31 December 1968, p. 28; "Vladimir W.P. Tytla", *Variety*, 1 January 1969, 55.

6. *Variety*, 2 April 1930, 10; *Variety*, 18 March 1931, 57; "Several Parties Given at Woodmere; Personal News", *Brooklyn Daily Eagle* (N.Y.), 13 August 1933, p. 2 B-C; "Why the Hollywood Dancing Kosloffs Did A Split Over Those Lovely Pupils", *Miami Daily News*, 24 November 1934, Magazine section, p. 2; *Variety*, 13 October 1937, 2; *Variety*, 26 November 1937, 2; *Variety*, 31 January 1940, 49; Olivier Amiel, *Samuel Fuller* (Paris: Henri Veyrier, 1985); Samuel Fuller, *A Third Face: My Tale of Writing, Fighting and Filmmaking* (New York: A. Knopf, 2002).

7. Very little is known about Sherman although he worked for Terry at the Terrytoons studio in the early 1930s before working for the Van Beuren studio beginning in 1933.

8. John Grant, *Encyclopedia of Walt Disney's Animated Characters*, 3rd ed. (New York: Hyperion Books, 1998); Frank S. Nugent, "The Screen in Review; "Pinocchio", Walt Disney's Long-Awaited Successor to "Snow White", Has Its Premiere at the Center Theatre – Other New Films", *New York Times*, 8 February 1940, p. 24; "Daisy Winner of Dog 'Oscar' for 2nd Year", *The Binghamton Press* (N.Y.), 24 February 1941, p. 10; "Hollywood Inside", *Variety*, 2 December 1941, 2. Obituaries: *Variety*, 5 November 1957, 10; *Variety*, 13 November 1957, 79.

9. "Obituary Notes", *New York Times*, 12 December 1928, p. 30.

10. Hicks Lokey, interview, 4 May 1990, J. Michael Barrier collection, 3, 6.

11. Ibid., 4.

12. Denig, "Cartoonist Bray with Paramount", *Moving Picture World*, 11 December 1915. Cited in: Crafton, 156.

13. Terry, interview, 14 July 1970, 132. "Agreement", Signatories: John R. Bray (for the Bray-Hurd Process Company, Inc.) and Paul H. Terry, 29 July, 1926, 2, Paul Terry Papers.

Chapter 12 • A Decade of Drawing Mice

14. Terry, interview, 13 June 1970, 99.

15. Ibid., 101.

16. See also "Hirliman, George A.", *The International Motion Picture Almanac, 1944–45*, 187.

17. Terry, interview, 13 June 1970, 101.

18. Hirlagraph Motion Picture Corporation, "Hirlagraph Motion Picture Corporation: First Mortgage 7% Gold Bonus", New York, New York, Paul Terry Papers.

19. Terry, interview, 13 June 1970, 102.

20. Charles Herliman and George A. Herliman, Promissory Note to Paul Terry, Fort Lee, New Jersey, 15 April 1922, Paul Terry Papers.

21. Share Transfer Agreement, Signatories: Charles Hirliman, Paul H. Terry, George A. Hirliman, Charles de Moos, January 1923, Paul Terry Papers.

22. Hirlagraph Motion Picture Corporation, "Hirlagraph Motion Picture Corporation: First Mortgage 7% Gold Bonus", 1.

23. Terry, interview, 13 June 1970, 102. "George A. Hirliman, Made Films for TV", *New York Times*, 2 April 1952, p. 29:2. See generally Slide, "Consolidated Film Industries", 78.

24. Terry, interview, 20 December 1969, 23–24.

25. Terry, interview, 14 July 1970, 123.

26. "Bud Barsky", *Variety*, 27 December 1967, 43, 55; "Bud Barsky", *NY Times*, 21 December 1967, p. 37:4.

27. Terry, interview, 14 July 1970, 123.

28. Ibid., 124–125.

29. "In and Out of Town", *Motion Picture News*, 14 January 1928, 131.

30. Joseph T. Terry, *Genealogy of Our Family*, 4.

31. "In the Rough", Review of Aesop's Fables (Animated Cartoons), *Variety*, 9 February 1927, 17.

32. George J. Reddy, "War Brides (Pathe One-Reel)", Review of Aesop's Fables (Animated Cartoons), *Motion Picture News*, 19 May 1928, 1707.

33. George J. Reddy, "Grandma's House (Pathe One-Reel)", Review of Aesop's Fables (Animated Cartoons), *Motion Picture News*, 16 February 1929, 502.

34. "Aesop's Fables", in *The Motion Picture Almanac 1929*, ed. Martin J. Quigley (Chicago: The Quigley Publishing Company, 1929), 214.

35. Norman M. Klein, *Seven Minutes: The Life and Death of the American Animated Cartoon* (New York: Verso, 1993), 11.

36. Gifford, *American Animated Films: The Silent Era, 1897–1929*, 143.

37. "First Animated Cartoon Seen With Sound", *Motion Picture News*, 25 August 1928, 614.

38. "Now Well Hear Those Funny Fables Animals", *Exhibitor's Herald and Moving Picture World*, 18 August 1928, 42; Crafton, *Before Mickey*, 211.

39. Walt Disney, letter to Roy Disney and Ub Iwerks, no date, quoted in Bob Thomas, *Walt Disney: An American Original* (New York: Simon and Schuster, 1976), 91–92.

40. "Entire Product of Van Beuren Will Be Made Sound Pictures", *Exhibitor's Herald and Moving Picture World*, 17 November 1928, 49.

41. "House Cleaning Time", Review of Aesop's Fables (Animated Cartoons), *Motion Picture News*, 3 August 1929, 478.

42. "Jail Breakers", Review of Aesop's Fables (Animated Cartoons), *Motion Picture News*, 6 July 1929, 125.

43. Skating Hounds", Review of Aesop's Fables (Animated Cartoons), *Motion Picture News*, 27 April 1929, 1410. See also: "Van Beuren Dialogue", *Exhibitor's Herald and Moving Picture World*, 22 December 1928, 47.

44. "10 Die, 18 Hurt in Film Studio Blaze; Panic Costs Lives of Four Chorus Girls as Quick Fire Cuts Off All But One Exit", *New York Times*, 11 December 1929, p. 1; "Survivors Dazed at Escape in Fire", *New York Times*, 11 December 1929, p. 2. Obituaries: "Carl Edouarde of the Films Dies", *New York Times*, 9 December 1932, p. 28:4; "Carl Edouarde", *Variety*, 13 December 1932, 55.

45. Marguerite D'Alvarez, "The Men Who Have Loved Me", *Buffalo Sunday Courier Magazine*, 18 May 1924, p. 6–7; "Zuro Musical Director for Pathé Sound Films", *Motion Picture News*, 3 November 1928, 1384. Obituary: "Josiah Zuro Killed When Auto Upsets", *New York Times*, 21 October 1930, p. 29:5.

46. Crafton, *Before Mickey*, 192.

47. "Memorandum of Agreement between Paul H. Terry and Fables Pictures, Inc.", 28 June 1928, Paul Terry Papers.

48. "Frank H. Moser – Plaintiff – Direct", *Case on Appeal from Judgment*, 131.

49. Davis, interview, 9e. Davis was likely referring to the contractual clause where Terry was guaranteed a percentage of the net profit of the earnings. It appears RKO had made some adjustments to their accounting methods to deny Terry financial gain he had been receiving earlier.

50. Another version: On June 5th, 1929, Paul Terry declined to sign a new contract offered by Van Beuren and RKO that no longer granted him the publicity and percentage of ownership he'd previously enjoyed as studio director. Terry was forced to sell his share in the studio.

51. Amedee J. Van Beuren (Fables Pictures, Inc.), Correspondence to Paul Terry, 25 May 1929. Terry was given one week's salary in lieu of notice after nine years with Fables.

52. Ibid.

53. Paul H. Terry, Release of Fables Pictures, Inc. and The Van Beuren Corporation for all legal claims (General Release – 158), 13 June 1929, Paul Terry Papers.

54. John B. Nash, Correspondence from the law firm of Breed, Abbott & Morgan to Mr. Paul Terry, 13 September 1929, Paul Terry Papers.

Chapter 13

Sweat Equity is the Best Start-up Capital: The Founding and Early Development of the Terry-Toons Studio, 1929–1932

Although now unemployed, Terry had little financial worries. Since 1921, he had accumulated a significant amount of financial equity through his lucrative employment contracts with Fables Pictures, Inc. and subsequent severance pay, his sale of 10 percent ownership in the studio, his generous returns on investments through the Hirlagraph Laboratories, and his profits from the Terry Trading Corporation. He had taken about eight months off to ponder his future in animation while Van Beuren continued to release the *Aesop's Fables* sound shorts he had directed.[1] In August 1929, a restless Terry telephoned Frank Moser and asked him to meet him at Grand Central Station. At their meeting, Terry proposed that both parties enter into a business partnership to produce animated cartoons of a general nature on a straight 50-50 profit sharing relationship.[2] The partnership would be known as Moser & Terry.

After Moser expressed interest in the idea, Paul asked him if he could approach Audio-Cinema in Long Island City, the westernmost residential and commercial neighborhood of the New York City borough of Queens, to inquire whether they would be interested in financing the operation for two years. Audio-Cinema was located in a small studio at 161 Harris Avenue. The studio had become the only Western Electric licensee in the east and had high quality recording technology. The president of Audio-Cinema was Joseph Wilfred Coffman. Coffman had a background in science education. He was head of the science department in Moultrie (Ga.) High School (1916), principal of the Anniston (Alabama) High School (1920), head of the science department, Ensley High School, Birmingham, Alabama (1921), and Supervisor, Visual Education, Atlanta Public Schools (1922–1923). He moved into film becoming production manager, Graphic Films Corporation, Atlanta (1924) before becoming an executive with Carpenter-Goldman Labs, New York City (1925–1929) (vice-president, 1927–1929).[3] Audio-Cinema, Inc. was the successor to Carpenter-Goldman Labs in 1929. During the 1920s, Coffman had become an expert and consultant on sound film technology.[4]

As early as September 1929, the Audio-Cinema studio was producing Bruce Bairnsfeather's "Old Bill" shorts starring Charles Coburn and began work on the *Sheriff Crumpet* series the following March. After a short period of negotiations between Moser and Coffman, Audio-Cinema agreed to an arrangement where they would furnish the studio for the animation crew to work in, the sound equipment, the animation production materials, and the musicians. Terry and Moser were to provide "sweat" equity, to give all of their time without pay until Audio-Cinema's advanced money was returned. After that Moser and Terry were to secure $300 a week each for their services, and following that, profits would be shared equally between

124

Chapter 13 • Sweat Equity is the Best Start-up Capital

Fig. 13.1 – 35mm film drying (c. 1930).

Audio-Cinema and Moser & Terry.[5] This contract entered in October 1929 between Audio-Cinema and Moser & Terry granted each party the right to renew the agreement after one year by guaranteeing the other party $25,000 per year above costs.

In November 1929, Audio-Cinema provided Picart Studios, Inc. located at 254 West 54th Street in New York City with a finished print of the first animated cartoon and the instructions to secure a distribution contract.[6] Picart Studios, Incorporated, on behalf of Audio-Cinema, approached Educational Pictures, Inc. and Earle Wooldridge Hammons (1892–1962), vice-president and general manager of Educational Pictures, Inc., and inquired whether Educational would be interested in distributing the cartoon product. Educational agreed to sign a distribution contract with Audio-Cinema to distribute the Terrytoons, for which Picart by securing the distribution contract, received 10 percent of the gross receipts under the contract between Audio-Cinema and Educational. This agreement was entered into between Joe Coffman on behalf of Audio-Cinema, Incorporated and Louis Jacobson, President of Picart Studios, Incorporated.[7] On January 27, 1930, Audio-Cinema and Educational Pictures entered into an agreement wherein Educational would distribute the Terrytoons produced by Moser & Terry at the Audio-Cinema studio facilities.[8]

Interestingly enough, Terry had known Hammons for about 13 or 14 years, since about 1917 but Hammons appears not to have had a central role in these negotiations.[9] Hammons' background prior to his entry in the film business was wide-ranging and he possessed strong management skills. He was a customs agent (Mexican National Railways), and building commissioner (New York Fire Department, Brooklyn; E. L. Ranlett of Marshall, Spader & Company, New York stock brokers, 1903–1907). He ventured next into real estate (Dean Alvord and Company, 1908–1909; Woodmere Realty Company; United States and Mexican Trust Company, 1910; Jamaica Union Land Company and Jamaica Bay Building Company, 1911; Howard Estates Development, 1912).[10] Hammons formed Educational Pictures in 1915[11] with George A. Skinner, President of Educational Pictures, Inc.[12]

Hammons had been attracted to the film industry as an independent experimenter in educational short subjects, comedy, and novelty reels. For the next 45 years he campaigned for motion-picture shorts, particularly those devoted to educational subjects.[13] Shortly after Paul's entry into the animation business in 1915, Educational became a distributor of cartoons featuring Happy Hooligan and Tad's Silk Hat Harry, made by Gregory La Cava. In the 1920s, Educational distributed such series as *Sketchografs* (1921–1926), *Tony Sarg's Almanac* (1922–1923), *Pen and Ink Vaudeville* (1924–1925), *L. B. Cornwell Productions* (1924–1925), *Life Cartoon Comedies* (1926–1927), and most notably John Terry's *Judge's Crossword Puzzles* (1925).[14] Terry and Hammons likely first met in a professional capacity as both were involved in the animation business, one as animator-producer and the other as distributor.

After having secured the financing, studio facilities, and distributor for the animated cartoons, Terry and Moser set about gathering together an animation crew. Calling on his old friends at the Fables studio, Terry was able to assemble one of the most talented groups of animation artists in the country. Headlining the group was master animator Bill Tytla. Tytla had spent 1929 in Europe touring the continent and studying drawing and painting. Tytla had returned to the United States intent on bringing to life some of the figures he had seen in the paintings of such masters as Flemish Renaissance painter Pieter Breughel (1525–1569). Tytla's desire was to incorporate his rich knowledge of art he had absorbed in Europe into his animation.[15]

Upon Tytla's return to Yonkers, New York, Terry sent him a letter offering him a job at the new studio. Tytla was excited to return to animation with the new challenge of sound cartoons. He also had other motivations not related to artistic aspirations, primarily financial ones. He had spent a considerable amount of money in his sojourn in Europe and was running out of money.[16] Complicating his economic situation was the recent troubles on Wall Street which was sending the nation into the Great Depression.[17] On October 24 ("Black Thursday"), the market lost 11 percent of its value at the opening bell on very heavy trading. On October 29, 1929 ("Black Tuesday"), about 16 million shares were traded, and the Dow lost an additional 30 points, or 12 percent.[18] The nation's financial institutions were collapsing and corporations and businesses both small and large were going bankrupt sending millions into bread lines.

Sometime during this period, Terry claims he was at a party he had been hosting and had been informed that his stock investments had been wiped out in the series of market crashes that had occurred. Not wanting to disturb the festivities, Terry quietly left the party and his guests who continued to dance and took a walk along the Hudson River line in the Bronx. He stopped along the river's edge, reached into his pocket, and took out his last dime and threw it into the Hudson River in order to "to start from scratch".[19] While there is evidence from family records that Terry had a habit of investing significant financial capital in stocks on the New York Stock Exchange,[20] there is no evidence to support his account that he was wiped out financially as a result of the 1929 Crash. Although he may have taken a heavy hit to his finances, family correspondence, financial reports, and personal papers reveal that he had enough diversification in his investment portfolio to carry on with the comfortable lifestyle he had been accustomed to.

The Audio-Cinema team of animators and artists that Terry and Moser put together included Arthur Babbitt, Thomas Bonfiglio, Tom Byrne, Mannie Davis, George Gordon, Ferdinand Huszti Horvath, Jack King, Isidore Klein, Frank Little, Frank Moser, Ralph Pearson, Connie Rasinski, Charles Sarka,[21] Sculia,[22] Frank Sherman, Larry Silverman, Paul Sommer, Hugh Shields, John Terry, Ralph Tiller, and Cy Young.[23] Davis, Horvath, King, Moser, Sherman, Shields and John Terry were all former animators from the Fables studio. Babbitt, Bonfiglio, Byrne, Gordon, Little, Pearson, Rasinski, Charles Sarka, Sculia, Tiller and Young were relative newcomers to the animation business. As there were other major animation studios in the New York area at the time (e.g. Van Beuren, Fleischer), Terry and Moser had to provide competitive compensation in order to keep their more experienced artists from moving to another studio.

Complicating efforts to retain a gifted group of artists was that since the birth of animation and through the "Golden Age of American Animation"[24] experienced and talented animators were always in short supply. In the silent film period, Bray Studios didn't pay their production staff until Monday because Mrs. Bray feared that the artists would spend all their money on alcohol over the weekend and possibly not show up for work Monday morning. Mrs. Bray was not inclined to release her animation crew for tardiness or abandonment because they would be difficult to replace.[25] By 1935, trade magazines had begun reporting that animators were in short demand and those that were skilled artisans were receiving high salaries driving up studio production costs.[26]

The shortage in animators was so severe that a *Variety* news article reported: "This is the only known

Chapter 13 • Sweat Equity is the Best Start-up Capital

Fig. 13.2 – Theatrical poster for Paul Terrytoons *2000 B.C.* (1931).

business where an actual shortage of man-power is holding back production".[27] Fleischer Studios was bold enough to put a sensational advertisement in *Variety* looking for 5,000 animators when the national unemployment rate was over 21 percent. By 1935, Disney was unable to find enough skilled talent on the west coast and therefore sent representatives to New York to interview 1,000 applicants thereby tapping into the home grown artistic talent of Terrytoons and Fleischer Studios.[28] However, as Disney was developing a reputation for investing more money and critical attention into his animation, animators with strong creative aspirations were moving to Disney for less money than Terry, Fleischer, Van Beuren, or Leon Schlesinger was paying them.[29]

Terry would later admit that he could not retain the talent at his studio. The love of sunshine and the attractions of Hollywood lured many talented artists to head west.

A lot of the talent I developed ended up on the coast. I could never compete with the coast because the climate and the chance to go to California. It was like a magnet. And I know that Disney copped a lot of good men from me like the fellow [Norm Ferguson] that developed, created Pluto was my man. I developed him from a nobody. He was a clerk.[30]

Adding to the shortage of artists during the 1930s was Metro-Goldwyn-Mayer's decision to start animation production in 1937 with the hiring of Fred Quimby to set up the department.[31] Not surprisingly the August 15, 1937 edition of *The New York Times* noted that the "new cartoon unit at Metro is experiencing difficulty in locating animators".[32]

With quality animators in short supply, Terry and Moser were challenged with locating artists with animation experience. Right from the opening of the studio there was constant employee turnover as artists headed elsewhere for better opportunities. Studio artists worked Monday to Friday as well as a half-day on Saturday and one evening, in essence a six day work week.[33] Prior to his work for Terry, Arthur Babbitt (1907–1992) worked for years in various jobs to help his family survive while he studied the writings of Sigmund Freud and dreamed of becoming a psychiatrist. At the age of 17, he decided to turn to commercial art as he was unable to afford medical school. A talent for drawing eventually led to a graphics job in an advertising agency. He was an animator of medical films and commercials between 1924 and 1928. He left for Walt Disney Studios in 1932. During his career, he received over 80 awards as animation director and animator, and also created the character of Goofy. Babbitt worked as an animator or animation director on such films as *The Three Little Pigs* (1933), *Snow White and the Seven Dwarfs* (1937), *Fantasia* (1940), and *The Incredible Mr. Limpet* (1964), among others.[34]

Another veteran animator from the Fables studio working at the Audio-Cinema studio was Paul's brother John. John's animation on these early Terrytoons varies in look from scene to scene. Certain scenes are in Terry's classic drawing style, while others appear to have been heavily touched up by Frank Moser. Certain scenes even appear to have one character animated by Moser interacting with another handled by John Terry. Terry left the studio in late February 1930, after animating on the seventh Terrytoons short, *Hawaiian Pineapples* (His other cartoon credits included *Hot Turkey* (1930), *Indian Pudding* (1930), *Roman Punch* (1930)). In 1930 he was living with his wife at 189 – West 10th Street in Manhattan. His short stay at Terrytoons makes it seem likely that he was only there to do his younger brother a favor, although Larry Silverman's claim that the brothers were not getting along at this time may have something to do with it as well.[35]

Larry Silverman (1908–1995) graduated from high school in 1926 and on the same day he started working for the Carpenter-Goldman studio on Madison Avenue. Silverman worked for three days washing and opaquing cels in the production of industrial animated films for the United States Navy. He then got a job for a few days working with Burt Gillett and Tom Palmer making Mutt and Jeff cartoons. After searching for work, he returned to the same studio where John Terry had returned from an illness and was producing Krazy Kat cartoons for producers George Winkler and Charles B. Mintz. Apparently, director Bill Nolan wasn't able to keep up with the production schedule for Winkler and Mintz and had to farm some work out to John Terry. He found work from John Terry opaquing cels for six months. Silverman then went to work for the *New York Sun* as a copy boy. He attended law school for two years and then went to work for the *New York Journal* for a few months. He worked for a while for John R. McCrory and a half-day for Max Fleischer but left because he felt he couldn't do the work.

When Terry and Moser opened up their studio in Long Island City in 1929 Silverman worked for the partnership (*Hungarian Goulash* (1930), *Irish Stew* (1930), *Jumping Beans* (1930), *Salt Water Taffy* (1930), *Golf Nuts* (1930), *Pigskin Capers* (1930), *Popcorn* (1931)). By 1930, he was in charge of the inkers and painters at the Terrytoons studio that had moved to the Bronx. When Scoop Scandals Ltd., a cartoon studio in Los Angeles, offered him nearly twice what he was earning from Moser & Terry, he decided to come to California to work for the company. He returned to work for Paul Terry in the late 1930s and remained with the studio until about 1950, later returning in 1956.[36]

George Gordon (1906–1986), along with his older brother Daniel Gordon, pursued a career in architecture. George became trained as an architectural draftsman while his brother Dan pursued a career as an architectural designer. After the stock market crashed in 1929, George and his brother Dan could not find architectural work. George moved into a career in animation in 1930 and began working for Paul Terry and Frank Moser at their studio. George started as a painter and inker but lasted in that position for only about half-a-week because his hand was too shaky. He was moved into the camera department and worked photographing the cartoons. As he had difficulties in the department, he remained in that position for about a week. He then began inbetweening animation for Frank Moser for about six weeks. He was then promoted to the position of animator in 1931 despite his lack of training because Terry was desperate for skilled film cartoonists.[37]

Cyrus Young (1900–1964) undertook artistic training at the National Art Academy and Art Students League in New York. He

Chapter 13 • Sweat Equity is the Best Start-up Capital

Fig. 13.3 – Film processing department (c. 1930–1932).

was employed with the art department at the American Tobacco Company based in Honolulu, Hawaii where he designed posters, calendars, newspaper advertisements, and animated movie intermission trailers. He moved to New York City where in 1924 he became employed for John Randolph Bray. At Bray he learned the use of animation cels from David Hand. He was also with Dr. A. Carpenter at the Annapolis Naval Academy assisting in technical animation for teaching purposes in 1924. From 1926 to 1928 Young worked on medical animation for the Tuberculosis Society of America under Dr. Teasdale and Dr. Sheehan. He was employed as an animator for Fleischer, Vitaphone, and Eastman Kodak Co., and was with RKO on a feature picture.[38]

Thomas Bonfiglio (1909–1984), who later changed his surname to Goodson, attended the Night School of Art at Cooper Union, New York City, 1927–1930, where he won a prize for freehand drawing, fourth year class, May 1930. He joined the studio in 1930 with little or no animation experience and spent a year there before moving to work for the Fleischer Studios.[39] Thomas Byrne (1905–1982) had started as an animator at the Pat Sullivan Studio in the 1920s and was working on the Felix the Cat series for Sullivan in 1925 eventually leaving Sullivan around 1929 to work for Terry and Moser.[40] Frank Patrick Little (1907–1997) attended the Art Students League before working for a brief period of time as a commercial artist with his father. In 1930 he started working for Paul Terry and Frank Moser at the Audio-Cinema facilities until 1931. At the Audio-Cinema studio he animated the Dr. Seuss cartoon 'Neath the Bababa Tree (June 1931) for Warner Bros.[41]

Paul Sommer (1912–2011), who worked in animation for a number of production studios including Terrytoons, MGM, Columbia, Walter Lantz, Swift-Chaplin, TV

129

Fig. 13.4 – Paul Terry (c. 1936).

Spots, Ray Patin, Song Ads, Hanna-Barbera Productions, Pantomime, Bakshi-Krantz, DePatie-Freleng and Filmation Associates, began his career at the age of 18 for Terry and Moser at the Edison studio, located in the Bronx, in the summer of 1930. He was inspired to apply after watching Terry's *Aesop's Fables* cartoons as a kid.[42] He started as a cel painter (opaquer) then worked as a cameraman for the studio for a short period. He advanced to the role as an inker and then inbetweener (*Dancing Mice* (aka *Club Sandwich*) (January 25, 1931)). By 1934, he was still inbetweening for Terrytoons and later moved into animating that year.[43]

Isidore Klein (1897–1986) was the most experienced animation artist on staff who had not worked at the Fables studio although his time at the Moser & Terry studio was brief. He studied at the Sara A. Fawcett Drawing School (Newark, New Jersey) (re-named Fawcett School of Industrial Arts), National Academy of Design and the Art Students League. I. Klein, also his pen name, started cartooning at age 15. He undertook duties as animator and story man for William Randolph Hearst's International Film Service first as a tracer in early 1918 (likely was there as early as 1916 working there until 1918) (becoming a full-fledged animator after only a few months) animating and doing story work on a number of series starring a variety of cartoon and comic strip characters (Judge Rummy, Katzenjammer Kids, Krazy Kat, Happy Hooligan, Silk Hat Harry), later after IFS closed down, performing similar duties at the Barré-Bowers studio (Mutt and Jeff), 1918-1925.

In 1925, he left animation to concentrate on illustrating cartoons for magazines. He was an illustrator of cartoon books and a contributor of gag cartoons to the *New Yorker* beginning in 1925, its first year of publication, and contributed over 250 cartoons to the publication over the next 10 years. He also illustrated cartoons for *New Masses, Collier's, Judge, Life* (*Miss Fiditch* series, 1928), *Saturday Evening Post*, and *College Humor*. He returned to animation in 1930 working for Ted Eshbaugh as an inbetweener. In 1931 he started working briefly as an animator at the Terrytoons studio with cartoons produced at the Audio-Cinema facilities in the Bronx (*The Explorer* (1931)). He remained at the studio until 1934 before moving to work for Van Beuren. He returned to Terrytoons in 1940 and became a member of the story department.[44]

John Conrad "Connie" Rasinski (1907–1965) and his brother Joe (1905–1984) who would later join Terrytoons as a cameraman were raised in Connecticut. Both were forced to leave Torrington High School to find jobs as machinists at the Hendey Machine Company in Torrington. Connie began studying under Norman Rockwell at the Phoenix Art Institute in New York. Upon the advice of Rockwell, he decided to pursue a career in cartooning. He undertook newspaper work in Waterbury, Connecticut and then devoted time to freelancing work for the Bell Publishing Company along with a number of humorous publications. He was noted for his newspaper political cartoons and caricatures of local politicians.

In 1930 Connie found employment at Terrytoons and began working as an inker/opaquer and then received his first animation duties as an inbetweener under Frank

Chapter 13 • Sweat Equity is the Best Start-up Capital

Fig. 13.5 – Left to right: Philip Scheib, Frank Moser, and Paul Terry.

Moser on two scenes in *Pigskin Capers* released on December 28, 1930. He slowly began to work his way through all stages of animated cartoon work. He worked as an assistant animator under Moser on the next short released *Popcorn* (January 11, 1931), as well as on *Dancing Mice* (January 25, 1931), *Razzberries* (February 8, 1931), *Go West Big Boy* (February 22, 1931) and *Quack Quack* (March 8, 1931). He worked as an assistant animator under Bill Tytla on *Clowning* (April 5, 1931) and *Sing Sing Song* (April 19, 1931) before working alone as an animator on *The Fireman's Bride* (May 3, 1931). While he later worked as an assistant under Moser again on *A Day To Live* (May 31, 1931), and *Blues* (June 28, 1931) (working as an animator between these two shorts on *2000 B.C.* (June 14, 1931)), by the next short *By The Sea* (July 12, 1931) he had gained full animator's status. Rasinski's expressive and energetic animation quickly drew attention from Paul Terry and his fellow animators and he would spend his entire career at the studio.[45]

Another young artist that was employed for Terry, although briefly, was Frank Tashlin (1913–1972). After dropping out of high school in New Jersey at age 13, Tashlin moved from job to job. In 1930, he started working for Paul Terry as a cartoonist on the cartoons starring Farmer Al Falfa, then worked briefly for Amadee J. Van Beuren, but he was just as much a wanderer in his animation career as he had been as a teenager. Tashlin joined Leon Schlesinger's cartoon studio at Warner Bros. as an animator in 1933, where he was noted as a speedy animator. Tashlin moved on from animation in 1946 to become a gag writer for the Marx Brothers, Lucille Ball, and others, and as a screenwriter for stars such as Bob Hope (*The Lemon Drop Kid* (1951)) and Red Skelton. His live-action films still echo elements of his animation background. Tashlin peppers them with unlikely sight gags, breakneck pacing, and unexpected plot twists. His films include *The*

131

TERRYTOONS: The Story of Paul Terry and His Classic Cartoon Factory

Girl Can't Help It (1956), with its satirical look at early rock and roll, the Dean Martin and Jerry Lewis film *Hollywood or Bust* (1956), *Will Success Spoil Rock Hunter?* (1957), starring actress and Playboy model Jayne Mansfield, and six of Jerry Lewis' early solo films (*Rock-A-Bye Baby*, *The Geisha Boy*, *Cinderfella*, *It's Only Money*, *Who's Minding the Store?*, and *The Disorderly Orderly*).[46]

The total number of staff employed by Terry and Moser during the first years of the studio was somewhere between 30 and 40 people. The animation department consisted of animators and inbetweeners, but no assistants. The animators cleaned up their own extremes, and just left the inbetweens. Depending on the scene you might have one inbetween or seven inbetweens. Moser would do the character layouts. There were no background layouts. There was no background department. Rather, each animator would do his own backgrounds. The studio was unusual in that character layouts were given to the animators with no indication of the backgrounds, only a rough sketch of the background at times.[47] There were no storyboards for the animators to work from. Rather Moser would assign one scene at a time for each animator to animate.

Terry would close himself up for a few days and write the stories with musician Philip A. Scheib (1894–1969). Scheib would write the music, an original score, for each cartoon. As a young man Scheib went to Germany to study music and graduated from the University of Berlin in Germany where he studied piano, violin, composition, and conducting. He completed a four-year musical course at the Stern Conservatory of Music in Berlin and graduated with an honorary diploma and a degree of pedagogy in 1914. He toured as conductor with the "Chocolate Soldier" company and a musical company sent out by the Thomas A. Edison Company during World War I. After the tour, he found work as a violinist and assistant conductor at the Strand theater.[48]

For over 10 years he was a composer and musical director for a Broadway chain of theaters, with headquarters at the Adelphi Theater, and for musical comedies and vaudeville. With the advent of motion pictures having soundtracks came the closing of theaters and the disbanding of theater orchestras, Scheib became the musical director for Audio-Cinema and producer-director David W. Griffith. Scheib wrote the original musical score for D. W. Griffith's motion picture *The Struggle* (1931).[49] In 1929, he joined the Terrytoons animation studio unit working at Audio-Cinema.[50] From the very first animated short, all the music was written before the cartoon went into production. Paul claimed he was the one of the first to prerecord the sound.[51] The orchestra used was somewhere between 12 and 15 men, depending on what was required.[52]

Through the use of original music, Terry and Moser avoided paying out on any music royalties and related fees. *Home on the Range* was the only piece of music the studio was ever sued for using. Terry was sued by the Southern Music Co. and paid them for the use of the music only to find out that they did not own it. To Terry's chagrin, the company did not return the money.[53] Another reason Terry preferred his studio to create its own music was because if they used a popular song in their cartoon, by the time the animated cartoon was produced and exhibited, many months later, the popular piece of music was no longer on the charts and a top selling song.[54] At one point Terry had contemplated using the nonsense song *Three Little Fishes* (1939) by *The Smoothies* in his cartoons but eventually chose not to.[55]

While Terry concentrated on writing the stories, Moser was in charge of the animation. Moser was a prolific animator and he could on average animate half the animated cartoon himself. A stock set of backgrounds were kept locked away in an archive which were reused. With Moser doing a large share of the animation, the studio reusing background art, and Scheib writing original music, production costs were kept down.[56] Each Terrytoon short took three weeks to animate, and was released 10 weeks later. Unfortunately, Terry's practice of making a soundtrack first and then animating to fit the sound denied the artists the chance either to revise their original thoughts or to develop scenes, and the predictable results left animators like Art Babbitt increasingly disappointed.

On February 8, 1930, *Motion Picture News* reported that

Chapter 13 • Sweat Equity is the Best Start-up Capital

Fig. 13.6 – Left to right: Philip Scheib, Paul Terry, and Frank Moser.

Educational would distribute "Terry-Toons", a series of sound cartoons produced at Audio-Cinema's Long Island facility with one short being released each alternate week. The first cartoon announced was *Caviar* to be released February 23.[57] The review of the first entry in the series by *Motion Picture News* was positive: "If the balance of these subjects measure up to the standards of this one, Educational has a real bet in this new series of Paul Terry cartoons".[58] The reviewer for *Variety* was a little less enthusiastic and noted: "Average cartoon comedy material in the new Terrytoons series. Opening is novel with silhouette effect of musicians playing apparently for skaters".[59]

While the animation and visual aesthetics of the cartoons were generally very good, which should not come as a surprise considering the studio could brag about employing artists like Tytla, Moser, Horvath, and later Davis, the cartoon shorts in the early 1930s suffered from a lack of originality in the storylines. Time and again Terry resorted to his same bag of tricks – humor and characters that carried him successfully during his years at Fables. The reviewer for *Scotch Highball*, released November 16, 1930, wrote:

> Nothing to make it stand up or even reach par. Two years ago it might have been good, but all the tricks used have been seen before, so it's no go for the present day showing. To make it worse, there's a song which serves to spoil any illusion created.[60]

Although there were notable exceptions ("Cartoon of above average merit with many novel angles and considerably more action than most"[61] (*Variety*); "Another topnotcher in Paul Terry's series of musical cartoons. It's speedy and catchy and will click anywhere"[62] (*Motion Picture News*) – *Hawaiian Pineapples* (May 4, 1930)), the majority the reviews criticized the cartoon shorts for their insufficient humor, lack of originality and plodding action ("Far from quality that might be expected from cartoons" (*Hungarian Goulash* (June 15, 1930)); "Dozen snickers and two or three laughs from good but familiar material"[63] (*Monkey Meat* (August 10, 1930)); "One or two minor laughs" (*Fried Chicken* (October 19, 1930));[64] "Disjointed story ... Only a filler for minor programs" (*Blues* (June 28, 1931));[65] "Usual animal gyrations, but not enough for laughs and not in action either"[66] (*Spanish Onions* (March 23, 1930)). In reviewing *Roman Punch* (April 20, 1930), the *Variety* reviewer writes: "Slight in action ... lacking in originality, same old mice love, animal athletic meet and chase".[67]

Another issue plaguing the early Terrytoons was poor sound

133

quality and uneven synchronization ("Recording isn't always clear (*Blues* (1931)); "Score okay, synchronization somewhat off (*Hungarian Goulash* (1930)). Terry eventually hired musical arranger Alexander N. Ivanoff (1886–1938) who began employment at the studio on November 23, 1931. Ivanoff was educated at the Petrograd Institute of Technology and the Imperial Conservatory of Music. He undertook work as a ballet dancer and later a ballet director with the Russian Ballet Russe immigrating to the United States in 1913 [1912]. By June 5, 1917 he was employed for a "Russian ballet studio" at 616 St. Paul Avenue, Los Angeles, California. In 1920, he was residing at 545 South Figueroa Street in Los Angeles working as a musician at a dance school. At Terrytoons, he was sound editor, synchronizer, and track mixer during the 1930s and early 1940s and greatly improved the sound quality and synchronization of the animated cartoons. He was a gifted music editor and was noted for having the ability to read with the naked eye the (optical) soundtrack recorded on the 35mm film.[68] Another complication was the antiquated animation camera which Terry was unwilling to replace. Among its problems was that it could not track or pan meaning the drawings had to slide back and forth under the camera.

The Moser & Terry studio continued producing cartoons at the Long Island studio for about 10 months when they moved to the old Edison studio in the Bronx, a large brick building at 2826 Decatur Avenue, the corner of Oliver Place and Decatur Avenue.[69] The area is a hilly location, one block away from an elevated train station, not too far from the Bronx Zoo. Under the elevated train platform was a saloon where the staff would go for lunch. If you bought beer you were given free lunch. The studio was located upstairs while on the main level was a sound stage where the live-action motion pictures were shot. Terry would also use the sound stage to record the sound for his animated cartoons.[70]

By June 1930 Coffman had taken over the Edison studio completely announcing ambitious plans to remodel the main stage (125 x 96 x 40 feet) and establish a smaller stage to be used for film scoring and recording.[71] Construction at the Edison studio occurred during the summer of 1930 with occupancy set for September 1930.[72] The move to the new studio was largely motivated by the fact that it had become too small to handle the production requirements at the Long Island facility. In a bizarre accident which highlights the cramp quarters at the Long Island studio, Coffman's head cameraman, Al Wilson, received several scalp wounds when he was struck in the head with a knife thrown by actor Roy D'Arcy during the filming of *The Gypsy Code*. The knife then ricocheted off Wilson cutting his assistant Paul Rogalli on the shoulder.[73]

On June 24, 1930, Picart Studios, for reasons unknown but possibly linked to economic issues, assigned their rights under the January 29, 1930 contract with Audio-Cinema over to the Bank of America National Association. All monies that would thereafter become due and payable to Picart were to be paid directly by Audio-Cinema to the Bank of America.[74] On October 16, 1930, the Moser & Terry partnership was formally entered into through a written contract extending the already existing partnership for 10 years. The contract respected the same terms and conditions of the Audio-Cinema agreement that was entered into in October 1929 and the parties continued business begun in August 1929.[75] The partnership agreement terms included a small $250 investment by each partner, and the option to draw $300 a week on the account of the accruing share of the net profits for the current year.[7]

After working for a year to make the operation a success, Terry and Moser declined not to take advantage of the one-year $25,000 renewal option with Audio-Cinema and inquired whether Audio-Cinema desired to renew the contract at the same price. Terry and Moser were hoping that the studio might secure another renewal for $25,000 on the fear that if they did not take advantage of the opportunity the cartoon producers would find another studio.[77] In a letter dated October 17, 1930, from Audio-Cinema to Terry and Moser, F. Lyle Goldman, Secretary, rejected Terry and Moser's request for a guarantee of $25,000 per year while adding that the company had invested very heavily into animated cartoon production with "only a slight

Chapter 13 • Sweat Equity is the Best Start-up Capital

hope of recovering our bare costs on these subjects".[78] In the end, both parties decided to work together and neither party profited from the renewal option.

With Picart Studios no longer involved in securing distribution contracts, Terry and Moser agreed to secure distribution agreements for the cartoon product, both in domestic and foreign markets. On or about November 28, 1930, a distribution contract between Educational Films and the partnership was renegotiated for the one year period beginning February 1931 whereby the partnership agreed to produce a series of 26 animated cartoons over the next year and stipulating that Educational was to receive a commission of 40 percent (United States), 50 percent (Canada), and 20 percent (International) of the gross receipts received while Picart Studios received 10 percent of the remaining balance after deducting advertising and censor fees.[79]

In November 1930, Terry and Moser agreed to have Joseph W. Coffman, President of Audio-Cinema, enter the partnership to produce the cartoons under the name Terry-Moser-Coffman.[80] Although, the addition of Coffman as a co-partner reduced both Terry and Moser's financial stake in the company, the benefits of having Coffman as a partner outweighed the loss in any control. First, Coffman would be motivated to strengthening the relationship between Moser & Terry and Audio-Cinema as he had a financial interest in both sides, even possibly securing better

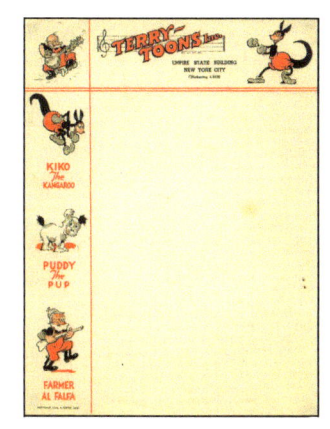

Fig. 13.7 – Terrytoons letterhead.

financial terms from Audio-Cinema in subsequent renegotiations. Second, Coffman's expertise in film sound and work as a consultant on processing motion picture film could help the partnership in improving the sound quality of their films while ensuring that the processing costs were kept at a minimum. Third, Coffman's extensive contacts in the motion picture industry could prove helpful if Audio-Cinema began to experience financial difficulties or Moser & Terry required outside assistance to meet production deadlines.

By the end of 1930, Terry began to explore foreign markets for their cartoon product. In producing for the foreign markets Terry would rely on pantomime and humor found in silent films in order to carry most of the cartoon content to foreign countries as dubbing in foreign languages was cost-prohibitive at the time.[81] In a letter dated December 8, 1930 from J. C. Barnstyn on behalf of Audio-Cinema, to Terry, Moser, and Coffman, a duplicate of which was signed by all parties, the threesome agreed to handle the distribution and sale of the second series of 26 Terrytoons for the foreign market which included the entire world, exclusive of the United States of America and Canada. Terry, Moser and Coffman were to receive 20 percent of the gross receipts and agreed to remit 80 percent of the said gross receipts back to Audio-Cinema. Terry, Moser and Coffman guaranteed that the gross sales would be a minimum of $5,000 and promised to remit to Audio-Cinema any shortfalls in gross sales.

By guaranteeing gross sales, Terry, Moser and Coffman were confident that the foreign market would generate at least $5,000 in gross sales. Further to the correspondence, Audio-Cinema agreed to deliver one negative and whatever positive prints the cartoon producers required at the laboratory price. Audio-Cinema also agreed to deliver whatever posters the domestic distributor may be able to furnish at a price of cost plus 10 percent. Finally, Terry, Moser and Coffman were allowed to grant distribution rights for each specific territory for a period of five years from the date of delivery of each subject to such territory.[82] This agreement was the first step in establishing the studio's presence overseas. The foreign market would provide significant revenues for Terry over the next three decades.

In 1931, the motion picture industry struggled through the effects of the Depression as "theaters were beginning to sharply feel the sting of nationwide economic

135

misfortune".[83] Many theatrical managers lowered their admission prices at the beginning of the year to attract admissions. A shortage of film stock and dual billing caused a scarcity of films. During the summer there was a significant drop in box office grosses resulting in many theaters being forced to close.[84] Bankers began to demand collateral for motion picture production. The Hays organization found that attendance had dropped by 40 percent by year end making 1931 the worst year financially in the history of motion pictures.[85]

By 1931, Audio-Cinema was experiencing significant financial problems despite the best efforts of their comptroller William Weiss. Bill Weiss (1907–2001) started his career with Wolf & Berger, a chain of theaters in Philadelphia, in various capacities over a six-year period before becoming home office representative for Universal Pictures Corporation. While with Universal Pictures he represented them in the field and this work entailed checking their contracts in their various branches. He was educated at the University of Pennsylvania (Wharton School of Finance and Commerce) earning a B.S. in economics in 1929 with a thesis on the motion picture industry titled "Accounting and Auditing Phases of the Motion Picture Industry". During his studies, Weiss had studied economics, finance, and law. His years in the theatrical business helped him in his source material for his thesis. Weiss interviewed company treasurers from the various film distributors and along the way became good friends with many of the exchange bookers. Upon graduation in 1929, he started working as a comptroller for Audio-Cinema Inc. located in Long Island City.[86]

In 1931, Audio-Cinema was quite successful in industrial-type shorts and medical films, but began to experience financial problems when moving into feature length live-action motion pictures.[87] The company produced two major feature-length theatrical sound productions: *I Pagliacci* (1931) and *The Struggle* (1931), both films failing miserably at the box office. *I Pagliacci*, directed by Coffman beginning March 1930, was the first feature length opera. The film, 80 minutes in length and all in Italian, was performed by the San Carlo Grand Opera Company (150 members) and the San Carlo Symphony orchestra (75 members) and premiered in New York at the Central Park Theatre on February 20, 1931.[88]

While ticket prices for premiere seats went as high as $5.50 ($80-$90 in current dollars), there was little box office interest in the musical production and plans to produce Gioachino Antonio Rossini's 4-act opera *William Tell* never materialized.[89] *I Pagliacci* starring Fortune Gallo was also received poorly by the critics. The film critic for *Time* magazine noted: "It is a courageous piece of pioneering and reveals a fact many producers had guessed but none had proved: grand opera is never likely to be successful cinema".[90] Similarly, *The Struggle*, the only sound film directed by D. W. Griffith, "was laughed off the screen".[91] Part of the problem with the film lay in the uneven script, largely the product of D. W. Griffith's habit of each morning re-writing what he was going to shoot during the day. The end result was not just problems with the story but increased production costs.[92] Griffith ended up borrowing in excess of $200,000 in order to finance a negative that cost around $300,000 and would return only about $100,000.[93]

Another financial obstacle was that Audio-Cinema was under license from Western Electric to use their sound and had reached a maximum license fee which they were unable to renegotiate.[94] According to Weiss, Audio-Cinema was losing money on the cartoon production because they were paying Western Electric both for sound recording and for clearing the use of the music through their subsidiary, Electrical Research Products Inc. (ERPI), in the range of $3,000 per cartoon.[95] ERPI was a major name in the design, improvement, sale, and service of sound equipment during the pioneering years of sound motion picture and was a subsidiary of the Western Electric Company and conducted and coordinated much of the research into sound on film and sound on disc on behalf of Western Electric and the Bell Telephone System.[96] Weiss noted that Audio-Cinema was basically a company of engineers, sound engineers and consultants for all the major companies including Eastman Kodak, Consolidated Film and Bell Telephone Labs. "And they made their money in engineering and wasted it in film production."[97]

Evidently, in September 1931

Chapter 13 • Sweat Equity is the Best Start-up Capital

Fig. 13.8 – Moser & Terry studio group, 1932 (left to right). Back Row: (unknown), Frank Moser, Jerry Shields, Connie Rasinski, (unknown), Jose Carreon, Bill Tytla, Renee McLaughlin, Ralph Pearson, Ed Cohen (King), Ted Waldeyer. Front Row: Art Babbitt, (unknown), Charles Sarka, (unknown).

Terry and Moser became concerned about revenues received and to be expected from the production of the Terrytoons shorts. A statement of "Returns to be Expected on 'Terrytoons'" was drafted on September 24, 1931 indicating that Moser & Terry was expected to generate $60,000 in revenues for production on Series I and Series II.[98] An examination of the Audio-Cinema Inc. financial statements for the Terrytoons produced during the period from March 1, 1930 to September 30, 1931 (Series I: March 1, 1930 – February 22, 1931; Series II: February 22, 1931 – September 30, 1931), a period covering the production of 43 shorts, by Patterson & Ridgway, certified public accountants, found that for Series I Moser and Terry and Audio-Cinema, Inc. shared equally (50 percent) a net profit of $33,484.01. Furthermore, Moser and Terry drew $34,094.70 in salaries from Series I. In addition, the "estimated additional income" (based on the fact that Educational will gross $13,000 per picture) generated a net profit of $28,489.30 to be shared equally between Moser & Terry and Audio-Cinema, Inc.

With respect to Series II, Moser & Terry drew $8,339.74 in salaries from foreign income, a further $28,303.79 in salaries from the estimated additional income, and a net profit of $21,660.81 to be shared equally between Moser & Terry and Audio-Cinema, Inc. In short, one does not have to be a mathematical genius to realize that the Terrytoons shorts were generating substantial revenues for both Audio-Cinema and Moser & Terry. Therefore, Weiss's statements that Audio-Cinema was losing money on cartoon production cannot be verified as the financial statements reveal a significant net profit.

Further, Weiss's statements that sound recording and fees for clearing the use of the music through Western Electric's subsidiary accounted for $3,000 per cartoon short cannot be confirmed. For Series I, the production costs for the musical director and musicians were $13,001.55, royalties on foreign income was $8,565, music fees on foreign income was $2,129.09, royalties for United States and Canada was $14,875, and copyright music fees was

$875.69 for a total of $39,446.33 or $1,517.17 per short, about half the figure quoted by Weiss.[99]

Therefore, based on the financial statements, the Moser & Terry division of Audio-Cinema's film production was operating at a profit. Accordingly, both parties' desire in 1931 to continue the business relationship without the necessity of addressing the $25,000 option is understandable. Educational Pictures was eager to continue the relationship with Moser & Terry. On May 19, 1931, with profits rolling in for all parties, Educational Pictures wrote a letter to Paul requesting whether Educational would increase their existing contract from 26 to 39 Terrytoons thereby adding 13 cartoons to their existing contract.[100] This extension was negotiated by Paul Terry who discussed the matter directly with Hammons.[101]

Meanwhile, Audio-Cinema was experiencing continuing financial problems as a result of their involvement in full-length live-action film production.[102] Both Moser and Terry agreed to enter a studio rental arrangement with the production company as a means to distance themselves from the studio's financial problems and continue operations.[103] With financial problems for Audio-Cinema Inc. continuing to mount, the company was meeting production deadlines for the distribution of shorts by Educational Films by borrowing a total of $134,911.34 during 1931 from Consolidated Film Industries.[104]

By September 24, 1931, $21,023.60 was still outstanding on the account.[105] A statement of "Pressing Accounts" revealed that over $18,000 was still outstanding by September 24, 1931, most of the accounts related to Audio-Cinema's motion picture production costs and studio overhead, although just over $3,200 was due and owing to Moser & Terry.[106] The key player in negotiating these series of loans was Coffman who had a lengthy and trusted relationship with Consolidated Film Industries. In an agreement dated September 28, 1931, Coffman negotiated another loan between Consolidated Film Industries and Audio-Cinema Inc. in the amount of $20,000, with Coffman personally guaranteeing payment of the loan on behalf of Audio-Cinema.[107] The loan helped further production at the studio for a short duration but with costs continuing to mount the end was near. Coffman remained a partner for about a year but with the studio troubles continuing, terminated his relationship with Paul Terry and Frank Moser in late 1931.[108] In July 1931, Terry and Moser renegotiated a distribution contract with Educational Films Corporation whereby Educational was to receive a 50 percent commission on gross rentals.[109] This arrangement was amended in December 1931 whereby Educational Films received 40 percent for distribution commission instead of 50 percent, and 35 percent of the net profits.[110]

With Audio-Cinema nearing bankruptcy and creditors approaching Audio demanding payment, Terry visited a trusted friend, Ben Goetz, and both decided it was best that Terry and his partner terminate the business relationship.[111] In early 1932, Terry negotiated an arrangement to produce in Harlem at the new studio address of 203 West 146th Street, New York City.[112] The rental space occupied was owned or previously rented by Consolidated Film, likely arranged through Terry's relationship with Coffman.[113]

The Moser & Terry relationship with Audio-Cinema was apparently quite lucrative for the partnership but Terry and Moser were well aware of the financial problems Audio-Cinema was having, information cycled back to them through Audio's comptroller Weiss and friend Goetz.[114] As Weiss would later declare, "When the sheriff moved in on Audio-Cinema, Terry and Moser moved out". Finally, when Audio-Cinema failed to make payments on the Western Electric sound royalties on the films they produced, Audio-Cinema was reorganized. The Eastern Services Studio, Inc. was organized by Audio-Cinema as a subsidiary to operate the studio and supply Western Electric sound service to the trade.[115] Terry and Moser offered Scheib and Weiss the opportunity to join them at Terrytoons, an offer both gladly accepted. Scheib took over as the composer for the studio while Weiss started as the company's auditor.[116]

Chapter 13 • Sweat Equity is the Best Start-up Capital

Notes

1. "Paul H. Terry – Defendant – Direct", *Case on Appeal from Judgment*, 515.

2. "Frank H. Moser – Plaintiff – Direct", *Case on Appeal from Judgment*, 108.

3. Head of Carpenter-Goldman Laboratories was Frank Lyle Goldman. Goldman would spend a good part of his career in animation at the Jam Handy organization in Detroit, Michigan as manager of the animation department and special effects. "Goldman, Frank Lyle", *Who's Who in the Midwest, 1976–1977*, 15th edition (Chicago: Marquis Who's Who, Inc., 1976), 260.

4. "Coffman, Joe W.", in *Who's Who in America*, volume 27, 1952–1953 (Chicago, Illinois: The A.N. Marquis Company, 1952), 476; Joe W. Coffman, "The Motion Picture in Science", *Society of Motion Picture Engineers, Transactions*, volume 11, 25 April 1927, 208–210; Joe W. Coffman, "Art and Science in Sound Film Production", *Society of Motion Picture Engineers, Journal* (Easton) 14 (1930): 172–179.

5. "Frank H. Moser – Plaintiff – Direct", *Case on Appeal from Judgment*, 109; Terry, interview, 20 December 1969, 49, 81.

6. Letter from Louis Jacobson, President of Picart Studios, Inc. to Joseph Coffman, Audio-Cinema Inc., 22 November 1929, Paul Terry Papers.

7. Memorandum of Agreement between Joe W. Coffman and Louis Jacobson, 29 January 1930, Paul Terry Papers.

8. Clause 3, "Memorandum of Agreement between Consolidated Film Industries, Inc. ("Consolidated") and Audio-Cinema, Inc. ("Producer") and Joe W. Coffman and F. Lyle Goldman ("Individuals")", 18 September 1931, Paul Terry Papers.

9. "Earle W. Hammons – Defendant – Direct", *Case on Appeal from Judgment*, 333.

10. "Hammons, E.W.", *The 1944–45 Motion Picture Almanac*, 164.

11. "Hammons, Earle Wooldridge", *Who Was Who in America*, vol. I, 1897–1942, 514; "Hammons, Earle Wooldridge", *Who Was Who in America*, vol. IV, 1961–1968, 401; "Hammons, Earle Wooldridge", *Who's Who in America*, volume 27, 1952–1953, 1026.

12. "George Skinner Dies; Film Company Head", *New York Times*, 22 December 1935, p. N11; "George F. Skinner", *Variety*, 25 December 1935, 55.

13. Obituaries: "Earle Hammons, Film Pioneer, 75", *New York Times*, 2 August 1962, p. 25: 3; "Earle W. Hammons", *Variety*, 8 August 1962, 63.

14. "Educational Pictures, Inc.", in *Slide, The American Film Industry*, 108; "Educational Enthusiastics", *Moving Picture World* 85, 26 March 1927, 384.

15. Canemaker, *Vladimir Tytla: Master Animator*.

16. "Satan-That Chap in Fantasia – Made By Former Yonkers Man", *Herald Statesman* (Yonkers, NY), 6 December 1940, p. 11.

17. Ibid.

18. Robert C. Goldston, *The Great Depression; The United States in the Thirties* (Indianapolis, IN: Bobbs-Merrill, 1968), 39–40.

19. Marchionni, "Paul Terry, At 82, Still Calls the Toon", 28. According to family sources, Paul and Irma had taken the walk together and had stopped near the Grand General National Memorial at 12th Avenue and W. 123rd Street. They both walked over to the banks of the Hudson River. Paul reached into his pocket and pulled out a dime. He remarked: "Well Irma, you know there is enough to buy us each an apple tonight". Irma responded: "Paul, throw it in the river because if you are going to be broke, you might as well be flat broke" (Leahy and Lazar, interview, 3).

20. The Paul Terry Papers contain a number of financial and banking records detailing Terry's investments in various financial instruments.

21. At the time of publication, the general scholarly consensus is that "Sarka" refers to Charles Nicholas Sarka (1879–1960), painter and illustrator.

22. First name unknown.

23. Production information on the first 47 Terry-Toon cartoons is found in the Paul Terry Collection, a 2 box collection at the Film Study Center, Museum of Modern Art, New York City. The collection features 47 sketchbooks with each book featuring scene drawings and artists assigned to animate each scene for each of the first 47 cartoons produced by the partnership. Accompanying the sketchbooks is "Schedule A" listing the sketchbook number, and title, production dates and contents (characters, synopsis) for each sketchbook.

24. There is a general agreement among historians that the "Golden Age" began with the advent of sound production, about 1928–1929. However, the end of the "Golden Age" period for animated cartoons is a bit more controversial. While the general consensus among historians is that the "Golden Age" period ended when theatrical cartoons were slowly losing popularity with the growth in television cartoons, there is no agreement as to an exact date when this occurred. For the purposes of this monograph, the author will follow the time period accepted by noted animation historian J. Michael Barrier who has established himself as one of the premier scholars on the "Golden Age" period in animation. Barrier's "Golden Age" time period is from 1928 to 1966 (Barrier, *Hollywood Cartoons*, xi).

25. Tom Sito, "'So What Was It Like?' The Other Side of Animation's Golden Age", *Animation World Magazine* 1, no. 4 (July 1996): 37–41.

26. "Animated Cartoon Prod. Is Now The Big Coin for Sketch Artists", *Variety* 119, no. 9, 12 February 1935, 2:4.

27. "Wanted – 5,000 Cartoonists; No Kiddin'", *Variety* 115, no. 2, 26 June 1934, 1:2, 51:5.

28. ""Mickey Mouse" is Eight Years Old: Disney's Squeaky Star Played to 468,000,000 in 1935", *Literary Digest* 122, 3 October 1936, 18.

29. William Monroe Weiss, interview by Harvey Deneroff, New Rochelle, New York, 15 June 1970. John Canemaker Animation Collection, Fales Library, Elmer Holmes Bobst Li-

139

brary, New York University, New York City, 8c.

30. Terry, interview, 13 June 1970, 117.

31. See generally Barrier, *Hollywood Cartoons*.

32. Douglas W. Churchill, "Hollywood Turns Back The Clock", *The New York Times*, 15 August 1937, p. 141.

33. Paul Sommer, interview by Milton Gray, 30 March 1977, North Hollywood, California, J. Michael Barrier collection, 17.

34. John Canemaker, "Art Babbitt: The Animator as Firebrand", *Millimeter* (September 1975): 7–10; John Canemaker, "Art Babbitt", *Cartoonist Profiles* (December 1979): 8–13; Charles Solomon, "Artist Still Gives Life to His Work", *Los Angeles Times*, 15 February 1985, p. L18; Klaus Strzyz, "Art Babbitt Interview", *Comics Journal* (March 1988): 77–87. Obituaries: Joseph McBride, "Animator Arthur Babbitt, 85, Dies", *Variety*, 6 March 1992, 8; Myrna Oliver, "Arthur Babbitt, 84; Hollywood Animator", *Los Angeles Times*, 7 March 1992, p. 26; "Arthur Babbitt, 85, Artist Who Created Cartoon Characters", *New York Times*, 7 March 1992, p. 32; *Variety*, 16 March 1992, v. 346, no. 2, 75.

35. Lawrence Silverman, Interview by Milton Gray, 3 December 1977, Woodland Hills, California, J. Michael Barrier collection, 1.

36. Silverman, interview, 3 December 1977, 1–12.

37. Obituary: "George Gordon", *Variety*, 27 June 1986, 16; *Variety*, vol. 323, 2 July 1986, 78–79.

38. For more on Young see: Frank Thomas and Ollie Johnston, *Disney Animation: The Illusion of Life* (New York: Abbeville Press, 1984).

39. By 1933 he joined the Walt Disney Studio (he is listed as staff at Disney on January 1, 1933), as an assistant animator (Mickey Mouse (*The Mail Pilot* (1933), *Mickey's Mechanical Man* (1933))) but remained there briefly before returning to Brooklyn to work as a commercial artist. He later worked for Terrytoons after his military service in 1945. "Cooper Union to Graduate 354: Diplomas and Certificates to Be Presented at School's Exercises Tonight. 37 Win Scholarships Medals Also Will Be Awarded at Commencement – Col. M.C. Rorty Will Deliver Address", *New York Times*, 10 June 1930, p. 15; "RoseMary Goodson: Sketching Her Way Through Life", *South Dakota Magazine* (September/October 2001): 36–46.

40. He also worked at Fleischer Studios as an inbetweener in the early 1930s. He then moved west to California in 1932 to work at the Walt Disney studio as an assistant animator on the *Silly Symphonies* shorts. He worked as an animator for the Harman-Ising studio, 1934–1935 before returning to Disney to work on the *Silly Symphonies* cartoons as animator (*Woodland Café* (1937)). He worked alongside Bill Hanna and Joseph Barbera at MGM before the two left to start their own studio. From the mid-1960s to the early 1970s he was working as an animator for Walter Lantz Productions until his retirement (Stacey Byrne-Gibbs, correspondence to author, 7 September 2010).

41. His other animation credits included the Van Beuren studio (1932–1934), Loucks & Norling (1935–1936), Terrytoons (1937–1943), and Famous Studios (1943–1945). He undertook technical animation work at Cineffects studio in the mid-1950s and then moved to work at the Fletcher-Smith studio in 1957 doing television commercials. From 1957–1970 he worked as an animator on technical animation at the Signal Corps Photographic Center (Army Pictorial Center) in Astoria, Long Island. Over his career, Little became a specialist in animating the "heavy stuff" or the crowd scenes involving lots of characters. He worked for the *Brooklyn Daily Eagle* doing newspaper illustrations and gag cartoons and was a writer and comic artist for the Bernard Bailey shop, 1944–1945. He was also a writer and did pencil art for the Iger (comic) shop, 1943–1958. He also illustrated record jackets for Lincoln Records, Treasure Records, and Willada Records from 1956[59]–1963. Frank Little's obituary was published in ASIFA's the *Peg-Board* (October 1997).

42. Sommer, interview, 30 March 1977, 14.

43. "In Memoriam". *The Peg-Board*, vol. 40, no. 7 (July 2011), p. 14; Sommer, interview, 30 March 1977, 13–14.

44. *Who's Who in American Jewry. Incorporating The Directory of American Jewish Institutions*, 1980 edition (Los Angeles: Standard Who's Who, 1980); I. J. Carmin Karpman, ed., *Who's Who in World Jewry. A Biographical Dictionary of Outstanding Jews* (Tel-Aviv, Israel: Olive Books of Israel, 1978); Dorothy B. Gilbert, ed., *Who's Who in American Art* (New York: R.R. Bowker, 1959); Horn, *The World Encyclopedia of Cartoons*; Falk, *Who Was Who in American Art*; Horn, *Contemporary Graphic Artists*, volume 3 (Detroit: Gale Research, 1988); Bill Janocha, *The National Cartoonists Society Album 1996* (Buffalo: American Color, 1996); I. Klein, "Cartooning Down Broadway", *Film Comment* XI, no. 1 (January – February 1975): 62–63; I. Klein Papers (1926–1981), Special Collections Research Center, Syracuse University Library, Syracuse, New York.

45. "J.C. Rasinski, Terrytoons Director Dies", (Obituary News), *The Standard-Star* (New Rochelle, NY), 14 October 1965, p. 2; 20th Century-Fox Film Corporation, "Experts Are Born: Connie Rasinski", *Dynamo* (Terrytoon Section), 15 April 1940, Chicago, Illinois, 8B; "J. Conrad "Connie" Rasinski", in *The National Cartoonists Society Album 1996, Fiftieth Anniversary Edition*, Bill Janocha, ed. (Buffalo, New York: National Cartoonists Society, 1996), 363.

46. Roger Garcia, *Frank Tashlin* (London: British Film Institute Publishing, 1994); Claire Johnston and Paul Willeman, *Frank Tashlin* (London: Society for Education in Film and Television, 1973); Peter Bogdanovich, "Frank Tashlin – An Interview and an Appreciation", *Film Culture*, no. 26 (Fall 1962): 21–23. "Obituaries: Frank Tashlin, 59, Movie Director: Master of Slapstick Dead – Made Jerry Lewis Films", *New York Times*, 9 May 1972, p. 44; Peter Bogdanovich, "Frank Tashlin", *New York Times*, 28 May 1972, p. D9.

47. Paul Sommer, interview, 30 March 1977, 13.

48. 20th Century-Fox Film Corporation, "Terrytoon Who's Who: Philip Scheib", *Dynamo* (Terrytoon Section), 15 April 1940, Chicago, Illinois, 4B; Elizabeth Cushman, "New Rochellean Contributes the Music for Talkie-Cartoon Feature in the Movies; Is Com-

Chapter 13 • Sweat Equity is the Best Start-up Capital

poser of Noted Ability (Our Famous Neighbors: A Series of Articles of Westchester's Outstanding Citizens, no. 149 – Philip A. Scheib)", *The Standard-Star* (New Rochelle), 16 July 1932); "Scheib, Philip A.", *International Motion Picture Almanac* 1968, ed. Charles S. Aaronson (New York: Quigley, 1967), 264. Obituaries: "Philip Scheib", *The Standard-Star* (New Rochelle, NY), 12 April 1969, p. 2; "Philip A. Scheib", *The International Musician* 67 (June 1969): 14; "Philip A. Scheib", *Variety*, vol. 254, 7 May 1969, 263.

49. "The Struggle", in *The American Film Institute Catalog. Feature Films, 1931–1940*, vol. F3, ed. Patricia King Hanson (Berkeley, California: University of California Press, 1993), 2083–2084.

50. "Philip Scheib", *The Standard-Star* (New Rochelle), 12 April 1969, 2; "Scheib, Philip A." *International Motion Picture Almanac*, 264.

51. Weiss, interview, 15 June 1970, 8c.

52. Ibid., 9c.

53. Terry, interview, 20 December 1969, 55.

54. Ibid.

55. Ibid.

56. Weiss, interview, 9c–10c.

57. "Educational to Handle Terry Sound Cartoons", *Motion Picture News*, 8 February 1930, 72.

58. "Caviar. Has Laughs", *Motion Picture News*, 22 February 1930, 41.

59. "Caviar", *Variety*, 19 February 1930, 21.

60. "Scotch Highball", *Variety*, 23 June 1931, 18.

61. "Hawaiian Pineapples", *Variety*, 28 May 1930, 21.

62. "Hawaiian Pineapples", *Motion Picture News*, 24 May 1930, 119.

63. "Monkey Meat", *Variety*, 8 April 1931, 18.

64. "Fried Chicken", *Variety*, 29 September 1931, 14.

65. "Blues", *Variety*, 30 June 1931, 15.

66. "Spanish Onions", *Variety*, 23 March [1930], 20.

67. "Roman Punch", *Variety*, 23 April 1930, 24.

68. Terry Ramsaye, ed. *International Motion Picture Almanac* (New York: Quigley Publishing, 1937), 483; 20th Century-Fox Film Corporation, "6,000 to 10,000 Separate Drawings For One Cartoon", *Dynamo* (Terrytoon Section), 15 April 1940, Chicago, Illinois, 6B. Obituaries: "A.N. Ivanoff, 63, Dies Suddenly", *The Standard-Star* (New Rochelle, N.Y.), 30 March 1942, p. 2; "Alexander Ivanoff", *Variety*, 1 April 1942, 54; "Sound Expert Dies in Storm", *New York Times*, 31 March 1942, p. 19:5.

69. Studio records indicate that while the company was located in Long Island City in August 1930, it had moved to the Bronx by October 1930. A letter dated August 8, 1930 from Breed, Abbott, Morgan to Paul Terry requested whether Terry wanted the photostat copy of his registered trademark delivered to his Larchmont home address or his business address in Long Island City. A letter dated October 17, 1930 from Terry to F. Lyle Goldman has the Audio-Cinema's Long Island City stationery address typed over with the new Bronx address indicating a recent move (The studio records and letters form part of the Paul Terry Papers collection, Fayetteville, North Carolina).

70. Sommer, interview, 30 March 1977, 13–14.

71. Koszarski, Richard, *Hollywood on the Hudson: Film and Television in New York from Griffith to Sarnoff* (New Brunswick, N.J.: Rutgers University Press, 2008), 257.

72. "Before the "Mike" in N.Y. Studios", *Motion Picture News*, 9 August 1930, 42.

73. "Two Cameramen Hurt", *Film Daily*, 10 July 1930, p. 2.

74. Assignment of Contract from Picart Studios to the Bank of America National Association, 24 June 1930, Paul Terry Papers.

75. This contract forms part of the Paul Terry Papers collection, Fayetteville, North Carolina.

76. Clauses 2 and 5 of Memorandum of Agreement between Paul H. Terry and Frank H. Moser dated 16 October 1930, New York, New York. The agreement also recognized the "Paul Terry-Toons" trademark consisted of the familiar "Paul Terry-Toons" lettering printed diagonally across a five line musical staff between a G-clef and two half notes. The trademark was applied for by Terry through his lawyer John B. Nash and issued August 5, 1930 (trademark number 273,389). See Letter from John B. Nash (Breed, Abbott & Morgan) to Paul H. Terry, 8 August 1930, Paul Terry Papers.

77. Letter from Frank H. Moser and Paul H. Terry to Audio-Cinema, Inc., 17 October 1930, Paul Terry Papers, Fayetteville, North Carolina.

78. Letter from F. Lyle Goldman, Secretary of Audio-Cinema, to Paul Terry and Frank Moser, 17 October 1930, Paul Terry Papers, Fayetteville, North Carolina.

79. Letter from Paul Terry, Frank Moser and Joe Coffman to J.C. Barnstyn, 8 December 1930, Paul Terry Papers, Fayetteville, North Carolina. Case on Appeal From Judgment, *Frank H. Moser v. Paul H. Terry, William M. Weiss, Earl W. Hammons, and Terrytoons, Inc.*, 9.

80. The business relationship between Coffman and the Moser-Terry partnership in the form of contracts and correspondence is detailed in the Paul Terry Papers. At the time of his 1970 interview Terry had much respect for Coffman as a businessman and sound expert. Terry, interview, 20 December 1969, 86.

81. Terry, interview, 20 December 1969, 65.

82. Letter from J.C. Barnstyn on behalf of Audio-Cinema to Paul Terry, Frank Moser and Joseph Coffman, 8 December 1930, Paul Terry Papers.

83. Roy Chartier, "Hard Year for Films", *Variety* 105, 29 December 1931, 12.

84. Chartier, "Hard Year for Films", 12.

85. Tom Waller, "The Year in Pictures", *Variety* 105, 29 December 1931, 4.

86. 20th Century-Fox Film Corporation, "Treasurer: William Weiss", *Dynamo* (Terrytoon Section), 15 April

141

1940, Chicago, Illinois, 4B; Terry Ramsaye, ed., *International Motion Picture Almanac, 1949–1950* (New York: Quigley, 1949), 362; Charles S. Aaronson, ed. *International Motion Picture Almanac, 1958* (New York: Quigley, 1957), 295; Richard Gertner, ed., *International Motion Picture Almanac, 1977* (New York: Quigley, 1977), 298. Obituary: "Weiss, William M.", *New York Times*, 13 November 2001, p. C19. Interviews: William Monroe Weiss, interview by Harvey Deneroff, New Rochelle, New York, 15 June 1970, John Canemaker Animation Collection, Fales Library, Elmer Holmes Bobst Library, New York University, New York City; William Monroe Weiss, interview by Wynn Hamonic, New Rochelle, New York, August 1996, Terrytoons Collection, Victoria, B.C., Canada.

87. Weiss, interview, 15 June 1970, 2c.

88. "Pagliacci", in *The American Film Institute Catalog. Feature Films, 1931–1940*, vol. F3, ed. Patricia King Hanson (Berkeley, California: University of California Press, 1993), 1608.

89. Ibid.

90. "The New Pictures", *Time*, 2 March 1931, vol. 17, issue 9, 30.

91. Roberta Hershenson, "When Griffith Filmed in Mamaroneck", *The New York Times*, 29 December 1996, p. WC1.

92. Weiss, interview, 15 June 1970, 3c.

93. Richard Schickel, *D.W. Griffith: An American Life* (New York: Simon & Schuster, 1984), 561.

94. Weiss, interview, 15 June 1970, 4c.

95. Ibid., 5c–6c.

96. Slide, *The American Film Industry*, 109.

97. Weiss, interview, 15 June 1970, 2c.

98. "Returns to be Expected on 'Terrytoons'", Audio-Cinema, Incorporated, 24 September 1931, Paul Terry Papers.

99. Calculated using the U.S. Bureau of Labor Statistics inflation data. Audio-Cinema, Incorporated, Terrytoons – Series I – 26 Reels – Released at the rate of one (1) every two (2) weeks starting March 1, 1930 (Financial Statement prepared 11 November 1931); Audio-Cinema, Incorporated, Terrytoons – Series II – 17 Reels – Released at the rate of one (1) every two (2) weeks starting February 22nd, 1931 (Financial Statement prepared 11 November 1931), prepared by Patterson and Ridgway, Paul Terry Papers, Fayetteville, North Carolina.

100. Letter from A. S. Kirkpatrick to Paul Terry, 19 May 1931, Paul Terry Papers.

101. "Frank H. Moser – Plaintiff – Direct", *Case on Appeal from Judgment*, 110–111.

102. Weiss, interview, 15 June 1970, 4c.

103. Ibid., 5c.

104. Consolidated Film Industries began as a film-processing laboratory around 1924. It was acquired by Herbert J. Yates (1880–1966), best known as the head of Republic Pictures, who began his film career by acquiring Hedwig Film Laboratories and Republic Film Laboratories in his teens. In the 1920s, Consolidated acquired two New York laboratories, Erbograph and Craftsman. Sidney Solow would become its long-time head for 33 years. Slide, *The American Film Industry*, 78.

105. Statement of Loans Account for Consolidated Film, Audio-Cinema, Inc., 24 September 1931.

106. "Pressing Accounts", Audio-Cinema, Incorporated, 24 September 1931 (68 accounts listed), Paul Terry Papers.

107. "Memorandum of Agreement between Consolidated Film Industries, Inc. ("Consolidated") and Audio-Cinema, Inc. ("Producer") and Joe W. Coffman and F. Lyle Goldman ("Individuals")", 18 September 1931, Paul Terry Papers, Fayetteville, North Carolina.

108. Terry, interview, 14 July 1970, 127–128.

109. Memorandum of Agreement between Frank H. Moser and Paul H. Terry doing business as a partnership known as Moser and Terry ("Producer") and Educational Films Corporation of America ("Distributor"), 8 July 1931, Paul Terry Papers.

110. Letter from E.W. Hammons (Educational Film Exchanges, Inc.) to Moser & Terry, 30 December 1931, Paul Terry Papers, Fayetteville, North Carolina. Letter from E.W. Hammons (Educational Film Exchanges, Inc.) to Moser & Terry, 18 January 1932, Paul Terry Papers.

111. Terry, interview, 14 July 1970, 87.

112. Studio records from the Paul Terry Papers collection indicate that in December 1931 the studio was located in the Bronx, but by May 1932, the new studio address was 203 West 146th Street, New York City.

113. Weiss, interview, 15 June 1970, 5c.

114. Terry, interview, 14 July 1970, 87.

115. "Captain Baynes Heads Eastern Service Studios", *The Film Daily*, 15 March 1932, p. 2.

116. "Frank H. Moser – Plaintiff – Direct", *Case on Appeal from Judgment*, 121.

Chapter 14

Enduring Adversity: The Early Struggles at the Studio, 1932–1935

The move from the Bronx to 203 West 146th Street occurred very quickly, almost overnight, and the studio was at the new location before February 21, 1932.[1] Soon the studio was in full production. The films were now being synchronized at the Atlas Sound Studios in Long Island City, New York, a recording concern headed by Ben Berke.[2] Moser and Terry formed an incorporated company, designated Moser & Terry, Inc., on January 20, 1932 with both producers having an equal share and control in the company.[3] The idea to incorporate was Terry's who thought that forming a corporation would relieve them of any personal liability.[4] Terry's other objective in forming the corporate entity was to seize control of the company by majority control. Soon after the incorporation Terry began making demands to Moser that he have a controlling interest in the new company. According to Moser, Terry wanted 101 shares and proposed to Moser that he should have 99 shares. Moser was contacted by Mr. Stockton, a lawyer for Breed, Abbott & Morgan and a close friend of Terry, who informed him that corporations always work better when one person is in control and added that Paul being in charge was a good thing for the corporation.

Terry sweetened the offer by promising Moser that if he was given control that he would contact Earl Hammons and make sure that Moser got his fair share of the publicity.[5] However, after discussions with his lawyer Moser wisely refused to yield a controlling interest in the incorporated company to Terry and the frustrated Paul decided that they should then return to a partnership arrangement.[6] The corporation was then dissolved and an agreement was signed between Moser and Terry to form a partnership, Moser & Terry, on May 18, 1932[7] with the partnership agreement of October 16, 1930 being reaffirmed.[8] Terry's insistence on corporate control arose naturally from his desire to make the final decisions of the corporation regarding operations and strategic planning, including capital allocations, acquisitions and divestments, top personnel decisions, and major marketing, production, and financial decisions.

After the move to Harlem, complaints began to surface from their distributor Educational regarding the quality of the pictures. Both Terry and Moser disagreed on how to address the complaints. The consistent pattern surrounding these quarrels was that Moser would suggest a number of necessary and costly changes to improve the quality of the cartoons. Terry would then resist these changes considering them unnecessary and suggest less expensive alternative methods to improve cartoon quality. These disagreements resulted in a series of escalating incidents over the next four years that were difficult to keep private from the artists and studio staff. Eventually the constant bickering and bitter animosity between Terry and Moser caused Phil Scheib to tender his resignation on November 20, 1932. Scheib planned to resign after the completion of Terrytoons cartoon numbered T79.[9] Scheib never carried out on his promise as he was convinced by the partners to stay with the partnership.

Although Moser insisted on spending capital to make the necessary changes that would bring the cartoons up to a standard that would satisfy their distributor, he was also very tight with his money. In the opinion of some Terry staff, Moser was more of a miser with his money than Terry. Moser saved cels, he conserved pieces of paper, and he watched over the animation department to ensure there was little or no waste. A common practice in the industry was to wash cels and reuse them on later productions. However, Moser took this practice to extremes by insisting on the continual reuse of cels until they were so wrinkled and damaged they should have been discarded.[10] Sometimes the cels had scratches on them, and old ink lines.[11]

When the animators asked for a model and an instructor to improve their animation and life drawing skills, Moser (and Terry) wouldn't entertain the idea. The result was some of the animators, like Bill Tytla, hired a model themselves. Most of the lead animators were great at animating cat and mice but had difficulty animating a human figure. A few animators went to dance school to ask for a few routine steps to help them animate dance sequences. When Tytla and his fellow students were ridiculed by their co-workers for their art school approach to animation, they stopped using models to learn how to animate the human form.[12] The key difference between Terry and Moser was not with their money management practices as each producer was very frugal with their funds. Rather the difference was with the relative fear attached to the loss of their distributor Educational Pictures.

Each was fully aware that keeping their distributor happy was a key to survival in the competitive business of animated film production. Both appreciated that the most important relationship external to an animation studio was the animation production studio's business dealings with the distributor. Almost since the birth of animated cartoons, animated shorts were played prior to the exhibition of the feature length live-action film. Each major animated film production company had a contractual relationship with a distributor and major film company guaranteeing bookings for the animated shorts before each live-action film. Without this relationship, the completed shorts would only gather dust sitting on a studio shelf. In the early years of the Depression, Disney's distributor was Columbia Pictures (1930–June 1932) and United Artists (June 1932–1937).[13] Fleischer Studios' distributor was Paramount Pictures, Van Beuren Studios (1928–1936) had a contractual relationship with RKO to distribute, Walter Lantz Productions (1929–1972) hooked up with Universal Studios, and Harman-Ising Productions (1930–1933) and Leon Schlesinger Productions (1933–1944) both had Warner Bros. as their distributor. In 1934, Columbia formed its own cartoon unit under the Screen Gems brand.[14]

There were a number of problems for an animation studio head in the Golden Age to overcome in attracting, negotiating, and retaining a distribution contract. First, there were just a dozen or so major Hollywood feature film production companies that were potential suitors to distribute animated cartoon shorts during the Golden Age while the number of producers of shorts (newsreels, animated cartoons, and 20-minute short subjects) was large and competitive.[15] Second, the animated short that preceded each feature film would sometimes be passed over either for a double-billed feature or for other non-animated short subjects making the exhibition of animated shorts unnecessary.[16] Third, opinions began to form in the industry whether there was a cost-benefit in exhibiting an animated cartoon before a main feature.[17] The end result was that many producers of animated shorts had weakened bargaining positions and entered distribution contracts under less than favorable terms to keep their studios in production.

Moser admitted under oath that by 1935 there were no other companies available to distribute their product other than Educational Pictures. He feared that if they lost their contract to Educational and were also turned down by Fox, no other company would want to distribute their films.[18] If the stakes were so high for Terry, why then did he not comply with making the required changes suggested by the

Chapter 14 • Enduring Adversity

Fig. 14.1 – Paul Terry bookplate.

distributor? The relationship between the partnership, Moser & Terry, and Educational Pictures was critical to the ongoing success of the animation studio, a fact Terry later publicly acknowledged.[19] The answer may be found in Terry's relationship with Hammons. Terry had a very close and trusting relationship with Hammons for nearly 20 years.[20] Quite possibly Terry had established a business and personal association with Hammons where he felt comfortable with the status quo. Unless informed by Hammons that his contract was in jeopardy, Terry was not convinced that the changes were absolutely necessary.

Terry may have had other reasons. Generally, distributors demanded inexpensively produced shorts and, other than Disney who ran consistently over budget,[21] most studio budgets were tight and keeping costs at a minimum was a necessity. In order to satisfy his distributor, Terry produced cartoons on a tight budget, avoided innovation, and kept his product routine and predictable.[22] Exhibitors were seeking conventional formulaic cartoons because predictable cartoons obviated "the need for screening the product carefully or even thinking much about it".[23]

Despite the complaints by Educational Pictures with respect to the quality of the cartoon product, an agreement dated June 14, 1932 was entered into for one year between the distributor and Moser & Terry. The agreement was on the same terms and conditions of the December 1931 agreement in that of the gross receipts and rentals received by the Educational from the leasing, licensing and/or exhibition of the animated cartoons, the distributor would retain 40 percent for its distribution fees and 60 percent would be retained by the producer, and that the 60 percent would be retained until such time as the Distributor had recouped all its advances made. For distribution to Canada, Educational's percentage from gross rentals and receipts was 10 percent more than in the United States.[24]

Terry and Moser were responsible for overseeing the production of one animated cartoon every two weeks. After the move from the Bronx, Moser's responsibilities at the new Harlem studio remained the same. He continued as supervisor of the 28 employees in the animation department while also completing animation himself. Each animator was responsible for about 35 feet a week, or about 560 drawings (112 drawings a day based on 16 frames per foot), a heavy workload for even the most experienced of animators.[25] At the Harlem studio, Paul would continue to be a one-man story department. He would spend three to five days of the two weeks at his desk writing the stories. Terry

145

understood the importance of the story to the success of a cartoon and from 1929 to 1937 rarely trusted others with preparing story materials. Terry's opinions on the importance of stories to an animated cartoon were captured in his interview in 1969.

> If the story is good it has everything in there. If it captures the imagination of the public and the picture will be successful. Some stories are so good you couldn't spoil them if you wanted to. And some stories are so bad that you couldn't do anything with them no matter how you try. You can take the finest actors and the finest directors and if it isn't in that script you are sunk.[26]

Since Terry understood that entertaining cartoons had to feature wonderful stories and great gags, he took on the crucial job of writing humorous and engaging cartoons for his studio. He believed he was the mastermind behind all the great gags, even those jokes not originating from his pencil.

Terry followed the practice of having either he or his staff screen the cartoons live with a studio audience. If the audience laughed loudly at a gag in a cartoon then he would work the same joke in again on another short. In his office he had a gag file of hundreds of jokes he would draw upon when writing his stories.[27] Paul was also very stubborn when it came to the story content. Sometimes a director or animator would have to argue with Terry to put some of his own ideas into the animated short.[28]

Paul would also spend a day in New York City with Phil Scheib when the scorings were made. A small orchestra would be used along with a sound effects man, Max Manne, who blew, shook, squeezed, rattled, and spun a variety of noisemakers. The conductor would start and everything would be recorded on one track. The studio could have gone into the more expensive three-track system, but Paul wouldn't have anything to do with it. Director George Gordon tried to convince Paul that they needed a separate track for the vocals and another track for the music but Terry thought that the idea was too radical.[29] According to Gordon, Terry's common response to change involving increased costs was, "My way is the best, it's the cheapest way to do it".[30] As a result of the use of the one track system, Gordon was forced to go into a room where he would use an instrument called the moviola, a device that allows a film editor to view film while editing, and punch a beat out (mark the film with a grease pencil) because if he had a dog barking, the only way he would bark would be on a beat.[31]

A moviola was also used to conduct pencil tests at the studio. At the Walt Disney studio, they would shoot a test of the drawings and you looked at it and if you wanted to change something, if you had subtle moves you wanted to add or you wanted to change the approach, you were able to do that. At Moser & Terry you would do the scene, it would be inbetweened, they would photograph it, they would look at it, and that was the test. Although small changes would be made, rarely were major changes allowed.[32] Besides writing stories and overseeing the recordings, Terry completed some animation. Terry stopped animating cartoons about 1933.[33] All of the business outside of production was handled by Terry and Weiss.[34]

Although Terry and Moser operated the studio on a very tight budget, this was the norm for the business. Except for Walt Disney, nearly all of the other major studio heads adopted measures to keep very strict control on expenses. To produce an animated short is an expensive process because a significant proportion of the work is completed through time consuming manual labor involving a variety of highly skilled artists and production personnel. Animation has been described as the most labor-intensive form of Hollywood film production.[35] In the infancy of animation, animated shorts were too expensive to produce to become an economic force in the film industry. Due to their inability either to produce animated films in large quantities or to control costs of producing such films, early practitioners like Emile Cohl and Winsor McCay were gone from animation by 1921.[36] In 1936 while passing his last years in Paris, pioneer French animator Emile Cohl was forced to live off $7 a month given to him by public charity.[37]

John R. Bray streamlined the process with the creation of identical printed background scenes using a zinc etching process, added the moving components of the animated cartoon to the blank centre, thereby significantly reducing the number of skilled artists needed to complete an animated cartoon short, and applied Taylorist principles and compartmentalized the animated filmmaking process through an assembly-line type method of skilled artists specializing in various tasks thereby further reducing time and labor costs.[38] With the creation of departments each animator had more time to pursue creative work[39] while the most repetitive and rudimentary tasks could be minimized and completed by semi-skilled labor, most of whom were paid far less than skilled cartoonists.

With the invention of celluloid by both Bray and Hurd, the number of drawings was gradually reduced because celluloid allowed the animator to draw only that part of the body which moved. However, by the 1930s, with the development of sound, speech and lip movements, the number of drawings required was increased once again driving up production costs.[40] During the 1930s, the assembly-line animation process began to fully develop with the establishment of separate departments not limited to animation (i.e. story, background, inking, camera, music, sound), and this organizational system[41] was employed by all Golden Age studios and would remain virtually the same until the introduction of computer technology.[42]

Based on the number of studio bankruptcies, receiverships and closings from the birth of animation to 1930, producing animated shorts for a profit during the early years of animation was a difficult endeavor requiring strong money management practices and strict financial control. When Disney built his studio in Burbank in 1939 which covers several acres, he designed the structures so that in the event the animation business didn't work out the studio could be converted into a hospital.[43] Hearst financed and operated an animation studio at a loss simply for the publicity value he could give his syndicated comic strips.[44] By the time litigation ended in the Bray-Hurd cartoon suit in 1930, half of the dozen defendants had gone out of business in the five-year interim.[45]

At the studio of John McCrory, he didn't have a darkroom. You had to load the magazine in the washroom. McCrory's wages

Fig. 14.2– Kiko the Kangaroo theme song.

were so paltry that artists had a difficult time making ends meet. McCrory used short ends of old films so you never knew if there was something on it or not. You considered yourself lucky if there was nothing else on it after you got back from the lab.[46] During the 1930s, some studio heads like Max Fleischer and Leon Schlesinger went to extreme lengths to reduce production overhead by equipping their studios with used office furniture and kitchen tables purchased at flea markets and garage sales.[47]

At New York's Raoul Barré Studio in the 1920s, there were no curtains, rugs or heat during the winter, and animators went home when their fingers got too cold to draw.[48] In the mid-1930s, animators had a six day work week. At many studios, the hours were 9:00 a.m. to 6:00 p.m., Monday through Friday, and 9:00 a.m. to 1:00 p.m. on Saturday. If the employee had problems working on Saturdays, Max Fleischer or Walt Disney would allow the employee to work Thursdays until 11:00 p.m. to make up the time. In January 1941, Disney and most studios went to 40 hours a week in an attempt to prevent their artists from unionizing.[49]

Time clocks were standard in the animation industry. At Metro-Goldwyn-Mayer, there was an electric bell that let the artist know when he could get up from his desk for a coffee break, and also told him (15 minutes later) when to come back to work. At Hanna-Barbera Productions in the late 1970s, the time clock was out of use due to employee sabotage, but the timepiece remained in effect at the Disney studio up until *The Little Mermaid* (1989). Hanna-Barbera had "The Late Book", in which the security guard would write the employee's name if he arrived five minutes past the 8:30 a.m. check-in time; the powers that be would supposedly read it at the end of the month and meet with the employee for disciplinary purposes.[50]

Van Beuren Studios fought production costs by asking the staff for "voluntary" unpaid overtime, "which was in fact something less than voluntary".[51] At first Van Beuren provided "dollar supper money" which enabled his overtime staff to eat dinner before heading back to work in the evening but then that perk was cut out.[52] Every studio had a footage quota. In the early 1930s, as earlier noted, the footage quota at the Moser & Terry studio was 35 feet-a-week. At Schlesinger's in 1940, it was 23 feet-a-week and at Disney's it was five. When Metro-Goldwyn-Mayer went union the same year, Fred Quimby angrily raised the quota to 25 feet-a-week and kept his dreaded "footage book"; this ledger, of course, could then be used against the artist when he went in to ask for a raise.[53] At Disney's, until *The Great Mouse Detective* (1986) employees had to pitch in money to pay for coffee and bottled water, and each staff member parking their motor vehicle on the studio lot had to pay rent for a parking space.[54]

In an attempt to reduce errors, some studios used large charts that featured every animator's name. If an artist made a production error, a mark was placed next to his name and artists that had too many errors were disciplined.[55] In 1976, at the Richard Williams studio, the employer wouldn't pay the staff until Friday at 5:00 p.m., because he distrusted the staff to stay all day.[56] In the 1930s, vacation pay was non-existent and overtime was rarely paid. On *Snow White and the Seven Dwarfs* (1937), in the deadline rush to complete the film, the studio demanded three hours extra a night and the only pay was a 55 cent dinner ticket to Blackie's Steakhouse on Sunset Boulevard.[57]

The working conditions at the Walter Lantz studio at Universal during the 1930s and into the 1940s were very poor. The studio only had two or three moviolas for the animators to use and during the 1930s the studio did not have pencil tests. The only way Walter Lantz or Bill Nolan could see what the animators were doing was by manually flipping the animation. Many times they would not even look at the work before sending the animation off to the ink and paint department. The animators were trained to do it right the first time and there was no room for experimentation. If the timing was incorrect or the pan was moving too fast, there was no budget to correct the errors. Lantz did not want to spend the money to reshoot the animation. If the scene had numerous production errors, possibly the artists got to rework it. There was also no character layout to guide the animators.

Chapter 14 • Enduring Adversity

Fig. 14.3 – Patricia Terry and her dog Puddy, the inspiration and model for the cartoon character.

Similar to the production demands at Metro-Goldwyn-Mayer, Leon Schlesinger's and Van Beuren, the film footage pressures at the Lantz studio were enormous, about 25 feet-a-week. There were three locations for the Lantz studio in the 1930s, a bungalow or cottage building, the old Universal dressing rooms along the side in a brick or masonry building (the studio was located on the 2nd floor), and then a new building. In the first two locations there was no air conditioning. During the summer months, the staff would sit in the studio practically stripped down to their shorts. The studio would be hotter than heck, and the fans would be going all the time. In the wintertime, you would almost freeze with the electric heaters plugged in. When Lantz moved into the new animation building, the facility had heaters and air conditioning. However, the air conditioning didn't work and Lantz wouldn't have the system fixed.[58]

Financial problems in the film industry continued in 1932 as theaters and motion picture studios continued to either languish or go bankrupt as a result of problems borne out of the Depression and those endemic to the film industry. Some of the solutions proposed to shave down operating costs were reorganization of theaters and exchange systems, and holding down flexible film costs such as studio costs, film production costs, and salaries.[59] The year 1933 was also a dark year for the film business as bankruptcies of film interests rose sharply, both RKO and Paramount-Publix sank into receivership,[60] many theater chains reduced the salaries of their employees by 50 percent,[61] film production costs were reduced to meet the grossing possibilities of the theaters,[62] banks refused to back film productions, prices were cut at the theaters affecting about 8,000 film showings, and Warner Bros. closed some theaters rather than reduce admissions.[63] Despite the poor economic outlook, the partnership of Moser & Terry renegotiated another distribution contract with Educational Films Corporation of America for 1932–1933.[64]

In early 1932 [late 1931] Terry hired Thomas James Morrison (1908–1978) who joined the studio as an apprentice washing and cleaning animation celluloid and working the camera. Morrison would become one of Terry's most loyal employees. His cousin was the Hollywood screen actress Claire Trevor.[65] As a child, Morrison enjoyed acting in theatrical productions with ambitions of working in motion pictures and he was a child speaker in the Liberty Loans drives during the First World War that brought him accolades from the U.S. Government, the Liberty Loan Committee and the Boy Scouts of

149

America. After studying at New York University and the Damrosch Conservatory of Music,[66] he found his first job as an usher at the Rivoli Theatre in New York.[67] However, his father, Thomas John Morrison, always wanted him to be in Wall Street and arranged for him to start working in the banking industry with Sutro Brothers & Company. He was with the company just a short while before the 1929 Crash that made Morrison determined never to work in the finance and banking sector again.[68]

His father was a long-time friend of Paul Terry's, and the Morrison family lived next door to the Terry family in Larchmont. Tom Morrison Sr. was born in Ireland and immigrated to the United States when he was 18 years old. He entered the restaurant business and operated the Archambault Restaurant at 101st Street and Broadway in New York City for a number of years. He began suffering from a debilitating illness and retired from the restaurant industry in the early to mid-1920s to dabble in the construction industry. By April 1930, Tom Jr. was unemployed and living with his father (then a builder of private homes), mother (Christina), and sister (Mildred E.). Tom Morrison Sr. was also a friend of Joe Schenck, the 20th Century-Fox executive living in California. After the October 1929 stock market collapse, Tom Morrison Sr. wrote Schenck a few letters requesting work for his son but didn't receive a response. Meanwhile Paul Terry offered Tom Morrison Jr. a job at Terrytoons that his father told him he better take. With no response from Schenck, Tom Morrison decided to take Terry's job offer. Just shortly after starting work at the cartoon studio, Schenck responded with a job offer but Tom Morrison, despite his big screen aspirations, decided to stay at Terrytoons.[69]

Tom Morrison wanted to work writing cartoon scripts but there was no story department at Terrytoons at the time.[70] Paul Terry wrote all the cartoon scripts and accepted input from other Terrytoons staff. After working in the camera department, Morrison headed up the inking and painting department, 1934–1935, moved to do some inbetweening work and eventually worked briefly as an assistant animator.[71] Morrison then became production manager, a position he did not enjoy, taking care of the records and activities of the staff. He appointed the tasks to be performed, checked that the duties were being completed and controlled the flow of production.[72] After Tom's father's death on July 28, 1942,[73] Terry paid for the funeral services and all of the medical bills. As Tom's mother was struggling financially, Terry offered her a job in the camera department where she was employed by 1943 according to studio records.

One employee that allegedly was interviewed by Terry early on was Michael Maltese (1908–1981) but there is no evidence from Maltese's archival papers to support this claim.[74] If Maltese was indeed interviewed by Terry, then Paul made a serious oversight in not hiring the story writer and gag man. According to the most reliable sources, Maltese began his career at Fleischer Studios in 1935. He later joined Leon Schlesinger and had a stellar career as a writer on scripts for Warner Bros. He teamed up with Chuck Jones on such classics as *For Scent-imental Reasons* (1949), *Bully for Bugs* (1953), *Rabbit of Seville* (1950), and the classic *What's Opera, Doc?* (1957) considered by many film historians to be one of the greatest cartoons ever produced.[75]

In late 1932 Paul decided that the studio needed to improve the entertainment value of their cartoon product to pacify his distributor as to the quality of the shorts. Paul's idea was that the studio should start producing some cartoons as comic operettas and others as "musical mellerdrammers".[76] The chief figures of the latter were drawn figures of humans. The most notable of the "musical mellerdrammers" produced during the 1930s was a series of shorts starring Fanny Zilch (the Banker's Daughter), the villain Oil Can Harry, and J. Leffingwell Stronghearl – stalwart, handsome, big-chinned, Fanny's lover and constant rescuer. Most of the dialogue was sung and not spoken, typical of operas. These shorts took their cues from the same old-time music hall melodramas – still a viable genre when the early silent movie serials were made, but an object of widespread parody by the 1930s. The three cavorted through a landscape that included sawmills, railroad tracks and other staples of the old-time serials.

Chapter 14 • Enduring Adversity

The Banker's Daughter (June 25, 1933) was the first in the series. In the short, Fanny, a young, beautiful blonde girl, is kidnapped by the dastardly Oil Can Harry, a tall, moustachioed male who dressed in a top hat, vested suit, and flowing cloak. During the action the characters sang mock opera songs (Pearl is a soprano, Oil Can Harry a bass-baritone, Strongheart a tenor) while Cole Porter's *The Villain Still Pursued Her* was overheard in the score. *Film Daily* wrote a glowing review of the cartoon short:

> The opera idea combined with the burlesque meller makes this a real laugh number that will appeal to grown-ups with its cleverness and be received with delight by the kids. It is the first of a series of four. If the new technique catches on, it is liable to create a new slant in the animated field.[77]

This short was also well received by audiences and was followed by *The Oil Can Mystery* (July 9, 1933), *Fanny in the Lion's Den* (July 23, 1933), *Hypnotic Eyes* (August 11, 1933), and *Fanny's Wedding Day* (September 22 [October 6], 1933). The series was revived in 1935 (*Foiled Again*, October 14) and 1937 (*The Villain Still Pursued Her*, September 3; *The Saw Mill Mystery*, October 29).

On May 11, 1933, *Film Daily* reported that Terry and Moser had planned to produce other operetta cartoons they developed earlier that season.[78] As a result, operetta and musical cartoons began appearing more frequently in the Terrytoons releases during 1933 and 1934. In *Jealous Lover*

Fig. 14.4 – Pershing Square Building, c. 1940s.

(January 8, 1933) a tenor mouse and his girlfriend are chased across the city by a team of gangster cats when he outwits the felines to take his sweetheart home. *Robin Hood* (January 22, 1933) is a burlesque opera featuring Robin Hood and his merry men rescuing a heroine captured and imprisoned in a castle. The short received a very favorable review in the *Film Daily* where the reviewer opined that the short was "cleverly executed in all departments".[79] In *Gypsy Fiddler* (October 6, 1933), to the tune of *A Gypsy Life*, a gypsy dog wins the heart of the king's daughter and steals her from her father carrying her off on a flying carpet. In *Holland Days* (January 12, 1934), a musical cartoon involving singing cows, dairy maidens and buckets of milk set in Holland, a struggle between a farmer and the mice for control of

151

the cheese ends with the mice winning out.

Many of these operetta cartoon shorts followed a predictable story line of a male character rescuing a female from the clutches of some villain. In *The Pirate Ship* (April 30, 1933), an operetta singing sailor mouse rescues a young female mouse from a ship of pirates. In *A Mad House* (March 23, 1934), an evil mad scientist living in a house full of skeletons drinks a potion to make himself invisible and then kidnaps a young female dog character before she is rescued by her doggy boyfriend. Another innovation Terry touted in the press, likely to further convince his distributor that the studio was moving in directions to improve the quality of the shorts, was a "new technique in cartoon story development". In the *Film Daily* article, the innovation was compared to the "narratage" in William K. Howard's live-action feature *Power and the Glory* (1933) except that in the Terry short *The Three Bears* (January 26, 1934) the central character (the father bear) has a comical set-to with the narrator over the manner in which the narration is being handled.[80]

In August 1933, Mannie Davis re-joined Terry at the Harlem Studio after many years with Terry at the Fables Studio in New York City and a short time with the Van Beuren Studios.[81] Bill Weiss had been promoted to business manager. He completed all of the financial work (i.e. accounts payable, accounts receivables, payroll) for the partnership, purchased all of the supplies and materials, and handled contracts with suppliers including the agreements with the distributor Educational Films Corporation and Fox Film.[82]

While many employees considered the move from the Bronx studio as a step up, the studio location was in upper Manhattan in the heart of Harlem, a major African-American residential, cultural and business center. Some of Terry's all-White animation staff were afraid to venture out at lunchtime, and a few feared for their lives. The studio was located on some upper floors, and the back windows of the studio looked out onto a vacant parking lot between two apartment houses. The children would build bonfires against the wall of the building and then urinate on the flames. The foul-smelling smoke from the fires would cause a number of the staff to gasp for fresh air. When some of the artists yelled at the children, they were met with hostility by the parents of the kids and were told to shut up.[83]

By 1933, the effects of the Depression had caught up with Educational Films as the company had begun to experience financial problems and, as a result, the distributor negotiated a distribution arrangement with Fox Film. Effective January 30, 1933 Fox Film would take over the sale and distribution of all Educational and World Wide films by way of a sub-contract agreement between Educational Films Corporation of America and the Fox Film Corporation. Hammons was the last of the short subject producers to surrender any part of his independence. Hammons believed that the hook-up would save him a million dollars annually.[84] Later in January 1933, Educational Films closed its 36 exchanges throughout United States and Canada and, by sub-contract, appointed Fox Film as its sales agent to distribute the cartoons now known as Terry-Toons in these two countries.[85] In March 1933, the 1932 distribution contract between Moser & Terry and Educational Film Corporation of America was continued for a period of one year, with the permission being given to appoint Fox Film Corporation as its agent in the distribution of the animated shorts of the partnership.[86] The renewal contracts between Moser & Terry, Inc., and Educational Films, all were on a yearly basis expiring about July 31 of each year. The renewals were usually signed several months in advance of the termination date.

By 1933, when the Great Depression reached its nadir, some 13 to 15 million Americans were unemployed (about 27 percent of all Americans) and nearly half of the country's banks had failed.[87] When asked about whether the Depression caught up with Terrytoons, Terry was first to stress the effect of the economic downturn on Educational Films and how its fall led to his long-term relationship with Fox.

> Yes, the depression caught up with everything. And Educational Films were in trouble with the banks. So the banks forced Educational Films to release through Fox. So that threw me over into Fox's lot. And I stayed there. Educational Films moved out

Chapter 14 • Enduring Adversity

and went with some other company which didn't last. But I stayed with Fox.[88]

Despite the financial adversity, Moser and Terry reported to *Film Daily* in July 1933 that they had increased the salaries of their Terry-Toons staff by 10 percent. Terry proudly commented on the raise in pay exhorting others to follow his lead, "This entire economic situation is a Mental Condition on the part of employers. If every organization large and small would increase salaries today, the nation would experience Prosperity automatically tomorrow."[89] During the troubled economic times of the 1930s Terry appreciated the difficulty the nation's unemployed were having in locating and maintaining employment. Therefore, he made it his personal policy not only to retain all his staff, but create positions for other artists and technicians looking to enter the animation business. Terry achieved these objectives as the staff at Terrytoons during the 1930s continued to grow.

On or about June 24, 1933, Joseph Rasinski (1905–1984), the older brother of Connie, started working at Terrytoons in the camera department. He soon became head of the department (about 1934) training other cameramen, and would remain with the studio in this position until his retirement in 1971.[90] Paul Terry would later recognize him as a fine cameraman and an integral member of his animation crew.[91] Joining the staff in 1934 was Dan Noonan (1911–1982) who started as a cel painter

working for $11.50-a-week. After nearly two years at Terrytoons, he moved west and had a distinguished career at the Walt Disney studio.[92]

Harvey Eisenberg (1912–1965) worked at the Fleischer Studios as an inker and assistant animator, 1930–1931, and at the Van Beuren studio in the 1930s. By 1934 he was employed at Terrytoons as an inker at the studio. He was later promoted to work as an inbetweener at Terrytoons. Eisenberg was a fantastic draftsman, designer and calligrapher. He could draw a character and a background from any angle, no matter how difficult. On the side, he did lettering and calligraphy work for theater advertisements and promotional materials. He left Terrytoons to move to Hollywood, California and work as production designer and layout artist at Metro-Goldwyn-Mayer, 1942–1945.[93] Other animation artists at the time included Philip Santry (1911–1976), Kin Platt (1911–2003), Robinson McKee (1911–1993) and Ralph Pearson.

Kin Platt was an American writer-artist best known for penning radio comedy and animated television series, as well as children's mystery novels, for one of which he received the Mystery Writers of America Edgar Award. He additionally wrote and drew comic books (creating an early funny-animal superhero, Supermouse) and comic strips. Kin Platt's long and varied career began with the drawing of theatrical caricatures in the 1930s. His caricature of Hitler in the *Brooklyn Daily Eagle* was one

of the first anti-Hitler cartoons in U.S. newspapers. In 1934, Kin Platt began working as an opaquer at the Terrytoons animation studio.[94]

By the end of 1933, Paul's brother John was very ill with tuberculosis. After leaving Terrytoons in 1930, John Terry produced freelance work for *Collier's*, and then sold *Scorchy Smith*, a daily adventure strip, to AP Newsfeatures. The comic strip character Scorchy Smith was modeled after Charles Lindbergh for the Associated Press Feature Service. The boy aviator strip became a huge success and was printed in newspapers throughout the United States. By 1933, *Scorchy Smith* had become Associated Press's bestselling strip. The strips were quite crudely drawn, a shocking contrast from the elegant illustration work he was producing in the teens.

Not wanting to tamper with the strip, feature editor Wilson Hicks looked around the art department for somebody to ghost the strip until John recuperated. He selected Noel Douglas Sickles (1910–1982), then in his middle twenties, to ghost the strip. Sickles, who was doing political cartoons and general art for Associated Press, found the strip poorly drawn, although how much of this poor artwork can be attributed to health issues as John Terry was ill from tuberculosis at the time is left to conjecture. Around the end of November 1933, John moved to Florida to recuperate from a kidney ailment as well as tuberculosis. The first *Scorchy* strip that Sickles worked

153

on ran on Monday December 4, 1933. Unfortunately, Terry did not recover. Suffering from the disease, he died abruptly on February 28 [February 27], 1934 in Coral Gables, Florida[95] and thereafter Sickles was able to sign his own name to the strip.[96] Although Paul and his brother had not been in the best of terms over the last few years leading up to John's death, Paul would deeply grieve his loss and 35 years later credited him with inspiring him to enter the world of comics, cartoons, and animation.

With a large growth in the Harlem studio staff in the fall of 1933, Paul began to look around for larger studio space and decided on leaving New York City for a location near his home in Larchmont. The site Paul chose for the new studio was a relatively new office building in New Rochelle, New York, a 13-story art deco edifice known as the Pershing Square Building (or the "Schiff" Building after its developer) located at 271 North Avenue at the northeast corner of North Avenue and Huguenot Street, on what was believed to be the former home of Paul Revere.[97] The brick, limestone and terra-cotta structure was designed by the architectural firm Schwartz & Gross and constructed by Harry Schiff & Sons.

Harry Schiff (1870–1939), a Russian immigrant in 1888, began working as a New York City street peddlar, entered the general merchandising business, before moving into real estate. Schiff also built several apartment houses on Central Avenue, as well as the Hotel Monterey (Broadway and 94th Street) and the Embassy.[98] The cornerstone for the Pershing Building was placed on September 30, 1929,[99] and the building was completed in 1930 at a cost of one million dollars. The building was later re-named "Kaufman" by a later landlord, the owner of Kaufman Studios in Queens, New York.[100]

The new site was an ideal location, about a seven minute automobile drive from his home, and the city where he first found success in the industry after selling his first animated short in 1915. At the time, New Rochelle had a population of about 54,000.[101] The city is largely suburban emphasized by parks, golf courses, and shoreline recreational activities. The town was settled by refugee Huguenots (French Protestants) in 1688 who were fleeing persecution (such as Dragonnades) in France. Quite fitting was that many of the settlers were artisans and craftsmen from the city of La Rochelle, France, thus influencing the choice of the name of "New Rochelle".[102]

By the time Paul had signed a lease agreement in the summer of 1934 to rent the entire 7th floor of the Pershing Square Building, the studio staff had almost doubled from the previous year. The move to the new location occurred about August 1, 1934[103] and by late August, the studio had produced its first short *Mice in Council* (released August 24, 1934) from the new location[104] In March 1936, Terry had signed another lease agreement at the Pershing Square, this time for the entire 13th floor thereby doubling his studio space.[105] On the 7th floor were Paul Terry's office, the reception area, story department, music department, background department, and animators. On the 13th floor, a gorgeous penthouse, the cel inkers and painters, largely a female staff, were located.[106]

In early 1934 Terry began contemplating once again incorporating with the end goal of having controlling interest in the company. Terry told Moser that he had devised a "new and cheap process for use of color so cheap that it would cost no more than black and white cartoon pictures which we produced"[107] He promised Moser that he would place this invention at the benefit of the corporation if given control of the newly formed company. Further, Terry promised that after the corporation was formed he would go to Hammons and secure a contract for four years.[108] Terry also suggested to Moser that he should oust Theodore Kelly as his attorney, and threatened Moser that unless such control were given to him "he would bust up our partnership and go to Earl Hammons and get the contract for himself".[109]

On May 7, 1934 a second corporation was organized and was designated as Moser & Terry, Inc. with an authorized capital stock of 200 shares, no par value, with two classes of stock designated as Class A and Class B, each class of stock having 100 shares and each class of stock having the same rights and privileges. Moser and Terry were equal owners of the capital stock of the new corporation Moser &

Chapter 14 • Enduring Adversity

Terry, Inc. In this new organization, Moser was the president, Terry was the vice-president and treasurer and William Weiss was Secretary. The directors were Moser, Terry, Theodore Kelly, and Phil Scheib.[110] After the incorporation of the company, Terry failed to secure the four-year contract and did not produce the invention because there was no final product.[111] Rather Terry's invention was in the form of an idea that he planned to develop.[112]

Later on May 14, Moser and Terry signed another one-year contract with Educational Films Corporation of America to have them distribute the Terrytoons cartoon product.[113] Prior to the execution of this contract there was talk of a four-year contract with Educational. However, Harvey Day, general manager in charge of sales and distribution, was advised by John D. Clark, general sales manager of Fox Film, not to sign a four-year contract. Clark believed that Educational was always ready to renew because Fox was doing all of the work, and this was all gravy to Educational. Clark promised Day that if Educational was ever to drop out that Fox would be glad to give them a direct contract.[114] Terry and Moser would sign another one-year contract with Educational on February 20, 1935 and another again on March 2, 1936 carrying the business relationship between both parties through to 1937.[115] ✐

Notes

1. Harry N. Blair, "Short Shots from Eastern Studios", *Film Daily*, 21 February 1932, p. 5.

2. "Atlas Not Closing", *Film Daily*, 8 July 1933, p. 2.

3. A corporate chronology of the early years of Moser and Terry can be found in Moser's Complaint. Case on Appeal from Judgment, 6–31. Care must be taken in the interpretation of the documentary evidence as the matter was obviously highly contentious.

4. "Frank H. Moser – Plaintiff – Direct", *Case on Appeal from Judgment*, 111.

5. Ibid., 113.

6. Ibid., 7, 114.

7. Memorandum of Agreement between Moser & Terry, Inc. ("Corporation") and Frank H. Moser and Paul H. Terry ("Individuals"), 18 May 1932, Paul Terry Papers.

8. Letter from D. Theodore Kelly (Kelly, Hewitt & Harte, Attorneys and Counsellors at Law) to Frank Moser, 20 April 1934; Letter from the law firm of Breed, Abbott & Morgan to Paul H. Terry, 1 May 1934. Case on Appeal from Judgment, 7.

9. Letter from Phil Scheib to Paul Terry and Frank Moser, 20 November 1932, Paul Terry Papers.

10. Dan Noonan, interview by Milton Gray, 12 December 1977, Pasadena, California, J. Michael Barrier collection, 1.

11. Ibid.

12. Canemaker, *Vladimir Tytla: Master Animator*.

13. See generally: Neal Gabler, *Walt Disney: The Triumph of the American Imagination* (New York: Vintage Books, 2006).

14. The relationships between the various animated production studios and their distributors have been briefly explored in a number of monographs (Leonard Maltin, *Of Mice and Magic: A History of American Animated Cartoons* (New York: McGraw-Hill, 1980); Barrier, *Hollywood Cartoons: American Animation in Its Golden Age*; Charles Solomon, *Enchanted Drawings: The History of Animation* (New York: Wings Books, 1994).

15. For a list of film studios, distributors, and animation production companies during the 1930s the author checked the annual copies of the *Motion Picture Almanac* published by Quigley Publications.

16. Andy Seiler, "Tall talent in short films; TCM celebrates its 'Added Attractions'", *USA Today*, 5 February 2002, D3.

17. Beginning in the 1930s, prior to the release of a short to the public, Disney adopted the practice of assessing the quality of a short by first screening the cartoon at an obscure theater for audience responses. If the short was found to lack entertainment value, the required changes were made to the cartoon back at the studio ("Big Bad Wolf, The (The Silly Symphony)", *Fortune* 10 (5) (November 1934): 88–93, 95, 142, 145–146, 148). Most animation studios did not have the budget to make further changes to a short after the cartoon had been produced and a print had been made. The modus operandi of these film executives was to release the short to the public and then rely upon critical reviews in the media to gauge the success of a cartoon in entertaining audiences. A general assumption in the film industry at the time was that if a short received good media coverage, then theater attendance would be enhanced by having the short accompany the main feature. While the author was unable to locate any empirical studies that directly examined the relationship between animated shorts and theater attendance during the Golden Age of Animation, verbal discussions with a few Terry personnel revealed that they understood that film studios were beginning to take a more scientific approach to determining the economic value of an animated short to their bottom line. Further there was internal documentation to indicate that there was little value in adding one animated short to the theater billing (Paul Terry Papers). For a more thorough analysis of this subject, see Stefan Kanfer, *Serious*

155

TERRYTOONS: The Story of Paul Terry and His Classic Cartoon Factory

Business: The Art and Commerce of Animation in America from Betty Boop to Toy Story (New York: Scribner, 1997).

18. "Frank H. Moser – Plaintiff – Cross", *Case on Appeal from Judgment*, 209.

19. Terry, interview, 20 December 1969, 82.

20. "Frank H. Moser – Plaintiff – Direct", *Case on Appeal from Judgment*, 125.

21. John McDonald, "Now the Bankers Come to Disney", *Fortune* LXXIII, no. 5 (May 1966): 138–141, 218, 223–224, 226, 228, 230.

22. Maltin, *Of Mice and Magic*, 135.

23. Richard Schickel, *The Disney Version: The Life, Times, Art, and Commerce of Walt Disney* (New York: Simon and Schuster, 1985), 102.

24. Memorandum of Agreement between Frank H. Moser and Paul H. Terry doing business under the firm name and style of Moser &Terry ("Producer") and Educational Films Corporation of America ("Distributor"), 14 June 1932, p. 6, Paul Terry Papers, Fayetteville, North Carolina.

25. George Gordon, interview by Milt Gray, Hollywood, California, 4–5 January 1977, Michael Barrier Collection, 24.

26. Terry, interview, 20 December 1969, 80–81.

27. Gordon, interview, 4–5 January 1977, 20.

28. Ibid., 25.

29. Ibid., 22.

30. Ibid., 21.

31. Ibid.

32. Silverman, interview, 3 December 1977, Woodland Hills, California, 2–3.

33. "Frank H. Moser – Plaintiff – Direct", *Case on Appeal from Judgment*, 125.

34. Ibid., 126.

35. Eric Smoodin, Eric, *Animating Culture: Hollywood Cartoons from the Sound Era* (New Brunswick, N.J.: Rutgers University Press, 1993), p. 119.

36. Mark Langer, "Institutional Power and the Fleischer Studios: The Standard Production Reference", *Cinema Journal* 30, no. 2 (Winter 1991), p. 5.

37. "Inventor of Animated Cartoons Now on Dole", *Variety* 121, no. 7, 29 January 1936, 1:5.

38. John Canemaker, "Profile of a Living Animation Legend: J.R. Bray", *Filmmaker's Newsletter* 8, no. 3 (January 1975), p. 28–31.

39. Harvey Deneroff, "'We Can't Get Much Spinach'! The Organization and Implementation of the Fleischer Animation Strike", *Film History* 1 (1987), p. 2.

40. "How Funny 'Looney Tunes' Are Made", *Variety* 99, no. 11, 25 June 1930, 14:3.

41. For a good overview of the animation process: Shamus Culhane, *Animation from Script to Screen* (New York: St. Martin's Press, 1988), p. 11–21.

42. Deneroff, 2.

43. Harriet Polt, "The Death of Mickey Mouse", *Film Comment* 2, no. 3 (Summer 1964), p. 36. The story developed as a result of Disney telling his dad how he could get his money back out of the studio in the event the animation company failed. See: Richard Greene and Katherine Greene, "The Burbank Studio", The Walt Disney Family Museum, Disney.com, http://disney.go.com/disneyatoz/familymuseum/exhibits/articles/burbankstudio/ (Accessed: 20 February 2008).

44. Joe Adamson, *Tex Avery, King of Cartoons* (New York: Popular Library, 1975), p. 20.

45. "Bray-Hurd Win Cartoon Suit". *Variety* 97, no. 13, 8 January 1930, 79:3.

46. Silverman, interview, 3 December 1977, Woodland Hills, California, 2–3.

47. Tom Sito, "'So What Was It Like?' The Other Side of Animation's Golden Age", *Animation World Magazine* 1, no. 4 (July 1996), p. 40.

48. Sito, 'So What Was It Like?', 40.

49. Ibid., 38.

50. Ibid.

51. Ibid., 39.

52. Lokey, interview, 4.

53. Sito, 'So What Was It Like?', 40.

54. Ibid.

55. Ibid.

56. Ibid.

57. Ibid.

58. Fred Kopietz, Interview by Michael Barrier, April 29–30, 1991, West Sedona, Arizona, J. Michael Barrier Collection.

59. Sam Shain, "Problems of the Film Industry", *Variety* 109, 3 January 1933, 12. For a detailed analysis of the effects of the Great Depression on Hollywood: Tino Balio, "Surviving the Great Depression", in *Grand Design: Hollywood as a Modern Business Enterprise, 1930–1939* (Berkeley: University of California Press, 1995), 13–36.

60. See generally Adolph Zukor, *The Public Is Never Wrong: The Autobiography of Adolph Zukor*, with Dale Kramer (New York: G.P. Putnam's Sons, 1953); John Douglas Eames, *The Paramount Story: The Complete History of the Studio and Its Films*, with additional text by Robert Abele (New York: Simon & Schuster, 2002); Lee Server, *Robert Mitchum: "Baby, I Don't Care"* (New York: St. Martin's, 2002).

61. Roy Chartier, "The Year in Pictures", *Variety* 113, 2 January 1934, 3.

62. Ibid.

63. Ibid.

64. Memorandum of Agreement between Frank H. Moser and Paul H. Terry ("Partners") and Educational Films Corporation of America, 14 June 1932, Paul Terry Papers.

65. "Thomas James (Tommy) Morrison", interview by Harvey R. Deneroff, transcript, New Rochelle, New York, 15 June 1970, John Canemaker Animation Collection, Fales Library, Elmer Holmes Bobst Library, New York University, New York, New York, 1d.

66. Obituary: "Thomas Morrison of Terrytoons Dies", *The Standard-Star* (New Rochelle, N.Y.), 3 March 1978, p. A8.

67. 20th Century-Fox Film Corporation, "Experts are Born: Thomas Morrison", *Dynamo* (Terrytoon Section), 15 April 1940, Chicago, Illinois, 4B.

Chapter 14 • Enduring Adversity

68. Thomas James (Tommy) Morrison, interview, 15 June 1970, 1d.

69. Ibid., 14d–15d.

70. Ibid., 2d.

71. Ibid.

72. Ibid., 8d.

73. "Thomas J. Morrison", *New York Times*, 30 July 1942, p. 21.

74. According to the story, when Maltese decided that plumbing wasn't the career he wanted, he set off down the street looking for an opportunity. After wandering awhile he stumbled across a sign for Terrytoons wanting "inbetweeners" for their animation department. Maltese had no idea what the job was, but he rode a rickety elevator up to the 18th floor and interviewed with Paul Terry. During this interview he jokingly suggested a slogan for the elevator he had ridden: "Good to the last drop".

75. For more information: The Michael Maltese Papers, 1907–1981, OCLC No.: 45811692, American Heritage Center Archives, University of Wyoming, Laramie, Wyoming.

76. "Cartoon 'Mellerdrammer,'" *Film Daily*, 10 June 1933, p. 9.

77. "Reviews of the Latest Short Subjects: "The Banker's Daughter"", *Film Daily*, 10 June 1933, p. 4.

78. "38 Musical Subjects on Educational Lineup", *Film Daily*, 11 May 1933, p. 1, 4.

79. "Short Subject Reviews: Robin Hood" (animated short review), *Film Daily*, 12 January 1933, p. 7.

80. Chas. Alicoate, "Short Shots from Eastern Studios", *Film Daily*, 26 January 1934, p. 11.

81. "Mannie Davis Joins Terry", *Film Daily*, 23 August 1933, p. 4.

82. "Frank H. Moser – Plaintiff – Direct", *Case on Appeal from Judgment*, 122.

83. Paul Sommer, interview, 30 March 1977, 16.

84. "Fox Film in New Link-Up", *New York Times*, 25 January 1933, 23; "Hammons' Reasons for Fox Deal; – His Educat Co. Will Save Million Dollars", *Variety*, 31 January 1933, 3.

85. "Earl W. Hammons-Defendant-Direct", Case on Appeal from Judgment, 330. Directions as to distribution arrangements can be found in Letter from Educational Films Corporation of America to Moser and Terry, 21 March 1933, Paul Terry Papers.

86. "Complaint", Case on Appeal from Judgment, 9.

87. Cory Gunderson, *The Great Depression* (Edina, Minnesota: ABDO Publishing, 2004), 29.

88. Terry, interview, 20 December 1969, 82.

89. Phil M. Daly, "Along the Rialto", *Film Daily*, 26 July 1933, p. 4.

90. Obituary: "Joseph G. Rasinski", *The Standard-Star* (New Rochelle), 3 May 1984 (also funeral notice). Interview: Conrad Joseph Rasinski, telephone interview by author, 31 October 1997, Kelowna, B.C., Canada, Terrytoons Collection, Victoria, B.C., Canada.

91. Terry, interview, 14 July 1970, 141.

92. He began in the role as an inker and opaquer at the Walt Disney studio, 1934–1935, then as an inbetweener primarily on Mickey Mouse shorts for the studio, 1935–1936. He was promoted to assistant animator in 1936 and worked on the Disney features *Snow White and the Seven Dwarfs* (1937) and *Dumbo* (1941). He was made an animator at the Disney studios between 1940–1941 working on *Bambi* (1942). His animation career also included work for Hanna-Barbera, Filmation Studios, and Sanrio. Outside of animation, he was a comic book artist on the staff of Western Publishing, c. 1943–c. 1951. From about 1951 to 1957, Noonan completed magazine illustrations for *Collier's, Bluebook, Coronet, Reporter, This Week*, and others. He also undertook work as an artist for album covers (*Fantasy Illustrated/Graphic Story Magazine*, 1969, and *Graphic Story Magazine* #9, Summer, 1968). Noonan, interview, 12 December 1977.

93. Noonan, interview, 12 December 1977, 1. He later worked sporadically as an assistant animator and animator at MGM, 1937–1945. He worked as a character designer and on animation models, layouts and storyboards for Hanna-Barbera, 1960–1965.

94. In the late 1930s he worked in the story departments of the Disney, MGM and Universal shorts units. In the 1960s he worked as a storywriter on the animated cartoons of Hanna-Barbera. Platt began writing children's books and young-adult mysteries in 1961. He eventually published more than 30 books, including general-reader mysteries. In the early 1960s, he would return to write stories for CBS-Terrytoons cartoons. *Authors & Artists for Young Adults*, volume 11 (Detroit: Gale Research, 1993); Martha E. Ward et al., *Authors of Books for Young People*, third edition (Metuchen, NJ: Scarecrow Press, 1990); Ann Evory and Linda Metzger, ed., *Contemporary Authors, New Revision Series. A Bio-Bibliographical Guide to Current Writers in Fiction, General Nonfiction, Poetry, Journalism, Drama, Motion Pictures, Television, and Other Fields*, volume 11 (Detroit: Gale Research, 1984), 407–408 (entries also found in volumes 17–20, 1st revision); Kevin S. Hile, ed., *Something About the Author*, vol. 86 (Detroit, Michigan: Gale research, 1996), 181–185.

95. "John C. Terry Will Be Buried On West Coast; Died in South", *The Standard-Star* (New Rochelle, NY), 2 March 1934; "John C. Terry". *Varlety*, March 6, 1934, 71.

96. John Terry married Bessie Spratt of Anaconda, Montana on June 1, 1903, in Butte, Montana. He later was divorced and re-married (Alexa) and had three children including John D. Terry (b. August 5, 1904, Anaconda, Montana), Augustus Perrin Terry (b. January 3, 1909, Anaconda, Montana), and Virginia Terry (b. July 31, 1910, San Francisco, California). John Terry's internment took place in California.

97. "Razing Old Landmark", *New York Times*, 4 March 1928, sec. XIII, p. 18:6.

98. "Harry Schiff, 70, Real Estate Man", *New York Times*, 21 October 1939, p. 15:4.

99. "Tall Suburban Edifice", *New York Times*, 29 September 1930, sec. XII, p. 22:78.

100. At the time of the writing the building is still standing, although in

157

the 1980s the tower began to shiver and quake. Causes for these tremors have yet to be determined. "The Quivering Tower of New Rochelle", *The Standard-Star* (New Rochelle, N.Y.), 24 May 1988.

101. U.S. Department of Commerce, Bureau of the Census, "Table 4-Population of Counties By Minor Civil Divisions 1930, 1920, and 1910 – Continued", *Population, Volume 1. Number and Distribution of Inhabitants. Total Population for States, Counties, and Townships or Other Minor Civil Divisions; For Urban and Rural Areas; and For Cities and Other Incorporated Places* (Washington, D.C.: GPO, 1931), 765.

102. New Rochelle (N.Y.). Chamber of Commerce, *New Rochelle, the City of the Huguenots* (New Rochelle, N.Y.: The Knickerbocker Press, 1926); Barbara Davis, *New Rochelle* (Charleston, South Carolina: Arcadia Publishing, 2012).

103. "Frank H. Moser – Plaintiff – Direct", *Case on Appeal from Judgment*, 141.

104. Charles Alicoate, "Short Shots from Eastern Studios", *Film Daily*, vol. LXVI, no. 45, 23 August 1934, p. 8.

105. "More Space for Terry-Toons", *Film Daily*, 18 March 1936, p. 2; Warren Hawkinson remembered that there were four floors occupied by Terry, the 7th, 13th, and two others, one of which was the 10th or 11th floor. Warren Hawkinson, telephone interview by author (transcript), 3 January 1998, Kelowna, B.C., Canada, Terrytoons Collection, Victoria, B.C., 1–2.

106. Hawkinson, interview, 3 January 1998, 1–2; Angelo Tarricone, telephone interview by author (transcript), 26 October 1997, Kelowna, B.C., Canada, Terrytoons Collection, Victoria, B.C., Canada, 7; Mary Zaffo Mathewson, telephone interview by author (transcript), 11 January 1998, Kelowna, B.C., Canada, Terrytoons Collection, Victoria, B.C., 1.

107. "Frank H. Moser – Plaintiff – Direct", Case on Appeal from Judgment, 116.

108. Ibid., 116–117.

109. "Frank H. Moser – Plaintiff – Direct", *Case on Appeal from Judgment*, 115.

110. "Complaint", Case on Appeal from Judgment, 7–8.

111. "Frank H. Moser – Plaintiff – Direct", Case on Appeal from Judgment, 116–117.

112. "Thomas F. Thompson – For Defendants – Direct", Case on Appeal from Judgment, 620.

113. "Frank H. Moser – Plaintiff – Direct", *Case on Appeal from Judgment*, 119.

114. Ibid., 120.

115. Ibid., 121.

Chapter 15

A Rising Storm and a Studio in Distress: The Search to Improve the Entertainment Value of the Cartoon Product, 1935–1936

On July 30, 1932, Walt Disney released the short, *Flowers and Trees*, the first commercially exhibited film to be produced in full-color three-strip Technicolor. The short would win the first ever Academy Award in the category "Short Subjects, Cartoons". Two years later most of the other animation studios had begun releasing their first colorized animated cartoon. In 1934, Fleischer Studios (*Poor Cinderella*) and Walter Lantz (*Jolly Little Elves*) produced their first color cartoons, the former in the two strip Cinecolor process and the latter in two-color Technicolor.

That same year Van Beuren started producing the colorized *Rainbow Parade* shorts, the first being *Pastry Town Wedding*, Columbia began releasing their *Color Rhapsody* series with *Holiday Land*, while Schlesinger for Warner Bros. release completed his first color *Merrie Melodies* short, *Honeymoon Hotel*.[1] Despite the fact that most of the other cartoon studios had moved to colorized shorts, Terry remained adamant that his studio should continue to produce in black and white. Frank Moser had been trying as early as 1934 to convince Terry to produce in color in order to keep pace with the other studios.[2]

By late 1935 Moser had changed his tactics with Terry and suggested that the company produce one or two cartoons in color "to see what success we would have with them". Terry, still intransigent, said "to forget about it".[3] Although by September 1935 nearly all of the other major cartoon studios except one or two had moved to producing in color,[4] Terry didn't buy into the argument that they needed to compete with them on the basis of colorized cartoons.[5] The general consensus among Terry's staff including Moser as to why he was so hesitant about going into color was that Terry believed that the colorization process was too expensive and he was trying to keep his production costs at a minimum.[6] Even when he started to produce in color in 1938 he did so reluctantly. Terry's opinion was that he never saw much benefit in color[7] because the added expense from colorizing the shorts did not provide any return on investment to his studio.[8]

Moreover, Terry felt that color added very little to box office receipts for theater owners because the movie-going public weren't paying to see the cartoon but rather the feature film. Terry compared the business of producing animated cartoon shorts to the restaurant business. When you go to a restaurant for a meal and they serve you bread and butter before the meal, that is fine, but you don't go to the restaurant for the bread and butter. Terry equated his cartoon product with the bread and butter and the feature film to the meal.[9]

Terry was correct that colorization was a very expensive process. The Technicolor process was very costly because there was no laboratory on the east coast to process the film requiring the studio to ship the celluloid out to California to be color

159

TERRYTOONS: The Story of Paul Terry and His Classic Cartoon Factory

Fig. 15.1 – Grumpy Paul Terry overlooking nervous storyboard staff – Panel 1.

processed. With respect to colorization, Scheib was in support of Terry as he didn't think that colorized cartoons were an option for the studio due to the processing costs.[10] Producing colorized cartoons in the early-to-mid 1930s was a very expensive and risky enterprise considering the failure of other technologies (i.e. two-color Kinemacolor, two-color Prizmacolor, three-color Chronochrome, two-color Technicolor), the high print cost for color, the dwindling receipts and declining production budgets that came with the Depression,[11] and "the fact that musicals, the genre with which two-strip Technicolor had become closely associated, were suddenly considered box-office poison".[12] With very few Hollywood live-action films produced in color by the mid-1930s (*La Cucaracha* (1934), *Becky Sharp* (1935)), color was seen as a novelty effect making color conversion less of a priority.

By 1935, the film industry had experienced the worst of the economic effects of the Depression and was in a process of restoration as most of the bankruptcies and receiverships were discharged. Paramount, Pathé, and Fox-Metropolitan successfully reorganized,[13] RKO received new investors, and attendance at movie theaters increased with the major problem facing the industry being the overhead required to meet the demand.[14] Film budgets were raised, more money was spent on marketing films, and extensive campaigns to push the bigger pictures were common indicating renewed confidence in the industry.[15] While increased box office receipts heralded good news for Hollywood in 1935, it was early that year that the quality of the Terrytoons cartoons became an issue with their distributor.

During the mid-1930s to help draw publicity to his cartoon studio, Terry began to speak publicly on the topic of animated films and filmmaking at community and social gatherings, a considerable challenge for a man with a speech disorder. He was a guest speaker at a motion picture course held at New York University on March 1, 1935

Chapter 15 • A Rising Storm and a Studio in Distress

Fig. 15.2 – Grumpy Paul Terry overlooking nervous storyboard staff – Panel 2.

where alongside Irma Williams of Trans-Lux who lectured on newsreels he spoke on shorts.[16] On April 9, 1936, Terry addressed the Metropolitan M. P. Club, comprising amateurs, on the topic of cartoon making.[17] In January 1937 he was a guest speaker at the Philadelphia Motion Picture Council explaining how animated cartoons are made and why the cartoon has reached its present level of popularity.[18]

On March 23, 1935, Herman Wobber,[19] manager of the Western division for Fox Film, wrote a letter to John D. Clark,[20] vice-president and general manager of distribution for 20th Century-Fox, explaining that the increase in distribution and sales of Terrytoons was not due to any increased quality but rather that "we are jamming shorts along with features". Wobber argued that Terrytoons cartoons were not keeping pace with Disney or Fleischer's Popeye. He suggested that the studio produce a series based on the popular *Henry* comic strip.[21] On March 25, 1935, John D. Clark wrote a letter to Harvey B. Day,[22] general manager in charge of sales and distribution for Terrytoons, with the words, "Herman (Wobber) has spoken to me three or four times regarding this matter and I really believe that with the volume of business that you are doing now that you probably can afford to make a more saleable and attractive cartoon than you are making – and I am certain that our returns will justify any improved quality that you can create".[23]

On September 11, 1935, William Sussman,[24] assistant to Clark and later Eastern division sales manager in 1936, wrote a letter to John D. Clark informing him that exhibitors are complaining about the lack of color in the Terrytoons cartoons.[25] By a letter dated September 16, 1935, John D. Clark forwarded the Sussman letter of September 11, 1935 to Harvey B. Day for his attention.[26] On September 18, 1935, William J. Kupper, Fox Film's Western sales manager, followed with another letter to Day after visiting exhibitors in the Southwest and Midwestern United States.

According to Kupper, exhibitors were complaining about the similarity in the cartoon stories and wanted some kind of change.[27] When Terry approached

Fig. 15.3 – Grumpy Paul Terry overlooking nervous storyboard staff – Panel 3.

an exhibitor, the producer was told that Terrytoons cartoons were exhibited after the feature to let the audience know that the program was over. The children would stay and watch the cartoon but the adults would not remain in the theater.[28] This feedback was further evidence to Terry that his cartoons needed improvements in the entertainment quality. On September 26, 1935, Sussman wrote Clark suggesting that Terrytoons produce their cartoons in color and feature some well-known character running through the cartoon "rather than the hit and miss characters they are using at the present time".[29] Clark responded to Sussman in a letter dated September 27, 1935 agreeing with him on improving the cartoons by producing in color and with an established character as well as suggested he talk to Day about his concern about the falling off of business which he was unaware of.[30]

In early 1936, problems related to lack of color cartoons came to a boiling point for the partnership when Educational began receiving complaints about the lack of color in their cartoons that if not corrected could potentially jeopardize a renewal of the distribution contract.[31] Moser began to pressure Terry even more about moving to color. Terry's response was the same, that "there was not enough money in the pictures to do color with".[32] Harvey Day also wanted to keep away from color because of the expense involved making it "practically prohibitive for us to go into color".[33] John Clark also believed Terrytoons could not afford to produce in color.[34]

Earle Hammons, manager of Educational Pictures, and Jack H. Skirball, general sales manager for Educational Films Corporation, found the entertainment quality of the cartoons more of a concern than the fact they were not colorized.[35] Terry, trying to avoid the use of color, suggested to Hammons that if the partnership created more humorous and entertaining cartoons, then the lack of colorization could be offset,[36] a suggestion supported by Day[37] and William Sussman.[38] Despite the complaints from the sales and distribution contacts at Fox and Educational, Terrytoons

Chapter 15 • A Rising Storm and a Studio in Distress

Fig. 15.4 – Grumpy Paul Terry overlooking nervous storyboard staff – Panel 4.

cartoons were continuing to receive positive reviews. For example, in early 1936, *Film Daily* found *The Mayflower* (December 27, 1935) to have "plenty of laughs" and "clever gags".[39]

When Moser made a number of other suggestions to improve the quality of the cartoons, he once again met with opposition from Terry. One of the suggestions was to establish a main character so that the public would become familiar with it. He wanted half of the animated cartoons produced each year to feature a main character.[40] Terry's response was that they were "not doing characters, they were producing Terrytoons".[41] Moser also recommended a moviola at a cost of $1,000 for a new machine or $400 for a second-hand machine. Since the studio recorded the sound first, the moviola would assist the cartoonists by allowing them to hear the sound before they were expected to draw the cartoon to match the noise effect. Further, the animators would be able to better synchronize the sound with the action of the characters that they were expected to draw. Terry's response was that the moviola would cost too much. Since the studio employed 12 to 14 animators, if all of them wanted to use the moviola to assist in animating the characters with the soundtrack, then the animation of individual scenes would take longer and production costs would rise.[42] Terry's attitude toward his animators was: "When I hire a man to animate, I want him to know how!"[43]

Moser also suggested that the cartoons have fewer scenes in them with big crowds to cut down on the amount of animation involved in each frame of action. The overworked Moser described his daily toil in the animation department.

> We started with 20 people and sweat from morning until night to get the pictures out. I was there at 8:30 in the morning and kept working until 5:30, and when I went home I was tired out.[44]

He later added, "I just did the best I could, and I sweat blood to deliver those pictures to Earl Hammons every second week".[45] Terry did not provide an immediate

163

response to Moser's proposal and wasn't interested in his suggestions in the form of a letter from him.[46]

Despite Terry's unreceptive attitude towards the letter, on February 14, 1936, Moser sent Terry another letter with his suggestions on how to improve the entertainment quality of the animated cartoons.[47] Besides fewer scenes with crowds, the purchase of a moviola, and the establishment of a story department, he suggested in his letter to keep the action in rhythm, synchronize more action with the melody, lengthen the number of scenes from 30–40 to 40–50, use stories that concentrate on one main subject or idea, and when heavy voices are used the characters should be drawn close-up or at least semi-closeup. He also recommended that they should carry the stories more nearly to completion before Scheib is asked to fit the music to them, use a main character and assistant characters that are developed, copyrighted and owned by the studio and not borrowed from any newspaper feature owned by others, and keep records of all animators, tracers and opaquers after each second picture (i.e. monthly). He also favored the dismissal of Don McKee, Terry's long-time friend, due to his lack of interest in the animation work.[48]

In late 1935, Bill Weiss went to Terry and asked him that he do something to improve the cartoons to address the complaints of Educational Films and suggested they begin by improving the stories but Terry wasn't interested in the idea.[49] At one time Weiss enjoyed going down to Fox Film to screen the animated cartoons being projected but by 1935 he was so ashamed to visit Fox because of the complaints they were receiving that he stopped going.[50] In September of 1935 Frank Moser confided with Terry that he thought their animation and general production was as good as their competitors but that their cartoons could be improved by introducing a story department. Moser told Terry that he was willing to spend as much as $200 a week if necessary. Terry did not give any answer until several months later.[51] By February 1936, Terry had changed his mind and he and Moser rented a room next to John Foster's office which they would use as the location for the new story department.[52]

In the early part of February 1936, Moser heard Harvey Day tell Weiss, in the presence of Terry, that it was about time to get the renewal contract from Educational – "that it was only a matter of exchange of letters as usual".[53] Moser did not attend to such matters because he was in charge of the animation of the cartoons and Terry and Weiss handled all of the outside contracts.[54] Terry scowled at Day, did not say a word and went into his private office.[55] Thereafter, Moser asked Terry about this matter, and Terry responded it was "too early" to ask for a new contract; that the contracts were usually renewed later, and that it was none of Day's business.[56] The significance of this episode is that Day evidently regarded the renewal of the contract as a matter of course, and was in a position to know, for he was the contact man between Educational and Fox on the one side, and Moser & Terry on the other, and had his office with Fox in its place of business.[57]

About February 18, Terry suggested to Moser that they should go to Hammons and try to get a new contract on the following Monday, February 24.[58] Thereafter, on Monday, February 24, 1936, Moser and Terry called on Hammons at his office respecting the renewal of their current contract for an additional period of one year.[59] Hammons stated he did not intend to renew, and left him with that impression definitely in their minds. It appears that Hammons refused the new contract because he (Hammons) had received so many complaints from Fox about the lack of color in Terry-Toons, and Hammons said that most of the complaints had come from Sussman, who had been made Eastern Sales Manager of Fox.[60]

Moser told Hammons that he made a number of recommendations for the improvement of the cartoons which he wished to show Hammons, but Hammons told Moser that it was too late for all that now, that Fox wouldn't permit a renewal, and he said he was sorry.[61] Hammons said he could not renew the contract because of complaints about the quality of the pictures.[62] Hammons' comments were more in the nature of a "hedge", for he testified on his examination before trial "that I had practically made

Chapter 15 • A Rising Storm and a Studio in Distress

Fig. 15.5 – Grumpy Paul Terry overlooking storyboard staff and having temper tantrum – Panel 5.

up my mind not to renew the contract but I did not definitely tell them that absolutely under no condition whatsoever would I not renew the contract".[63] When Moser and Terry returned to their place of business at New Rochelle, they told Weiss that Hammons had turned them down, and Weiss said nothing. Moser suggested taking up the matter with other distributors, but Terry said, "No other distributor would want us after Fox had turned us down".[64]

During the next few days, they were various discussions and conferences between Moser and Terry, in which Weiss participated. On February 25, the day following the refusal of renewal, Moser said that Terry wanted to know how to settle up the matter, and Moser replied they still had a considerable number of pictures to complete.[65] Weiss seemed interested only in what would happen to the "valuable" 16 millimeter rights.[66] On February 26, Moser went down to see his attorney, Mr. Theodore Kelly, in the morning. When he returned in the afternoon, Weiss told Moser and Terry that their business had fallen off badly; that their withdrawals had been too heavy; that a substantial amount of money was needed at once, at least $30,000 to $40,000.[67] Moser claimed that Terry wanted him to furnish all this additional capital though this is in dispute.[68]

On February 27, Terry said that something had to be done fast, and asked Weiss "how we stood".[69] Thereupon, Weiss stepped into his own room, and in about 15 to 20 minutes returned with a typewritten statement dated February 26, 1936, detailing liabilities and expected income from August 1, 1936 (when the current contract with Educational ended) to July 31, 1937 and showed this statement to Moser and Terry.[70] Terry then asked Moser if he would sell his interest to Terry if Terry could get his friend Morrison interested, to which Moser replied asking how much he would get. Terry said "Just what Mr. Weiss's statement shows".[71] Weiss then referred to his statement and said, "That would be half of $41,400 or $20,700".[72] Thereupon there was

165

some talk about payment for equipment (fixtures) and trademark, together with attorneys' fees in the event that there should be a sale.[73] The parties arrived at a figure of $24,200.[74]

Of note, the most significant part of Weiss's statement is that it entirely omitted two of the most important items of assets in connection with the partnership and corporation business, namely the amounts of cash and accounts receivable totalling $28,828.74. This total accounted for more than half of the amount as figured by Weiss[75] and this total would have greatly entered into the liquidation value of the business. Moser was an artist from a rural farming community in Kansas with little knowledge of accounting and finance. He trusted Weiss implicitly with providing an accurate representation of the sale value of the company. Weiss always prepared his income tax, reconciled his personal check account and bank statements, advised him on all his investments, and took lunch with him daily.[76]

On the following day, February 28, Moser met Terry at Terry's office in their place of business. Terry had Tom Morrison with him and they looked around the place.[77] On the afternoon of that day, Terry told Moser that Morrison would help him; that he hoped that Morrison would not change his mind, and Moser responded that he was satisfied; to which Terry replied that it was too bad that they couldn't finish up the deal that day.[78] That evening, Weiss and Terry discussed in detail the financial statement presented to Terry and Moser by Weiss.[79] Moser and his lawyer Kelly made an appointment for the next day and arranged with Terry to have Weiss get in touch with Moser so that he (Weiss) might be present.[80]

On February 29, 1936, Moser sold his interests in the partnership and corporation for $24,200 to Terry.[81] The closing took place in Kelly's rooms in the Hotel Shelton, to which he was confined by illness.[82] The parties were present, together with Weiss, and their respective attorneys. Weiss had with him and showed to Kelly the relevant financial documents.[83] Weiss later claimed he discussed these papers in detail with Kelly. He claimed that he even discussed the subject of cash in the banks. Kelly told a different story. He said he first saw the Weiss statement on February 29.[84] Kelly stated that nothing was said to him by Weiss regarding either cash in the banks or accounts receivable.[85] Kelly asserted he did not see the trial balance as of January 31, 1936, or the financial statement for the business for 1935.[86] Kelly claimed he also never saw the cash items on hand.[87] Moser had asserted repeatedly his implicit confidence in Weiss.[88] Terry would testify at trial that during the week of February 14 that cash and accounts receivables were not mentioned.[89] The deal was consummated, the papers exchanged and the money passed.[90] Terry now owned the company outright. He remembered what his father told him to never have a partner after having gone through a number of failed partnerships in San Francisco in the 1870s.[91]

On March 1, Terry went to the country home of Hammons, and there urged him to renew the contract. He painted a beautiful word picture of the improvements he would make in the pictures, and that Hammons was practically convinced to renew on that day, but not to have given Terry the final definite word. The explanation Hammons gave for his sudden change of attitude towards the renewal is that he had confidence in Terry, that when he learned Terry had bought out Moser there would be no longer any fighting between the two producers like a "house divided", and that Terry was going to improve the pictures, he, Hammons, then felt "very favorable toward renewing the contract with him".[92] Terry promised, "As far as I am concerned I don't care whether I make a dime for the next two years. What I want to do is to get the name of Paul Terry back to where it was." Terry told him that he would put forth every effort and spend every available dollar to make his cartoons a success. However, Terry asked for a two-year contract as he thought he would need a little more time to recoup his investment.[93]

On March 2, 1936, the contract with Educational Films was formally renewed.[94] The renewal of the contract took place at a conference with Terry at Hammons' office in New York City at 3:00 p.m., just 24 hours after Moser had been removed from the equation.[95] On that same day, Moser went to the business office

Chapter 15 • A Rising Storm and a Studio in Distress

of Moser & Terry, Inc., in New Rochelle, saw Terry there, and Terry told him that he had informed the employees he had bought out Moser.[96] On the following day, March 3, Terry gave a dinner to the entire staff of employees of Moser & Terry, at the Skyport Restaurant in New Rochelle.[97] Moser saw Terry and Weiss at the dinner but Terry neither mentioned to him the new contract which had been obtained from Hammons.[98] After the dinner, Moser went with Weiss to Weiss's office where Weiss completed Moser's income tax statements due on the following March 15, and again saw Moser on the same matter a week later and also just a day or two before March 15 but Weiss said nothing about the renewal.[99]

Weiss's salary was increased on the same day of the dinner of March 3 – by Terry, from $82 per week to $100 per week, effective as of the preceding week, and shortly thereafter Weiss became the Treasurer of the corporation, succeeding Terry, and began signing all checks.[100] On March 3, 1936, *Film Daily* reported the reorganization of the studio and the departure of Moser.[101] The article reported that Harvey Day was elected vice-president in charge of sales, Scheib was named second vice-president, and Weiss secretary-treasurer. Thereafter, Moser took a vacation trip of 11 days and returned late in March 1936.[102] Upon his return from his vacation, Moser read about the new two-year renewal contract in the March 18 edition of *Film Daily* wherein it was reported that Terry had doubled

Fig. 15.6 – Inkers and opaquers (c. 1940). Front to back: Unknown, Esmeralda Fernandes, Rocco Eletto, Norm Polansky, Dottie Loth, Milton Stein.

his studio space after being stimulated by a new contract from Educational.[103]

On the whole, Terry made good on his promise to Hammons. While still holding out to produce in black and white, Terry was now wondering whether not going into color was a mistake.[104] Besides doubling his studio space and founding a story department, he made significant increases in the number of artists he employed. On March 31, 1936, *Film Daily* reported an increase of 15 percent in production personnel at the studio.[105] Earlier in March he promoted George Gordon to the position of head of the animation department in place of Moser.[106] In early April, Terry announced that Mannie Davis was to head the newly formed story department.[107] At the end of April 1936, Terry announced that he was introducing a number of new characters which would appear consistently giving a new continuity in characterization.[108]

One of Terry's closest neighbours in the animation business was Van Beuren Studios, based in New York City and headed by Terry's former boss Amedee Van Beuren. The studio was responsible for producing the popular *Rainbow Parade* color cartoons featuring such characters as the Parrotville Parrots, Molly Moo Cow, and the Toonerville Trolley gang. The distributor for Van Beuren was RKO. On April 2, 1936, *Film Daily* announced that the completion of the deal for RKO to distribute the Van Beuren cartoon product for another year was pending the

167

return from Hollywood of A. H. McCausland, Irving Trust Company representative and RKO trustee.[109]

Unfortunately for Van Beuren, McCausland returned with bad news as RKO had switched studios to distribute cartoons produced by Walt Disney. With no outlet to distribute his animated shorts, Van Beuren looked around for a distributor, found no one interested, then decided to close his studio. Displaced animators and other production artists who wanted to remain in the business had a decision to make whether to remain in New York and look for work at Fleischer Studios or Terrytoons or head west to California to seek employment for Walt Disney, Ub Iwerks, Universal (and Walter Lantz) or Leon Schlesinger and Warner Bros.

In May 1936 Terry seized on the opportunity and made a telephone call to former Van Beuren animator Jack Zander who was living in Manhattan at the time and asked if he was interested in a job. Zander took the train up to New Rochelle and met Paul. Terry let Zander know he wanted to improve his cartoon product and they agreed on a salary. Terry then asked Zander if he knew anybody else that would like to come up and talk to him about a job. Zander recommended story man Ray Kelley and animators Joseph Barbera, Carl "Mike" Meyer, and Dan Gordon (George Gordon's brother).[110] All would end up joining the studio. Terry hired Barbera because he was heading to California to work for Disney and Paul, in the view of Barbera, hated Disney and was just trying to keep Joe from working for Disney.[111]

One day as Terry was in the projection room screening one of his cartoons and wasn't completely satisfied with the end result he told Zander, "It's okay with me. Walt Disney is the Tiffany's of the business and I am the Woolworth's".[112] Terry's Woolworth quote has since been commented upon by a number of animation historians and film scholars. Leonard Maltin in *Of Mice and Magic*, his seminal book surveying American animation studios during the Golden Age, opines that Terry's quote is evidence that Paul was a businessman producing cartoons on an uncompromising schedule with no love for the product he was producing.[113]

Adrian Bailey, as noted in his work *Walt Disney's World of Fantasy*, views the famous quote as Terry admitting "to being more interested in quantity than in quality".[114] In his quote, Terry was most likely referring to his practice of producing a product on volume and price much like Woolworth. While the cartoon Terry and Zander were viewing did not meet his artistic standards, he was working on a schedule and had production deadlines to meet. He could not afford to spend months on one cartoon creating a masterpiece. He had a schedule and budget to meet.[115] Long-time staffer Tommy Morrison is quoted as saying: "I think from our operation that Terry's principle was volume and price. I had heard the remark that 'We're in the five-and-ten-cent business'".[116]

In Terry's defence, he was on a tight production schedule and had very little time to experiment with and improve his product. He was locked into a contract and had to produce his cartoons on budget and deliver one animated short every two weeks 26 times-a-year to 20th Century-Fox. He was never paid in advance for his work. Rather, he had to invest in his product (salaries, animation supplies, film processing costs), wait for his distributor to distribute the cartoons and have them exhibited, and then months later collect on the terms of his contract with 20th Century-Fox.[117]

Outside of the studio Terry was noted for stating to family and relatives: "Anything but perfection is rank failure".[118] He admired the artistic and technical brilliance of Walt Disney animation and after Moser's departure ploughed back profits into his cartoon product and continually sought the improvement of his film product while keeping a firm control over expenditures and budgets. Terry was a realist. His cartoons were never going to look like Disney's product but for the budgets assigned to each cartoon short, Terry sought to maximize every penny spent.

After establishing a story department and putting Davis in charge of the department, Terry wasn't finished. At the end of May 1936 he hired John Herman, long-time assistant for cartoonist Rube Goldberg, to create gags and ideas for the stories.[119] In mid-June, Terry announced the addition of Jack Zander, Dan Gordon and Carlo Vinciguerra,

Chapter 15 • A Rising Storm and a Studio in Distress

former "ace members" of Van Beurens' staff, to the animation studio. Herb Roth was hired to create more gags and ideas for the stories. *Film Daily* noted that the organization was now 60 percent larger than it was when Terry began the reorganization after Moser had been bought out.[120]

During the first six years of the studio's operations, Terry was a firm believer in producing a variety of animated cartoons, miscellaneous pictures with no central stars.[121] Other than the odd Farmer Al Falfa cartoon produced each short featured different characters. However, Moser had been encouraging Terry to begin developing a stable of cartoon characters. During late spring 1936, Terry decided to create three new characters that he hoped would catch the imagination of youngsters and become established characters for the studio. His choices were Kiko the Kangaroo, Puddy the Pup, and Ozzie the Ostrich.

Kiko was the brainchild of Roger Ferri, a sales promotion director with 20th Century-Fox.[122] Terry thought that his suggestion was a valid one and decided to produce a few cartoons. Kiko first appeared in *Farmer Al Falfa's Prize Package* (July 31, 1936) as a pet sent from Australia to the farmer by the latter's brother Hank. Many of the Kiko cartoons featured the kangaroo coming to the rescue of others by using his long tail and powerful legs to defeat the enemy. In *Kiko and the Honey Bears* (August 21, 1936), he saves some cubs from a pack of hunting dogs. In *Kiko Foils the Fox* (October 2, 1936), Kiko saves a little bird from a fox. In *Kiko the Kangaroo in Red Hot Music* (March 5, 1937), Fireman Kiko goes to the rescue when a "red hot" band catches fire.

Terry was excited by the idea of a cute, overly friendly and heroic marsupial cartoon character and invested substantially into marketing and producing product merchandise, including inflatable rubber dolls (made by the Miller Rubber Co.) and plush toys, featuring the character. Kiko is also among the few characters of the studio to have a theme song. In September 1936, as part of the marketing strategy to popularize Kiko the Kangaroo more than 80 radio stations across the United States broadcasted Paul Terry's offer to send a photograph of Kiko to anyone who requested it. Every picture was specially prepared for the person receiving it and included his name. Along with the picture of Kiko were included a couple of the lines from the Kiko the Kangaroo theme song written by Philip Scheib.[123] Unfortunately, despite Terry's best efforts the character was never well-received by movie-going audiences.

Joe Barbera's first storyboard was for a proposed Kiko the Kangaroo cartoon, the story of a coast-to-coast air race between Kiko and a handlebar-moustachioed version of Baron von Richthofen involving comic aerial combat featuring machine gun fire whittling the aircraft down to nothing. Barbera thought that Kiko as a cartoon character was "just terrible".[124] Several reasons can be highlighted for Kiko's lack of popularity. He never spoke nor had much of a personality and therefore it was difficult for the audience to identify with the character. His character was based on an animal foreign to American soil that was not very likeable. He wasn't warm, cuddly or cute. If Terry was looking for an adorable Australian animal to base his cartoon upon, why not a koala bear? The Kiko stories were also pretty tame affairs. For example, the problem that Kiko spends a good portion of the animated cartoon trying to manage in *Kiko's Cleaning Day* (September 17, 1937) is an out-of-control vacuum cleaner. With 10 cartoons having been released and plans being made to create another cartoon featuring the marsupial, Terry decided to drop the unlikeable character. The character was dropped by the winter of 1937.[125]

Like other animation producers, Terry was looking for a character that audiences would find appealing and memorable. An appealing character would help the 20th Century-Fox sales and marketing team promote product merchandise featuring the screen star. Terry is quoted as saying, "Making cartoons is like delivering milk. People expect the bottles at the door every morning. If you miss a morning, people get upset. I see to it that we don't miss a morning and nobody gets upset".[126] What Terry was referring to in the quote was his relationship with his distributor 20th Century-Fox. Production deadlines needed to be met or "people get upset" so that entailed standardizing animation production processes and releasing some cartoons that

169

probably should have been kept in production a little longer before release. Distributors demanded consistency in the product, in terms of production standards, quality of animation, and wanted cartoons with recognizable characters that audiences have become familiar with. Exhibitors and audiences would come to recognize a Terrytoons cartoon by association to the character and cartoons would be easier to market to the public if they contained characters audiences enjoyed watching.

Ozzie the Ostrich was no better a creation than Kiko and the bland cartoon character appeared briefly with Kiko in a few cartoons. Paul attempted to develop his own series on the character with *Ozzie Ostrich Comes to Town* (May 28, 1937) but movie audiences showed little interest in Ozzie's antics. Puddy the Pup, Farmer Al Falfa's dog, had appeared as early as February 8, 1935 in *The Bullfight* and in 1936 Terry decided to make him a regular character in his own series of shorts to capitalize on the appeal of cartoon canines such as Disney's Pluto. Puddy was a frisky little white dog with a black ear and was similar in appearance to the generic dogs Terry had been featuring in his cartoons since the early 1930s. Puddy was modelled after a little dog that Terry had at the time.[127] Between 1935 and 1942, Puddy would appear in no less than 13 cartoons. Similar to the Kiko shorts, some of Puddy's adventures end up with him as the hero. In *Puddy the Pup and the Gypsies* (July 24, 1936), he chases off gypsies raiding Farmer Al Falfa's farm house. In *Puddy the Pup in Cats in a Bag* (December 11, 1936), he saves some kittens from the rapids.

Other cartoons have the canine helping Farmer Al Falfa look for treasure, (*Puddy the Pup in Sunken Treasure* (October 16, 1936)), dreaming of traveling to Bookland where he is menaced by the giant in *Jack and the Beanstalk* (*Puddy the Pup in the Bookshop* (February 5, 1937)), dreaming it's his coronation day (*Puddy's Coronation* (May 14, 1937)), upsetting an Italian restaurateur (*The Dog and the Bone* (November 12, 1937)), becoming a star act in a "no dogs allowed" circus (*The Big Top* (May 12, 1938)), and disciplining a mischievous kitten (*The Big Build-Up* (September 4, 1942)), his last cartoon. While Puddy was a step up from Kiko in terms of personality, unlike Disney's Pluto he wasn't able to endear himself to audiences. One of the features of Disney's Pluto that made him so popular was his ability to display human-like emotion. Pluto is one of the first cartoon characters that is actually shown to have thought processes. He surprises, delights and charms through his wiles, jealousy and vulnerabilities the audience can relate to. Conversely, Puddy goes about his day in predictable doggy fashion solving problems with a methodical routine. ✦

Notes

1. Webb, *Animated Film Encyclopedia*, 166, 225, 229, 390, 256, 364.

2. Weiss, interview, 15 June 1970, 13c.

3. "Frank H. Moser – Plaintiff – Direct", *Case on Appeal from Judgment*, 130.

4. Ibid., 132.

5. "Harvey B. Day – for Defendants – Recross", *Case on Appeal from Judgment*, 605.

6. Alexander Hume Anderson, telephone interview by author (transcript), 9 November 1997, Kelowna, B.C., Canada, Terrytoons Collection, Victoria, B.C., Canada, 17e; Davis, interview, 17e; "Frank H. Moser – Plaintiff – Direct", *Case on Appeal from Judgment*, 130.

7. "Paul H. Terry – Defendant – Cross", *Case on Appeal from Judgment*, 558–559.

8. "Paul H. Terry – Defendant – Recross", *Case on Appeal from Judgment*, 578.

9. Patricia (Terry) Leahy, interview by author, 24 August 1996, Fayetteville, North Carolina, Terrytoons Collection, Victoria, B.C., Canada, 18; Eve Oakley, "Pat Leahy Was There in New York For Salute To Dad's Terrytoons", *Fayetteville Observer* (Fayetteville, North Carolina), 9 March 1982.

10. "Philip A. Scheib – for Defendants – Direct", *Case on Appeal from Judgment*, 608.

11. J.P. Telotte, "Minor Hazards: Disney and the Color Adventure", *Quarterly Review of Film and Video* 21, no. 4 (October/November/December 2004): 273–274.

12. Gorham Kindem, "Hollywood's Conversion to Color: The Technological, Economic and Aesthetic Factors", In *The American Movie Industry: The Business of Motion Pictures*, ed. Gorham Kindem, 146–158 (Carbondale: Southern Illinois University Press, 1982), 150.

13. Roy Chartier, "Year in Pictures", *Variety* 121, 1 January 1936, 6.

14. Charles F. Morgan, "Picture Prospects and Profits", *Magazine of Wall Street* 58, 15 August 1936, 522–523.

15. Chartier, "Year in Pictures", 6.

Chapter 15 • A Rising Storm and a Studio in Distress

16. Phil M. Daly, "Along the Rialto", *Film Daily*, 27 February 1935, p. 15.

17. Phil M. Daly, "Along the Rialto", *Film Daily*, 10 April 1936, p. 4.

18. Charles Alicoate, "Short Shots from Eastern Studios", *Film Daily*, 30 January 1937, p. 6.

19. "Wobber, Herman", *Who Was Who in America: With World Notables*, volume IV: 1961–1968 (Chicago: Marquis Who's Who, Inc., 1968), 1028; Obituary: "Herman Wobber", *Variety*, 23 June 1965, 71.

20. Obituaries: "John D. Clark, 47, Movie Executive", *New York Times*, 2 June 1938, p. 23:5; Roy Chartier, "No Immediate Successor to John D. Clark; Industry Notable Dies at 47", *Variety*, 8 June 1938, 4.

21. "Defendants Exhibit L", *Case on Appeal from Judgment*, 913.

22. Biography: Terry Ramsaye, ed., *International Motion Picture Almanac* (New York: Quigley Publishing, 1949), 58; "Harvey B. Day", *Variety*, 28 November 1951, 63; "Harvey Day Dead; Movie Sales Aide", *New York Times*, 25 November 1951, p. 86:5.

23. "Defendants Exhibit L", *Case on Appeal from Judgment*, 912.

24. Obituary: "William Sussman", *New York Times*, 8 October 1968, p. 47:2.

25. "Defendants Exhibit L", *Case on Appeal from Judgment*, 918.

26. Ibid., 917.

27. Ibid., 914.

28. Terry, interview, 20 December 1969, 85.

29. "Defendants Exhibit L", *Case on Appeal from Judgment*, 916.

30. Ibid., 915.

31. "Frank H. Moser – Plaintiff – Cross", *Case on Appeal from Judgment*, 211–212.

32. "Frank H. Moser – Plaintiff – Direct", *Case on Appeal from Judgment*, 141.

33. "Harvey B. Day – for Defendants – Direct", *Case on Appeal from Judgment*, 591.

34. "Harvey B. Day – for Defendants – Recross", *Case on Appeal from Judgment*, 604.

35. "Earle W. Hammons – Defendant – Direct", *Case on Appeal from Judgment*, 328–329; "Earle W. Hammons – Defendant – Cross", *Case on Appeal from Judgment*, 359; "Jack H. Skirball – For Defendants – Direct", *Case on Appeal from Judgment*, 656–659.

36. "Paul H. Terry – Defendant – Direct", *Case on Appeal from Judgment*, 521.

37. "Harvey B. Day – for Defendants – Direct", *Case on Appeal from Judgment*, 591.

38. "Harvey B. Day – for Defendants – Recross", *Case on Appeal from Judgment*, 604–605.

39. "The Mayflower" (animated cartoon review), *Film Daily*, 7 January 1936, p. 11.

40. "Frank H. Moser – Plaintiff – Direct", *Case on Appeal from Judgment*, 130, 142.

41. Ibid., 130.

42. Ibid., 130–131.

43. Canemaker, *Vladimir Tytla: Master Animator*.

44. "Frank H. Moser – Plaintiff – Cross", *Case on Appeal from Judgment*, 197.

45. Ibid.

46. "Frank H. Moser – Plaintiff – Direct", *Case on Appeal from Judgment*, 136.

47. Ibid.

48. "Plaintiff's Exhibit 7", *Case on Appeal from Judgment*, 833–835.

49. Ibid., 131.

50. Ibid., 133.

51. Ibid., 132.

52. Ibid., 137–138.

53. "Frank H. Moser – Plaintiff – Direct", *Case on Appeal from Judgment*, 139.

54. Ibid., 126–127.

55. Ibid., 139.

56. Ibid., 139–140.

57. "Harvey B. Day – For Defendants – Direct", *Case on Appeal from Judgment*, 586–588.

58. "Frank H. Moser – Plaintiff – Direct", *Case on Appeal from Judgment*, 138–139.

59. Ibid., 141–142.

60. Ibid., 141; "Plaintiff's Exhibit 5", *Case on Appeal from Judgment*, 831–833.

61. "Frank H. Moser – Plaintiff – Direct", *Case on Appeal from Judgment*, 142.

62. "Paul H. Terry – Defendant – Direct", *Case on Appeal from Judgment*, 522.

63. "Nathan Vogel – For Plaintiff – Recalled in Rebuttal – Direct, "*Case on Appeal from Judgment*, 671.

64. "Frank H. Moser – Plaintiff – Direct", *Case on Appeal from Judgment*, 143.

65. Ibid., 144.

66. Ibid., 144.

67. Ibid., 144–146.

68. Ibid., 147.

69. Ibid., 147–148.

70. "Plaintiff's Exhibit 8", *Case on Appeal from Judgment*, 836.

71. "Frank H. Moser – Plaintiff – Direct", *Case on Appeal from Judgment*, 150.

72. Ibid., 150.

73. Ibid., 150–152.

74. Calculated as follows: ½ of amount of Weiss's statement ($20,700), ½ of the equipment (fixtures) ($950.00), ½ of trademark value ($2,500), attorney's fee ($50.00).

75. "Nathan L. Vogel – for Plaintiff – Direct", *Case on Appeal from Judgment*, 248–249; "William M. Weiss – Defendant – Cross", *Case on Appeal from Judgment*, 473; "Plaintiff's Exhibit 13", *Case on Appeal from Judgment*, 844.

76. "Frank H. Moser – Plaintiff – Direct", *Case on Appeal from Judgment*, 122–123; "Frank H. Moser – Plaintiff – Cross", *Case on Appeal from Judgment*, 187; "Frank H. Moser – Plaintiff – Redirect", *Case on Appeal from Judgment*, 215.

77. "Frank H. Moser – Plaintiff – Direct", *Case on Appeal from Judgment*, 153.

78. Ibid., 154.

79. "William M. Weiss – Defendant – Cross", *Case on Appeal from Judgment*, 454–455.

80. "Frank H. Moser – Plaintiff – Direct", *Case on Appeal from Judgment*, 154.

81. "Plaintiff's Exhibit 9; Exhibit "B" Attached to Complaint", *Case on Appeal from Judgment*, 29–31.

82. "Frank H. Moser – Plaintiff – Direct", *Case on Appeal from Judgment*, 156.

83. (1) The Moser & Terry, Inc. Trial Balance as of January 31, 1936 ("Plaintiff's Exhibit 29", *Case on Appeal from Judgment*, 893–894); (2) The 1935 Financial Statement of the Business, bearing date December 31, 1935 ("Plaintiff's Exhibit 4", *Case on Appeal from Judgment*, 759–830); (3) Weiss's Statement of February 26, 1936 "Plaintiff's Exhibit 8", *Case on Appeal from Judgment*, 836; "Plaintiff's Exhibit 32", *Case on Appeal from Judgment*, 899).

84. "D. Theodore Kelly-For Plaintiff in Rebuttal Direct", *Case on Appeal from Judgment*, 672, 678.

85. Ibid., 673–675.

86. Ibid., 679–680.

87. Ibid., 679.

88. Ibid., 681.

89. "Paul H. Terry – Defendant – Recross", *Case on Appeal from Judgment*, 586.

90. "Frank H. Moser – Plaintiff – Direct", *Case on Appeal from Judgment*, 157.

91. Leahy and Lazar, interview, 4.

92. "Earl W. Hammons – Defendant – Direct", *Case on Appeal from Judgment*, 333.

93. "Paul H. Terry – Defendant – Direct", *Case on Appeal from Judgment*, 536.

94. Ibid., 535–536.

95. "Earl W. Hammons – Defendant – Direct", *Case on Appeal from Judgment*, 335–336.

96. "Frank H. Moser – Plaintiff – Direct", *Case on Appeal from Judgment*, 158.

97. Ibid., 158.

98. Ibid., 160; "Frank H. Moser – Plaintiff – Redirect", *Case on Appeal from Judgment*, 673–674; "William M. Weiss – Defendant – Cross", *Case on Appeal from Judgment*, 459; "Paul H. Terry – Defendant – Cross", *Case on Appeal from Judgment*, 575.

99. "Frank H. Moser – Plaintiff – Direct", *Case on Appeal from Judgment*, 159–160; "Frank H. Moser – Plaintiff – Recross", *Case on Appeal from Judgment*, 226.

100. "Nathan L. Vogel – For Plaintiff – Direct", *Case on Appeal from Judgment*, 242–243.

101. "Moser-Terry Cartoon Unit Undergoes Reorganization", *Film Daily*, 3 March 1936, p. 1, 9.

102. "Frank H. Moser – Plaintiff – Direct", *Case on Appeal from Judgment*, 160.

103. Ibid., 160; "More Space for Terry-Toons", *Film Daily*, 18 March 1936, p. 2.

104. "Frank H. Moser – Plaintiff – Direct", *Case on Appeal from Judgment*, 140.

105. "Increase Terry-Toon Production", *Film Daily*, 31 March 1936, p. 2.

106. "George Gordon Promoted", *Film Daily*, 24 March 1936, p. 2.

107. "Heads Terry-Toon Story Dept.", *Film Daily*, 4 April 1936, p. 2.

108. "New Educational Lineup Names Set", *Film Daily*, 28 April 1936, p. 24.

109. "To Set Van Beuren Deal", *Film Daily*, 2 April 1936, p. 1.

110. Jack Zander, phone interview by author (transcript), 13 December 1997, Kelowna, B.C., Canada, Terrytoons Collection, Victoria, B.C., Canada, 2.

111. Joseph Barbera, *My Life in Toons: From Flatbush to Bedrock in Under a Century* (Atlanta: Turner Publishing, Inc., 1994), 54.

112. Zander, interview, 13 December 1997, 2.

113. Maltin, *Of Mice and Magic* (1987), 125.

114. Adrian Bailey, *Walt Disney's World of Fantasy* (New York: Everest House, 1982), 55.

115. Wynn G. Hamonic, ""Disney is the Tiffany's and I am the Woolworth's of the Business": A Critical Re-Analysis of the Business Philosophies, Production Values and Studio Practices of Animator-Producer Paul Houlton Terry", (Ph.D. dissertation, Brunel University, 2011).

116. Thomas James (Tommy) Morrison, interview, 15 June 1970, 13d.

117. Howard Beckerman, interview by author (transcript), August 1996, New York City, Terrytoons Collection, Victoria, B.C., 2.

118. Leahy and Lazar, interview, p. 25.

119. Charles Alicoate, "Short Shots From Eastern Studios", *Film Daily*, 28 May 1936, p. 7.

120. "Four More Artists Added to Terry-Toon Staff", *Film Daily*, 16 June 1936, p. 2.

121. Thomas James (Tommy) Morrison, interview, 15 June 1970, 11d.

122. Richard Gertner, ed., *International Motion Picture Almanac* (New York: Quigley Publishing, 1978), 84; Obituary: "Roger Ferri", *Variety*, 19 July 1978, 291: 108. Tom Morrison remembers that Kiko was suggested by one of the Australian exhibitors or salesman. Thomas James (Tommy) Morrison, interview, 15 June 1970, 21d.

123. "80 Radio Stations In Tieup on Kiko", *Film Daily*, 16 September 1936, p. 24.

124. Barbera, *My Life in Toons*, 55.

125. Terry, interview, 20 December 1969, 76.

126. Barbera, *My Life in Toons*, 54.

127. Thomas James (Tommy) Morrison, interview, 15 June 1970, 21d.

Chapter 16

Cartoons Go to Court: A House Divided, the Moser–Terry Trial, and Terry Takes Control, 1936–1938

While Terry was busy reorganizing his studio, Moser was working with his lawyers and laying the groundwork for a lawsuit. On December 2, 1936, both *Film Daily* and the *New York Times* reported that Moser had filed in the Supreme Court of the State of New York (Westchester County) a claim that Paul H. Terry, president, and William M. Weiss, secretary-treasurer, of Terrytoons Inc., and Earle W. Hammons, president of Educational, conspired to defraud him of a 50 percent interest in the Terrytoons cartoon business. The plaintiff Moser was seeking $500,000 or his restoration of half-interest in the firm.[1] The action was begun on July 21, 1936 by the personal service of the Summons and Complaint on the defendants Terry, Weiss, and Terrytoons, Inc. and on August 1, 1936 on the defendant Hammons.[2]

In his Complaint, Moser plead that he was induced to enter the contract of sale of February 29, 1936, as the result of misrepresentations by the defendants which were fraudulent and material. Moser claimed that the statements were known to be false when made by the personal defendants, were made with intent to induce Moser to act thereon and with intent to deceive and defraud him, and the same was part of a plan on the part of the defendants to induce him to dispose of and part with his interest in the partnership and corporation at a small fraction of its real value (paragraph 55 of the Complaint). The remedy sought here was monetary damages.

Alternatively, Moser plead that if there was no fraud, and if the concealments were innocent or inadvertent and the defendants had reasonable grounds for believing that their false statements were true, then the remedy of rescission is available to him,[3] the purpose of which is to put the parties back into a position as if the contract had never taken place.[4] Moser plead that numerous complaints about the animated cartoons had not been made (paragraph 57), that Educational Films Corporation of America at no time intended to terminate its business relations with Moser & Terry, Inc. (paragraph 58), that Educational Films Corporation of America at all times intended to enter into a new contract or to renew the contract terminating on or about July 1936 (paragraph 59), that neither the capital of the business, corporate or partnership, nor the earnings power thereof had been impaired (paragraph 61), and that real earnings and assets of the business were much greater than represented (paragraph 62). Moser also claimed that Terry be required to account for and directed to pay to him all income salaries, dividends and profits received by Terry while his interest in the partnership and stock was in Terry's possession.[5] The defendants responded by filing their Answers, a pleading which addressed each of allegations contained within the Complaint.[6]

The trial was heard over six days on May 13, 17, 18, 19, 20, and 21, 1937 before Raymond Elbert Aldrich (1888–1947) Supreme Court Justice for the 9th Judicial District of New York. He was elected to the bench in 1933 after

173

Fig. 16.1 – 1937 Terrytoons Studio Group. (left to right) Front Row Seated: Jose Carreon, George Cannata, Edwin Donnelly, Connie Rasinski, Hugh M. Shields, Paul H. Terry, Philip A. Scheib, Mannie Davis, William M. Weiss, George Gordon, Al Ivanoff. Second (Middle) Row: Paul J. Sommer, J. Alan Klein, Joseph Rasinski, Philip Santry, Julie Dean, Carl O. Sacks, Mike Prendergast, Harvey Eisenberg, Esmeralda Fernandes, Vincent Eletto, Carl Meyer, Thomas J. Morrison, Rocco Eletto. Top (Back Row): Ralph Pearson, John Foster, Vivie Risto, Lou Marcus, Dan Ward, Robinson McKee, Armand D'Angelo, Raymond Kelley, Frank Schudde, Walter Gleason.

having received the unanimous endorsement of the Republican county committees and the nomination of the judicial convention. Aldrich had a background in banking and was a graduate of Albany (N.Y.) Law School in 1909 (LL.B.). On November 23, 1909, he was admitted to the New York bar. Aldrich clerked for Judge Morschauser. From 1910 to 1915 he practiced independently before being elected district attorney of Dutchess County in 1916. He was re-elected to that office twice, but resigned in December 1922 and then organized the firm of Aldrich, Morschauser (Joseph, Jr.) & Haas (Edward K.) practicing until 1933.[7] As an attorney he was upright, fearless, and honest and was considered to have a keen legal mind along with having a good deal of patience, courtesy and human understanding.[8] With Aldrich's experience, credentials, and character, all parties to the legal proceedings would be assured of receiving an impartial, well-reasoned and discerning judgment.

The attorney for Frank Moser was Emanuel Luria (1902–1996), a graduate of New York University Law School and admitted to the bar in 1929.[9] Luria was a rising talent in the New York legal community and the case would provide him with a little media coverage to help promote his career. At trial, Samuel A. Shacter[10] (b. 1902), a graduate of law school at New York University and who was admitted to the bar in 1927, conducted the direct examinations of Moser and cross-examinations of the defendants at trial. Prior to trial, examinations were conducted by Shacter of some of the defendants, including Bill Weiss. Earle Hammons' attorney was originally Norman C. Nicholson (1900–1966)[11] who filed much of the pleadings leading to trial but was replaced by the distinguished Henry R. Barrett (1869–1940). Barrett, who was 67 years of age at time of trial, graduated A.B. at Lafayette College in 1890. He studied law at White Plains, New York. He was an authority on condemnation matters, his practice growing out of watershed rights in the Hudson Valley. In 1918 he founded the White Plains Publishing Co. He was a leader in

Chapter 16 • Cartoons Go to Court

Fig. 16.2 – Al Ivanoff, sound editor.

civic life in White Plains, New York and drafted the city's charter.[12]

Barrett was not experienced in civil litigation and personal injury matters. Therefore, Barrett's associate, Arthur D. Brennan, handled much of the trial work including the cross-examinations of Moser and Terry. Brennan (1899–1993), a graduate of Syracuse University (LL.B., 1923), possessed a brilliant legal mind and would lead a stellar career in law. Mr. Brennan was elected a judge of the Westchester County Court in 1951. Two years later, he was elected a justice of the New York State Supreme Court for the Ninth District. In 1960, he was named an associate justice of the Appellate Division for the Second Judicial Department, where he served until he retired in 1976.[13] Hugh S. Williamson (1896–1965), a partner of the firm Breed, Abbott & Morgan, a graduate of Columbia University in 1922 where he received his law degree three years later,[14] handled the trial work and examinations for Terry and Weiss.

The trial received considerable media attention and opened with Frank Moser taking the stand under direct examination by his attorney Shacter. Moser provided a history of the early years of the studio, his struggles with a stubborn Terry to improve the cartoons, the complaints received from their distributors, Hammons refusal to renegotiate the contract, and the eventual sale of his 50 percent share of the business to Terry.[15] In his direct examination, Moser emphasized his ignorance in financial and business matters, his trust in Weiss with respect to his personal finances, and that it was Terry and Weiss who handled the business affairs outside of production.[16] He provided evidence that Terry and Hammons had known each other intimately for years thus laying suspicion that both conspired to deceive him into selling his half-interest in the business.[17]

Under cross-examination by Williamson, the wily attorney attempted to elicit from Moser that he was aware of many of the financial and business matters related to producing an animated cartoon but the lawyer met with difficulty in doing so.[18] Williamson's intent was to obtain evidence that Moser wasn't ignorant or naive about the company's net worth and that he had the knowledge and ability to determine the value of the company prior to the sale. Moser denied awareness of what the corporation's income had been, the corporate receipts from distribution of the films, and the cost of producing an animated cartoon.[19] He did admit knowing that he received one-half interest from the company's income, but denied receiving financial statements of the corporation.[20] Moser informed the court that his focus was on the animation and left the business and financial matters to Terry and Weiss.[21]

Moser was then briefly cross-examined by Brennan on issues with respect to Moser's belief, although mistaken, that Fox Film could have prevented Educational Pictures from renewing the contract. Moser held firm to his understanding that since all other distributors had contracts for cartoons to distribute that Educational was the only source through which the animated cartoons could have been distributed.[22] Moser admitted that he never asked Terry to join with him in an attempt to find some other distribution company to distribute the product after Educational informed them that they were not

175

Fig. 16.3 – Animation background, attributed to Johnny Vita.

going to renew.[23] Moser seemed to believe that such efforts would prove futile. On the redirect, Shacter focused on the issue of Weiss's failure to include cash in the bank and the accounts receivable in the estimation of the value of the company prior to the sale.[24] He also was able to demonstrate to the court that Weiss did not keep accurate records of Moser's income tax records.[25] Williamson then tried to bring forward admissions by Moser that he kept detailed records of his own financial matters, but again Moser denied keeping track of his bank accounts, and that he was never given financial statements of the company.[26]

The next to take the stand was Moser's witness Nathan Vogel, an experienced certified public accountant who had been practicing since 1918.[27] Vogel had conducted an audit of Terrytoons and prepared financial statements quite different from Weiss's work. Vogel's financial statements indicated that the company was worth considerable more than Weiss had estimated at the time of the sale of Moser's share to Terry. Vogel testified that Mr. Weiss's salary was increased after the sale of the business thereby implying that Weiss was rewarded for his duplicitous work.[28] Mr. Vogel also testified that at the time of the sale of the business the company had significant amounts of cash in the banks and outstanding accounts receivables which were not included by Weiss in his financial statements forwarded to Moser. Shacter also successfully elicited from Vogel that the income generated from the business was significantly more than what was reported by Weiss.[29] Other issues were discussed including valuations of company revenues, trademarks, and goodwill, all of which with the intent of demonstrating to the court that the company was significantly undervalued by Weiss at the time Moser sold his 50 percent stake to Terry.[30]

Under cross-examination by Williamson, the attorney first tried to discredit Vogel for having no experience with the system of accounting used generally in the motion picture business including

Chapter 16 • Cartoons Go to Court

Fig. 16.4 – Paul Terry residence, 40 Ocean Avenue, Larchmont, New York.

amortizing costs and liquidation.[31] Williamson questioned whether he would change his opinion based on the fact that 75 percent of the distribution on the animated cartoons was on a selective basis whereby the theater owner could choose to exhibit them. Vogel said, "No".[32] However, Williamson was able to hammer home the point that Vogel did not factor in the effect of liquidation of the business and its effect on the net worth of the company.[33] Williamson also attacked Vogel's accounting on the fact that he did not take into account income differences with respect to international distribution. He asked the accountant whether the company had outstanding debts not accounted for which Vogel replied in the negative.[34] Williamson also drove home the point that while Weiss got a salary increase after the sale, so did a number of other Terrytoons animation staff.[35]

The next witness to take the stand was Earl Hammons. His testimony was crucial in the determination of whether there was any misrepresentation on behalf of the defendants. The issue before the court was: Did Hammons make a factual misrepresentation, knowing that it is false (fraudulent misrepresentation) (or had reasonable grounds for believing that his false statement was true (innocent misrepresentation)) and intending it to be relied on by the recipient? There was little question before the court that Moser relied upon and acted upon the representation (i.e. the distribution contract was not going to be renewed) to his detriment. His lawyer, Arthur Brennan, began the direct examination and Hammons outlined the history of complaints received with respect to the Terrytoons shorts.

Hammons stated the reason why he did not renew the contract, "When they told me they had come to see me about the renewal of the contract I informed them that I didn't believe that I could renew the contract because I had been complaining for months about the quality of the product they were delivering, and that while they had promised me to improve the product yet they had not done so, and I did not see my way clear at that time to give them a renewal of the

177

Fig. 16.5 – Mannie Davis (left) and Tom Morrison (right) in the story department.

contract".[36] The main problem Hammons pointed out was that the cartoons were of poor entertainment quality.[37] Hammons also described in considerable detail Terry's visit with him after he had purchased Moser's share and what convinced him to change his mind:

> He (Terry) stated that he and Mr. Moser had not been getting along well together, that he wanted to do one thing and that Mr. Moser would not permit him to do so, and that they were constantly fighting, and that he was at his wits end, and he finally determined to buy him out and had done so, and that he wanted a renewal of the contract because he would make good pictures for us, he was going to increase his facilities a great deal and was going to a lot of expense, and that he could produce good pictures. Well, I have known Mr. Terry for over 20 years, or about 20 years at least, and I knew for a great many years he had produced good pictures, and I knew that a house divided and fighting amongst itself, as he told me they had, and I had had a suspicion that they were doing it, and the elimination of that, that he probably could and would make good pictures, and I told him that under those conditions that I felt very favorable toward renewing the contract with him, but that I had to talk to my associates at the office because we had almost decided not to renew the contract, but that I would explain to them the extra expense that he was going to and we would consider it favorably.[38]

Hammons then explained that he discussed the matter with Jack Skirball, general sales manager, and a few other principals and the contract was renewed. Terry was able to convince Hammons to renew for two years considering the extra capital Terry was investing in the cartoon product.[39] Hammons was quick to point out that although he had known Terry for about 20 years that his meetings with Terry were infrequent, and that Educational Films had no other financial interest in Moser & Terry, Inc.[40]

Under cross-examination by Mr. Williamson, the attorney requested Hammons provide his opinion on what the goodwill of Moser & Terry, Inc. would be of the company without a distribution contract and Hammons replied, "Nil".[41] In an attempt to draw evidence that the Terrytoons business was valuable to Educational Films despite the poor quality of the films, Shacter tried to clarify how much of the Terrytoons business accounted for Educational Films gross and net profit which Hammons confirmed to be less than 18 percent on the gross.[42] However, on further questioning Hammons admitted that Terrytoons receipts accounted for 22 percent of total receipts.[43] This was an important admission because it brought into question whether Hammons was being truthful in stating that Educational Films was not going to renew the contract because why would Hammons want to decline a renewal when Terrytoons cartoons encompassed a significant percentage of their gross sales and income?

Shacter then tried to bring to the court's attention whether Hammons and Terry could have conceivably conspired against Moser based on the closeness of their relationship. After much

Chapter 16 • Cartoons Go to Court

questioning, Shacter was able to draw from Hammons that he was very good friends with Terry.[44] Shacter also was able to enter as evidence photographs and marketing which excluded Moser and featured Terry prominently with the intention of showing a prejudicial attitude of Educational towards Moser.[45] Moser's attorney also called Hammon's attention to a *The Motion Picture Daily* article that was published before the renewal of the contract. The article reported that Educational planned the same quota of 26 Terrytoons cartoons for the 1936–1937 season. Hammons had no comment.[46] Shacter than had Hammons repeat what he told Terry and Moser on February 24, 1936 with respect to his statements regarding not renewing the contract. Hammons kept his calm and did not change his retelling of the incident that on that day he was definitely not going to renew the contract.[47]

Norman C. Nicholson, the assistant treasurer and secretary of Educational Pictures, Inc., was next to take the stand. Originally, he was the attorney for Hammons. He testified that Educational Films Corporation of America derived 15 percent of the gross from the product manufactured by Moser & Terry, and then he detailed in great length the overhead including advertising, contract, play date, sales, auditing, accounting, music and title, and legal departments.[48] The objective of these questions was to downplay the profitability of the Terrytoons shorts to Educational's bottom line thereby providing justification for

Fig. 16.6 – Voice artist Arthur Kay (born Albert Kalfus) (standing left) and John Foster (standing right).

Hammons and management to not renew the shorts. On cross-examination, Shacter was able to have Nicholson clarify that of the receipts mentioned earlier by the assistant treasurer that there is an additional item for Canadian receipts and that in the years Educational has been acting as distributor for Terrytoons there has never been a penny of loss in the accounts receivables.[49]

William Weiss took the stand and explained how he arrived at the totals in the statement of February 26 which Moser relied upon.[50] Weiss chronicled the events on the day the deal was consummated, February 29. The day began with meeting Moser at Grand Central Station where Moser told him he was going to sell his interest to Terry. The two then went to see Moser's attorney Theodore Kelly at the Hotel Shelton where Weiss answered various questions regarding the statements he prepared including, according to Weiss, disclosing the cash in the banks to Kelly. Weiss then explained that after Moser told him to wait in the lobby of the Shelton, Moser later came back and let Weiss know that he and Kelly discussed the matter and that he intended to sell his share to Terry. Moser then retrieved his stocks from the bank a contract of sale was drafted and signed, and money exchanged.[51]

Weiss also gave evidence that he showed Moser charts of the weekly gross business for all of the United States and Canada. According to Weiss, Moser was shown all of the financial statements prepared by him including the budgets and foreign business.[52] Weiss also testified that in the latter part of 1935 Moser said that considering the business had dropped in the previous months that he was not going to put any more money into "if it didn't make a go on its own feet", as well as said that "I would never put another nickel into a business with Terry if it was the last thing I did".[53]

179

When Weiss was cross-examined by Shacter, Weiss admitted he left out cash and accounts receivables on the statement but that he had no intent to conceal any part of the assets, that Moser was aware of these omissions, and that his estimate was simply a conservative guess.[54] Weiss admitted under heated cross-examination that he never said anything to Moser about the cash on hand, cash in the bank, and accounts receivable.[55] Shacter went through his statement of February 26 and asked Weiss how he arrived at the various totals in his statement while questioning the methodology used in arriving at the totals.[56] Shacter pointed out that Weiss had used older financial statements when compiling averages for his statement, a period of time when the studio was still growing and revenues were not as strong.[57]

Weiss was allowed to correct his answers from his earlier testimony. He admitted that he saw Terry late on the evening of the 28th to discuss the February 26 financial statement he had prepared, a sign he may have been hiding something from the court.[58] Weiss also admitted using the total expected revenues of $75,000 rather than what the company had recently been earning ($105,000 to $125,000) because he thought the business was going to be liquidated.[59] Weiss also admitted eliminating foreign income in the event the liquidation went beyond his original estimate on the domestic as any foreign income would take care of an additional drop in the domestic income.[60] He testified he left out cash because of compensating items (payroll, accrued interest, taxes).[61]

With a little bravado, Paul Terry began his testimony with a meticulous and lengthy overview of his early career in animation before being abruptly interrupted by his own counsel who advised him to begin at the time when he and Moser first went into a partnership.[62] Paul, drawing on his great memory, wrapped his recollections with a tremendous amount of background information while sporadically injecting a little humor into his retelling. He was relaxed and focused on recollecting the events of the week leading up to the purchase of Moser's stake. He didn't appear to be a man being sued for a half million dollars with the future of his studio at stake.

Terry corroborated much of the earlier testimony from the other defendants. He testified that Moser was not ignorant of company finances. He was regularly informed of the weekly grosses, and was aware of the production costs.[63] When describing the events surrounding Moser's departure, Terry told the court that Moser appeared glad to leave and was anxious to travel and enjoy time with family after 19 years in the animation business.[64] According to Terry, once Hammons had informed the partners that Educational was not going to renew the contract Frank wanted to close the studio down as soon as possible, while he wanted to keep the business going for sake of the staff and their families.[65] In Moser's testimony, it was Terry who wanted to close the deal soon, while in Terry's evidence it was Moser who was pressuring him to purchase his stock.[66] After the purchase of Moser's shares, Terry corroborated Hammons' testimony by recollecting that he let Hammons know that he was prepared to plow back every available dollar that was earned back into the business, and that it was this promise that convinced Hammons to renew the contract.[67]

Under cross-examination, Shacter questioned Terry why on February 24, 1936 he didn't make the same attractive promises (i.e. to spend money and make improvements and turn out a better cartoon) to Hammons as he did after he bought Moser's stock. Terry's response was that his relationship with Moser made that impossible.[68] Terry testified that it was his idea to rent a room for a new story department and that Moser was against the idea. Terry testified that Moser never wanted to invest in the studio, "he was only interested in taking it out".[69] Terry closed his testimony with answers to a series of questions from the court, the most significant being his assertion that after purchasing Moser's stock he believed he was taking a chance on finding a distributor. Terry stated: "There had been no contract signed and the only thing I had to go on was the faith in myself, and feeling quite confident that if I didn't put it over with Mr. Hammons I could put it over with somebody else".[70]

Harvey B. Day provided testimony on the quality of the Terrytoons shorts and feedback received from

Chapter 16 • Cartoons Go to Court

Fox executives. Day, a witness for the defendants, provided evidence that would support the inference that Hammons would have cause to refuse to renew the distribution contract. Day recollected the large number of complaints received from the sales and distribution organizations and bookers and that some shorts were so poor that when screened in front of an audience they never even generated a single snicker or laugh.[71] By 1935, Day was afraid that the inferior quality of the cartoons was beginning to erode the goodwill of the Fox Corporation. Day also believed like Terry did that entertainment quality was more important than whether the short was colored.[72] With respect to liquidation, Day testified that a company gets about 50 percent of the value of the company compared to if it was a going concern.[73] Day also testified that it was Terry that wanted to "put in everything he possibly could and make a special effort to build up the products", and it was for this reason he received a two-year contract.[74] On re-cross, Day admitted that a liquidated company will take in 60 to 65 percent of the previous year's income on the product released the year of its liquidation.[75]

Philip Scheib, a witness for the defendants, provided brief testimony on the complaints received on the Terrytoons cartoons and the heated friction between Moser and Terry as to whether the studio should produce cartoons in color. Moser felt color was necessary to keep pace with other studios and Terry disagreed.[76] On cross-examination, Shacter got Scheib to disclose that Moser wanted the moviola which Terry did not feel was necessary and because there was no room for the machine.[77] Scheib also testified that Moser was regularly informed about the gross receipts.[78] On re-direct examination by Williamson, Scheib informed the court that Moser was not prepared to put any money in "any crazy idea of Paul's".[79]

Thomas F. Thompson (1901-1999),[80] a witness for the defendants and a certified public accountant, provided evidence that from an accounting perspective a company in liquidation would have a considerably lower book value than a going concern thereby providing support for Weiss's conservative estimate of the net worth of the company as contained in the financial statement of February 24.[81] Thompson also provided his own financial statements that aligned with figures from Weiss's statement. On cross, Shacter questioned Thompson's lack of experience in the film business and then tried to obtain from Thompson admissions that tended to show that Weiss was too conservative in his net worth estimate and failed to take into account certain income streams using various hypothetical scenarios, anticipation of earnings, and contingent liabilities.[82]

Jack Skirball, general sales manager with Educational Films Corporation of America, was called to testify about the complaints received about the Terrytoons product and that he recommended to Hammons that the contract should not be renewed. He also testified that after talking with Hammons he agreed to the two-year renewal as Terry had promised to make significant investments in the studio to improve the product.[83] Nathan Vogel was then recalled in rebuttal to provide further testimony on various accounting issues such as bad debts and anticipated revenues that supported the conclusion that Weiss's financial estimations of net worth were too conservative.[84]

Finally, D. Theodore Kelly[85] (1882–1962) was called for rebuttal. Kelly was a graduate of New York Law School, admitted to the New York bar in 1905, was the founder and senior partner of the New York law firm of Kelly, Hewitt & Harte. He was president and board chairman of the Lumber Mutual Casualty Company. As previously noted, Kelly was present during the negotiations leading up to the sale of Moser's share and testified that no mention was made by Weiss to Moser as to the cash in the bank or the accounts receivable.[86] Kelly advised Moser that an audit by a third party should be made of Terrytoons before he agreed to sell his share, a recommendation from a senior attorney with over 30 years experience which Moser unwisely did not act upon.[87] All parties then rested and Williamson closed with submission of a Notice to Dismiss on the grounds that the causes of action alleged had not been proven by the

Fig. 16.7 – Testing the negatives to spot errors in the animation (Lester Schudde at camera).

plaintiff against the defendants. Decision on that motion was reserved.[88] The trial was both a lesson in the financial accounting methods of a 1930s animation studio as well as sombre reminder of the precarious business of producing animated cartoons during the Golden Age of Animation when the fortunes of a studio were so closely tied to securing and maintaining a contract with a distributor. As previously noted, when Van Beuren Studios lost their distributor RKO in 1936, there was no choice except to close the production facility. While much of the testimony focused on tedious financial matters, there was still considerable courtroom drama as Moser's attorney attempted to uncover evidence of a conspiracy among Terry, Weiss and Hammons to induce Moser to sell his share in the business. Terry's motivation to buy out his partner is not difficult to understand. With Moser out of the equation, he would have full control of studio operations and could set about producing cartoons he believed would best entertain audiences. Certainly there was motivation for Hammons to deceive Moser. Educational was receiving a significant portion of their revenues from the distribution of Terrytoons. The quality of the shorts had fallen off in 1935 and Hammons was taking complaints about the cartoons from Fox executives. Hammons had suspected that Moser and Terry were bickering among themselves and that these disagreements were disrupting efforts to improve the quality of the shorts. With Moser bought out there was every reason to believe that Terry would invest in his studio and the quality of the shorts would improve.

The decision of Justice Aldrich was eagerly expected by the media and was rendered on September 20, 1937, when the judge granted judgment in favor of the defendants with costs to the defendants against the plaintiff. Justice Aldrich held that the defendants did nothing and said nothing with any design to cheat

Chapter 16 • Cartoons Go to Court

Fig. 16.8 – Walter Addison, sculptor, creating cartoon character models.

the plaintiff in any way, nor was there any misrepresentation or concealment on their part without intention to deceive or fraudulently represent any fact. The statement made by the defendant Hammons on February 24, 1936, to the plaintiff and the defendant, Terry, to the effect that he did not intend to renew the contract with Moser & Terry, Inc., in the opinion of Aldrich represented an honest expression of his then belief and opinion in good faith. In making these statements Aldrich decided that Hammons was trying to protect the interests of Educational Films Corporation of America to the best of his ability. The statement was a truthful expression of his then conviction. The fact that he reached a different conclusion on March 2, 1936 and renewed the contract did not change the fact that the defendant made no fraudulent representation on February 24, 1936.[89]

Aldrich further found that the first time Hammons had any knowledge of the purchase or intention to purchase Moser's share was on March 1, 1936.[90] Aldrich held that William Weiss gave the best information he could under the circumstances and honestly believed in the reasonable accuracy of the figures shown on the statement.[91] Further, Terry did nothing and said nothing with any design to cheat Moser in any way and entered into the agreement with the plaintiff in good faith.[92] Aldrich found that the contract with Moser & Terry, Inc. was not a substantial part of the profitable business of Educational Films Corporation of America.[93] The renewal of the contract for two years was brought about by the commitment of Terry to invest additional funds in the business and to keep it invested and to afford the defendant Terry to cash in on the increased overhead.[94]

In his written opinion, Aldrich's reasoning for his decision was explained. Aldrich could find no evidence to substantiate a claim against Hammons. Hammons had no interest in Moser & Terry, Inc., or in the partnership. With respect to Weiss, he was a very competent accountant, his books and records accurately reflected the true condition of the corporation and of the partnership. The written statement of Weiss never purported to be a balance sheet. It was merely an estimate and an expression of opinion by Weiss based on his experience and knowledge of the books as to what Moser and Terry might be reasonably expected to salvage in the way of money upon the liquidation of the business, in the event that the elimination of the distribution outlet through Educational Films Corporation required such liquidation.[95]

As to Terry, Moser wasn't even prepared to see the current contract out until the end of the year while Terry was not prepared to quit. Moser sold his share and Terry was animated by optimism that induced him to continue rather than give up. Each of the parties was acting in good faith. Moser received as much as he could have received viewed from the standpoint of a potential liquidation. Terry went back to Hammons to persuade Hammons to change his mind and this was not a suspicious circumstance under the conditions established. Terry obtained the renewal based on his perseverance and persuasion. Each of Moser and Terry made his bargain in good faith and at arm's length and with the full knowledge of the situation as it then appeared to exist.[96]

Wanting further legal redress, Moser, as plaintiff-appellant, filed

183

an appeal in the New York Supreme Court, Appellate Division, Second Department. The Notice of Appeal was filed on October 28, 1937 by Emanuel Luria.[97] The brief of the plaintiff-appellant, submitted by Luria and Shacter and argued by I. Maurice Wormser, was filed and in the argument cited relevant common (case) law. Moser argued on four points of law. He argued that the plaintiff was induced to enter into the contract of sale of February 29, 1936, as the result of fraudulent and material misrepresentations by defendants, which necessitate a rescission of the contract (Point I).

To further this argument he argued that that actual conspiracy may be inferred from the circumstances. Next, he argued that Terry was unjustly and unconscionably enriched by reason of the innocent misrepresentations, the minds of the plaintiff and defendant Terry did not meet, as they contracted on the basis of misapprehension and misunderstanding of highly material matters of fact including the omission of cash and accounts receivable from Weiss's statement, that income accruing was radically underestimated, and that the full cost of producing the last 13 animated cartoons, from start to finish, was not properly chargeable, and the cost could not amount to any such sum (Point II).

Moser further argued that serious error was committed by the exclusion of evidence offered by Moser which would have shown Hammons' consistently prejudicial attitude towards Moser and his favoritism and partiality to Terry, in disregard of the terms of the contract between Moser & Terry and Educational Films Corporation Moser should have been afforded reasonable leeway to develop his claim of fraudulent conspiracy, and should have been allowed to show Hammons' bias in favor of Terry (Point III). Finally, he argued that the judgment of the Special Term should be reversed, with costs, and judgment directed to be entered for the plaintiff; or, a new trial should be ordered. [98]

The appellate brief of Hammons was submitted by Henry Barrett and was argued by Arthur D. Brennan. The appellate brief of the respondents Paul H. Terry, William M. Weiss and Terrytoons, Inc. was submitted by the firm of Breed, Abbott & Morgan and was argued by Hugh S. Williamson. Moser, as appellant, also filed an Appellant's Reply Brief in response to the two briefs of the defendants. The Reply Brief further advanced an argument of collusion between Terry and Hammons drawing upon the trial testimony and related evidence. On June 6, 1938, the judgment of the Supreme Court, Appellate Division, Second Department, New York (five members: Lazansky, P.J., Hagarty, Carswell, Adel and Close, JJ.) dismissed the complaint unanimously affirmed, with costs against the plaintiff-appellant.[99] A motion for leave to appeal to the Court of Appeals, New York State's highest court, was denied on October 7, 1938 by Lazansky, P.J., Hagarty, Carswell, Davis and Johnston, JJ.[100]

Moser was now at the end of his appeals. Most likely the attorney fees and court costs he incurred in bringing and litigating his claim had taken a big bite out of the funds he received from his 50 percent share of the business. In later years, Moser resided with his artist wife Isabel Moser[101] and was chiefly involved in landscape and portrait painting, in both oils and watercolors, and he exhibited his work at galleries in New York City and in White Plains and Westchester County, including those of the Yonkers and Hudson Valley Art Associations.[102] Frank Moser made the correct decision not to sell his nearly worthless stocks and investments after the 1929 stock market crash like other investors had done and when the stock market recovered he was able to live off of his investment income and his artwork he sold, sometimes based on commission.[103] He found recreation in fishing and collecting Indian arrowheads.[104] With Moser out of the picture, Terry could now divert all of his energies towards developing a cartoon product having an entertainment value that would satisfy movie-going audiences. ❧

Chapter 16 • Cartoons Go to Court

Notes

1. "Suit Filed Over Sale Of Cartoon Interest", *New York Times*, 2 December 1936, p. 6:4; "$500,000 Asked in Cartoon Suit Against Paul H. Terry", *Film Daily*, 2 December 1936, p. 4.

2. "Summons", *Case on Appeal from Judgment*, 5; "Complaint", *Case on Appeal from Judgment*, 6–31.

3. "Complaint", *Case on Appeal from Judgment*, 16–17; "Brief of the Plaintiff-Appellant", *Case on Appeal from Judgment*, 16.

4. Prior to *Hedley Byrne v Heller* [1964] A.C. 465 where the court found that a statement made negligently that was relied upon can be actionable in tort, all misrepresentations that were not fraudulent were considered to be innocent. The Court in *Hedley Byrne* found that a statement made negligently that was relied upon can be actionable in tort.

5. "Complaint", *Case on Appeal from Judgment*, 16–20.

6. "Answer of Defendants Paul H. Terry, William M. Weiss and Terrytoons, Inc.", *Case on Appeal from Judgment*, 32–33; "Answer of Earl W. Hammons", *Case on Appeal from Judgment*, 34–35.

7. "Aldrich, Raymond Elbert", *The National Cyclopaedia of American Biography*, volume XXXIV (New York: James T. White & Company, 1948), 83–84. Obituary: "Justice Aldrich Is Dead of Stroke", *New York Times*, 23 January 1947, p. 23.

8. "Justice Inducted Amid Flowers, Flowery Talk", *The Daily Argus* (Mount Vernon, New York), 3 January 1934, p. 9; "Aldrich Takes Post on Bench; Disowns Praise", *The Herald Statesman* (Yonkers, New York), 3 January 1934, p. 5.

9. *Martindale-Hubbell Law Directory*, volume II, Eightieth Annual Edition (New York: Martindale-Hubbell Law Directory, Incorporated, 1948), 1073.

10. *Martindale-Hubbell Law Directory*, volume II, Eighty-Second Annual Edition (Summit, New Jersey: Martindale-Hubbell Law Directory, Incorporated, 1952), 1201.

11. Obituary: "Norman C. Nicholson", *New York Times*, 11 December 1966, p. 88:8.

12. "Barrett, Henry Robertson", *The National Cyclopaedia of American Biography*, volume XXIX (Ann Arbor, Michigan: University Microfilms, 1967), 398–399. Obituary: "Henry R. Barrett of White Plains, 70", *New York Times*, 5 February 1940, p. 17:5.

13. *The Lawyer's Directory 1946* (Cincinnati, Ohio: The Lawyer's Directory, Inc., 1946), 319; *Martindale-Hubbell Law Directory*, volume II, Eighty-Second Annual Edition (Summit, New Jersey: Martindale-Hubbell Law Directory, Incorporated, 1950), 1823. Obituary: "Arthur D. Brennan: Judge, 94", *New York Times*, 15 November 1993, p. D14.

14. Obituary: "Hugh S. Williamson", *New York Times*, 13 May 1965, p. 37:4.

15. "Frank H. Moser – Plaintiff – Direct", *Case on Appeal from Judgment*, 107–164.

16. Ibid., 122–123, 126.

17. Ibid., 125.

18. "Frank H. Moser – Plaintiff – Cross", *Case on Appeal from Judgment*, 164–208.

19. Ibid., 166–167.

20. Ibid., 169.

21. Ibid., 179.

22. Ibid., 208–209.

23. Ibid., 210.

24. "Frank H. Moser – Plaintiff – Redirect", *Case on Appeal from Judgment*, 217.

25. Ibid., 233–237.

26. Ibid., 221–224.

27. "Nathan L. Vogel – for Plaintiff – Direct", *Case on Appeal from Judgment*, 242.

28. Ibid., 242–243.

29. Ibid., 248–257.

30. Ibid., 257–285.

31. "Nathan L. Vogel – for Plaintiff – Redirect", *Case on Appeal from Judgment*, 285–288.

32. Ibid., 287.

33. Ibid., 290.

34. Ibid., 305–308.

35. Ibid., 312.

36. "Earl W. Hammons – Defendant –Direct", *Case on Appeal from Judgment*, 328.

37. Ibid., 329.

38. Ibid., 333.

39. Ibid., 336.

40. Ibid., 337.

41. "Earl W. Hammons – Defendant – Cross", *Case on Appeal from Judgment*, 345.

42. Ibid., 350–351.

43. Ibid., 375.

44. Ibid., 356.

45. Ibid., 364–370.

46. Ibid., 377–378.

47. Ibid., 392.

48. "Norman C. Nicholson – for Defendants – Direct", *Case on Appeal from Judgment*, 405–409.

49. Ibid., 410–411.

50. "William M. Weiss – Defendant – Direct", *Case on Appeal from Judgment*, 412–415.

51. Ibid., 418–422.

52. Ibid., 423–427.

53. Ibid., 429.

54. "William M. Weiss – Defendant – Cross", *Case on Appeal from Judgment*, 432, 447–448.

55. Ibid., 440.

56. Ibid., 433–512.

57. Ibid., 446.

58. Ibid., 447.

59. Ibid., 466.

60. Ibid., 469.

61. Ibid., 501.

62. "Paul H. Terry – Defendant – Direct", *Case on Appeal from Judgment*, 516.

63. Ibid., 517–518.

64. Ibid., 522–523.

65. Ibid., 526.

66. Ibid., 528.

67. Ibid., 536.

68. "Paul H. Terry – Defendant – Cross", *Case on Appeal from Judgment*, 537.

69. Ibid., 554.

70. "Paul H. Terry – Defendant – Recross", *Case on Appeal from Judgment*, 581–582.

71. "Harvey B. Day – for Defendants – Direct", *Case on Appeal from Judgment*, 587–588.

72. Ibid., 591.

73. Ibid., 592.

74. "Harvey B. Day – for Defendants – Redirect", *Case on Appeal from Judgment*, 597.

75. "Harvey B. Day – for Defendants – Recross", *Case on Appeal from Judgment*, 598–599.

76. "Philip A. Scheib – for Defendants – Direct", *Case on Appeal from Judgment*, 609.

77. "Philip A. Scheib – for Defendants – Cross", *Case on Appeal from Judgment*, 613–614, 616.

78. "Philip A. Scheib – for Defendants – Direct", *Case on Appeal from Judgment*, 609–610.

79. "Philip A. Scheib – for Defendants – Redirect", *Case on Appeal from Judgment*, 619.

80. Biography: "Thompson, Thomas Frederick", *Who's Who in the East, 1981–1982* (Chicago, Illinois: Marquis Who's Who, Inc., 1981), 781.

81. "Thomas F. Thompson – for Defendants – Direct", *Case on Appeal from Judgment*, 621–627.

82. "Thomas F. Thompson – for Defendants – Cross", *Case on Appeal from Judgment*, 627–641.

83. "Jack H. Skirball – for Defendants – Direct", *Case on Appeal from Judgment*, 655–658.

84. "Nathan Vogel – for Plaintiff – Recalled in Rebuttal – Direct", *Case on Appeal from Judgment*, 662–666.

85. Obituary: "D. Theodore Kelly", *New York Times*, 11 November 1962, p. 88:8; *Martindale-Hubbell Law Directory*, volume II, Eighty-Second Annual Edition (Summit, New Jersey: Martindale-Hubbell Law Directory, Incorporated, 1950), 1382.

86. "D. Theodore Kelly – for Plaintiff – Recalled in Rebuttal – Direct", *Case on Appeal from Judgment*, 673–675.

87. Ibid., 681.

88. "Notice to Dismiss", *Case on Appeal from Judgment*, 699.

89. "Decision", *Case on Appeal from Judgment*, 102–103.

90. Ibid., 100.

91. Ibid., 97.

92. Ibid., 97.

93. Ibid., 102.

94. Ibid., 101.

95. "Opinion", *Case on Appeal from Judgment*, 945–948.

96. Ibid., 948–950. These findings of fact and conclusions of law are found in: "Defendants' Terry, Weiss and Terrytoons, Inc. Proposed Findings of Fact and Conclusions of Law", (*Case on Appeal from Judgment*, 36–39), "Defendant Earl W. Hammons Proposed Findings of Fact and Conclusions of Law", (*Case on Appeal from Judgment*, 40–45), "Plaintiff's Proposed Findings of Fact and Conclusions of Law", (*Case on Appeal from Judgment*, 46–93). "Court Dismisses Moser's Complaint Following Trial", *Film Daily*, 13 July 1937, p. 1, 13.

97. "Notice of Appeal", *Case on Appeal from Judgment*, 3–4.

98. "Brief of Plaintiff-Appellant", *Case on Appeal from Judgment*.

99. 254 A.D. 873; 6 N.Y.S. 2d 345; 1938 N.Y. App. Div. LEXIS 8119.

100. 255 A.D. 783; 7 N.Y.S. 2d 220; 1938 N.Y. App. Div. LEXIS 5296.

101. "Moser, Isabel Fairclough", *Who's Who of American Women (and Women of Canada): A Biographical Dictionary of Notable Living Women of the United States of America and Other Countries, 1968–1969*, 5th ed. (Chicago: The A.N. Marquis Company, 1969). Moser was married twice, the first time on June 6, 1914 in New York City to Anna Augusta Margareta Hård (Nilsson) (b. abt. 1888, Stockholm, Sweden), a registered nurse. By this marriage, he had two children: John Frank and Marjorie. Marjorie died at age 14 from tubercular meningitis in August 1929. She contracted the disease during the summer of 1929 while at a camp in Vermont. Despondent over her daughter's death, Anna Moser committed suicide on December 9, 1929. She had poisoned herself with gas that was released from the kitchen range. He was married the second time in New York City, September 1, 1932, to Isabele [Isabel], daughter of Edward Fairclough of that city. Paul Terry was best man at the wedding. Frank Moser was animating the Bud and Susie shorts for Bray Productions where he met Isabel, who was working as an inker and tracer at the time. Frank Moser was a Republican politically. Frank Moser died on September 30, 1964 in Dobbs Ferry Hospital, Dobbs Ferry, New York. Obituaries: "Frank Moser, Co-Founder of Terrytoons", *The Standard-Star* (New Rochelle, NY), 2 October 1964, p. 2; "Frank Moser Dead; Cartoonist Was 78", *New York Times*, 2 October 1964, p. 37.

102. "Moser, Frank H.", *National Cyclopedia of American Biography*, vol. 52 (N.Y.: James T. White and Co., 1970), 607.

103. Tragedy struck Moser on May 4, 1939, when while driving an automobile, he accidentally struck 5 1/2- year-old Manfried Hauptmann, the son of Bruno Richard Hauptmann (who was electrocuted four years earlier for the kidnapping of Charles Lindbergh's baby). In February 1940, the jury of the Bronx Supreme Court awarded damages of $23,500 to Manfried who had suffered a leg injury, and $2,000 to Mrs. Hauptmann. In July 1940, Mrs. Hauptmann requested a reduction of the damage award in an attempt to avoid prolonged litigation. The final settlement figure was never released to or reported by the media. "$25,500 to Hauptmanns", *New York Times*, 2 February 1940, p. 19:1; "Aids Mrs. Hauptmann", *New York Times*, 12 July 1940, p. 17:8.

104. His wife provides a good profile on her husband in an interview conducted by Harvey Deneroff in 1970. Isabele F. Moser, interview by Harvey Deneroff, New Rochelle, New York, 2 July 1970. John Canemaker Animation Collection, Fales Library, Elmer Holmes Bobst Library, New York University, New York City.

Chapter 17

A Studio Transformed: Gandy Goose, Dinky Duck and New Directions for Terrytoons, 1938–1942

While Paul Terry was adamant about not producing in color due to high production costs, he decided in October 1937 to produce one cartoon in sepia tone, a less expensive option than full Technicolor, and then measure the audience response to determine whether the other 38 Terry cartoons from the 1937–1938 season should also be produced in the same fashion.[1] Sepia tone is a type of reddish brown monochrome tint. The picture appears in shades of brown as opposed to greyscale as in a black-and-white image. It was originally produced by adding a pigment made from the Sepia cuttlefish to the positive print of a photograph taken with any number of negative processes.[2] The first sepia-toned animated cartoon was the Puddy the Pup animated cartoon short *The Dog and the Bone* (November 12, 1937).

The reviews of the cartoon were very favorable and Terry was so encouraged by the results he decided to move gradually into color.[3] By the end of March 1938, Terry had decided to produce at least six animated cartoons in color from the 26 Terrytoons produced each season.[4] Announcement of the six Technicolor cartoons was made in the April 27, 1938 edition of the *Film Daily*.[5] In the May 13, 1938 edition of *Film Daily*, the shorts were again announced along with news that the studio had been completely equipped to make color cartoons.[6]

In search of another cartoon character to replace Kiko, Terry drew upon the success of a goose character named Willie who first appeared in *Gandy the Goose* [*The Gandy Goose*] released on March 4, 1938. In the short, Willie runs away from home and arrives at a lunch stand run by a sly fox. The fox invites him to his home and immediately puts a pot on the stove to make him some goose stew. The fox proposes a game of hide and seek and suggests the goose hide in the pot and then puts the cover over him. The goose gets smart and hops out of the pot as the fox is seasoning him with salt and pepper. After a terrific fight with the fox, the goose escapes back to safety of the farm.

In the cartoon Willie speaks in an expressive vocal parody of radio comedian Ed Wynn with a fluttery, giggly, and wavering voice. Willie was Terrytoons' response to the popularity of Warner Bros.' new rising star Daffy Duck created by Tex Avery and appearing first in *Porky's Duck Hunt* released about 11 months earlier on April 17, 1937. Daffy established his status by jumping into the water, hopping around, and yelling, "Woo-hoo! Woo-hoo! Woo-hoo! Hoo-hoo! Woo-hoo!" The early incarnation of Willie looked very much like Daffy with black feathers, long neck and bill, and goofy grin.

Willie was voiced by the relatively unknown Arthur Kay, born Albert Kalfus (1896–1968), who was a retailer of fine leather goods through his company Kalfus-Mond Inc.[7] Terry chose Kay for the vocals because the cartoons featuring his vocal talents were very successful with theater audiences. When Kay voiced a character who declared "Fe Fi Fo Phooey. Something here's a little

187

Fig. 17.1 – 1939 studio staff (left to right) Front row: Peggy Roberts King, Saul Kessler, Martha Cochrane, Esmeralda Fernandes, Ralph Lodge, Clifford Augustson, Carlo Cuccinata, Mark Brennan, Joseph Rasinski, Mar Zaffo, Charles Perrin, Volney White, Philip Scheib, William Weiss, Paul Terry, Harvey B. Day, Mannie Davis, Connie Rasinski, Ed Donnelly, John Foster, (unknown), (unknown), Carmen Eletto, Norm Polansky, Dottie Lot (unknown). Middle row: Walter Gleason, Kamma Noring, Edna May Regal, Vincent Eletto, Frank Little, Bob Ro Frank "Sparky" Schudde, (unknown), Matthew Gentilella, (unknown), Warren Hawkinson, George May, Al Sta Frank Carino, Arthur Bartsch, Tom Morrison, Marty Taras, Gordon Whittier, Donald McKee, Robinson "Robert McKee, Marge Dwiggins, (unknown), (unknown), Dan [Dennis] Ward, Johnny Vita, (unknown), Mike Prenderg Larry Silverman. Back row: (unknown), Mildred Bishop, Constance Quirk, Rocco Eletto, Walter Addison, Lloyd White, (unknown), (unknown), Lester Schudde, (unknown), Joe Bathgate, (unknown), Joe Moran, (unknown), James, (unknown), James V. Whipp, Anderson Craig, Thurlo Collier, George Zaffo, Carlo Vinci, (unknown), Jo Gentilella, (unknown), John Phelps, Theron Collier, C. Renza, George McAvoy, Donald Figlozzi, Milton Stein, D Peters, Steve Gattoni, (unknown).

screwy" in a Jewish accent, the studio received some nasty letters from rabbis thinking Terry was poking fun at the Jews. Terry turned the letters over to Kay who answered the letters and Terry never heard anything more about it.[8] The credit goes to John Foster for creating the character of Gandy Goose. There is the possibility that Foster developed Gandy out of an earlier effeminate goose character seen in many early 1930s Fables cartoons. Kay would retire from the cartoon business after his leather goods business got busy. Tom Morrison then took over the voice of Gandy from Kay.[9]

The first cartoon starring Willie screened well with audiences so Terry decided to feature the goose in another cartoon *The Goose Flies High* (September 9, 1938) (both of the first two animated Willie cartoons were directed by John Foster), a story about Willie asking a wolf impersonating Clark Gable to teach him to fly a plane. The first cartoon featuring a goose named Gandy was the colorized *Doomsday* (December 16, 1938), which follows the Chicken Little storyline. The character is now drawn in the familiar white color with Kay still doing the voice work. After *The Frame-Up* (1938), Terry decided to introduce another character into the stories,

Chapter 17 • A Studio Transformed

Sourpuss the Cat, a cat who talks like Jimmy Durante.

Terry admitted to "running into a brick wall" with Gandy[10] and Sourpuss added a fresh new dimension to the cartoons as each character played off each other, both appearing together for the first time in *The Owl and the Pussycat* (January 13, 1939) (Sourpuss is named George in the cartoon). Usually Gandy ended up getting himself and his feline friend into trouble. Many of the cartoons featured the two characters going to bed at the beginning of the cartoon, having dreams involving magical or fantasy elements, and then both waking up in an awkward position or in an action mimicking a dream state event. Thoroughly embarrassed, Sourpuss would say, "Keep me out of your dreams!"

In *Aladdin's Lamp* (October 22, 1943), Gandy and Sourpuss are in the army and drift off to sleep where they have adventures in China with Aladdin. They end up dancing with a Chinese girl and both wake up to find they are holding each other's hand. In *Comic Book Land* (December 23, 1949 [January 1950]), Gandy reads some comic books before he falls to sleep sending both he and Sourpuss into a land of comic book characters (including Mighty Mouse). The short ends with Sourpuss chastising Gandy for reading too many comic books. In *The Frog and the Princess* (1944), both fall asleep listening to a radio program. Gandy finds his princess and kisses her. Sourpuss wakes up first and discovers that the sleeping Gandy is kissing his tail. Sourpuss decides not to wake the amorous Gandy up because "it would be a shame". In *Post War Inventions* (March 23, 1945), Gandy falls asleep while reading a book titled *Post War Inventions* and with Sourpuss both go off into discovering a world of fantastical inventions including a pill that turns into a full course meal after a drop of water falls on it. The cartoon ends with Gandy and Sourpuss fighting a bear. When they wake up both are hitting each other with pillows.

One of the superior entries in the series is *The Magic Pencil* (1940) directed by Volney White (1907–1966). Prior to working at Terrytoons, White was employed for Romer Grey Pictures Limited, Leon Schlesinger Studios, and Fleischer Studios on the feature *Gulliver's Travels* (1939). Around 1939, Paul Terry hired him to

189

Fig. 17.2 – Anderson Craig painting an animation background.

work in the story department at Terrytoons and his work was so good Terry promoted him to a director. By 1940, he was working at Terrytoons both as an animator and director. He later worked at TV Arts Productions on Alexander Anderson's *Crusader Rabbit* cartoons until 1951. By the early 1960s he was working for UPA on the motion picture *Gay Purr-ee* (1962). Volney White also undertook work as a comic book artist.[11]

In *The Magic Pencil*, Gandy sends off 2,000 box tops and 10 cents to a radio program and receives a magic pencil. With pencil in hand, Gandy's magic drawings cause all kinds of problems for him and Sourpuss. When Sourpuss goes to hit Gandy over the head with a board, Gandy draws a spring over his head causing the board to spring back and hit the cat. Gandy draws a beautiful cat for Sourpuss to fall in love with. When Gandy draws an evil villain, Sourpuss gets a knock over the head and the scoundrel runs away with the girl. Gandy uses an eraser to erase the villain engaged in a swordfight with Sourpuss. When Sourpuss starts to kiss the girl, the pretty cat disappears into Gandy's pencil much to the frustration of the feline. The cartoon short was well received by critics and was given a great review in *Film Daily*.[12]

While Gandy Goose has never been considered a superstar in the class of Bugs Bunny or Mickey Mouse he would become one of Terrytoons more popular cartoon characters and was featured in 48 Terrytoons shorts from 1938 to 1955, his last being *Barnyard Actor*. His popularity sprung from his magical surreal adventures, wacky personality, and hilarious capacity to get him and his co-star Sourpuss into trouble. The shorts featured fast paced action, lavish production values and great voice work. The reviews from critics were generally very positive ("Swift moving laugh piece" and "surprisingly funny"[13] (*Gandy Goose in the Outpost* (1942)); "Good Technicolor Reel",[14] (*The Home Guard* (1941)); "hectic, hilarious charms"[15] (*Peace-Time Football* (1946)); "Amusing" and "several good laugh situations"[16] (*The Golden Hen* (1946)).

While Paul was busy churning out animated shorts, Disney was working on his masterpiece feature *Snow White and the Seven Dwarfs*. On December 21, 1937, the film premiered at the Carthay Circle Theatre, followed by a nationwide release on February 4, 1938. The film was a box office sensation with international earnings of $8 million during its initial release ($130 million adjusted for inflation). The film briefly assumed the record of highest grossing sound film at the time.[17] The popularity of the Walt Disney motion picture had 20th Century-Fox thinking about releasing its own successful animated feature film. Eventually, a Fox representative approached Paul and asked whether he would be interested in producing a feature. Terry thought about the idea for a while and then approached banker Attilio Henry Giannini (1874–1943), head of the Bank of America. Paul would occasionally meet with Attilio to discuss financial matters. They had developed a very cordial and warm relationship. Paul had a banking relation with Giannini's bank for 20 to 30 years.[18]

Attilio was the president of the bank located in New York City at 40th Street and Broadway. Dr. A. H. Giannini was the younger brother of Amadeo Pietro Giannini (1870–1949), the American banker who founded the Bank of

Chapter 17 • A Studio Transformed

America. A. P. Giannini had earlier rented Paul's sister's house in Burlingame, California and Terry would play with A. P.'s children.[19] The Giannini brothers were one of the first to gamble on movie makers and their constant need for short-term loans. They evidently judged each industry segment on character and performance and decided the film business was as good a risk as most others.[20] Walt Disney had asked Attilio for a loan to complete *Snow White* and the banker was very skeptical. Although Disney had run $2 million over budget, Attilio was persuaded by Walt to provide the loan.[21]

At their meeting Terry brought up the possibility of Giannini's bank financing a loan for a Terrytoons feature. Giannini's advice was to "never make a cartoon feature" because it was too hazardous.[22] Terry trusted the opinion of his banking friend and after discussions with William Weiss decided not to produce a feature. When Disney had to go sell public stock to raise funds after the box office disappointments of *Fantasia* (1940) and *Pinocchio* (1940), and Fleischer Studios closed after the flop of their feature *Mr. Bug to Town* (aka *Hoppity Goes to Town*, 1941), Terry was convinced that making a feature was too risky.[23] Even in his 80s and after the success of Disney films in the 1950s and 1960s Terry was still convinced he would never make a feature in animation, although he would be open to producing a live-action motion picture.[24]

Terry believed that adults, unlike children, were not willing to

Fig. 17.3 – Arthur Bartsch, layout artist.

accept an animated film that was longer than 10 or 15 minutes. While children can watch many cartoons at a single sitting, adults can only watch one, much like reading a book of short stories. An adult reads one short story and they don't want anymore. Terry found animated cartoons to be less relaxing than live-action features.[25] Terry summed up his opinion of producing an animated feature film: "It's a very lucrative business if you're right. It's very disastrous if you're wrong".[26]

Although Terry was not prepared to risk millions to produce a feature, he made smaller investments in his animation production in 1938 to improve the entertainment quality of his cartoons. In April 1938, marking a new trend in production Terry produced the first Terrytoons cartoon, *Robinson Crusoe's Broadcast*, using a Spanish dialect soundtrack as opposed to the usual dubbing. The cartoon was aimed at Spanish speaking countries that the studio served.[27] That same month, Terry began to expand his efforts into foreign distribution of his cartoons and invited Walter J. Hutchinson,[28] the 20th Century-Fox director of foreign distribution and members of the foreign department of 20th Century-Fox to a luncheon and inspection of the new studio facilities. On August 26, 1938, Terry finally released his first color cartoon, *String Bean Jack*, a short directed by John Foster concerning a re-telling of "Jack and the Beanstalk". In addition, Paul Terry as an individual and Terrytoons as a company were elected to the Hays Office in June of that year.[29]

As early as 1936, Terry had been working with inventor Carl Louis Gregory on a method of combining animation with live action, a process which was patented in 1939 ("Method and apparatus for the production of motion picture films of the animated cartoon type" – US2174931 A).[30] The invention combined animated drawings with natural photographs (movie-film) used as backgrounds to produce a film

191

Fig. 17.4 – Inkers and Opaquers (c. 1939).

featuring an animated cartoon character moving in a natural environment. The process involved using an animation cel (featuring a cartoon character), a projector that casts the image of a natural photograph on a reflecting prism which reflects the image through condensing lenses below the animated drawing. A motion picture camera above photographed the combined image of the animation cel with the reflected natural photograph. The invention was featured in the December 1940 edition of *Popular Science*.[31] Terry only made one cartoon short, *The Last Indian* (June 24, 1938), with the invention as the process was too labor intensive and expensive for the results achieved.

The studio was not without its share of excitement in 1938. In early-September of that year, a storm that formed on the Atlantic Ocean near the coast of Africa became a Category 5 hurricane on the Saffir-Simpson Hurricane Scale. At 9:00 a.m. on September 21 the Washington office issued northeast storm warnings north of Atlantic City and south of Block Island and southeast storm warnings from Block Island to Eastport, Maine but the advisory underestimated the storm's intensity and said the storm was farther south than it actually was. At 10:00 a.m. the bureau downgraded the hurricane to a tropical storm. The 11:30 a.m. advisory mentioned gale force winds but nothing about a tropical storm or hurricane. At the Terrytoons studio, it was business as usual that morning as production staff were busy producing their next cartoon. However, by 2:30 p.m., the hurricane made landfall as a Category 3 hurricane on Long Island and the storm struck Westchester County with a vengeance.[32]

As the power began to go out across Westchester County, for safety precautions the elevator of the Pershing Square Building was closed.[33] The structure first began

Chapter 17 • A Studio Transformed

to sway slightly as gusts of wind well over 100 miles per hour hit the structure. As the storm picked up in intensity and gusts hit 150 miles per hour, the building began to rock like a pendulum swaying back and forth. For Terry's employees on the top floor, the rocking of the building caused many to fear the building was going to topple over. Terry ordered an immediate evacuation of all studio employees down the stairs. Mary Zaffo, at the time a secretary for the studio, and her brother, background artist George Zaffo, had safely reached street level, got into their automobile and began to make their way to their home on Rich Avenue, Mount Vernon while the trees were toppling all around. As many of the roads were blocked with fallen trees George was forced to drive on people's lawns. What should have taken them 10 minutes to get home, took a couple hours.[34]

The hurricane was estimated to have killed between 682 and 800 people, damaged or destroyed over 57,000 homes, and caused property losses estimated at US$306 million ($5.2 billion adjusted for inflation). Fortunately, none of the Terrytoons studio personnel were killed or injured in the disaster. Even as late as 1951, damaged trees and buildings were still seen in the affected areas. It remains the most powerful and deadliest hurricane in recent New England history, eclipsed in landfall intensity perhaps only by the Great Colonial Hurricane of 1635.[35]

By 1939, Terry had become increasingly upset over the

Fig. 17.5 – Max Manne, sound effects expert.

increase in the number of employees talking to one another during work hours. One time an inker sitting next to animator Larry Silverman struck up a conversation with the artist. Terry walked in and scolded her for talking to Silverman telling her she was stealing money out of his pocket by taking his time.[36] Eventually, Terry instituted a rule that all employees were to refrain from talking to each other unless the conversations were for work related purposes. Despite the new rule, artists continued to converse amongst each another so Terry put his relative, 60-year-old Charles F. Perrin, in a large room with the other animators. Perrin's job was to act as policeman. Terry was paying his employees to work and not to chat and Perrin was there to make sure they did just that. If you needed another pencil or if your light bulb burnt out at your desk, you came to Perrin for a replacement.[37] Another of Perrin's jobs every Christmas was to go around with a list with everybody's names on it and write

down what each person gave to Paul Terry's Christmas gift. According to one source, after everyone had been canvassed for the money, Perrin would take the list back to Terry's office for Paul to see how much each employee gave to his Christmas gift.[38]

Soon after Perrin was placed in his new position as "studio policeman", Terry had another temper tantrum over wasted time, a result of further talking among employees, this time outside of the visual range of Perrin.[39] As a result, a platform about four feet high was built for Perrin ensuring that he had eye contact on all of the staff working in the room. Perrin's job was also to perform duties as the studio's treasurer. When asked why a platform was built for Perrin, he responded that it was to ensure that people couldn't look over his shoulder when he was making out the cheques.

With Perrin's constant surveillance over the employees, the atmosphere to some animation staff became quite oppressive.[40]

193

Fig. 17.6 – Mannie Davis animating.

For animators like Silverman, there were not many opportunities in the profession in the New York area. People were scared about losing their jobs and there was no unemployment insurance. Terry never exhibited an eagerness to hire employees even if he wanted to employ them. He requested that they come back a little later. As a result, at their next meeting Terry was in a better position to negotiate a salary more favorable to his studio.[41]

Terry had a habit of always having a cigar in his mouth as he made his rounds in the studio. There is little doubt that Terry enjoyed the taste of a good cigar. He developed the habit of smoking cigars as a teenager in San Francisco. Many Chinese funerals, such as the one on September 23, 1903 for Tom Kim Yung (1858–1903), military attaché to the Chinese Legation to the United States, were well-attended affairs both by the Chinese community and other citizens of San Francisco.[42] Paul and a few of his school friends would attend the ceremonial portion of Chinese funeral processions and then follow the parade of mourners out to the cemetery while picking up discarded cigars along the street to smoke.[43] However, as he got older his cigar smoking habit caused the development of a hiatus hernia and he had to give up smoking in favor of chewing on the end of the cigar. Terry's mood could be judged by the angle of the cigar in his mouth, the cigar serving as a barometer for his frame of mind. If the cigar pointed downwards he was in a very bad mood. If the cigar pointed upwards, he was in a very good mood.[44] Each morning the secretary would see the angle of the cigar and would report back to Frank "Sparky" Schudde whether or not Paul was in a bad mood.[45]

In the early afternoon, Terry would retire to his office for a nap which he claimed provided him with the energy necessary to finish his day at the studio. Many times his staff would see him exit his office with his hair messed up having slept on it in the sofa in his office.[46] Terry has been quoted as saying: "Whenever I feel the need to exercise, I lie down until it goes away". Although Terry has been given credit for the origination of the quote, the more plausible source is Robert Maynard Hutchins (1899–1977), an educational philosopher, dean of Yale Law School, and president of the University of Chicago.

Film footage pressure, common in the industry although rarely present at the Disney studio, put significant strain on a number of animators at the studio. No matter how many drawings you were producing many animators felt the output was never enough to satisfy Terry. Silverman was doing 25 to 30-feet-a-week working with an assistant and possibly an inbetweener and this pace to even the most talented animators was hard, steady

Chapter 17 • A Studio Transformed

Fig. 17.7 – Phil Scheib conducting the Terrytoons orchestra.

work.[47] Eventually, Perrin wanted each animator to provide him with the footage completed each day. This was difficult to do at times such as when you were roughing out a scene. Therefore, many times the footage provided by the animators was just an estimate. Perrin then put a chart up on the wall and wrote the number of feet completed by each artist at the end of each week. A couple of animators decided to have a competition to see who could complete the most footage. Perrin decided to put a star up alongside the animator who completed the most footage that week. This incentive inspired a few animators to try and get the star even though there wasn't any financial benefit for achieving more footage.[48]

During the early part of 1939, Terry began working on using the two-headed giant in a number of animated cartoons as well as a cartoon character named Captain McDoodle.[49] These characters found limited success. On October 6, 1939, the studio released *The Orphan Duck*, an animated short directed by Connie Rasinski and featuring their newest cartoon character creation, Lucky Duck. In *The Orphan Duck*, Lucky tries to be adopted by hiding in an empty eggshell. When he emerges from the shell he is welcomed by the hen but chased away by the rooster. After Lucky rescues a chick from drowning, he is welcomed into the family of the hen and rooster. The animated cartoon was given a great review in *The Film Daily*.[50] *Film Daily* reported in their March 21, 1940 edition that Lucky was developing "a big public following" with toy and novelty shops "growing keener 'bout him".[51] For most of his appearances, Lucky was a young black feathered duck who resided on a farm with ducks, chickens and other typical farm animals. Sometimes he was an orphan who simply wanted a place to call home; on other occasions, he would perform some heroic deed and help restore calm to the barnyard when adult animals quarreled.

In *Much Ado About Nothing* (March 22, 1940), Dinky's second appearance, a squabble between Dinky's parents and a rooster and hen is resolved after they see their children, Dinky and a chick, embracing as friends. In *Life With Fido* (August 21, 1942) Dinky (in the short still called Lucky Duck) befriends a hunting dog, the dog watches over his little friend on

195

Fig. 17.8 – Tom Morrison heading the story department.

the farm, Dinky flies off with some geese, Fido gets sad over his lost friend, then Dinky returns to the farm with some other duck friends. In *The Lucky Duck* (September 6, 1940) Dinky is scared away from other ducks by a hunter, and falls in with a rooster, hen and their three chicks. Dinky tries to fit in but the rooster chases him away. When he rescues one of the chicks that has fallen into a well, he is welcomed into the rooster's family. In *Welcome Little Stranger* (October 3, 1941) Dinky brings a rooster and hen back together after they had been quarrelling by having them work together to prevent him from leaving.

In *The Beauty Shop* (April 28, 1950) a vulture operating a beauty shop on wheels captures a group of hens. Despite his diminutive size, Dinky chases down the vulture and beats him up knocking off his feathers. In *Flat Foot Fledgling* (January 25, 1952), Dinky cannot fly because his feet are too big and wings too small. A weasel operating a flying school intends to make Dinky his dinner but forest creatures come to help scare the weasel off. Dinky eventually learns to fly after being scared off a cliff by a swarm of bees. In *Featherweight Champ* (February 6, 1953) Dinky uses quick thinking to rescue three hens and a goose trapped in a cave by a sly fox.

The problem with the Dinky cartoons was not found in the aesthetics of the shorts. Dinky was a cute adorable little duck which character many young children found endearing. The problem with many of the Dinky cartoons was that the stories relied on the same basic storyline of a homeless duck welcomed into the family of a rooster and hen after performing a heroic act. Since Dinky never spoke it was difficult for an audience to explore the character's personality. Famous Studios' Casper the Friendly Ghost was another character just trying to make friends but Casper speaks and is quite personable. Unlike Dinky who is featured primarily in a farm environment, Casper's adventures take him to a variety of interesting settings. Dinky never became popular, appearing in a total of only 15 cartoons between 1939 and 1957. He was such a minor character that when, in 1942, Marvel Comics licensed the studio's properties for comic books, Dinky wasn't even included. Dinky's final appearance was in *It's a Living*, a CinemaScope cartoon, in which he

Chapter 17 • A Studio Transformed

sheds his cute farmyard duck persona and instead takes on the role of a disgruntled animation actor who quits his cartoon character job to try his hand in television commercial acting.

Terry's busy production schedule did not keep him from pursuing recreational pursuits. In June 1939, *Film Daily* reported that Terry recorded back-to-back holes-in-one at a local New York golf course, a feat that happens once in a lifetime for a golfer.[52] Terry announced that 10 of the 26 Terrytoons produced for the 1939–1940 season would be in color and that their budget would be the biggest ever. Exhibitors were to exploit each individual Terrytoon cartoon in planning for future productions.[53] In July 1939, Fred Siegelstein (b. March 27, 1915, New York), formerly on the editorial staff of the *Journal-American*, joined the story department to write scripts for Paul Terry.[54] On October 16, 1939, Paul Terry celebrated his 25th anniversary as a cartoonist and 10th birthday of Terrytoons.[55]

On November 17, 1939, Terry released *A Wicky Wacky Romance*, a story about a pretty young hula dancing mouse captured by a band of pirate cats. The girl is rescued by a muscular Tarzan mouse who takes her away on his swordfish. The animated cartoon is significant for featuring a muscular mouse hero who rescues a damsel in distress, the theme found in most Mighty Mouse cartoons produced in the decade to come. On December 18, 1939, *Film Daily* announced that 30 former artists associated with Terrytoons and Fleischer Studios

Fig. 17.9 – Connie Rasinski overseeing the musical work of Phil Scheib.

had formed a studio, East Coast Animation Studios, Inc. located at 1600 Broadway in New York City, the old address of Fleischer Studios before the studio moved to Miami, Florida. Byron Rabbit was president of the organization.[56] Little is known of this studio although it did not survive in the competitive animation market for very long.

With respect to hiring policies, Terry was never one to discriminate based on race, age, or sex. One of his animators employed at the studio in 1939 was Margaret (Peg) Roberts (1918–1977), the daughter of New Rochelle mayor George I. Roberts. Roberts attended Holy Family Grammar School then went to the Ursuline School for Girls on a scholarship in 1931, taking a four-year course and majoring in art. In 1935, she graduated from Ursuline, and took a post-graduate course, including arts and crafts, at New Rochelle Senior High School. Terry hired Roberts shortly thereafter as an opaquer. She progressed to tracer, inbetweener (in 1938) and finally animator. In September 1939, at the age of 21, she was of one of only four women animators in the United States (others would include Lillian Friedman promoted in 1933 to full animator's status by Max Fleischer and probably the first woman animator in United States theatrical films, La Verne Harding, Hollywood's first woman animator, and Retta Scott Worcester, Disney's first female animator). In 1939, Roberts was one of 14 animators in Paul Terry's studio.[57] Her animation was well rendered and her contributions were highly valued by Terry and the studio management.

Terry continued to increase the number of Technicolor cartoons produced each year. After producing eight color cartoons in 1939–1940 and 10 in 1939–1940, for the 1940–1941 season, 12 of the 26 cartoons

197

TERRYTOONS: The Story of Paul Terry and His Classic Cartoon Factory

Fig. 17.10 – Surveying the wax records of the music and sound effects.

were produced in color. For the 1941–1942 season Terry produced 15 Technicolor cartoons.[58] In February 1940, Paul Terry hired prominent film publicist Gordon Stowe White to promote the Terry cartoons. White was valuable to Terry because he had experience in the script end of the shorts.[59] Stowe, like Terry, had a career as a newspaperman. He was a reporter and copy editor for the *St. Louis Globe*, *The St. Louis Democrat*, *The Chicago Herald* and *The Chicago Daily News*.[60]

By March 1940, over 10,000 theaters across North America had contracted to exhibit Terrytoons cartoons.[61] On March 18, 1940, *Film Daily* reported that Paul Terry was planning a two-reel animated cartoon in Technicolor.[62] For reasons left to conjecture, although likely related to financial matters, the two-reeler was never produced. By 1940, Paul had doubled his staff since the time he had first signed his distribution contract with 20th Century-Fox and had increased his budget by 20 percent from the year before.[63] That year Terry had an organization that numbered 125 employees.[64] From July 3 to 15, 1940, the studio shut down allowing the staff to vacation simultaneously.[65] On October 31, 1940, Paul Terry was feted by Academy of Motion Picture Arts at a luncheon held at the Edison Hotel in New York City on the occasion of his 25th anniversary in cartoons.[66] By this time, Terry had hired A. Rutgers Neilsen to promote his studio's product and image to the general public. Previously, Neilsen had directed publicity for J. Amedee Van

Beuren, C. C. Burr Enterprises, Pathé Pictures (including the merged Pathé and RKO enterprise), as well as RKO-Radio Pictures abroad from 1951 to 1955.[67]

In July 1940, Terry began to issue full color 8" x 10" still photographs of all Technicolor cartoons produced by the studio starting with *Billy Mouse's Akwakade* (August 9, 1940).[68] On July 29, 1940, Terry signed a long-term four-year renewal with 20th Century-Fox for 104 Terrytoons cartoons.[69] He hired sculptor, illustrator and muralist Walter Nichols Addison (1914–1982) to create small sculptures of Dinky Duck, Gandy Goose and other Terry cartoon characters for the animation artists to use as models. Addison had studied at the National Academy of Design, 1932–1935

Chapter 17 • A Studio Transformed

and worked as staff illustrator for the Bronx Zoo, 1937–1938. He created animal murals such as the watering hole at Gov. Clinton Hotel, New York City. He would create all the animal figures for the General Motors Exhibition Hall, "The World of Tomorrow", New York World's Fair, 1964.[70] In 1941, Terry began considering the establishment of a cartoon studio in Laguna Beach, California. Terry had been considering a studio in the Los Angeles vicinity for a number of years. Little is known why the project was not undertaken.[71]

Passing through Terry's doors in 1941 was Charlie Thorson. From 1935 to 1946 he worked for Walt Disney, Harman-Ising, MGM, Warner Bros., Fleischer, Terrytoons, Columbia/Screen Gems, and George Pal's studio. Thorson was hired by Walt Disney in early 1935 where he designed characters for *Elmer Elephant*, *The Old Mill*, *Wynken, Blynken and Nod*, *The Country Cousin*, *Toby Tortoise Returns*, and most importantly, *Little Hiawatha*. For Disney he also worked on *Snow White and the Seven Dwarfs* (1937). For Harman-Ising Studios he worked on Captain and the Kids cartoons. At Warner Bros., he designed a prototype for Bugs Bunny. For Chuck Jones he created the Sniffles the Mouse characters, Inki, the Little Lion Hunter, and his nemesis, the Mynah Bird, and the curious puppy and pals. At Fleischer Studios, he worked on *Gulliver's Travels* and *The Stone Age* cartoon series. After working successfully as a children's book illustrator and in billboard and magazine advertising

Fig. 17.11 – Terrytoons machinist.

in New York for a while, Thorson returned to animation at Terrytoons but little is known of his contributions while at the studio.[72]

In February 1941, Nat Falk wrote *How to Make Animated Cartoons; The History and Technique* (New York: Foundation Books) with a foreword written by Paul Terry. On July 24, 1941, *Film Daily* reported that 20th Century-Fox had over 400 employees serving in the military both in the United States and abroad. The highest ratio of men in service to total number of employees was Terrytoons studio where seven men were in uniform.[73] Terrytoons employees in the military at the time included Carmen J. Eletto, Clifford Augustson, and Joseph L. White.[74] Tragedy struck the Terrytoons studio in April 1942 when music editor Alexander Ivanoff died of a heart attack on the way home during a storm.[75] In May 1942, Terry signed a contract with Timely Topics where his cartoon characters were to appear in book form.[76] In

August 1942, *Film Daily* announced the launch of *Terrytoons Comics* created by Paul Terry.[77]

On August 7, 1942, Paul Terry released a masterwork of animated filmmaking, the cartoon short *All Out For "V"* directed by Mannie Davis.[78] The short depicts the war activity of all living things of a woodland community after their habitat had been bombed by an enemy power. Everyone participates to help meet the menace. The cartoon contains a very catchy song by Phil Scheib "We're Working For Defense" that will leave the viewer humming the tune long after the cartoon credits roll. The animated short was given rave reviews by the critics in the trade magazines. The reviewer for *Film Daily* writes: "Paul Terry has produced a war cartoon that deserves heavy booking everywhere. Any praise of it, however, is not limited to its value in promoting the nation's defense program. It is above, everything else, superb entertainment into which has gone a lot of cleverness

199

Fig. 17.12 – Mike Prendergast drying films.

and inventiveness. Laughs are numerous and strong".[79]

The animated short was nominated for an Oscar® in the category "Short Subjects, Cartoons" which award was handed out at the 15th Academy Awards, held in the Cocoanut Grove at the Ambassador Hotel in Los Angeles on March 4, 1943. This would be Terry's first of three Oscar® nominations in the category. Upon hearing the news of the nomination, Terry never jumped up in the air, clapped his hands and shouted out expressions of joy.[80] That was not his personality. Rather, Terry took the nomination in stride with a feeling that his studio had accomplished something very special keeping his satisfaction to himself. The other nominees included *Der Fuehrer's Face* (Walt Disney Productions, RKO Radio – Walt Disney), *Blitz Wolf* (Metro-Goldwyn-Mayer – Fred Quimby), *Juke Box Jamboree* (Walter Lantz Productions, Universal – Walter Lantz), *Pigs in a Polka* (Leon Schlesinger Productions, Warner Bros. – Leon Schlesinger), and *Tulips Shall Grow* (Paramount – George Pal). Terry's short was in tough that year against some great cartoons. The winner of the coveted Oscar® was Walt Disney's *Der Fuehrer's Face* directed by Jack Kinney. In 1994, the Disney cartoon was voted Number 22 of "the 50 Greatest Cartoons" of all time by members of the animation field.[81] However, because of the propagandistic nature of the short, and the depiction of Donald Duck as a Nazi (albeit a reluctant one), Disney kept the film out of general circulation after its original release.

In April 1942, in the continuing search for a cartoon character with box office appeal, Paul decided to purchase the rights to Ernie Bushmiller's popular *Nancy* comic strip characters.[82] The first Nancy cartoon produced was *School Daze* (September 18, 1942), the story about children convincing their teacher that *Nancy* comic books help them more with their lessons on National Defence than textbooks. The reviews of the cartoon were generally mixed as reviewers judged the cartoon as passable in terms of entertainment quality. Some of criticisms of the cartoon from the trade magazines were that Nancy was a tough, homely looking character, she was "not the type to ingratiate herself with audiences easily", and the laughs in the cartoon were mild and scattered.[83] Terry produced another Nancy cartoon, *Doing Their Bit* (October 30, 1942), where Nancy and Sluggo raise funds for USO using various tricks and gimmicks such as releasing mice in a woman's home and then selling her a cat to get rid of the mice.

Unfortunately for Terry, the Nancy cartoons never caught the imagination of the public.

Chapter 17 • A Studio Transformed

The two Nancy cartoons are mildly pleasant shorts to watch. The two main characters, although not drawn precisely to model, were recognizable as Bushmiller's comic strip stars. Both cartoons featured a delightful Nancy theme song and the plots contained enough humor to make them watchable. The Nancy cartoons are similar in concept and structure to Famous Studios' popular Little Lulu cartoons based on the comic strip character created in the mid-1930s by Marjorie Henderson Buell. After receiving less than favorable reviews from the critics Terry decided not to produce more cartoons starring the character. That is a shame as it would have been interesting to see where he would have taken the characters.

Notes

1. "Terry-Toon Tests Sepia", *Film Daily*, 25 October 1937, p. 12.

2. Annette Kuhn and Guy Westwell, *A Dictionary of Film Studies*, 1st ed. (Oxford: Oxford University Press, 2012).

3. "The Dog and the Bone" (animated cartoon review), *Film Daily*, 22 November 1937, p. 10.

4. "Thorgersen and Lehr Named Talley's Aides", *Film Daily*, 30 March 1938, p. 1, 8.

5. "Here is the Short Product", *Film Daily*, 27 April 1938, (Advertising insert).

6. "20th-Fox 1938–39 Shorts Sales Near Feature Total", *Film Daily*, 13 May 1938, p. 3.

7. Contemporary sources have Arthur Kay incorrectly listed as Arthur Kay (1882–1969), the musician-conductor who became the assistant conductor of the Boston Symphony.

8. Terry, interview, 20 December 1969, 77.

9. Thomas James (Tommy) Morrison, interview, 15 June 1970, 25d.

10. Ibid.

11. 20th Century-Fox Film Corporation, "Terrytoon Creators: Volney L. White", Dynamo (Terrytoon Section), 15 April 1940, Chicago, Illinois, p. 5B. His funeral notice was published in the *Los Angeles Times* on December 26, 1966.

12. "The Magic Pencil", (animated cartoon review), *Film Daily*, 28 November 1940, p. 9.

13. "Gander Goose in the Outpost", (animated cartoon review), *Variety*, 24 June 1942, p. 8.

14. "The Home-Guard", (animated cartoon review), *Film Daily*, 17 April 1941, p. 7.

15. "Peace-Time Football", (animated cartoon review), *Film Daily*, 17 June 1946, p. 12.

16. "The Golden Hen", (animated cartoon review), *Film Daily*, 17 April 1946, p. 10.

17. Leonard Maltin, *The Disney Films*, 3rd ed. (New York: Hyperion, 1995).

18. Terry, interview, 14 July 1970, 150.

19. Ibid., 149

20. Richard Dyer MacCann, *The First Tycoons* (Metuchen, N.J.: The Scarecrow Press, 1986), 57–59.

21. Dana Haight Cattani and Angela B. Haight, *A.P. Giannini, The Man With the Midas Touch* (Bloomington, Indiana: AuthorHouse, 2009), 95–96.

22. Terry, interview, 14 July 1970, 149.

23. Ibid., 149–150.

24. Ibid., 150.

25. Terry, interview, 20 December 1969, 25.

26. Terry, interview, 14 July 1970, 151.

27. "Terrytoon Reel Produced With Spanish Soundtrack", *Film Daily*, 27 June 1937, p. 7.

28. Obituary: "W.J. Hutchinson, Fox Official, Dies", *New York Times*, 12 April 1942, p. 45; "Walter J. Hutchinson", *Variety*, 15 April 1942, 54.

29. "Industry's Fair Role Before MPPDA Board", *Film Daily*, 16 June 1938, p. 1, 5.

30. Paul Houlton Terry and Carl Louis Gregory, "Method and Apparatus for the Production of Motion Picture Films of the Animated Cartoon Type", US Patent 2,174,931 A, filed June 18, 1936, and issued October 3, 1939.

31. "New Cartoon Camera Combines Drawings and Photographs", *Popular Science*, December 1940, p. 98–99.

32. R. A. Scotti, *Sudden Sea – The Great Hurricane of 1938* (Boston: Little, Brown & Co., 2003).

33. Mary Zaffo Mathewson, telephone interview by author (transcript), 22 November 1997, Kelowna, B.C., Canada, Terrytoons Collection, Victoria, B.C., 5.

34. Mary Zaffo Mathewson, telephone interview by author (transcript), 11 January 1998, Kelowna, B.C., Canada, Terrytoons Collection, Victoria, B.C., 5.

35. For more on the disaster: Everett S. Allen, *A Wind to Shake the World: The Story of the 1938 Hurricane* (Boston: Little, Brown and Company, 1976). The hurricane was covered extensively in the *New York Times*: "Hurricane Sweeps Coast; 11 Dead, 71 Missing, L.I. Toll; 80 Die in New England Flood", *New York Times*, 22 September 1938, p. 1.

36. Silverman, interview, 37.

37. Irene Scagnelli, telephone in-

201

terview by author (transcript), Kelowna, B.C., Canada, 22 January 1998, Terrytoons Collection, Victoria, B.C., 3.

38. Jordan Caldwell, telephone interview by author (transcript), Kelowna, B.C., Canada, 25 October 1997, Terrytoons Collection, Victoria, B.C., 5.

39. Mathewson, interview, 11 January 1998, 8.

40. Silverman, interview, 37.

41. Ibid., 38–39.

42. Robert W. Bowen and Brenda Young Bowen, *San Francisco's Chinatown*, Postcard History Series (San Francisco, CA: Arcadia Publishing, 2008), 24.

43. Leahy and Lazar, p. 2.

44. Marchionni, "Paul Terry, at 82, Still Calls the Toon", p. 28.

45. Patricia Leahy, interview by author (transcript), Fayetteville, North Carolina, 24 August 1996, Terrytoons Collection, Victoria, B.C., 14.

46. Vinnie Bell, telephone interview by author (transcript), Kelowna, B.C., Canada, 23 February 1998, Terrytoons Collection, Victoria, B.C., 6.

47. Silverman, interview, 45.

48. Ibid., 45–46.

49. "14 Shorts in Color Among 20th Fox's 52 Next Year", *Film Daily*, 31 March 1939, p. 1, 6.

50. "The Orphan Duck", (animated cartoon review), *Film Daily*, 12 October 1939, p. 8.

51. Phil M. Daly, "Along the Rialto", *Film Daily*, 21 March 1940, p. 4.

52. Charles Alicoate, "Putts and Takes", *Film Daily*, 23 June 1939, p. 11.

53. "Record TerryToon Budget for 1939–40", *Film Daily*, 1 June 1939, p. 17.

54. "Siegelstein With Terry", *Film Daily*, 31 July 1939, p. 14.

55. "Double Terry Birthday", *Film Daily*, 17 October 1939, p. 2.

56. "30 Artists Launch New Animation Studios Here", *Film Daily*, 18 December 1939, p. 2.

57. "George I. Roberts Seeks Mayoralty as Promotion After Decade in Council", *The Standard-Star* (New Rochelle, NY), 10 October 1939, p. 3; "Roberts Dies; Former City Councilman", *The Standard-Star* (New Rochelle, NY), 27 December 1960, p. 1; "Miss Roberts' Job is to Put a Motion Before the House", *The Standard-Star* (New Rochelle, NY), 1 September 1939, p. 4.

58. "15 Terrytoons in Color", *Film Daily*, 10 January 1940, p. 6.

59. "White With Terry-Toons in Promotional Capacity", *Film Daily*, 28 February 1940, p. 8.

60. He later became director of the Advertising Code Administration of the Motion Picture Association of America, popularly known as the Hays Office. In the early 1940s he had a running battle with Howard Hughes over the censoring of advertising of *The Outlaw* starring Jane Russell. The battle lasted five years, but the ban stood. Obituaries: "Gordon S. White Sr., Served Hays Office", *New York Times*, 16 February 1969, p. 76:6; "Gordon S. White", *Variety*, 19 February 1969, 79.

61. "10,000 Terry-Toon Sales Give Series Record High", *Film Daily*, 11 March 1940, p. 2.

62. "Terry Plans Color 2-Reeler", *Film Daily*, 18 March 1940, p. 7.

63. "Paul Terry Boosts Year's Budget 20%", *Film Daily*, 20 May 1940, p. 4.

64. Theodore Strauss, "Mr. Terry and the Animal Kingdom", *New York Times*, 7 July 1940, IX, p. 3:2.

65. "Terry-Toon Studio Closes July 3–15 for Vacations", *Film Daily*, 26 June 1940, p. 2.

66. "AMPA to Waive Dues of All Members in Armed Services", *Film Daily*, 25 October 1940, p. 2.

67. Obituary: "A. Rutgers Neilsen", *New York Times*, 3 November 1974, p. 79:1; "A. Rutgers Neilsen", *Variety*, 6 November 1974, 71.

68. "Still Photos in Color Plug Terry-Toons", *Film Daily*, 31 July 1940, p. 6.

69. "20th Century Renews Deal For Paul Terry Reels", *Film Daily*, 29 July 1940, p. 1, 8.

70. "Addison, Walter Nichols", in *Mantle Fielding's Dictionary of American Painters, Sculptors & Engravers*, ed. Glenn B. Optiz (Poughkeepsie, New York, 1986), 6.

71. "Film Studio May Locate in Laguna", Paul Terry Papers.

72. "Thorson, Charles", *The Canadian Who's Who, 1949–1951*, volume V (Toronto, Ontario: Trans-Canada Press, 1951), 992; Joseph Thorson, "Charles G. Thorson", *The Icelandic Canadian*, volume XXV, no. 4 (Summer 1967): 68–71. Best source on Thorson's life and work: Eugene P. Walz, *Cartoon Charlie: The Life and Art of Animation Pioneer Charles Thorson* (Winnipeg: Great Plains Publications, 1998).

73. "400 20th-Fox Men Now Wear Uniforms", *Film Daily*, 24 July 1941, p. 7.

74. Charles Alicoate, "Hollywood of the Army", *Film Daily*, 11 August 1941, p. 6.

75. "Lakewood Funeral Today for Alexander N. Ivanoff", *Film Daily*, 1 April 1942, p. 2.

76. Phil M. Daly, "Along the Rialto", *Film Daily*, 18 May 1942, p. 4.

77. Phil M. Daly, "Along the Rialto", *Film Daily*, 3 August 1942, p. 3.

78. His daughter provides a glowing tribute in: "A Creative Force in Animated Cartoons", *New York Times*, 28 February 1982, section 11, p. 18.

79. "All Out For V", (animated cartoon review), *Film Daily*, 14 August 1942, p. 8.

80. Leahy and Lazar, interview, 18.

81. Jerry Beck, ed., *The 50 Greatest Cartoons: As Selected by 1,000 Animation Professionals* (Atlanta: Turner Publishing, 1994).

82. "Nancy, Post's Comic, As Terrytoons Series", *Film Daily*, 29 April 1942, p. 2.

83. "School Daze", (animated cartoon review), *Film Daily*, 22 October 1942, p. 9.

Chapter 18

Here I Come To Save The Day!: The Mouse that Saved a Cartoon Studio, 1942–1945

In mid-1942, most of the major cartoon studios had at least one popular and bankable cartoon character in their animation stable. The common belief shared by film distributors and theater owners was that cartoon characters that were popular with audiences would help sell box office tickets to the main feature. Walt Disney had Mickey Mouse (1928), Donald Duck (1934), and Goofy (1932), characters immensely popular with audiences. Warner Bros. was having tremendous success distributing cartoons starring Bugs Bunny (1940), Daffy Duck (1937), and Porky Pig (1935). Walter Lantz had created Woody Woodpecker (1940) to boost his company's fortunes. Fleischer Studios produced cartoons starring the lovable Betty Boop (1930) and the crowd-pleasing spinach-eating Popeye (1933) before Paramount assumed full ownership of the studio on May 25, 1941. Columbia Pictures had recently introduced their star team of the Fox and Crow on December 5, 1941 in the *Color Rhapsody* short *The Fox and the Grapes*.

Metro-Goldwyn-Mayer had been creating Tom and Jerry cartoons since 1940. As for the Terrytoons studio, Paul Terry was left with star wannabes Gandy Goose and Dinky Duck.

Like most animation studios, at Terrytoons the creation of new cartoon characters began in the story department. While in 1936, Terry had placed Mannie Davis in charge of the newly created story unit, he did not last for long. About a year later Mannie was moved back to working as a director and Tom Morrison was placed in charge of the department. The first short he wrote was the sepia-toned *The Dog and the Bone*.[1] Around 1938, the more experienced John Foster was made the head of the Terrytoons story department. During the first half of the 1940s, the story department at Terrytoons comprised John Foster, Donald McKee, Al Stahl, and I. Klein.

Foster and Terry were long-time friends. In June 1929 after Terry had been released at the Fables Studio, Foster had assumed Terry's position as studio head. His name replaced Terry's as the first credit on each and every cartoon produced by the studio over roughly the next four years. Mannie Davis and Harry Bailey were chosen as Foster's initial two directors. Therefore a cartoon credited "By John Foster and Mannie Davis" is actually de-facto directed by Davis. Foster's creative role during this time would have mostly been reserved to story work and working with the musical director, although he also contributed animation to a fair amount of the cartoons. "Bunny" Brown, a nephew of a top RKO shareholder, was appointed business manager of the studio in 1933 and butted heads with Foster resulting in Foster's dismissal. George Stallings was promoted to head of the animation department in his place. In February 1934, Foster was hired at Frank Goldman's studio Audio Productions, Inc.

To accommodate increased activity in the trick photography and animation field, Audio Productions, Inc., moved its production headquarters from the Bronx to the Fox studios on 56th

203

TERRYTOONS: The Story of Paul Terry and His Classic Cartoon Factory

Street. Foster was in charge of animation. In 1934, Foster animated for Audio Productions/Ashton B. Collins. Foster's stay at Audio seems to have been a short one. Foster joined the staff of Paul Terry's Terrytoons sometime later in 1934, his animation first appearing in *Jack's Shack*, a November 1934 release. By 1937 Foster began directing at Terrytoons beginning with *The Billy Goat's Whiskers* (Dec. 1937) followed by *Bugs Beetle and His Orchestra* (Jan. 1938). As previously noted Foster created the character Gandy Goose. Foster also directed the first color Terrytoons cartoon *String Bean Jack* (August 26, 1938) and the first two Gandy Goose cartoons (*Gandy the Goose* (March 4, 1938), *The Goose Flies High* (September 9, 1938).[2] Donald McKee was also a long-time friend of Paul Terry from their days in California. McKee was a significant contributor of animation for the Fables Pictures studio during the 1920s. He then moved to work for Terry in the early 1930s.[3]

Al Stahl (1916–1999) started his career in animation working for Van Beuren Studios as an errand boy around 1933. He was gradually promoted to an opaquer, inker, and inbetweener. He eventually worked up to the position of assistant animator working under Joe Barbera helping to animate the *Toonerville Trolley* series and Molly Moo Cow character. After the Van Beuren studio closed in 1936, Stahl then moved to Fleischer Studios as an assistant animator working on Popeye shorts. At Fleischer he met Gill Fox whom he would later work for in the comic book industry. Around 1936, Stahl started doing comic book artwork for about year. In 1937, he was an artist on the syndicated *Happy Trailings* comic strip. In 1938 Stahl found work at Terrytoons in the story department, a position he had never held before in the animation industry. Paul Terry hired Stahl based on his comic strip experience and his ability to create stories in a comic strip storyboard format.[4]

Klein had worked previously for Terry in the early 1930s. After he had left the Terry-Moser studio about 1932, Klein was offered a job at Charles Mintz's Screen Gems studio but turned the offer down to remain in New York City to keep in contact with the magazine editors of *The New Yorker*. His friend Bill Tytla suggested he apply for work at the Van Beuren animation studio as his old friend Burt Gillett (they had worked together 10 years earlier at Associated Animators in Long Island City) was in the process of reorganizing the studio. There were three directors working under Gillett: Jim Tyer, Steve Muffati, and Ted Eshbaugh. Klein was assigned to work under Eshbaugh. He worked at the Van Beuren Studios, 1934–1935 [1932/33–1935], animating a number of series (Burt Gillett's *Toddle Tales*; *Rainbow Parade*) as well as working on storyboards/stories for the studio.

In 1935, Klein quit the Van Beuren studio to go back to magazine cartooning. However, due to the effects of the Great Depression, most magazines were not purchasing his cartoons any longer although *The New Yorker* was buying the occasional cartoon. He then left New York City and traveled to Hollywood joining the staff of the Charles Mintz studio, cartoons distributed by Columbia Pictures, as animator and story man (Krazy Kat; Scrappy; Barney Google; *Color Rhapsody*). In 1936, he moved over to the Walt Disney studio as an animator and occasional story man (*Silly Symphonies*, 1936–1938; Donald Duck, 1937; Mickey Mouse, 1937–1938; Goofy) before joining Terry.[5]

Tom Morrison also contributed plots and ideas on a sporadic basis. During this period Terry and Foster's ideas tended to make up the lion's share of each story. While the head of the department was John Foster, it was Paul Terry who was active as the headman making all final approvals on scripts. I. Klein had returned to New York City in April 1940 and started his Terrytoons career about two weeks later. He got the job after he brought along a reel of his animation which he had completed in Hollywood. Terry offered him a job and then the two chatted about some laughs Klein received from an animated cartoon that he had seen the night before at a movie theater. The cartoon was about dinosaurs and cavemen and Klein described some of the gags. Terry listened to Klein with an amused smile.[6]

Terry suddenly asked Klein if he would consider working in the story department for a couple of days before plunging into animation. Klein accepted the

Chapter 18 • Here I Come To Save The Day!

Fig. 18.1 – Demon Cat from *The Green Line* (1944), Bill Tytla artwork.

offer since he had some experience at other studios in the story department, most notably at the Disney studio. Klein was introduced to William Weiss and then led to the story room. On two of the walls were large fiber boards, about eight feet long and four feet high. These boards were used to pin up the story sketches. There was a large conference table around which sat the story crew of four men. Each had a clamp board that held his sketch paper. Each had a cigar box that held his supply of pencils, erasers, and some colored crayons. This was each man's "office". Klein was introduced to the other story artists and told he was going to start on Monday (Klein's interview was on a Friday morning). After the studio tour, Terry and Klein went down the elevator together. On the ground floor Terry shook hands with Klein and he went on his way.[7]

On his first day of work, Klein arrived at the studio, sat in his "office" waiting for instructions, and was ignored by the other three story artists in the room. When Foster put a gag sequence on the storyboard, Klein realized that he was to do the same thing. Cooking up gags was nothing new in his life, and in a little while a spark struck him. He made some sketches and pinned them up on a corner of the large storyboard. Terry entered the room looked at the story material on the board, made random remarks unrelated to the story sketches, and walked out. The next morning, Terry came in and pinned up on the board a magazine article on dinosaurs and cavemen. Stahl, McKee, and Foster took down their story sketches. Klein decided to do so as well. Evidently Terry wanted a cartoon based on cavemen and dinosaurs.[8]

During the balance of the week, Klein began putting up story sketches on the caveman-dinosaur theme. He soon became aware that the board parallel to the long table was the Foster acceptance board. The other board was rejection or possibly "maybe or if" board. John Foster would go to the main board and lift off a gag sequence onto the other board. Those shifted sequences were never his gags. Terry would come into the room once in a while with gag sketches on small note paper and pin them onto the board. To Klein, these Terry sketches looked more like bird feet markings on sand. Foster never moved them to the secondary board. On Monday of the second week of the story, the director assigned to the picture joined the story crew and threw in his talent on the assignment. By the end of the second week the story was always finished. The final shape up of the story was made between Foster and Terry. All of Paul Terry's gags were kept. Most of Foster's remained and a sprinkling of the work of the other artists completed the opus. The story sketches were then numbered in their proper order, and the director would take them to his room to continue the other stages of the animation production process.[9]

Terry took an active part in the story work. Klein noted: "He considered himself Mr. Story Department for Terrytoons, from whom all ideas originated. Other people's ideas were merely fillers. Nevertheless, he expected and demanded support from the 'backfield'."[10] Terry enjoyed collecting gags and kept a joke archive file in his office containing thousands of humorous wisecracks on which he would rely upon. In 1954, shortly after Bud Fisher's funeral, Terry bought the large joke file of over 100,000 gags from radio and vaudeville comedian Joe Laurie, Jr. (1892–1954).[11] Both Terry and Laurie, Jr. believed that jokes are never an original creation as people borrow a little from different sources when developing

the gags.[12] Terry would screen all his cartoons in front of a live theater audiences. Gags which received hearty laughs and plenty of chuckles from the audience during screening were reused in other cartoons. For example, one common gag Terry relied upon since the silent days has the title card (in the case of silent film) or narrator (for the sound cartoons) exclaiming that it was "raining cats and dogs" followed by cats and dogs raining down from the sky (*Noah's Outing* (January 24, 1932), *Johnstown Flood* (June 28, 1946)).

Another gag was the "ambulance joke". This gag has an unconscious and injured individual being picked up in a stretcher by an ambulance crew and hastily put in the back of the ambulance. As the ambulance speeds away, the force of the vehicle accelerating from a stationary position slides the patient out the rear doors. The suddenly conscious patient gets up off the ground, raises his arm up in the air to try and flag the ambulance, and then starts running after the vehicle (*The War Bride* (April 20, 1928), *Barnyard WAAC* (December 11, 1942), *Throwing the Bull* (May 3, 1946), *Prescription for Percy* (April 1954)).

In *Farmer Al Falfa's 20th Anniversary* (November 27, 1936) a very fat pig dancing with his back to the viewer turns around to reveal that the large swine is dancing with four smaller dogs, a joke also found in *The Glass Slipper* (October 7, 1938) (using a large woman and three young men) and the Mighty Mouse

cartoon *Mother Goose's Birthday Party* (December 1950) (using a hippo and three cats). The sequence of a hapless character bouncing off of turrets and towers on the top of a castle like a pinball in a pinball machine is used both in *Beanstalk Jack* (December 20, 1946) and *Mother Goose's Birthday Party*.

A common joke found in many Heckle and Jeckle cartoons (*The Intruders* (May 9, 1947)) has the birds handing a large fizzing explosive to their victim. The victim drops the object and hides for cover. The explosive safely "pops" open rather than explodes peeling back a smaller version of the bomb. Through a series of minor pops, the device becomes successively smaller in size until it is tiny and appears harmless. When the magpies' victim approaches the apparently safe object and picks it up the tiny bomb explodes with a terrible force. Another common gag involves a tire blowing or a wheel falling off a moving vehicle such as a stagecoach or motor vehicle. Instead of replacing the damaged part with another wheel or tire, the driver of the vehicle hastily uses a hospital crutch and the transportation device hobbles along with the crutch (*No Sleep for Percy* (March 1955)).

To Klein, Terry was a sight to behold. He always had a cigar in his mouth. He always wore a vest and a jacket-type sweater. He wore the sweater unbuttoned. His vest appeared to Klein to have more than the usual number of buttons, which might have been due to his stout figure. When he remained in the story room for

Chapter 18 • Here I Come To Save The Day!

more than a walk-through, he would sit on an ancient wooden chair with a leather seat stuffed with horsehair. The underside of the chair's bottom was worn with age so that the cloth and horsehair dangled from below. One time when Terry had ripped some story sketches from the board, did some hollering, and walked angrily from the room, Foster went over to the "throne", an object that so much represented Terry, and kicked it while he swore a blue streak.[13]

At the start of a new story period, Terry would come in and look at the sketches on the storyboard of suggested story ideas, then walk out again. If by Wednesday there was nothing to his satisfaction, he'd act mad and holler complaining to his story crew, "What's going on here. This is Wednesday! No brains here!"[14] Sometimes he would look at the stuff in a good-natured way with a smile on his face, but that was only on a Monday or Tuesday. It was not very often Terry found an acceptable idea on the story board, even if there were brilliant drawings pinned on the board. Eventually he would come into the story room with a small batch of scratchy sketches, pin them onto the board, and that was the theme for the next story.[15]

Terry's ideas were often about mice and cats. One day he came into the story room with the major announcement that the studio was finished with using mice in their cartoons. However, when MGM introduced their star cat and mouse team of Tom and Jerry in 1941, Terry's interest in cartoon mice was revived. Klein sometimes was moved into the animation department for brief periods of time. Once when he approached the door to the story room he was greeted by Terry exiting the room with a big, pleasant smile on his face. When Klein entered the room Foster was complaining how Terry had fiercely attacked his story crew. Because Terry was smiling Klein wondered whether Paul's outbursts were just put-ons to impress the story crew that he was boss and brains of the story department.[16] What the outburst likely signified was nothing more than Paul having a few chuckles at the expense of his story crew.

After the first few weeks at the studio, Klein ventured and turned Terry's chicken-track hieroglyphics story sketches into real drawings for the storyboard. Since Foster gave out no real directives and Terry made no objections, Klein continued this practice and Terry soon showed that he liked the idea. This left Klein working with the directors laying out their shorts during the first week after they picked it up. During that week he laid out backgrounds and extremes for animation. He would cover as much as he could during that period. By that time another story would be underway, and Terry insisted Klein be back in the story department. The routine of spending every other week in laying out backgrounds and animation did not develop until Klein had worked at the studio for about two years. Terry used Klein as an animator when the animation belt hit a snag or slowed down for some reason and he needed Klein to ensure that the production was completed on schedule. His activity would only be for several weeks at the most. Sometimes he remained in the animation bullpen a little longer than a few weeks and this included when he had to take over for an animator who suffered a skiing accident, and when Peggy Roberts had to absent herself as she was having a baby.[17]

One day Klein was putting up ideas for a cartoon on the storyboard. It crossed his mind that a spoof of the new comic-strip sensation *Superman* would be a great subject for a Terrytoons cartoon. Since most of the animated cartoon characters of that period were humanized animals and insects, Klein thought that a super-fly would be a character that would draw audience interest. Klein had read that a fly, for its size, had super strength. With cartoon license, this strength could be multiplied many times over. He started by sketching a fly wearing a Superman type of cape holding up with one arm an enormous pole, which, related to his size, seemed like a telegraph pole. He was really balancing an ordinary pencil. In his second sketch, he drew the super fly flying against the front of an automobile, causing the radiator to buckle and bringing the car to a forced halt. He did not discuss this with the other story men, Foster, McKee, Morrison, and Stahl. He just pinned the sketches on the storyboard.[18]

These two sketches attracted Terry's attention when he came into the room. He asked for an explanation. Klein told him about

207

the popular new comic strip called *Superman* and described the basic idea of that strip. Terry looked impressed, agreed that he had a good idea, but instead of a fly, the studio would make it a mouse – a super mouse! Terry must have suddenly visualized a super-mouse hero for all of his cartoon mice of the past. Thereupon, after briefly discussing the possibilities of this new character, Terry said, "The hell with it. Let's forget it." Later that day Terry tapped Klein on the shoulder and let him know that they were running behind on their animation quota and asked if he could pitch in to help them along. Klein agreed and picked up the sequence to animate from one of the directors. He continued animating for the rest of the week and several weeks thereafter.[19]

On the following Monday, Tom Morrison came to see Klein at his animation desk. Morrison was laughing and said that Terry had brought in Klein's idea of Super Mouse without mentioning his name. He had tacked up some ideas on the board and the story crew was going to work on it. Later that day, Klein went into the story room and found Terry's scratchy sketches on the board with a mouse in a Superman-type cape in some sort of rescue situation, saving some mouse from a big villainous cat. Klein remarked, "I see where Terry has approved of my 'takeoff' on Superman". Foster made no response, while Stahl, McKee and Morrison nodded and smiled. Terry never directly acknowledged that it was Klein that sparked the Mighty Mouse character.[20]

Terry's use of a mouse over an insect is not surprising considering his reliance on the rodent as a character staple of his cartoons since his first years in animation. He had already used a heroic mouse in such shorts as *One Mouse in a Million* (November 3, 1939) and the previously mentioned *Wicky Wacky Romance* (November 17, 1939). Terry's opinion was that a mouse is an appealing cartoon character because of its diminutive size. He believed that keeping many of his characters small, it gave the audience the feeling of being superior.[21]

The first Super Mouse cartoon produced was *The Mouse of Tomorrow* directed by Eddie Donnelly and released on October 16, 1942. In the cartoon short, in a small quaint village the mice are living in fear as the cats are watching over each and every little mouse hole. Precisely at 1:00 p.m., the mice sprint from their holes trying to make a break for liberty. The mice are unsuccessful, but avoid being captured retreating back to their homes. The cats use gas to force the mice from their mouse holes and round them up. But one little mouse breaks free. He burrows into a supermarket and bathes in super soap, eats super soup, chews on super celery, and dines on super cheese. Burrowed inside the dairy product, the cheese spins and explodes revealing Super Mouse, a muscular mouse wearing a Superman costume, blue tights and a red cape and underpants.

Knowing he has a job to do, Super Mouse flies off, smashes through the supermarket wall, increases his speed "to that of light itself", and uses his super powers to battle the cats. His super abilities in the first cartoon include super strength, the ability to fly, and a type of telekinesis involving pointing his fingers to emit a force that repels the felines. Super Mouse ends up trapping the cats in a shed and lifting the shack high into space where it becomes stuck on a pointy end of a star. The cats fall through the shed floor and land on the crescent moon. Super Mouse is welcomed back to the village cheered on by his fellow mice. The narrator exclaims: "What a mouse, what a mouse!"

The cartoon was an instant success with critics and theater audiences. The reviewer for *Variety* considered the cartoon as "just misses being outstanding".[22] Terry knew he had a hit on his hands and the second Super Mouse film produced was *Frankenstein's Cat* released on November 27, 1942 and directed by Mannie Davis. The film took advantage of the then current Universal Studios monster craze that was sweeping theaters across the country. In the short, a horde of angry village mice and birds plan to storm Frankenstein's castle and destroy the monster that had kidnapped an innocent little bird. One of the mice telephones Super Mouse at his Super Market headquarters and the hero flies off to vanquish the evil creature rescuing the helpless bird. The third Super Mouse cartoon, *He Dood It Again* released February 5, 1943 and directed by Eddie Donnelly, has our hero rescuing the mice inhabitants of Sol's Diner just down the street from the Super

Chapter 18 • Here I Come To Save The Day!

Market from a gang of evil cats. The cartoon received a lukewarm review from the *Film Daily* calling the short "strictly kid stuff".[23]

The film suffers from a lack of a spectacular villain but features a nice Lindy-hop jitterbug dance sequence with a group of mice and like the previous two cartoons and most of the Super Mouse/Mighty Mouse cartoons that followed had voice-over narration which some reviewers found irritating.[24] The fourth cartoon in the series, *Pandora's Box*, released June 11, 1943, has the mouse battling bat-winged cat demons. In this cartoon, his origination changes as he consumes Vitamins A through Z to become Super Mouse. A similar instance occurs three years later in *The Johnstown Flood* (June 28, 1946) wherein a mouse ranger drinks from a jug labelled "Atomic Energy" before he becomes Mighty Mouse. In *Super Mouse Rides Again* (August 6, 1943), our hero vanquishes a mob of evil cats. At the beginning of the cartoon Super Mouse greets his mice fans and signs autographs. Interestingly enough, he signs his name "Supermouse" (as one word like "Superman") rather than his titled two word character name. The cartoon received a "no better than fair" review by the critic from *Film Daily*. The reviewer found the plot line predictable although he conceded "the kids will find the cartoon entertaining".[25]

Down with Cats (October 7, 1943) has Super Mouse rescuing some ice skating mice from a gang of cats while *The Lion and the Mouse* (November 12, 1943), is a

Fig. 18.2 – Harem Girl from *The Sultan's Birthday* (1944), Bill Tytla artwork.

re-imagining of the Aesop's Fable with Super Mouse in the role of the mouse. In the short, a mouse drunk from hard cider and filled with a "false sense of values" approaches a lion who traps him and agrees to free him as someday he may be able to help him. Super Mouse makes good on his promise rescuing a lion trapped in a net at the bottom of a pit and surrounded by three angry hunting dogs. Similar to the review given for *He Dood It Again*, the *Film Daily* reviewer found this short "Okay" although "the kids especially will find something to laugh about in this short".[26]

In 1944, Super Mouse received a name change to Mighty Mouse. The reasons for this change have never been conclusively determined. I. Klein's story is that Paul Terry changed the name Super Mouse to Mighty Mouse under pressure from the owners of the *Superman* character, National Periodicals, or its forerunner Detective Comics, Inc. (DC Comics). Detective Comics Inc. had launched a new title, *Action Comics*, the premiere of which introduced Superman in *Action Comics* #1 (June 1938). However, recent investigation has shown that DC has no record of any such legal action.[27] If DC had threatened legal action, most certainly Terry would not only have changed the character name but the blue costume and red cape and underpants as well, an outfit which wasn't redesigned until June 1944.

The other theory is that the name was changed as a result of a comic book entitled *Coo Coo Comics* published by Standard Comics (Nedor Publishing, Inc.), featuring a similar character named Super Mouse. The comic was published in October 1942, the same month that *The Mouse of Tomorrow* was released. The creator of Standard Comics' Supermouse was Kin Platt (birth name: Milton Platkin), formerly associated with the Terrytoons studio in the early 1930s. The comic book Supermouse was married to Mabel. Other regular characters who appeared were his nephew named Roscoe and Terrible Tom who was his arch-enemy. Supermouse gained his extraordinary powers by eating super cheese. The super cheese in turn derived its powers from the milk of a super cow, from which it was made from. Supermouse proved a popular character outliving *Coo Coo Comics* and gaining his own title in 1948. This character ran until Standard Comics folded in 1958.[28]

According to this explanation, Standard Comics managed to copyright the name before Terrytoons could, and Terry was forced to change the name of his star character to avoid legal liability. Once again, there is no evidence to support the contention that Terry was aware of any copyright violation or that Standard had threatened legal action. Most likely, Terry simply decided to change the name of his character to avoid confusion with the comic book character. The benefits for Terry by differentiating his character from Standard's included avoiding any association to qualities of the comic book character that the studio did not want to become associated with and capitalizing on the market advantages from a character the consumer identifies as unique.

The first official Mighty Mouse cartoon with the newly titled character is *The Wreck of the Hesperus* released February 11, 1944 which adapts the famous Henry Wadsworth Longfellow poem to the cartoon format with Mighty Mouse rescuing the captain, his daughter, the crew and the ship from the storm. The next cartoon *The Champion of Justice* (March 17, 1944) tells a story of a kind elderly couple, Mr. and Mrs. Plushbottom, who leave their fortune to their pet mice causing their nephew Willie the Spendthrift to take the matter to court. When he loses in court, he uses his 1890s boneshaker bicycle to tow the mansion off a cliff before Mighty Mouse, perched on the scales of justice, shows up to rescue the home and mice. Interestingly enough, in the short, Mighty Mouse uses a pistol on his adversary.

In *Mighty Mouse Meets Jeckyll and Hyde Cat* (April 28, 1944), directed by Mannie Davis, a small group of mice come in from the storm to the deserted house of Dr. Jeckyll. The doctor's cat befriends them then betrays them. Unable to catch them on his own, he enters Dr. Jeckyll's laboratory and consumes his evil potion turning himself into the monstrous Mr. Hyde Cat who captures and is about to devour the mice until "The Champion of Justice" arrives to defeat the fiend feline. The cartoon is noteworthy for the work of master animator Bill Tytla who designed and animated the Mr. Hyde Cat character.

Tytla's animation of Grumpy in *Snow White and the Seven Dwarfs*, Stromboli in *Pinocchio*, Chernabog in the "Night on Bald Mountain" sequence from *Fantasia* and the title character in *Dumbo* helped elevate his status and reputation in the animation industry as one of the foremost talents in the business. Tytla had supported the employees in the 1941 Disney strike. After the strike, there was too much tension and electricity in the air and Tytla resigned from the Disney studio on February 25, 1943. Paul Terry made a special trip out to California to try and convince Tytla to return to the studio. He wined and dined Tytla and his wife at posh restaurants in the Los Angeles area. He even called upon movie actress Claire Trevor, the cousin of Tommy Morrison, to dine with them in efforts to convince Tytla to head east. Terry's efforts were rewarded as the Tytlas moved to their 160-acre farm in Connecticut on March 1, 1943, and Tytla returned to Terrytoons as a director of animation.[29]

In *Wolf! Wolf!*, released June 22, 1944, a wolf dressed as Bo Peep tries to lure a flock of innocent lambs into a trap while playing a hot swing tune on his clarinet. For the first time, Mighty Mouse no longer sports the outfit colors of Superman as he now dons a red outfit and yellow cape and underpants. *Eliza on the Ice* (June 16, 1944) is an adaptation of

Chapter 18 • Here I Come To Save The Day!

Uncle Tom's Cabin and has Simon Legree and his bloodhounds chasing Eliza during a race. It's up to Mighty Mouse to save the day. The cartoon is notable for being the first to show Mighty Mouse as a resident of the stars where he streams down from the heavens to save the day.

The Green Line (July 7, 1944) directed by Eddie Donnelly tells the story of a town divided in two by a green line, with the cats living on one side and the mice on the other. Both sides live peacefully until an evil feline demon/spirit appears and stirs up a battle between both sides. The cat demon is magnificently animated by Bill Tytla. Mighty Mouse takes care of the evil demon and his magic powers. The cats and mice end up kissing and making up. The idea behind the story came from Terry's travels in Europe and northern Africa when he went to Algiers in 1913. On one side the Moors lived and on the other side was the quite cosmopolitan French. From this experience he got the idea of the green line up the middle of the street separating two ways of life, each remaining in their own territory while living peacefully with the other inhabitants.[30] In *The Two Barbers*, released September 1, 1944, hungry cats tie up a barber, the protector of the mice, and proceed to chase after the mice before being defeated by Mighty Mouse.

The Sultan's Birthday (October 13, 1944), directed by Bill Tytla, tells the story of a mouse kingdom being invaded on the Sultan's birthday by a rival nation of sinister Arabesque felines on flying carpets. Seemingly undefeatable they are beaten when the Mouse of Tomorrow comes to the rescue. The cartoon is noteworthy primarily for the sequence of the veiled dancing mouse girl. Tytla personally animated the dancing girl sequence and his depiction of force vectors and his mastery of animating the human form in motion is very much in evidence. Many years later Terry said: "I remember a dancing girl in that picture. The dancing girl really made the picture. Of course, she danced before this sultan. A beautiful piece of animation."[31] Terry would later reuse the sequence in several other films long after Tytla had left his studio.

The cartoon is also noteworthy for featuring the first appearance of the redesigned fuller bodied Mighty Mouse in his familiar yellow outfit with red cape and underpants. The original character looked more like a super rat with buc:kteeth, spindly legs, and long whiskers. The redesign was undertaken by Connie Rasinski who was rapidly proving to be one of the finest of the Terrytoons directors. By the mid-1940s Rasinski's reputation spread across the continent to California where Walt Disney offered him the opportunity to join his company as animator. Rasinski declined the invitation preferring to remain on the east coast near his families.

During World War II, Rasinski completed security animation films for the United States Army, Navy and Marines while working at Terrytoons. He worked on animated television commercials. Rasinski undertook studies for two years at the Art Students League. Connie Rasinski loved to teach the art and craft of animation. For many years, once a week in the evening at the studio he would teach animation techniques to fledgling artists at Terrytoons.[32] The last Mighty Mouse short produced during 1944 was *At the Circus* (November 17) involving the rescue of a circus acrobat, Mademoiselle Fifi, from the clutches of a hungry lion.

From the moment of his creation to the day Terry retired, Mighty Mouse would be the studio's most bankable cartoon star. Terry attributed the popularity of the cartoon character on several factors. First, children could identify with a character "who is a little insignificant something" and who tackles enemies much larger than him. In schoolyards across America, Mighty Mouse provided hope for all the small kids bullied by the much larger school bully. To add a more human quality to him, capable of being defeated, Terry followed the cinematic plot devices of director D. W. Griffith and had the superhero knocked down a few times before vanquishing his foe. Terry remarked, "The tougher you made it for him to win the more important it was when he did win".[33]

Another motif that ran through most Mighty Mouse cartoons was a religious one and based on the theme which Terry referred to as "Man's extremity is God's opportunity". Terry described this concept as follows:

> When a man is sick, or down, or hurt, you say, "There's

211

Fig. 18.3 – Inking and Opaquing department, early 1940s.

nothing more we can do. It's in God's hand". And he either survives or he doesn't according to God's plan. Right? So, "Man's extremity is God's opportunity". So, taking that as a basis, I'd only have to get the mice in a tough spot and then say, "Isn't there someone who can help?" "Yes, there is someone; it's Mighty Mouse!" So, down from the heavens he'd come sailing down and lick the evil spirit, or whatever it was. And everything would be serene again. And it was a pattern-made-thing.[34]

As the Mighty Mouse series progressed during the mid-to-late 1940s, the superhero's most commonly located domicile would be on a star, moon or in the clouds, in a place among the heavens. In essence, Mighty Mouse became a Christ-like figure, a savior of all "mouse-kind". Terry would take the theme to overt displays of hero worship. Sometimes the characters seeking his protection would get on their knees with their hands clasped together in a prayerful position pleading heavenward to the super mouse to come to the rescue, such as a sheep in *The Crying Wolf* (January 10, 1947). With the use of a prayerful sheep in the cartoon the Mighty Mouse–Jesus Christ metaphor becomes even more credible when considering the pericope of John 10:1–21, in which Jesus Christ is depicted as the Good Shepherd who lays down his life for the sheep.

Terry found that the most popular cartoons starring Mighty Mouse involved the superhero battling a flesh and blood adversary like a cat. The animated cartoons involving Mighty Mouse coming up against the forces of nature such as *Mighty Mouse in Krakatoa* (December 14, 1945) where the mouse rescues the rodent population of a south sea island from doom and destruction and fiery molten lava after a volcano erupts or *The Johnstown Flood* (June 28, 1946) featuring Mighty Mouse rescuing a little mouse village outside Johnstown from the flood in 1889 were unpopular shorts with movie audiences.[35] In devising new story ideas Terry followed a routine. He would go to bed early and get a good night's rest and when he awoke his mind was fresh. He would then try and do all his creating and planning before he arrived at work and then he delegated his duties.[36]

A total of seven Super Mouse and 73 Mighty Mouse cartoons were produced at the studio from 1942

Chapter 18 • Here I Come To Save The Day!

to 1961. The voice of Mighty Mouse was provided by Roy Halee, Sr. Royal Walter Halee (1899–1960) was a tenor, singing dialectician, composer, and voice artist. In his youth, Roy's ambition was to be an operatic tenor. However, one of his voice teachers convinced Halee that his versatile vocal range allowed him to move beyond the restrictions of opera. He began as a singer in Broadway musical productions, most notably musical comedies, in the early 1920s, and for church. In 1930 he began performing on radio. His voice was soon heard nationally in the United States and he appeared as a soloist on many radio programs including *The Voice of Firestone*, *The Telephone Hour* and *The Harvest of Stars*. He was a character actor, singer, and member of a number of leading quartettes in many commercial radio programs over a 20-year period.

He was a member of the Rondaliers Quartet and Fred Waring's Pennsylvanians. He began doing cartoon voice work for the cartoons of J. R. Bray. He was hired by Paul Terry and did the voice of Farmer Al Falfa, the tenor singing voice of Mighty Mouse, and the sometimes the voices of both Heckle and Jeckle (when Dayton Allen wasn't available) along with other Terrytoons cartoon characters. His voice can be heard in most of the Mighty Mouse operatic cartoons that featured Oil Can Harry and Pearl Pureheart. Halee and his quartet did all the voices in these operatic melodramas.[37] He was hired as a voice artist for children's recordings for Lincoln

Fig. 18.4 – Super Mouse from *Mouse of Tomorrow* (1942).

Records, Inc. In many of these recordings he would voice all the characters including the animals and the sound effects. He also did voice work for children's recordings that appeared on the Capital, Victor, Golden and Prom record labels. He undertook work in filmed commercials (both voice-over and on camera) including work for Minoco and Educational shorts.[38] When Mighty Mouse moved to television with the *Mighty Mouse Playhouse* in 1955 and on commercials, Tom Morrison did the speaking voice of the cartoon character.[39]

With the onset of World War Two, eligible men were drafted to support the war effort. By 1942, men from every Hollywood and New York cartoon studio were entering the military. The studio contributed about 45 men to the armed forces with 25 serving in the Signal Corps.[40] The Army Signal Corps had established its first small animation unit and many men from these studios were put to work making training

and educational films. Despite the manpower loss, Terry was able to continue meeting production deadlines and had no problems with paper or celluloid shortages as foresight had allowed Terry to stockpile production work and cartoon shorts.[41]

The United States military also used animation studios to spread their message, such as buying war bonds and donating scrap metal, in an entertaining manner. The government also used animation studios to encourage people to pay their taxes promptly and highlight the importance of the American farmer. Animation was co-opted in the 1940s for training and instructional purposes. Some films showed how the regular G.I. should behave. Animation was quickly appropriated for political campaigning. The phrase, 'lights out,' was a popular saying during the war, especially in major cities to encourage people to turn off their lights to hinder targeting by potential enemy bombers.[42] In 1943 and 1944, 50 percent of the

213

footage shot by the studio was related to the war effort.[43]

Terry decided not to use his new star character, Mighty Mouse, to directly support the war effort. Rather, Terry relied on his next most popular cartoon character, Gandy Goose, as a weapon in the propaganda war. *The Home Guard* (March 7, 1941) has Gandy joining the home guard, a bunch of misfit barnyard creatures that mostly march and drill. At one point, Gandy is menaced by a fifth columnist, who travels in a literal fifth column from a porch. In *The One Man Navy* (September 5, 1941), Gandy fails the eye exam and is rejected by the military. Therefore, he creates his own navy and with the help of some hens defeats an enemy sub. In *Sham Battle Shenanigans* (March 20, 1942), Gandy appears on the "Dunker's Donuts" radio show and recalls a disastrous day when he and Sergeant Sourpuss were training for combat. In *Night Life in the Army* (October 2, 1942) at the army base one night, Private Gandy and Sergeant Sourpuss are sleeping and Gandy, who wants to learn how to fly a plane, has a series of nightmare involving Sourpuss who wants out of his dreams. In *Scrap for Victory* (January 22, 1943) Private Gandy and Sergeant Sourpuss and a group of animals help in the efforts to collect scrap for the war effort.

Barnyard Blackout (March 5, 1943) has Gandy and Sourpuss as air raid wardens involved in some hilarious antics trying to get Henry the Rooster to shut out all light in his home when the siren sounds. In *The Last Round Up* (May 14, 1943) an exploding shell sends Private Gandy and Sergeant Sourpuss outside Hitler's Bavarian mountaintop home. Soon they are engaged in a gun battle with Hitler (a shrieking pig) and Mussolini (Hitler's pet monkey) turning the home into rubble. Terry also created a few cartoons involving some of his minor characters to spread the government message. *Barnyard WAAC* (December 11, 1942) has the hens joining the Women's Army Auxiliary Corps leaving Hank the Rooster to take care of the children. In *Keep 'Em Growing* (July 28, 1943) the barnyard animals do their bit for the war effort by volunteering to assist in crop production and harvesting.

One of the finer cartoons produced by the studio during 1944 was *My Boy Johnny* released on May 12. This short is based on predictions of things to come in the world after the end of World War II. To the tune of "When Johnny Comes Marching Home", the short takes a humorous poke at what every "G.I." Johnny can expect when he returns home to civilian life (planes with outdoor swimming pools, helicopters for every child, and homes with automatic appliances such as hands that wash and dry you off). The short was nominated for an Academy Award in the "Short Subjects, Cartoons", Terry's second nomination for the coveted Oscar®.

The other nominees in the category included the Tom and Jerry cartoon *Mouse Trouble* (Metro-Goldwyn-Mayer – Fred Quimby), *And to Think That I Saw It on Mulberry Street* (Paramount – George Pal), *Dog, Cat and Canary* (Screen Gems, Columbia – Raymond Katz), *Fish Fry* (Walter Lantz Productions, Universal – Walter Lantz), *How to Play Football* (Walt Disney Productions, RKO Radio – Walt Disney), and *Swooner Crooner* (Warner Bros. – Edward Selzer). The Academy Awards ceremony was held on March 15, 1945 at Grauman's Chinese Theater, Hollywood, California. The winner of the Oscar® was *Mouse Trouble*, in the opinion of most critics today the most deserved of the Oscar® among the nominees. The plot concerns Tom's use of a book on how to catch mice and his hilariously unsuccessful attempts in doing so.

My Boy Johnny was directed by Eddie Donnelly. Donnelly (1896–1979) completed art studies at the Art Students League. His first position was as a cartoonist on the staff of the Morse Dry Dock Company illustrating advertisements for the company's sales magazine. He then spent three years as a newspaper (political) cartoonist for such newspapers as the *New York World*. In the early 1920s (about 1923–25), he worked as a cartoonist for the newspaper *The New Era*, which later became the *South Shore Press*. Donnelly started his animation career as a tracer for Fable's Pictures working on the *Aesop's Fables* series and Farmer Al Falfa animated shorts as early as 1923. When Paul Terry and Amedee Van Beuren parted company in 1929, Donnelly remained with Van Beuren Studios as an animator through the early 1930s working on the Cubby Bear series of shorts. He had an interim

Chapter 18 • Here I Come To Save The Day!

period of a year animating at Walt Disney Studios on the *Silly Symphonies* shorts but served the Aesop's Fables unit for nine years. In 1933, he moved back east and joined Terrytoons as an animator and in 1937 was promoted to directorial status.[44]

By June 1944, all of the Terrytoons cartoons were being produced in color. The move to colorizing all of the cartoons added a further 25 percent to the studio budget. The number of cartoons for the 1944–1945 season was reduced from 26 to 20 as a result of raw stock curtailment incidental to the war effort. With respect to color, Terry decided to remain with Technicolor rather than switch to Monopak feeling the former more perfectly met the requirements of an animated cartoon. Terry also announced publicly that he had no plans to produce a cartoon feature believing that the cartoon's place in the feature field is in connection to a story utilizing human actors. Terry stated that the cost of a cartoon feature is about the same as a Hollywood live-action feature. During the summer of 1944, Terry was approached by advertising agencies with a view to making shorts for the new medium of television but Terry was not interested. As for producing animation for the visual training field, Paul also had no plans to enter it in 1944.[45]

The year 1945 was a banner year for Mighty Mouse as some of the cartoon character's best cartoons, nine in total, were produced by the studio. Animation historian Will Timbes Friedwald considers *Mighty Mouse and the Pirates*

Fig. 18.5 – Technicolor paint room at the studio.

(January 12), directed by Connie Rasinski, as the greatest Mighty Mouse cartoon ever.[46] In the cartoon, when a crew of cat pirates led by a rotund peg-legged captain spots an alluring and sexy jungle mouse princess on her tropical island home, they capture the beauty with the intent on ravishing her. Mighty Mouse shows up to dispatch the crew and rescue the maiden in distress. The film is notable for being the first Mighty Mouse cartoon to use an operetta-like score, a tune which sounds much like Gilbert & Sullivan music reminiscent of *H.M.S. Pinafore*. *The Port of Missing Mice* (February 2) is set in old San Francisco where a bunch of rowdy sailor mice are shanghaied by several crew cats with a vacuum cleaner who carry them off in the back of a truck and drive off into the rolling hills until Mighty Mouse arrives to save them. In *Raiding the Raiders* (March 9, 1945), old Doc Owl (animated by Bill Tytla) helps the stork deliver a litter of baby bunnies to Mr. and Mrs. Rabbit. A tribe of vulture Indians steals the youngest of their offspring and flies off with it, leaving Mighty Mouse to rescue the bunny.

In *The Kilkenny Cats* (April 13), the mice in a big city are being ravaged by a vicious gang of cats led by the notorious gang leader Kilkenny. The mice create assembled military units (tanks, planes and infantry) to take on the cats ... but they fail, and Mighty Mouse must rescue them. In one of the poorer entries of the year, *The Silver Streak* (June 8), mice living in a shack are protected by a dog named Rover until one day Rover is trapped by the cats leaving Mighty Mouse to rescue the mice. In *Mighty Mouse and the Wolf* (July 20), a wolf is repeatedly foiled in his attempts to catch Red Riding Hood, Bo Peep and the Three Pigs by an anonymous character (Mighty Mouse) who does not reveal himself until the end of the film. By this time the wolf has called in other wolves on the Atlantic City boardwalk for reinforcements.

On August 3, Terry released what many critics consider to be one of the greatest Mighty Mouse cartoons ever produced: *Mighty Mouse in Gypsy Life*. The plot

215

Fig. 18.6 – Mighty Mouse model sheet.

involves a dancing gypsy mouse girl captured by a horde of evil bat-winged felines. She is rescued by Mighty Mouse but not before nearly being eaten by a crocodile. The cartoon features the song *Gypsy Life* (first heard in *The Gypsy Fiddler* (1933)), a terrifically catchy, memorable, and hummable tune. The short was nominated for an Academy Award in the "Short Subjects, Cartoons", Terry's third nomination for the coveted Oscar®. The ceremony that year was held on March 7, 1946 at Grauman's Chinese Theater, Hollywood, California.

Besides *Gypsy Life*, also vying for the coveted prize were *Quiet Please!* (Metro-Goldwyn-Mayer – Fred Quimby), *Donald's Crime* (Walt Disney Productions, RKO Radio – Walt Disney), *Jasper and the Beanstalk* (Paramount – George Pal), *Life with Feathers* (Warner Bros. – Edward Selzer), *The Poet and Peasant* (Walter Lantz Productions, Universal – Walter Lantz), and *Rippling Romance* (Screen Gems, Columbia – Raymond Katz). The other nominees that year were far from stellar productions. *Rippling Romance* was a forgettable *Color Rhapsody* short about a swan so enamored with itself she overlooks gentlemen suitors. *The Poet and Peasant* is a mediocre Andy Panda short featuring Andy conducting the *Hollywood Washbowl Orchestra* (an ensemble of farm animals, on a farm) in the title tune. *Life with Feathers* is a Sylvester the Cat cartoon. A love bird's wife has left him. He wants to end it all and tries to force Sylvester to eat him. Sylvester thinks there's something fishy about the situation and refuses to eat the bird.

Jasper and the Beanstalk is a George Pal stop motion puppet film with Jasper in the role of Jack. In *Donald's Crime*, Donald has a date with Daisy, but has no money. He raids his nephews' piggy bank, but his guilty conscience catches up with him. The short is mildly amusing at best and a far reach from such Donald Duck masterpieces as *Der Fuehrer's Face* (1943) and *Chef Donald* (1941). The Tom and Jerry nominee *Quiet Please!* is an entertaining cartoon but not in the same class as the Tom and Jerry cartoons *The Yankee Doodle Mouse* (1943) or *The Cat Concerto* (1947). The short concerns a bulldog wanting to take a nap and being kept awake by Tom chasing Jerry around the house. While Terry must have believed he had a good shot at the Oscar®, once again it was the Tom and Jerry short that took home the prize.

On November 9, the studio released *Mighty Mouse Meets Bad Bill Bunion*. In the cartoon, Mighty Mouse rescues the "Belle of the Golden West" from the evil clutches of one of the studio's greatest villains, the notorious desperado Bad Bill Bunion. The review from *The Film Daily* found the cartoon "should prove amusing to all".[47] The last short released in 1945 was the previously described *Mighty Mouse in Krakatoa* (December 14). The highlight of the cartoon is the magnificently dancing hula girl animated by Carlo Vinci. The lyrics to the hula song are cleverly contrived:

> She's Krakatoa Katy
> She ain't no lady
> When she starts to shake her sarong!
> Even down in Haiti
> They've heard of Katy;
> When Katy starts to shake and sway,
> They declare a holiday!
>
> She's Krakatoa Katy
> She ain't no lady,
> When she starts to shake her sarong.
> Katy, Katy, Krakatoa Kate.

The short is directed by Connie Rasinski and is considered one of his masterpieces. The film received an excellent review from *The Film Daily*.[48]

At a very early age Vinci demonstrated great artistic talent. During his childhood he developed and refined his artistic skills with support from family and friends. His efforts were rewarded. After he graduated high school, he was granted a scholarship at the National Academy of Design, New York City. Over the next four years he devoted his life to the study of art of the classical painters and was rewarded by graduating with honors. In 1929, the Tiffany & Co. Foundation awarded Carlo a silver medal (Tiffany Foundation Fellowship), the highest award given for craftsmanship. In 1921 he began working as an artist in commercial art drawing murals, and designing landscapes for residential homes and business offices. Carlo also worked on commercial stained glass. In 1933 he heard about the growing animated cartoon field, applied for a job at the Terrytoons studio and began working there.

He left Terrytoons to work at Van Beuren Studios. He moved back to Terrytoons after Van Beuren Studios closed in 1936. He soon developed a special talent for animating dance sequences and was assigned by Terry to animate many of the dancing numbers in the cartoons. Carlo's animation exhibits brilliant timing. When he animated a dancing sequence he would use a metronome to help choreograph the sequences and many times would go through the dance motions standing by his desk with pencil in hand. To capture the correct facial expressions he would use a mirror at his desk and put his face through various contortions.[49]

He was also an exceptional animator for scenes requiring graceful movement of characters and acting. He never followed the rules of animation but rather tried to advance the art form into new directions. Rather than follow the "straight-line" forms of Disney his characters would be drawn in "zig-zagged" poses with knees, ankles and wrists in flexible "bent" or "crooked" positions. His character's facial expressions were many times filled with vibrant emotion. Vinci would remain with the studio for nearly 20 years. Meanwhile, in 1945, Bill Tytla, unhappy with the schedule that was tight, efficient, and fast moved to work for Famous Studios but found the production pace about the same at that studio.

Shortly after the creation of Super Mouse, in late 1942 (or possibly very early 1943), story man Al Stahl was unexpectedly fired by Terry. The story behind his dismissal has been re-told so frequently in the animation industry that it has developed its own mythology. The most common version of the event has Stahl opening a window on the seventh floor of the Pershing Square Building and dropping a water balloon nearly striking Terry as he was either exiting or entering the building. An angry Terry storms upstairs to the seventh floor and like a drill sergeant commanding his troops tells his animation crew working in the room where the window was located to line up in a row.

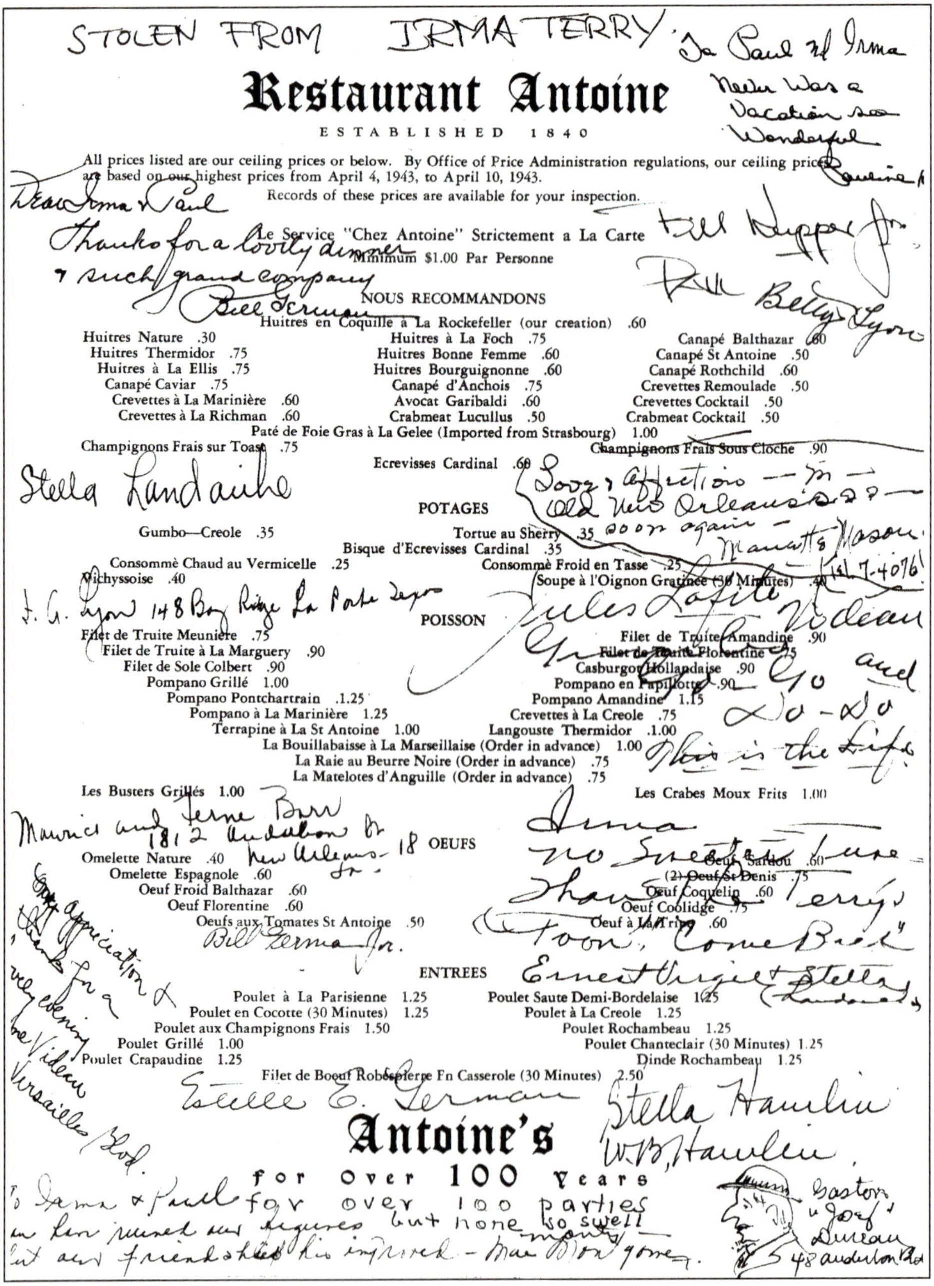

Restaurant Antoine

ESTABLISHED 1840

All prices listed are our ceiling prices or below. By Office of Price Administration regulations, our ceiling prices are based on our highest prices from April 4, 1943, to April 10, 1943. Records of these prices are available for your inspection.

Le Service "Chez Antoine" Strictement a La Carte
Minimum $1.00 Par Personne

NOUS RECOMMANDONS

Huitres en Coquille à La Rockefeller (our creation) .60

Huitres Nature .30	Huitres à La Foch .75	Canapé Balthazar .60
Huitres Thermidor .75	Huitres Bonne Femme .60	Canapé St Antoine .50
Huitres à La Ellis .75	Huitres Bourguignonne .60	Canapé Rothchild .60
Canapé Caviar .75	Canapé d'Anchois .75	Crevettes Remoulade .50
Crevettes à La Marinière .60	Avocat Garibaldi .60	Crevettes Cocktail .50
Crevettes à La Richman .60	Crabmeat Lucullus .50	Crabmeat Cocktail .50

Paté de Foie Gras à La Gelee (Imported from Strasbourg) 1.00

Champignons Frais sur Toast .75   Champignons Frais Sous Cloche .90

Ecrevisses Cardinal .60

POTAGES

Gumbo—Creole .35   Tortue au Sherry .35

Bisque d'Ecrevisses Cardinal .35

Consommè Chaud au Vermicelle .25   Consommé Froid en Tasse .25

Vichyssoise .40   Soupe à l'Oignon Gratinée (30 Minutes) .40

POISSON

Filet de Truite Meunière .75	Filet de Truite Amandine .90
Filet de Truite à La Marguery .90	Filet de Truite Florentine .75
Filet de Sole Colbert .90	Casburgon Hollandaise .90
Pompano Grillé 1.00	Pompano en Papillotte .90
Pompano Pontchartrain 1.25	Pompano Amandine 1.15
Pompano à La Marinière 1.25	Crevettes à La Creole .75
Terrapine à La St Antoine 1.00	Langouste Thermidor 1.00

La Bouillabaisse à La Marseillaise (Order in advance) 1.00
La Raie au Beurre Noire (Order in advance) .75
La Matelotes d'Anguille (Order in advance) .75

Les Busters Grillés 1.00   Les Crabes Moux Frits 1.00

OEUFS

Omelette Nature .40	Oeuf Sardou .60
Omelette Espagnole .60	(2) Oeufs Denis .75
Oeuf Froid Balthazar .60	Oeuf Coquelin .60
Oeuf Florentine .60	Oeuf Coolidge .75
Oeufs aux Tomates St Antoine .50	Oeuf à La Tring .60

ENTREES

Poulet à La Parisienne 1.25	Poulet Saute Demi-Bordelaise 1.25
Poulet en Cocotte (30 Minutes) 1.25	Poulet à La Creole 1.25
Poulet aux Champignons Frais 1.50	Poulet Rochambeau 1.25
Poulet Grillé 1.00	Poulet Chanteclair (30 Minutes) 1.25
Poulet Crapaudine 1.25	Dinde Rochambeau 1.25

Filet de Boeuf Robespierre En Casserole (30 Minutes) 2.50

Antoine's
for over 100 years

Fig. 18.7 – Autographed menu of dinner guests at Paul and Irma's 20th wedding anniversary dinner held at the legendary Antoine's in New Orleans, Louisiana.

Terry then threatens to fire a number of potential suspects unless the perpetrator confesses to his crime. Stahl steps forward to admit he is the guilty party and to the surprise of many of those gathered is fired on the spot by a still fuming Terry.

Chapter 18 • Here I Come To Save The Day!

In the author's discussions with Stahl 55 years later, a different version of the story is told. According to Stahl he had thrown a paper airplane made from a sheet of animation paper out the window. Terry was walking along the street and had spotted the object. He picked it up and knew the airplane had come from his studio because of the peg holes in the paper. In his office, one-by-one Terry quietly questioned each of his employees about the airplane. After Stahl was taken into Terry's office, shown the paper airplane, and asked if he threw it out the window, he admitted to the dastardly deed and was then dismissed.[50]

The question is which version of the incident is the correct account? Likely, we will never know the truth. Usually the answer is a bit of both stories. What we do know is that Stahl threw an object out the window; Terry discovered he had done so, and Stahl was fired. If Stahl had thrown a water balloon out the window aiming the object at Terry, then the firing would make sense. A heavy object, even a water balloon no more than a pound in weight, falling from a seven story height (about 120 feet)[51] and striking an individual could cause serious injury even death. Terry had little choice but to hand out a severe penalty to send a message to the other staff that the behavior would not be tolerated.

If Stahl had thrown a paper airplane out the window, then why would Terry react so strongly to childish behavior and a pardonable stunt? Was Terry so concerned about Stahl throwing company materials out the window that he deserved to be fired? Or was Terry so upset that one or more of his staff was engaging in non-work related activities during working hours that he felt a dismissal was an appropriate punishment? Possibly the firing was the direct result of a mixture of bad timing and an ongoing personality conflict between the two men. At the time of the incident, Terry was under a great deal of pressure from his distributor to create a cartoon product that would compete on an entertainment level with the animated cartoons produced by other studios. Terry was likely under a great deal of stress and not in the mood for games. Mighty Mouse had yet to become the cartoon superstar that would change studio fortunes.

At the time of the incident, Stahl's relationship with Terry was probably not in good standing. Stahl had a habit of engaging in buffoonery, practical stunts and getting under the skin of fellow co-workers, behavior he considered all in good fun. The young story man had a dangerous habit of being very candid with those he worked for and already had a number of confrontations with Terry prior to the incident. During a poker game involving a considerable amount of pocket change, Terry warned the other players at the table that if they raised or bet the pot they would be fired. Stahl's stinging response was: "Well, I'm betting that I have four aces against your four kings. You can fire me right now." He then proceeded to lay down his cards and collect the pot much to Terry's ire.[52]

Stahl was a very good story man and created a large number of extremely humorous situation gags. He was not shy about expressing his opinions and would frequently criticize Terry on his approach to story material. Stahl would have several confrontations with Terry over his habit of reusing gags in his cartoons pleading with the producer to use fresh material. When Terry ran into a storyline situation involving the villain and was unable to come up with new ideas, he habitually inserted the "ass kicking gag" into the cartoon. This involved a situation where the villain, after having been made a fool of or having been outwitted by the protagonist, uses a boot attached to a lever nailed to a tree. The villain pulls on the rope attached to the lever and the boot kicks him repeatedly in the rear thereby punishing himself for his stupidity.

To make his point clear to Terry, Stahl created a gigantic storyboard with dozens of ways to punish a villain he titled "Everything you can do to a villain except kick him in the ass". He put the storyboard on the wall. Despite the clever material, Terry's response was that he would look it over and someday use the material.[53] Stahl was constantly creating fresh, inventive and humorous material for Terry but the producer would never use it. When Terry was in a story conference with the story artists and Stahl would mention some funny situation gags, Paul would write them down then days later suggest the very same gags

219

to his crew insisting the gags were his. When Stahl argued with Terry that those gags were created by him, Terry would argue otherwise insisting the gags were his creation.[54]

Terry also liked to borrow gags from other cartoons. He understood that to take a big bite out of any one source is plagiarism and you're a thief. So he and John Foster had a saying: "Never steal more than you can carry".[55] In 1949, Terry had his daughter work in a separate office and take good jokes out of radio programs for use in the cartoons.[56] During the early 1950s, Terry would rely on assistant animator Ralph Sancier (1911–1984) to visit the local theaters, screen the cartoons of the other studios, and gather the gags used in the cartoons. For each cartoon, Sancier would list the cartoon title, running time, production company, theater where he viewed the cartoon, provide a one line synopsis of the cartoon, type an approximate 500-word outline of the short, list the jokes used, sketch out each of the gags, provide his opinion on the audience responses to the gags, and then provide his review of the short.[57] Sancier had started his career with the Fleischer Studios in Miami, Florida in the late 1930s before moving to work for Terry. Sancier would be employed at Terrytoons for 25 years when he chose to become semi-retired and worked part-time for the Westchester Federal Savings Bank in New Rochelle.[58]

Terry was not just interested in gathering gags from these cartoons, he was also interested in studying the reactions and responses of movie and theater audiences. Terry wanted to understand what was funny and why. In a 1955 *TV Guide* article, Terry tells the reader why children laugh. Terry found that children will laugh at a character that falls down, provided they know he can get up again. They will laugh at small objects, those that they feel mentally and physically superior to. He believed that tastes in humor never change and gags that were funny 2,000 years ago are still funny today if done in modern dress. Terry also espoused the belief that sight gags were popular and became less dated over time as opposed to jokes that appealed to the mind.[59]

The author's interview of Stahl highlighted a popular misconception that still persists today, the belief that Terry, as studio mogul, was incredibly wealthy, lived in luxurious surroundings and enjoyed the finest things that money could buy. When Terry invited Stahl over to his home the story man noticed what he thought was a gold-plated kitchen sink. Stahl asked Terry why he gold-plated the kitchen sink calling the behavior "foolishness" considering he could remodel the entire kitchen with new fixtures for the same price. According to Stahl, Terry's response was: "You know, old things are new things, new things are old things".[60] By these words, Terry likely meant that he need not remodel the kitchen and buy a new sink but simply coat the old sink with a thin layer of gold because there is not much difference between old sinks and new sinks.

The fact is Terry never had a gold plated kitchen sink in his residence. What Stahl had observed was a small copper-plated butler's pantry sink that was in the house when Terry had purchased it.[61] Terry, possibly chuckling beneath his breath, was probably turning the tables on some of Stahl's earlier pranks by playing along with Stahl's mistaken belief. The simple truth is Terry and his family lived a comfortable upper middle-class lifestyle without pretension. There was no posh mansion, swimming pool in the backyard, water fountain in the driveway, Rolls Royce in the garage, army of servants at beck and call, memberships to the Larchmont Yacht Club, and global vacations to the Caribbean or the French Riviera.

Rather, Terry preferred to live a life marked with prudence, thrift, and economy. His most expensive indulgence was an annual winter vacation to Florida with his wife, a trip he took many Decembers in the 1940s and 1950s to enjoy some sun. He visited Europe on just a few occasions but after discovering that the cities were generally quite dirty as compared to American cities chose to confine his travel to the United States.[62] Terry drove an automobile during his life but as he got older he hired a chauffeur which decision may have been due partly to his vision restrictions. For his chauffeur, Larry Fortune,[63] Terry would periodically reward him with bonuses and even during illnesses would always have a cheque for him.[64] He sent his daughter to a private school to receive a first-class education which he believed was important for a child. He also belonged to a number of clubs such as the Westchester Country Club where he occasionally played golf but found it would form bad habits.[65] However, a typical weekday for Terry was not much different from most upper middle class American husbands. After getting home from the studio, he would have dinner, read the newspaper, and spend time with his wife and daughter.

Terry was by his very nature a frugal person. The *Merriam-Webster Dictionary* defines frugal as "characterized by or reflecting economy in the use of resources" with the etymology from the Latin "fruit", "value" or "virtue".[66] The *Oxford English Dictionary* defines frugality as "moderate or sparing expenditure or use of provisions, goods, etc.".[67] James A. Nash in "On the Subversive Virtue: Frugality", describes frugality as denoting "moderation, temperance, thrift, cost-effectiveness, efficient usage, and a satisfaction with material sufficiency".[68] Frugality "thrives not only on restrained consumption but also on conscientious conservation, optimal technical efficiency, comprehensive recycling, and an insistence on built-in durability and repairability".[69]

Frugality is considered a personal virtue and an excellent trait or habit of individual behavior and is not the means to prosperity.[70] "Though it is not miserliness or hoarding, frugality surely includes saving and investing – reserving and increasing resources for future plans and needs, such as educational expenses or retirement".[71] "But frugality also has a more comprehensive purpose, which includes just and generous sharing".[72] Frugality can be viewed as a revolt against the society of consumption. "For the sake of personal, social, and ecological well-being, frugality rejects the gluttonous indulgence, compulsive acquisitiveness, conforming and competitive consumerism, casual wastefulness, and unconstrained material growth promoted by the peddlers of economic progress – and embraced in different degrees by all of us who have known the enticements of affluence".[73]

Frugality is not pure deprivation but reflects short-term sacrifices in buying and using consumer goods in order to achieve idiosyncratic goals in the longer term. "Frugality is a uni-dimensional consumer lifestyle trait characterized by the degree to which consumers are both restrained in acquiring and in resourcefully using economic goods and services to achieve longer-term goals".[74] Therefore, frugality involves careful spending of money and both restraint and discipline in acquisition. A study by Shoham and Brencic found that frugal consumers tend to be less impulsive and more disciplined in how they spend money compared to other users.[75]

Terry's frugality is evidenced by the clothes he wore and shoes on his feet. He would be seen frequently walking the corridors of his animation studio with tattered attire. He wore his shoes down until there were holes in the soles and then rather than discard them he would insert cardboard inside the shoe to obtain maximum usage from the footwear.[76] Once as a single young man he was invited to a black tie affair in New York City. He put on his woollen trousers to wear to the event and noticed that there were moth holes in one of the legs. Rather than go out and purchase a new pair of pants he painted one of his legs with black Indian ink and went to the social gathering wearing the trousers.[77] At the studio, Terry reused, repurposed and repaired animation equipment until it was no longer functional. It was not uncommon to see chairs held together by wire.[78]

With the profits he generated from his studio, Terry wisely invested them in a diversified financial portfolio of cash, stocks, bonds, and real estate to ensure that in the event of tough economic times his family had food on the table and his studio would continue to operate and produce the animated film product. Terry stated:

> To be prepared is the key to all success. That's the reason you have fire departments. That's the reason you have insurance policies. And you make sure you build up a bank account to be prepared for the unexpected. Then so when these things happen you're prepared for them. Then you go on from there.[79]

Terry would best be described as a "shrewd" money manager, one who amasses wealth by wisely using cunning, knowledge, foresight and balanced judgment. His financial management skills followed the dictionary definition of "shrewd" by exhibiting marked wisdom or judiciousness, clever discerning awareness, and hard-headed acumen highlighted by circumspection.[80] Terry spent wisely on his animated cartoons ensuring that production costs were under control and budgets were not exceeded.

Conversely, Walt Disney spent lavishly on his animated cartoons and theatrical features. As a result of the technical and artistic brilliance of his cartoon product Disney won the Oscar® in the category "Short Subjects, Cartoons" the first eight years the award was handed out, 1932–1939, and another five times by 1970. Disney's solution to the rising costs of animated cartoon production during the 1930s and early 1940s was "to make his shorts so good that the public would demand them forcing exhibitors to pay higher rentals".[81] However, this method was largely unsuccessful because distributors were unwilling to pay Disney more for a short despite the favorable critical response and were only interested in keeping costs at a minimum.[82] While Terry refused to make an animated feature, Disney chose to continue making features after the critical and box office successes of *Snow White and the Seven Dwarfs* (1937) but after *Bambi* (1940) (cost: $1.7 million) and *Fantasia* (1940) (cost: $2.3 million), the Disney family had incurred $3.5 million in debt[83] forcing the company to go public in 1940 when Disney lost his foreign market as a result of the Second World War.[84]

A little known narrative about Terry, even within family circles, is his involvement in moving Jews out of Germany during the troubling years leading up to the Second World War. For Pat Terry, the daughter of Paul, the story only came to light during the mid-1990s after she had discussions with one of her cousins. According to the cousin, Terry and his wife Irma along with Irma's half-brother Milton and his family were actively involved in helping Jewish families escape the country. From the evidence gathered it appears Paul financed part of the operation and worked alongside Milton with government officials to process entry visas by hiring Jewish couples to work at his residence in various capacities. After a short period of time with the Terry family, the couple would relocate to employment elsewhere in the United States allowing Terry the opportunity to begin the immigration process again to assist with the relocation of other Jewish families out of Germany.

As a child of eight or nine, Pat remembers a Jewish woman working for her parents telling her about the harrowing process of leaving Germany. The woman recounted to the young Ms. Terry stories about life in Germany under Hitler with German military parades and "armies that went on forever". At the time, the little Ms. Terry didn't make anything from the fact that German-Jewish couples would periodically come and go from the household on a regular basis. Pat also remembers the book *Mein Kampf* lying near her parent's bed. The book stood out to Pat because her mother was not one to read historical and political works but rather restricted her readings to novels. Possibly Adolf Hitler's anti-Semitism and his plans for the Jews written on the pages of the book sent off alarm bells to her parents to help the Jews in Germany.[85] Irma may have been particularly disturbed and moved to assist since her parents were both European Jews. Irma's parents, the Heimlichs, were from the mighty Austro-Hungarian Empire at the turn of the century. Her father was Hungarian while her mother was Austrian. While the story of Paul's involvement will never be fully made known and the stories behind the lives of the people he helped rescue from a regime bent on their destruction lost, the tale makes an interesting sub-plot to the Terry legacy.

On February 2, 1945, Harvey Day, vice-president and general sales manager at Terrytoons, who had been with Terrytoons since 1932, resigned his post.[86] No immediate replacement for Day was announced. On March 26, 1945, *Film Daily* reported that Paul Terry was celebrating his 30th anniversary in animated cartoons, and his 10th anniversary with 20th Century-Fox.[87] 20th Century-Fox hosted a cocktail party for Terry at the St. Moritz Hotel's Sky Garden Room on December 28.[88] About 300 guests were in attendance including officers and executives of 20th Century Fox.[89] An article in the January 2, 1946 edition of *The Film Daily* listed a veritable "Who's Who" of 20th Century-Fox who attended the event. Bill Weiss was the master of ceremonies.[90]

In retrospect, the arrival of Mighty Mouse could not have occurred at

Chapter 18 • Here I Come To Save The Day!

a better time for the studio. When Bill Tytla came east from the Disney studio to join the Terrytoons staff as another director in 1943, after the Mighty Mouse series was well underway, Terry gave Tytla a restaurant dinner party as a welcoming gesture. The directors, story crew, and several other people of the staff gathered in the story room at 5:30 p.m. after working hours before heading to dinner. The group sat around talking for a while. Terry did most of the talking, directing his conversation to the new director. Terry said that in 1942 the prospect of a renewal of a release contract with 20th Century-Fox looked very bleak. Terry noted that 20th Century-Fox was losing interest in the Terrytoons cartoon product. Then we, Terrytoons, came up with Mighty Mouse. Their interest was rekindled and a new contract was signed. Mighty Mouse had saved the studio. When Terry said, "When we came up with Mighty Mouse", he nodded in Klein's direction. Klein doubted if anyone was aware of that nod except himself.[91]

Notes

1. Morrison, interview, 15 June 1970, 10d.

2. 20th Century-Fox Film Corporation, "Terrytoon Creators: John Foster", *Dynamo* (Terrytoon Section), 15 April 1940, Chicago, Illinois, 5B.

3. Falk, ed., *Who Was Who in American Art, 1564–1975*; Opitz, *Mantle Fielding's Dictionary of American Painters, Sculptors & Engravers*; Opitz, *Dictionary of American Sculptors: "18th century to the Present"*.

4. Alvin Stahl, phone interview by author (transcript), 24 November 1997, Kelowna, B.C., Canada, Terrytoons Collection, Victoria, B.C.

5. For more on I. Klein see The I. Klein Papers (1926–1981) that are held at the Special Collections Research Center, Syracuse University Library.

6. I. Klein, "On Mighty Mouse", in *The American Animated Cartoon: A Critical Anthology*, ed. Gerald Peary and Danny Peary (N.Y.: E.P. Dutton, 1980), 172.

7. Ibid., 172–173.

8. Ibid., 173–174.

9. Ibid., 174.

10. Ibid., 174.

11. Terry, interview, 20 December 1969, 41; Obituary: "Joe Laurie, Jr., 62, Comedian, Is Dead: Career Spanned Period 'From! Vaude to Video' – Known for Theatre Writings", *New York Times*, 30 April 1954, p. 23.

12. Terry, interview, 20 December 1969, 41; Robert Schiffer, "His Jokes Are Old: Joe Laurie Says There Are No New Gags and Illustrates His Point With Whiskers Laurels Final Proof", *New York Times*, 29 July 1945, p. X5.

13. Klein, "On Mighty Mouse", 174–175.

14. Ibid., 175.

15. Ibid.

16. Ibid.

17. Ibid., 175–176.

18. Ibid., 176.

19. Ibid., 176–177.

20. Ibid., 177.

21. Terry, interview, 20 December 1969, 68.

22. "Mouse of Tomorrow", (animated cartoon review), *Variety*, 2 December 1942, 8.

23. "He Dood It Again", (animated cartoon review), *The Film Daily*, 14 May 1943, p. 8.

24. The reviewer from *Variety* referred to the narration as "faulty" (*Variety*, 2 December 1942, 8), while Friedwald in his survey of the Terrytoon Mighty Mouse cartoons commented similarly: "slightly irritating narrator". Will Timbes Friedwald, "Of Mighty Mouse & Men", *Mindrot*, no. 16 (28 February 1980): 19.

25. "Super Mouse Rides Again", (animated cartoon review), *Film Daily*, 1 September 1943, p. 10.

26. "The Lion and the Mouse", (animated cartoon review), *Film Daily*, 24 November 1943, p. 12.

27. Jim Korkis, "Suspended Animation: Mighty Mouse and Company", *Comics Journal* (June 1980): 4.

28. Gina Renée Misiroglu and David A. Roach, ed., *The Superhero Book: The Ultimate Encyclopedia of Comic-book Icons and Hollywood Heroes* (Canton, MI: Visible Ink Press, 2004), 221; *Contemporary Authors, New Revision Series. A Bio-bibliographical guide to Current Writers in Fiction, General Nonfiction, Poetry, Journalism, Drama, Motion Pictures, Television, and Other Fields*, volume 11 (Detroit: Gale Research, 1984) (entries also found in volumes 17–20, 1st revision).

29. John Canemaker, "Vlad Tytla: Animation's Michelangelo", in *The American Animated Cartoon: A Critical Anthology*, ed. Gerald Peary and Danny Peary (New York: E.P. Dutton, 1980), 88.

30. Terry, interview, 20 December 1969, 57.

31. Ibid., 73.

32. "J.C. Rasinski, Terrytoons Director Dies", (Obituary News), *The Standard-Star* (New Rochelle, NY), 14 October 1965, p. 2; 20th Century-Fox Film Corporation, "Experts Are Born: Connie Rasinski", *Dynamo* (Terrytoon Section), 15 April 1940, Chicago, Illinois, 8B; Conrad Rasinski, interview by Author (transcript), 31 October 1997, Terrytoons Collection.

33. Terry, interview, 20 December 1969, 70.

34. Ibid., 57.

35. Ibid., 70.

36. Ibid., 71.

37. Thomas James (Tommy) Morrison, interview, 15 June 1970, 26d.

38. Rosaleen Doherty, "1,000-Voice

223

TERRYTOONS: The Story of Paul Terry and His Classic Cartoon Factory

Singer Plugs Mother Goose", *New York Daily News*, c. 1941; "Obituary: Roy Halee, 59, Singer, Actor", (newspaper unknown, c.1960); Paul Terry Papers.

39. Thomas James (Tommy) Morrison, interview, 15 June 1970, 26d.

40. "50% of Terry's Pix For Armed Forces", *Film Daily*, 19 June 1944, p. 7.

41. Ibid.

42. Michael S. Shull and David E. Wilt, *Doing Their Bit: Wartime American Animated Short Films, 1939–1945*, 2nd ed. (Jefferson, N.C.: McFarland, 2004).

43. "50% of Terry's Pix", p. 1, 7.

44. 20th Century-Fox Film Corporation, "Terrytoon Who's Who: Eddie Donnelly", *Dynamo* (Terrytoon Section), 15 April 1940, Chicago, Illinois, 4B. Polly Bourne Donnelly, phone interview by Author (transcript), 1996, Terrytoons Collection.

45. "50% of Terry's Pix", p. 1, 7.

46. Friedwald, "Of Mighty Mouse & Men", 22.

47. "Mighty Mouse Meets Bad Bill Bunion", (animated cartoon review), *Film Daily*, 19 February 1946, p. 11.

48. "Krakatoa", (animated cartoon review), *Film Daily*, 19 February 1946, p. 11.

49. Angelo "Terry" Tarricone, telephone interview by author (transcript), Kelowna, B.C., Canada, 26 October 1997, Terrytoons Collection, 2.

50. Stahl, interview, 3–4.

51. The Pershing Square Building is 247 feet high. From the 7th story of the edifice, about half way up, the distance would be about 120 feet.

52. Stahl, interview, 5

53. Ibid., 4.

54. Ibid., 5.

55. Terry, interview, 13 June 1970, 99.

56. Leahy and Lazar, interview, 14.

57. A large number of Sancier's cartoon reviews are found in the Paul Terry Papers.

58. Obituary: "Ralph Sancier", *The Standard-Star* (New Rochelle, NY), 20 December 1984, p. 4.

59. Paul Terry, "A Cartoonist Tells the Brutal Truth On: How to Make Children Laugh", *TV Guide*, April 16–22, 1955, 16–17.

60. Stahl, interview, 4.

61. Caron Lazar, electronic correspondence to the author, 2 August 2015.

62. About 1946 Terry traveled to Mexico. On a few occasions he and his wife went to Mardi Gras to visit friends in New Orleans. In 1948 Terry and his family toured Europe. He later went to Scandinavia in the early 1950s. According to family sources his European vacations were partly business related. Apparently there was difficulty with receiving outstanding receipts due on the rentals of film prints to his European clients which necessitated Terry visiting with his business associates overseas to resolve these issues (Leahy and Lazar, interview, 30).

63. The 1955 New Rochelle City Directory lists Larry Fortune's address at 71 Remington Place in New Rochelle, New York while Terry's address was in Rye, New York (*Polk's New Rochelle (Westchester County, N.Y.) City Directory 1955*, vol. XLVII (Boston, Massachusetts: R.L. Polk & Co., 1955), p. 200. Larry Fortune was not required to live on the Terry family property in his capacity as chauffeur.

64. Leahy and Lazar, interview, 16.

65. Ibid., 20.

66. Merriam-Webster Online, *Merriam-Webster's Online Dictionary*, s.v. "frugal", http://www.m-w.com/dictionary/frugal (Accessed: 10 December 2007).

67. *The Oxford English Dictionary*, 2nd ed., vol. VI, prepared by J.A. Simpson and E.S.C. Weiner, s.v. "frugality" (Oxford: Clarendon Press, 1989), 228.

68. James B. Nash, "On the Subversive Virtue: Frugality", in *Ethics of Consumption: The Good Life, Justice, and Global Stewardship*, David A. Crocker and Toby Linden, eds. (Lanham, Maryland: Rowman and Littlefield, 1998), 421.

69. Ibid.

70. A number of books promoting frugality have appeared on the marketplace, most notably: Amy Dacyczyn, *The Complete Tightwad Gazette: Promoting Thrift as a Viable Alternative Lifestyle* (New York: Villard, 1998).

71. Nash, "On the Subversive Virtue: Frugality", 424.

72. Ibid., 424–425.

73. Ibid, 420–421.

74. John L. Lastovicka et. al., "Lifestyle of the Tight and Frugal: Theory and Measurement", *Journal of Consumer Research* 26 (June 1999): 88.

75. Aviv Shoham and Maja Makovec Brencic, "Value, Price Consciousness, and Consumption Frugality: An Empirical Study", *Journal of International Consumer Marketing* 17, no. 1 (2004): 55–69.

76. Leahy and Lazar, interview, 1.

77. Ibid.

78. Ibid., 16.

79. Terry, interview, 13 June 1970, 116.

80. Merriam-Webster Online, *Merriam-Webster's Online Dictionary*, s.v. "shrewd", http://www.m-w.com/dictionary/shrewd (Accessed: 10 December 2007).

81. "Mickey Mouse and the Bankers", *Fortune* 10(5) (November 1934): 94.

82. Richard Schickel, *The Disney Version: The Life, Times, Art, and Commerce of Walt Disney* (New York: Simon and Schuster, 1985), 102.

83. McDonald, "Now the Bankers Come to Disney", 218.

84. Ibid., 223.

85. Leahy and Lazar, interview, 9.

86. "Harvey Day Resigns Posts at Terrytoons", *Film Daily*, 1 February 1945, p. 1, 4.

87. "A Dual Anniversary for Producer Terry", *Film Daily*, 26 March 1945, p. 11.

88. "Party for Paul Terry", *Film Daily*, 20 December 1945, p. 4.

89. "Terry Cocktail Party Today", *Film Daily*, 28 December 1945, p. 9.

90. "Industry Honors Terry's 30th Anniversary in Pix", *Film Daily*, 2 January 1946, p. 2.

91. Klein, "On Mighty Mouse", 177.

Chapter 19

Those Magnificent Mischievous Magpies: Heckle and Jeckle and the Terrytoons Labor Strike, 1946–1947

On January 4, 1946, Terrytoons released *The Talking Magpies*, considered by most animation historians to be the first Heckle and Jeckle short, although in the cartoon both magpies were prototypes of the classic duo. The cartoon featured Farmer Al Falfa and his dopey dog, a developing version of Dimwit, being pestered by a pair of magpies, a noisy husband-and-wife couple looking for a new home. *Listen to the Mockingbird* (1855), an American popular song of the mid-19th century with lyrics composed by Septimus Winner under the pseudonym "Alice Hawthorne", and music by Richard Milburn, would become their unofficial signature theme, played over the opening titles. At this point the pair was still unnamed (one of them is addressed as "Maggie" in the cartoon), and had white beaks. While one magpie had a vaguely New York-like accent, the other had no trace of a British accent at all – and was female, wearing a ladies hat. The contemporary reviews of the short were very positive. *The Film Daily* reviewer found the short "fast-moving and quite humorous" with "a big appeal for the kids because of its chatter and slapstick".[1]

At the time of the release of the short, little thought was given to capitalizing on their audience appeal and using the characters in subsequent cartoons. In fact, it was nearly 11 months later when the next magpie cartoon was released. All succeeding episodes (beginning with *The Uninvited Pests* released November 29, 1946) portrayed both characters as males, and featured their now-familiar colors and characterizations. The idea for two identical magpies that looked exactly alike came from Terry who "thought there might be some fun in the idea".[2] Further, having two identical characters simplified the drawing and made animating the short less complex. The cartoons were directed on a rotating basis by Connie Rasinski, Eddie Donnelly and Mannie Davis. Unlike Bugs Bunny, who retaliates against a foe only after repeated provocation, the magpies' comic aggression is often unprovoked, and in a number of Heckle and Jeckle cartoons (*Moose on the Loose* (November 1952), *Free Enterprise* (November 23, 1948), *The Power of Thought* (December 31, 1948 [January 1949]), *Hula Hula Land* (July 1949)) their foes win in the end.

Although both birds are identical in appearance, they are differentiated by their voices. Jeckle speaks with a slightly falsetto English accent, and his dialogue is somewhat more cultured. Heckle is more coarse around the edges, and speaks with a more informal, slangy vernacular and gruff New York City (Brooklyn) dialect. However, the two magpies are far more alike in temperament than they are different. The two birds were voiced almost exclusively by Dayton Allen although Sid Raymond, Roy Halee, and Ned Sparks provided some voices when Allen was not available.[3] Dayton Allen later claimed that he was the inspiration behind the idea of using British and Bronx accented magpies.[4] The first Heckle and Jeckle cartoon where the birds speak in British and Bronx accents was the fifth short,

Cat Trouble (April 11, 1947). Whether Allen voiced the characters prior to this short is uncertain.

Paul Terry hired Dayton Allen in 1947 to do the voices of the two birds, and he would end up creating voices for many other Terrytoons characters. Allen would work for Terrytoons for 20 years. Allen's career in voice work started shortly after graduating from high school at 15 years of age. Allen found a full-time job as a projectionist of 16mm movies that were shown as recreation at hospitals, summer camps, and prisons. The other part of the program was an act by an Indian chief that included his tribal dance. Allen began introducing the man, who was named "Swift Eagle", and soon was doing impersonations. In 1935, the radio station WINS hired him as a disc jockey. From 1936 to 1940, he undertook a number of motion picture road shows. From 1940 to 1941, he worked for WINS as a writer of vaudeville comedy bits. "Uncle Jim" Harkins hired him as a comedy writer for Fred Allen, whom he managed. Allen also made frequent appearances on the star's network radio show. He also performed stand-up comedy during this period.

During 1941 through to 1945, Allen was a radio comic, puppeteer and did voice work. After finding work for Terry, Dayton discovered a lucrative market in voiceovers and cartoon voices for television. Beginning in 1948, Allen was hired as the voice of various New York based children's show characters using his vocal talents on television. He was the voice of the puppet star of *The Adventures of Oky Doky*. In 1949, Bob Keeshan, who was playing Clarabell the Clown on *The Howdy Doody Show*, asked Buffalo Bob Smith if Allen could do some of the voices on the show and soon Allen began playing Phineas T. Bluster, Howdy Doody's nemesis, later Flub-a-Dub and about 11 other puppets including Ugly Sam the Wrestler, Lanky Lou the Cowhand, Sir Archibald the Explorer, and Pierre the Chef. He also did voices of cartoon characters on the Saturday morning television show *Winky Dink and You* for five years, 1953–1957, with Mae Questel doing all the lines for Winky Dink (Allen voiced the character of Mr. Bungle, the landlord). He also did voice work for television commercials.

In late 1958, Dayton first appeared as a last-minute substitute for the double-talking comedian Al Kelly. In a sketch in which he was interviewed as Congressman Dudley, Pat Harrington, Jr. asked him an unscripted question and he ad-libbed "Why not?" Allen recalled "Skitch Henderson fell on the floor" and "the audience howled". He became one of the regulars within weeks and the "Why Not?" was heard everywhere. Allen used the expression for television commercials and saw novelty toys, a book and a record spin off (both titled Why Not?) of the "Why Not?" phenomena. British Airways used the slogan in an ad campaign.

In the 1960s, for CBS-Terrytoons Allen was doing the voices for Luno, Astronut, Possible Possum, Deputy Dawg (Allen originated Deputy Dawg's voice), Muskie the Muskrat, Ty Coon the Raccoon, Vincent Van Gopher and Pig Newton and stayed at CBS-Terrytoons until the studio stopped producing cartoons in the late 1960s. Allen used to ad-lib a good portion of the material using his experience doing club work. As his reputation grew, so did his salary. When he started at Terrytoons in the mid-1940s he was being paid $25 a cartoon and when he left in the late-1960s he was being paid $500 a short.[5]

In their cartoons, Heckle and Jeckle seldom referred to each other by name, leading to some confusion as to which one was which. Heckle usually refers to Jeckle familiarly, as "pal" or "chum", while Jeckle often calls Heckle "old chap", "old boy", "old thing", or "old featherhead", revealing his British background while indicating a close friendship between both birds. Among the few occurrences where the two birds are positively identified, they clearly refer to each other by name. In the short *Bulldozing the Bull* (March 11, 1951), the Brooklyn accent belongs to Heckle and the British accent belongs to Jeckle. In the cartoon *Stunt Men* (November 23, 1960), Jeckle, in a British accent, again calls Heckle by name. In *Rival Romeos* (November 7, 1950 [January 1951]), the magpies, after being simultaneously love-struck by the same female, race home to get dressed. They are shown to occupy two sides of the same tree, and each character's home is marked with a sign – Heckle is

Chapter 19 • Those Magnificent Mischievous Magpies

Fig. 19.1 – Arthur Bartsch, layout artist.

clearly designated as the Brooklyn magpie with his jaunty porkpie hat, and Jeckle sports a British-looking bowtie, monocle and straw boater. *Rival Romeos* is also one of the only cartoons where the magpies are at odds with each other rather than united against a common adversary (usually either of two series "regulars": Dimwit, a moronic hound dog, or Chesty, a belligerent, disagreeable bulldog).

While both magpies are essentially brash, cynical and confrontational, Heckle may be more openly antagonistic, and Jeckle slightly more wily and deceitful. Both may deliberately annoy their mutual foils with insults, slapstick violence and rudeness, but Heckle is more likely to make his intentions clear from the outset. Conversely, Jeckle often treats enemies politely at first, in order to lull them into a false sense of security before unleashing magpie mayhem. They are alternately cast as a pair of confidence men actively out to swindle an unsuspecting dupe – or just freeloading opportunists, idly in search of a free ride or mooching a meal. However, even when they're gainfully employed (as in *The Super Salesmen* (October 24, 1947) or *Pill Peddlers* (April 1953)), there's often a hint of hucksterism or prankishness involved. In *Sappy New Year* (November 10, 1961), they're a couple of inveterate, compulsive practical jokers trying (unsuccessfully) to turn over a new leaf.

The characters' pert and mischievous personas occasionally extended to impromptu song routines, such as *Give Us a House to Wreck* in *House Busters* (August 1952), and *Come to Our Diner* in *Blue Plate Symphony* (October 29, 1954). In *Taming the Cat* (January 1948), they stop the action just to perform a lively version of *Get a Couple of Songbirds Today* on piano, in the style of Jimmy Durante. Other

227

impersonations of Hollywood and radio favorites included Humphrey Bogart, Walter Winchell, Edward G. Robinson, Hugh Herbert, Bert Lahr, and Groucho and Harpo Marx.

The animated pair was extremely popular with audiences. Paul Terry considered Heckle and Jeckle to be the best cartoons the studio produced.[6] A total of 52 Heckle and Jeckle animated cartoons were produced at the Terrytoons studio from 1946 to 1961. The high point of any Heckle and Jeckle cartoon was arguably the climactic chase sequence, often interspersed with witty banter between the two magpies. The duo bested their foes by outsmarting them, all the while indulging in wry commentary that made their adversaries appear even more stupid. Heckle and Jeckle often received their comeuppance before the fadeout, however, as they were usually the instigators of the conflict in the first place.

Although they've wound up inside a jail cell on occasion, for some (usually unspecified) offense (*Out Again In Again, Free Enterprise, A Merry Chase*), other episodes portray the pair ostensibly on the side of law and order (*The Hitch Hikers, 'Sno Fun, Hair Cut-Ups*), instead of fleeing from it. In the short *Blind Date* (1954), Heckle is able to forcibly disguise the unwilling Jeckle as a girl, indicating that Heckle is physically stronger than Jeckle. In *The Power of Thought* (1948), it is Jeckle who self-reflexively discovers the unlimited possibilities of being a cartoon character, although Heckle is quick enough to go along when this is pointed out to him.

Mighty Mouse cartoons continued to dominate the release schedule in 1946 when a total of 11 shorts were released. In *Svengali's Cat* (January 18), a sinister feline mesmerist has hypnotized a girl mouse into sweetly singing "Oh don't you remember sweet Alice / Ben Bolt" over and over, and then puts her out on the sidewalk where she lures innocent male mice into a trap for him and his cat gang. *The Wicked Wolf* (March 8) features the memorable scene of an animator drawing the superhero (Mighty Mouse: "Hurry up, I have a job to do!") before he flies off to the rescue. Mighty Mouse helps the hero in *My Old Kentucky Home* (March 29) win the Kentucky Derby so he can give Little Nell the money to a Zoot-suited wolf to pay off the mortgage on her grandfather's plantation. *The Trojan Horse* (July 26) is an animated version of the classic work with the mice as the Greeks and the cats as the Trojans.

Winning the West (August 16), directed by Eddie Donnelly, involves a vicious tribe of injun cats attacking a wagon train full of settlers. After General Custer, Stonewall Jackson, Daniel Boone, and Buffalo Bill all fail, Mighty Mouse flies in to rescue the mice. The short begins with an effective sequence of the shadows cast by Indians dancing around the campfire. Bad Bill Bunion returns in *The Jail Break* (September 20) escaping from Alcatraz Prison and committing foul deeds that get worse and worse until he steals the football from the Army-Navy game before he is stopped by Mighty Mouse. These last two shorts received "very good" reviews in *The Film Daily*.[7] Mighty Mouse rescues a little mouse village from a massive flood outside Johnstown in *The Johnstown Flood* (June 28), battles a robot dinosaur in *The Electronic Mousetrap* (September 6), overcomes the evil magic of a king's wicked (cat) wizard in *The Crackpot King* (November 15), and in *The Hep Cat* (December 6) rescues mice who are kidnapped by a cat playing a hot Benny Goodman-Artie Shaw style solo on his clarinet.

The animated gem of 1946 was *Throwing the Bull* (May 3) directed by Connie Rasinski. In the cartoon, a rich Spaniard offers his daughter's hand in marriage to any matador that can defeat the bull in the ring. The bull defeats all matadors who challenge him. Mighty Mouse enters the ring and pummels the bovine sending the animal to the butcher shop thereby winning the daughter's hand. Numerous scenes of accurately rendered animation, expressive character animation, detailed costume designs that offer a wide range of colors and hues (e.g. toreadors), consistent casting of shadows by characters with appropriate directional lighting, and many close-ups of character faces with life-like emotions provide outstanding examples of high quality animation. Cycled artwork is limited to few distant crowd scenes and is almost imperceptible.

Excellent depth cues are provided such as when the bull brags that he can beat Mighty Mouse, the

Chapter 19 • Those Magnificent Mischievous Magpies

clouds in the background move. The use of chiaroscuro for symbolic purposes occurs when the matadors, unable to exit the room, are waiting nervously for their next turn to fight the bull. The shadows of prison cell bars are cast on the floor and the corner wall of the room where they sit symbolizing their trapped and claustrophobic predicament.

The backgrounds are meticulously painted evident by the many objects that fill the interior spaces. More impressively, the high overhead wide shot of the bullring features intricate design work. Despite the distance, tiny houses, flags, roads, people and trees, most of which cast shadows, are all clearly discernible. Most of the cartoon is sung in opera borrowing from Donzetti's sextet (chi mi frena tal memento) from *Lucia di Lammermoor* using powerful tenor voices. The cartoon also uses a Spanish speaking bull, witty language and a few clever puns (evident by the title) to carry the dialogue.

During the production of the Mighty Mouse cartoon, the studio produced a reel on how cartoons are made. The one reel live-action short was shot by photographer and background man Johnny Vita and offers rare glimpses into studio life during the 1940s.[8] Heading into 1947, Paul Terry had his strongest lineup of cartoon celebrities and he spent little effort on producing shorts not featuring his main stars. Of the 21 shorts released in 1947, all but three were either a Mighty Mouse or a Heckle and Jeckle cartoon, *One Note Tony* (October 22), *Mexican Baseball* (March 14), a Gandy Goose short about Gandy and Sourpuss taking on the entire Mexican Bulls baseball team, and *The Wolf's Pardon* (December 5).

The third magpie short *McDougal's Rest Farm* (January 31) has Dimwit (now without Farmer Al Falfa) keeping watch over a rest farm for animals. The magpies arrive to build a new home and begin making all sorts of construction noise and mayhem. *Happy Go Lucky* (February 28) is a showcase for the vocal artistry of Sid Raymond who as Heckle and Jeckle does a large number of impressions of famous celebrities and historical figures. In the short the birds terrorize a farm guarded jealously by a dog but end up with their feathers blown off after a firecracker they had disguised as a birthday candle and given to the dog explodes. *Cat Trouble* (April 11), featuring the magpies having to protect a small bird from a hungry cat, is notable for being the first short where Jeckle speaks with a British accent.

In *The Intruders* (May 9), the magpies invade a private mansion guarded by a bulldog (eventually named Clancy) and begin to pester the intellectually inferior canine. By the end of the short, after a bomb explodes, the trio ends up by the Pearly Gates with the bulldog guarding the entryway and bragging that no one will get by the gates. However, the magpies, having snuck through the gates and behind the dog, have the last laugh by knocking the canine over the head with a large mallet. *Flying South* (August 15) has the magpies trying to freeload off grandmother, but the home turns out to be the residence of a wolf with a French accent. The wolf chases after the birds planning on making magpie stew. After the usual chase sequences Heckle and Jeckle are trapped in a stove so they give the wolf a stopwatch as a present. The timepiece explodes. With the wolf fleeing and their feathers blown off they both decide to head south for the winter. Other 1947 releases include *Fishing by the Sea* (September 19) (the magpies annoy Dimwit, a fisherman), *The Super Salesmen* (October 24) (the magpies peddle hair tonic on park grounds causing Dimwit and the bulldog to pick up the chase ending with the birds in prison), and *The Hitch Hikers* (December 12) (the birds invade the hideout of two robbers (Dimwit and the bulldog)).

Terrytoons released 10 Mighty Mouse cartoons during 1947, five of which are worth mentioning. *Crying Wolf* (January 10) is noteworthy because of the ugly gag of the wolf sharpening his axe on the little lamb's tongue. *Dead End Cats* (February 14) features a gangster (Edward G. Robinson caricature) cat dealing in black market mice who with his henchman place a sleeping Mighty Mouse in a safe encased in concrete and toss it into the river. In *Aladdin's Lamp* (March 28) Mighty Mouse rescues the Aladdin's daughter after defeating three beasts summoned from the lamp, a giant-flying warthog, an airborne saber-toothed tiger, and a winged fire-breathing dragon, and the wolf who had conjured the monsters. *Mighty Mouse Meets Deadeye Dick* (May 30) has the

229

Fig. 19.2 – Heckle and Jeckle model sheet.

superhero luring the villain (a one-eyed cowboy wolf with a tombstone under his eye patch) out of town by dressing up as a busty girl. This is the first cartoon to feature Mighty Mouse in disguise as "The Mysterious Stranger", a dark little figure wearing a trench coat, shades and a porkpie hat, who does not reveal his true identity until the end of the film.

The cartoon gem of 1947 is *A Fight to the Finish* (November 14), an animated short that revived the classic operetta style "mellerdrammers" of the silent film serials, and were earlier parodied at the studio in the 1930s in cartoons starring Oil Can Harry, Fannie Zilch, and the dashing young hero Strongheart. In *A Fight to the Finish*, Oil Can Harry was redesigned into a creature that had been Mighty Mouse's long-time enemy, the cat. The character sported a handlebar mustache, black top hat, vested suit, and flowing cloak. Fannie Zilch was replaced by a blonde little mouse girl named Pearl Pureheart (sometimes called Little Nell). She was known as Mighty Mouse's girlfriend and appeared in a series of shorts as the object of desire for Oil Can Harry. These cartoons had a liberal helping of camp humor and self-parody. The narrated cartoon opens with Mighty Mouse tied to the railroad tracks with a bomb on his head and the 5:15 train due any minute.

The short features great action (gun fight, sword duel), truly hilarious dialogue, and a cliffhanger ending with Mighty Mouse rescuing Pearl before she is sawed in half by a buzzsaw.

While the studio released some entertaining cartoons in 1947, the year would not be remembered for the cartoons the studio produced but rather for an intensely bitter nine-month labor strike. The first powerful labor action in animation came at the Fleischer Studios. In the late 1930s the New York studio had a harsh "job shop" atmosphere. The employees toiled hard for little benefits under an uneven pay structure. In an effort to achieve an improved working environment the artists began

Chapter 19 • Those Magnificent Mischievous Magpies

investigating the idea of joining the Commercial Artists and Designers Union (CADU). The Fleischer brothers (Max and Dave) were very anti-union, concerned about what the workers' demands would do to their company. The brothers saw their staff as family and couldn't understand why the employees had taken these 'family problems' to a third party. By 1937 tensions on both sides were at a fever pitch. In March of that year Max Fleischer fired two employees who were union activists.

In an attempt to bring the situation to a close, the CADU seized the tension and approached the Fleischers and asked to be recognized as the union of the employees. The Fleischers retaliated by firing 13 union member employees. The workers could not sit idle anymore and on May 7, 1937 they went on strike. The strike became a truly integrated one as people from across related fields came in to assist. The musicians union refused to do soundtracks for the studio while union projectionists across the United States declined to exhibit what Fleischer films they had. After five months of picketing, intense union pressure and influence from Paramount (the Fleischers' film distributor), the Fleischers begrudgingly recognized the union and their demands.

The Motion Picture Screen Cartoonist's Guild, then known as the Hollywood Screen Cartoonists, held their first union meeting in 1937. A year after the Fleischer victory, the Painters, Decorators and Paperhangers Union chartered the Screen Cartoon (later Screen Cartoonist's) Guild, Local 852. A formal constitution was drafted in 1939, and the name Screen Cartoonist's Guild was adopted. The Guild allied with the Conference of Studio Unions (CSU), a group that contended with the International Alliance of Theatrical Stage Employees (I.A.T.S.E.) for control of film workers in Hollywood. In 1940, William Littlejohn became the Guild's president. While the Screen Cartoonist's Guild cast their lot with the International Brotherhood of Painters, Decorators and Paperhangers of America, an affiliate of the American Federation of Labor, they had to battle with I.A.T.S.E. for union recognition. The Hollywood Cartoonists then became Local 852 of the Painters Union.

Under the leadership of Herbert Sorrell, the Guild made some general headway but didn't really reach any substantial amount of power until 1941 when the employees of MGM, Walter Lantz Studios and Screen Gems all became members. Over at the Warner Bros. studio, animation head Leon Schlesinger was very worried about the effects unionization would have on his staff. In an effort to ward off any potential union/strike activities, Schlesinger locked several guild employees out. Immediately, Schlesinger began to feel serious pressures and so six days later, he ended the lock-out and signed a contract with the Guild.

The Walt Disney Studios had always been the benchmark to which other artists compared their work. To reach the artistic perfection that the Disney films often achieved, the Disney artists were often forced to toil long hours under less than perfect conditions and in an unequal pay structure. Further, they never received screen credit for their work. The Screen Cartoonist's Guild began to talk to the employees about organizing together to address these issues. Some employees did sign with the Guild while others took their issues directly to Disney. Disney countered the Guild's activities by forming a union of his own, the Federation of Screen Cartoonists, an in-house (company sponsored) union which, in Disney's benefit, was unaffiliated with any other labor organization. Of the 602 employees at Disney, 568 of them joined the Federation with Art Babbitt as President.

Unequal pay meant that the differences between what two animators could make in a week could be 200 percent or more. Raises were handed out and salaries cut in the same day. There was also the issue of residuals. Disney had promised to share the profits of *Snow White and the Seven Dwarfs* with his employees. Although the film was profitable, the pay-share was a promise that never came to be. Disney argued that the studio's finances were on shaky ground. World War II brought a shrinking distribution market. Babbitt decided to quit his position in the Federation and joined the Guild, encouraging other employees to do the same. Respecting Babbitt's opinions, employees began signing up en masse.

Both Disney and Babbitt felt hurt by each other's attitudes and stance on the labor issues. Due to weak finances, in May of 1941 the studio started to lay off employees. The Guild feeling that perhaps all was not what it seemed, immediately called a meeting where they discussed the possibility of a strike against Disney. The next day, Disney fired a small group of employees including Art Babbitt. The following day, May 28, about 300 Disney employees went on strike. As the strike proceeded, the strikers became more bitter and their number ballooned to 1,200. To put pressure on the studio, they picketed the opening of *The Reluctant Dragon* (1941).

As the strikers grew angrier and Disney more defiant, President Roosevelt sent in a federal mediator to try and get both sides together but the result was a standoff. Finally after nearly four months, Disney relented and the strike was ended. The strikers returned to work triumphantly, but in a very different and divided work environment (as not every employee had joined the picket lines). The Disney culture had changed. Disney became more distant, suspicious and vengeful. The results of the strike can be correlated to Disney's later appearance before the House Un-American Activities Committee and the blacklisting of a number of industry workers.[9]

In 1943, with help from the Screen Cartoonist's Guild in California, the Screen Cartoonists Local 1461 (Brotherhood of Painters, Decorators and Paperhangers – A.F.L.) was organized on the east coast with an office at 800 Riverside Drive, New York. Most animation studios, with the exception of the Walt Disney Studio, had less than ideal working conditions prior to unionization. Terrytoons was no different. Paul Terry was intent on minimizing his overhead while producing a cartoon product that would entertain audiences and satisfy his distributor.

At the Terry studio, monthly incentives and Christmas bonuses for his employees were bags of Florida oranges, one bag per employee. His animation equipment was never state of the art and probably the most antiquated in the industry. Keeping with his frugal nature, his furniture was functional but in a state of disrepair. Equipment that was considered essential at other studios (e.g. a moviola) was in short supply at the studio. Artists were told to take their artistic training on their own time which schooling was never funded by the studio.[10] Employees were encouraged to avoid discussing non-work related issues during work hours. Terry wanted every minute to count as deadlines needed to be met.

The wages for Terry's friends on staff, senior members of the crew, artists difficult to replace, and those Terry considered essential to studio success (e.g. Bill Tytla, Connie Rasinski, Philip Scheib, Mannie Davis, John Foster, Carlo Vinci) were compensated at or above industry averages for persons with similar experience, skills and abilities. However, for most others, especially those employees Terry could replace with little training, such as the inkers and opaquers, wages were less than optimal.

From the beginning of the organizational drive of Local 1461, Terry fought the union bitterly. Terry's opinion was that unionization at his studio would only drive up production costs. At the Terry studio, unionization would benefit those in the lower brackets of pay (e.g. tracers, colorers) as those in the higher wage brackets (e.g. animators, directors) were already being well compensated.[11] Terry had very little incentive to increase the pay of inkers and opaquers, workers he could easily replace and retrain. Prior to the strike, inkers and opaquers were earning $16-a-week while the union rate was $43.75 for exactly the same type of work. When Jim Logan was hired in 1942 to work at Terrytoons, he was making $15-a-week as an opaquer. He then went into the military to serve during World War II and when he returned two years later, he was shocked to discover the wage for opaquers at the studio was just $20-a-week. He went into Terry's office and asked for a wage increase and was denied a boost in earnings by the producer. These incidents galvanized Logan to fight for a union shop.[12]

On or about March 15, 1943, Local 1461 informed Terrytoons, Inc. by letter that it represented a majority of its production employees and requested a conference for the purposes of collective bargaining. Terrytoons, Inc. did not reply and refused to recognize Local 1461 as a bargaining agent unless and until it was duly certified by the

Chapter 19 • Those Magnificent Mischievous Magpies

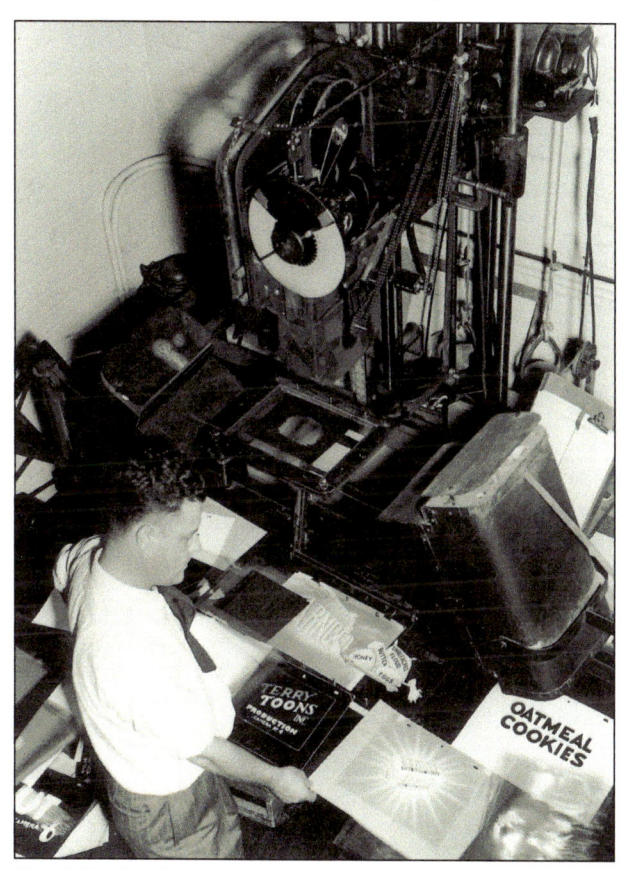

Fig. 19.3 – Joe Rasinski photographing the animation cels.

National Labor Relations Board (NLRB). On May 3, 1943, a decision of the NLRB directed that a secret ballot be conducted to ascertain representation for the purposes of collective bargaining.[13] After a vote on May 17 in which 53 of the 77 eligible voters cast their ballots in favor of representation by Screen Cartoonists Local 1461, A. F. of L., on June 16, 1943, through a "Supplemental Decision and Certification of Representatives", Local 1461 was certified by the NLRB as the exclusive representative of all such employees.[14]

When the President and Vice-President of Local 1461 were involved in organizing a union shop at the studio, they were fired by Terry. Terrytoons was subsequently held to have committed unfair labor practices by the NLRB and required to reinstate the two employees.[15] One of Terry's first responses to the growing labor unrest in 1943 was to avoid the issue altogether by failing to respond to employee suggestions that management and staff meet to discuss unionization. By using delay tactics Terry was able to postpone for about a year coming to some agreement with his employees. Eventually Terry agreed to a one-year contract with his employees in June 1944 that did not include a union shop clause.

When the contract expired on June 30, 1945, the employees were left without another agreement. The union had earlier forwarded a proposed contract on May 19 to Paul with a request for a negotiation meeting, but after a meeting on May 24 and June 5 Terry rejected the union demands. On June 16, by way of a letter, the company submitted a counter proposal suggesting an extension of the existing contract for one more year but this proposal was rejected by the union on June 19. The President of Local 1461 contacted Terry on June 30 to set up another meeting but Terry advised that he could not meet until September 5. When Terry met with the union representatives on September 5, he rejected all of their proposals. The two key issues throughout the negotiations were wage rates equal to the standard in the animated cartoon industry and the union shop clause. Another meeting on October 2 brought similar results. At the October 23 meeting Terry asked for a copy of the recently signed Disney labor agreement before meeting again.

On November 5, 1945, the Disney contract was forwarded to Terry. Representatives from Local 1461 and Terry met on November 26 to review the Disney contract with the intent of agreeing on the various issues. On November 27, Terry sent Local 1461 his proposed contract with the same conditions as the previous contract without the union shop clause. In January 1946, the union signed a contract with Famous Studios, the main competitor of Terrytoons in the New York area, which terms were exactly the same as the Disney contract, the standard in the industry. In a tight vote, on January 24 Terry's proposed contract was rejected by the union, nine against eight. Throughout much of February there were continued discussions among the members of Local 1461 to sign the proposed Terry contract. However, the union, in particular the General Membership in New York, felt that it had to maintain its position of fighting for a standard contract in the industry and it therefore could not sign a contract with Terrytoons, Inc. that did not contain the standard rates and a union shop clause.

On February 7, a motion not to strike was passed by 20 people (five voted against it). Discussions with Herb Sorrell in California during the second week of May left Local 1461 with little options but to demand the union shop clause in any future agreement. By now it had become apparent to the union they would need the assistance of their parent organization, the Brotherhood of Painters, Decorators and Paperhangers (A. F. of L.) in order to reach an agreement. This need was emphasized when the union received instructions from the Conference of Studio Unions in Hollywood (an organization of motion picture unions including the Cartoonists) not to sign any contract which did not include a union shop clause.

On May 28, 1946, Terry took the position that his company already had a one-year contract based on a verbal agreement between the studio and some of its employees and contended that an agreement was implied when increases and retroactive pay were accepted by its employees. The union denied that any verbal agreement was in place. On June 7, Terry declined to accept the proposed contract. In order to reach an agreement, the Local held meetings with the Industrial Relations department of 20th Century-Fox, the distributor of the animated cartoons. Through June and July 1946, meetings were held with the union and 20th Century-Fox. Very little was achieved on their June 24 meeting with 20th Century-Fox and it was finally resolved that Fox could offer little assistance in the labor dispute.

On July 15, the union and Terry met again. At this meeting Terry agreed to the union shop idea but refused any of the other demands. On July 18, Sorrell advised the Local not to sign with only the union shop clause and not the standard wage rates. By the end of July 1946, a tentative agreement was reached. Meetings were suspended until after the summer vacation as Terry was away from the studio.

On September 12 Terry changed his mind again and the company reneged on the tentative agreement. In the fall of 1946, the Conference of Studio Unions and the Screen Cartoonists in Hollywood obtained a 25 percent increase in wage rate, thereby setting a new standard and the union submitted a new proposal to the company. After several meetings with the company, which resulted in no agreement, the union filed a strike notice with the Labor Department. In January 1947, Local 1461 signed another contract with Famous Studios at the standard rates in the cartoon industry, again leaving Terrytoons, Inc. as the only studio in the country which did not pay standard rates and which did not have a union shop. On February 22, 1946, a conciliator was assigned by the Labor Department to mediate the matter.

On March 26, 1947, the union and the company met at the office of the U.S. Conciliation Service (operating within the Department of Labor) with Commissioner Frank Walsh in attempt to mediate the matter. During the mediation, the union conceded on all of its demands except the standard wage rates and union shop clause. On March 29, Terry and the union agreed informally on the union shop clause and standard wages clause. On April 2, 1947, the company met with the union Negotiation Committee of 12 members and stated unequivocally, before them all, that it agreed to the wages proposed and to the union shop clause. An agreement was made to sign an amendment to the 1943–1944 contract between the parties extending that agreement for one year and amending it to include the proposed wages and union shop clause. The union attempted to get the contract signed immediately but Terry became ill and the signing was delayed for about 10 days.

On April 14, 1947, Terry informed the union that his agreement to a

Chapter 19 • Those Magnificent Mischievous Magpies

Fig. 19.4 – Patricia Terry, Paul Terry's daughter, working at the studio on the presentation artwork.

union shop did not include non-members now working at the studio. To speed up the signing of the contract, the negotiating committee union agreed to Terrytoons, Inc.'s version of the union shop clause and to several unsatisfactory changes on classification of personnel. On April 17, 1947, Terrytoons, Inc. suddenly decided after the agreement was reached that it could not sign it unless the contract was for two years. The Executive Board of the union feeling it had no authority to sign a contract with the company's proposed changes after the General Membership had already approved an agreement, called a meeting for the Terrytoons unit the following afternoon to give them an opportunity to act on the company's new proposals.

On April 18, the union met and within one hour sent a committee to meet with Terry and conclude an agreement once and for all. The Terrytoons unit decided to remain in session until the committee could bring a definitive answer so that they could act upon it without delay. However, Terry was not available to meet and Bill Weiss promised to contact Terry and to wire the union as to when a meeting could be called during that weekend. Terrytoons, Inc. did not contact the union during that weekend.

On Sunday April 20, U.S. Commissioner Frank Walsh contacted the union and asked the members to be at work Monday morning and to allow him an opportunity to arrange for a conference. On Monday, the Terrytoons Unit decided that rather than wait for the company to keep its promises and arrange for an early meeting they would adjourn their meeting and continue to work while U.S. Commissioner Walsh attempted to arrange the conference. At 9:30 a.m. the group returned to the studio and found that the doors were locked and that they could not obtain entrance to go to work.[16] On April 22, charges were brought against Terry by the Local at the NLRB.

On May 1, the NLRB required Terry to pay back salary to the workers and the next day, all

235

employees returned to work. On May 10, Terry informed the union by way of a letter that he would be laying people off the following week. At the General Membership on May 14, a decision was made to strike on Friday May 17 before the members received their layoff notices. However, Terry discovered the move and on May 15 laid five people off. On Thursday May 16, the workers went out on strike again charging the management with "stalling tactics" in the negotiations.[17]

The strike was instigated, organized, and coordinated by Pepe Ruiz. Ruiz was born Jose Maria Ruiz in Cuba on March 19, 1906 to Spanish speaking parents. He had immigrated to the United States attaining his citizenship in 1935. While never attending school to study labor, management or business school, he was a key figure in the organizing of the Screen Cartoonist's Guild in Hollywood, California in 1943. He became assistant business manager for the guild helping to organize Motion Picture Screen Cartoonists, Local 841. He later came to New York City and organized the workers there becoming business agent for the Screen Cartoonists Local 1461 (New York City) (c.1945–1967). By the time of the Terrytoons strike in 1947, he had eight years of practical experience with the labor movement. He was also involved as an artist with the Fleischer Studios in the 1930s and later Warner Bros. He also undertook comic book artwork for Eastern Color Printing (*Famous Funnies*) (*Jingle Jangle* (cartoon), 1943).[18]

Ruiz was influential in convincing the Terry unit members to take up their picket signs. He heralded his successes in California and the Local was convinced that the time was ripe for a strike. However, Tommy Morrison tried to convince the Terry members not to strike. He informed members that over the last few years Terry had been anticipating a strike and by drawing the negotiations out had piled up a backlog of animated shorts that could keep the studio going for at least a year. Morrison knew that the strike would be "deadly" for anybody working there, that they would be out for a long time, and that they would gain nothing by a strike. When the union wouldn't listen to reason, Morrison sent in his membership and resigned from the union. Rather than accept the resignation, the union voted Morrison out.[19]

After the strike was called, not all of the Terrytoons staff walked the picket lines, about 20 non-members of the union continued to work throughout the strike including layout artist Arthur Bartsch, background department head Anderson Craig, story sketcher (and Terry's nephew) Alex H. Anderson, director Mannie Davis, director Eddie Donnelly, story department head John Foster, director Connie Rasinski, head of the painting department Frank Schudde, head of the camera department George McAvoy, and background painter Douglas "Uncle Bill" Hilliker. A total of 36 workers went out on strike.

With the strike in force, Terry's plan was to continue to meet his contractual commitments by releasing the cartoon shorts for distribution by 20th Century-Fox from his backlog of films. To keep production moving, Terry carried on employing those staff who were not in support of the strike and needed the work to support their families. He welcomed back most employees who were willing to cross the picket line, and he engaged the services of other qualified artists from outside the studio who were applying for jobs. Since the studio was a non-union shop, artists from other studios and organizations took the jobs of those that were picketing out on the street.[20] Terry also went out and rehired former inkers and opaquers he had released and paid them $30 week, a significant increase from the salary of $16 a week he was paying prior to the strike.

The labor dispute caused Terry to adjust slightly his typical work schedule. The studio would open up at 8:30 a.m. and close at 5:30 p.m. Terry was always at the studio every day before the doors opened, and was there when the doors closed. He took his lunch down the street at the local lunch shop with many of the other employees, although during the strike this practice changed to avoid confrontations with disgruntled picketers. After lunch, which was about an hour from 12:00 to 1:00 p.m., Terry took a 20 minute nap in his office which he felt helped make him more efficient and creative. He generally was absent from the animation department leaving the

Chapter 19 • Those Magnificent Mischievous Magpies

supervision to people like Tom Morrison and Frank Schudde but enjoyed peeking in on his story department to offer his creative input when he felt necessary.[21]

The strike was a family affair as Terry had a habit of hiring relatives. Some employee siblings took differing opinions whether to support the labor movement. Many times the result was one family member would man the picket line while the other continued to work for Terry. Tempers sometimes flared making family gatherings and life outside the studio difficult. Connie Rasinski as a non-member of the union would work throughout the strike while his brother Joe would walk the picket line until he was financially unable to continue striking and returned to work in November 1947.

Theron Collier worked during the strike while his brother Thurlo would strike but eventually crossed the picket line for family reasons. Rocco, Carmen and Vincent Eletto were three brothers who differed on the issue; the first two were inkers and continued working during the labor dispute. Vincent, an animator, walked the picket line. Tommy Morrison's mother Christina worked as a test cameraman. Christina never became a union member and like her son never joined the strikers. Frank Schudde was a non-member of the union and continued working while his brother Lester, a cameraman, walked the picket line. Polly Bourne, a painter, would marry director and non-member Eddie Donnelly. Both were not part of the strike action. Alex Anderson, story and sketch artist, was the nephew of Paul Terry. He was a non-member. Opaquer, later film editor, John "Jack" S. MacConnell was Charlie Perrin's son-in-law. He was also a non-member. Perrin was the cousin of Paul Terry and did not strike.

Local 1461 began reaching out to a disparate and extensive number of local unions for financial assistance for the strike fund recommending that their members not attend movie theaters that exhibited Terrytoons films. These union organizations included the American Union of Telephone Workers, Local No. 1, Workers Party (New York Local), Glaziers' Local Union 1087, Bakery & Confectionery Workers' Int'l Union, Local No. 1, Newspaper Guild of New York, United Scenic Artists, United Public Workers of America, C.I.O., Sign-Pictorial & Display Union, Brushmakers Union Local 16303, Industrial Insurance Employees Union Local 30, Window Cleaners Union Local 2 (New York, N.Y.), and Beltmakers Union Local 40. Pepe Ruiz took it upon himself to write a letter to Rev. Father Thomas Darby from the College of New Rochelle for his feedback and assistance in an effort to settle the strike.

From their New Rochelle office, the Terry unit of Screen Cartoonists Local 1461 published the weekly trade circular *On the Line* where they provided updates to their striking members on local union and studio activities. The publication used especially vituperative language while referring to Paul Terry as "The Great White Father". For most publications, the Terry unit published their own "Aesop's Fable" creating new fables to poke fun at Terry's labor practices. For example, the story of "The Goat-Herd and the Wild Goats" offers the moral that one should not treat newcomers (scabs) better than one's own flock (his long-time employees).

Paul Terry began recruiting from local high schools to fill positions as inkers and opaquers. In response, Local 1461 began writing to local schools requesting that they encourage their students not to cross the picket line to obtain work at the studio. By the eighth week of the strike, Ruiz used a sound truck in a verbal campaign to try to humiliate Terry. Many of the announcer's remarks were directed to Terry who when walking down the street avoided the truck by walking in the opposite direction.[22] Ruiz looked into using a sound truck again but was denied a second-day permit because of the many complaints City officials and police had received.[23] The permit refusal drew heavy criticism from the American Party of Labor asserting that the refusal was a threat to freedom of speech and was interpreted by the union as "interference in favor of the employer".[24] During the 10th week of the strike the cartoonists and artists out on strike began distributing handbills to passersby in the Pershing Square area. The handbills urged "all civic-minded people" to write or telephone Terrytoons protesting the strike and demanding immediate settlement.[25]

Also on the 10th week of the

237

> **TERRYTOONS INC**
> 271·NORTH AVENUE
> NEW ROCHELLE·NEW YORK
>
> Registered Return Receipt Requested
>
> May 9, 1947
>
> Screen Cartoonists
> Local Union 1461
> 800 Riverside Drive
> New York 32, N. Y.
>
> Dear Sirs:
>
> We find that prevailing business conditions do not justify the continuance of a full working staff. Accordingly, we are going to lay off some of our employees beginning Friday May 16, 1947.
>
> Although we are not presently obligated so to do, the lay-offs will be made in accordance with departmental seniority. When business conditions improve, we will notify such employees to return, also in accordance with seniority. In the event any employee fails to return after forty-eight (48) hours notice to his or her last known address, we shall regard such employee as having permanently left our employment.
>
> We believe that this procedure is in accordance with the spirit of our past contracts, and are proceeding accordingly.
>
> Notices of lay-off will be delivered to the individual employees as the occasion requires.
>
> Very truly yours,
>
> TERRYTOONS INC.
>
> By *Paul H. Terry*
> President

Fig. 19.5 – Paul Terry's layoff notice to staff during labor strike.

strike against Terrytoons, Inc. the strikers held a monster "anniversary party" in front of the Pershing Square Building. The New Rochelle unit of Local 1461 having an office on the fifth floor of the Frost Building at 481 Main Street called on five other New York City units of the local for aid. The New Rochelle Unit was able to send 100 union members into a huge picket line as participants in the "party". Horns and hats were distributed to the union workers and a huge dummy anniversary cake, complete with 10 candles was carried around the area by one of the picketers. The party was watched over by the local police without incident.[26]

Attorney David Halper represented the Terrytoons firm who negotiated with Pepe Ruiz with respect to the strike. As the weeks passed by, both sides were inflexible on the union shop clause issue. Terry did make concessions with respect to increases in the general wage including a $6-a-week increase, $2 above the firm's previous offer, but the offer would still make Terrytoons below the wage standard for the rest of the country. In the "war of words", Halper contended that there is the possibility that the studio would not be able to continue in business if it approved the increases demanded by the Local. Halper made known that of the 36 striking cartoonists and artists, 26 new employees were hired to replace them. Ruiz was quick to point out that some of their strikers were finding temporary work in New York City and were prepared for a long strike.[27]

By the end of June Local 1461 began picketing theaters exhibiting Terrytoons cartoons. After the Roxy Theatre exhibited a Terrytoons cartoon, picketing by approximately 50 cartoonists at the theater occurred the following two weekends.[28] That month, Gordon Whittier was unanimously elected President of the Local. Muriel Gushue, after a five week absence from the group for personal reasons, decided to cross the picket lines and return to work. She never wanted to go on strike. She didn't vote for the strike and kindly asked Paul if she could have her job back. Terry graciously allowed her to return to work.[29] In the first week of July, a citizens committee called the

Chapter 19 • Those Magnificent Mischievous Magpies

Fig. 19.6 – Paul Terry and business associate flexing muscles like Mighty Mouse.

Citizens Committee to Investigate the Terrytoons Strike, composed of representatives of four New Rochelle organizations was formed to investigate the seven-week-old strike, while the third conference at the U.S. Conciliator's office of Commissioner Charles Steutel at 341 Ninth Avenue, New York City was held where some progress was reported.[30] Bill Littlejohn, who co-founded and served as the first president of the Screen Cartoonists Guild Local 852 in 1938, wrote a letter to the Local encouraging them to continue in their strike action. A meeting was held in early September at the U.S. Conciliation Office, New York, but the stalemate was never broken as additional proposals were left on the table.[31]

At the September 3 meeting, a tentative agreement was reached providing for an election, since the company wanted proof that the union represented the employees. The union stressed three main points. The NLRB was to determine which employees are bona-fide replacements. In the event the union won, to submit to arbitration the wages and union shop for future employees. In case the union lost, to pull out their picket lines. Terry's five-page document containing 11 clauses included the offer that the election was to take place at 271 North Avenue (thereby forcing union members to cross their own picket lines). Second, the employers should restore strikers to former positions only as they saw fit, and third, that current employees (scabs) should have seniority rights over striking members. Terry's offer was not seriously considered by the Local and was deemed a rude violation of the fair play principles.[32]

In mid-October, a number of current employees filed a petition with the NLRB in New York City requesting "decertification" of Screen Cartoonists Local 1461, AFL, as the bargaining unit for Terrytoons workers.[33] With financial pressures mounting for most workers, by mid-November

239

1947 they were forced to cross the picket lines and ask Terry for their jobs back. These workers included Steve Gattoni, Carlo Vinci (November 17), Constance Quirk, James Tyer (November 12), Thurlo Collier (November 17), and Joseph Rasinski (November 12). Gattoni and Quirk were not offered their jobs back but the others were given employment positions at the studio. At a January 7, 1948 Executive Board meeting of Screen Cartoonists Local 1461, Eddie Rehberg as Chairman of the Terrytoon Unit, all six members were found guilty violating Section 302(2) and (13), and Sections 303 and 304 of the Constitution of the Brotherhood of Painters, Decorators and Paperhangers of America. Due to mitigating circumstances in the case of Quirk and Collier's previous records as union members, they were suspended for six months while the other four were expelled from the union.

During early December negotiations were underway around a proposal to hold an election at Terrytoons to determine the bargaining agent for the employees. Both the union and management agreed that an election should be held but differed on how the election should be conducted and who would be eligible to vote. On December 19, 1947, one of the longest strikes in the history of New Rochelle, and the longest animation strike in the United States ended with the announcement from both union and management that Screen Cartoonists Local 1461 had terminated its labor dispute against Terrytoons, Inc. The union withdrew in the middle of a hearing at the regional office of the NLRB in New York City to determine if the union was to be decertified as the bargaining agent of Terrytoons employees. Ruiz declared that 28 of the 36 artists and cartoonists that were called out May 16 had since been placed in other jobs by the union and that eight [seven] had returned to work at Terrytoons with applications from four others.[34] After the Local was unsuccessful in forming a union, it was officially decertified pursuant to a decision and order by the NLRB on May 5, 1948.[35]

One of the main reasons the strike failed was that the union was not part of the I.A.T.S.E. but rather a smaller union not affiliated with the motion picture industry. The I.A.T.S.E. would have been integral in preventing the Terrytoons cartoons from being exhibited at theaters through picketing by their members. Rather, since the Brotherhood of Painters, Decorators and Paperhangers (A.F. of L.) had been in a jurisdictional battle for union recognition with the I.A.T.S.E. and won, the I.A.T.S.E. ignored requests by the Brotherhood of Painters for support during the strike. Without the I.A.T.S.E., the Terry unit had very little influence on motion picture exhibitors. As Morrison had correctly predicted, the workers had gained absolutely nothing from their employer and the strike was doomed to fail. ❧

Notes

1. "Talking Magpies", (animated cartoon review), *Film Daily*, 19 February 1946, p. 11.

2. Thomas James (Tommy) Morrison, interview, 15 June 1970, 13d.

3. Ibid., 26d.

4. Dayton Allen, telephone interview by author (transcript), Kelowna, B.C., Canada, 4 October 1997, Terrytoons Collection, Victoria, B.C., Canada, 7.

5. Richard Lamparski, *Whatever Became Of ... ? All New Ninth Series: 100 Profiles of the Most Asked About Personalities From Television Series, Documentaries, and Movies*, volume 9 (New York: Crown, 1985); Richard Gertner, ed., *International Motion Picture Almanac*, 1977 edition (New York: Quigley Publishing Co., 1977), 4; Ronald L. Smith, *Legends in Their Own Time* (New York: Prentice Hall General Reference, 1994); *Who's Who in Comedy: Comedians, Comics, and Clowns from Vaudeville to Today's Stand-ups* (New York: Facts on File, 1992). Articles: Robert Metz, "Market Place: Comedian Buys Mining Stocks", *New York Times*, 26 April 1969, p. 42; Richard F. Shepard, "Factory for Television Funnies", *New York Times*, 29 October 1961, p. X1. Obituary: "Dayton Allen, 85, Cartoon Voice Actor", *New York Times*, 18 November 2004, p. A29.

6. Terry, interview, 20 December 1969, 56.

7. "Winning the West", (animated cartoon review), *The Film Daily*, 11 September 1946, p. 10; "The Jail Break", (animated cartoon review), *The Film Daily*, 11 September 1946, p. 10.

8. Terry, interview, 20 December 1969, 59.

Chapter 19 • Those Magnificent Mischievous Magpies

9. For a great overview on the history of the animation labor movement: Tom Sito, *Drawing the Line: The Untold Story of the Animation Unions from Bosko to Bart Simpson* (Lexington, Ky.: University Press of Kentucky, 2006).

10. As previously noted, director Connie Rasinski was always willing to teach artists the art and craft of animation. One evening a week he would spend time with staff interested in acquiring animation skills.

11. Terry, interview, 14 July 1970, 126.

12. Jim Logan, telephone interview by author (transcript), Kelowna, B.C., 20 November 1998, Terrytoons Collection, Victoria, B.C., Canada, 1.

13. Decision and Direction of Election, In the Matter of Terrytoons, Inc. and Screen Cartoonists Local 1461, Affiliated With the Brotherhood of Painters, Decorators and Paperhangers of America, A. F. of L., Case No. R-5199, Decided May 3, 1943, *Decisions and Orders of the NLRB, Volume 49, April 22, 1943, to May 31, 1943*.

14. Supplemental Decision, In the Matter of Terrytoons, Inc. and Screen Cartoonists Local 1461, Affiliated With the Brotherhood of Painters, Decorators and Paperhangers of America, A. F. of L., Case No. R-5199, Decided June 16, 1943, *Decisions and Orders of the NLRB, Volume 50, June 1, 1943, to June 30, 1943*.

15. Terrytoons, Inc. and Screen Cartoonists Local 1461, NLRB, Case No. 2-C-5108.

16. A comprehensive history of the Terrytoon, Inc. labor negotiations and 1947 strike is found in: The Motion Picture Screen Cartoonists Guild, Local 839 Collection, 1937–1951, Special Collections and Archives, Oviatt Library, California State University, Northridge. This collection contains historical records relating to the organization of the Guild, jurisdictional disputes, and its support and involvement in union strikes. The bulk of the material found in the collection consists of by-laws, cartoons and sketches, correspondence, memorabilia, minutes, newspaper clippings, newsletters, notes for speeches, organizational leaflets and strike photographs. Of particular significance are the handbills, leaflets and photographs from the Walt Disney Strike of 1940/1941, extensive correspondence between union organizers Herb Sorrell and Pepe Ruiz, and records detailing the Terrytoons Strike of 1947. The collection has been divided into four series: Screen Cartoonists Guild, Local 839 (1939–1951), Federation of Screen Cartoonists (1939–1941), Walt Disney Studios' Strike (1941–1946), and Terrytoon, Inc. Strike (1944–1948). Series IV, Terrytoon, Inc. Strike, documents the strike's history through contracts, correspondence, financial records, minutes, newsletters and press releases. The series is arranged alphabetically according to the nature of the material and chronologically thereafter.

17. "In, Out Again at Terrytoon As Firm Fires 5 Cartoonists", (Newspaper clipping), *Trade Union Courier*, 2 June 1947, The Motion Picture Screen Cartoonists Guild, Local 839 Collection, 1937–1951.

18. Pepe's biography can be found in The Motion Picture Screen Cartoonists Guild, Local 839 Collection, 1937–1951.

19. Morrison, interview, 19d.

20. Ibid.

21. Leahy and Lazar, interview, 19.

22. "Striking Artists Use Sound Truck" (newspaper clipping), *The Standard-Star* (New Rochelle, NY), 8 July 1947, The Motion Picture Screen Cartoonists Guild, Local 839 Collection, 1937–1951.

23. "Permit Refused for Sound Truck" (newspaper clipping), The Motion Picture Screen Cartoonists Guild, Local 839 Collection, 1937–1951.

24. "Permit Refusal Draws ALP Fire", (newspaper clipping), *The Standard-Star* (New Rochelle, NY), 10 July 1947, The Motion Picture Screen Cartoonists Guild, Local 839 Collection, 1937–1951.

25. "Terrytoons Union Seeks Public Help", (newspaper clipping), The Motion Picture Screen Cartoonists Guild, Local 839 Collection, 1937–1951.

26. "Cartoon Strikers Hold 'Party' To Mark 10th 'Anniversary,'" *The Standard-Star* (New Rochelle, NY), 24 July 1947, (newspaper clipping), The Motion Picture Screen Cartoonists Guild, Local 839 Collection, 1937–1951.

27. "Terrytoon Strike Still Unsettled", (Newspaper clipping), The Motion Picture Screen Cartoonists Guild, Local 839 Collection, 1937–1951.

28. "Cartoonists Picket Roxy For Showing Terrytoon Shorts", (Newspaper clipping), *AFL Journal*, 30 June 1947, The Motion Picture Screen Cartoonists Guild, Local 839 Collection, 1937–1951.

29. Muriel Gushue, telephone interview by author (transcript), Kelowna, B.C., Canada, 24 November 1997, Terrytoons Collection, Victoria, B.C., 6.

30. "Citizens Group Forms to Help Settle Dispute At Terrytoons", *The Standard-Star* (New Rochelle, N.Y.), 2 July 1947, The Motion Picture Screen Cartoonists Guild, Local 839 Collection, 1937–1951.

31. "Terrytoons Strike Conference Fails", *The Standard-Star* (New Rochelle, N.Y.), 9 September 1947, The Motion Picture Screen Cartoonists Guild, Local 839 Collection, 1937–1951.

32. "Fantastic Company Demand Rejected by Cartoonists", *Trade Union Courier*, 22 September 1947, p. 16, The Motion Picture Screen Cartoonists Guild, Local 839 Collection, 1937–1951.

33. "Move to 'Decertify' Cartoon Union Filed", *The Standard-Star* (New Rochelle, N.Y.), 15 October 1947, The Motion Picture Screen Cartoonists Guild, Local 839 Collection, 1937–1951.

34. "Strike is Ended at Terrytoons", *The Standard-Star* (New Rochelle, N.Y.), 19 December 1947, The Motion Picture Screen Cartoonists Guild, Local 839 Collection, 1937–1951.

35. Decision and Order, In the Matter of Terrytoons, Inc., Employer and Joshua Levine, Petitioner, Case No. 2-RD–9, Decided May 5, 1948, *Decisions and Orders of the NLRB, Volume 77, April 12, 1948, to June 25, 1948*.

241

Chapter 20

Rounding Out the Cast: Little Roquefort, the Terry Bears and the Glory Years of Terrytoons, 1948–1951

While Terry succeeded in temporarily avoiding a union shop at the studio, he did so at a cost. While his core group of veterans remained with him after the strike, he lost some promising talent to union shops in the New York area. Four years later, in 1951, the animated cartoonists at Walt Disney, Warner Bros. and Walter Lantz voted to join the I.A.T.S.E. The Animation Guild, I.A.T.S.E. Local 839 (Los Angeles) and 841 (New York) were chartered in 1952. Only after the animation guilds were chartered and they had significant influence over whether the Terry cartoons would be exhibited at theaters across North America was Paul forced to sign a contract and the studio finally became a union shop.[1]

During the years 1948 and 1949, Terry continued to focus his efforts on producing the majority of his cartoons starring his superstars. Of the 39 shorts produced, 12 were Mighty Mouse cartoons, 12 were Heckle and Jeckle films, three were Gandy Goose and/or Sourpuss shorts, and the remaining 12 featured no recurring character. There were a number of cinematic pearls during this period. The Mighty Mouse short *Magic Slipper* (December 1948) has a deliciously delightful Lindy dance sequence involving the prince and Cinderella, a swing number animated by master animator Carlo Vinci. Terry featured the trio of Oil Can Harry, Pearl Pureheart, and Mighty Mouse in six "mellerdrammer" cartoon shorts during these two years. *Loves Labor Won* (September 1948) involves Harry kidnapping innocent Pearl as well as a canine justice of the peace to marry them. Mighty Mouse chases them through sawmills, railroad trains and over ice-covered rivers. *The Mysterious Stranger* (October 1948) has Harry pursuing Pearl ("Little Nell"), a circus acrobat, with the intent on marrying her. The "mysterious stranger" exposes his true identity as Mighty Mouse and sends Oil Can off into the distance in a deflating hot air balloon.

Triple Trouble (November 1948) begins with an iconic scene of Mighty Mouse bound and gagged on the Mojave Desert entirely surrounded by vultures. The old Colonel, Pearl Pureheart's father, had just been tossed off the Brooklyn Bridge and below, the East River is swarming with crocodiles. Meanwhile, on top of the Empire State Building in her beautiful penthouse suite, Pearl Pureheart is being pursued by Oil Can Harry. In this cartoon operetta even the vultures get in on the operatic score. After breaking free from his ropes, Mighty Mouse rescues Pearl's father before he falls into the East River, then dispatches Harry trying to escape in a helicopter. *A Cold Romance* (April 1949) takes place at the North Pole where Harry continues his pursuit of Pearl while he trades naïve seals some fish for their furs.

The Perils of Pearl Pureheart (October 1949) is probably one of the finer cartoons from this series and has Pearl being hypnotized by Harry and forced to sing *Carry Me*

Chapter 20 • Rounding Out the Cast

Fig. 20.1 – Terrytoons Studio, 38 Centre Avenue, New Rochelle, New York.

Back to Old Virginny at a saloon while the greedy Oil Can vacuums up the coins thrown on the stage by the cowboys weeping at Pearl's touching solo. The cartoon ends with a terrific fight between Harry and Mighty Mouse aboard a stagecoach. Inside the carriage Pearl is still hypnotized and singing, ignorant of her plight as the stagecoach is rolling towards a cliff. The cartoon's great musical score and camp humor, sometimes unintentional, make this cartoon a classic. *Stop, Look and Listen* (December 1949) has Pearl tied to the tail of a bull while her father, Colonel Pureheart, is drilling for oil in his basement to pay his daughter's ransom.

Another standout is *The Catnip Gang* (July 1949) where at Station W.O.O.F. the National Bureau for Mouse Protection is presenting the radio program *Racket Busters*. The program chronicles the story of the Catnip Gang. The gang consists of Julius "Pinhead" Schlabotka (8'9", 310 lbs, tattoo on upper left arm), "No Chin" Charlie (5'3", 99 lbs, tail bent in several places due to gunshot wounds), and Shorty the Runt (3'2", 120 lbs, highly skilled criminal mind and the brains of the gang). The radio host recounts the story of the gang's evil doings. The three criminals break out from the city pound, steal a used car, round up some black market mice in a bag, and hold up in their hideout. The police, tipped off by mice dropping out of a hole in the bag, surround the hideout but are unable to defeat the gang after a vicious gun battle. Mighty Mouse streams down from the sky to capture the gang and for his efforts is rewarded with a whole host of radio prizes including an ocean going yacht and a model subway train with a year's supply of tracks.

The studio also released some very creative and entertaining Heckle and Jeckle cartoons during the same time period. *Taming the Cat* (January 1948) has the birds trapping a cat in a shower stall with the water running, outwitting him in a game of pool, and sucking him up in a vacuum. By the end of the cartoon, the cat is hanging from the ceiling, a prisoner of the same cage he tried to capture some songbirds with, while the two magpies play *Get a Couple of Songbirds Today* on piano, in the style of Jimmy Durante. *Free Enterprise* (November 1948) has the birds breaking into prison to sell pneumatic drills to the prisoners. The magpies victimize a guard dog with their gags but their antics eventually catch up to them as they end up by the close of the cartoon as permanent inhabitants of the prison. *Out Again In Again* (November 1948) has the birds breaking out of prison. In their attempt to elude the bulldog warden they pose as North American Indians, African savages, and a mother and her

243

baby. Their gags again get the better of them as a train engine they are stoking explodes rocketing them back into prison.

In *Goony Golfers* (December 1948), when an errant golf ball smashes through their window, the magpies get revenge by offering their services as the caddies to the bulldog golfer that sent the ball into their home and then go about ruining his golf game. *The Power of Thought* (January 1949) has Jeckle realizing that since he is a cartoon character he can be whatever he wants to be (mouse, puppy, one man band). Heckle joins in the fun and both end up menacing a police dog. *The Lion Hunt* (March 1949) has the two magpies on a lion hunt and pulling a series of gags on the king of the jungle. They knock him out with a boxing glove that is ejected from a camera. After a popcorn machine explodes knocking the lion unconscious he awakes and is put on trial for the death of Jeckle (who is of course faking his death). The lion gets the last laugh as he traps the birds in the same cage they were using to capture him. *The Stowaways* (April 1949) features the birds, planning on visiting Africa, as stowaways aboard an aircraft. In his attempt to get the magpies off the plane, the bulldog captain becomes the victim of a number of gags. The captain wins out in the end as he pushes a button sending the magpies through the floor of the aircraft where they fall into a large cooking pot surrounded by hungry dancing African natives.

Joining the Terry studio in mid-1946 after eight years at Famous Studios was Terry's old

Fig. 20.2 – Terrytoons poster celebrating 30 years of cartoons.

friend, animator James "Jim" Tyer (1904–1976). His first job in the animation business was for Paul working at the Fables Pictures studio beginning around 1926 where he remained with the studio for the rest of the silent era. After Terry left in 1929, Tyer stayed with Van Beuren throughout the early thirties and when George Stallings was appointed director of Van Beuren Studios in 1933, Tyer was made an animation director. Tyer first began animating and occasionally directing (with Stallings) on the cartoon series based on Otto Soglow's *The Little King* comic strip, 1933–1934. When Burt

Gillett was brought in as the new manager, Tyer was assigned to work on the *Toddle Tales* series as director.

In early 1935, Tyer left Van Beuren to work at Walt Disney Studios in the effects animation department where he stayed for a few months leaving after being upset over unrealistic demands of effects department manager, Cy Young. He moved to Harman-Ising Studio working as a gagman and storywriter for Rudy Ising's unit. In 1937, Tyer and his family moved to Detroit where he worked for the Jam Handy studio staying a few months. By the end of

Chapter 20 • Rounding Out the Cast

1938, Tyer had moved to Florida to work for the Fleischer brothers on a number of the Fleischer shorts remaining with the studio after Paramount Pictures took the studio out from underneath the Fleischers and moved it back to New York and renamed it Famous Studios.

At Terrytoons, he animated all the major and most minor characters. He also worked in the story department doing story sketches and gags and did comic artwork for all the Terry characters beginning in the late 1940s. Tyer eschewed the Disney style of realistic animation. In his approach to animation Tyer was a pure cartoonist. Tyer animated cartoons for the main reason that cartoons should exist- to be wacky looking. His cartoons are instantly funny to look at, and his characters do impossible things and move in crazy, imaginative ways. Tyer's loose animation style can best be described as a squash, stretch and mangle style of animation. He paid little attention to model sheets and animating proper mouth movements for the characters.

Tyer's animation characters were rubbery and they frequently feature dramatic changes in eye size and wobbly loose-lipped mouths. While at Terrytoons Tyer was given liberty to roam through a cartoon and transform the rather arbitrary scenes he was assigned into displays of graphic ingenuity.[2] Tyler was an efficient animator and he did not require an inbetweener. He animated straight ahead.[3] After he had finished animating he would pick up his sheets and flip them and would sit there laughing and telling himself how funny the scenes were. Other animation crew sitting nearby would think he was putting on a show for them because he knew they were listening over the partition. Sometimes he would stop and take off his glasses and wipe the tears from his eyes because he was laughing so much.[4]

Fig. 20.3 – Animation background for *A Fight to the Finish* (1947).

Much of his animation mirrored his personality and habits. Tyer was a notorious practical joker and many times his fellow workmates would fall victim to his outlandish pranks.[5] In one animation sequence he drew a man in a nightgown proceeding across the screen with his nightgown flapping in the tailwind. When production manager Frank Schudde walked by Tyer's desk and was flipping through the sequence of drawings he was mortified at what he saw exposed below the nightgown.[6] While the sequence of drawings gave Schudde a little shock Tyer had created the drawings just for laughs. Tyer's rampant eccentricity was tolerated because he could animate fast and his work was fun to look at. He was usually given scenes in which extreme facial expressions, body transformations, or physical contortions of the characters were required to highlight the on-screen action. To catch a glimpse of Tyer's work one need to look no further than the opening scenes of the Mighty Mouse cartoon *Prehistoric Perils* (March 1952) or the witch-turned-vulture scene from the Mighty Mouse cartoon *Hansel and Gretel* (June 1952).

In July 1949, Paul Terry moved his studio to a new location, a two-story 17,000-square-foot building located at 38 Center Avenue in New Rochelle, the former home of the Knights of Columbus. On October 12, 1915, the cornerstone was laid for the building, north of Huguenot on land purchased from William Kahn in 1914. The building of brick construction with a 70-foot

245

TERRYTOONS: The Story of Paul Terry and His Classic Cartoon Factory

Fig. 20.4 – Bill Weiss (left) and Paul Terry (right) with character models.

frontage on Center Avenue is located on a plot 100 by 150 feet which included a large parking lot. Earlier in April 1946, the Knights of Columbus structure was bought by Nicholas Mayer for resale to an appliance manufacturer. Mayer renovated the building and installed a sprinkler system.[7]

In 1947 Mayer sold the building to the 38 Center Avenue Realty Corporation who rented it to an electrical appliance manufacturer. Milton Cohen, president of the corporation, then sold the building to Terry. The building was a vast improvement on the previous location both in terms of studio space as the Pershing Square Building studio had 10,000 square feet of space and design. The sound studio was located on the second floor of the building. No longer would the musical director, composer, musicians, voice actors and other sound personnel have to travel to New York City to do the recording. Other benefits included owning a real property investment which increased in value. Paul no longer had to concern himself with negotiating commercial lease agreements with a landlord.

By 1950, Terry was looking to add a few more cartoon celebrities to his roster of stars. With the critical success and audience appeal of MGM's Tom and Jerry, Terry thought that it would be a good idea to create his own cat and mouse team.[8] He had his story department work on developing rodent and feline cartoon characters. The result was Little Roquefort, a spritely, mischievous and bucktoothed brown mouse, and his feline adversary Percy Puss, a black house cat with whom he shared residence. The series features comedic fights between the two characters.

The plots of each short usually center on Percy's numerous attempts to capture Roquefort and the mayhem and destruction that follow. Percy rarely succeeds in catching Little Roquefort, mainly because of Roquefort's cleverness, cunning abilities, and luck. Unlike Tom and Jerry they rarely display genuine friendship and concern for each other's well-being. The pair are true rivals pursuing their own self-interests. Many cartoons end with Roquefort getting the better of Percy. In *The Haunted Cat* (December 1951) Percy thinks he has killed Roquefort but the mouse returns to play a series of ghostly tricks on the feline. In *Mouse Meets Bird* (March 1953) Roquefort foils Percy's efforts to eat a yellow canary bird ending with the house owner chasing Percy down the street with a broom.

While Connie Rasinski would direct the first cartoon, Mannie Davis would be credited with director on 11 of the 19 shorts produced. Both Roquefort and Percy were voiced by Tom Morrison, who was also the voice of Mighty Mouse's adversary, Oil Can Harry. The first in the series

Chapter 20 • Rounding Out the Cast

was *Cat Happy* (September 1950). In the cartoon Percy finds Roquefort stealing some cheese. In the process of chasing after the mouse he accidentally ingests some catnip and becomes Roquefort's overly affectionate friend. When the catnip wears off, Roquefort makes sure he has another dose. *Seasick Sailors* (July 1951) has Percy following Little Roquefort aboard an ocean liner to convince him to come home or he will lose his job as the house mouse catcher. In *City Slicker* (March 1952) Roquefort visits his cousin Elmer on his farm but finds country life more hazardous than life with Percy. In *Hypnotized* (June 1952), Percy learns the art of hypnosis and hypnotizes Roquefort into believing he is a bird and then a dog much to the feline's amusement. Roquefort snaps out of his hypnotic state and gets revenge by hypnotizing a bunch of dogs to think they are cats who then become overly affectionate to a bewildered Percy.

Good Mousekeeping (October 1952) has Roquefort redecorating his mouse hole with a new paint job and in the process makes a mess of the family home despite Percy's best efforts to keep the home clean. In *Flop Secret* (December 1952) Roquefort has a dream that ends up with him awakening to find he has pushed Percy down a flight of stairs. Percy makes Roquefort eat the comic book which caused the dream. *Pastry Panic* (October 1951) has Roquefort baking a cake. Percy is intent on getting the better of the mouse but after thinking he has squashed him with

Fig. 20.5 – Connie Rasinski with Thomas Morrison voicing a character.

a fly swatter, a relieved and repentant Percy discovers Roquefort is alive. Thankful for the birthday cake, he joyfully feeds the mouse forkfuls of the pastry. In *Friday the 13th* (July 1953), Percy decides that since it is Friday the 13th he should make Little Roquefort's life miserable.

In *Runaway Mouse* (January 1954) Little Roquefort, tired of being chased by Percy, leaves home to go to the local zoo where he is enlists the help of two squirrels to help "teach him the ropes". Roquefort ends up receiving rough treatment from the squirrels and returns home where although he is chased again by Percy he realizes that "there is no place like home". Percy points a large cannon at Little Roquefort in *Cat's Revenge* (September 1954) but his conscience, a little Percy, tells him not to set the cannon off. Percy then has a series of flashbacks of Roquefort causing him problems including interrupting his romantic interlude with his girlfriend. Percy, now more determined than ever to destroy the pesky mouse, lights the cannon fuse. However, his conscience points the cannon at Percy, the cannon fires and the cat is knocked into a fountain. His conscience turns out to be Roquefort in disguise who comments, "That cat has lots to learn".

The final cartoon in the series is *No Sleep for Percy* (March 1955) where Roquefort is keeping Percy awake by listening to a car radio at a garage. After a series of chases, the two get caught in a runaway automobile that send both to the hospital where much to Percy's chagrin Roquefort turns on the radio. The Little Roquefort cartoons were generally very entertaining shorts with solid production values. The cartoons featured slapstick comedy, original storylines with first-rate gags, and excellent chemistry between the two stars. The series received favorable audience

TERRYTOONS: The Story of Paul Terry and His Classic Cartoon Factory

Fig. 20.6 – Terry Bears model sheet.

feedback but would be discontinued after Terry had sold his studio and left the animation business. Had Terry remained in the business we most assuredly would have been treated to more cartoons from the series.

Another two of Terry's new character creations in 1950 were Dingbat and Sylvester the Fox, characters created by Connie Rasinski.[9] Dingbat is a yellow canary who wears a sailor's hat and has a goofy grin, small pointy beak, and a giggly laugh. He first appeared in the Gandy Goose cartoon *Dingbat Land* (February 1949). Paul Terry's inspiration for the characters was the canary Tweetie Pie from the *Looney Tunes* series, and his nemesis Sylvester the Cat. The series lasted just two cartoons before it was dropped. *All This and Rabbit Stew* (July 1950) has Dingbat foiling the efforts of two vultures intent on catching a rabbit. *Sour Grapes* (December 1950) has Dingbat nailing some grapes to a tree branch and foiling Sylvester's efforts to obtain the fruit. Dingbat often resorted to physical violence and took pleasure from the discomforts of his enemies. There was little originality in these shorts which may have played a part in the series' short run. Another 1950 cartoon character creation was Victor the Volunteer who appeared in the one-shot cartoon *Better Late Than Never* (March 1950), a short about a volunteer firefighter late to arrive at a raging inferno but just in time to fortuitously rescue a girl falling from a fiery building.

In 1951, Terry introduced Half Pint, a little white baby elephant and a Disney Dumbo knock-off, who appeared in two cartoons. *Stage Struck* (February 1951) has Half Pint trying to become a circus star. *The Elephant Mouse* (May 1951) has the elephant annoying a cat, a champion mouse catcher, who thinks the elephant is a large mouse. Another one-shot cartoon character was Nutsy the Squirrel, a take-off on Walt Disney's popular Chip 'n' Dale cartoon series. In *Squirrel Crazy* (January 1951) Nutsy outwits a dog to raid the canine's home of a bounty of edibles.

Terry's other noteworthy cartoon series of the 1950s was the Terry Bears, starring two mischievous bear cub twins finding trouble just by being kids. The conflict was

Chapter 20 • Rounding Out the Cast

provided by Papa Bear who possessed a violent temper, was pompous toward his children, and in his efforts to make his kids behave got himself into trouble. While it was clear he loved his two children (who didn't have individual names), that didn't prevent him from trying to punish them for their misdeeds. In the end, it was usually his two boys who had the last laugh on dear old dad.

There were 17 series cartoons produced from 1951 to 1956. The first of their outings was *Tall Timber Tale*, directed by Connie Rasinski and released during July 1951. In the short, the two Terry Bears cause mischief (e.g. runaway outboard motor, saw on the loose) while Papa is out cutting trees. In the end, the boys get credit by their mother for chopping the wood as she thinks her unconscious husband lying in the hammock is sleeping. The next in the series was *Little Problems* (September 1951), directed by Eddie Donnelly, and concerns Papa's efforts to unsuccessfully keep his two boys from misbehaving. Despite following the instructions in a book on how to raise children, he ends up sitting at the bottom of a lake where he angrily tears the manual apart. *Nice Doggy* (October 1952) has Papa Bear thrown in jail after a St. Bernard dog that his two boys want to keep lands him in trouble with the law.

Boastful Papa Bear takes his Terry Bears cubs on a camping trip in *Picnic With Papa* (December 1952) and, since he claims to be an expert camper, he sets out to give the cubs the benefits of his camping skills. He immediately proceeds to spend his time going from the frying pan to the campfire, while the cubs prove that they are the expert campers. Similarly, in attempting to teach his children how to take award winning photographs in *Snappy Snapshots* (March 1953), Papa ends up sore and upset because his sons did not follow his orders. All turns out well because a photograph of Papa's misfortune while trying to take a picture wins the first prize in the contest.

In *Plumber's Helpers* (May 1953) Papa's efforts to fix a plumbing problem with the help of the two cubs results in him being spit out through the pipes into a frozen lake while his children, in an attempt to help their father with the leak, reassemble the plumbing into a confusing maze of pipes. *Baffling Bunnies* (April 1956) is the last in this series and concerns the boys' efforts to teach their dog Pago how to hunt rabbits. The usual chaos ensues with Papa falling from a tree and coming back home to scold his children only to have the wind-up toy rabbit that was used to try and teach the dog how to hunt fall apart.

While *The Terry Bears* series featured great animation and splendid background art, the series suffered from predictable plots, cheap laughs, and shallow characterization. Papa Terry Bear was voiced by Doug Moye (1914–1986), one of the few African-Americans working in the animation industry in the early 1950s. Moye was an accomplished drummer and headlined his own bands such as Doug Moye and his Rhythm Ramblers, Doug Moye and his Glee Club Orchestra, and Dougie Moye's Club Sky Vue Orchestra during the 1930s and 1940s. His bands would play for large crowds of 250 or more in Westchester County featuring swing, jazz and music from Harlem. In his thirties Moye began suffering kidney

Fig. 20.7 – Paul Terry and his most famous cartoon characters.

TERRYTOONS: The Story of Paul Terry and His Classic Cartoon Factory

Fig. 20.8 – Philip A. Scheib.

problems and fell on hard times. Terry, aware of Moye's health problems, hired him and helped to train him as a cameraman.[10] He was employed at the studio for over 20 years. During this time he would also provide voices when called upon for various Terry characters.

Like the other Terry characters, they were spun off into comics. St. John Publishing, which had earlier done comic book versions of the Famous Studios characters (Casper, Baby Huey, etc.), was licensing the Terrytoons properties just then, and included the Bears in *Paul Terry's Comics*, sometimes on the cover. St. John also gave them their own title for three issues in 1952–1953. There was little if any other licensing. The studio changed hands in 1955, and most of the old characters were left behind including the Terry Bears.

From the late 1930s until the day Paul Terry sold his studio nearly 20 years later, the studio would produce some of the most gorgeous and detailed background art in the animation industry, art that was clean, stylish, colorful, and unpretentious. When the studio opened in 1929, there was no background department. In the mid-to-late 1930s, about 1936, the background department was headed by Art Bartsch (1904–1971). Bartsch attended the Pratt Institute, New York, and studied architecture. He later undertook art classes at the Metropolitan Art School, Grand Central Art School and the Phoenix Art Institute in New York City. His early art training was in advertising with the Stanley E. Gunnison advertising agency where he was eventually promoted to art director of the agency.[11]

He began his career in animation at the Van Beuren Studios as a background designer and layout person working primarily on the *Rainbow Parade* series, 1934–1936. In 1936, around the time the Van Beuren Studios closed, Bartsch moved over to Terrytoons where Paul Terry hired him to undertake the role of head of the background and layout department in charge of all layout work including the background design, selection of colors and other related duties. Bartsch remained in that role until portrait artist Anderson Craig began working at Terrytoons. Craig assumed the role as the background department supervisor around 1939 moving Bartsch into strictly designing layouts. In 1940 Craig, George Zaffo and John Vita formed the background department. While Bartsch was employed as layout artist at Terrytoons for most of the 1940s he also undertook animation of the cartoons. After Terry sold Terrytoons to CBS in 1955, Bartsch was assigned directorial duties on a number of Terrytoons character shorts beginning in 1958 until the studio wound down operations in 1967 and 1968.

Background artist Anderson Craig (1904–1964) undertook design and illustration courses at the Kansas City Art Institute and School of Design, Kansas City,

Chapter 20 • Rounding Out the Cast

Missouri, October 1922 – July 1923 and June – July, 1925. While at the Kansas City Art Institute and School of Design, Craig studied under painter, lithographer Randall Vernon Davey (1887–1964). While in Kansas City he lived just two blocks from Walt Disney's Laugh-O-Grams studio and likely was first acquainted with animated cartoons at that time. He moved with his new wife to New York City after their marriage in 1926 where during 1928 Craig had executed a dozen important portrait commissions.[12]

Craig founded the Experimental School of Art at his home studio located at 20 West Eighth Street and undertook the position of director at the studio.[13] He closed the studio by 1930 and with his wife returned to Kansas City, Missouri to work as a portrait artist for a brief period before returning to New York City. Eventually, the economic problems of the early 1930s caused problems in locating painting commissions. Craig began looking for a permanent full-time employment position and found one working at Fleischer Studios as a background artist in the mid-1930s. In the late 1930s, he moved to work as a background artist at the Terrytoons studio. At Terrytoons, Anderson Craig and John Vita would soon be considered two of animation's finest background artists. Their brilliantly rendered detailed backgrounds done in watercolor tempera resulted in vibrant colorful landscapes that melded seamlessly with the animated characters.

John Vita (1917–1988) was raised in Port Chester and graduated from Port Chester High School in 1935. He attended night school at Pratt Institute in Brooklyn, where he studied art, 1937–1938. In the late 1930s Vita began working at the Terrytoons studio painting animated cartoon backgrounds. He worked at Terrytoons until induction into military service in March 1941. While in the military he made training films in the field (rather than at bases in the United States). Seeking more adventure he became a Signal Corps combat cameraman and photographer. After forming part of the Anzio beachhead offensive and pushing back the German forces, he was assigned to photograph the crowds in the Piazza Venezia in Rome.

On June 6, 1944, Staff Sergeant Vita climbed up onto Mussolini's balcony and made a speech while mocking Mussolini. Thousands of Rome's residents cheered as Vita fulfilled a promise he had made to his mother that he would speak from Mussolini's balcony when he arrived in Rome with the American forces. Vita also filmed the liberation of the Dachau concentration camp and was allegedly the first U.S. serviceman to walk through the camp as he photographed some of the most haunting and memorable photographs of the conflict. Wounded twice during the war, Vita was awarded a Purple Heart, as well as several medals of valor. He teamed up with John Huston as cameraman for the wartime documentary *The Battle of San Pietro* (1945).

After the war, Vita worked as a commercial photographer in New York City then went back to Terrytoons working as a background artist (and with slide films) leaving shortly thereafter. Vita then worked as a freelancer on television commercials for Walt Disney Productions. In the early 1960s, Vita was working for Joe Oriolo with Trans-Lux Productions on the Felix the Cat series. When CBS-Terrytoons got busy in the early to mid-1960s after the departure of background artist John Zago, Terrytoons background department head Bill Focht would ask Vita to come in and help.[14]

George John Zaffo (1916–1984) graduated from (Bridgeport) Central High. Zaffo attended Pratt Institute and also apprenticed under Norman Rockwell. In 1937, at the age of 20, he graduated from Pratt Institute and was employed as an artist for the D. Ozene Advertising Agency He began as a layout and background artist at the Terrytoons studio later that year. He worked at Terrytoons as a background artist for about six years until, like Vita, his induction into the military in 1942. During World War II, after enlistment on August 8, he served in the U.S. Army Signal Corps at Fort Monmouth, Monmouth, New Jersey teaching animation later transferring back to New York state where he worked on animated training films. After the war, he worked for an advertising agency as an art director.

He then worked for about 18 months on animated television commercials. In the late 1940s, about 1948, he started to

Fig. 20.9 – Paul Terry overseeing the work of Jim Tyer.

concentrate on book illustration. He was the author and illustrator of a number of children's books. His credits included *The Big Book* series (all self-illustrated picture books for children) published by Grosset (e.g. *The Big Book of Real Trains* (1949); *The Big Book of Real Fire Engines* (1950)), and *The How and Why Wonder Book* series published by Grosset and later Wonder Books (e.g. *The How and Why Wonder Book of Flight*, (1961); *The How and Why Wonder Book of Science Experiments* (1962)). He won two *Herald-Tribune* awards for his artwork in the books including the New York *Herald Tribune* Spring Book Festival Award picture book honor, 1951, for *The Big Book of Real Building and Wrecking Machines*.[15]

Around 1943, with the loss of Vita and Zaffo to the military, Douglas "Bill" Hilliker (1891–1986) joined Anderson Craig in the background department. By the mid-1940s, Craig was supplementing his Terrytoons income by working evenings as a freelance advertising artist illustrating magazine advertisements. Craig and Hilliker were joined briefly in the background department by W. M. Stevens (1943) and Robert Blanchard (mid-1940s). Around 1954, after about fifteen years as head of the background department, Craig left the studio and moved to New York City where he opened his own art studio in an expensive apartment at 129 West 52nd street doing portraits, figures and commercial artwork.

By 1956, Craig was heading Anderson Craig Studios producing film animation for television commercials for clients such as Canada Dry. When Craig left Terrytoons, Bill Hilliker assumed the position as head of the department. By 1960, after accepting a position in commercial animation for CBS-Terrytoons, Craig and his family moved to work in Agawam, Massachusetts. By September 1961 the Craig family's residence was in West Springfield, Massachusetts. Anderson was employed as an art director for the Bay State Film Productions, a motion picture and slide production company for business industry and television located in Agawam, Massachusetts.

Bill Hilliker began his art studies at the age of 11 in San Francisco at the Mark Hopkins Art Institute where he remained for at least four years. At the age of 14, Hilliker, like Terry, experienced the April 1906 earthquake. By 1910 he was working as an artist for the *San Francisco Chronicle* newspaper. During this period, he became friends with Paul. In 1914–1915, he was an artist on the University of California at Berkeley yearbook. By 1915, he had moved to New York City where he was residing at 20 Gramercy Park and was employed as an illustrator. In 1917, he had enlisted in the United States Army (Company 14, 18th Provisional Training Regiment) at Plattsburgh, a New York training camp in upstate New York on the banks of Lake Champlain. During World War I, he was promoted to major in charge of an Afro-American regiment.

After the war, he became a freelance painter and moved back to New York City. His paintings were used as covers for such magazines as *Collier's* and *Saturday Evening Post*. He painted pictures of movie actors and actresses and completed illustration work for motion picture posters and other

Chapter 20 • Rounding Out the Cast

advertisements earning a large income at a time when employment was difficult to find. During the 1930s he worked as a commercial artist and did artwork for 20th Century-Fox. Through his work with Fox he was reacquainted with Paul Terry who had his animated cartoons distributed by the film studio. While in New York City, he was a frequent illustrator and contributor to *Railroad Magazine*, a pulp magazine devoted to railroad stories and railroad history. In the early 1900s, he built a cabin with no indoor plumbing (and handcrafted most of the furniture inside the cabin) in the isolated community of Beaver River, New York, a tiny village with no road access and located in the six million acre Adirondack Park. Paul Terry would visit Hilliker on a number of occasions in Beaver River. Prior to beginning work for Terry in 1943 Hilliker tried to re-enlist in the military but was refused admittance due to his age and physical condition.[16]

Terry continued to rely heavily on his main stars during 1950 and 1951 producing nine Mighty Mouse shorts, a Gandy Goose featuring Mighty Mouse (*Comic Book Land* (January 1950)), and eight Heckle and Jeckle cartoons of the 46 produced during the two years. The best of the Mighty Mouse cartoons include *Law and Order* (June 1950) and *The Cat's Tale* (November 1951). In *Law and Order*, once again as told on the "Racket Busters" radio program by Clancy, Chief of the Mouse Protection Bureau, the Catnip Gang (Shorty, Charlie, and Pinhead Schlabotka) have escaped from jail

Fig. 20.10 – Frank "Sparky" Schudde.

and returned to their old career in crime re-naming themselves "The Deep Freeze Gang". Using a peep show ("Have you seen Lulu?") containing dancing girl footage from *The Sultan's Birthday*, they trap the male mice, freeze them, and turn them into Mouseicles in various fruit flavors which they sell to the fellow cats. Clancy and the Bureau corner them and engage in a shootout but it seems the culprits are winning this battle until Mighty Mouse comes to aid the police.

The Cat's Tale features another alternate origin of Mighty Mouse. A baby mouse is abandoned on a mouse couple's doorstep. He grows up to discover he has superpowers to become the Champion of Justice. The age of the cats on Earth was ending. Now cometh the age of the mouse. His fame spreads around the globe. However, the cats produce a giant cat, Power Puss, to take on Mighty Mouse. After a spine-tingling battle, Mighty Mouse pounds the monster cat

into the Earth with such force that it sucks in the ground and land for miles around. During 1950 and 1951, the Oil Can Harry-Pearl Pureheart-Mighty Mouse trio were featured in three shorts: *Beauty on the Beach* (November 1950) set on Coney Island, *Sunny Italy* (March 1951) set in Pisa, Venice, Rome, and at Mt. Vesuvius, and *A Swiss Miss* (August 1951) set in the Swiss Alps. All three were enjoyable cartoon operettas with memorable music and lyrics by Phil Scheib.

Some of the more notable Heckle and Jeckle shorts during the same period are *Steeple Jacks* (September 1951) involving the two magpies being chased by the bulldog watchman perilously high above and along the steel girders of a tower being constructed at the Ajax Construction Company site. *A Merry Chase* (May 1950) have Dimwit and his bulldog friend chasing the two magpies through the forest and along the way the two birds get the best of both of their pursuers. A classic scene

253

from the cartoon has Jeckle removing the false teeth from Dimwit's mouth and using them as clackers in order to perform a Latino dance. In *Bulldozing the Bull* (March 11, 1951), Heckle and Jeckle invade a bullfighting stadium to sell tamales and end up coming up against the bull, El Toro Pantso, outwitting the beast through a clever array of pantomime, disguises and trickery.

As 1951 closed, with a stable of cartoon superstars, a strong business relationship with his distributor 20th Century-Fox, and steady marketing and commercial revenues from comic books, toys and other merchandise starring his characters, Paul Terry could lay claim to having one of the most profitable and financially sound studios in the industry. At the Walt Disney Studios, only after the release of *Cinderella* (1950) which grossed $4 million domestically did the production company become solvent again.[17] However, a new threat had emerged in the marketplace which would forever change the way the public spent their entertainment dollar and would lead to Paul Terry's exit from the animation business. ✎

Notes

1. Thomas James (Tommy) Morrison, interview, 15 June 1970, 20d.

2. *Cartoonist PROfiles #47*; Will Friedwald, "Mighty Jim Tyer: The Animator Who Broke the Rules", *Animation Blast* 6 (Spring 2001): 29–37, 44–46, 50–51; Jerry Beck, "Comical Tyer", *Animation Blast* 6 (Spring 2001): 38–39; Mark Mayerson, "The Curly Howard of Cartoons: Mark Mayerson Analyzes the Art and Style of Tyer", *Animation Blast* 6 (Spring 2001): 40–43; Ralph Bakshi, "Ralph Bakshi on Jim Tyer", *Animation Blast* 6 (Spring 2001): 50.

3. Animating "straight ahead" means animating sequentially, creating pose after pose, frame after frame, "straight ahead", from the first to the last in a sequence.

4. Doug Crane, telephone interview by author (transcript), Kelowna, B.C., 18 October 1997, Terrytoons Collection, Victoria, B.C., Canada, 4.

5. Beckerman, interview, 5.

6. Bill Kresse, telephone interview by author (transcript), Kelowna, B.C., 5 October 1997, Terrytoons Collection, Victoria, B.C., Canada, 2.

7. "New Studio Due For Terrytoons", *The Standard-Star* (New Rochelle, N.Y.), [1949], clippings file, New Rochelle Public Library, New Rochelle, N.Y.

8. Paramount Pictures would follow in 1952 with their own cat and mouse duo of Herman and Katnip.

9. Terry, interview, 20 December 1969, 75.

10. Leahy and Lazar, interview, 10; "Westchester County Section: New Rochelle, N.Y.", *The New York Age*, 21 May 1937, p. 12; "Douglas Moye's Band Wins At Scout's Benefit Dance", *The New York Age*, 5 June 1937, p. 12.

11. 20th Century-Fox Film Corporation, "Terrytoon Creators: Arthur Bartsch", *Dynamo* (Terrytoon Section), 15 April 1940, Chicago, Illinois, 8B); "Art Bartsch", in *The National Cartoonists Society Album 1996, Fiftieth Anniversary Edition*, Bill Janocha, ed. (Buffalo, New York: National Cartoonists Society, 1996), 316.

12. "Craig, Anderson", in *Who Was Who in American Art, 1564–1975*. Obituaries: "Anderson Craig", *Springfield Union*, 22 February 1964, p. 24; "Anderson Craig, Sr.", *Sunday Republican* (Springfield, MA), 23 February 1964, p. 18A.

13. "Craig, Anderson", in *Mantle Fielding's Dictionary of American Painters, Sculptors and Engravers*, 185.

14. Jerry Rosco, "Area Artist Hits the Jackpot", *Mamaroneck Daily Times*, 17 August 1972; Elaine Bissell, "Italian 'Dictator' Re-lives Glory", *The Herald Statesman* (Yonkers, N.Y.), 28 April 1975, p. 30. Obituary: "Johnnie N. Vita, Famous Painter, Photographer, Dead at 71", *The Standard-Star* (New Rochelle, N.Y.), 27 June 1988, p. A6.

15. Dolores Blythe Jones, *Children's Literature Awards & Winners: A Directory of Prizes, Authors, and Illustrators*, 1st ed. (Detroit, Michigan: Gale Research Company, 1983), 480; "Zaffo, George J.", in *Something About the Author: Facts and Pictures about Authors and Illustrators of Books for Young People*, vol. 42, ed. Anne Commire (Detroit, Michigan: Gale Research Company, 1986), 208–209. Articles: "Painting of 'Grandpop' Judged Most Popular at Art Exhibit", *The Daily Argus* (Mount Vernon, N.Y.), 26 May 1947, p. 11; "Mount Vernon Artist Exhibits Railroad Paintings at Library", *The Daily Argus* (Mount Vernon, N.Y.), 30 March 1950, p. 12. Funeral Notice: *The Standard-Star* (New Rochelle, N.Y.), 29 March 1984, p. 4. Interviews: Mary Zaffo Mathewson, telephone interview by author (transcript), 22 November 1997; Mary Zaffo, telephone interview by author (transcript), 11 January 1998; Tom Zaffo, telephone interview by author (transcript), 20 November 1997.

16. Biographical data for Mr. Hilliker was primarily compiled from reminisces of Hilliker by Beaver River residents (Pat Thompson, *Beaver River: Oasis in the Wilderness* (Eagle Bay, New York: Beaver River Press, 2000)), and interviews of his co-workers as found in the Paul Terry Papers and Terrytoons Collection. A short biographical entry can be referenced in: Hughes, *Artists in California, 1786–1940* (Sacramento, CA: Crocker Art Museum, 2002). Funeral notice: *New York Times*, 9 April 1986, p. D23.

17. John McDonald, "Now the Bankers Come to Disney", *Fortune* LXXIII, no. 5 (May 1966): 224.

Chapter 21

Relinquishing the Reins: The New Challenge of Television, the Sale of Terrytoons to CBS, and the Retirement of Paul Terry, 1952–1956

The television era of animation began in 1949 with *Crusader Rabbit*, the first cartoon series produced specifically for television release. *Crusader Rabbit* was the brainchild of Alex Anderson, the nephew of Paul Terry. After graduating from University High School in Oakland, California, Alex moved east to New Rochelle, New York in December 1937 to work at his uncle's animation studio. In 1938, Anderson worked for about eight months in a number of positions including an assistant in the camera department, an inbetweener, and a story critic assigned to viewing the Terrytoons cartoons screened at local theaters to make note of the audience's response to the cartoon gags.[1] Gags which generated laughter from audiences were reused by Terry in other cartoons.

After studying journalism for two years at the University of California Berkeley, working summers at the studio for his uncle, studying at the California School of Fine Arts, and spending about four years in the military, Anderson returned to Terrytoons in early 1946 to work full-time. While at Terrytoons, after viewing the "Baby Weems" segment from Disney's *The Reluctant Dragon* (1941), Anderson began to think there was a way to do comic strips for television with just enough movement to sustain interest and having a narrator tell the story. After talking about his ideas with Art Bartsch and other Terrytoons staff, Anderson proposed to his uncle the idea of producing an animated series for television. Terry was not interested in the idea because he viewed television as the enemy to the theatrical cartoon market.

Terry was concerned that if he tried to produce cartoons for television that his distributor, 20th Century-Fox, might not renew his contract. Terry's words to his nephew were very clear: "Alex, if I had anything to do with television, 20th Century-Fox would cancel our contract like that".[2] In the 1940s, the stance among studios towards television was mostly non-cooperative. "Nearly everyone reacted to television merely by praying that it would go away. A few saw in TV production a chance to use up overhead through facilities rental, but on the whole the studios were late getting into TV with shows of their own".[3] Terry's fear of upsetting his distributor robbed him of the claim of having the first animated series produced specifically for television.

By 1951 television networking in the United States was linked coast to coast and the new medium was growing as more households purchased television sets. While only 0.5 percent of U.S. households had a television set in 1946, 55.7 percent had one in 1954.[4] By the early 1950s, most Hollywood studios began adapting to the challenge television posed by producing entertainment that could not be offered by the tube including wide-screen productions (i.e. CinemaScope, Cinerama, Techniscope, VistaVision, etc.),

255

Fig. 21.1 – Connie Rasinski (sitting) and Arthur Bartsch (standing).

increasing the amount of color productions, creating adult fare with violence, partially clad bodies, and strong language, and introducing gimmicks (i.e. 3-D viewing with cardboard glasses, Smell-O-Vision, etc.). Some studios tried to find further revenue streams by investing in Broadway shows, developing merchandising campaigns around their film stars, speculating in the real estate market, and divesting themselves of some of their real estate holdings (e.g. selling ranches where they once had filmed westerns; selling backlots of a main studio for real estate development or oil exploration purposes).[5]

While Terry was at first hesitant to embrace television, by the early 1950s he understood that in order for his studio to meet the challenges posed by the new media required adaptation. John Grant notes: "He was one of the first animation producers to realize that television was going to kill the animated theatrical short, and that one must come to some arrangement with the new medium or in due course perish".[6] Both live-action and animation studio heads began to seek ways to capitalize upon the new entertainment medium. By the late 1940s, television animation was being produced by independent animation studios such as Fletcher Smith Studios, Zac-David (Tempo), Transfilm Inc., Shamus Culhane Productions, and Film Graphics.[7] Live-action studios also began to sell portions of their theatrical film libraries to other companies to sell to television.[8] Likely Terry sensed an opportunity for his studio to take advantage of the medium by making his film library available for television.

Terry noted in his 1969 interview the value of television with regards to long-time producers of animated shorts:

> The great boon, as far as I'm concerned, was when television came along and made all this old stuff valuable again. Otherwise, you'd never would have heard of Terrytoons. It was just a hand to mouth business. You made a living. Sure, you paid the bills and enough to go ahead for another year, like most businesses do. But we kept laying those negatives up. And then television came along, they were hungry for material.[9]

By 1953, Terry had decided to take a more assertive role and approached 20th Century-Fox with his desire to make his cartoon library available for the television market. Fox was open to the possibility as long as they were satisfied that the broadcasted cartoons would not represent competition to the theatrical Terrytoons shorts being currently released.

Schickel writes that while many studios were late getting into television production, they "compounded the first error with a second – selling sizable chunks of their film libraries to the competing medium, which improved cash flow of the studios and kept their balance sheets looking good temporarily but placed the studios in the unenviable position of allowing their old products to compete with their new ones, often to the latter's disadvantage".[10] Fox was intent on not making the same mistake. Therefore, Fox stipulated that only the much older black-and-white shorts from the 1930s could be televised (e.g. Kiko the Kangaroo, Farmer Al Falfa, Puddy the Pup) and not the newer theatrical cartoons (e.g. Mighty Mouse, Heckle and Jeckle, Gandy Goose). Further, the

Chapter 21 • Relinquishing the Reins

production credits were to be camouflaged by re-filming the opening credits. As a result, Terrytoons' most popular character from the 1930s, Farmer Al Falfa, was renamed Farmer Gray.[11]

Terry was able to interest General Foods in purchasing the television rights to a large package of shorts from the early film library. In late 1953, Terry negotiated a licensing deal with CBS for 112 sound cartoons from his film library to be viewed on the television network for $140,000.[12] The cartoons became part of *Barker Bill's Cartoon Show*, which premiered on CBS November 18, 1953 and ran to November 25, 1956. The program featured 200 Terrytoons shorts, 42 of which were Farmer Al Falfa shorts.[13] The show host was a stationary picture of Barker Bill, a chubby circus ringmaster sporting a long black handlebar moustache and dressed in a traditional suit with white gloves and a top hat. Barker Bill's voice came from an off-camera announcer introducing the cartoons. By successfully negotiating a deal, Terry ensured that Terrytoons was "the first major animation studio to sign up for television".[14] The program was also television's first weekly cartoon series.[15] The 15-minute cartoon show was sponsored by Post Sugar Jets and was seen twice a week although some local stations showed both episodes together as a single 30-minute program.

While Terry started to make inroads into the television market, he continued to produce his animated shorts on schedule

Fig. 21.2 – Anderson Craig, background artist.

meeting his contractual commitments with Fox. In March 1952, Terry was honored by the Museum of Modern Art for producing his 1,000th animated cartoon with a week's showing of nine representative shorts he had made in the past 30 years.[16] From 1952 to 1954, the studio produced 10 more Mighty Mouse cartoons, the last cartoons starring the superhero before Terry sold his film library to CBS. Four of these cartoons starred the trio of Oil Can Harry, Pearl Pureheart and Mighty Mouse. *Prehistoric Perils* (March 1952) has Oil Can Harry kidnapping Pearl and taking her in a time machine back to prehistoric times where Mighty Mouse must fight both Harry and dinosaurs. *Happy Holland* (November 1952) involves Mighty Mouse rescuing Pearl (as a little Dutch girl) from being crushed by a huge grinding wheel after first having to plug a leak in a dike. In *A Soapy Opera* (January 1953) Oil Can Harry beats up a Mighty Mouse doll in front of Pearl so she will think he is beating up on the superhero. She agrees to work in the "Busted Seam Laundry" if he will stop pounding her hero, but soon the real Mighty Mouse shows up to beat, bleach, and starch Oil Can Harry. *When Mousehood Was in Flower* (July 1953), set in medieval times, features Oil Can Harry as the Black Knight who plans to marry Pearl so she can pay off her father's debts if no one can defeat him. Mighty Mouse takes on the challenge.

During the same period of time, Terry produced a number of very entertaining Heckle and Jeckle shorts. *Movie Madness* (January 1952) has the birds sneaking onto a motion picture studio lot disguised as directors. When their disguises are exposed, they try and avoid being chased off the lot by the watchman by sneaking onto production sets and taking on various performance roles while in costume. *Off to the Opera* (May 1952) has the two magpies trying to sneak into an opera house during a performance of *The Barber of Seville* and being chased around by the bulldog manager while assuming various disguises to avoid detection before flooding the building. In *Ten Pin Terrors* (June 1953) the magpies are trying to get some sleep but the noise from the bowling alley downstairs is keeping them awake. The birds decide to solve their problem by sabotaging the bowling game of the noisemaker ending with the bowling alley blowing up. *Blue Plate Symphony* (October 1954) has the magpies managing a roadside diner, the Indigestion Inn, and thwarting the attempts of two thieves from robbing the establishment by using various restaurant tools and equipment.

With the comical success of Dimwit the Dog and Clancy the Bulldog evident in the Heckle and Jeckle cartoons, Terry decided to star each character in their own cartoons. Dimwit headlined two cartoons, *How to Keep Cool* (October 1953), where he unsuccessfully battles the heat and *How to Relax* (February 1954) where the canine calamitously tries some hobbies to relax. Both cartoons rely on the plot motif of the unfortunate mishaps of a stressed out canine attempting to solve a problem. Clancy appeared in *Police Dogged* (July 1956), a spoof of the film noir crime films of the period. The cartoon features the bulldog battling master criminal Pinhead Schlabotka. Unfortunately, without the magpies as their foils, the cartoons starring these canine characters lacked the humor, spontaneity, and inventiveness found in the Heckle and Jeckle shorts.

Borrowing from the inspiration of John R. Bray's Heeza Liar cartoons from the silent period, the character, Phony Baloney, starred in *The Tall Tale Teller* (May 1954). When Phony Baloney, an Irishman with a great imagination, is caught drinking water from a public water fountain and dragged off to court, he explains to the judge that the public fountain is in fact the fountain of youth. He then proceeds to tell a fanciful and far-fetched tale as to how he came about this discovery. The judge does not appear amused with Baloney's tale but dismisses the charges after he is a sprayed with the fountain water and turned into a baby. This short featured one of the more promising new characters created by Terry during the first half of the 1950s and he would reappear later in *African Jungle Hunt* (March 1957) where Phony recounts another farfetched tale of his African adventures and capture by pygmies.

Another one-shot cartoon, *Pride of the Yard* (August 1954), introduced Percival Sleuthhound. In the cartoon, Limehouse Harry and his pal escape from prison but they cannot avoid getting rid of the ever present Percival, a crime dog from "Scotland Backyard". When they send Percival on a rocket ship to Mars, the Martians return the hound back to Earth. When they try to blow Percival up they only end up blasting themselves up into the air. They fall through the roof and land in front of a judge with Percival standing nearby telling the court they were good sports. Another character, Willie the Walrus, was featured in *Arctic Rivals* (June 1954) and *An Igloo for Two* (March 1955). In the first short he vies with his rival Dennis the Dogfish for the affections of Suzy the Seal winning her heart but ends up doing the wash with Suzy watching over him with a rolling pin. In the latter cartoon, muscular Walter the Walrus tries to use Willie's singing to capture the heart of Suzy but after Willie rescues Walter from a polar bear, Suzy teams up with Willie for a duet.

In April 1955, the studio introduced Good Deed Daly in a short by the same name. Three cartoons were produced from the series; all directed by Connie Rasinski. The Good Deed Daly shorts were premised on the idea of a model Boy Scout determined to do a good deed daily. Although his help is not needed, in his eager efforts to do a good deed he unwittingly foils the plans of criminals. In the first cartoon from the series, Good Deed captures bank robber Desperate Dumkopf "Fiend of a Thousand Faces" who can transform himself into anything he wants, including a lamppost and ham sandwich. *Scouts to the Rescue* (April 1956) has Good Deed Daly and his fellow scouts capturing Mexican bandit Chico Pico attempting to steal a buffalo from a national park. In this short, the character was voiced by Conrad Rasinski, the son of Joe Rasinski, the Terrytoons cameraman, and nephew of director Connie Rasinski. In *Cloak and Stagger*

Chapter 21 • Relinquishing the Reins

Fig. 21.3 – Camera Department, circa 1952. Clockwise from bottom left: (unknown female), Joe Rasinski, Walter Gleason, Conrad Rasinski, George Davis, Doug Moye.

(August 1956) Good Deed Daly unwittingly thwarts the plans of two criminals intent on blowing up the city's water works.

Like the other major cartoon studios during the "Golden Age of American Animation", Terry was active in licensing and merchandising his cartoon characters. During the 1930s to the 1950s, Terry licensed a variety of character related products including comic books, toys, games, clothing (T-shirts, Halloween costumes), puzzles, dolls, coloring books, handkerchief, children's jewelry, and records. However, despite a broad range of character merchandise, only the comic books were successful. Terry later admitted regretting licensing his characters. "I think we wasted too much time and thought on it. And then it makes the stuff rather commonplace".[17] Terry did create a number of framed animation art presentation pieces in the mid-to-late 1940s that were sold or given away to members of the public. These presentation pieces were watercolor-on-paper cut-outs of Mighty Mouse, about 4–5 inches in height, that were fixed to an animation background from a Mighty Mouse Terrytoons cartoon which was then framed and the matte signed by Paul Terry. These pieces were created in-house by Bill Fox and Paul's daughter, Patricia Terry. Paper cut-outs of the character were preferred over animation cels because they were deemed to be less fragile and would age better than cels. A few of these pieces occasionally turn up on the market commanding significant sums.

With respect to comic books, the company's characters were initially licensed to Timely Comics, a predecessor of Marvel Comics, in the early 1940s. Terry published comics featuring such characters as Mighty Mouse, the magpies Heckle and Jeckle, Gandy Goose, Dinky Duck, Little Roquefort, and the Terry Bears. The first *Terry-Toons Comics* was published in October 1942. Timely published *Terry-Toons Comics* until August 1947 (issue #59). St. John Publications took over the licensing from September 1947 to 1951 (#60–83), then from June 1952 to November 1953. *New Terrytoons* was published by Dell (June-August 1960 – May 1962), then by Western (October 1962 – January 1979).

Mighty Mouse had his own comic book, *Mighty Mouse*, first published by Timely in Fall 1946 (and is the most valuable and collectible of all the Terry comics) and continued for three more issues until Summer 1947 (#4). St. John Publications then took over publication until 1956 (#5–67). First, St. John published 21 issues from August 1947 to 1951 (changed to *Paul Terry's Mighty Mouse Comics* at issue #19). St. John published *Paul Terry's Mighty Mouse Comics* from 1951 to February 1956 (through to issue #67). Pines took over (March 1957 – June 1959 (issues #68–83)), then Western (October 1964 – September 1965), and Dell (March 1966 – October 1968).

St. John also published *The Adventures of Mighty Mouse* (renaming of *Paul Terry's Comics*, where Mighty Mouse appeared) from January 1952 to May 1955, and then from August 1955 to November 1955 (#126–128). Pines took over (April 1956 – August 1959) (#129–144), then Dell (October-December 1959 – July-September 1962) (#145–155), Western (October 1962 – October 1963) (#156–160), and then *Dell Comics* (#161–172) (1964–1968)). St. John's Terrytoons comics include the field's first 3-D comic book, *Three Dimension Comics* #1 (Sept. 1953 oversize format, Oct. 1953 standard-size reprint), featuring Mighty Mouse. According to Joe Kubert, co-creator with the brothers Norman Maurer and Leonard Maurer, it sold an exceptional 1.2 million copies at 25 cents apiece at a time when comics cost a dime.

Paul Terry's Terry-Toons Comics featured one issue published by Toby in 1950. St. John published three issues of *Paul Terry's Terrytoon Comics* in 1951. St. John then published 41 issues of *Paul Terry's Comics* from March 1951 to May 1955. Pines published four issues of *Paul Terry's Mighty Mouse* in 1956. Mighty Mouse's first comic book appearance was in *Terry-Toons Comics* #38 (November 1945), published by Timely Comics. Mighty Mouse was featured in: *Terry-Toons Comics* #38–85 (1945–1951) and *Paul Terry's Comics* #86–125 (1951–1955).

Heckle and Jeckle appeared in their own comic book, *Heckle and Jeckle*, published by St. John (22 issues: October 1951 – October 1955), Pines (10 issues: Fall 1956 – June 1959), Western (four issues: November 1962 – August 1963), and Dell (three issues: May 1966 – 1967). Gandy Goose appeared in his own comic book published by St. John (four issues: March 1953 – November 1953) and Pines (two issues: Fall 1956 – Summer 1958). Dinky Duck appeared in his own comic book published by St. John (14 issues: November 1951 – September 1955) and Pines (two issues: Fall 1956 – Summer 1958). St. John published *Terry Bears Comics* (three issues: June 1952 – March 1953) and Pines published *Terrytoons, The Terry Bears* (one issue, Summer 1958). St. John published *Little Roquefort Comics* (nine issues: June 1952 – October 1953) and Pines published an issue in the summer of 1958.

Although not a risk taker by nature, Terry took a stance on a major political investigation sweeping the film industry that may have jeopardized his relationship with his distributor and damaged his reputation in the film industry: the blacklisting of artists in Hollywood. The decision to take a position on the matter was not difficult for Terry to make. He possessed deeply entrenched views on the freedom of a man to think and do as he pleased and regarded human beings as the master of their own destiny. Paul believed that only God has supreme authority over humans, because he created mankind and put humans on Earth to survive and prosper. According to Terry, the right of God to rule over the United States populace can be found in the United States Constitution which document was founded on principles of the sovereign authority of God over the peoples of the United States.[18] During the Vietnam conflict, Paul made it known that he was opposed to U.S. involvement in the war on the grounds that the U.S. had no right to use military force to tell the Vietnamese peoples how to run their lives.[19]

In 1941, producer Walt Disney took out an ad in *Variety*, the industry trade magazine, declaring his conviction that "Communist agitation" was behind a cartoonists and animators' strike. According to historians Larry Ceplair and Steven Englund, "In actuality, the strike had resulted from Disney's overbearing paternalism, high-handedness, and insensitivity".[20] In October 1947, drawing upon a list of names in the *Hollywood Reporter*, the House Committee on Un-American Activities, an investigative committee of the United States House of Representatives

Chapter 21 • Relinquishing the Reins

Fig. 21.4 – Barker Bill comic strip drawn by Paul Terry taken from the *New York Mirror* in 1954.

originally created in 1938 to uncover citizens with Nazi ties within the United States, subpoenaed a number of persons working in the Hollywood film industry to testify at hearings. It had declared its intention to investigate whether Communist agents and sympathizers had been planting propaganda in U.S. films.

The hearings opened with appearances by Walt Disney and Ronald Reagan, then president of the Screen Actors Guild. Disney testified that the threat of Communists in the film industry was a serious one, and named specific people who had worked for him as probable Communists.[21] The first systematic Hollywood blacklist was instituted on November 25, 1947, the day after 10 writers and directors, the "Hollywood Ten", with suspected political beliefs, associations, memberships or sympathy with the Communist Party USA were cited for contempt of Congress for refusing to testify to HUAC, and subsequently fired by a group of studio executives, acting under the aegis of the Motion Picture Association of America.[22] Eventually, more than 300 artists – including directors, radio commentators, actors and particularly screenwriters – were boycotted by the studios. Actors Charlie Chaplin, Orson Welles, and Paul Robeson, and lyricist Yip Harburg, left the U.S or went underground to find work.[23]

By 1950, Robeson, an outspoken supporter of Communism, was beginning to have difficulty locating work in the entertainment industry. That year NBC canceled Robeson's appearance on Eleanor Roosevelt's television program.[24] Subsequently, the State Department denied Robeson a passport to travel abroad and issued a "stop notice" at all ports because it believed that an isolated existence inside United States borders would afford him less freedom of expression.[25] In 1952, Robeson was awarded the International Stalin Prize by the Soviet Union.[26] Unable to travel to Moscow, he accepted the award in New York.[27] In April 1953, shortly after Stalin's death, Robeson penned *To You My Beloved Comrade*, praising Stalin as dedicated to peace and a guide to the world: "Through his deep humanity, by his wise understanding, he leaves us a rich and monumental heritage".[28] Robeson's opinion on the Soviet Union kept his passport out of reach and stopped his return to the entertainment industry and the civil rights movement.[29] In his opinion, the Soviet Union was the guarantor of political balance in the world.[30]

How and when Terry became acquainted with Paul Robeson is unclear and all evidence gathered by the author has been strictly anecdotal after conversations with Terry's family.[31] What appears certain is that Terry was well-acquainted with Robeson's work as a singer and enjoyed his music and magnificent voice before he met him. However, Terry did not care for Robeson's political beliefs and pro-Communist stance. According to family sources, Terry offered Robeson the opportunity to provide his vocal and singing talents to Terrytoons cartoons. Despite Robeson's pro-Communist leanings, Terry believed that the actor-singer had a right to self-expression without victimization and should not have to live his life based on the ideas, beliefs and values imposed by others. Following Terry's policy on

261

Fig. 21.5 – George McAvoy, sound editor.

film credits for his artists, Robeson's name did not appear on film. Whether Robeson's work for Terry took place in the late 1930s, or mid-1950s is unknown but if Disney had discovered the Terry-Robeson employment relationship, there is little doubt that HUAC, the F.B.I. or other officials within the U.S. Government would have been alerted to the relationship and the matter thoroughly investigated. As to the extent of Robeson's involvement with the studio and which cartoons he provided his immense voice talents, the matter is deserved of further research by scholars and critics.

The pressures of ensuring his studio produced one animated cartoon every two weeks didn't keep Paul from writing lyrics to sacred and inspirational music composed by his musical director Philip Scheib. In 1951 he wrote the lyrics to *The Miracle* in which the lyrics strike the note: "Every day's a miracle to me".[32] In 1952, he wrote the lyrics to *Never Let Satan's Foot Get in the Door*, music composed by Phil Scheib, with words warning the listener to be careful and avoid those doing the devil's work. These songs were deeply personal to Terry as they were drawn from his childhood experiences and religious upbringing.

By early 1955, Terry was seriously contemplating retirement from the cartoon business and selling his cartoon studio. Theatrical animated cartoons had become very expensive to produce and had very little drawing power for exhibitors as Terry noted in his 1969 interview:

> Well, the cartoon never demanded a price. And it got to be too expensive to make them. Production costs continued to rise and you could never get any money from the exhibitor for your product. The cartoon has no drawing power in a theater. You go to the theater and you enjoy the cartoon, to be sure, but you'd pay the same amount of money to see the show if they didn't have a cartoon.[33]

Terry was also aware of the problems his distributor was having with selling the cartoon shorts. Theater owners would sign contracts to exhibit 26 animated cartoons. However, since the public was paying to see the main feature and not the cartoon some of the exhibitors never exhibited all of the animated shorts they had contracted for. The result was the distributor would have to cancel the contract in order to persuade the theater owners to sign a new contract for the following year.[34] At the same time, the rise of television was causing a decline in box office revenues as theater audiences remained home for their film entertainment. The result was movie studios were suffering financially and becoming less willing to pay for animated cartoons which were being exhibited before each feature.

To add further impetus to sell his cartoon library, his main New York competitor, Famous Studios under their owner Paramount Pictures, was making the move to television. In December 1955, Paramount sold most of their pre-October 1950 shorts and cartoons, except for the Popeye and Superman shorts, to U.M. & M. TV Corp. for television distribution. Represented by A. W. Schwalberg, a former Paramount sales executive, U.M. & M. won the bid buying 1,600 short subjects for $3.5 million.[35] The Popeye cartoons were acquired by Associated Artists Productions, and the Superman cartoons had already reverted to Superman's

Chapter 21 • Relinquishing the Reins

owners National Comics after the studio's film rights to the character had expired. In October 1956, Famous Studios was downsized and reorganized. Paramount assumed full control of the studio, integrating it into the Paramount Pictures Corporation as a division named Paramount Cartoon Studios. Paramount sold their remaining cartoon film library and the rights to their established characters to Harvey Comics in 1959.[36]

With a drop in theatrical attendance, the rise in production costs, and cartoons appearing more frequently on television, Terry had become a firm believer that the theatrical animated cartoon was about to end. After the sale of Paramount's cartoon assets his wife Irma was concerned that if Paul did not sell his studio assets soon they may not be a market left to sell the Terrytoons film library. She would occasionally remark to Paul: "We want you alive to spend it". When the sale was finally made, she was visibly relieved.[37] On February 19 of that year, he had turned 68 years old and had been in the business for 40 years. In October 1955, New Rochelle renamed the city Terrytown for a day in honor of Paul Terry. The media at the time reported that the Terrytoons studio had been in New Rochelle for 25 years but in fact it had only been in the city since 1934.[38]

In 1956, *Barker Bill's Cartoon Show* ended and was replaced by a syndicated program, *Terry Toons Club* (later re-titled *Terry Toons Circus*), hosted by Claude Kirchner on WWOR-TV New York.

Fig. 21.6 – Roy Halee, the singing voice of Mighty Mouse.

Farmer Al Falfa also got his name back in 1956 with the syndicated *Farmer Al Falfa and His Terrytoon Pals* featuring Farmer Al Falfa cartoons as well shorts from the Aesop's Fables series. The success of CBS's *Barker Bill's Cartoon Show* was the incentive for CBS to sit down with Terry in 1955 and discuss the purchase of his entire film library to the television network.

Terry put Bill Weiss in charge of negotiating with CBS. Weiss had been with Terry for over 20 years, and he trusted Weiss, who was educated both as an accountant and lawyer, to obtain the best deal for his studio. At the time, NBC was also interested in purchasing the Terrytoons film library although little is known about the details of their negotiations with Weiss. Negotiations with CBS heated up in late 1955. On January 2, 1956, *Broadcasting, Telecasting*

magazine reported that CBS was in the final stages of a transaction with Terrytoons Inc., under which CBS would acquire the assets of the film animation company for about $5 million, which included the 1,100 cartoon library and the merchandising-licensing rights to the characters.[39] The final sales price for the cartoon library along with the merchandising and licensing rights on the characters was identical to the one negotiated by Paramount with U.M. & M. TV Corp., $3.5 million.[40] Along with the deal Bill Weiss had obtained a secure tenured position with Terrytoons, a new division of CBS Films Inc.

As Terry began to pass landmarks both in terms of years in the industry and number of cartoons his studio produced, he began receiving honors and awards from the film industry. One award was a very expensive gift certificate to

263

one of the more luxurious clothiers in New York City. Upon visiting the store with his daughter, keeping with his frugal nature he was unable to bring himself to purchase any of the expensive items considering the merchandise much too extravagant for his tastes. Eventually after much prodding by his daughter, Terry purchased a Vicuña jacket consisting of fabric made from hairs gathered from a rare animal that lives only in the high Andes.[41]

As Terry was moving his thoughts towards a life outside the studio during the early to mid-1950s, he began promising his studio assets and positions of authority to some of his employees, veterans including Tom Morrison, Mannie Davis, Connie Rasinski, and Eddie Donnelly. These promises were taken seriously by the veteran staffers who had worked industriously for Terry for more than 20 years. Right up to the day Terry walked into the studio and told them that he had sold his cartoon assets his devoted senior staff labored earnestly expecting some reward for years of dedicated service. Although Weiss had negotiated a plum position for himself after Terry had sold the studio, none of the other employees would receive any financial benefits from the studio sale.

During 1954 and 1955, Terry had begun experimenting with new ways to reach the public with his animated product. He was approached by an individual with the idea of creating what he later referred to as "Terryscopes". These machines were similar to a kinetoscope (peep show) machine. For a nickel or a dime, the spectator could view a 3-D Terrytoons color cartoon.[42] Terry invested $50,000 into the operation (although he claimed ten times that amount). He leased them to supermarkets, amusement parks and locales where parents and children visited. While mother would shop, her children could watch the cartoons in a corner of the supermarket. However, the cost in producing the 3-D cartoons (requiring animating in three different colors) along with difficulties in marketing the machines caused Terry to lose money on this venture in what some of his staff would refer to as "Terry's Follies".[43]

As Terry stepped out of the studio spotlight and into a comfortable retirement with his newfound fortune, he did so with a sense of pride and accomplishment. During his career he produced over 1,100 animated cartoons over the 40-year period he was in animation and is considered one of the most prolific film producers in history. With respect to the quality of animation, Paul had no misconceptions that the aesthetic qualities of his cartoons were on par with those of Disney. But he never viewed the other studios as competition. In fact, he applauded the work of those in the industry who produced beautiful animation as they were an asset to the industry. He saw studios working together to develop the animated cartoon as an art form and as an entertaining product for audience consumption. Paul felt that there never was enough quality animation produced.[44]

He could be proud of creating one of the most famous cartoon characters in animation history, Mighty Mouse, as well as the popular duo of Heckle and Jeckle. These characters would be part of his legacy to animation. While at sometimes cautious and reluctant to spend money on his cartoons, both directly and indirectly through his pioneering work in animation he helped advance the medium as art and entertainment. Terry launched the careers of a number of animation greats who may never have followed careers in the field had it not been for Paul, artists such as Norm Ferguson, Connie Rasinski, Jim Tyer, George Gordon, Ferdinand Horvath, and through the assistance of his brother, Bill Tytla.

After the studio expansion in the late 1930s, his studio employed over 100 personnel and played an important function in Westchester County from the mid-1930s until the mid-1950s by boosting the economic activity in the city of New Rochelle and surrounding areas. While Terry at times endeavored to always get the most out of his staff, he was loyal to his employees and made it a practice to hire family members of his studio personnel. He kept his staff busy even during the bleak economic times of the 1930s when bread lines were just a few blocks down the street. An example is mechanic Dan Ward who became a fixture at the studio repairing studio equipment as well as experimenting on new projects such as the photographic system he developed in 1939 to combine live-action film with animation.[45] Terry had met Ward

Chapter 21 • Relinquishing the Reins

in Washington about 1917 when Terry was producing animation to record the medical history of the First World War. Terry brought Ward along with him to Terrytoons. Terry had bought a drill press and lathe and Ward taught him how to use the equipment as he wanted to learn how to make camera stands.[46] Terry would keep Ward employed until his untimely death in the 1940s.

During his four-decade career, Paul Terry produced scores of highly entertaining shorts, three of which were nominated for Oscars®. His cartoons, although not masterpieces of animation art, rivaled the aesthetics found in the cartoons of most other Hollywood animation studios. With animation from Bill Tytla, Connie Rasinski, Mannie Davis, Eddie Donnelly, Carlo Vinciguerra, and Johnny Gentilella, Terry could argue that his small studio had some of the finest artists in the business. His animation background art from artists Anderson Craig, Johnny Vita, George Zaffo, and Bill Hilliker is considered by industry professionals to have been some of best in the animated short business. Today his cartoons streaming over the Internet are being viewed by millions around the world and his characters today emblazoned on all types of product merchandise are instantly recognizable by children generations removed from the first theatrical release of these cartoons.

After CBS purchased the Terrytoons film library from Paul Terry in very late 1955, the network used the collection to create *The Mighty Mouse*

Fig. 21.7 – Animation background for *The Green Line* (1944).

Playhouse. The series featured one or two Mighty Mouse adventures plus an assortment of Paul Terry cartoons. Beginning in December 1955, the cartoon show was shown regularly on Saturday mornings. Each half-hour program opened with the Mighty Mouse theme song.

> Mister Trouble never hangs around,
> When he hears this Mighty sound:
>
> *"Here I come to save the day!"*
>
> That means that Mighty Mouse is on the way!
> Yes sir, when there is a wrong to right,
> Mighty Mouse will join the fight!
> On the sea or on the land,
> He's got the situation well in hand!

Marshall Barer (1923–1998),[47] a writer/producer for Golden Records, the famous U. S. children's record label of the 1940s to 1950s, wrote the lyrics, while Terrytoons long-time studio musician, Philip Scheib, composed the music.

The *Mighty Mouse Playhouse* was a phenomenal success and despite challenges from other cartoon programs such as Hanna Barbera's *Ruff and Reddy* series which first aired in December 1957, the program remained a staple of network television through 1966. Throughout the program's 12-year run on CBS, *The Mighty Mouse Playhouse* relied solely on the theatrical Terry cartoons as the producers were reluctant to tamper with the program's popularity by adding the made-for-television shorts. *The Mighty Mouse Playhouse* was so popular that the program maintained an average 11.6 rating with a 45.8 percent audience share throughout its 12-year CBS run. The series strongly impacted the cartoon industry as cartoon studios began to follow the success of the show with their own fully animated series. The series also revived the career of the super mouse and earned CBS a fortune through character toys, books and other merchandise.[48]

265

Notes

1. Anderson, interview, 4.
2. Ibid., 6.
3. Schickel, *The Disney Version*, 26.
4. Cobbett Steinberg, *TV Facts* (New York, N.Y.: Facts on File, 1985).
5. Schickel, *The Disney Version*, 26–27.
6. John Grant, *Masters of Animation* (New York: Watson-Guptill Publications, 2001), 189.
7. Karl Cohen, "The Development of Animated Television Commercials in the 1940s", *Animation Journal*, 1, vol. 1 (Fall 1992): 44–46; For a good overview of television advertising in the late 1940s and 1950s, refer to: Lawrence R. Samuel, *Brought to You By: Postwar Television Advertising and the American Dream* (Austin: University of Texas Press, 2001).
8. See generally Tino Balio, *Hollywood in the Age of Television* (Boston: Unwin Hyman, 1990).
9. Terry, interview, 20 December 1969, 87–88.
10. Schickel, *The Disney Version*, 26.
11. Hal Erickson, *Television Cartoon Shows: An Illustrated Encyclopedia, 1949 through 1993* (Jefferson, N.C.: McFarland & Company, 1995), 14.
12. *Variety*, 11 November 1953, 4.
13. George W. Woolery, *Children's Television: The First Thirty-Five Years, 1946–1981, Part I: Animated Cartoon Series* (Metuchen, New Jersey: The Scarecrow Press, Inc., 1983), 34–35.
14. Grant, *Masters of Animation*, 189.
15. Note should be made of the "Commonwealth Cartoon Package" a short-lived 30-minute television program that premiered in 1951 and featured cartoon classics such as Ub Iwerks' "Flip The Frog" and "Willie Whopper", Paul Terry's "Aesop's Fables", and even some Walt Disney vintage shorts along with other cartoon favorites offered for local programming (See generally Woolery, *Children's Television: The First Thirty-Five Years, 1946–1981, Part I: Animated Cartoon Series*).
16. *Variety*, 12 March 1952, 13.
17. Terry, interview, 14 July 1970, 143.
18. Terry, interview, 20 December 1969, 45.
19. Ibid., 46.
20. Larry Ceplair and Steven Englund, *The Inquisition in Hollywood: Politics in the Film Community, 1930–1960* (Urbana and Chicago: University of Illinois Press, 2003), p. 157–158.
21. Karl F. Cohen, *Forbidden Animation: Censored Cartoons and Blacklisted Animators in America* (Jefferson, N.C.: McFarland, 1997), p. 167.
22. See generally, Edward Dmytryk, *Odd Man Out: A Memoir of the Hollywood Ten* (Carbondale, IL: Southern Illinois University Press, 1953).
23. See generally, Reynold Humphries, *Hollywood's Blacklists: A Political and Cultural History* (Edinburgh: Edinburgh University Press, 2008).
24. "Mrs. Roosevelt sees a 'Misunderstanding'", *New York Times* 16 March 1950, p. 33.
25. Charles Wright, *Paul Robeson: Labor's Forgotten Champion* (Detroit: Balamp Publishing, 1975), p. 97.
26. "Paul Robeson is Awarded Stalin Prize", *The News and Courier*, 22 December 1952, p. 6.
27. "Paul Robeson Gets Stalin Peace Prize", *The Victoria Advocate*, 25 September 1953, p. 5.
28. Philip S. Foner, ed., *Paul Robeson Speaks: Writings, Speeches, Interviews, 1918–1974* (Larchmont: Brunner/Mazel, 1978), p. 347–349.
29. Martin Bauml Duberman, *Paul Robeson* (New York: New Press, 1998), p. 354.
30. Foner, *Paul Robeson Speaks*, p. 236–241.
31. Leahy and Lazar, interview, p. 10.
32. Muriel Fischer, "Every Day's a Miracle to Paul Terry", *New York World-Telegram and Sun*, 7 July 1951, p. 4.
33. Terry, interview, 20 December 1969, 82.
34. Ibid., 84.
35. *Box Office*, 3 December 1955, p. 36.
36. Maltin, *Of Mice and Magic* (1980, rev. 1988), 316–319.
37. Leahy and Lazar, interview, 23.
38. *The Kane Republican* (Kane, Pennsylvania), 6 October 1955, p. 7; "TV Chatter", *The Hartford Courant*, 30 October 1955, p. F7.
39. "$24 Million Worth of Films Involved in Transactions", *Broadcasting, Telecasting*, 2 January 1956, p. 44.
40. Weiss, interview, 15 June 1970, 18c.
41. Leahy and Lazar, interview, 15.
42. "Broadway", *Record-Eagle* (Traverse City), 28 June 1955, p. 4:2.
43. Davis, interview, 28 July 1970, 18e–20e.
44. Terry, interview, 20 December 1969, 24; Val Adams, "Kingsley Signed to C.B.S. Contract: Playwright Joins Network as Producer, Writer and Director for 5 Years", *New York Times*, 29 December 1955, p. 41.
45. Davis, interview, 28 July 1970, 20e.
46. Terry, interview, 20 December 1969, 61–62.
47. Stephen Holden, "Marshall Barer, 75, Lyricist For "Mattress" and Mighty Mouse", *New York Times*, 28 August 1998, p. A23; "Marshall Barer: Lyricist Wrote Musicals, "Mighty Mouse" Theme", *Chicago Tribune*, 28 August 1998, p. 10; Myrna Oliver, "Obituaries; Marshall Barer; Lyricist for 'Mattress'", *Los Angeles Times*, 27 August 1998, p. 24.
48. Erickson, *Television Cartoon Shows*; Jeff Lenburg, *The Encyclopedia of Animated Cartoons* (New York, New York: Facts On File, 1991).

Chapter 22

Paul Terry's Cartoon Legacy: A Comparative Analysis of Golden Age Animation

How do the Terrytoons cartoons produced by Paul Terry rank against the animated shorts distributed by the other American animation studios? The answer depends on what production elements you are comparing, and what criteria you are applying. Just as important is what time period you are making the comparison as the production quality of cartoons produced by the studios varied over time. If the measuring stick is artistic and technical merit as judged by the Academy of Motion Picture Arts and Sciences, then by the end of 1959 when the Golden Age of American Animation was drawing to a close, Walt Disney Productions had garnered 11 Oscars® in the "Short Subjects, Cartoons" category, Metro-Goldwyn-Mayer had won eight Oscars®, Warner Bros. was awarded five, United Productions of America won three, and John and Faith Hubley (Storyboard) earned one Oscar®.[1]

The other Golden Age studios, Walter Lantz Productions, George Pal (Paramount), Columbia Pictures, Fleischer Studios, and Terrytoons, all failed to win an Academy Award in the "Short Subjects, Cartoons" category, the award for the best animated cartoon of the year.[2] By AMPAS standards, Terrytoons, Lantz, Fleischer (and its successor Famous Studios), George Pal, and Columbia fall far short. However, are the number of Oscars® handed down by AMPAS in the category "Short Subjects, Cartoons" an accurate reflection of which studios were better able to produce animated shorts of a higher technical and artistic merit? If so, then conclusions can be drawn that studios such as Terrytoons, Walter Lantz, and Columbia Pictures produced animated cartoons that were inferior in terms of technical and artistic merit than studios such as Disney and Warner Bros.

A compelling argument can be made that the lack of success at the Academy Awards for New York-based studios such as Terrytoons and Fleischer could be related to distribution and access problems with the animated cartoons. Long before the arrival of the Internet in an age of radio with no television, members of the Academy of Motion Picture Arts and Sciences would have found great difficulty in viewing even a small number of shorts produced globally. For east coast studios such as Terrytoons and Fleischer, their distance from Hollywood may have played an integral factor in access to these shorts in the nomination process.

There is also the distinct possibility that not all of the members who cast their votes for the best cartoon short viewed all of the nominated shorts. In 1978 the voting precedents for the Academy Awards were changed for the animated and live short subjects where only peer groups were allowed to cast votes for the winners. This was a great improvement over previous years where, although peer groups would nominate nominees, the final voting was thrown open to the entire Academy, many of whom had not even seen the short subjects.[3] Today, members can vote only after attesting they have seen all of the nominated films in the Animated Short Film category.[4] Another possibility is

267

Fig. 22.1 – Paul Terry, circa 1950.

that the motion picture studios that distributed the shorts such as Educational Pictures/20th Century-Fox (Terrytoons), Paramount (Fleischer), and Universal (Walter Lantz) may not have effectively marketed their products to the Academy to ensure that the voters were able to view the animated product.

Since the first day the studio opened, critical opinions on Terry's body of film work have been mixed. While during the late 1920s and 1930s there were a number of very complimentary newspaper articles published in the *New York Times* and a few flattering columns in the New Rochelle *Standard-Star* on Terry and his studio,[5] the first work that took a serious look into the inner workings of Terrytoons was the book *How To Make Animated Cartoons* by Nat Falk with a foreword by Paul Terry. Published in 1941, the book featured information from all of the major studios of the day including Disney, Warner Bros., Terrytoons, Fleischer, Screen Gems, Lantz and Harman-Ising. The first chapter of the book details the early history of animated cartooning and the "Big Four" (J. R. Bray, Earl Hurd, Paul Terry, Raoul Barré) who pioneered the art form.

In his book, Falk highlights the 1915 Terry-Selznick incident and casts Terry as an aspiring young producer trying to interest the elder film mogul in purchasing a "masterpiece". In rejecting Terry's offer, Selznick is cast as a poor businessman "blind to the possibilities of this new medium".[6] Falk writes that in the making of animated cartoons Terry has made "countless revolutionary changes" including a number of creative accomplishments. Terry was "the first ever to use celluloid for action drawings", and "the first screen artist to draw animal characters in humanized form".[7]

Eighteen years later, Stephen Becker wrote a relatively substantial (i.e. four to five page) biographical portrait of Paul Terry in Chapter IV "Added Attractions" of his book *Comic Art in America*, published in 1959. Generally, Becker had positive remarks for the Terry cartoon product and summed up Terry's managerial style as follows: "An intelligent businessman, Terry proved a boon to many foreign distributors: he was scrupulously fair, helped them often when business slumped and never called for advance guarantees. He was therefore personally liked and admired".[8] Similarly, Les Daniels' comments on Paul Terry's executive capacities in his 1971 published work *Comix: A History of Comic Books in America* were positive ones. Daniels viewed Terry as a wise businessman who consolidated the concepts of the animated film business "into a consistently marketable commodity".[9] With respect to the Terrytoons cartoon product, he found the adventures of both Mighty Mouse and Heckle and

Chapter 22 • Paul Terry's Cartoon Legacy

Jeckle highly energetic and entertaining.[10]

Ralph Stephenson in his widely distributed 206-page book *The Animated Film*, published in 1973, examined the history of international animation from silent film to time of writing. In his short (approximately 200-word) review of Paul Terry and the Terrytoons studio, he found the Terry product "very average" while the shorts (e.g. *Flebus* (1957), *The Juggler of Our Lady* (1958)) produced after Terry sold to CBS to be "excellent" cartoons.[11] The first chapter written on Terry (albeit a small eight-page overview titled "Mr. Terry's Toons") in any monograph must be credited to Donald Heraldson for his work *Creators of Life* published in 1975. Heraldson's critical opinion of Terry and his cartoon product is generally favorable.

Heraldson does gives Terry credit for experimenting with "new ideas for the medium" including "trying cross marks on the paper sheets for registration".[12] Heraldson's opinion is that the cartoons of Terry and "Barrié" (referring to Raoul Barré) in the late 1910s were the best drawn of the era.[13] He also found the vocal parts in the "Terry Toons" of the early 1930s as "excellent".[14] By 1940 Heraldson opined that Terrytoons had "reached a quality of artwork similar to the other studio output; color and animation had weathered the crudity period and now were excellent".[15] However, Heraldson notes that later the Terrytoons product began to become less artistic.

Heraldson did not find Scheib's music impressive being very repetitious sounding with "an overindulgence in saxophones and cymbals in every cartoon".[16] Further, Heraldson also mentions the story of the theater owners not having to pay Terry for unprojected cartoons and gives credit to Terry for his fairness in not holding the theater owners to their contractual obligations. Heraldson also notes that Paul Terry also allowed distributors to cancel their contracts when overseas business fell in World War Two and by doing so "Paul Terry was escalated immensely in popularity overseas by such business practices".[17] Heraldson included one former Terrytoons animator's comment that Terry remained small for a purpose: to avoid any temptation of having to do something underhanded to survive.[18]

With regards to the cartoon product, Heraldson states that Terrytoons "were never really works of art" some of which were drawn by unskilled students. He saw Terry as never refining his product and conceiving no great "firsts" in film cartoons. Further, Heraldson was not aware of any "pioneering" or research for improvement in the cartoon product. The animation and color could both be near perfection and near disaster in the same cartoon. Heraldson concludes that Paul Terry had great respect for Disney but did not try to copy him and "Terry was well liked, and his product, like Disney's, retains his name even after he no longer was associated with it".[19]

More contemporary critical reviews of the Terry body of film work have not been as kind. In 1980, film historian Leonard Maltin wrote the first definitive source book on both well-known and obscure American cartoon studios, *Of Mice and Magic: A History of American Animated Cartoons*.[20] He argued that Terry was reluctant to spend money on his animated cartoons with the Terry cartoons of the 1950s not looking much different from the Terry cartoons of the 1930s.[21] With respect to the overall quality of the Terry product, according to Maltin the character animation and design was primitive, only the backgrounds had some visual distinction, and Philip Scheib's music scores did not change through the years.[22] Maltin's overall impression of Terry was a producer that had little love for the cartoons he produced and was more interested in turning a healthy profit than producing cartoons with high production values.

In 1994, film historian Giannalberto Bendazzi published *Cartoons: One Hundred Years of Cinema Animation*, a detailed chronological history analyzing animated film on a global scale. In the book, the career of Paul Terry is briefly mentioned. Terry is described by Bendazzi as a "modestly gifted artist" and "a hard-headed independent spirit" who persevered in the animation business despite setbacks.[23] In his 1997 book *Serious Business: The Art and Commerce of Animation in America from Betty Boop to Toy Story*, author and long-time editor of *Time* magazine, Stefan Kanfer, closes his comments on Paul Terry by detailing Terry's sale to CBS in 1955 then stating that he left no

269

creative or artistic legacy to the animated film genre, and that his biggest claim to fame was being a survivor.[24]

Lawyer, journalist, political aide, and animated film historian Michael Barrier authored *Hollywood Cartoons: American Animation in its Golden Age* published in 1999. While Barrier devoted the greater portion of the text to the Hollywood studios, he did spend some time analyzing the personalities and animated products of the New York studios (i.e. Terrytoons, Van Beuren Studios, and Fleischer Studios), if only for purposes of placing the California studios in greater context to the United States animation industry. Barrier gave some credence to Maltin's assertions about Terry's reluctance to spend money on the cartoons he produced by noting that Terrytoons had only half as many employees as other studios with comparable output and these other studios were spending twice as much on each cartoon.[25] Like Maltin, Barrier was also unimpressed with the quality of the Terry cartoon product. For example, he found the short *Two Headed Giant* (1939) a disappointing and awkward copy of Disney's *Brave Little Tailor* (1938).[26]

The majority of scholarly research or critical commentary into animated cartoons has concentrated on textual matters such as audience effects, violence, sex roles, racial stereotypes, adult themes, war-time propaganda, how animated cartoons are created, and computer-generated

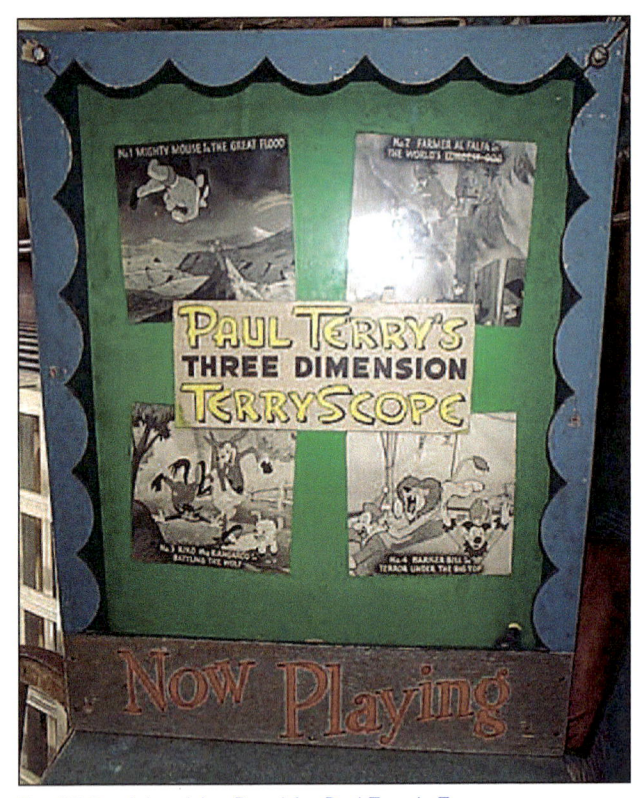

Fig. 22.2 – Advertising Board for Paul Terry's Terryscope.

animation.[27] Until the 1990s, there was a complete absence of any serious study into evaluating and comparing the quality of the cel animation produced by various animated cartoon studios during the Golden Age. In 1994, *The 50 Greatest Cartoons: As Selected by 1,000 Animation Professionals*[28] was published, the first attempt to explore and rate the production output of animated shorts from various animation studios. The book, edited by animated cartoon historian Jerry Beck, showcased the 50 greatest cartoons of all time as judged by a panel of more than 1,000 cartoon historians and animation professionals. By taking votes from people working in the

animation industry, Beck attempted to make the list an authoritative compilation of the best cartoon shorts produced.

Of the top 50 shorts listed in Beck's book, 43 were produced during the first 32 years of the Golden Age of American Animation, attesting to the decline in quality of cartoons over the last half of the 20th century. Categorizing the shorts by studio, 17 cartoons were produced by the Warner Bros. studio, nine shorts were created by Walt Disney Productions, seven manufactured by Metro-Goldwyn-Mayer, five turned out by Fleischer Studios, four by United Productions of America, three by the National

Chapter 22 • Paul Terry's Cartoon Legacy

Film Board of Canada, and one each by Winsor McCay, Walter Lantz Productions, Pat Sullivan, Marv Newland, and Sally Cruickshank. None of the over 1,000 shorts produced by Paul Terry during his 40-year career in animation (1915–1955) made the list.

The editor's only submission requirements were that each cartoon on this list had to be under 30 minutes long and cel animated (with *Gertie the Dinosaur* (1914) being the only exception noted in the book). Those that took part in the poll were primarily members of the San Francisco, Portland, New York and Hollywood chapters of ASIFA (Association Internationale du Film D'Animation).[29] All those polled were asked to rank their favorite cartoons from numbers 1–50.[30] There was no definition given to the term "greatest" and how this should be measured. Rather, Beck asked those he polled one question when making a decision as to whether to include the cartoon in their personal top 50: "Is this a classic cartoon?".[31]

What it seems Beck was attempting to measure were "great" cartoons in terms of his pollsters' personal favorites, their entertainment value, rather than animated cartoons that achieved some level of artistic and technical brilliance. Of significance, there is a weak correlation between what the Academy judged as a cartoon featuring strong production values and what pollsters in 1994 considered to be a "classic" cartoon. Of the 230 animated cartoon shorts nominated for an

Fig. 22.3 – Mighty Mouse balloon at Macy's Parade, New York City.

Oscar® by the end of the 1980s, only 14 of Beck's 50 "greatest" cartoons were Oscar®-nominated shorts, and only seven of these garnered the coveted Oscar® over the 63 years the award was handed out for best cartoon short.

When comparing the level of artistic talent at the Terrytoons studio during its approximate 40 years of operation with that found at the other studios, it is not difficult to argue that Terry employed some of the finest artists and technicians in the animation business.[32] Animators such as Tytla, Tyer, Rasinski, Kuwahara, and Donnelly had either worked at Disney or were being actively courted by the Burbank studio sometime during

their careers. Other animators such as Carlo Vinciguerra and Mannie Davis were considered to be some of the best and brightest in the industry during the 1940s to 1960s.

Terry could also boast as employing some of the finest background painters in the business all of whom at one point in their careers had earned an income outside of animation as painters, designers, and illustrators. The backgrounds painted by John Vita, George Zaffo, Anderson Craig, Art Bartsch, and Bill Hilliker were richly decorated with objects and filled with strong vibrant hues resulting in strikingly attractive works of art. Today Terrytoons

271

backgrounds are highly sought after by collectors in the animation art marketplace. While Terry had a practice of saving all of his backgrounds for possible later use in other cartoons, it is difficult to detect the reuse of these backgrounds in other shorts even after multiple viewings.

The same year that the Beck book was published, Jeffrey Neal-Lunsford submitted to the faculty of the graduate school at Indiana University in partial fulfillment of the requirements for the degree Doctor of Philosophy in the Department of Telecommunications, his doctoral dissertation *Cel Aesthetics: A Method for the Analysis of Animated Cartoons*. The overall goal of the study was to establish a framework that could be "used by critics and scholars to analyze animated cartoons in terms of their cel aesthetics qualities and to show how this framework can be applied to evaluate individual cartoons, particularly in terms of comparison with other cartoons".[33]

Neal-Lunsford was able to identify five cel aesthetics elements (i.e. motion, space, light, time, and sound). For each of these cel aesthetic elements he listed features which are linked to increased studio costs and higher production values.[34] Neal-Lunsford claimed that by examining a cartoon short in relation to his criteria one can identify cartoon shorts with strong production values. The author found that by applying Neal-Lunsford's cel aesthetic elements the Terry cartoons (for the most part), especially those cartoons produced after he had gained control of the studio in 1936, featured strong production values with complex character animation, lush background design, and varied camerawork. Terry was able to maintain high standards while controlling production costs by keeping his cartoons just over six minutes in length, a full 60 seconds shorter than the average length of cartoon produced by the other Golden Age studios.

The Terry shorts did feature recycled animation but this practice was common at all of the Golden Age studios even at Disney where, for example, scenes from *Dumbo* (1941) and *Bambi* (1942) were recycled for scenes for *Fun and Fancy Free* (1947), or the scene of the Great Danes, Tiger and Talbot, licking Wart in *Sword in the Stone* (1963) which were later recycled for the scene of the two dogs licking Mowgli in *Jungle Book* (1967). Terry never invested into expensive technological processes to create innovative camera technology such as at Disney (multiplane camera) or the Fleischer Studios (Stereoptical Camera). Nevertheless, his cameramen used a broad panorama of camera pans, tilts and zooms to create interesting photographic effects for his cartoons. His films were also smartly edited to aid in storytelling.

As for the music, Philip Scheib was a highly educated and capable musician with many years of experience as a composer prior to his tenure at Terrytoons. The background music and the rhythmic pacing in the Terry cartoons such as found in the highly frenetic and fast-paced Heckle and Jeckle shorts is as outstanding as any of the music Carl Stalling and Scott Bradley did. For many of the Mighty Mouse cartoons he borrowed from classics from stage and opera rewriting lyrics and changing beat and tempo to delightfully parody the on-screen action between Mighty Mouse and his nemesis Oil Can Harry.

However, over time, Scheib's music did develop that "sameness" for which many contemporary film historians have criticized his work. In composing his music Scheib failed to experiment with different forms, sounds, themes, and textures resulting in many of his pieces sounding eerily similar. Likely this similarity was partly due to the frenetic pace of having to compose an original composition every two weeks. Had he been given the time, he may have produced such wonderful pieces such as his music for the short *The Juggler of Our Lady* (1958).

Just as problematic the sound effects library suffered regrettably from a limited collection of noises. No matter the size or shape of a character or at what height he fell from you will always hear the same "splash". Sometimes sound sources were mismatched to the object on screen such as found in the cartoon short *String Bean Jack* (1938) where a piano is used to imitate the sound of a harp. And yet who is to say that the mismatching of sounds to objects was not intentionally done by Terry or Scheib for comic effect? Despite Scheib's shortcomings, during his tenure at Terrytoons, he

Chapter 22 • Paul Terry's Cartoon Legacy

was able to create original music for over 750 Terrytoons shorts, a substantial body of creative work for one artist under tight studio deadlines where one cartoon was produced every two weeks.

Many of the Terry cartoons have been criticized by film historians for being dull, humorless "potboilers".[35] Critics have noted that outside of the Mighty Mouse and Heckle and Jeckle cartoons, many of the shorts suffered from weak storylines with very few gags. Terry recognized the value of a good story going so far as to say that "... some stories are so good you couldn't spoil them if you wanted to. And some stories are so bad that you couldn't do anything with them no matter how you try".[36] Despite Terry's strong belief in the importance of an engaging story, it was not until 1937 before the story department was established at the studio.

The reason for Terry's indifference towards establishing a story department was that he considered himself "The Story Department" at the studio. Only after receiving numerous complaints from his distributor Educational (beginning as early as 1935) with respect to the entertainment quality of the cartoons was a department finally established two years later. Prior to 1937 Terry preferred to rely upon his creative spark and an old archive of gags he had been amassing since his days at Fables Studio. Gags which cartoon audiences found humorous would be used again in other cartoons. Despite the formation of a story department he would continue with this practice up to the date of the sale of his studio to CBS.

Although in the early days Terry seemed to have a knack for creating great gags for his Fables cartoons, by the early 1930s he was having difficulty coming up with humorous storylines. Jack Zander (1908–2007) who worked for Terry in 1936 and 1937 found Terry's sense of humor to be "a little skimpy". It seems by middle age Terry's creative spark had been extinguished and his personal "reservoir of gags" had run dry. Terry had another problem in that he had a very different take on what most audiences would consider humorous.

In 1936 or early 1937 animator

Fig. 22.4 – Paul Terry wearing a Mighty Mouse mask.

Dan Gordon, a very good story artist who later was a key story man for Fleischer Studios and Hanna-Barbera, had put a storyboard up on the wall. The story involved a mouse and the mouse did something very, very funny. Terry asked his story crew "Is that funny?" The story crew, consisting of Gordon, Zander and Joe Barbera, responded that the gag was hilarious as they all nearly died laughing. Terry's response was: "Put in two mice". A puzzled Gordon said: "Well yeah, but two mice don't fit in the story Paul". Paul's response was: "One mouse is funny. Two mice are twice as funny." So the story crew added another mouse to the scene.[37]

Fig. 22.5 – *The Miracle* sheet music, words by Paul Terry, music by Philip Scheib.

Zander, Gordon and Joe Barbera would do storyboards in their spare time before the department was established in 1937. During this period, Gordon created a number of fantastically funny storyboards at Terrytoons but following the Terry studio philosophy he wasn't given credit on the cartoons he wrote. Another problem Terry had was holding onto talented story men. Gordon left Terrytoons in mid-1937 with a few other Terrytoons defectors such as Barbera, Carl Meyer, and

Chapter 22 • Paul Terry's Cartoon Legacy

Ray Kelley all of whom joined Zander, who had left Terrytoons a short time earlier, in California at the new MGM cartoon unit. Gordon's brother George would follow him to MGM about a month later. I. Klein, a very talented story man who worked for the studio beginning in 1942 and created the Mighty Mouse prototype Super Mouse, left Terrytoons in 1945 to work for Terry's New York rival, Famous Studios.

Terry has been criticized for losing some of his top artists because of a failure to pay them fair wages for their services.[38] A deeper analysis of the primary research sources on the studio reveals otherwise. When Joe Barbera threatened to pack up and head to California, Terry gave him raise. However, the boost in pay was not as much Barbera had expected and he decided to head to California after all.[39] Zander's opinion was that Terry had no problem paying his more valued artists a good wage:

> He didn't throw his money around but he wasn't [cheap]. He was fairly generous. He'd give you a raise if he thought you deserved it.[40]

The problem Terry had to face was talent hunters from the Disney studio making trips to the east coast to scoop his homegrown artists. The other problem was the lure of California and the great sun-drenched weather the Los Angeles area had to offer. Terry explained:

> Of course, in those days, people used to make passes and steal your talent. You'd bring in a young fellow and

Fig. 22.6 – Carlo Vinci overseeing the work of Connie Rasinski.

you'd develop him, he'd become pretty good. Then they'd hear about him. Of course, from California they always made raids on us.[41]

As the years progressed, animation studios in New York found it increasingly difficult to retain talented artists. By the mid-1960s the opinion among many top media executives looking for studios to produce television animation was that the best artistic talent was found in California.

The difficulty in finding great story artists and gag writers was not isolated to Terrytoons. The problem was endemic throughout the industry during the Golden Age. One just needs to watch a few Mickey Mouse cartoon shorts to realize that even Walt Disney was struggling to find good story material. For example, in *A Gentleman's Gentleman* (1941)

after Pluto serves Mickey Mouse breakfast in bed he is instructed by his master to fetch a newspaper. After losing his coin down a storm drain and retrieving it, Pluto purchases a newspaper and ends up jumping onto Mickey's bed a muddy mess.

This wonderfully animated cartoon short by such talents as Basil Davidovich, Eric Gurney, Emery Hawkins, Kenneth Muse and George Nicholas, and directed admirably by Clyde Geronimi, has little humor to offer the viewer and has a predictable ending. The end result is the cartoon is thoroughly forgettable. The few gags in the short seem to be forced upon the viewer and there are no witty surprises awaiting the audience. The only gag that might crack a smile is found in the scene of Pluto tripping over his own feet while pompously walking with his nose in the air in front of a number of pedestrians.

275

While Disney had an unwavering commitment to quality and brought a level of character to cartoons that no one had ever seen before, he was always struggling to find great gags to include in his films and paid his animators by the gag. On his first animated feature, *Snow White and the Seven Dwarfs* (1937) he paid $5 and $10 for every gag that was accepted and used in the film, this was during the Depression when you could buy a great dinner for 35 cents.[42] At the time animator Kendall O'Connor was working on the short *Mickey's Circus* (1936), the staff were being paid $4 a gag.[43]

The value of a good story man to the success of a cartoon is evident in the work of such story masters as Michael Maltese, Rich Hogan, Heck Allen, and Warren Foster. Of Beck's top 50 "greatest" cartoons, five of the top 12 were scripted by Warner Bros.' Maltese (*What's Opera, Doc?* (1957) (#1), *Duck Amuck* (1953) (#2), *Duck Dodgers in the 24 1/2th Century* (1953) (#4), *One Froggy Evening* (1955) (#5), *Rabbit of Seville* (1950) (#12)). Warner Bros.' Warren Foster was responsible for scripting *The Great Piggy Bank Robbery* (1946) (#16) and *Coal Black and de Sebben Dwarfs* (1943) (#21). MGM's Rich Hogan was responsible for the story for Tex Avery's *Red Hot Riding Hood* (1943) (#7), *Bad Luck Blackie* (1949) (#15), and *Little Rural Riding Hood* (1949)). Heck Allen was the story man for *King-Size Canary* (1947) (#10).

When making a comparison of the Terry cartoon product with the cartoons produced by the other studios, Terry can proudly claim that he produced shorts featuring animation which was on par with Golden Age Hollywood animation studios such as Columbia, Walter Lantz, and Warner Bros. When called upon Scheib was able to produce some great scores and his music for the Mighty Mouse and Heckle and Jeckle shorts are as good as it gets. The Terrytoons story department should be commended for creating three classic cartoon icons, Mighty Mouse and Heckle and Jeckle, as well as the stories for over 110 entertaining animated cartoons these characters appeared in. While Terry has been vilified for producing hundreds of tedious cartoons, one should understand that animated shorts lacking in humor and good storytelling was the rule rather than the exception in animation. Across the entire Terry cartoon library there are enough cute, charming cartoons with a healthy sprinkling of gags to keep audiences engaged for hours on end and keep any cartoon connoisseur of Golden Age animation happy. ❧

Notes

1. Walt Disney Productions had garnered 11 Oscars® (on 35 nominations), Metro-Goldwyn-Mayer had won eight Oscars® (on 22 nominations), Warner Bros. was awarded five (on 20 nominations (one was withdrawn)), United Productions of America won three (on 14 nominations), and John and Faith Hubley (Storyboard) earned one Oscar® (on one nomination).

2. During the three decade period Walter Lantz Studios earned 10 nominations, George Pal had seven nominations, Columbia Pictures garnered six nominations, Fleischer Studios had four nominations, Terrytoons Studio earned four nominations, National Film Board of Canada had one nomination, and Pintoff Productions was given one nomination. All failed to win an Academy Award in the category.

3. Joan Irving, "Co Hoedeman: Castles in the Sand", *Cinema Canada* 46 (April/May 1978): 28–31.

4. The Academy's entire active membership is eligible to select Oscar® winners in all categories, although in five – Animated Short Film, Live Action Short Film, Documentary Feature, Documentary Short Subject, and Foreign Language Film – members can vote only after attesting they have seen all of the nominated films in those categories. For an explanation of the decision rules in the voting process: William V. Gehrlein and Hemant V. Kher, "Decision Rules for the Academy Awards Versus Those for Elections", *Interfaces* 34, Issue 3 (June 2004): 226–234.

5. "Aesop on the Screen", 3; Theodore Strauss, "Mr. Terry and the Animal Kingdom", *New York Times*, 7 July 1940, IX, p. 3; Edgar W. Brown, "Film Comic Drawn Here Tickles World", *The Standard-Star* (New Rochelle, N.Y.), 26 October 1934.

6. Nat Falk, *How to Make Animated Cartoons*, with a foreword by Paul Terry (New York: Foundation Books, 1941), 16.

7. Ibid., 17.

8. Stephen Becker, *Comic Art in America* (New York: Simon and Schuster, 1959), 102.

9. Les Daniels, *Comix: A History of Comic Books in America* (New York: E.P. Dutton & Co., 1971), 50.

10. Ibid., 53.

11. Ralph Stephenson, *The Animated Film*, The International Film Guide Series (New York: A. S. Barnes & Company, 1973), 42.

12. Donald Heraldson, *Creators of Life* (New York: Drake Publishers,

Chapter 22 • Paul Terry's Cartoon Legacy

1975), 212. Please note that Heraldson's work has a large number of historical inaccuracies bringing his research methodology into question.

13. Ibid., 213.
14. Ibid., 216.
15. Ibid., 217.
16. Ibid.
17. Ibid., 218.
18. Ibid.
19. Ibid., 219.
20. Maltin, *Of Mice and Magic*. Table of Contents for the book: Chapter 1: Silent Era; Chapter 2: Walt Disney; Chapter 3: Max Fleischer; Chapter 4: Paul Terry and Terrytoons; Chapter 5: Walter Lantz; Chapter 6: Ub Iwerks; Chapter 7: The Van Beuren Studio; Chapter 8: Columbia: Charles Mintz and Screen Gems; Chapter 9: Warner Bros.; Chapter 10: MGM; Chapter 11: Paramount/Famous Studios; Chapter 12: UPA; Chapter 13: The Rest of the Story.
21. Ibid., 141–142.
22. Ibid., 142.
23. Giannalberto Bendazzi, *Cartoons: One Hundred Years of Cinema Animation* (London: John Libbey; Bloomington: Indiana University Press, 1994), 22.
24. Kanfer, *Serious Business*, 181.
25. Barrier, *Hollywood Cartoons*, 385.
26. Ibid., 384.
27. Representative books include: Christopher P. Lehman, *The Colored Cartoon: Black Representation in American Animated Short Films, 1907–1954* (Amherst, Massachusetts: University of Massachusetts Press, 2007); Nicholas Sammond, *Birth of an Industry: Blackface Minstrelsy and the Rise of American Animation* (Durham, North Carolina: Duke University Press Books, 2015); Kanfer, *Serious Business*; Rolf Giesen and J.P. Storm, *Animation Under the Swastika: A History of Trickfilm in Nazi Germany, 1933–1945* (Jefferson, North Carolina: McFarland & Company, 2012).
28. Jerry Beck, ed., *The 50 Greatest Cartoons: As Selected by 1,000 Animation Professionals* (Atlanta, Georgia: Turner Publications, 1994).
29. Ballots were also mailed to members of the Society for Animation Studies, 100 animation studios, and film critics at more than 100 periodicals. No mention is made as to whether these were located outside North America. Beck, *The 50 Greatest Cartoons*, 6.
30. Ibid.
31. Ibid.
32. Refer to Appendix 1 for in-depth biographies of the key artists.
33. Jeffrey Neal-Lunsford, "Cel aesthetics: A method for the analysis of animated cartoons", Ph.D. diss., Indiana University, 1994.
34. Animated cartoons with high production values have the following production elements: (1) Motion: characters in a constant state of motion, character motion that is life-like, natural and fluid, character movement along the z-axis; (2) Space: copious amounts of camera movements, little or no reused or cycled animation, realistic backgrounds, consistent application of depth cues, panoramic wide shots, scene transitions by fades, dissolves, and wipes (as opposed to cuts, use of angles in camera shots, the use of depth cues (e.g. relative size of objects, overlapping planes, the application of linear perspective, and utilization of shadows), use of unusual technological practices (e.g. Stereoptical process) for special effects and enhancement of video space; (3) Light: application of directional lighting, consistent application of chiaroscuro and shadows in the character animation, three-dimensional characters, use of a broad spectrum of colors in character animation and background art, special use of color (e.g. to establish mood, indicate emotional states, define and articulate space, provide symbolism, describe the visual character of objects, depict weather conditions or time and day, and guide viewer attention to certain screen areas), execution of much detail in the character animation usually found in facial features and clothing, execution of much detail in the background art with a naturalistic look to the objects, consistent application of color from cel to cel; (4) Time: efforts that increase the clock time of an animated cartoon, screen time that reinforces the mood of the production, rapid editing/cutting rhythm to the action; (5) Sound: character dialogue that complements on-screen action, accurate lip synchronization, vocals that identify personality traits and define characterization, creative use of sounds (e.g. effective descriptive sound effects to reinforce visual images, aid in the articulation of space, and decorate scenes), a large library of sound effects that accurately represent the action on screen, creation of unique sounds rather than relying on a sound effects library, greater use of music and sounds to help describe the action, creation of original orchestral scores specifically for each individual short, original creation of a musical arrangement, use of music to establish mood, and use of music to establish or supplement the rhythmic structure of screen events by parallelism, stabilization, or counterpoint.
35. Hal Erickson, *Military Comedy Films: A Critical Survey and Filmography of Hollywood Releases Since 1918* (Jefferson, North Carolina, McFarland and Company, 2012), 371; Shamus Culhane, *Talking Animals and Other People* (New York: St. Martin's Press, 1986), 392.
36. Terry, interview, 20 December 1969, 80.
37. Zander, interview, 13 December 1997, 3.
38. Maltin, *Of Mice and Magic*, 122.
39. Barbera, *My Life in 'Toons*, 58.
40. Zander, interview, 13 December 1997, 3.
41. Terry, interview, 13 June 1970, 117.
42. Richard Holliss and Brian Sibley, *Walt Disney's Masterpiece Snow White and the Seven Dwarfs* (Walt Disney Home Video, 1994), 15.
43. Don Peri, *Working with Walt: Interviews with Disney Artists* (Jackson, Mississippi: University of Mississippi Press, 2008), 100.

Chapter 23

A Studio in Transition: The Gene Deitch Years and the Animation Renaissance, 1956–1958

With the new studio, CBS-Terrytoons, a division of the CBS Television Films Sales Inc. subsidiary, required new creative direction. In June 1956, CBS executive Newt Schwin approached 31-year-old Eugene "Gene" Merril Deitch and offered him the position as its creative (and supervising) director and a carte blanche to bring the studio to CBS standards. The young illustrator, animator and film director was an unusual choice for the position as he was at least 20 years younger than most of the directors and senior crew. He also had a background in the stylistic design of United Productions of America (UPA) which eschewed the ultra-realistic Disney style which Terrytoons was trying to emulate. UPA animation was characterized by flattened perspective, abstract backgrounds, strong primary colors, and "limited" animation.

Although a young man, Deitch had about 10 years of experience in animated film production after having become familiar with animation as a young teen. With the encouragement of a teacher, he made his first animated cartoon at the age of 13 in a Disney-organized class project at Venice (California) Junior High School. After graduation from Los Angeles High School in 1942, he was drafted into the United States Air Force. Upon his return to civilian life, he worked for a while as assistant to the art director at CBS Radio in Hollywood, 1945–1946. In June 1946 he started as an apprentice production designer to John Hubley and an assistant to production designer Bill Hurtz at UPA studios based in Hollywood, California. He worked up to production designer status and became Bobe Cannon's layout man/designer.

While at UPA he worked on the Air Force Flight Safety series for Bobe Cannon. He worked as an assistant production designer on the *Fox and Crow* and *Mister Magoo* cartoon series for Columbia Pictures. Within five years he was Creative Director of UPA's New York studio, where he directed the famous Bert & Harry Piels beer commercials. Deitch was also responsible for animating the first NBC color peacock. Before that, in 1949, he had moved to Detroit to work for Jam Handy where he directed his first film, *Building Friends for Business*, and within a year was working as animation department head producing industrial and commercial films.[1]

In mid-1951, UPA head Steve Bosustow flew to Detroit to lure Deitch back to UPA as an established staff member at their New York City studio and to help organize a branch studio in New York in the position of supervising director. While at UPA Deitch was the creative head of all television commercial production and educational and entertainment films in the studio. He directed many animated advertising films and shorts. He also wrote and directed the cartoon *Howdy Doody and His Magic Hat* (1952), and *Pump Trouble* (1952) for The American Heart Association. His animated TV commercials were the first ever shown at the New York Museum of Modern Art; an entire month of daily screenings in 1954 (including a kinescope of his

Chapter 23 • A Studio in Transition

Fig. 23.1 – Opaquing Department, 1957.

CBS TV coast-to-coast appearance on the *Let's Take a Trip* show on which he was host and studio guide). He also won the New York Art Directors Gold Medal twice for his work on television commercials.

He went to work for John Hubley's new studio Storyboard Films as a film director and story adapter for about six months but found little creative work to accomplish. In early 1956, Deitch left Storyboard Films to move to the position of creative advisor for Robert Lawrence Productions, a commercial film studio. United Features Syndicate had also given him a contract for his daily and Sunday comic strip, *Terr'ble Thompson!* which he was only able to maintain for a year, due to the increasing demands of his animation work. After being with Robert Lawrence Productions for just two weeks CBS executive Newt Schwin visited his office and offered Deitch the Terrytoons job.

Deitch didn't know why CBS had come to him with the offer, and he certainly didn't ask. Deitch considered it a dream position to remake one of the world's most recognizable animation studios into the best. Although in Deitch's own opinion it turned out to be his greatest failure, while at the studio he created his most famous cartoon character, Tom Terrific. It was the CBS name and image that drew Deitch to take up the offer to join Terrytoons. One of his first jobs after World War Two was the previously mentioned assistant art director position at CBS Radio in Hollywood. Deitch noted that they had a magnificently modern building, and the highest graphic standards in the business, guided by their great art director, William Golden, designer of the famous CBS-eye logo. Deitch was proud to work for CBS. He had always held them in awe.

What Deitch did not know was that Bill Weiss had a tenure contract with CBS and that the executive producer had little love for UPA style animation. Weiss had the job of juggling the Terrytoons cartoons from the Terry studio into weekly kiddie

279

TERRYTOONS: The Story of Paul Terry and His Classic Cartoon Factory

shows on CBS-TV. Deitch was given the golden job of reshaping CBS-Terrytoons into his vision of a winning cartoon studio. Deitch had complete freedom to reinvent Terrytoons, to make a creative renaissance. There were 18 CinemaScope cartoons to produce each year for 20th Century-Fox, and CBS would use the cartoons as their source for television programming. While Deitch wanted to invest the company's money in first-class animation projects that would in time raise the Terrytoons image, Weiss was simply packaging the old library into CBS television programming. This was easy and quick money.

When Deitch was first recruited by CBS, the executives delayed as long as possible taking him out to the Terrytoons studio, until they felt sure he would accept the job. Deitch felt CBS thought he would be dismayed, and turned off when he finally was introduced to Bill Weiss. When Deitch was introduced to Weiss immediately the new director was disappointed with the executive producer finding him crude, cultureless, and bitter at feeling Terry had left him without financial recompense for years of service. Weiss told Deitch that Terry had promised him 10 percent but in fact he did not get a nickel. Weiss was bitter that Terry just took the money and ran. Connie Rasinski was another long-time employee of the studio who was promised a share of the sale proceeds and never received anything. Rasinski was rightly upset with Paul and he was not shy about discussing this betrayal for many years after Terry had left the studio.[2]

Schwin had downplayed Weiss's position, describing him as a "business manager" of minor importance, and that he would have CBS support continuously in weekly staff meetings, which Schwin would always attend. Deitch was only interested in the position if he had a secure written contract. However, he was informed that nobody had a contract at CBS, only later to find out that Weiss had a five-year contract with CBS. Terry had insisted on Weiss obtaining the contract as a condition of sale of the studio. Terry had made promises to Weiss that he would cut him in on a portion of the sale payment from CBS, and the contract was used by Terry to get out of his earlier verbal promise to Weiss. Since the sale was premised on the contract, to CBS executives the Weiss contract "did not count". In his enthusiasm for creating something great at CBS-Terrytoons, Deitch took the position without the security of a contract. This decision would cost him dearly.

Weiss was cleverly patching together cartoons to make each week's installment seem like a new show. This cost virtually nothing to get on the air, and the programs were getting amazingly good ratings for CBS. Meanwhile Deitch was creating 20th Century-Fox Cinemascope cartoons for an increasingly weakening theatrical market, with only a long-range hope of creating enough films to go onto television. So while Deitch was working feverishly trying to make a "renaissance", Weiss was taking the train each week to CBS headquarters in Manhattan, and making it clear to the executives just who was spending their money and who was making money for them.

Deitch felt he inherited a studio full of disgruntled, underpaid veterans who had been led to believe by Terry that when he eventually sold the studio they would all get a cut. According to Deitch, the morning the sale was announced, Tommy Morrison approached Terry asking him whether it was true that the studio had been sold. According to Deitch, Terry told Morrison that it was none of his business and walked out of the studio. Many artists felt that he would be firing them all, and they would be out in the cold. There was no champagne for Deitch's arrival. Nevertheless, Deitch informed everyone that he was not going to fire them. His desire was to reform them not release them. Deitch also insisted on giving the production staff the full screen credits they deserved, which Terry never done.

Deitch perceived Weiss to be a threat to his position. In fact, there was no love lost between both men. If Deitch had his way he would have gotten rid of Weiss almost immediately. After meeting the staff, Deitch's opinion of Terry as an animated film producer was negatively impacted. The animators told Deitch that in the early days Terry would go around the studio, from animator to animator, carrying a ruler. He would measure each animator's stack of drawings, and when the pile was high enough, he'd say,

Chapter 23 • A Studio in Transition

"That's enough, put a 'The End' sign on it!"

Deitch had the studio remodeled, and had work areas rebuilt to create a more ergonomically friendly atmosphere. The interior of the studio was configured like a huge auditorium. All the workers – animators, inbetweeners, inkers and painters, were all lined up in rows in one huge mass. Deitch found the studio dark and gloomy. CBS gave the studio money for renovations to their standards. Deitch had the place painted, and provided cubicles for the animators, and little rooms for the directors, so there would be a modicum of privacy. While not everyone was thrilled with the changes, they soon got used to it, and some expressed their appreciation to Deitch. Deitch also personally designed a new Terrytoons logo. The original Terry-Toons logo, with musical notes, was part of the studio's old image, and one of the first things Deitch did was to create a logo that would reflect a new vision and artistic approach. The design was a reference to the smiling, movie-screen-shaped Greek theater mask, with the word "Terrytoons" scribbled as its hair.

Shortly after Deitch's arrival, Terry showed up at the studio but did not take a look around at the new production facility. He invited Deitch out to lunch at his exclusive club driving him there in his big Cadillac. Over lunch, Terry suggested to Deitch that he should create a character based on Charles Lindbergh, who Terry considered one of the greatest heroes of all time. Deitch kept his thoughts to himself as he felt that

Fig. 23.2 – Gene Deitch drawing Tom Terrific, publicity photograph.

in the 1950s very few remembered Lindbergh except that his baby was kidnapped. Terry argued that the style and humor of the early part of the 20th century was still relevant and funny. Once again, Deitch disagreed with this assessment but kept his opinions to himself. Terry talked much about his new fortune, his last few years at the studio, and his future financial plans. After meeting with the former producer, Deitch's opinion of Terry both as a businessman and artist did not improve.

As Deitch's overriding goals were to reinvent Terrytoons, to create a new reputation, to win the support of the disgruntled staff, to revise, where practical, films in production, without interrupting workflow, and mainly to rebuild the story department, bringing in fresh talent such as Jules Feiffer, and Al Kouzel, to inspire Tommy Morrison, Larz Bourne, Eli Bauer, and others already on the story staff to venture into fresh territory. Deitch spent most of his time with the story staff in their department working on story and characters. He also hired new talent to inject new artistic approaches and fresh ideas including R. O. Blechman, Tod Dockstader, Ray Favata, Ralph Bakshi, Ernest Pintoff and others.

Eli Bauer (1928–1998) studied at the School of Industrial Art, New York, graduating in 1947, and later pursued advanced studies at the Art Students League in New York. His first job was with established cartoonist Harry Lampert. After nine months cleaning brushes and learning the business, Bauer left Lampert. He undertook art studio work (comic book filler artwork, brochure artwork) and was associate art director & designer, Demael Greeting Cards, 1953–1954. He then worked as a freelance artist for NBC doing television promotion artwork and also did work for major advertising art agencies on Madison Avenue. He soon began to do gag cartoons on a freelance basis.[3] He sold his first cartoon in

1949 to *American Magazine*, a women's publication similar to *Good Housekeeping*. The drawing, which earned Bauer a hefty $90, showed a bride working in a kissing booth at her own wedding. In the caption she was explaining to her husband that the venture would help them make the down payment on a house.[4]

Bauer started selling other cartoons to *Collier's, American Magazine, Saturday Review* followed by *Playboy, Omni, The Saturday Evening Post, Penthouse, Punch, Park East, American, 1,000 Jokes* and *National Lampoon*, among many other publications. He also created the comic strips *Kermit the Hermit, Norman*, and *Don Patrol*.[5] Bauer was a comic book artist for DC Comics and Fawcett Publications. He started in animation for television spots working as a story man and layout designer for Ray Patin Productions on Sunset Boulevard, Hollywood, California, 1956–1957. While in California, he was encouraged by animation legend Art Babbitt to pursue a career in animation. After being hired, Bauer worked as a story designer and layout artist, CBS-Terrytoons, 1957–1967. His first job was doing layout and design on the *Tom Terrific* series working under project head Tom Golden.

At the age of five Jules Feiffer won a gold medal in an art contest inspiring him to pursue an artistic career. After high school he enrolled at the Art Students League of New York in 1946 and attended drawing classes at Pratt Institute in Brooklyn from 1947–1948 and 1949–1951.

From 1949 to 1951 Feiffer also drew a Sunday cartoon-page feature called *Clifford*, which ran in six newspapers. Beginning in 1951 Feiffer served two years in the Signal Corps spending his recreational periods drawing anti-military cartoons and during this time developed the character of Munro, the four-year-old boy drafted by mistake, into the Army. He turned out a book of cartoons called *Sick, Sick, Sick*. Feiffer's *Sick, Sick, Sick*, subtitled *A Guide to Non-confident Munro* was later renamed simply *Feiffer*.[6]

His cartoon strip, *Feiffer*, appeared in the *Village Voice* from 1956 to 1997. Feiffer's cartoon featured monologues or dialogues revealing the speakers' psychological or sexual angst using from six to eight comic strip panels. Robert Hall syndicated the strip in 1960. While at Terrytoons he completed design and layout work on a number of characters (Foofle, John Doormat). In 1961, the cartoon *Munro* (1960), produced by Rembrandt Films and written by Feiffer, was awarded the best short-subject cartoon by the Academy of Motion Picture Arts and Sciences. Feiffer's other animation credits included writing the scripts for Rembrandt's *The Nudnik Show* (1991) series and the songs for Bill Plympton's *Boomtown* (1985).[7]

Under Deitch's supervision and direction, the studio created a number of innovative cartoon characters such as John Doormat, Clint Clobber, Foofle, Sidney the Elephant, and Gaston Le Crayon. *Topsy TV* (January 1957) was the first of four John Doormat cartoons; also the first Terrytoons produced under Gene Deitch's supervision. John Doormat was developed from a new character the studio was already working on named "John Doe", a harassed husband; a completely stock character. Feeling the name "John Doe", meaning the average man, was not copyrightable, too generic, and didn't say anything to indicate his character, a browbeaten husband, Deitch changed the name to John Doormat.

Al Kouzel (1923–1990) created a new model, and directed two of the shorts. Kouzel graduated from the University of California Los Angeles with a M.S. degree in art history and illustration. At UCLA, he produced several award winning films and then he began his career in animation. He started working for Transfilm under animation department head Jack Zander animating television commercial advertisements. He then left Transfilm and worked as a junior animator at a studio operated by ex-Disney animator Lars Calonius. Calonius ran a small highly productive operation hiring people when needed and letting them go during slack season and avoiding high overhead items. During a periodic layoff at Calonius' studio, Kouzel produced several short films he had been planning to produce since his time at UCLA. He took these films to Deitch who had just been hired as the creative director at Terrytoons. He started working for Terrytoons under Deitch in 1958 as a color coordinator to give the animated shorts a new look. He was moved into doing

Chapter 23 • A Studio in Transition

Fig. 23.3 – Larz Bourne at a story meeting.

layouts and character design and eventually directing.[8]

At CBS-Terrytoons, Kouzel is credited with creating the final model for the John Doormat character and directing what Deitch considered the best film of the series, *Another Day, Another Doormat* (March 1959). He also worked on and directed *The Fabulous Firework Family* (August 1959), a cartoon adaptation of a story by magazine art director, children's book author and illustrator, painter, and storyboard artist James Flora (1914–1998). The animated cartoon faithfully transfers Flora's story of Pepito, Amelia, and their mother and father, titled the "Fabulous Firework Family" because they make the finest fireworks in their Mexican village, into the animated medium. They've been asked to create a grand fireworks display to honor the village's patron saint. In brilliant animation, full of color and excitement, Kouzel perfectly captures the wonders of feast day and a glorious fireworks display.

In *Topsy TV*, directed by Connie Rasinski, John Doormat is addicted to television. His wife Jane does her best to keep him from watching including blowing up the television but John has other sets hidden around his home which he takes great satisfaction in hiding from his spouse. He ends staying up late to watch television. On the way back to work the next morning he falls asleep on the way to the bus. *Dustcap Doormat* (June 1958), directed by Al Kouzel, has John being given advice from his neighbor to be more assertive and not to do anymore housework. John's wife ends up clobbering her husband for his unwillingness to assist in the household chores as well as walloping the nosy, troublemaking, hypocritical neighbor. In *Another Day Another Doormat*, directed by Kouzel, John is a raging bull when he returns a defective pipe back to the department store but becomes weak and whiny when in the presence of his wife. This series was a delightful and quirky look at your typical henpecked husband, a subject that has been in some form of entertainment since the dawn of time.

Clint Clobber, named De Witt Clinton Clobber, was an overweight apartment house superintendent, who beneath his grouchy exterior was a man passionate about his job and his shabby apartment house. Deitch made a special Terrytoons promotional film with the character. Doug Moye's booming voice was the inspiration for the character. The story department began to develop and deepen the character. Recording sessions for the new Clobber films proved that even with his funny deep voice, Doug Moye did not have the acting talent to provide the emotion the character required, so Deitch brought in his old friend and colleague Allen Swift to take over the voice.

Swift's acting talents and voice artistry was crucial to the success of Deitch's cartoons. As a grade school student, Allen Swift (1924–2010), born Ira Stadlen, would mimic other school teachers and instead of being reprimanded for his actions he was encouraged to imitate the other instructors. After World War II, he appeared on radio serials (*Gangbusters*; *Casey, Crime Photographer*). He worked as a stand-up comedian and magician, appearing in nightclubs and in comedy sketches on *The Bob Hope Show* and Milton Berle's *Texaco Star Theater*. His earliest

283

television appearance was on the *Robert Q. Lewis TV Show*, c. 1950–1953. He began his career as a vocal artist portraying a talking flashlight battery for a 1954 television commercial. During his career Swift worked on more than 30,000 television and radio commercials for products such as Hostess Twinkies and Ho Hos, Eveready (as the battery), Vita's Beloved Herring Maven, and Drano (as a toilet plunger). He portrayed over 50 characters on the *Howdy Doody Show* including the voice of Howdy Doody. He was Captain Allen Swift (host), *Popeye* (cartoon show), WPIX-TV (New York City), 1956–1960. He is probably most famous for providing cartoon voices on *King Leonardo and His Short Subjects* (1960) (voices of Odie Colognie, Itchy Brother, Tooter the Turtle), *Tennessee Tuxedo and His Tales*, 1963 (voice of Tooter the Turtle), *Underdog*, 1964 (voices of Simon Bar-Sinister, Riff-Raff, Goggle the Zok Man, Odie, Itchy Brother, and others), and *Tom and Jerry*, 1965 (entire cast).[9]

There were seven Clobber shorts produced for the series, most of them revolving around a problem Clobber has to correct while on duty as a superintendent. The first in the series was *Clint Clobber's Cat* (July 1957). In the short a nearsighted old lady thinks a dog that has taken refuge in her apartment is a cat and feeds it. The dog realizes he has it good so he behaves like a cat, even meowing. Clobber wants the dog to leave as no pets are allowed in the apartment but when the old lady begins to weep after Clobber grabs the mutt, he has a change of heart and returns the "cat" to her. In *Camp Clobber* (July 1958), an old general in Apartment 2A is blowing his bugle keeping the tenants awake. Clobber hands the general an old newspaper about the 1917 mobilization and the soldier heads off to war in his tank. *Signed, Sealed and Clobbered* (November 1958) has Clobber becoming mixed up as "Clown Clobber" in a trained seal act headed by "Happy Ed".

Old Mother Clobber (September 1958) has Clobber babysitting a talkative and destructive girl Penelope who ends up causing enough damage to convince her parents when returning to the building not to live in the run-down apartment. *Clobber's Ballet Ache* (January 1959) has Clobber offering his attic to the "The Champ" to train for his boxing match but the current tenant, a ballet dancer, knocks out the boxing title holder by using fancy footwork. In *Flamboyant Arms* (April 28, 1959), Mr. Flamboyant, the owner of the apartment, phones Clobber and informs him of an upcoming inspection. However, Clobber's hasty clean-up attempts only cause damage to the apartment. When an awning under the weight of a build-up of water collapses on Mr. Flamboyant causing his suit to shrink, Clobber threatens to quit until he hears the tinkling chandelier calling his name and hears the water hissing and crying and decides to stay.

Gene Deitch had the reputation around the studio as a clumsy, arm-waving enthusiast, dangerous to be near. When he entered a directors' room each morning for discussion, he would automatically move his coffee cup out of harm's way. When some important visitors were coming to visit, Deitch decided to wear a necktie to work, and while leaning over the moviola, his tie became threaded into the sprocket wheel, yanking his head downward and almost knocking his teeth out. This event was amusing and startling enough to get him started on a disaster-prone character. Foofle, Deitch's original character, was born from this ineptness, as well as the inspiration from a long line of pantomime, loser-type characters.

Eli Bauer refined Deitch's original sketches of Foofle. Years later, in Prague, he redeveloped the idea for Paramount, and called his new character Nudnik. Deitch made 12 episodes for Paramount theatrical release. The first one was nominated for an Oscar®. For CBS-Terrytoons, Deitch supervised the production of three Foofle animated cartoons. *Foofle's Train Ride* (May 24, 1959) has the unlucky character taking a scenic train ride and enduring a series of unfortunate events aboard the train. *Foofle's Picnic* (March 1960) features Foofle involved in some picnic misadventures. He gets caught up in a hammock, loses his lunch in the river, has his inner tube explode, and ends up going over the waterfall. *The Wayward Hat* (July 1960) has the character chasing after his new hat blown away by a gust of wind. After falling victim to a series of calamities he finally retrieves his hat only to discover it has been damaged.

The cartoon character Gaston Le Crayon was Deitch's parody on an

Chapter 23 • A Studio in Transition

Fig. 23.4 – Tom Morrison (left) and Robert Kuwahara (right).

exuberant, flamboyant, but untalented French artist. Eli Bauer drew the ultimate model for him. Deitch originally wanted to call him "Gaston le Garbage", pronounced as a French word, "Gar-BAZH", but Bill Weiss rejected the name. There were five shorts produced from the series. These cartoons not only poked fun at the flamboyant world of painters and fine artists but also satirized the world of modern art. The first in the series, *Gaston is Here* (May 1957) has Gaston intruding on an Alfred Hitchcock movie set. Believing the actors are in trouble, Gaston uses his paint brush to paint objects that come to life while exclaiming "Have no fear, Gaston is here". His good intentions only end up ruining the shoots causing the director to send a guided missile at him. A couple hires Gaston to babysit in *Gaston's Baby* (March 1958) while they go to a fancy dress party. As the husband is dressed as a baby, Gaston thinks he must paint his portrait and won't let him leave for the party.

Wanting to leave America and return home, Gaston stows away aboard a French luxury liner in *Gaston Go Home* (May 1958). The artist uses his paintbrush to try and keep one step ahead of the captain intent on throwing him overboard. In *Gaston's Easel Life* (October 1958) the artist's easel is splashed with motor oil from a passing automobile causing a rich art patron to admire the painting and ask Gaston to paint another; a feat he cannot accomplish.

Gaston's Mama Lisa (June 1959) features the famous Da Vinci painting stolen by two thieves. Gaston thinks he painted the portrait in his sleep but is unable to sell the painting, even for 50 cents.

Another new talent Deitch recruited was Ernie Pintoff (1931–2002) who joined the studio in 1957. Pintoff was educated at Syracuse University majoring in art. He started out as a jazz trumpeter and later studied painting and design for two years at Michigan State University graduating with a Master of Fine Arts degree in 1953 and eventually going to teach at the university (art history and studio courses) for three years. While waiting for a teaching position at

285

the University of Southern California, Pintoff was hired at Disney as an inbetweener but left after a few days because he was more interested in the contemporary look of UPA films. He was hired by UPA in 1955 as an apprentice inbetweener. Almost immediately he became a co-director with John Whitney on *The Gerald McBoing Boing Show*, the first animated program made especially for network television. Over the next year Whitney and Pintoff produced a number of inventive and amusing animated shorts for the show such as *Aquarium, Lion Hunt, Blues Pattern, Fight On For Old* and *Performing Painter*. Pintoff worked at UPA Hollywood on *The Gerald McBoing Boing Show* until the program folded.[10]

Pintoff was a very unique character in the Terrytoons studio. He had little to talk about with the majority of the old guard, and pretty much kept to himself in his little director's cubicle. He always had his trumpet with him at work, and would play the blues, while waiting for inspiration. Deitch didn't care how crazy or other-worldly he seemed to the older animators. What was important to Deitch was the new breath of creativity he brought to the place. One animator with whom he bonded, and who caught the challenge Ernie presented was Jim Tyer.

At CBS-Terrytoons, Pintoff got started almost immediately on the Flebus character who he named "Willy", but Deitch didn't think that name funny enough. On his way to work one day Deitch heard a talk on his car radio about the disease, phlebitis. Never having suffered from the pain of that ailment, Deitch thought the word was funny, and suggested the name Flebus as an amusing and original non-sequiter name. Pintoff suddenly left the studio while the film was still in the early pencil test stage, so Deitch had to take over and finish it according to the color models Pintoff had left. Deitch was saddened when Pintoff suddenly decided to leave. Although Weiss hated the character Deitch took over the Flebus project and was determined to see it brought to completion just as Pintoff had laid it out. Jim Tyer did the key animation on Flebus.

Flebus (August 1957) tells the story of the titled character, a man who never had any problems making friends. "Everybody likes Flebus". When he meets Rudolph and offers him an ice cream cone but is told that he is not interested in being his friend, Flebus offers him a flower but achieves the same response. When he offers Rudolph a fish, he gets walloped. Unable to win Rudolph's affections, Flebus can't sleep at night, takes pills and eventually goes to see a psychiatrist and is told he is neurotic. Rudolph, unhappy with the way he treated Flebus, goes to the same psychiatrist and is also told he is neurotic. When Flebus and Rudolph both admit to each other that they are neurotic their shared disorder bonds the two characters and they become friends forever.

The Terrytoons short won first prize at the San Francisco Film Festival, 1958, and "Best Animated Film", Brussels World's Fair, 1958. Deitch considers the short to be one of the landmark productions at CBS-Terrytoons (1957). Pintoff left in 1958 to start a studio with Robert Lawrence who at the time had one of the largest commercial studios in the city and worked on television commercials. After a few months Pintoff left Lawrence and set up his own animation studio, Pintoff Productions, where he created ads for companies. He is most famous for his animated shorts the Oscar®-nominated *The Violinist* (1959), *The Interview* (1959), and the Academy Award winning *The Critic* (1963).[11]

At the time, CinemaScope seemed to be the current rage in the movie industry. CinemaScope, an anamorphic lens series, was used for shooting wide screen movies from 1953 to 1967 and was created in 1953, by the president of 20th Century-Fox, Spyros P. Skouras. The system marked the beginning of the modern anamorphic format in both principal photography and movie projection. Terrytoons had been releasing a few cartoons in CinemaScope since 1955 and would release all of their cartoons in the format in 1958 and 1959. They would continue releasing CinemaScope cartoons until the end of 1963.

After Deitch started working with this format he was faced with some depressing truths in that his goals and those of CBS and 20th Century-Fox, were all at odds. CBS was primarily interested in the vast cartoon library to fill their small screen programming. CBS wanted cartoons to be produced that could run on TV. So they

Chapter 23 • A Studio in Transition

insisted that all the essential action be within the central portion of the screen – within the limited TV field – and that the wide sides of the screen could be cut off without losing the essential action. 20th Century-Fox was the inventor of CinemaScope and insisted henceforth that all Terrytoons should be produced in that format, and thus give their cartoons a box office edge, promoting the CinemaScope format and thus 20th Century-Fox. Deitch wanted to raise the level of artistic creativity. He wanted to exploit the entire wide screen area to bring an added dimension to movie cartoons, and to widen their effect.

These three divergent goals could not be successfully reconciled but it did not stop Deitch from trying. The creative benefits of a very wide screen were markedly diminished by the limitations posed by the television field because Deitch could not use the most fundamental of dramatic camera moves, rotating angle shots. The moment he would rotate the camera, the wide edges of the animation field would swing out of camera range. The cameramen could only rotate the camera at very small field sizes where the production crew would lose image sharpness. So basically, the studio could only handle straight-on shots. Another limitation was the same as in live-action CinemaScope movies. The very wide screen favored long shots, and made close ups jarring. It drastically limited the most basic element of the craft: film editing. Deitch had to stay with

Fig. 23.5 – John Gentilella, animator, 1957.

longer running shots, with action within the frame, and limit cuts and close-ups. In Deitch's opinion, with all the conflicting demands of TV and distributors, CinemaScope was more a hindrance than a blessing.

In spite of all this, he did his best to fight it. He was determined to sneak as much benefit as he could from the CinemaScope format he was stuck with. There were just two films that gave Deitch a chance to really exploit the wide screen format, the Dinky Duck film, *It's a Living* (February 1958) and the R. O. Blechman story, *The Juggler of Our Lady* (April 1958). Dinky Duck was the only standard Terrytoons character that Deitch ever used, and just that one time. With the story that Tommy Morrison, the story staff and Deitch created, the studio had a chance to do a satire on the old Terrytoons shtick, and to call direct attention to the CinemaScope screen shape. The short begins with Dinky being unhappy about being chased (as he is in the Terry cartoons) by a crocodile so he leaves the cartoon screen into the audience and walks into a world of the Deitch style UPA design cartoon format. Dinky exclaims "I should have quit years ago". After being given a screen test, he signs a movie contract but is put through an assortment of on-screen travails. Unable to accept the abuse, he decides to return to the theater and enter the on-screen cartoon to continue to be chased by the crocodile exclaiming, "It's a Living".

After reviewing R. O. Blechman's little book, *The Juggler of Our Lady*, with every word, including the title and copyright notice hand written in Bob's tiny and shaky style, Deitch thought that here was the greatest opportunity he would ever have to really work the CinemaScope format, playing off those tiny nervously scribbled figures against the vast expanse of that very wide screen. Fortunately, he was able to convince Bill Weiss of the value of such a film to the studio's image, as well as persuade Blechman to adapt and design his book for the animated short.

Blechman was terrified that the studio would convert his little juggler into Mighty Mouse. Blechman made two conditions for his participation in the project: he was to act as director and he could choose his composer.[12] Deitch was on the phone with Blechman for nearly a year trying to convince Blechman to participate and allow the studio to use his story. The secret to his participation was Al Kouzel. Deitch knew that Kouzel could get Bob Blechman's images unscathed onto the big screen. Al was a talented and dedicated artist who worked with Deitch for many years in many locations, even in Prague. He was able to earn Bob's confidence that he would faithfully recreate Blechman's work[13] and that long-time Terrytoons musical director, Phil Scheib, would compose wonderfully appropriate music for the cartoon. It was a prodigious undertaking, and Bob himself came into the studio to work with Kouzel on the layouts. Deitch monitored and guided the visual staging development each day. Deitch knew this had to work and bring the studio needed prestige, or he would be finished immediately.

Deitch spent many hours working with Scheib and assuring him that he would be allowed to break out of the restrictions he had been working with for so long. According to Deitch, Terry had insisted that if he was paying for a 30-piece orchestra, he wanted every musician to be playing all the time. The result was some wacky, over busy arrangements. As Scheib was a former piano player for silent movie theaters, he had developed a heavy-handed anachronistic output. When allowed to break out of his routine, Scheib surprised Deitch who found him to be a great musician who could create spare, funny, and lovely film scores. Deitch considers Scheib's *Juggler* music to be one of the finest scores used in his animated productions, creating a wonderful medieval woodwind quintet. Bob Blechman gives much of the credit for the success of the cartoon short to Scheib, music he termed "glorious".[14]

Deitch considers his greatest inspiration for the film was in the choice of Boris Karloff as the narrator. Deitch was jeered at for choosing this typecast movie monster for such a delicate story as "The Juggler", but he had a hunch from hearing him speak on the radio, and realizing that he was actually a gentle and cultured Englishman. He immediately felt that he was the one, and when Deitch contacted him, Karloff was eager to do it, and breakout of his stereotyped monster image.

The film's full title was *The Juggler of Our Lady: A Medieval Legend* and was directed by Kouzel. Blechman based his book on *Le Jongleur de Notre Dame*, a religious miracle story by the French author Anatole France, published in 1892 and based on an old medieval legend. It tells the story of a juggler turned monk who has no gift to offer a statue of the Virgin Mary except for his ability to juggle well. Upon doing so, he is accused of blasphemy by the other monks, but the statue comes to life and blesses the juggler. In the cartoon, also set in medieval times, Candlebert, a juggler, has little success in attracting attention to his juggling; he puts on a hair shirt and becomes an ascetic, but attracts only a few other ascetics. Finally, in desperation, he becomes a monk. He visits the other monks, who all glorify the Lady with their skills: composing, cooking, painting, and sculpture. He tries helping them, but is unsuccessful. A festival is held for the Lady, and each of the monks offers his gift, but the juggler has nothing. Frustrated, he juggles for her, all night, alone and collapses in exhaustion. Inspired by Candlebert's gift, all the monks become jugglers. The film was a success with the critics and was nominated for a BAFTA award in 1959.

During his first year at the studio,

Chapter 23 • A Studio in Transition

Deitch got a call from the office of CBS's *Captain Kangaroo* show. They wanted a new animated serial created for the show, and they needed the product quickly. Deitch was invited to have lunch with Bob Keeshan, (Captain Kangaroo), and his business manager, Marvin Josephson, at the posh Plaza Hotel in Manhattan. Deitch was surprised to see that the "old" Captain was a crew cut young man of 31. While Deitch was still creative director at UPA he was writing and drawing a daily and Sunday comic strip for United Features Syndicate on the side, titled, *Terr'ble Thompson!* The strip was about a little boy who had his "World Heddquarters" in a tree house, and who traveled back in time and was called upon by the great figures of world history to help them solve various desperate problems. Deitch had to give up his comic strip just before he joined Terrytoons, but he still owned the copyright. Deitch decided to use the strip as a basis for an animated serial, assuming he would be there forever. He reworked it of course to fit the needs of animation, with Terr'ble Thompson becoming Tom Terrific.

In adapting the strip to animated film, a great deal of simplifying was necessary, and also, a purely animation device. Whereas Terr'ble Thompson was an adventurous little boy, who just ran energetically into situations that needed to be saved, Deitch felt that Tom Terrific, who also lived in a treehouse, needed to have something magic about him, which would take advantage of the possibilities of animation.

Fig. 23.6 – Tom Terrific and Mighty Manfred, animation cel.

Deitch was always fascinated with metamorphosis, so he decided that Tom had the ability to quickly change his shape into any kind of form that could solve the problem at hand. Tom transformed himself into anything he wanted thanks to his magic, funnel-shaped "thinking cap", which also enhanced his intelligence. He also gave him a sidekick he had not yet introduced into the comic strip, Mighty Manfred the Wonder Dog, an anti-hero who was neither mighty nor wondrous, except in the eyes of his loving master. Tom gave Manfred credit for every idea that he himself thought of. Manfred was only interested in food and sleep. He had an arch-foe named Crabby Appleton, whose motto was, "I'm rotten to the core!" Other foes included Mr. Instant, the Instant Thing King, Captain Kidney Bean, Sweet Tooth Sam, the Candy Bandit and Isotope Feeney, The Meany.

The cost and production time restrictions were formidable but he wanted to use as much real animation as possible, taking advantage of the large Terrytoons staff of animators. To reduce production costs, Deitch's solution was to eliminate opaquing the cels, letting the characters be transparent, and making the backgrounds simple enough so it wouldn't matter. He wanted to get the greatest possible dynamics out of the soundtrack – mainly the voices, as he also had to keep the music to a minimum. The choice was the use of an accordion, (which Deitch hated, but it gave the cartoons a mini-orchestral sound). There were plenty of sound effects and probably for the first time in TV animation, a Trinidadian steel drum.

He then worked out every imaginable way to stretch out the animation time. With Tommy Morrison, he created a *Tom Terrific* song opening, to start off each episode. Taking a cue from the old Saturday movie serials, at the end of each episode, he created teaser previews, and at the beginning of each following episode, he made recaps of what happened yesterday. The previews and recaps were printed as negatives to separate them from the actual story sections. With all of these gimmicks, Deitch was able to almost double the effective

289

playing time of most of the animation. Deitch was disappointed that he couldn't do *Tom Terrific* in color. The *Captain Kangaroo* show was still in black & white, and no one seemed willing to look ahead during the mid-1950s.

Tom Terrific ran in a series of five-minute cartoons created specifically for the *Captain Kangaroo* show from 1957 to 1959, and was rerun on *Kangaroo* for years thereafter. For several years after 1962, *Tom Terrific* would be broadcast every other week, alternating with *Lariat Sam*, another Terrytoons creation. There were 26 stories produced, the first 13 filmed in 1957, the remaining 13 filmed in 1958. Each story was split into five parts for broadcast each weekday morning. During the years that *Captain Kangaroo* was also broadcast on Saturday mornings, the episodes would be re-edited into two parts (with cliffhangers and recaps from the daily versions eliminated), the first part broadcast during the first half-hour, the conclusion during the second half-hour. All the voices were performed by Lionel Wilson. *Terrific* was ranked #32 by *TV Guide* magazine among its "50 Greatest TV Cartoon Characters".

Deitch's other theatrical cartoon series featured Sidney the Elephant. Deitch assigned Jim Tyer to work on an idea for a new series starring a "neurotic elephant" character. Deitch enjoyed working with Jim Tyer who did amazing things with Sidney, Tom Terrific, and Flebus. Deitch considered his animation as sometimes being weird, but it was always inventive, and always funny. For Deitch, Tyer was not only permitted to draw and animate in his wildest fashion, but was actually encouraged to. He could take his animation as far as he wanted with Deitch's blessing.

Sidney was originally the "sick, sick, sick" elephant character in a *Tom Terrific* episode. Deitch had drawn an elephant with a fat trunk, that he sucked on like an overgrown baby. Lionel Wilson, who did all the voices for Tom Terrific, had a funny Ed Wynn voice take-off for Sidney, and Deitch decided to make him a new Terrytoons character. The first in the series was *Sick, Sick Sidney* (August 1958). The cartoon concerns the efforts of a whiny and self-absorbed elephant, Sidney, who has become irritated by the jungle noises. Sidney tries to get captured by some hunters and taken back to civilization where he can get some peace and quiet and three square meals a day. Despite his best efforts, the hunters leave the jungle without Sidney leaving the poor elephant feeling alone and abandoned.

The next in the series was *Sidney's Family Tree* (December 1958). In this hilarious and inventive animated short, Sidney, 44-years-old and insecure, begins to complain that everyone in the jungle has a mom except for him. He starts to plead with various animal moms to take him as their child. The hippo and giraffe turn him down, but a monkey that drops a coconut on Sidney's head takes him in (though her husband isn't completely sold on the idea). The husband tries several times to get rid of Sidney, to no avail. Finally, a girl elephant walks by, and Sidney chases after her but then brings her home, asking if they can move in for a while. When the two elephants sit on a tree branch alongside their new monkey family, the branch breaks sending all four animals falling to the ground.

Sidney's Family Tree was nominated for an Oscar® in the "Best Short Subject, Cartoons" for 1958, the winner receiving the award at the 31st Academy Awards ceremony held on April 6, 1959 at the Pantages Theatre in Hollywood, California. This would be Terrytoons fourth and last Oscar® nomination. The competition that year was weak, just two other nominees, *Knighty Knight Bugs*, a fairly mediocre Bugs Bunny Warner Bros. cartoon directed by Friz Freleng and produced by John W. Burton, and certainly not one considered by critics to be one of Bugs' more memorable and entertaining cartoons, which honors would go (according to Jerry Beck's *50 Greatest Cartoons*[15]) to such cartoons as *What's Opera, Doc?* (1957), *Rabbit of Seville* (1950), *Rabbit Seasoning* (1952), *Ali Baba Bunny* (1957), and *Little Red Riding Rabbit* (1944). Both *Ali Baba Bunny* and *What's Opera Doc* were not even nominated for an Oscar® the year before. The other nominee was *Paul Bunyan*, directed by Les Clark and produced by Walt Disney Productions, a likeable but not entirely memorable documentary on the famous giant lumberjack.

The morning after the nomination was announced, Bill Weiss was waiting for Deitch in the

Chapter 23 • A Studio in Transition

Terrytoons parking lot as he drove in to work. As Deitch got out of his car, Weiss strode up to him and said, "Gene, I want you to understand that if Sidney wins the Oscar®, I will be the one to pick it up!" Deitch could hardly restrain an ironic laugh. Weiss wanted to catch Deitch before he got inside the studio and received congratulations from the staff. After this incident, Deitch considered Weiss his enemy. In all fairness to both parties, it had been the practice in the animated cartoon category for the producer rather than the director to accept the coveted Oscar®. Weiss made the trip to Hollywood, California in March 1959, but it was Burton rather than Weiss who was awarded the coveted hardware.

Sidney would become Deitch's most successful Terrytoons theatrical character, with 19 films produced from 1958 to 1963, more shorts than were produced for Dinky Duck, and the same amount of Little Roquefort cartoons released by the studio. Much of the humor from the Sidney cartoons revolved around Sidney's neurotic behaviors and the trouble these behaviors cause his two friends Stanley the Lion, Cleo the Giraffe and the other jungle animals. In *Tusk, Tusk* (April 3, 1960) Sidney is worried he has no tusks so he creates ones and is captured by hunters. In *Hide and Go Sidney* (January 1960), he has no one to play with and befriends a couple of hungry vultures intent on eating him. In Sidney's eagerness to make friends, he ends up injuring the birds. In *Send Your Elephant to Camp* (July 4, 1962), Sidney does

Fig. 23.7 – Eli Bauer (left) and Jules Feiffer (right).

not want to go to summer camp and when he arrives he whines that he is lonely. When he is picked up by his friends to take him home he decides he likes the camp life after all. In *Banana Binge* (1961) Sidney has a banana habit he can't break which has him consuming most of the plantation owner's crop.

A familiar theme in the cartoons involves Sidney's attempts to achieve a goal or reach out to others, efforts that usually end up in disaster. In *Really Big Act* (1961), Sidney attempts to be accepted by the circus expedition but his acts flop and he scares off the leaders of the circus caravan. When he is captured by a lumberman in *Tree Spree* (1961) and forced to work in a lumber camp, he ends up destroying a saw mill. In *Driven to Extraction* (June 28, 1963), Sidney's efforts to help a rhino get rid of a troublesome horn only ends up injuring the rhino. In *Two Ton Baby Sitter* (September 4, 1960), Sidney starts a babysitting service but loses a pair of kookaburra birds as a result of his sneeze. The Sidney cartoons were some of the most entertaining shorts produced by the studio in the late 1950s and early 1960s.

In 1957, under Deitch CBS-Terrytoons released three one shot cartoons. *Gag Buster* released in March featured Spoofy (a small red fox). *A Bum Steer* introduced Beefy (a bull) and was also released in March. *The Bone Ranger* released in April starred Sniffer (a dog). *Gag Buster*, the best of the three shorts, has the fox as a sheriff in a western cartoon using a pencil to change the circumstances of the cartoon eventually capturing the outlaw. After drawing a beautiful girl to be his sweetheart, the newly created character runs off with the cuffed criminal. The second animated short concerns a small bull who rescues his dad during a bullfight from Panhandle Peter, the world's greatest bullslinger. In the latter cartoon, Sniffer pursues an elusive bone that he just can't sink his teeth into.

Deitch oversaw a long animated promotional film for CBS-TV at Terrytoons, titled *Depth Study* (1957), with design by Cliff Roberts, a brilliant graphic artist he discovered in Detroit, and brought with him to UPA New York. Deitch promised CBS a UPA-quality film, and was able to get the assignment for CBS-Terrytoons. To ensure the UPA look and sound, along with Cliff Roberts, Deitch brought in another UPA era colleague, Irwin Bazelon, to compose the music. The film's animation director was Ray Favata. After graduating from high school Favata was drafted into the United States Army serving in the Quartermaster Corps, 1942–1946. He was recruited to do some acting with the Special Services but with only one high school art course as training he ended up as the official camp cartoonist at Camp Lee, Virginia.

After being discharged from the military, he completed some freelance work for various studios producing commercials until he was given the opportunity in 1951 to do storyboards at Tempo Productions in New York City after the storyboard designer was forced to take an extended leave. Favata had never done storyboards and so was given a crash course and quickly adapted. At Tempo, Favata worked with animation director Bill Tytla whom he would later work with off and on for 10 years after Tytla started his own animation studio. Favata remained at Tempo for about a year [three] years until Hilberman was blacklisted in 1952 by the McCarthy investigation with help from evidence given at the hearings by Walt Disney. According to Favata, there was acrimony between Disney and the two founders of Tempo as both Hilberman and Schwartz had worked for Disney and were involved in the Disney strike. Favata was then hired at Academy Pictures, and also worked with Jordan Caldwell, another Terrytoons artist.

Many of the Terrytoons animators were unable to maintain the sophisticated shapes of Roberts' designs; the responsibility for fixing the animation fell on Favata's shoulders. Several of the more experienced Terrytoons animators took to Cliff's complex characters, and gave him some classy animation. The film's story was the post-war emergence of television as the prime advertising and sales medium. Deitch used the term "Bronze Age" in the story to symbolize the immediate post-war period. During World War II, discharged soldiers received a little bronze eagle honorable discharge lapel pin. Deitch considers the cartoon one of the best industrial animated shorts he produced.

In March or April 1958 Bill Weiss did not like the direction the studio was headed and decided to fire Deitch and bring back some of the old cartoon characters such as Mighty Mouse and Heckle and Jeckle. Weiss and CBS decided to put economics ahead of art and revert back to Terry's original idea of efficiently producing children's animation rather than Deitch's meticulous approach for each individual film. The firing should not have come as a surprise to Deitch. He made the mistake many young producers make in failing to recognize the important contributions of the senior crew. What Deitch had done was split the studio in two with the young artists loving Deitch's approach to animation while the older artists despising his new design aesthetics.[16] With Deitch out, good friend Tyer left on November 18 of that year. With Deitch gone, the studio was going "limited" the same way that Paramount had already gone. In fact, it looked like New York animators would be turning out limited animation from here on out.

At the time of Deitch's ousting in 1958, he had a brilliant serial being worked up by Jules Feiffer. It was about a group of tiny kids with large perceptions, forty years in advance of *The Rugrats*. Deitch was a great fan of ragtime music, and had a ragtime musical theme planned for them, so he named the serial after a Scott Joplin piece, *The Easy Winners*. Deitch considered the failure to produce the series as a great loss for the development of primetime TV animation. After leaving Terrytoons, Deitch was then hired by the New York Advertising firm

Chapter 23 • A Studio in Transition

of Cunningham & Walsh as an external creative consultant. His former business manager Marvin Josephson then helped Deitch set up his own studio, Gene Deitch Associates, Inc., in May 1958.

Notes

1. Biographical information on Gene Deitch and his time at CBS-Terrytoons from 1956 to 1958 was compiled from a press release ("Gene Deitch Named Creative Supervisor of Terrytoons", Press Information Release, CBS Television Network, 26 June 1956), as well as a completed questionnaire and some electronic correspondence found in the Terrytoons Collection, Victoria, B.C., Canada.

2. Ralph Bakshi, telephone interview by author (transcript), Kelowna, B.C., Canada, 25 March 1998, Terrytoons Collection, Victoria, B.C., 4; Arnie Levey, telephone interview by author (transcript), Kelowna, B.C., Canada, 19 October 1997, Terrytoons Collection, Victoria, B.C., 10.

3. Falk, *Who Was Who in American Art*; Walker and Janocha, *The National Cartoonists Society Album*; Erickson, *Television Cartoon Shows*.

4. Jules Feiffer, *Backing into Forward: A Memoir* (New York: Doubleday, 2010); "Aniforms Process Used by Best Foods", *Broadcasting*, v. 64, 1963; "A Look Back on the 'Golden Days'", *Herald-Statesman*, 5 January 1973, p. 8; Anne Anable, "4 Families: Life Dictates Style; For 4 Fashionable Families, Life Dictates Style", *New York Times*, 25 September 1977, Section New Jersey Weekly, p. 540.

5. Randall V. Berlage, "Mighty Mouse Saved Day for Studio", *Pittsburgh Press*, 11 April 1982, p. G6; "Eli Bauer", *News-Times, The* (Danbury, CT), 8 January 1998.

6. *Current Biography Yearbook*, 1961 edition (New York: H.W. Wilson Co., 1961).

7. Ian Herbert, ed., *Who's Who in the Theatre. A Biographical Record of the Contemporary Stage*, 17th edition (Detroit: Gale Research (also 15th and 16th editions); *Contemporary Authors, New Revision Series. A Bio-bibliographical Guide to Current Writers in Fiction, General Nonfiction, Poetry, Journalism, Drama, Motion Pictures, Television, and Other Fields*, volume 129 (Detroit: Thomson Gale, 2004) (also vol. 59 from New Revision Series); Thomas Riggs, ed., *Contemporary Dramatists*, sixth edition (Detroit: St. James Press, 1999 (also 5th (1993) edition)); *Encyclopedia of World Biography*, second edition, seventeen volumes (Detroit: Gale Research,1998); *Something about the Author. Facts and Pictures About Authors and Illustrators of Books for Young People*, volume 157 (Detroit: Thomson Gale, 2005) (also volume 111).

8. Obituaries: "Alfred Kouzel Dies; Film Cartoonist, 67", *New York Times*, 19 September 1990, p. B6; "Alfred Kouzel; Academy Award-Winning Cartoonist", *Los Angeles Times* (Southland Edition), 21 September 1990, p. 26; "Alfred Kouzel; Leading Cartoonist", *Los Angeles Times* (Home Edition), 25 September 1990, p. 24.

9. Myron Kandel, "Advertising: $300,000 a Year For a Voice", *New York Times*, 3 August 1962, p. 26; Marjorie Rubin, "Versatile Voice: Spokesman for Products Finds Success on TV His Method Local Boy", *New York Times*, 8 September 1963, p. X15; "If It Makes a Sound Al Swift Can Mimic It", *The Hartford Courant*, 22 October 1967, p. 48A; Jerry Buck, "Allen Swift: 'The Man of 1,000 Voices'", *The Hartford Courant*, 2 June 1968, p. 4J; "Mimic Completes His 45,000th Air Commercial", *The Hartford Courant*, 23 November 1969, p. 64A; Jerry Buck, "'Voices' Bring Him a Good Living", *Chicago Tribune*, 26 May 1968, p. f17; Mel Gussow, "Theater: 'Checking Out' Opens: A Situation Comedy About Dying by Allen Swift", *New York Times*, 15 September 1976, p. 53; A. Kent MacDougall, "Super Salesman: TV's King Con Cashes In on Golden Voice King Con Thrives on Anonymity as Ads Sell Competing Products", *Los Angeles Times*, 15 April 1978, p. 1. Allen Swift's obituary was published in the *New York Times*, 28 April 2010, p. B18.

10. *Contemporary Authors. A Bio-bibliographical Guide to Current Writers in Fiction, General Nonfiction, Poetry, Journalism, Drama, Motion Pictures, Television, and Other Fields*, volume 203 (Detroit: Gale Group, 2003) (entries also in volumes 17–20, 1st revision and volume 12); Adam Abraham, *When Magoo Flew: The Rise and Fall of Animation Studio UPA* (Middletown, Conn.: Wesleyan University Press, 2012); Ernest Pintoff, *Animation 101* (Studio City, CA : M. Wiese Productions, 1999); Ernest Pintoff, *Directing 101* (Studio City, CA : M. Wiese Productions, 1998); Amid Amidi, *Cartoon Modern: Style and Design in Fifties Animation* (San Francisco: Chronicle Books, 2006); Eugene Archer, "At Home With Ernest Pintoff's 'Fireman'", *New York Times*, 3 May 1964, p. X9; Louis Chapin, "Middleman, Fireman", *The Christian Science Monitor*, 10 August 1965, p. 2.

11. Obituaries: "Ernest Pintoff, 70, Director Who Won an Oscar for Animated Film", *New York Times*, 4 February 2002, p. B7; "Ernest Pintoff, 70; Animator Won Oscar", *Los Angeles Times*, 7 February 2002.

12. R. O. Blechman, letter to author, 10 September 1995, 2.

13. Blechman was given the credit as "Consultant Director".

14. R. O. Blechman, letter to author, 10 September 1995, 3.

15. Beck, *The 50 Greatest Cartoons*.

16. Bakshi, interview, 4.

Chapter 24

A New Cast of Characters: Hashimoto Mouse, Hector Heathcote, Deputy Dawg, Luno, and Astronut, 1959–1964

The decision to return to producing animated shorts starring the cartoon characters that established the studio as a major player in theatrical animation during the 1940s and 1950s was welcomed by many of the veterans on staff. Conversely, the artists that Deitch had brought on board who were looking to the studio as a "UPA New Rochelle" were less than thrilled by the decision, some finding the move to be a step back. While Weiss opted to go back to producing cartoons starring established stars, he chose to only produce cartoons featuring their most famous creations, Mighty Mouse and Heckle and Jeckle, and then only infrequently. Only three Mighty Mouse and nine Heckle and Jeckle cartoons were produced by CBS-Terrytoons after Terry had left the studio.

Two of the three Mighty Mouse cartoons had a space age theme, a popular topic in the late 1950s and early 1960s. In *Outer Space Visitor* (November 1959) the mice of Cheeseville are having a Saturday night barn dance when they receive a visit from a little baby robot (complete with diapers!) from outer space who looks and sounds harmless until a scientist uses a "fish and monster gurgle interpreting machine" to translate the little character's language, and finds out that his father is planning to invade the earth and destroy Cheeseville. When the creature's father comes looking for him, he is 20 feet tall, 10 feet wide and breathes fire. Mighty Mouse is called upon to solve the mystery of why children all over the world are vanishing in *The Mysterious Package* (January 1961 [December 15, 1961]). Turns out the children are receiving space helmets that when worn are used to attract the youngsters to a castle on a distant planet.

In *Cat Alarm* (December 31, 1961) the mice of Cheeseville protect themselves with an alarm that warns them of the approach of their feline foes. The cats plot to capture the mice by faking a news broadcast to Mighty Mouse that the Mouseville dam has burst and a gigantic flood is headed for the town. Flying back to Mouseville from a Florida beach, Mighty Mouse warns the populace of the approaching doom and sends the mice to a cave where the cats trap them. When he becomes aware of the deception, Mighty Mouse flies to the cats' mountain hideout where he clobbers the felines and traps them inside their own mountaintop hideout.

The three Mighty Mouse cartoons lacked the special charm and artistic craftsmanship found in the shorts produced during the Terry years. Gone were Oil Can Harry, Pearl Pureheart, the colorful villains (e.g. Pinhead Schlabotka), the witty dialogue between characters, and the corny yet strangely endearing operetta scores of Phil Scheib. Just as important, missing were the lush, colorful, decorative and richly detailed backgrounds of Craig, Zaffo, and Vita. The last member of the Terrytoons background department from the 1940s, Bill

Chapter 24 • A New Cast of Characters

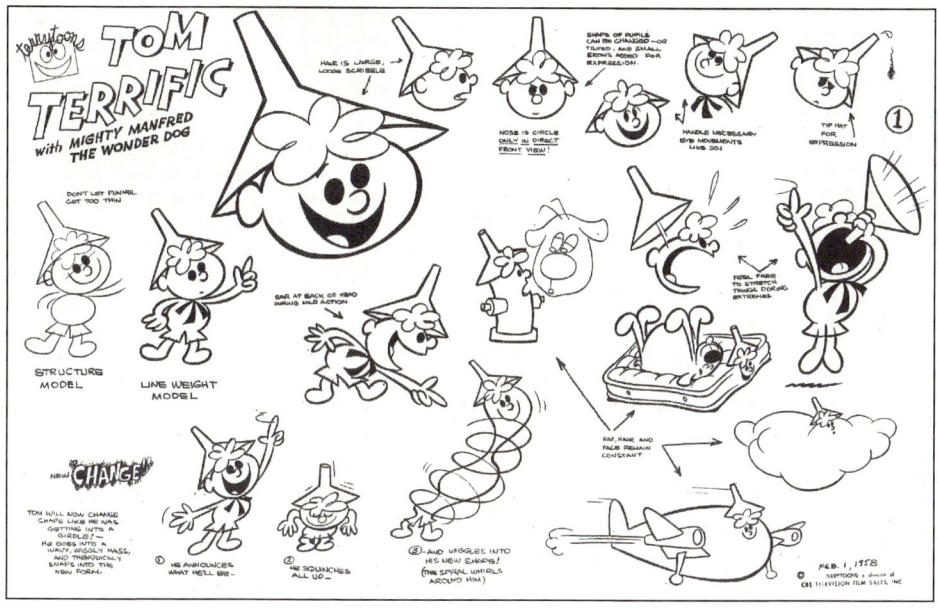

Fig. 24.1 – Model sheet - Tom Terrific.

Hilliker, had retired in 1959. Johnny Zago and Bill Focht were the key background artists for CBS-Terrytoons during the late 1950s and 1960s. Their work was competently rendered but minimalist in design keeping with the limited animation of the television age.

After his stint in the army during the Korean War, Focht enrolled at the Parsons School of Design in New York City, majoring in advertising and graphic design. At a lecture at the N.Y.C. Art Directors Club, Gene Deitch, then animation director at the Robert Lawrence Studio, N.Y.C., gave a lecture on animation and during the talk Deitch mentioned that he was looking for an assistant. At the end of the lecture, many of the students approached Deitch wanting the job as his assistant. Focht took a different approach. He rented a 16mm camera that weekend and with no film experience worked non-stop to create a one-minute commercial. Deitch viewed the film and Focht was offered the job.[1]

Focht arrived at the Lawrence studio but was told that Deitch had been hired away by CBS-Terrytoons as creative head. Focht caught a train to New Rochelle to enquire whether there was an opening at the studio. Upon his arrival, Deitch hired him on the spot. Focht's first assignment was to design a new Terrytoons logo, but when executive producer Bill Weiss returned from Europe, he told Deitch to stop wasting money and get Focht into some regular production work. Focht went to work in the background department under Bill Hilliker. The 65-year-old Hilliker, at that time the union shop steward, was uncomfortable with the new set-up at the studio after Paul Terry sold the studio to CBS in 1955. At the time, Deitch was producing the CBS promotional film *Depth Study*. When Hilliker couldn't adapt to the abstract style and his samples were rejected, it was decided to hire a freelancer.[2]

Someone suggested that newcomer Focht be given an opportunity. Focht did some samples and Deitch approved them. He put Focht in charge of creating the backgrounds for this rather extensive project, thereby creating a rift between Focht and Hilliker. At the end of this project, Focht was assigned to rendering the black and white backgrounds for the new *Tom Terrific* television series while Hilliker handled the theatrical backgrounds. Despite their differences, Hilliker, still finding it difficult painting in the non-realistic style, taught Focht

295

Fig. 24.2 – Animation cel and matching production background - Deputy Dawg.

the technical aspects of the craft. By the end of the *Tom Terrific* series, Focht and Hilliker were good friends.[3]

John Zago joined the department in 1958.[4] When Hilliker retired in 1959, Focht was made department head. In addition to handling all the ongoing theatrical properties, Focht and Zago, with Alan Shapiro and model makers Terry Guadagno and Mya Melvin, designed and completed the backgrounds for *Lariat Sam* (1961), a series created by Gene Wood for the *Captain Kangaroo* show. During his time at CBS-Terrytoons, Focht worked on all the series. His other responsibilities included designing and hand lettering all titles and credits and handling all advertising and promotional tasks. When CBS-Terrytoons got busy, background artists such as John Vita (who had worked for Terrytoons in the

1940s), Bob Owens, Dave Ubinas and Marty Strudler worked in the background department for short-term periods. Focht stayed at CBS-Terrytoons for 10½ years, leaving in 1966.[5]

In the animation department, the finely choreographed, well-gestured, full-animation of Carlo Vinci was also gone. He had moved to California in the late 1950s to create animation for Hanna-Barbera, scenes such as Fred Flintstone's tippy-toe bowling scenes from *The Flintstones*. The zany squash, stretch, and mangle animation of Tyer was also no longer present in these cartoons. He had left on November 18, 1958 to the newly organized Felix the Cat Productions to produce a Felix television series for Trans-Lux Television and then worked for Trans-Lux on a *Mighty Hercules* series.

The Heckle and Jeckle cartoons fared a little better in terms of entertainment quality during the post-Terry era. While the cartoon aesthetics were of a vastly inferior quality compared to the Terry cartoons of the 1940s, the stories were generally humorous, violent, and fast paced, everything you would expect from the magpie shorts. In *Thousand Smile Check Up* (January 1960) Heckle and Jeckle set up the "Last Chance Service Station" in the desert, but quickly find out that their business is in jeopardy when a tough bulldog wants to cut in on the action by opening up another gas station across the street. The two magpies begin a massive war with the canine (while always being quite polite, of course) – blowing up each other's station, stealing customers, and moving the stations past each other to claim the title of being the "last chance service station" until they run out of desert and end up in Los Angeles (changing the name to the "First Chance Gas Station" instead). Heckle and Jeckle are up to their old tricks again as they add some fuel to a live cannon shell the dog is riding on and wish him "Happy Motoring" before it continues its journey into the distance where it explodes with the force of an atomic bomb. The birds pump the dog with air sending him into space and paint his gas station with paint that makes it look like the road so that a truck drives through it. Finally, they drop him into the gas pump and pump him into the next customer's car.

In *Stunt Men* (November 23, 1960) when the movie studio heads plan to hire a new stuntman for their next series of films, resident stuntmen Heckle and Jeckle try to get rid of their competition (cowboy movie star Flint Locke) by putting him through a series of cruel stunts and embarrassing situations. The ploy backfires when the entire series of stunts are captured on film and the studio executives are pleased with the new stuntman's efforts. In *Sappy New Year* (November 10, 1961) in order to make friends, Heckle & Jeckle make a New Year's resolution to get rid of their pranks and never play a mean trick on anyone again. But their efforts to help people only result in the entire town angrily chasing the two magpies into the sunset.

Tragedy struck the Terrytoons family when voice artist Roy Halee died on May 31, 1960 in Garden City, Long Island, New

Fig. 24.3 – Opaquers (left to right) (1961): Ricki Cunningham, Barbara Puehl, Gloria Granata, Marianne Von Tucher.

York. Halee, the singing voice of Mighty Mouse, had voiced the two magpies after the absence of Dayton Allen in 1959. Allen returned to provide the voices for the two birds in the last Terrytoons Heckle and Jeckle cartoon *Messed Up Movie Makers* (March 1966). Jonathan Winters and Carl Reiner visited the studio occasionally to brainstorm gags and provide voice-overs.[6] Another voice actor that CBS-Terrytoons kept busy during the 1960s was Lionel Wilson (1924–2003) who completed voice work for Terrytoons from 1957 to 1967. Wilson was born Lionel Lazarus Salzer, raised in Brooklyn and educated at New York University, 1941–1942. He began acting on stage at the age of 14 when he appeared in *Dodsworth* on Broadway. He also completed touring in winter and summer stock productions. Wilson started acting in radio in 1949 on the radio series *The Aldrich Family* as George Bigalow and began his career as a voice artist in film at Terrytoons where his first credit

at the studio was for the animated short *A Bum Steer* (1957).[7]

His first big roles were the voices for all the main characters on the *Tom Terrific* series, 1957–1959 (Tom Terrific, Mighty Manfred, Crabby Appleton, Isotope Feeney, Silly Sandman, Captain Kidney Bean). His CBS-Terrytoons cartoon voice credits include work on animated shorts starring Clint Clobber, John Doormat (voice of John Doormat), Sidney the Elephant (the voices of Sidney and Stanley the Lion), Gaston Le Crayon, Astronut (voice of Astronut), Martian Moochers, Possible Possum (voice of Billy Bear, Owlawishus Owl, Macon Mouse, Possible Possum), and *The Mighty Heroes* series (voices of Strong Man, Rope Man, Cuckoo Man, Tornado Man). He provided various voices for the Terrytoons television series *The Deputy Dawg Show*, 1959 and *The Hector Heathcote Show*, 1963. Wilson always felt it was important to inspire children, and so he penned a number of fiction and non-fiction

Fig. 24.4 – Terrytoons group (c. 1960) (left to right): Front Row: Al Chiarito, Walter Gleason, Nick Alberti, Arthur Bartsch, Doug Moye, Terry Tarricone. Middle Row: Arnie Levy, Ralph Bakshi, John Paratore, Sal Greco, Bob Corelli, George Davis, Larz Bourne. Back Row: Don Caulfield, Jack MacConnell, Vinnie Bell, Cosmo Anzilotti, Ralph Rossburg, Joe Rasinski, Dave Tendlar.

children's books, sometimes pseudonymously.[8]

In 1945, 44-year-old Japanese-American Robert Kuwahara (1901–1964) was released from a Japanese internment camp, Heart Mountain Relocation Camp, in Wyoming, where he had spent three years teaching art to fellow camp mates. Kuwahara had become friends with Tommy Morrison who assisted Kuwahara in settling in Larchmont, New York. Morrison invited him to join Terrytoons. Kuwahara had graduated from the Los Angeles Polytechnic High School in 1921. He then studied drawing and painting for seven years at the Otis Art Institute in Los Angeles while working at a full-time job. During this time he had completed a number of portraits.[9]

In 1929, he graduated with an art degree from the Otis Art Institute and in May went off to New York City hoping to work as a portrait artist but ended up undertaking a position as a commercial illustrator. While in New York City, he met Tom Morrison. After the start of the Great Depression he returned to California and began his career as a story man/story sketch artist at Walt Disney Studios in 1932 working on the *Silly Symphonies* and Mickey Mouse shorts and the feature film *Snow White and the Seven Dwarfs* (1937). He moved to the new MGM cartoon unit and worked on sets/backgrounds there from 1937 to 1942. Kuwahara also worked on the first Tom and Jerry cartoon *Puss Gets the Boot* (1940) while at MGM where he remained until he was evacuated from the Pacific Coast after the start of World War II.[10]

In 1949, Kuwahara joined the Terrytoons studio as a character designer and story man. While at Terrytoons, Kuwahara's most notable creation was a mouse named Hashimoto who first appeared in *Hashimoto-San* released in September [October] 1959, the first cartoon Kuwahara directed for the studio. The cartoon received favorable reviews and a decision was made to produce more shorts starring the Japanese mouse. The backgrounds to the cartoons were painted in the style of Japanese

Chapter 24 • A New Cast of Characters

artist Hokusai Katsushika (1760–1849). Hokusai is best known as author of the woodblock print series *Thirty-six Views of Mount Fuji* which includes the internationally recognized print, *The Great Wave off Kanagawa*, created during the 1820s. Hashimoto was a Japanese house mouse and judo expert and was married to Hanako. The couple had two children: Yuriko and Saburo. The series pilot and subsequent adventures featured Hashimoto's reminiscences about the legends, folklores, and traditions of his beloved country for American newspaper correspondent G.I. Joe. In many of the cartoons, Hashimoto and his family had to overcome the evil plans of the local Japanese house cat. Each cartoon ended with a wise Japanese saying from a lesson learnt from the cartoon, usually in the form of a pun.

There were 17 Hashimoto Mouse cartoons produced (15 released theatrically) between 1959 and 1963, each cartoon so exquisitely crafted in the Katsushika Ukiyo-e style that the stories seem almost superfluous. Kuwahara would direct all of the cartoons in the series. The first entry has Hashimoto introducing his family to the viewers. After old friend G.I. Joe arrives, Hashimoto Mouse teaches him judo and then demonstrates his abilities by flipping a cat around. Joe returns home to America but his new martial arts skills are no match for the American house cat. *Hashimoto-San* was a critical success and selected for showing at Cannes. In *House of Hashimoto*

Fig. 24.5 – Terrytoons party (c. 1959) (left to right) Front Row: Larz Bourne, Tom Morrison, John Paratore, Dave Tendlar. Back Row: Joe Rasinski, Bob Corelli, Ralph Rossburg, Ralph Bakshi, Doug Moye.

(November 1960), Hashimoto tells Joe, now an American reporter, of how an invisible mouse defeated a giant cat terrorizing the mouse village. The wise philosophical saying that concluded the cartoon was, "He who is not seen is 'real gone man'".

In *So Sorry, Pussycat* (March 1961) Hashimoto is teaching his son to fish when they are attacked by a cat. Hashimoto ends up feeding the cat so much fish that the cat falls asleep. Joe and Hashimoto spend a night out in Tokyo in *Night Life in Tokyo* (February 1961) checking out the Geisha girls but end up fighting off a cat. In *Honorable Cat Story* (November 1961) Ichiro, Japanese house cat, tells the story why Japanese mice are masters of Japanese cats. Tachibara, Japanese sumo cat, is defeated by Hashimoto using martial arts. When Tachibara and his fellow cats learn jiu-jitsu and attack the mice they are again repelled because the mice have learned a more advanced martial art, ninjitsu.

In *Strange Companion* (May 1961), Hiroshi, a pet dragon raised by Taro in a village at the foot of Mount Fuji, becomes too big for the community so he is escorted out of town. When Mount Fuji erupts, the dragon saves the village from the slowly encroaching lava and plugs the crater with a big boulder. Hashimoto tells the story of the pearls that form part of the pearl necklace he has given his daughter in *Pearl Crazy* (May 1963). When Hashimoto rescues a cat trapped underwater by a giant clam, the grateful feline gives Hashimoto the pearls. In *Doll Festival* (February 1961) a large Japanese house cat invades a Hinamatsuri "Doll's Day" festival disguised as a Kabuki doll but the mice end up trapping the feline in a glass cage where it becomes a "living doll" and a festival exhibit. Hashimoto's wise saying at the end of the

Fig. 24.6 – Hector Heathcote animation cel.

cartoon is another corny pun, "He who lives in glass house can have shattering experience".

The Hashimoto cartoons introduced America to some of the culture, customs and traditions of Japan, a subject matter not commonly explored by the media in the early 1960s. All the cartoon characters in the Hashimoto cartoons were voiced by vocal artist, actor, and writer Johnny Myhers (1921–1992). Myhers was educated at the University of Rome where he received his Ph.D. (lit.), 1950. Prior to his work in animation Myhers had extensive experience in theatrical productions. He attended the MacPhail School of Music and Drama and studied directing and film writing at the Experimental Center of Cinematography, Rome, 1948–1952, graduating with a degree in directing. He is the founder, director, and acted for the Rome Theatre Guild, 1949–1952, and the Rome Playhouse. He appeared in numerous stage plays in Italy. He toured in *Kiss Me Kate*, 1952–1954. He appeared in Broadway shows, 1959–1960. He was a co-star and toured with the national company of *The Sound of Music*, 1961–1963 (playing the role of Captain Von Trapp). He has performed in over 1700 performances of *The Sound of Music*. He also appeared in minor roles in a number of motion pictures and TV series.[11]

At Terrytoons, Kuwahara directed a number of other series including Deputy Dawg, 1962; Lariat Sam, 1962; Astronut, 1965; Hector Heathcote, 1963; and the Martian Moochers, 1966 (prod. 1964). By 1960, Kuwahara as well as a number of studio artists, particularly the veteran staff, were becomingly increasingly disenchanted with the way CBS was operating the studio. With Paul in control, the studio was run like a family operation and there was a warm, supportive and friendly atmosphere. The tale is told of one Christmas party when the elevators of the Pershing Square Building were commandeered by members of Terry's staff, and everybody using the elevators that day ended up on the seventh floor party-whether they liked it or not.[12]

With CBS in control, to many artists the studio had become a cold, faceless corporate concern, possibly due to the increased production pressure caused by television. When the Hashimoto

Chapter 24 • A New Cast of Characters

cartoons were suddenly cancelled by CBS in late 1963 Kuwahara was upset and began to question CBS's programming decision. He struck up discussions with old friend Joe Barbera whom he had met while at MGM in the late 1930s and began to explore career options elsewhere. Barbera was trying to convince Kuwahara to come to California to work for him. During early 1964 Kuwahara was seriously contemplating moving back to California where he was raised as a child. Tragically, he would never get the opportunity as he was diagnosed with cancer and died very shortly after the diagnosis in December of that year.[13]

After televising 26 adventures of *Tom Terrific* over five years, in 1961 Bob Keeshan asked for a fresh cartoon series from Terrytoons for his *Captain Kangaroo* television show. A decision was made to produce a cartoon series based on a western hero. The series was titled *The Adventures of Lariat Sam* and Keeshan himself would have a role in developing the stories. Keeshan enlisted his writer (and future game show host) Gene Wood to produce and co-write with Terrytoons head writer Tom Morrison.

Like *Tom Terrific*, *Lariat Sam* was a serialized cartoon. Each of its 13 stories consisted of five "chapters" to tell its story. Each chapter was broadcast Monday through Friday to make a complete story each week. The stories were set in the Old West and usually centered on Lariat Sam's constant battles with arch-rival and nemesis, Badlands Meeney. Lariat Sam was a friendly, naive and honest cowboy who rode a poetry-reading derby-hatted horse named Tippytoes (also known as "Wonder Horse"). Sam was always cheerful and optimistic who tended to see the good in everyone he encountered.

Keeshan insisted that the cartoons be non-violent. Therefore, Lariat Sam intentionally didn't wear guns – preferring to use his magical lariat to round up the evil villains. Unlike *Tom Terrific*, *Lariat Sam* would be produced in color (though the *Captain Kangaroo* show itself would be broadcast in black & white until 1966). Bob Kuwahara, Dave Tendlar, Art Bartsch, and Connie Rasinski would share the directing duties. Dayton Allen provided all the voices (Gene Wood sings the theme song). The series premiered on CBS on September 10, 1962 and ran until August 27, 1965.[14] While *Tom Terrific* is best remembered by Baby Boomers, the Lariat Sam series has its own special charms. John Zago's backgrounds are graphically interesting, the plots featured engaging themes, and Dayton Allen had fun with the voices. To adults, the cartoons were a bit on the dull side but the program was primarily aimed at pre-schoolers and its three-year run on *Captain Kangaroo* is a testament to its appeal to younger children.

Another late 1950s character creation was Hector Heathcote, a Revolutionary War minuteman who had a habit of playing a key role in the major events of the America's history. Hector Heathcote was created by Eli Bauer and first introduced in the Terrytoon cartoon *Minute and ½ Man* (July 1959). Bauer had earlier pitched the idea to Gene Deitch, a story about a Revolutionary War figure who was always late to muster. Deitch liked the idea but was too busy with his own projects to seriously consider the character. Therefore, after Deitch had been released, Bauer approached Tommy Morrison and Bill Weiss with the idea and got the green light to produce an animated cartoon starring the character.[15] In the short, poor Hector wants to be a Minuteman, but no matter how hard he tries to muster within a minute he is always 30 seconds late. On one attempt to muster, he arrives at his station on time but because his suspenders were wrapped around his bedpost he springs back to his bed. Frustrated, he practices his mustering and devises a whole bunch of gadgets so that he can report on time but each contraption backfires. When the Redcoats land on shore, the bugle sounds for the Minutemen to muster. This time Hector's attempt to arrive on time ends up with him crashing into an ammunition dump and causing an explosion sending cannon balls at the British. The British retreat back to their ship and sail back to England. Hector manages to save the day by accident and becomes a hero.

Bauer wasn't completely satisfied with the end product as he felt that director Dave Tendlar had missed some gags and his timing was a bit off. He was also not pleased with the choice for the voice of Hector.[16] Despite Bauer's dissatisfaction with the final product, *The Minute and ½ Man* was a critical success and won first prize at the Venice Children's Film Festival (12th International Exhibition of Film for Children, Venice, 1960). After the success of the animated short, Morrison approached Bauer to create another Heathcote cartoon. The result was *The Famous Ride* and other entries in the series, a few of which won more awards at film festivals in Europe.[17] As the series progressed, the creators decided to have him reshape history at different time periods though the creators never divulged how Hector was able to travel through time to appear at these key events in history. However, this was never Bauer's intentions for his character wanting him to remain in the Colonial time period.[18]

Most of Hector's adventures took place during the Revolutionary War, but Hector always sported the 18th century tricorner hat regardless of the era he was visiting. Some episodes featured Winston, Heathcote's bulldog, who spoke in a Churchillian manner and provided wise advice to the befuddled Hector. Despite Hector's major accomplishments, he rarely received the credit he deserved, partly because he always seemed to stumble into these historical events and never achieved what he originally intended to accomplish (such as inventing the harvester when trying to invent the airplane).

Despite his clumsiness and bad luck, his efforts usually ended up producing unexpected positive results. He accidentally destroys a British fort during the War of 1812 (*Riverboat Mission* (May 1962)), sends a cannon shot at Jean Lafitte during the American Revolution causing the French to enter the war on the side of the United States (*He-Man Seaman* (March 1962)), restores peace with the American Indians (*Peace Pipe* (June 1973)), invents a primitive automobile (*The Hectormobile* (October 1973)), and helps Jean-Pierre Blanchard make the first manned flight of a balloon in America in 1793 (*First Flight Up* (October 1962)). He sends Paul Revere on his famous ride (*The Famous Ride* (April 1960)), forges a path for Daniel Boone (*Daniel Boone, Jr.* (December 1960)), sinks a British ship during the American Revolution (*The Unsung Hero* (July 1961)), saves the Pony Express mail from being robbed (*The First Fast Mail* (May 1961)), keeps Washington's boat from sinking as it crosses the Delaware River (*Crossing the Delaware* (June 1961)), and captures a British fort during the Revolutionary War (*Drum Roll* (March 1961)).

The character headlined the television show, *The Hector Heathcote Show*, which was comprised of recycled theatrical cartoons, premiered on NBC October 5, 1963, and ran to September 25, 1965. The program's other cartoon components included "Hashimoto" and "Sidney the Elephant". Of the 71 cartoons broadcast during the program's two-year run on NBC Television, only 39 had previously been seen in the theaters.

Another of the experienced talents on staff that was hired by Gene Deitch was Larz Eugene Bourne (1916–1993) born and raised in Knoxville, Tennessee. After studying at the Chicago Professional School of Cartooning, he got his start as a newspaper cartoonist's apprentice in Toledo, Ohio in the 1930s. He began work in the story department at the Fleischer Studios in Miami, Florida, where Max Fleischer had just moved, in 1937. He remained at the studio until 1942 working on Betty Boop and Popeye shorts as well as the feature *Gulliver's Travels* (1939). He was in a writing capacity with Famous Studios from 1942 to 1943. Between 1943 and 1945, Bourne served in the United States Navy in the South Pacific.

Following his discharge, Bourne returned to Famous Studios (the former Fleischer Studios now newly re-organized in New York City under Paramount control) where he worked on a number of animated productions such as the *Little Lulu* series and the original Casper cartoons from 1945 to 1958. He was hired by Deitch in 1956 and worked at CBS-Terrytoons until about 1965. He wrote the story on the last Dinky Duck cartoon (*It's A Living* (1958)) and did story work on Mighty Mouse (*Cat Alarm* (1961)) and Heckle & Jeckle cartoons during 1959 to 1960 and 1966. His most notable achievement at CBS-Terrytoons was creating the character of Deputy Dawg, the bumbling Mississippi sheriff that featured the vocal talents of Dayton Allen. The series was an instant hit, even garnering requests from theaters to show television cartoons, a reversal of

Chapter 24 • A New Cast of Characters

Fig. 24.7 – Model sheet - Mighty Mouse, CBS-Terrytoons version.

the usual sequence. Of the 104 shorts for the Deputy Dawg television series beginning in 1959 he scripted nearly every one over a one-year period.[19]

Deputy Dawg was a not-so-bright southern lawman who struggled to maintain law and order in the southern United States while being pestered by pranksters Vincent "Vince" Van Gopher, Ty Coon The Racoon, Moley Mole, Muskie The Muskrat, and Pig Newton. While trying to track down these mischief makers, Deputy Dawg was constantly attempting to please the Sheriff while simultaneously being the constant object of idol worship from Elmer, his lookalike little nephew. As the episodes progressed, the setting of the cartoons changed from Florida to Mississippi, and later to Tennessee.

Much of the humor in the cartoons is sight gag based with some jokes focused around humorous accents and stereotypical southern characteristics. Many of the storylines involve Deputy Dawg protecting his crops or eggs in the henhouse (*The Yoke's On You*; *Law and Disorder*; *National Spoof Day*) from Muskie and Vince, battling with some of the peculiar locals and trying to please the Sheriff. In *Cotton Pickin' Picnic*, Deputy Dawg is a watchdog over food at a cotton pickers' picnic and must fend off the attempts by Muskie and Vince to steal the food. However, most of the foul deeds committed by Muskie and Vince weren't treated seriously, and Deputy Dawg was on friendly terms with his varmint friends most of the time (except when he had to perform his duties as a lawman and keep them from causing trouble). Deputy Dawg

would have friendly fun with Muskie and Vince just as often as he would put them behind bars in the jailhouse, and the three amigos would often engage in their favorite pastime, fishing for catfish.

The Deputy Dawg cartoons were created by Terrytoons specifically for the television market. *The Deputy Dawg Show* debuted in October 1960 in over 47 television markets, primarily in the South and Midwest, principally in the 6 p.m. to 7 p.m. time slot. Many kids would end up watching these cartoons while having dinner. The rest of the country viewed the 104 Deputy Dawg cartoons as solo "fillers", minus the rest of the Terrytoons package. The television program was sponsored by the W. H. Lay Potato Chips company. A number of Lay potato chip commercials featuring Deputy Dawg were

303

produced to accompany the program.

The television series across the country aired on a weekly basis, from September 8, 1962 to May 25, 1963, with no episodes on December 8 to December 29, 1962, resuming on January 5, 1963. The cartoons were packaged three [four] at a time and shown as a half-hour program. There were also six additional titles that were released theatrically, for show in theaters and which were not part of the original television package.

The rigors of maintaining a heavy television production schedule was too much for the CBS-Terrytoons studio. The studio was never equipped to produce so many cartoons over a short time span. In addition, employees were required for CBS Animation, the unit headquartered in New York City that completed animation for television commercials. Consequently, Terrytoons was forced to go outside of the studio for directing and writing talent. The result was inconsistent stories and varying production values. Although the cartoons were produced using cost-effective limited animation, the productions were nicely stylized and the backgrounds well rendered.

The vocal talents of Dayton Allen were a key factor in the success of the cartoons. Deputy Dawg sounded like Frank Fontaine's "Crazy Guggenheim" character (whom Fontaine was calling "John L. C. Sivoney" in 1960). Vincent Van Gopher possessed the vocal sounds of character actor Percy Helton (1894–1971) (a voice that sounded like the cross between a squeak toy and a raspy gasp). The supporting character actors ranged from Groucho Marx (whom Allen would use quite effectively in the Heckle and Jeckle cartoons) to Hugh Herbert (1887–1952).

As a result of the success of the television series and from requests from theater managers across the country, most notably in Texas, CBS released some of the made-for-television cartoons theatrically in 1962. Unfortunately, the cartoons looked unfinished and inexpensively produced on the wider screen. Seven years later, Deputy Dawg premiered on NBC in a new series *The Deputy Dawg Show*. This new vehicle repeated episodes from the original series and featured two additional segments comprised of previously released Gandy Goose cartoons and *Terrytoons Classics*, many of which starred the Terry Bears. Deputy Dawg can claim the honor of starring in the most Terrytoons cartoons of any Terry character since the studio was founded in 1929, a testament to his popularity during the early 1960s.[20]

Appearing in one of the Deputy Dawg television cartoons titled *Astronut* was a space varmint by the same name. In the cartoon Astronut arrives from outer space and insists on trading his spaceship for the Sheriff's car driven by Deputy Dawg. The decision was made to star the character in his own theatrical series. In the series Astronut was a small friendly alien who was the loyal companion of Oscar Mild, a mild mannered bachelor who was constantly being berated by his boss, Mr. Nicely (later Mr. Bellow). There were 19 theatrical cartoons produced in the series. In the first cartoon of the series, *Brother from Outer Space* (March 1964), Astronut introduces himself to Oscar Mild and helps the office worker by zapping Nicely with his sweetness ray turning the boss from grouch to nice guy. Later Astronut foils the plans of three bank robbers and Oscar is given credit for the capture.

Many of the cartoons centered their plots on Astronut's ability to transform into other beings. In *Oscar's Moving Day* (January 1973) Astronut changes into Oscar Mild so that the real Oscar can go play golf. Unfortunately, in Oscar's absence Astronut ends up causing more problems at work than finding solutions. *Molecular Mixup* (December 1964) has Astronut transforming into a dog but unable to change back to his former self. When Oscar goes searching for a molecular energy pill to help his friend, a boy takes Astronut home with him. *Robots in Toyland* (August 1965) has Astronut changing his molecular structure into Oscar, a department store employee in a toy department, in order to help his friend impress his boss.

Another familiar plot device was the use of gadgets or objects from Astronut's planet to cause problems on earth. *Oscar's Birthday Present* (January 1971) features Astronut giving Oscar a mysterious flying rod for his birthday which sends a Soviet spy after the object. In *Outer Galaxy Gazette* (September 1964)

Chapter 24 • A New Cast of Characters

Fig. 24.8 – Model sheet - Hashimoto mouse and family with G.I. Joe.

Astronut's newspaper predicts a meteor impact and windstorms. In Oscar's attempt to warn the authorities of the upcoming disastrous events the police end up questioning his prophetic abilities. In *Weather Magic* (May 1965) a weather maker machine from Astronut's planet alters the Earth's weather providing Oscar with the opportunity to impress a weatherman with his predictive abilities but the machine eventually causes weather problems for the citizens of the planet. In *Hokey Home Movies* (September 1972) Astronut switches a film reel so that Oscar exhibits a home movie from the planet Mishagoss to the Home Movie Society. *The Invisibeam* (c. 1965) has a ray-type gun assisting Oscar in helping Mr. Bellow with getting ready for a backyard barbecue.

Another common story theme was creatures or beings from outer space causing Oscar problems on Earth. In *Jolly Jupiter* (c. 1965), Astronut's nephew arrives causing Oscar to keep the little alien from causing problems for Mild's neighbor Mr. Bellow. A large hungry and friendly blue dinosaur goes on an eating rampage in *Space Pet* (c. 1965). Other shorts have Astronut giving Oscar special powers such as the ability to lift things by just thinking (*The Sky's the Limit* (February 1965)), or to talk like animals (*Going Ape* (c. 1965)).

With the success of the theatrical run of cartoons, in August 1965, Astronut was featured in his own half-hour series for syndication and several Astronut cartoons were produced for the television program. In the late 1960s, Terrytoons stars Hashimoto Mouse, Sidney the Elephant, and Luno the Flying Horse (detailed below), each stars of their own theatrical film series, were made a part of the show. In the early 1970s, Viacom, the program's distributor, reprogrammed the series with supporting episodes from other Terrytoons favorites Possible Possum, Sad Cat, and James Hound.[21]

Another early 1960s cartoon character was Luno, the White Stallion, or simply Luno. The stories focused on a little boy named Tim who had a toy-sized figure of a winged horse, which was transformed into a full-sized, living winged horse when he said "Winged horse of marble white, take me on a magic flight". Luno would whisk him off on adventures in far off lands. The source of Tim's powers to transform his toy into a living horse, which transformation was performed in Tim's bedroom, was never explained. These magic flights weren't limited to present-day happenings. Luno often took Tim to historic or prehistoric times, or to worlds of myth or legend. The only thing necessary was that the destination be able to provide an exciting adventure for its young viewers. In that initial outing, Tim's voice was done by Norma MacMillan, who was also heard as Gumby and Davey. But in subsequent appearances, he was voiced by Dayton Allen. Luno was always done by Bob McFadden.

Bob McFadden (1923–2000) got his break as a singer and impersonator while stationed in Puerto Rico with the Navy during World War II. After leaving the Navy, he worked in a Pittsburgh steel mill, and got into show business as an opening act at hotels and nightclubs for the McGuire Sisters, Harry Belafonte and others. He met his wife in Boston in 1950 when the two were working together. While he sang onstage, she and her twin sister performed synchronized swimming exercises in a pool below. The McFaddens moved to Queens, N.Y. in the mid-1960s and McFadden became a voiceover talent in advertising and cartoons. He made hundreds of thousands of dollars selling his voice to advertise products for Ban deodorant, Campbell's soup, Ford, Frankenberry cereal, Geritol, Mountain Dew and Pepto-Bismol. He was a stable voice for Terrytoons and was best known as Cool McCool's "Pop the Cop" for King Features Syndicate in 1966. He was also Milton the Monster.[22]

Only six Luno cartoons were made for theatrical release, but the series was continued for about 11 more for television. There, Luno appeared as a back segment in shows starring Astronut, Deputy Dawg and others. The first Luno cartoon released theatrically was *The Missing Genie* (April 1963) which has Tim and Luno rescuing Aladdin's genie kidnapped by an evil magician. The next theatrical release *Trouble in Baghdad* (September 1963) has Luno and Tim capturing the 40 thieves and exonerating Ali Baba from the theft of the jewels. In *Roc-A-Bye Sinbad* (January 1964), the pair of adventurers help Sinbad defeat the Roc, a giant mythological bird of prey. *King Rounder* (April 1964) tells the story of Tim and Luno's efforts to return the crown of King Rounder that was stolen by a black knight riding a unicorn. *Adventure by the Sea* (July 1964) has Tim and Luno helping a cowardly Captain Ahab capture Moby Dick. In *The Gold Dust Bandit* (October 1964) the pair rescue a cowardly sheriff from a western outlaw, "The Gold Dust Bandit", in the Old West. Later in the mid-1970s, a few of the Luno television cartoons were released theatrically.

Other notable early 1960s

Chapter 24 • A New Cast of Characters

Terrytoons characters were Duckwood and Donkey Otie, two drifters, a beatnik duck and a donkey who talks like W. C. Fields. Three cartoons were produced starring these characters. *The Red Tractor* (February 1964) has the two characters as salesmen selling farm tractor attachments. When they demonstrate their equipment to the farmer they end up causing damage to his property. *Short-Term Sheriff* (May 1964) features the two taking the job as lawmen to go after two criminals. Despite their capturing the gangsters, they end up no better off financially than they were before. *Oil Thru the Day* (August 1964) has Duckwood and Donkey Otie breaking onto an oil construction site to join a company cookout and leaving with the food. With little chemistry between these characters and predictable plots, the cartoons are forgettable "fillers".

The last noteworthy Terrytoons cartoon character from the first half of the 1960s was Pitiful Penelope who starred in a one-shot cartoon *Search for Misery* (November 1964), an engaging and humorous spoof on the television soap operas of the period. The early 1960s was a period of time in which several memorable cartoon characters sprung to life at the studio. The latter half of the decade at the production house would see the rise of one of the most influential animated film directors and producers of the 20th century as well as the gradual winding down of the studio after nearly 40 years in operation. ✍

Notes

1. Bill Focht, phone interview by author (transcript), Kelowna, B.C., Canada, 30 October 1997, Terrytoons Collection, Victoria, B.C., Canada, 1.
2. Ibid., 3.
3. Ibid., 3–4.
4. Ibid., 5.
5. Ibid., 5–6.
6. Jacqueline Perelson, "Terry's works remain in tune", *The Standard-Star* (New Rochelle, N.Y.), 1 February 1982, p. B1.
7. *Contemporary Authors. A Bio-bibliographical Guide to Current Writers in Fiction, General Nonfiction, Poetry, Journalism, Drama, Motion Pictures, Television, and Other Fields*, volume 217 (Detroit: Gale Group, 2004) (entry also in volume 105); *Something about the Author. Facts and Pictures About Authors and Illustrators of Books for Young People*, volume 144 (Detroit: Gale Group, 2004) (entries also in volumes 31 and 33).
8. Lewis Funke, "News of the Rialto; Musical Will Lampoon Television Commercials – Sundry Other Items", *New York Times*, 7 May 1961, Section: Art, p. X1. Obituaries: "Lionel Wilson, Who Gave Voice To Tom Terrific, Is Dead at 79", *New York Times*, 24 May 2003, p. A30; "Lionel Wilson", *Pittsburgh Post-Gazette* (PA), 25 May 2003, p. C–8; "Obituaries; Passings; Lionel Wilson, 79; Voice of 'Tom Terrific,' Children's Author", *Los Angeles Times*, 27 May 2003, p. B.11; "Lionel Wilson. Voice of Tom Terrific and Crabby Appleton; 79", *The San Diego Union – Tribune*, 1 June 2003, p. B.7.
9. "Kawahara [sic], Cartoonist" (Obituary News), *The Standard-Star* (New Rochelle, N.Y.), 8 December 1964, p. 3.
10. "Bob Kuwahara", *The National Cartoonists Society Album 1996*, 350; Michel Kuwahara, interview by author, transcript of telephone recording, Las Vegas, Nevada, 8 November 1998, Terrytoons Collection, Victoria, B.C., Canada.
11. *Contemporary Authors. A Bio-bibliographical Guide to Current Writers in Fiction, General Nonfiction, Poetry, Journalism, Drama, Motion Pictures, Television, and Other Fields*, volume 105 (Detroit: Gale Research, 1982) (also entry in v. 137); Walter Rigdon, ed., *The Biographical Encyclopaedia and Who's Who of the American Theatre* (New York: James H. Heineman, 1966); "Music Man Is Planning Film Career. John Myhers To Be Actor-Author-Director", *The Pittsburgh Press*, 13 February 1963, p. 46; "'Sound of Music' in Santa Monica", *Los Angeles Times*, 2 September 1964, p. F12; "John Myhers to Return for Valley's 'Camelot'", *Los Angeles Times*, 25 June 1965, p. C8; "John Myhers, 70; Director, Actor, Screenplay Writer", *Los Angeles Times*, 30 May 1992, p. 22.
12. Dick Tracy, "A Look Back on the 'Golden Days'", *The Daily Item* (Port Chester, N.Y.), 5 January 1973, p. 4.
13. Kuwahara, interview by author, 6.
14. Erickson, *Television Cartoon Shows*, 15, 65.
15. Elias Bauer, interview by author (transcript), New Rochelle, New York, August 1996, Terrytoons Collection, Victoria, B.C., 8.
16. Ibid.
17. Ibid., 10.
18. Ibid., 10–11.
19. "Larz E. Bourne, 77; Drew Deputy Dawg", *New York Times*, 19 Mar 1993, p. A22; "Obituaries: Larz E. Bourne", *Variety*, 26 April 1993, 84.
20. Erickson, *Television Cartoon Shows*, 241–242.
21. Ibid., 99.
22. "Bob McFadden, 76. Actor Known for Role in Whisk Commercials Dies", *The Vindicator* (PA), 10 January 2000, p. B3; "Bob McFadden, Voice in TV Ads", *Sun Sentinel* (Fort Lauderdale), 10 January 2000, p. 7B; Douglas Martin, "Bob McFadden, Voice-Over Star, 76, Dies", *New York Times*, 12 January 2000; "Bob McFadden. Did Commercial Voice-overs", *Milwaukee Journal Sentinel* (Wisconsin), 14 January 2000.

307

Chapter 25

L'Enfant Terrible and the Twilight of Terrytoons:
Ralph Bakshi, the Adventures of Sad Cat, The Mighty Heroes, Possible Possum, and James Hound, and the Studio Closure, 1965–1968

L'Enfant Terrible ("terrible child", also enfant terrible) is a French expression, traditionally referring to a child who is terrifyingly candid by saying embarrassing things to adults, especially parents, "a child who embarrasses his elders by untimely remarks".[1] However, the expression has drawn another usage in the creative arts, a successful "genius" who is very unorthodox, striking, and in some cases, offensive, or rebellious. Classically, one who "thumbs their nose" at the establishment, or challenges it. If there ever was a poster boy for this expression, his name would be Ralph Bakshi.

Ralph Bakshi was born in Haifa, Mandatory Palestine (later Israel). His family immigrated to New York City in 1939 where he grew up in the Brownsville neighbourhood of Brooklyn.[2] In June 1956, after learning how to cartoon from Gene Byrnes' *Complete Guide to Cartooning*, Bakshi graduated from Manhattan's School of Industrial Art with an award in cartooning.[3] Bakshi's friend Cosmo Anzilotti was hired by Terrytoons when Bakshi was 18 years old. Anzilotti recommended Bakshi to the studio's production manager, Frank Schudde. Bakshi was hired as a cel polisher and commuted four hours each day to the New Rochelle studio.[4]

After a few months, Schudde was encouraged by the fact that Bakshi was still showing up to work despite the long commute, and promoted him to cel painter. Bakshi began to practice animating. To give himself more time to practice, he added 10 cels he was supposed to work on into the "to-do" pile of fellow cel painter, Leo Giuliani. Bakshi's trickery was not noticed until two days later, when he was called to Schudde's office because the cels had been painted on the wrong side. When Bakshi argued that Giuliani had made the mistake, a quarrel ensued between the three. Schudde eventually sided with Bakshi. By this point, the studio's employees were aware of Bakshi's drive to become an animator, and the young artist began to receive help and advice from established animators, including Connie Rasinski, Mannie Davis, Jim Tyer, Larry Silverman and John Gentilella.[5] His two favourites were Connie Rasinski and Jim Tyer. Bakshi found Connie to be a brilliant draftsman and a wonderful guy. Tyer was the most original animator that Bakshi had ever met in his life.[6]

Bakshi's wife Elaine detested his long work hours causing marital strife in the household. To parody his marital problems, Bakshi drew

Chapter 25 • L'Enfant Terrible and the Twilight of Terrytoons

Fig. 25.1 – Model sheet - James Hound and villains Dr. Ha-Ha and Igor.

Dum Dum and Dee Dee, a comic strip about a man determined "to get – and keep – the girl".[7] As he perfected his animation style, he began to take on more jobs, including creating design tests for Gene Deitch during Deitch's tenure at the studio. Deitch however was not convinced that Bakshi had a modern design sensibility. In response to the period's political climate and as a form of therapy, Bakshi drew the comic strips *Bonefoot and Fudge*, which satirized "idiots with an agenda", and *Junktown*, which featured "misfit technology and discarded ideals".[8] Bakshi's frustrations with his failing marriage and the state of the planet further drove his need to animate. In 1959, he moved his desk to join the rest of the animators; after asking Rasinski for material to animate, he received layouts of two scenes: a hat floating on water and Deputy Dawg running. Despite threats of repercussion from the animators' union, Rasinski fought to keep Bakshi as a layout artist. Bakshi began to see Rasinski as a father figure; Rasinski, childless, was happy to serve as Bakshi's mentor.[9]

Around 1963, the musical director at CBS-Terrytoons animation studio, Philip Scheib, decided to reduce his workload and was contemplating retirement. Bill Weiss decided to hire Jim Timmens (1920–1980) on a freelance basis to direct a number of cartoons and eventually Timmens took over the position when Scheib retired in 1965. During his 36-year career in animation, Scheib labored as a composer on over 750 animated cartoons for Paul Terry.[10] Jim Timmens was a jazz musician, orchestrator, conductor, and musical director. He was raised in a musical family. His father and brother both played the saxophone. He studied piano as a child and later attended the Eastman School of Music at the University of Rochester, Rochester, New York. He started his musical career as a musical arranger for dance bands. He came to New York City and studied with pianist Stefan Wolpe (1902–1972) who founded the Contemporary Music School in New York City in 1948.[11]

In New York City, Timmens began work in radio, television, and recordings. In 1952, he recorded as a member of the Sauter-Finnegan Orchestra. He wrote arrangements for *Porgy and Bess Revisited*; *Gilbert and Sullivan Revisited* (12 popular numbers recorded by Jim Timmens and his Jazz All-Stars) (Warner Bros.,

309

Fig. 25.2 – Model sheet - The Mighty Heroes and the villain The Junker.

1952); and *Off the Cuff* (Viking). He formed his own orchestra in the 1950s, the Jim Timmens Orchestra, and recorded children's music through the Golden Records label from the late 1950s through to the mid-1960s. At CBS-Terrytoons Timmens was assisted by jazz pianist and bandleader Elliot Lawrence (b. 1925).[12] He remained with the cartoon studio as a freelance musical director working at the Terrytoons studio (the studio was equipped with a sound studio allowing all recordings to be done on site) until cartoon production ended in 1968.

At age 25, Bakshi was promoted to director. His first cartoon directorial assignment was on the series *Sad Cat*. Bakshi and his wife had separated by then, giving him the time to animate each short alone. Bakshi was dissatisfied with the traditional role of a director at the studio. Under the supervision of Tommy Morrison, the story department controlled the storyboards and the voice tracks were pre-recorded leaving little opportunity for the director to become involved in the creative process. While the directors were removed from the creative aspects of filmmaking that didn't keep Bakshi from trying to gain more control over the production. He would edit, re-time, and mix-up the soundtracks, and do whatever he could to gain some artistic control over the film so he could make it his own.[13]

The studio produced 13 Sad Cat cartoons. Bakshi designed all the characters in these animated cartoons.[14] The premise of the series is based on the Cinderella fairy tale with a masculine twist. In the cartoons Sad Cat, a dreary looking male cat, has to take care of his two mean brothers Latimore and Fenimore. Like Cinderella, he has a godmother-like figure. In the first five cartoons (directed by Bakshi) that character was Gadmouse, the apprentice fairy. However, on the final eight cartoons (directed by Art Bartsch, as Bakshi had left the studio), Sad Cat was instead aided by his "Super Ego", a muscular, tougher version of himself. Bob McFadden voiced all the characters.

In the first entry from the series, *Gadmouse the Apprentice Good Fairy* (January 1965), in the city of Imagination lived Gadmouse whose one desire is to produce a happy ending for someone so that he may earn his wand as a full-fledged good fairy. Sad Cat, stuck in a Cinderella role, wants to go to the dance club but his

Chapter 25 • L'Enfant Terrible and the Twilight of Terrytoons

Fig. 25.3 – Model sheet - Sad Cat and his brothers.

two mean brothers won't let him join them. Gadmouse arrives and magically gives Sad Cat his magic dancing shoes but also in the transformation process he unintentionally attires him in a dress, long feminine curls, and curly eyelashes. Gadmouse bemoans his mistake but he attributes the error to the fact that he is only an apprentice. Sad Cat goes to the club and becomes a sensation, billed as "The Dancing Fool". However, his domestic situation does not change despite his stardom as his brothers have become his agent and he is still a miserable wretch cleaning their home.

In the next entry, *Don't Spill the Beans* (April 1965), Gadmouse mistakenly gives Sad Cat some defective magic beans. After being planted, rather than growing up into the clouds they grow deep into the Earth causing geysers of oil to erupt making the townspeople rich. The last bean is planted which grows up into the clouds where Sad Cat and his brothers must face an angry giant. In a contest for who is the best dressed "cat" in the kingdom, in *Dress Reversal* (July 1965) Sad Cat is beaten up by his jealous brothers leaving his fancy clothes torn. A judge passes by and finds Sad Cat's tattered appearance the new "Beat Look" and he is awarded first prize. However, once again, Sad Cat is still unhappy as he is now an overworked tailor and still a miserable unhappy slave of his two brothers.

In *The Third Musketeer* (October 1965) Gadmouse uses a can of magic musketeer dust to transform Sad Cat into the third musketeer so that he can join his two swashbuckling musketeer brothers. However, his brothers argue over who is the "first" musketeer leaving Sad Cat no better off than before. In the last Bakshi short *Scuba Duba Do* (June 1966), Sad Cat finally gets the better of his brothers. While scuba diving with his siblings searching for sunken treasure he says the magic words "Treasure Map" and wins prizes in an underwater game show, the "Sunken Treasure Jackpot Program", hosted by a sea monster. Sad Cat sails happily away on a cruise ship.

The eight Sad Cat cartoons

Fig. 25.4 – Model sheet - Possible Possum.

directed by Bartsch were more upbeat shorts with Sad Cat being assisted by his superego in triumphing over his two mean brothers during some type of competition. In *Big Game Fishing* (February 1968) Sad Cat wins a fishing contest thanks to a magic fishing rod given to him by his superego. Sad Cat's superego turns a sandwich into a racing car in *Grand Prix Winner* (March 1968) helping Sad Cat win a race. Sad Cat uses magic golf balls and a golf club to defeat his brothers in a golf tournament (*All Teed Off* (June 1968)), uses a magic rope to reach the summit of a mountain before his siblings (*The Abominable Mountaineers* (September 1968)), and has his superego use magic to help him win an airplane race despite his brothers' attempts to sabotage the other fliers (*Loops and Swoops* (November 1968)).

The cartoon world would suffer a "mighty" loss in 1965. In the early morning of Wednesday, October 13, Connie Rasinski had just returned from taking his sheepdog for a walk. He was gardening in the flower bed when he suffered a massive heart attack. He walked into his house, said two words to his wife ("heart attack"), and collapsed onto the sofa. Connie's wife Alma called a friend, Hope Cummings, to come over. Cummings attended the Rasinski house and phoned the doctor. By the time the doctor had arrived Rasinski had passed away. The death of Connie was quick to reach the studio as he was scheduled to be picked up by his brother at his residence where he carpooled to work.[15] The disbelief, shock and tears quickly spread throughout the studio and wise Weiss decided to give everyone a day off to mourn the loss of an animation giant.

Connie was with the studio almost since it opened in 1929. He had directed 200 animated cartoons for the studio, helped create dozens of cartoon characters, reshaped the look of Super Mouse into the now familiar Mighty Mouse, and had mentored scores of animation artists. Rasinski was instrumental in the development of Ralph Bakshi as an animator and director. His animation gifts have become legend among his peers. He could animate beginning with any part of the character's anatomy, a difficult feat to accomplish even among the best animators. He could render his cartoon characters so effortlessly

Chapter 25 • L'Enfant Terrible and the Twilight of Terrytoons

that some believed he could animate with his eyes closed.[16] While Rasinski could animate with the best from Disney he didn't believe in creating cartoons that were elegant if they lacked the spirit of the creator. Rasinski told Bakshi that it is not the slickness of the cartoon that matters which is evident in the cartoons of Walt Disney. Rather, what is important is the whether the cartoon has "heart", cartoons with characters that have a soul, cartoons that are instilled with the passion of the artist, something which Rasinski tried to embed in every one of his cartoons he animated and directed.

In March 1965, Possible Possum made his theatrical debut in the animated cartoon *Freight Fright*. The character was heavily inspired by the success of the popular *Deputy Dawg* series. Larz Bourne wrote the stories for the cartoons which followed plotlines similar to the Deputy Dawg series. Like the Deputy Dawg cartoons they were also set in the south, in the *Possible Possum* series in the sleepy town of Happy Hollow. The lead character is of course Possible Possum, who looks and acts very similar to Muskie Muskrat from the Deputy Dawg cartoons. Possible Possum gets his name from his catchphrase "it's poss-i-bull, it's poss-i-bull", which is a phrase Muskie used to say in some of the first theatrical Deputy Dawg cartoons.

Possible Possum has a weakness for dill pickles which he would do almost anything to get his hands on. Billy Bear is analogous to Deputy Dawg in appearance and mentality, though he is undeniably a sidekick. Mr. General (owner of the general store) looks very similar to the sheriff in Deputy Dawg and fills the same "only recurring human" role in the cartoon series. Macon Mouse meanwhile acts like Vincent Van Gopher, and fills a similar role as Possible Possum's sidekick. The owl, Owlawishus, is the only recurring character in this series which has no equivalent in the Deputy Dawg series.

CBS-Terrytoons produced 37 Possible Possum cartoons in the mid-1960s, 26 of which were released theatrically until 1974 long after the studio closed. The first entry in the series has Possible and his friends trying to deliver a freight of canned goods from the freight depot to the general store in exchange for some dill pickles. The General Store burns down in *Darn Barn* (June 1965) so Possible Possum and friends decide to rebuild it. When Hill the builder claims only he has the right to rebuild the store, Possible Possum and gang spend the rest of the cartoon trying to get by Hill who tries to stop them at every turn. In *Git that Guitar* (September 1965), an antique dealer wants Possible Possum's guitar.

The Pickle Pirate (c. 1965) has Possible Possum and gang trying to retrieve some barrels of pickles that were stolen by the swamp pirate Big Beard. *Watch the Butterfly* (October 1966) tells the story of Possible Possum and friends guiding Professor Flutter through the swamp in search of a rare butterfly. Their efforts fail to catch the rare insect. Back at the rail station, while eating corn pone some black strap molasses falls on the professor's head and the rare butterflies get stuck on it and are captured. In *Kooky Cucumbers* (November 1971), Possible Possum plans to make his own dill pickles. He and his friends try to prevent a factory from laying a pipe through his cucumber patch but when they blow up a dam to sabotage the new industrial unit the patch becomes flooded.

Hobo Hassle (December 1974) has the gang trying to evict a hobo from the railway station house. When a "northern" supermarket plans to build in Happy Hollow threatening to put the General out of business, Possible Possum scares away the builder but in the process causes an avalanche requiring him and his friends to clear the rocks to allow the General's customers to get through (*Southern Supermarket* (not released theatrically)). The Possible Possum cartoons had very simple plots usually involving the gang trying to overcome some problem or obstacle. The ending usually had a twist in it which made their previous efforts in solving the problem seem hasty, foolish or ill-advised. The cartoons are largely forgotten today except for Possible Possum's oft-repeated catchphrase.

Independent animation studios such as Hanna-Barbera and Filmation were selling shows to the networks (ABC, CBS, and NBC), but Terrytoons was a studio that was owned by CBS and therefore there was only one target client. The cartoons currently produced by the studio were declining in popularity and by 1966 CBS was demanding some new series that would capture the

Fig. 25.5 – Jim Tyer storyboard for an unproduced Terrytoons cartoon called "Blood is Thicker Than Water".

minds and hearts of children as well as become a launching pad to market commercial products such as breakfast cereal and toys. In 1966, Bill Weiss asked Ralph Bakshi to help him carry presentation boards to Manhattan for a meeting with CBS. At the appointment, the network executives rejected all of Weiss's proposals as "too sophisticated", "too corny", or "too old-timey". Clearly, Weiss was trying to market a cartoon series based on what had worked 20 years earlier.

As Fred Silverman, CBS's daytime programming chief, began to leave the office, an unprepared Bakshi pitched a superhero parody called *The Mighty Heroes*. He described the series' characters, including Strong Man, Tornado Man, Rope Man, Cuckoo Man and Diaper Man: "They fought evil wherever they could and the villains were stupider than they were".[17] The executives loved the idea, and while Silverman required a few drawings before committing to the series, Weiss immediately put Bakshi to work on the series' development. Once Silverman saw the character designs, he confirmed that CBS would greenlight the show, on the condition that Bakshi serve as its creative director.[18] The cartoons would appear as a segment of *Mighty Mouse Playhouse* on the network's 1966–1967 Saturday morning schedule; the series was renamed *Mighty Mouse and the Mighty Heroes* in recognition of the new segment.

The series is set in Goodhaven, a city in the United States that is continually plagued by various super villains. When trouble occurs, "a call goes out for the Mighty Heroes" as the city launches a massive fireworks display with the flag's stars and stripes and the Statue of Liberty lighting up the background of the Goodhaven cityscape to summon a

Chapter 25 • L'Enfant Terrible and the Twilight of Terrytoons

Fig. 25.6 – Heckle and Jeckle animation cel from *Messed Up Movie Makers* (1966) on a non-matching production background.

quintet of high-flying superheroes into action. The original show debuted on CBS, on October 29, 1966, and ran for one season for 20 episodes.

The five heroes are clumsy accident-prone bunglers who often find themselves in ridiculous predicaments. A typical occurrence has them hopelessly tangled together or possibly trapped together offering each other stock apologies, often while falling en masse into an even worse state of affairs. In combat, they are pathetically inept, continually getting into each other's way until they are all captured by the villain (who almost always has enormous V-shaped teeth). The narrator then recaps how the Heroes managed to find themselves trapped in their predicament. In the final episode, the villains somehow manage to escape the death trap, usually with the aid of Diaper Man's baby bottle and then fight with proper coordination to capture the villain and save the city.

Strong Man is the "Superman" of the quintet, who has incredible strength – if not invulnerability. He speaks with a friendly southern farm-boy type accent and holds a civilian job as a mechanic. His favorite fighting move is his "jet-propelled blow" where he flies into a villain fist-first. Rope Man is a sailor who works at the docks. A very cultured and intelligent man with a light British accent, his body is a seemingly unending length of rope. He has a habit of talking too much. He can use his hands like lassos, and can even weave himself into a net. The shortcoming to his powers is that he often gets tangled up or knotted, commonly around his own hero mates.

Tornado Man works as a television weatherman who can spin himself into a tornado. He often sucks the villains into his vortex then shoots them out towards the nearest wall inflicting damage. He speaks in a winded wheezy voice. Cuckoo Man is a bird shop owner whose powers are simply bird-based. Unlike the other heroes, who can fly with no effort, Cuckoo Man has to flap his arms almost constantly in order to keep aloft. Cuckoo Man changes into his costume by jumping up through the bottom of his store's cuckoo clock and popping out through the little door. He may be the least effectual of the heroes, but he is not useless.

Diaper Man is a red-headed, diapered, yet well-spoken articulate baby as well as the leader and brains of the group. His main weapon is his bottle, which by holding on to the rubber nipple, he can swing around forcefully (or shoot like a slingshot). The bottle can also shoot high pressure streams of baby formula. In emergencies, Diaper Man (and often Strong Man) will drink some formula from the bottle when extra strength is needed.

The character voices were provided by Herschel Bernardi, who provided those of Strong Man, Diaper Man, and Tornado Man, and Lionel Wilson, who provided those of Cuckoo Man and Rope Man. Bernardi was also the original provider of the "Ho Ho Ho" voice of the Jolly Green Giant and of StarKist's Charlie the Tuna voice in commercials. The series came to an end when Bakshi left Terrytoons in 1967.

The inspiration for the series came from Bakshi's love of *MAD* comics and the satirizing found within the periodical. Bakshi grew up on comic books and he loved reading stories starring Superman, Blue Beetle, Batman and especially the Green Hornet. Comic book heroes became a part of his vocabulary as a kid and then in the 1950s when *MAD* comics began to satirize Archie and other comic book characters and popular culture figures, Bakshi couldn't get enough of the magazine. The Mighty Heroes were a marriage of his love of the satirizing found in Mad with his passion for superheroes.[19]

The first character Bakshi drew from the quintet was Diaperman.

The inspiration for the character came from his newborn son. Bakshi had a child, Mark, in 1961 and he would sit in the crib and throw his bottle at his father when he wanted more milk. Bakshi's first idea was to have Diaper Man throw the contents of his diaper at the villains but the studio did not think that baby feces being hurled in the direction of the bad guys was a good idea so Bakshi went with the bottle instead.[20] Cuckoo Man was originally Chicken Man. Strong Man was based on the Superman concept. Tornado Man was designed to be a blowhard. Rope Man was homage to Popeye the Sailor whose cartoons Bakshi loved to watch as a child.[21]

The villains in the Mighty Heroes cartoons were colorful and campy. The Plastic Blaster uses a gun to plasticize his victims sealing them in a coat of plastic. The Frog lives in an underwater hotel in a murky swamp outside Goodhaven. His weapon was the "swamp lifter" which raises the level of the swamp to flood Goodhaven. The Junker has an army of small metal robots with large snapping jaws. The Shrinker speaks with a Peter Lorre accent and uses his ray helmet to shrink objects, including the Goodhaven National Bank. The Ghost Monster speaks in a Transylvanian or Eastern European accent and flies around Goodhaven scaring people.

The Stretcher is made of rubber and traps the Mighty Heroes inside the Vulcanizer, a large pot that coats the heroes in rubber. The Monsterizer creates ghoulish monsters from citizens by using his monsterizer machine. The Timekeeper has built a large cuckoo clock and wants Cuckoo Man to be the new cuckoo bird for the clock trapping him inside the gigantic time piece. The Raven commands a large flock of ravens and uses a "building buster" which when dropped on a building the walls fall off. The Drifter unveils a sinister new weapon: an anti-gravity gun so powerful that it lifts the entire town of Goodhaven 6,000 feet in the air.

The Shocker has an army of electrified robots. The Enlarger is an evil man who owns a machine which can take germs and enlarge them to the size of giants. Toy Man has the dim-witted heroes trapped inside a giant coil spring (an over-sized Slinky) guarded by an army of mean wind-up toys. The Big Freeze can freeze anything he points his finger at. The Time Eraser is a villain from outer space who appears with his "Frankenstein" pal flashing a ray gun which transports anything that he points it at back in time.

The Mighty Heroes cartoons were a hit with television audiences in 1966. Bakshi had received a pay raise for his contributions to the studio, but was not as satisfied with his career advancement as he had anticipated. Bakshi did not have creative control over *The Mighty Heroes*, and he was unhappy with the quality of the animation, writing, timing and voice acting. Although the series' first 20 segments were successful, Bakshi wanted to leave Terrytoons to form his own company. In 1967, he drew up presentation pieces for a fantasy series called *Tee-Witt*, with help from Cosmo Anzilotti, John Zago

Chapter 25 • L'Enfant Terrible and the Twilight of Terrytoons

Fig. 25.7 – Model Sheet - Sidney the Elephant.

and Bill Focht, but CBS passed on the series. When Paramount Pictures had recently fired Shamus Culhane, the head of the studio's animation division, Bakshi met with Burt Hampft, a lawyer for the studio, and was hired to replace Culhane.[22] After Bakshi left CBS-Terrytoons, the studio decided they had lost the creative force behind the cartoons and *The Mighty Heroes* shorts were no longer produced.

The Martian Moochers, characters who were spin-offs from the *Astronut* series, starred in two animated cartoons in 1966. The Martian Moochers are two mice from Mars who sport buck teeth and have voracious appetites. *Champion Chump* (April 1966) has a proud feline, a mouse catching champion, showing off to a hero worshipping kitten. When the Moochers arrive, they eat everything they can sink their teeth into and humble the cat before flying back off into space. In *The Cowardly Watchdog* (August 1966), the Martian Moochers hypnotize a cowardly dog being bullied by a cat to become brave and get the better of the feline.

On October 5, 1962, the James Bond British spy film *Dr. No* starring Sean Connery was released by United Artists to an astounding box office gross of nearly $60 million (1962 dollars). The feature was followed in rapid succession by three other Bond films: *From Russia With Love* (1963), *Goldfinger* (1964), and *Thunderball* (1965). The success of the four Bond films led Mel Brooks and Buck Henry to produce *Get Smart*, an NBC television series that satirized the secret agent genre. The series first aired on September 18, 1965 and was a hit with audiences of the little screen. Terrytoons thought that a cartoon series featuring a secret agent might also be a success and so set out to produce a series starring a canine secret agent, James Hound.

Seventeen James Hound animated cartoons were produced by CBS-Terrytoons and released from 1966 to 1967. Borrowing traits from the bumbling agent Maxwell Smart in *Get Smart*, James is a secret agent with karate skills who is somewhat clumsy. However, no matter how many mistakes he makes in his efforts to capture the bad guy, he usually winds up bagging the criminal and foiling his plans to take over the world. Ms. Q is the Agency's operator who notifies James of his next assignment and keeps track of his efforts. James'

317

nemesis in many of the cartoons is Professor Mad who always avoids capture threatening to return and take over the world.

The series featured James Hound in a variety of far-off exotic locales battling evil while using secret agent weapons, karate, and uttering an assortment of bad puns. The first cartoon in the series was *Dr. Ha-Ha* (February 1966). Dr. Ha-Ha has developed a gas that makes one laugh uncontrollably and has used it to steal gold from the world bank. Hound sneaks into the castle hideout to capture Dr. Ha-Ha and his servant Igor but not before all end up sniffing the gas and are so happy that Ha-Ha gives Hound the secret formula to the gas. *The Monster Master* (July 1966) has Professor Mad planting monsters all around the world with the ghouls impersonating as rock stars and football players. Hound infiltrates the command post in Mad's castle and then unintentionally destroys the generator powering the machine that creates the monsters.

In *The Phantom Skyscraper* (December 1966), Professor Mad sends an apartment building with rocket capabilities blasting off to the South Pole where the tenants are to be used as slaves on a penguin ranch. Hound breaks into Mad's penthouse and then ineptly runs into the control mechanism destroying the system and sending the apartment complex back home. James Hound and nephew Conrad capture Diamond Jill and cohort Charlton trying to smuggle diamond watches to Florida by using ducks in *It's For the Birds* (March 1967). In *The Heat's Off*

(April 1967), Professor Mad has turned the world's weather upside down. Mad has a giant underwater fan attached to his submarine to reverse the warm sea currents. James' scarf gets caught in the submarine's fan causing the underwater craft to explode. Mad escapes threatening revenge.

Mr. Winlucky (February 1967) has James Hound flying to the tiny island of Bounty Carlo to visit a crooked casino owned by Winlucky. Winlucky only accepts countries, kingdoms or principalities as bets on his rigged roulette wheel. James breaks the casino bank and captures the greedy and deceitful casino owner. *Fancy Plants* (July 1967) has Professor Mad planting deadly plants that attack people all over the city with plans to take over the world. Mad escapes by using a plant that works like a missile launcher. The James Hound cartoons were mildly entertaining spoofs of the secret agent genre of films produced during the 1960s. The animation was well-rendered in comparison to some of the theatrical and television cartoons being produced at the time. The theme song was memorable and there was enough gadgetry on display to keep any fan of secret agent cinema satisfied.

By the mid-1960s, the theatrical cartoon was almost dead as the costs involved in producing a seven-minute cartoon had become too expensive for most Hollywood studios. As studios such as Warner Bros. and Paramount weren't willing to absorb the production costs to have cartoons

featured before their live-action features, animators found work in creating television animation or animated theatrical features. Bill Weiss understood that the future lay in producing television animation. However, between 1965 and 1967, Weiss found it increasingly difficult to sell projects to the television networks and as a result staff layoffs were inevitable.

In 1968, CBS requested several Saturday morning pilots from Terrytoons. However, executive producer Bill Weiss had no animation crew at the New Rochelle studio to produce the cartoons. With the studio unable to find new animation work, many had moved to work at studios on the west coast, found work in related artistic fields, or had retired or died. Weiss had little choice but to farm production out to the west coast. Weiss contracted with director Fred Calvert, who in turn hired several Hanna-Barbera animators (including Jerry Hathcock and Iwao Takamoto) to produce two pilots: *The Ruby Eye of The Monkey God* and *Sally Sargent*.

Neither of these pilots was made into a series. *The Ruby Eye of The Monkey God* is a weak, uninspired jungle adventure cartoon. A guard has snatched the ruby eye of a monkey god from a magician who had stolen it from the temple. A little boy and girl and their jungle animal friends return the ruby back to the temple while avoid being captured by an evil magician thereby saving the guard from being turned into a monkey by the stone statue. This nine-minute short, with a *Jonny Quest* feel to

Chapter 25 • L'Enfant Terrible and the Twilight of Terrytoons

it, was later released theatrically by 20th Century-Fox in January 1969 – and eventually circulated to television in the Terrytoons television package syndicated in the late 1970s.

In the latter short, Sally Sargent is a 16-year-old girl secret agent, Agent G16, who possesses a keen wit, some nifty secret agent gadgets, and skills in the martial arts. The cartoon draws upon inspiration from the Nancy Drew stories. This 10-minute animated cartoon was the final new production that Bill Weiss produced. The short features a groovy sixties theme song and Gary Owens voice on the track making it a much better short than the other pilot. This short was eventually added to the Mighty Mouse/Deputy Dawg syndication package.

By mid-1968, after the failure of the two pilots, and with no animation production being currently undertaken in the studio and no new projects being given the green light by CBS, CBS-Terrytoons was on the brink of closure. According to Nick Alberti who was Manager of Business Affairs and in charge of production from 1957 to 1972, the animation action had moved to the west coast. Hanna-Barbera, Filmation and other television animation factories were located in California and therefore much of the talent in the industry was located in the state. The buyers for the television networks didn't think that the quality of the talent on the east coast was as good as that on the west coast.[23]

While production ceased at the New Rochelle studio in 1967,

Fig. 25.8 – Doug Moye, cameraman and voice actor.

Weiss and Alberti would continue to operate business affairs from New Rochelle as well as New York City until 1972. From 1968 to 1972, Weiss continued to confer with CBS management in New York City attempting to sell animation projects to network executives. Unfortunately, his efforts were without success. Eventually, Fred Silverman, who was promoted from Vice-President of Program Planning and Development to Vice President, Programs – heading the entire program department at CBS, made the final decision to close the studio which took place in August 1972.[24] Nick Alberti was ordered by CBS to auction off all of the equipment. *The Daily Item* reported on January 5, 1973:

Now, the story room, like the rest of the Centre Avenue studio, is empty. The few remaining pieces of furniture-a couch, a table, the fibreboard where artists pinned up their rough drawings-have been sold, given away or junked, gone the route of the special photographic equipment and the metal shelves where films were stored and the special desks where once animators

319

and background men, inkers and opaquers toiled to supply a public hungry for funny cartoons. All gone.[25]

In cleaning out the studio, Alberti gave the first 10 films ever produced by Paul Terry and Frank Moser to the Museum of Modern Art in New York City for archival and historical purposes.

CBS also ordered that all of the production materials, which would have included Paul Terry's famous archive of animation background art, were to be destroyed. Alberti discarded some of the materials in the waste container near the studio and made the decision to have most of the materials incinerated. This would include millions of dollars of collectible animation cels, storyboards, and background art.[26] Fortunately, at least one wise individual, having spotted some of the artwork in the dumpster, salvaged a treasure trove of materials from the container. These magnificent pieces of art now can be found on the market, in galleries, museums, and in private collections. Beginning in early 1973, Terrytoons operated out of the Manhattan offices of Viacom International, Inc., formerly a division of CBS and now the cartoon firm's parent company.[27]

CBS Films, Inc., the television syndication division of CBS established in 1952, was spun off and renamed Viacom in 1971, amid new FCC rules forbidding television networks from owning syndication companies[28] (the rules were later repealed). The film library, which Viacom had the underlying rights, was still being tapped into regularly re-releasing shorts to theaters by Fox until at least 1975 thus ensuring its existing cartoon library a long life in TV reruns. The Terrytoons cartoons (especially Mighty Mouse and Deputy Dawg) were syndicated to many local TV markets, and they were a staple of after-school and Saturday morning cartoon shows for over three decades, from the 1950s through the 1980s, until the television rights to the library were acquired by USA Network in 1989. ❧

Notes

1. "L'Enfant Terrible", in *Oxford English Dictionary*, 2nd ed., prepared by J.A. Simpson and E.S.C. Weiner (Oxford: Clarendon Press; Oxford; New York: Oxford University Press, 1989).

2. Jon M. Gibson and Chris McDonnell, *Unfiltered: The Complete Ralph Bakshi* (New York: Universe; Enfield: Publishers Group UK [distributor], 2008), 22–24.

3. Gibson and McDonnell, *Unfiltered*, 28–29.

4. Ibid., 32–33.

5. Ibid., 38–39.

6. Ralph Bakshi, telephone interview by author (transcript), Kelowna, B.C., Canada, 25 March 1998, Terrytoons Collection, Victoria, B.C., 4.

7. Gibson and McDonnell, *Unfiltered*, 38–39.

8. Ibid.

9. Ibid.

10. When asked by a parent what advice he can give to their child wanting to pursue a music career, the overworked Scheib stated: "Do not get into the business because it is too difficult". Cosmo Anzilotti, telephone interview by author (transcript), Kelowna, B.C., Canada, 26 March 1998, Terrytoons Collection Victoria, B.C., 5.

11. "Timmens, James F." in *The New Edition of the Encyclopedia of Jazz*, by Leonard Feather (New York: Horizon Press, 1960), 442.

12. Ibid.; See also: "Sunday D&C Features Article on S. Timmens", *Caledonia Advertiser* (Caledonia, New York), 21 May 1953, p. 7, 10; "Obituary: James Timmens", *Caledonia Advertiser* (Caledonia, New York), 22 May 1980, "Scottsville News", p. 4.

13. Gibson and McDonnell, *Unfiltered*, 43.

14. Rasinski, interview, 1.

15. Ibid.; Hope Cummings, telephone interview by author (transcript), Kelowna, B.C., Canada, 20 November 1997, Terrytoons Collection, Victoria, B.C., 5.

16. Mary Taracka, telephone interview by author (transcript), Kelowna, B.C., Canada, 23 November 1997, Terrytoons Collection, Victoria, B.C., 2.

17. Gibson and McDonnell, *Unfiltered*, 47–49.

18. Ibid.

19. Bakshi, interview, 2.

20. Ibid., 3.

21. Ibid.

22. Gibson and McDonnell, *Unfiltered*, 47–49.

23. Nick Alberti, telephone interview by author (transcript), Kelowna, B.C., Canada, 29 September 1997, Terrytoons Collection, Victoria, B.C., 5.

24. Ibid., 6–8.

25. Tracy, "A Look Back on the 'Golden Days'", p. 4.

26. Alberti, interview, 7.

27. Tracy, "A Look Back on the 'Golden Days'", p. 4.

28. "CBS transfers CATV to new public firm", *Broadcasting*, 27 July 1970, p. 48.

Chapter 26

Cartoon End Credits: The Retirement and Death of Paul Terry, 1956–1971

Paul Terry's exit from the studio in January 1956 was swift and quiet leaving behind a number of surprised, angry and bitter employees who had been promised a share of the studio upon his retirement. These studio artists would be Gene Deitch's inheritance. Why Terry made these promises is not difficult to fathom. His assurances would engender a greater sense of devotion to the studio and help ensure that his talented group of veterans remained with him until his retirement. Why these artists believed him is another matter. There was no precedent for this type of managerial change within the animation industry. Tom Morrison, Connie Rasinski, and Mannie Davis were loyal, dedicated, and tireless workers who spent a good portion of their careers working five days a week, Monday to Friday from 8:30 a.m. to 5:30 p.m., plus one evening a week and a half day on Saturday in the days before the union. But they were paid well for their services. Although they labored tirelessly, some for decades, were they truly deserving of a share of the sale of the studio for which Terry had risked everything to establish and manage for 26 years?

Of those that were not given some financial reward for their loyalty, it was probably Connie who had sacrificed the most to help develop studio talent and create an entertaining cartoon product. Outside of some weekend fishing and the mandatory vacation period during which time he resided in the Westchester community, Rasinski had never taken much of a vacation and spent many evenings, usually Thursdays, at the studio teaching and inspiring new artists. He had been with the studio almost since it first opened. Possibly it was the way Terry left the studio, without saying much of a goodbye or a thank you to his long-time friends and then disappearing into retirement.

As part of his deal with CBS, for about the next five years Terry was provided a salary and given the title of President.[1] In return, he was tasked with being a consultant for the new studio but he wasn't completely comfortable with that responsibility, possibly because this entailed returning to the studio and facing those same employees he had betrayed by reneging on his promise. Besides the $3.5 million payday, Terry was promised a new Cadillac every year for a number of years. However, he was not comfortable with that arrangement, primarily because he was frugal by nature, finding a new car every year to be an unnecessary luxury and a waste of money.[2]

To cast Terry as a prodigious budget-minded producer of hundreds of entertaining animated cartoons during the Golden Age of American Animation who thrived in a field where most other filmmakers have failed without highlighting his work as a man who genuinely cared for the lives of his family, friends, employees, and even those whom he had never met would be offering a one-dimensional portrait of the animation legend. During the 1930s and 1940s Terry provided employment opportunities to hundreds of untrained and lesser-skilled artists looking for opportunities they were unable to

321

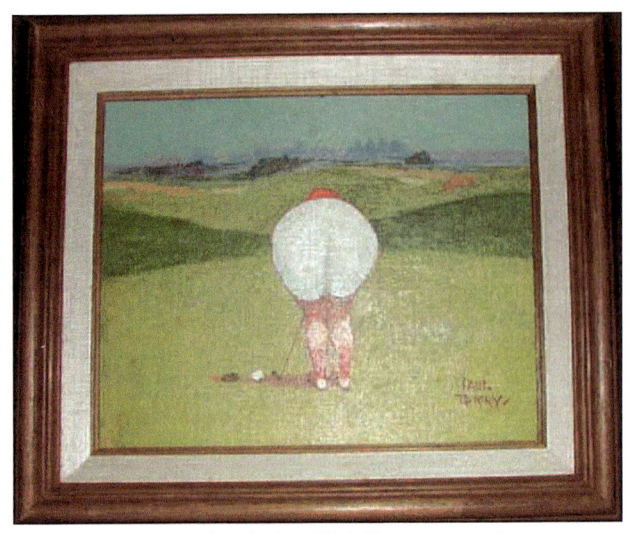

TERRYTOONS: The Story of Paul Terry and His Classic Cartoon Factory

Fig. 26.1 – Paul Terry's painting titled "Concentration".

obtain at other animation houses such as Disney or Fleischer and during the tough economic times of the Depression endeavored, and largely succeeded, in keeping all his staff employed. If an employee was struggling financially and became ill, Terry kept the paychecks coming during the illness long before there were any sick pay benefits.

Terry approached his studio as a family operation and would hire relatives of his staff whenever possible rather than seek help elsewhere. When some of his employees were struggling financially, Terry would make loans out to these employees. When some of these employees were unable to repay their loans back, Terry did not press the matter. Paul managed a studio on a tight budget where every penny did count and by doing so kept the operation afloat and his staff of artists and technicians employed. At home, he was financially generous not just to his close family but also to distant relatives, and could be relied upon for assistance especially in times of economic need.

Terry stayed true to his inner convictions that a man has a right to speak his opinions without penalty or discipline and hired Paul Robeson for a brief period of time when most other employers were turning their backs on the outspoken pro-Communist singer and actor. He hired one of the first Afro-Americans in the animation industry and trained him in the field of animation photography. Terry had a special place in his heart for the victimized and those with nowhere else to turn to. Prior to and during the early years of the Second World War, he struggled for and was successful in arranging the emigration of Jewish families out of Germany and their subsequent employment at his residence and by doing so saved lives and changed family destinies.

Despite retirement, Terry continued to be active artistically. In his sixth floor Westchester Country Club apartment he allocated a room for sculpture, a little painting and a workshop.[3] On a typical morning he might model clay to create a bust of a friend, such as he did in May 1965 for Dr. Irving Weinstein of New Rochelle. The same year he created a cast-metal sculpture of a couple dancing the twist. In 1964, he painted a mural showing a bull and bear playing golf on the grounds of the Westchester

Fig. 26.2 – Paul Terry with his painting.

Chapter 26 • Cartoon End Credits

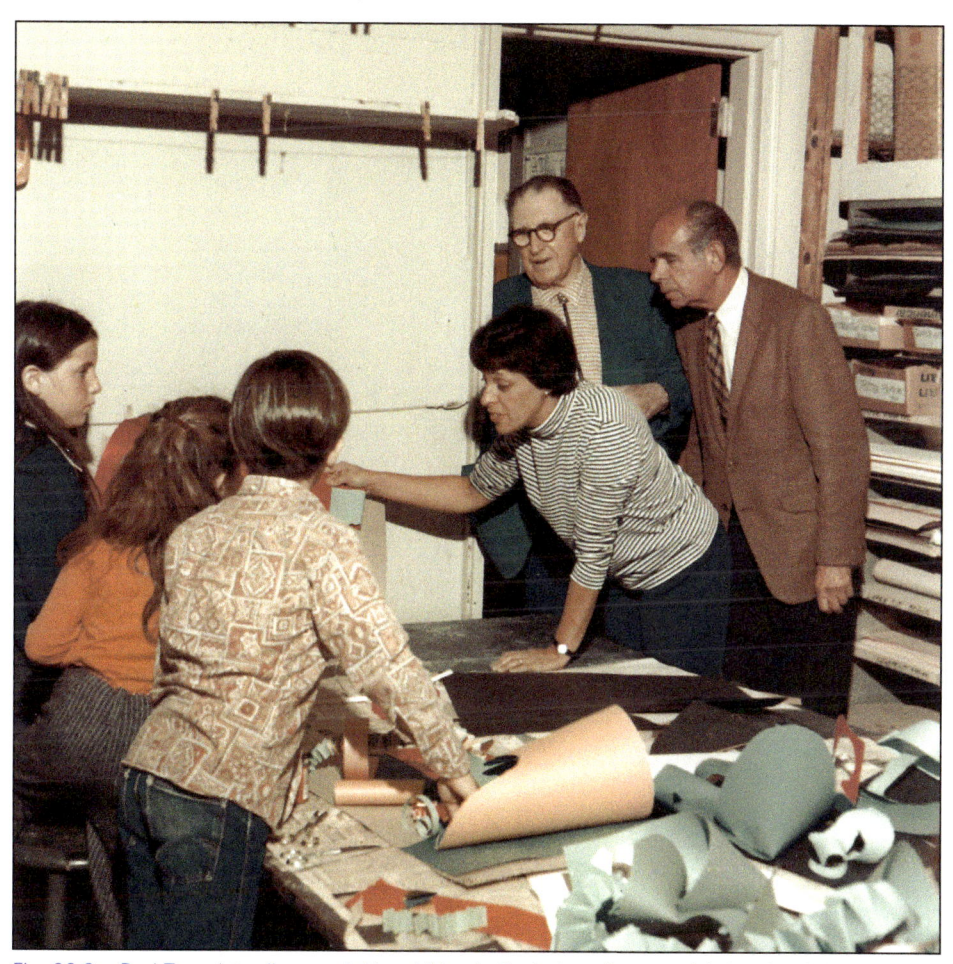

Fig. 26.3 – Paul Terry (standing rear left) and Mannie Davis (standing rear right) at the Children's Art Studio.

Country Club. The mural was hung in a New York stock broker's office, Ernst & Co.[4] He also completed a beautiful color painting of a grandchild of Edwin Goodman of the famed Bergdorf-Goodman.[5] In his preparatory work on his paintings, Terry was known to be very meticulous undertaking a number of studies before putting oil on canvas.[6] As homage to Marcel Duchamp's painting *Nude Descending a Staircase, No. 2* (1912), Terry created a sculpture.

In Terry's version, the nude is tumbling down the staircase with legs airborne. In 1969, he completed a bust of Roman Catholic priest Father Keller, head of the Christophers.[7] The sculpture was an excellent likeness of the clergyman.

He usually ate lunch at the club; possibly checked the stock market and his afternoon might be running a clay sculpture down to a foundry for casting in metal. He might be driven out to a social gathering to meet friends. He also took a Dale Carnegie Institute course on public speaking. He admitted to becoming more conservative the older he got. He initially agreed with the Johnson administration's intervention in the Dominican Republic to forestall the establishment of a Communist dictatorship (1965) and the U.S. fighting of the Vietnam War (1955–1975), but later changed his opinion on the conflicts.[8] He would jokingly comment that he spent a lot of time going to

323

Fig. 26.4 – Paul Terry viewing eight theater lobby cards.

funerals of old friends.[9] He would assert in his later years that he sold his studio for $5 million to CBS. He did not really want to sell, he claimed, but he had reached that age.[10]

As the years passed Terry devoted more time to charitable and philanthropic causes. He donated a small balance of money to the Larchmont Public Library and the Mamaroneck Public Library.[11] He went up to Massachusetts to put on a show for the diabetic camp of about 200 children where he exhibited some of his cartoons including the 1946 film showing how a cartoon is produced.[12] In December 1965, Terry and Father Keller spoke at a joint meeting of the executive board and the public relations committee of the Hutchinson River Council, Boy Scouts of America. The topic was the importance of sound community public information and public relations program, and the need for more effective communications with the boys in the 12 to 17 age group.[13] Terry also spoke on the importance of high standards and sound objectives on the part of adult Boy Scouters.[14] He also participated in a weekly public speaking class at the Westchester Country Club.[15] Terry also enjoyed playing cards, poker, canasta and gin. His wife Irma was an avid card player and together they would pass many hours over hearts, clubs, diamonds and spades.[16]

Right up until his passing Terry remained a member of the Hook and Ladder No. 1, the Larchmont Fire Department comprised of volunteer firemen.[17] He served on the board of trustees at the Industrial Arts School in New York City. He was President of the Museum of Arts and Industrial Crafts of Larchmont and Mamaroneck. He supported the Children's Studio, a private art school for children founded by Florence Weichsel that closed in 1972.[18] He donated funds to establish a Paul Terry Scholarship Award through the Florida Federation of Women's Clubs.[19] He gave many talks in New Rochelle and Larchmont to clubs and schools. At least once Terry was the guest speaker at the Rye Kiwanis Club. The Social Security Administration featured Terry in a film which was part of the television series *Social Security in America*. The film was produced in early 1967.[20]

About once a week, Terry would visit his daughter and four grandchildren, usually taking the children to the movies. Once a year he and his wife would take a weekly trip during the summer to the Westport, Connecticut Country Playhouse.[21]

He joined the National Cartoonists Society in the 1950s and won a NCS award in the Animation category. He also became a member of the Variety Club of New York and the Lambs Club. He was a member of the Speakers' Forum to address animation related issues to the Westchester County business community. In October 1966, Terry joined the (New Rochelle) Mayor's Conference on the Aging to discuss various aging-related issues.[22]

In August 1967, Terry traveled to Montréal, Québec, Canada to take part in the Retrospective Mondiale du Cinema Animation from August 13 to 19, a retrospective on world animation that formed part of the World's Fair held in the French-Canadian city. Seventeen programs consisting of 187 films, mostly animated shorts outside of Disney's *Dumbo*, Halas &

Chapter 26 • Cartoon End Credits

Batchelor's *Animal Farm*, film titles by Saul Bass and some educational animated films.

The films were exhibited at the Expo 67 Theatre. Terry's representative works formed part of the program on the 1930s animation held at 4:00 p.m. on August 16.

The attendees at the retrospective comprised a veritable who's who of international animation including Chuck Jones, Peter Foldes, Abe Levitow, John Halas, Ward Kimball, Ken Peterson, Shamus Culhane, Pete Burness, Ub Iwerks, I. Klein, Ian Popesco-Gopo, Carmen d'Avino, Bill Mathews, Len Lye, June Foray, Bill Hurtz, Spence Peel, Paul Frees, Steve Bosustow, Dave Hilberman, Art Babbitt, Feodor Khitruk, Fred Wolf, Ivan Ivanov-Vano, and J. R. Bray. Other animation notables included Walter Lantz, Otto Messmer, Dave Fleischer, Ruth Kneitel, Bruno Bozzetto, Bob Clampett, Karel Zeman, Dusan Vukotic, Bretislav Pojar, Jean Image, Grim Natwick, and Tissa David.[23] Terry became reacquainted with some of his old friends in animation and thoroughly enjoyed the seven-day retrospective.

In March 1969, Terry and old friend Bill Hilliker took a five-week motor trip to California.[24] In May 1970, Terry was the guest of honor of the City of Yonkers for his work in animation.[25] On February 8, 1971, the city of New Rochelle honored Terry at City Hall. The council resolution pointed out that Terry had made Aesop's Fables long before Walt Disney had made his first short. Visibly moved, Terry

Fig. 26.5 – Paul Terry at his residence with his sculpture.

acknowledged the citation by saying, "I owe New Rochelle more than New Rochelle owes me".

Then perhaps thinking of the first day he came to the city he added softly, "If anybody asks what you

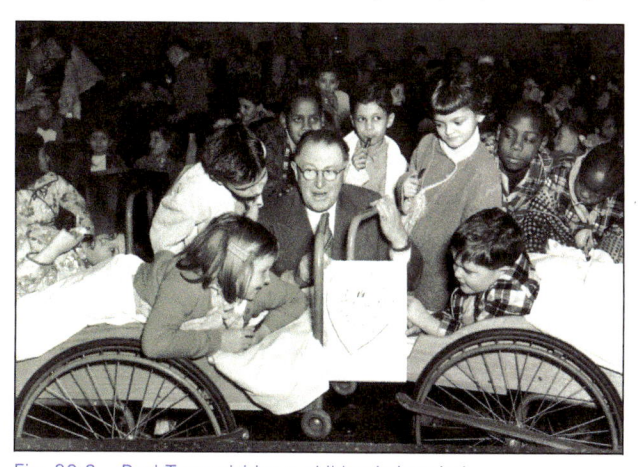

Fig. 26.6 – Paul Terry visiting a children's hospital.

Fig. 26.7 – Paul Terry and *Beany and Cecil* creator Bud Clampett.

did tonight, you just tell them you made an old man very happy".[26] Terry enjoyed viewing the animation produced by other studios and independent animators. When the avant-garde and experimental animation of Norman McLaren was exhibited at the Guggenheim in 1969, Terry attended the exhibition and found his work very humorous, interesting, and offering new lines of thought in animation and stop motion photography.[27]

By late 1968, Paul's wife Irma had suffered a series of heart attacks and was hospitalized at the United Hospital in Port Chester, New York. Paul accompanied her to the hospital and asked if he could stay with her in the same room but hospital policy strictly forbade a man and a woman sharing the same hospital room. Therefore, the hospital staff had a bed made up for him across the hall where he could stay. During his residence at the hospital Paul would walk into her room and spend some time with her telling the nurses that "he was going to see my girl".[28]

Paul's time with his wife after entering the hospital was brief. On January 7, 1969, Irma was close to death as her heart was very weak. Paul, well aware that his wife was near death, was summoned to the room. As he bent down to gently kiss her he said goodbye to her and she passed away. Irma wanted to be cremated quickly and so a funeral was held, which was attended by Alfred Benedict DelBello, later the 70th Lieutenant Governor of New York from 1983 to 1985.[29]

At the age of 82, Terry was still eager to live for another 20 or so years.[30] He found inspiration working with children helping them to become more creative at an early age and counted each day as a new blessing.[31] A year later, at age 83 he still desired to get back into the animation business but recognized his advanced age and that in seven years he would be 90, and "a fellow 90 years old, no matter who he is, I don't care who he is, he's not what he used to be".[32] He began paying thanks to some of his old friends and those that worked for him through financial gifts. Just a week before he died he wrote a $25,000 cheque to his accountant to reward him for many years of diligent work.[33]

As Terry moved into his late 70s, he continued to ignore the advice of his family physician to cut

Fig. 26.8 – Paul Terry (extreme left) and Father James Keller (second from right).

down on his fat intake as he became more obese. He had always consumed a diet rich in fat with little concern for the effects of obesity on his health and had a stout, portly figure. In his coffee he would take sugar and whole cream. His daughter Pat would watch him consume foods rich in fats and sugars and almost got ill looking at what her father was eating.[34] In October 1971 after complaining of abdominal discomfort Terry was admitted to the Memorial Hospital for Cancer and Allied Diseases for surgery on his intestines done under local anaesthetic.[35] He came through the operation fine but remained in the hospital under observation. Seventeen days later, on October 25, 1971, he died. Pat received a phone call from the hospital early that morning informing her that her father had passed away.

The cause of death was colon cancer and the likely culprit was years of chewing on the end of his cigar which would slowly disappear into his mouth during the course of a day. Medical research has found that digesting rather than smoking tobacco is a leading cause of oral cancer, pancreatic cancer, esophagus cancer, stomach cancer and colon cancer. The funeral was held at 11 a.m. on October 28 at the Rye Presbyterian Church in Rye, New York. Terry wanted a large funeral and he got one as family, friends, and members in the animation community arrived to pay their respects.[36] He was cremated and his ashes placed in an urn and the container is kept with the Terry family. In summing up his life Terry stated with a smile: "I wouldn't have missed this world for anything. I've had a wonderful life".[37]

Notes

1. Alberti, interview, 3.
2. Leahy, interview, 19.
3. Henry Null, "Cartoon Pioneer Retired ... Not Bored", *The Daily Item* (Port Chester, N.Y.), 19 June 1965.
4. "Something New", *The Daily Item* (Port Chester, N.Y.), 2 September 1964.
5. "Lunch With Paul Terry", *The Cartoonist*, p. 20.
6. Leahy and Lazar, interview, 27.
7. *Westchester Country Club News*, April 1969.
8. Null, "Cartoon Pioneer Retired... Not Bored".
9. Ibid.
10. Ibid.
11. Charles M. Baxter to Paul Terry, 4 February 1964, Paul Terry Papers.
12. Terry, interview, 20 December 1969, 59.
13. "Scout Staff To Hear Cartoonist and Priest", *The Daily Item* (Port Chester, N.Y.), 1 December 1965.
14. "Father Keller Honored By Scouts", *The Standard-Star* (New Rochelle, N.Y.), 17 December 1965, p. 19.
15. "Lunch With Paul Terry", *The Cartoonist*, p. 20.
16. Leahy and Lazar, interview, p. 21.
17. Terry, interview, 20 December 1969, 72.
18. Paul Terry to Florence Weichsel, undated, Paul Terry Papers.
19. Florida Federation of Women's Clubs to Paul Terry, 8 August 1959, Paul Terry Papers.
20. *Pelham Sun*, 31 August 1967, Paul Terry Papers.
21. "Lunch With Paul Terry", *The Cartoonist*, p. 20.
22. "Terrytoons Founder Joins Conference On The Aging", *The Standard-Star* (New Rochelle, N.Y.), 11 October 1966, p. 51.
23. Others in attendance were Manuel Otero, Edith Vernick, Don Bajus, Bill & Fini Littlejohn, Carl Bell, Gerald Baldwin, Gene Plotnick, Stan Van der Beek, Les Goldman, Jimmy Murakami, Mike Lah, Robert Breer, Tom Roth, Barrie Nelson, Andre Martin, Ed Smith, Dick Rauh, and John Whitney.
24. Marchionni, "Paul Terry, at 82, Still Calls the Toon", *Herald Statesman*, 28.
25. "Senior Citizens of Yonkers", *The Record of Yonkers*, 28 May 1970, p. 7.
26. Schetterer, "New Rochelle was home for Terry's cartoon genius", p. 1; Dick Tracy, "Paul Terry Honored By City; Animated Cartoons Born Here", *The Daily Item* (Port Chester, N.Y.), 9 February 1971.
27. Terry, interview, 20 December 1969, 60, 66.
28. Leahy, interview, 24 August 1996, 21.
29. Ibid.
30. Terry, interview, 20 December 1969, 63.
31. Ibid., 63–64.
32. Terry, interview, 14 July 1970, 151.
33. Leahy and Lazar, interview, 17.
34. Leahy, interview, 24 August 1996, 16.
35. Ibid.
36. "Paul H. Terry, 84, Drew Terrytoons: Animation Pioneer Created Tales of Mighty Mouse", *New York Times*, 26 October 1971, p. 44.
37. Terry, interview, 20 December 1969, 63.

327

Chapter 27

The Terrytoons Retrospective: A Meeting of Old Friends, 1982

In 1980, the idea began to germinate among a few of the former Terrytoons staff that a retrospective be organized in New Rochelle to commemorate the studio which was such an integral part of the community for nearly 40 years. Dianne, the wife of former Terrytoons story man Eli Bauer, was one of the first to step forward and begin planning the celebratory event. Both Dianne and Eli would become co-chairpersons of the Terrytoons retrospective. Soon animator and comic book artist Doug Crane joined the endeavor. Before long they realized the effort was too big for them so they contacted the New Rochelle Council on the Arts.[1]

The Arts Council agreed to participate as part of its continuing efforts to highlight the community's contributions to the fine and popular arts. Thea Eichler, Arts Council program chairwoman, and the other members of the planning committee began the task of contacting former studio employees, including Pat Terry, requesting their participation in organizing the event. Their recruitment efforts were successful. Others active in

Fig. 27.1 – Terrytoons theatrical poster.

Chapter 27 • The Terrytoons Retrospective

Fig. 27.2 – Edward G. Robinson cat from *The Racket Buster* (1949).

planning the event were Howard Beckerman, Nicholas Alberti, Ralph Bakshi, and Bill Weiss.[2]

The task of planning and organizing the festival was not easy, duties which included gathering artwork and memorabilia for the exhibition and contacting former staff members. There was talk of erecting a giant statue of Mighty Mouse downtown but nothing came of it. Another idea was to rename Memorial Highway, "Mighty Mouse Square". One of the biggest obstacles to overcome was to find samples of the studio's artwork for the exhibition. During the years CBS was in control of studio operations, some of the art was destroyed by the media giant. A significant quantity of the original artwork had been donated to the School of Visual Arts and was destroyed in a flooded storage area there. When the studio closed in the early 1970s, on orders from CBS, the rest of the artwork was either discarded or incinerated.

Fortunately, a number of studio artists had brought some of the artwork home with them during their tenure of employment and a few former staff members offered to lend some of their Terrytoons treasures for the exhibition. Pat Terry drove from North Carolina with a truck full of her father's effects. She was overjoyed with

Fig. 27.3 – Promotional leaflet cover for Terrytoons Retrospective (1982).

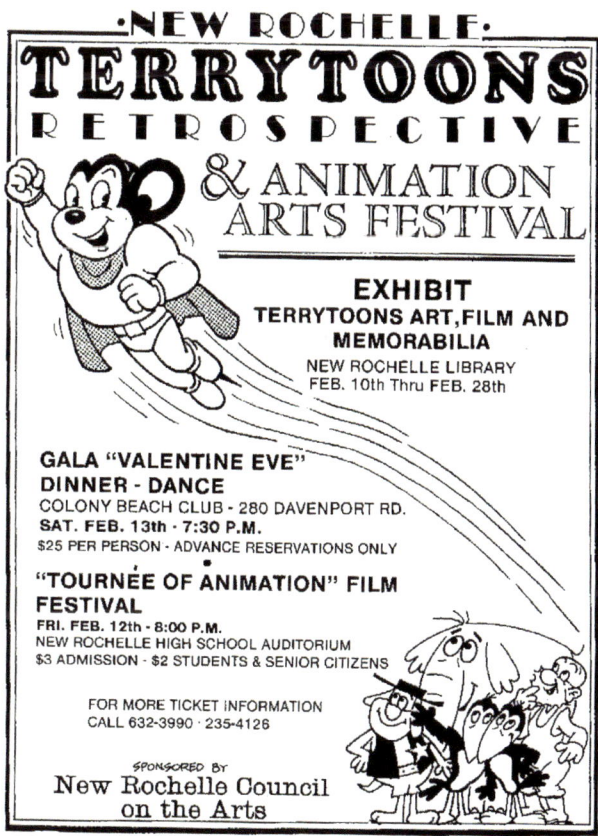

·NEW ROCHELLE·
TERRYTOONS
RETROSPECTIVE
& ANIMATION ARTS FESTIVAL

EXHIBIT
TERRYTOONS ART, FILM AND MEMORABILIA
NEW ROCHELLE LIBRARY
FEB. 10th Thru FEB. 28th

GALA "VALENTINE EVE"
DINNER - DANCE
COLONY BEACH CLUB - 280 DAVENPORT RD.
SAT. FEB. 13th · 7:30 P.M.
$25 PER PERSON - ADVANCE RESERVATIONS ONLY

"TOURNÉE OF ANIMATION" FILM FESTIVAL
FRI. FEB. 12th - 8:00 P.M.
NEW ROCHELLE HIGH SCHOOL AUDITORIUM
$3 ADMISSION - $2 STUDENTS & SENIOR CITIZENS

FOR MORE TICKET INFORMATION
CALL 632-3990 · 235-4126

SPONSORED BY
New Rochelle Council on the Arts

Fig. 27.4 – Terrytoons foreign exhibition poster.

the idea of a retrospective being given in honor of her father's studio. After her father's retirement from animation Pat had devoted herself to work as a political and cultural activist. In 1982 she was secretary of the Democratic Party in Fayetteville, North Carolina. She was a board member of Democratic Women and a Lafayette Society board member and was chairperson of

Chapter 27 • The Terrytoons Retrospective

Fig. 27.5 – Paul Terry with movie camera (c. 1960s).

Fig. 27.6 – Paul Terry relaxing at his residence (c. 1950s).

the April 16 Big Band Night for the Fayetteville Museum of Art.[3]

The Terrytoons studio had employed approximately 1,000 people during its nearly 40 years in New Rochelle so advertisements in national union newspapers, such as the one published by the Screen Cartoonist's Guild, elicited names and materials. The organizing committee was able to locate about 100 former Terrytooners.[4] The Terrytoons alumni who attended the retrospective were a veritable who's who of New York animation and included Dayton Allen, Clifford Augustson, Ralph Bakshi, Eli Bauer, Howard Beckerman, John Gentilella, Alfred Kouzel, Joe Rasinski, Ralph Sancier, Martin Taras, John Vita, and David Ubinas.[5]

The 19-day salute to Terrytoons was officially titled "Terrytoons Retrospective & Animation Arts Festival" and took place from February 10 to 28, 1982 in New Rochelle. The festival included a retrospective exhibit, demonstrations of the art of animation with artists and critics, and screenings of outstanding Terrytoons cartoons, all in the New Rochelle Public Library. Highlights of the celebration were the "Valentine Eve" celebration at the Colony Beach Club on Saturday February 13, and a "Tournee of Animation" on Friday, February 12. The Saturday supper party included a full course dinner, disco dancing, and entertainment starting at 7:30 p.m. at $25 per person. Cocktails were served from 7:30 to 8:30 p.m., dinner and dancing from 8:30 to 10:30 p.m., and then welcoming remarks by Dr. Robert Rosenbaum, chairman of the New Rochelle Council on the Arts, and introductions by Nicholas Alberti.[6] More than 30 of the partygoers at the Colony Club were once employees of Terrytoons.[7]

All proceeds from the dinner and dance benefited the New Rochelle Council on the Arts. The "Tournee of Animation", included 16 [15] of the latest in award-winning

331

TERRYTOONS: The Story of Paul Terry and His Classic Cartoon Factory

animated films from around the world screened at New Rochelle High School's Whitney M. Young Jr. auditorium. Films screened were *Confessions of a Stardreamer* (1978) by John Canemaker, Jean Francois Laguionie's *La traversee de l'Atlantique a la rame* (1978), and the National Film Board of Canada's *Why Me?* (1978) and *Special Delivery* (1978). There were also people in costumes dressed up as cartoon characters to delight the kids.[8]

On February 10, Leonard C. Paduano, Mayor of New Rochelle, proclaimed the dates of February 10 to 28 as "Terrytoons Studio Days". Included in the festivities were demonstrations ("chalk talks") on the art of animation by Doug Crane, panel discussions with guest artists and critics, and films were donated by Viacom, the owner of the Terrytoons film library at the time, which were exhibited. The exhibition, in the library's gallery, included photographs, posters, storyboards, cels, memorabilia and life size replicas of the cartoon characters. Comedian and voice artist Dayton Allen provided some entertainment.

The 19-day retrospective was a resounding success. Old friends got the opportunity to share stories and memories, the Westchester area was treated to the art and history of a legendary cartoon studio, and the artists and staff responsible for bringing to life cartoon characters such as Mighty Mouse, Heckle and Jeckle and Deputy Dawg were given due recognition and paid tribute. Doug Crane, a Terrytoons animator in the early 1960s, felt it was necessary to hold the exhibit fearing that history would someday forget the New Rochelle studio and its contributions to the history of animated film.[9] With hundreds of Terrytoons cartoons now available to be viewed over the Internet, it is unlikely the studio will be forgotten anytime soon.

For nearly 40 years a Terrytoons cartoons was shown before a feature film produced by 20th Century-Fox. The cartoons were distributed worldwide from Paris to Peking. Thanks to television, Mighty Mouse has become a cultural icon. Other Terrytoons cartoon characters such as Heckle and Jeckle, Deputy Dawg, and Tom Terrific are still being used to market hundreds of commercial products. From 1929 to 1967, the studio gave birth to and employed some of the most talented artists in the business, many of whom would shape the art of animation. The production house was founded by one of the most prodigious producers of animated cartoons. During his career, Terry produced more shorts than any other cartoon producer, including Walt Disney and his famed studio. With these laurels, Terrytoons can rightly be ranked as one of the giants of the animated cartoon studios of the 20th century. ஓ

Notes

1. Ian T. MacAuley, "Mighty Mouse (and Others) on the Way to Save the Day", *New York Times*, 7 February 1982, p. WC1.

2. June Schetterer, "What's going on: Terrytoons festival includes party, show", *The Standard-Star* (New Rochelle, N.Y.), 30 January 1982; Randall V. Berlage, "Animators Fondly Recall Creation of Terrytoons", *The Fayetteville Observer* (Fayetteville, North Carolina), 15 April 1982, p. 2B.

3. Oakley, "Pat Leahy Was There in New York For Salute To Dad's Terrytoons".

4. Larry Cole, "Cartoons are what's up, Doc", [*Standard-Star* (New Rochelle, N.Y.)].

5. New Rochelle Council on the Arts, "Gala "Valentine Eve" Dinner-Dance" (program brochure), Saturday February 13, 1982, Paul Terry Papers, Fayetteville, North Carolina.

6. Ibid.

7. Schetterer, "Partygoers celebrate birthday of legendary super mouse", *The Standard-Star* (New Rochelle, N.Y.), 15 February 1982.

8. June Schetterer, "What's going on: Terrytoons festival includes party, show", *The Standard-Star* (New Rochelle, N.Y.), 30 January 1982.

9. Perelson, "Terry's works remain in tune", B1.

Appendix 1

Terrytoons Who's Who: Biographies of The Key Players

ALLEN, Dayton (1919–2004). Dayton Allen, voice artist, comedian, and writer, was born Dayton Allen Bolke in New York, New York on September 24, 1919, the son of Solomon and Helen (née Freedman) Bolke. Allen was raised in White Plains, Jackson Heights, and Mount Vernon, New York, and attended Mount Vernon High School where his school peers voted him "the wittiest boy in class".

His first full-time job was a projectionist of 16mm movies shown as recreation at hospitals, summer camps, and prisons, where he also introduced an Indian (Swift Eagle) act and did impersonations. He was a disc jockey for radio station WINS (1935), undertook motion picture road shows (1936–1940), and wrote vaudeville comedy for WINS (1940–1941). He was a comedy writer for Fred Allen, made appearances on Allen's radio show, and performed stand-up comedy. He was a radio comic, puppeteer, and did voice work (1941–1945). Allen provided voices on *The Adventures of Oky Doky* (1948–1949), *The Howdy Doody Show* (four years), *Winky Dink and You* (1953–1957), and television commercials.

He began doing voices for Terrytoons cartoons in 1947 [1946] and was the originator of the Brooklyn and British accents for Heckle and Jeckle. Allen would work for Terrytoons until cartoon production ceased in 1967. His salary grew from $25 to $500 a show during this period. For CBS-Terrytoons (1956–1967) he was the voice of Sidney the Elephant, Luno, Astronut, Possible Possum, Muskie the Muskrat, Ty Coon the Raccoon, Vincent Van Gopher and Pig Newton. He did voices for *The Adventures of Lariat Sam* (1962–1965). Allen originated Deputy Dawg's voice and would ad-lib material for the cartoons. His cartoon credits include voices for Walter Lantz cartoons, Famous Studios (1960–1963), Hal Seeger (1963–1966), and Ernest Pintoff's *Old Man and the Flower* (1962).

He originated the "Why Not?" phenomena on *The Steve Allen Show* (1956) which expression was used for television commercials and merchandise. There were 135 five-minute *Dayton Allen Shows* shown on local television news shows featuring Allen delivering monologues (early 1960s). Allen

Fig. A1.1 – Dayton Allen

ran a real estate investment business in White Plains, New York (early 1970s) and became an expert in the international gold market (late 1970s). He also made appearances on the *Merv Griffin Show* and continued doing voice work in the 1980s to1990s. In 1986, Allen moved down to Florida to retire. His movie credits include Solly in *The Cotton Club* (1984). He married Elvi (née Daniels) Allen (1958). Allen is the brother of cartoon voice artist Bradley Bolke. Dayton's hobbies included playing the piano. Allen died on November 11, 2004 in Hendersonville, North Carolina.

References: Lamparski, Richard. *Whatever Became Of ... ?*, Volume

9. New York: Crown, 1985; *International Motion Picture Almanac*. 1975–1996 editions. New York: Quigley Publishing Co.; Smith, Ronald L. *Legends in Their Own Time*. New York: Prentice Hall General Reference, 1994; Smith, Ronald L. *Who's Who in Comedy: Comedians, Comics, and Clowns from Vaudeville to Today's Stand-ups*. New York: Facts on File, 1992; "Dayton Allen, 85, Cartoon Voice Actor". *New York Times*. November 18, 2004, p. A29.

BAKSHI, Ralph. Ralph Bakshi, animator, writer, producer and director of animated and live-action films, was born on October 26 [29], 1938 in Haifa, British Mandate of Palestine (later Israel), the son of Russian Jews who immigrated to the United States in 1939 to escape World War II to settle in Brooklyn, New York where Bakshi was raised. Bakshi attended Thomas Jefferson High School (Brooklyn) and graduated from Manhattan's High School of Industrial Art (June 1956) with the top cartooning award.

At 18, Bakshi was hired at CBS-Terrytoons as an animation cel polisher, promoted quickly to opaquer and inker, and was animating by 1959. At age 25, he was promoted to director (first short: Sad Cat cartoon (*Gadmouse, the Apprentice Good Fairy* (1965))), designing the series characters. He designed miscellaneous characters for the Deputy Dawg series, and the character James Hound. In 1966, he created the popular superhero parody series *The Mighty Heroes*. He moved to the animation division of Paramount Pictures in 1967 and started his studio, Bakshi Productions, in 1968 producing *Rocket Robin Hood* and *Spider-Man* (television series).

Through producer Steve Krantz, Bakshi made his debut film, *Fritz the Cat* (1972), the first animated feature to receive an X rating from the Motion Picture Association of America, and the most successful independent animated feature of all-time grossing over $100 million on a $1 million budget.

Over the next 11 years, Bakshi directed seven additional animated features, *Heavy Traffic* (1973), *Coonskin* (1975), *Wizards* (1977), *The Lord of the Rings* (1978), *American Pop* (1981), *Hey Good Lookin'* (1982) and *Fire and Ice* (1983). In 1987, Bakshi returned to television work, producing the series *Mighty Mouse: The New Adventures*, broadcasted for two years. After a nine-year hiatus from features, he directed *Cool World* (1992) starring Kim Basinger and Brad Pitt. Bakshi returned to television with the live-action film *Cool and the Crazy* (1994) and the anthology series *Spicy City* (1997). He founded the Bakshi School of Animation and Cartooning in 2003. Awards: Golden Gryphon (1980) for *The Lord of the Rings*, Giffoni Film Festival; ACT Achievement in Television Award (1988); Annie Award for Distinguished Contribution to the Art of Animation (1988); Maverick Tribute Award (2003), Cinequest Film Festival.

By 2000, Bakshi retired to

Fig. A1.2 – Ralph Bakshi

illustrate, paint and sell his artwork. He taught an undergraduate animation class, New York's School of Visual Arts. The Museum of Modern Art has added Bakshi's films to its collection for preservation.

Hobbies: collecting cartoon art (Harold Gray (1894–1968); Jay Irving (1900–1970)) and illustrated children's books (Arthur Rackham; N. C. Wyeth), medieval music. Favorite children's film: *Pinocchio* (1940). Bakshi married twice (Elaine, Elizabeth) (children: (first marriage) Mark; (second marriage) Preston, Victoria, Eddie)). Memberships: National Cartoonists Society, Writers Guild of America West, Directors Guild of America, Producers Guild of America, American Society of Composers, Authors, and Publishers.

References: *Current Biography Yearbook*. 1979 edition. New York: H.W. Wilson Co., 1979; Grant, John. *Masters of Animation*. New York: Watson-Guptill, 2001; Gibson, Jon M. and Chris McDonnell. *Unfiltered: The Complete Ralph Bakshi*. New York: Universe Publishing, 2008.

Appendix 1 • Terrytoons Who's Who

BARTSCH, Arthur E. (1911–1971). Art Bartsch, animator, layout artist, comic book artist, and commercial artist, was born on November 3, 1904 in Bergen County, New Jersey, the son of Robert E. and Margarethe (née Woll) [Wall] Bartsch. Bartsch was raised in Overpeck Township, New Jersey. He studied architecture at the Pratt Institute (New York City). He attended art classes at the Metropolitan Art School, Grand Central Art School and the Phoenix Art Institute in New York City. His early art training was in advertising with the Stanley E. Gunnison advertising agency in the early 1930s where he was promoted to art director of the agency.

He began his animation career at the Van Beuren studio in New York City as a background designer and layout artist working primarily on the *Rainbow Parade* series, 1934–1936. In 1936, around the time the Van Beuren studio closed, Bartsch moved to the Terrytoons as the head of the background and layout department. Around 1940, Anderson Craig assumed the role of background department supervisor moving Bartsch into designing layouts. By 1947, Bartsch was a layout artist and animator.

Bartsch is best noted for designing in 1947 the prototype for Crusader Rabbit, the star of the first animated series produced specifically for television by Paul Terry's nephew Alexander Anderson (Anderson's character was a donkey called "Donkey Otie" after crusader Don Quixote).

After Terry sold Terrytoons to

Fig. A1.3 – Arthur Bartsch

CBS in 1955, Bartsch became director on a number of Terrytoons shorts until the studio ceased production in 1968 (Sidney, 1958/1960–1963; Hashimoto, 1961; Hector Heathcote, 1961–1962; Lariat Sam, 1962–1965; Luno, 1964; Astronut, 1965; Sad Cat, 1967–1968; Possible Possum, 1968).

Bartsch worked at CBS Animation on Madison Avenue where he produced television commercials, 1961–1962. Bartsch illustrated children's books and Terrytoons comic books (panels and covers). His comic book credits include Terrytoons titles for St. John Publishing/Jubilee (Mighty Mouse (1947–1956), Little Roquefort (1950), and Gandy Goose (1954)). He completed comic book artwork for K.K. Publications/Dell Comics (Disney strips (1949–1954), Screwy Squirrel (1950–1953), Woody Woodpecker (1950–1953), Ugly Duckling (1951), Spotty Pig (1953)).

By 1968, he was working on a proposed cartoon series for Terrytoons based in Ancient Rome. With the New Rochelle studio closed, about 1969, Bartsch moved to Chicago to work as an art director in television. Bartsch was involved in helping to build playrooms and completed interior design work in many Westchester county homes.

Bartsch was married (Marguerite Catherine (Collins) Bartsch) and had a son (Arthur Daniel). Bartsch, who was ambidextrous with his artistic talent, was a member of the National Cartoonists Society. He enjoyed bowling, golf, model building, interior design, poker, photography and woodworking. Arthur Bartsch died from cirrhosis of the liver on February 13, 1971 at Columbus Hospital in Chicago, Illinois.

References: Fox's Dynamo (20th Century-Fox Film Corporation. "Terrytoon Creators: Arthur Bartsch". *Dynamo* (Terrytoon Section) (Chicago, Illinois). April 15, 1940, p. 8B; "Art Bartsch". In *The National Cartoonists Society Album 1996, Fifticth Anniversary Edition*, edited by Bill Janocha, 316. Buffalo, New York: National Cartoonists Society, 1996.

CRAIG, Anderson (1904–1964). Anderson Craig, portrait painter and animation background artist, was born on April 15, 1904 in Iowa City, Iowa, the son of Arthur Still and Melle Rosimin (née Campbell) Craig. He was raised in Kansas City, Missouri graduating from Central High School as "Central's foremost cartoonist". He completed design and illustration courses at the Kansas City Art Institute and School of Design, 1922–1925, studying under Randall Vernon Davey.

Fig. A1.4 – Anderson Craig

After marrying Adele McLain [Kennedy] at age 22, the couple moved to New York City where Craig executed freelance portrait commissions, including a series of about 15 portraits of celebrities (e.g. Theodore Dreiser, George Gershwin) for the Ferargil galleries. His auctioned works include: *Young Man From the Country* (1925) and *Self Portrait* (1930). In September 1928, as director, Craig founded the Experimental School of Art at his home studio. By mid-1929, the studio school had grown to 14 pupils and plans were being made to enlarge the school and endow it.

The 1929 stock market crash sent the couple back to Kansas City to reside before returning to Manhattan (early 1930s). In January 1933, he conducted weekend classes in painting and drawing at the Greenwich House Workshops. By 1935, Craig found stable work as a background painter for Fleischer Studios, New York City working on *Color Classics* cartoons (*Kids in a Shoe* (1935)). In the late 1930s, Craig moved to work for Terrytoons as head of the background department supervising artists George Zaffo and John Vita, later Douglas Hilliker (1943).

In 1942, Craig painted the portrait of Edward P. Stuart posing as Uncle Sam for a navy poster. The poster won a contest and was widely used during World War II. By the mid-1940s, Craig was supplementing his income as a freelance advertising artist. Around 1953, Craig left Terrytoons to open a Manhattan art studio doing portraits, figures and commercial artwork.

In 1956, Craig was heading Anderson Craig Studios producing film animation for television commercials (e.g. Canada Dry). By July 1959, Craig closed his studio and joined CBS-Terrytoons as Director of (Television) Commercials. By 1960 Craig had moved to work in Massachusetts as an art director for the Bay State Film Productions (Agawam, Massachusetts), a motion picture and slide production company for industry.

Craig was re-married (Catherine Cahill) (Son: Anderson Craig Jr.). Religion: Roman Catholic. Anderson Craig died on February 21, 1964 in Springfield, Massachusetts. Exhibitions: KCAI, 1923–1925; Ferargil Galleries, New York, 1929; Woman's City Club, Kansas City, Missouri, 1931; Artists and Writers Dinner Club, New York City, 1934.

References: "Craig, Anderson". In *Mantle Fielding's Dictionary of American Painters, Sculptors and Engravers*, 2nd ed., ed. Glenn B. Optiz, 185. Apollo: Poughkeepsie, New York, 1986; "Craig, Anderson". In *Who Was Who in American Art, 1564–1975: 400 Years of Artists in America*, edited by Peter Hastings Falk. Madison, Connecticut: Sound View Press, 1999; "Fates & Fortunes". *Broadcasting* (July 1959), p. 79–83; "Anderson Craig". *Springfield Union*. February 22, 1964, p. 24; "Anderson Craig, Sr". *Sunday Republican* (Springfield, MA). February 23, 1964, p. 18A.

DAVIS, Emanuel (1894–1975). Mannie Davis, animator and animation director, was born on January 23 [22], 1894 in Yonkers, New York, the son of Samuel and Sarah Rosa (née Berkowitz) Davidowitz [Davidovitz] (family name later changed to "Davis"). Davis is one of four brothers (others: Art, Phil, Sid) that became involved in animated film production.

Davis, raised in Yonkers, was a graduate of Cooper Union Art School (two years) and studied at the Art Students League (one year). He started with the art department of the American Press

Fig. A1.5 – Emanuel "Mannie" Davis

Appendix 1 • Terrytoons Who's Who

Association (APA) Syndicate doing decorative art and small sketches for stories. He saw his first animated cartoons at an artists' party (Castle Cove, NYC).

After the APA folded, he animated for Barré-Bowers on the *Mutt and Jeff* series with Bud Fisher, Edison studio (Bronx, NY), 1916. He served in World War I as a cartographer and Corporal (472nd Engineers), Washington, D.C. animating medical and training films (discharged: 1918).

He returned to Barré-Bowers managing the studio with Burt Gillett, 1918–1921. He is credited with being the first to combine live actors with animation on screen. He was with Pat Sullivan's "Felix the Cat" company, 1921–1922. He was an animator for Fleischer Studios (*Out of the Inkwell* series (Koko the Clown and Betty Boop)), 1922–1924.

He animated and directed (beginning 1927) *Aesop's Fables* shorts at Fables Pictures for producer Paul Terry and Amedee Van Beuren, 1924–1929. After Terry and Van Beuren parted company, he worked under John Foster as animator, character designer, and director (*Aesop's Sound Fables, Cubby Bear*) for Van Beuren Studios, 1929–1933. He created Cubby Bear (Brownie Bear) (1933).

Davis was married (1929) (Florence J. Goodstein). In August 1933 Davis joined the Terrytoons studio as animator, then was promoted to director alongside George Gordon (April, 1936) (sole director, May 1937). He animated and directed (with film credits) Terrytoons shorts until 1962.

In 1942, Mannie Davis directed *All Out for "V"*, an animated short that was nominated for an Academy Award and won special commendation from the United States government for wartime service. Davis retired from CBS-Terrytoons around 1963. Davis was a member of the National Cartoonists Society. Davis later divorced (children: James, Susan). In his later years, Davis was living in the Benjamin Franklin Hotel in New York City. Mannie Davis died on October 9, 1975 in New York Hospital, New York City.

References: Davis, Mannie. Interview by Harvey Deneroff. "Paul Terry Oral History Interview with Mannie Davis". Rough transcript, New York, New York, 28 July 1970, John Canemaker Collection, Fales Library, Elmer Holmes Bobst Library, New York University, New York, New York); "Emanuel Davis", (Obituaries). *Variety*. October 15, 1975, 78; "Emanuel Davis", (Obituary). *The Standard-Star* (New Rochelle). October 11, 1975, p. A20; 20th Century-Fox Film Corporation. "Experts Are Born: Emanuel Davis". *Dynamo* (Terrytoon Section) (Chicago, Illinois). April 15, 1940, p. 5B; "Mannie Davis Joins Terry". *Film Daily*. August 23, 1933, p. 4; "Mannie Davis". In *The National Cartoonists Society Album 1996, Fiftieth Anniversary Edition*, edited by Bill Janocha, 325. Buffalo, New York: National Cartoonists Society, 1996.

DONNELLY, Edwin Eugene (1896–1979). Edwin Donnelly, animator and director, was born on April 4, 1896 in Brooklyn, New York, the eldest son of William J. and Ann (née Sheridan) Donnelly. Donnelly's animation career spanned 40 years, 1923 to 1962, employed for Fables Studio, Van Beuren Studios, Walt Disney Studios, and Terrytoons. He was raised in Brooklyn and early on was a welder with the Todd Shipyard and a clerk for the Metropolitan Life Insurance Company (1917).

During World War One, he spent a year with the 832nd Aerial Squadron [833rd Aero (RPR) Squadron] at a training camp in Cranwell, England. He was injured aboard ship returning from England and was sent to a veteran's hospital in the United States. While in hospital recovering from his injuries, he found he had a talent for drawing. After release from hospital, Donnelly completed art studies at the Art Students League. By 1920, Donnelly was working as a clerk for an export company. His first artistic position was for the

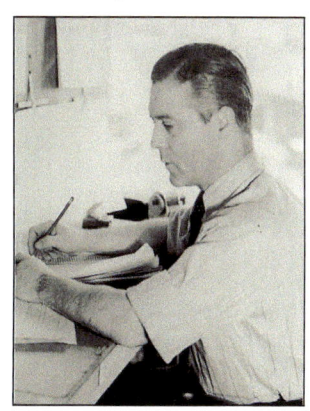

Fig. A1.6 – Edwin Donnelly

Morse Dry Dock Company illustrating advertisements for the company's sales magazine. He spent three years in the early 1920s as a political cartoonist for newspapers (*New York World*, *The New Era* (*South Shore Press*)).

Donnelly started his animation career about 1923 as a tracer for Fables Pictures working on the *Aesop's Fables* series starring Farmer Al Falfa. When Paul Terry and Amedee Van Beuren parted company in 1929, Donnelly remained with Van Beuren Studios as an animator through the early 1930s working on the *Cubby Bear* series among others. With an interim period of a year animating at Walt Disney Studios on the *Silly Symphonies* shorts (*King Neptune* (1932), *Babes in the Woods* (1932), *Elmer Elephant* (1936)), Donnelly served the Aesop's Fables unit for nine years.

In 1933, he joined Terrytoons as an animator. In 1937 he was promoted to director (first director credit: *Here's to Good Old Jail* (June 1938)). In 1955, Donnelly moved back to animating at Terrytoons until he retired around 1962. About 1955, Donnelly worked for a short period at a New York City commercial studio animating commercials and segments for the television show *Beat the Clock*.

Donnelly's most notable achievement was probably directing the Academy Award nominated Terrytoons short *My Boy Johnny* (1944). Donnelly's hobbies included playing cards, traveling, woodworking and miniature model making. His elaborate reproduction in miniature of the New York skyline and waterfront won him recognition in the New York press. He also made dollhouses, tables, desks, dressers, wall shelf units, wooden sleds, wagons and rockers.

He married twice ((1) Ellen (Sommers) Donnelly (1899–1949) (married in Brooklyn, April 1, 1918) (two daughters (Virginia M., Patricia Ann) and two sons (Edwin E., Raymond)); (2) Mary Bourne (1922–2003) (married June 9, 1956)). Ed Donnelly died on September 15, 1979 in Hewlett, Nassau, New York.

References: Donnelly, Polly B., Letter to W. Hamonic, 16 December 1997. Paul Terry Papers, Victoria, B.C.; 20th Century-Fox Film Corporation. "Terrytoon Who's Who: Eddie Donnelly". *Dynamo* (Terrytoon Section) (Chicago, Illinois), April 15, 1940.

FOSTER, John J. (1886–1959). John Foster, animator, animation director, and story man, was born in Hoboken, New Jersey on November 27, 1886, the son of John and Louise (née Daab) Foster. Foster was raised in Hoboken, New Jersey, quit school after 7th grade, worked in the upholstery business, and was a designer in a shirt house (1910). He never studied art but had a natural talent for comedy and was inventive with gags.

He was a pen and ink artist on Mutt and Jeff animated cartoons for Raoul Barré (Edison studio, Bronx, NY), 1915. He animated and completed story work on the *Katzenjammer Kids*, *Jerry on the*

Fig. A1.7 – John Foster

Job, and *The Shenanigan Kids* series (International Film Service), 1917. During World War One, he served in France (U.S. Army, 306th Field Artillery, 77th Division) (Battle of Argonne Forest), December 1917 – May 1919. He returned to IFS on the Goldwyn-Bray Comic series (*Happy Hooligan*, *Shenanigan Kids*, and *Judge Rummy* cartoons). He was next with Fables Pictures working for Paul Terry as story man, animator, and director (after 1927) on *Aesop's Fables* shorts, 1923–1929. After Terry left, Foster remained as director with Van Beuren Studios (*Aesop's Sound Film Fables*), 1929–1933. He was an animator, Frank Goldman's studio (Audio-Cinema, Inc./Audio Productions) (commercial animation), 1934.

Foster joined Paul Terry's Terrytoons in late 1934, his animation first appearing in *Jack's Shack* (November 1934). Foster began directing with *The Billy Goat's Whiskers* (December 1937). Foster created the character of Gandy Goose. In 1938, he directed the first color Terrytoons *String Bean Jack*

(1938) and the first two Gandy Goose cartoons (*Gandy the Goose*, *The Goose Flies High*). In 1938, Foster was put in charge of the story department replacing Tommy Morrison (who headed department, 1937–1938). Foster's first story credit: *Housewife Herman* (November 1938). Foster worked in collaboration with about three to four other writers that included Tom Morrison, Don McKee, Al Stahl, and Izzy Klein. Terry and Foster's ideas tended to comprise the bulk of each story. From 1938 to 1950, Foster was credited with story work for every Terrytoons cartoon, over 250 cartoons. In the story department, Foster was seen more as an idea and gag man rather than an artist.

In the late 1940s Foster began to develop Parkinson's Disease, soon crippling one of his legs. When Foster retired in late 1949 due to illness (last story credit: *Aesop's Fable: Foiling the Fox* (April 1950) [*Comic Book Land*, 1949]), Tom Morrison took over. In retirement, Foster worked for Terry from home recording radio shows that Terry could recycle gags from. John Foster was married (Grace Ashton Foster) (children: John J., Doris A.). Membership: American Legion Post 8, New Rochelle, NY. Religion: Episcopalian. John Foster died on February 16, 1959 in New Rochelle, New York.

References: "John Foster". *The Standard-Star* (New Rochelle). February 16, 1959, p. 2; "John Foster", (Obituary News). *The Standard-Star* (New Rochelle). February 18, 1959, p. 2; 20th Century-Fox Film Corporation. "Terrytoon Creators: John Foster". *Dynamo* (Terrytoon Section) (Chicago, Illinois). April 15, 1940, p. 5B.

HILLIKER, Douglas Hagar (1891–1986). Douglas "Bill" Hilliker, illustrator, fine art painter, commercial artist, poster designer, and background artist, was born on May 25, 1891 in San Francisco, California, the son of Nelson H. and Daisy (née Douglas) Hilliker.

He was raised in San Francisco, California. In August 1894, the Hilliker family along with wealthy grandfather James Douglas survived a spectacular fire in their mansion residence in Woodland, California. At age 11 he began art studies at Mark Hopkins Art Institute (four years), and experienced the horrors of the April 1906 earthquake and fire. By 1910 he was an artist for the *San Francisco Chronicle* befriending fellow artist Paul Terry. He was an artist, University of California (Berkeley) yearbook (1914–1915). By 1915, he had moved to New York City and became employed as an illustrator.

During World War I, he enlisted (1917) in the U.S. Army and was promoted to major in charge of an Afro-American regiment. He saw active engagements at Champagne, Marne, and Aisne-Marne (Overseas: January 1918 to August 1919) (honorably discharged: September 4, 1919).

After the war, as freelance painter his paintings were used for magazine covers (*Collier's*, *Saturday Evening Post*). He painted pictures of movie stars and illustrated motion picture

Fig. A1.8 – Douglas "Bill" Hilliker

posters and advertisements. During the 1930s he was a commercial artist for 20th Century-Fox (e.g. movie posters). He illustrated stories and covers for *Railroad Magazine*, a pulp magazine devoted to railroad stories and history (1937–1942). He was also a book illustrator (e.g. *You Can Live in an Apartment* (Farrar & Rinehart, 1939)).

In the 1920s, he built a cabin in isolated (no road access) Beaver River, New York, furnishing it with handcrafted Adirondack style furniture. During World War II, he was refused admittance to the U.S. military due to age and physical condition. In the early 1940s, he began working at Terrytoons as a background painter under department head Anderson Craig. In the early 1950s, Hilliker was promoted to department head after Craig left to establish his portrait studio. After Paul Terry sold the studio, Hilliker successfully adapted to the new visual style demanded by CBS-Terrytoons.

In 1959 [1960] Hilliker retired from Terrytoons to Beaver River with his motorboat and snowmobile, and later bought a 1968 Volkswagen Bug. Taking over in the CBS-Terrytoons background department were Bill Focht and John Zago. He pursued his hobbies of woodcraft, hunting, diagram (map) relief design, watching soap operas, and listening to talk shows on his battery powered radio.

Hilliker attributed his long life to his Beaver River outhouse named "Aunt Effie". Hilliker was married twice (first at the age of 21) (Mary) and had a daughter (Mary D.). Douglas Hilliker died on April 4, 1986 in New London, Connecticut.

References: Thompson, Pat. *Beaver River: Oasis in the Wilderness*. Eagle Bay, New York: Beaver River Press, 2000; Edan Hughes, Milton. *Artists in California, 1786-1940*. Sacramento, CA: Crocker Art Museum, 2002; "A Costly Conflagration. The Handsome Residence of J.A. Douglas Goes Up in Smoke". *Woodland Daily Democrat*. August 23, 1894, p. 3.

KUWAHARA, Robert S. (1901-1964). Bob Kuwahara, animator, director, and story artist, was born Rokuro Kuwahara, the son of Yoshi and Yushu Kuwahara, near Tokyo, Japan on August 12, 1901. In 1910, his family immigrated to the United States settling in Los Angeles, California. He graduated from Los Angeles Polytechnic High School, 1921. After seven years of study at Otis Art Institute (Los Angeles) funding his studies with full-time employment, he

Fig. A1.9 – Robert Kuwahara

graduated in 1929. Looking for commissions as portrait artist in New York City, he found work as a commercial illustrator (early 1930s).

He began his career as a story man/story sketch artist at Walt Disney Studios in 1932 working on the *Silly Symphonies* shorts, Mickey Mouse cartoons and the feature *Snow White and the Seven Dwarfs* (1937) until 1937. He worked on sets/backgrounds at the Metro-Goldwyn-Mayer cartoon unit, 1937-1942 (*Captain and the Kids*, others). Kuwahara worked on the first Tom and Jerry cartoon *Puss Gets the Boot* (1940) while at MGM.

During World War II, he spent three years (1942-1945) in a Japanese internment camp, Heart Mountain Relocation Camp, in Wyoming where he painted and taught art classes with Benji Okubo, Hideo Date and Shingo Nishiura. Kuwahara resettled to Larchmont, New York in 1945.

He created the comic strip *Little Miki* for the George Matthew Adams syndicate. The strip concerns a little boy who has what adults think is an imaginary companion called Uncle Harry. However, Uncle Harry is a real person only Miki can see who can do amazing things. The strip ran for five years in the United States and was popular overseas even longer. As a result of a United Feature Syndicate contest, he created the popular strip *Marvelous Mike* in 1956.

Kuwahara was employed at the Terrytoons studio as character designer and story man, 1949-1959. Kuwahara's most notable studio creation was Japanese house mouse Hashimoto-San. The backgrounds to the cartoons were painted in the style of Japanese artist Hokusai Katsushika. He also created the Lariat Sam character for the *Captain Kangaroo* television program.

He directed a number of series at Terrytoons (Hashimoto, 1959-1963; Deputy Dawg, 1962; Lariat Sam, 1962-1965; Astronut, 1965; Hector Heathcote, 1963; and the Martian Moochers, 1966 (prod. 1964)).

Kuwahara did artwork for Terrytoons comic books and the *Barker Bill* comic strip. In 1958 Kuwahara became a naturalized citizen. Bob Kuwahara was married (Julia Susuki [Suzuki]) (Sons: Denis J., Michel F.).

In 1964 Kuwahara was in negotiations with Joe Barbera to work for Hanna-Barbera Productions in California. Kuwahara died from cancer in New Rochelle, New York, on December 7, 1964. Award: Honor Medal, Freedom Foundation, Columbia University, 1951. Recreations: Golf. Memberships: National Cartoonists Society, Cartoonists Local 841.

Appendix 1 • Terrytoons Who's Who

References: "Kawahara [sic], Cartoonist", (Obituary News). *The Standard-Star* (New Rochelle, N.Y.). December 8, 1964, p. 3; "Bob Kuwahara". In *The National Cartoonists Society Album 1996, Fiftieth Anniversary Edition*, edited by Bill Janocha, 350 (Buffalo, New York: National Cartoonists Society, 1996); Kuwahara, Michel. Interview by W. Gerald Hamonic. Transcript of telephone recording. Las Vegas, Nevada, November 8, 1998 (Paul Terry Papers).

MORRISON, Thomas James (1908–1978). Thomas Morrison, story man and voice actor, was born April 22, 1908, in Brooklyn, New York [Larchmont, New York], the son of Thomas John and Christina Frances (née Heinzer) Morrison. As a child, Morrison acted in theatrical productions with ambitions of working in film. He was a speaker in Liberty Loans drives (First World War) receiving accolades from the U.S. Government, Liberty Loan Committee and Boy Scouts of America. He studied at New York University and the Damrosch Conservatory of Music. His first job was an usher at the Rivoli Theatre (New York). He was with the Sutro Brothers & Company briefly before the 1929 Crash resulting in losing his job.

Morrison joined Terrytoons in late 1931 [early 1932] washing animation celluloid and undertaking camerawork. Morrison headed the inking and painting department, 1934–1935, moved to inbetweening, worked as an assistant animator then

Fig. A1.10 – Thomas Morrison

became production manager which job he did not enjoy. In 1937, Morrison was appointed story department head co-writing his first story with George Gordon, a Puddy the Pup cartoon, *The Dog and the Bone*. In 1938, John Foster was appointed story department head and Morrison worked under him. Morrison wrote gags and song lyrics (including Oil Can Harry-Pearl Pureheart operatic cartoons) and did voices (narrator, Little Roquefort, Percy the Cat, Gandy Goose (after Arthur Kay left), Terry Bear child). He did the television voice of Mighty Mouse (commercials, *The Mighty Mouse Playhouse* (introduction)). After John Foster retired (late 1949), Morrison headed the story department (sole story credit beginning with *The Beauty Shop* (April 1950)).

After Terry left in 1956, Morrison shared story credits, wrote animated television commercials, and became voice director (directing dialog, acquiring voice talent, and sound work). He invented sound effects with noisemakers. He hired story writers. Starting in the late 1950s, Morrison began to edit stories written by the story department. Morrison wrote the comic strips *Barker Bill*, *Marvelous Mike* and *Miki*. He was an editor, St. John Publishing, 1949–1955 (most Terrytoons titles (cover material: Mighty Mouse, Heckle & Jeckle, Dinky, Little Roquefort)).

He wrote and directed plays, appeared in radio skits, dabbled in make-up, and wrote modern music (*It Must Be Love*). Morrison retired in 1973 after Viacom International Enterprises assumed control of Terrytoons. Morrison married Elizabeth (DuBois) (children: Thomas, Lynn, and Barbara). Memberships: Larchmont Shore Club, National Cartoonists Society, and communicant of Sts. John and Paul Church (Larchmont, New York). Tom Morrison died from prostate cancer in Cape Coral, Florida on March 1, 1978.

References: Morrison, Thomas James (Tommy). Interview by Harvey R. Deneroff. Transcript. New Rochelle, New York. John Canemaker Animation Collection, Fales Library, Elmer Holmes Bobst Library, New York University, New York, New York, June 15, 1970; 20th Century-Fox Film Corporation. "Experts are Born: Thomas Morrison". *Dynamo* (Terrytoon Section) (Chicago, Illinois). April 15, 1940, p. 4B; "Thomas Morrison of Terrytoons Dies". *The Standard Star* (New Rochelle). March 3, 1978, p. A8.

MOSER, Frank Herman (1886–1964). Frank Moser, animator, cartoonist, illustrator, fine art painter and teacher, was born in Oketo [Blue Rapids],

Fig. A1.11 – Frank Moser

Marshall County, Kansas on May 27, 1886, son of John Jacob and Alvina (née Krause) Moser. Moser was raised in Marysville, Kansas. He studied at: Albert T. Reid Art School, Topeka, Kansas (1907–1908); Cummings School of Art, Des Moines, Iowa (1908–1910); Art Students League of New York (1912); National Academy of Design, New York City; John Fabian Carlson, Woodstock, New York.

He was a sketch artist and cartoonist, *Des Moines Register & Leader*, 1909–1912; illustrator, *New York Globe*, 1912–1916 (daily: *In Our School*). Moser created the Sunday strip series *Fan Fanny in Sport*, (illustrated Sunday supplement, *New York Press*) and produced *Summer Kids*, panel, 1914. In 1915, he animated the *Animated Grouch Chaser* series (*Kid Kelly* cartoons) (Raoul Barré (producer), Edison Co.). In 1916 he animated the *Jerry on the Job* series (others), and established an animation department (supervising animator) for Hearst-Vitagraph News Pictorial series (*Joys and Glooms*, 1916; *Bringing Up Father*, 1916–1918; *Krazy Kat*, 1916–1917).

Moser animated the *Happy Hooligan* series, 1916–1919, *Little Jimmy* and *Judge Rummy* series (both IFS), 1918–1921. He wrote, animated and directed 26 *Bud and Susie* shorts, Bray Productions, 1918. He wrote, animated and directed shorts (Farmer Al Falfa) at Fables Pictures under Paul Terry and Amedee Van Beuren, 1921–1929 (430 cartoons).

In August 1929, Terry and Moser entered a partnership (Moser & Terry) producing Terry-Toon cartoons (Audio-Cinema, Long Island City (later the Bronx)) distributed by Educational Pictures, 1930–1934, partnering briefly with Joseph Coffman (Moser, Terry & Coffman, 1930–1931). Moser animated and managed the animation department. Terry (stopped animating, 1933), wrote stories. In 1934 the partnership moved to New Rochelle, New York continuing production.

In 1936, Moser resigned his position and sold his half-interest to Terry for $24,200, then sued Terry claiming he was induced by "misrepresentation, conspiracy and deceit" to sell his stake. Moser lost the lawsuit and appeal. At Terrytoons, Moser is credited as director (with Terry) on all shorts produced to *Off to China* (Mar. 1936), and the short *The Sailor's Home* (June 1936) (160 Terrytoons cartoons). In retirement he pursued landscape and portrait painting on commission.

Memberships: Salmagundi Club (exhibitions, prize, 1944), Yonkers Art Association (exhibitions), Hudson Valley Art Association (founder, treasurer, officer, historian) (exhibitions), Allied Artists of America (exhibitions), Westchester AC Guild and American Watercolor Society. Other exhibitions: National Arts Club; New York Water Color Club. Collection: New Britain (Conn.) Museum of American Art. He produced animated cartoon, National Wildlife Federation, 1938. Recreations: baseball, fishing, collecting Indian arrowheads. Married twice: (1) Anna Augusta Margareta Hård (née Nilsson) (1914–1929) (children: John Frank, Marjorie); (2) Isabel Fairclough (1932 – his death). Political: Republican. Frank Moser died on September 30, 1964, in Dobbs Ferry, New York.

References: *Encyclopedia of American Biography*. New Series. Volume 36. New York: American Historical Society, 1967; *The National Cyclopaedia of American Biography*. Volume 52. New York: James T. White & Co., 1970. Obituary: *The Herald Statesman* (Yonkers, N.Y.). October 1, 1964, p. 2.

RASINSKI, John Conrad (1907–1965). John Conrad 'Connie' Rasinski, animator and director, was born in Torrington, Connecticut on January 28, 1907, the son of Walter and Michalina (née Plaga) Rasinski. Connie Rasinski was raised in Torrington. His father was a brass mill worker and violinist (proficient in four instruments) who died c. 1917. His mother remarried (Teofil

Appendix 1 • Terrytoons Who's Who

Fig. A1.12 – John "Connie" Rasinski

Budney). As a child, Rasinski loved to cartoon demonstrating promising talent. To earn money, he delivered newspapers. Family financial problems forced Connie and his brother Joe to leave high school to work as machinists at the Hendey Machine Company. Connie became a promising pitcher in the industrial baseball league.

Rasinski studied under Norman Rockwell at the Phoenix Art Institute (New York). Upon Rockwell's advice, Rasinski pursued a career in cartooning. He completed artwork for newspapers (Waterbury, Connecticut), the Bell Publishing Company (freelance work) and humorous publications. He was noted for his newspaper political cartoons and caricatures of local politicians. Rasinski sold his first cartoon on May 20, 1927.

In 1930, while working in New York City as a newspaper cartoonist, Rasinski found employment at Terrytoons as an inker/opaquer. He received his first animation duties as an animation assistant under Frank Moser on the short *Pigskin Capers*. He also worked as an assistant under Bill Tytla. By July 1931 he had gained full animator's status (*By The Sea*). In 1937, Terry appointed him a director of animation. After Isidore Klein created Super Mouse (a super rat with buckteeth) first appearing in *The Mouse of Tomorrow* (1942), Rasinski redesigned the character into the more familiar Mighty Mouse. Rasinski declined a job offer to animate films for Walt Disney preferring to remain at Terrytoons. He was with the studio until his passing. His brother was a long-time cameraman for the studio.

During World War II, Rasinski completed security animation films for the United States military. He worked on animated television commercials. Rasinski worked as a comic artist (Terrytoons characters) for St. John Publishing, 1949–1954. Rasinski studied with the Art Students League (two years). Rasinski enjoyed teaching the art of animation to fledgling artists at Terrytoons.

Rasinski was married (Marie Agnes Byrne Gleason). After her death (1945), he married Alma K. Rasinski. He did not have children. Rasinski's hobbies included fly-fishing, stamp collecting, and making 16mm movies (sound film theater in his home). He produced amateur productions (e.g. biography on sculptor Michael Lantz, (1908–1988); documentary on how animated cartoons are produced at Terrytoons).

Religion: Roman Catholic. Memberships: National Cartoonists Society, Motion Picture Screen Cartoonists Local 841, Salmagundi Club, Patrol Company (Larchmont Fire Department). Connie Rasinski died on October 13, 1965 in Larchmont, New York.

References: "J.C. Rasinski, Terrytoons Director Dies", (Obituary News). *The Standard-Star* (New Rochelle, NY). October 14, 1965, p. 2; 20th Century-Fox Film Corporation. "Experts Are Born: Connie Rasinski". *Dynamo* (Terrytoon Section) (Chicago, Illinois). April 15, 1940, p. 8B; "J. Conrad "Connie" Rasinski". In *The National Cartoonists Society Album 1996, Fiftieth Anniversary Edition*, edited by Bill Janocha, 363. Buffalo, New York: National Cartoonists Society, 1996.

SCHEIB, Philip August. Philip A. Scheib, composer, conductor, and musical director, was born in Brooklyn, New York on April 14, 1894, the son of Philip and Augusta (née Lichtenberger) Scheib. Scheib was raised in Brooklyn, New York. He graduated from the University of Berlin

Fig. A1.13 – Philip Scheib

343

(Germany) where he studied piano, violin, composition, and conducting. He completed a four-year musical course at the Stern Conservatory of Music in Berlin graduating with an honorary diploma and a degree of pedagogy in 1914. He conducted the "Chocolate Soldier" company on tour across the United States followed by a three-year tour during World War I in the United States and Canada (primarily in Army camps) promoting Thomas A. Edison's invention, the phonograph. He then found work as a violinist and assistant conductor at the Strand Theater (N.Y.C.) conducting concerts before and after each film.

He was a musical director for Adelaide and Hughes, a composer and musical director for a Broadway chain of theaters over a 10-year period with headquarters at the Adelphi Theater, and composed music for musical comedies and vaudeville. In 1920, he introduced audience participation singing in vaudeville theaters, using song slides. He was musical director for a Canadian circuit of theaters. In 1929 Scheib became the musical director for Audio-Cinema adding music to film soundtracks writing the original score for D. W. Griffith's *The Struggle* (1931). Scheib was the musical director on two Dr. Seuss cartoons produced in 1931.

In 1929, he began composing music for the Moser-Terry studio at Audio-Cinema. Scheib was Terrytoons' only musical director composing, arranging and conducting almost 1,000 original cartoon scores remaining with the studio after Paul Terry sold his assets to CBS in 1955. He was the originator of several innovations for cartoons, and composed music for television commercials. His other duties included auditioning people for the dialogue to the animated cartoons.

Jim Timmens assumed most of the studio musical work in the early 1960s as musical director. Scheib officially retired in 1965. Scheib's published song hits as composer and lyricist include *Five Little Reasons for Happiness*, *Working For Defense*, *Have Y'Got Any Scrap?*, and *Keep 'Em Growing* (Terrytoons cartoons) and *In Old Havana*.

Scheib was a member of the Associated Musicians of Greater New York and the American Federation of Musicians, Local 802. His recreations included skeet shooting, golfing, and antique hunting. In 1934, he wrote a children's song *Blue Lullaby*. He was a frequent speaker at organizations in Westchester County.

He was married to Adelaide L. (Grahlfs) Scheib (daughter, Barbara Anna). Mrs. Scheib died in 1952. Scheib remarried his first wife's sister. He moved to Eastchester, New York in 1962 and was an elder of the Eastchester Presbyterian Church. Philip Scheib died on April 11, 1969 in New Rochelle, New York.

References: 20th Century-Fox Film Corporation. "Terrytoon Who's Who: Philip Scheib". *Dynamo* (Terrytoon Section) (Chicago, Illinois). 15 April 1940, p. 4B; *The Standard Star* (New Rochelle), July 16, 1932; "Philip A. Scheib". *The International Musician* 67 (June 1969): 14.

TYER, James Harold. Jim Tyer, animator, was born February 7, 1904 in Bridgeport, Connecticut, the son of John Francis and Mary E. (née Navin) Tyer. Tyer was raised in Bridgeport where he completed high school and then served in the United States Navy aboard the U.S. Olympia. Without art training, Tyer started working at Fables Pictures studio for Paul Terry around 1926. Tyer stayed with the studio and its successor, Van Beuren Studios, through 1934. In 1933, Tyer was appointed an animation director on shorts (*The Little King*, 1933–1934, and *Toddle Tales*, 1934).

In early 1935, Tyer left to work at Walt Disney Studios in the effects animation department on *Silly Symphonies* shorts then worked for the Harman-Ising studio as a gagman and storywriter for Rudy Ising's unit. In 1937, Tyer briefly worked for the Jam Handy studio in Detroit on commercial animation. By 1938, Tyer had moved to Florida to work for Fleischer Studios on cartoon

Fig. A1.14 – James Tyer

shorts moving back to New York City in 1942 animating for the newly reorganized studio under Paramount, Famous Studios. In mid-1946, Tyer left Famous Studios to animate cartoons for Terrytoons for 10 years. Occasionally he did story sketches and gags.

After Terry sold the studio to CBS in 1955, Tyer left for Shamus Culhane's studio serving as senior animator on commercial animation. In late 1956, Tyer returned to work for the new CBS-Terrytoons for Gene Deitch on theatrical cartoons and the *Tom Terrific* series. In 1958, Tyer moved to the newly organized Felix the Cat Productions animating a Felix television series for Trans-Lux Television then worked for Trans-Lux on the *Mighty Hercules* series until 1961. Tyer worked freelance for Treasure Films (a "Billy Bounce" pilot) and three series for Hal Seeger Productions (*Out of the Inkwell*, 1963; *Milton the Monster*, 1964; and *Batfink*, 1966–1967).

Tyer worked on Paramount's *Snuffy Smith* cartoons (1963). Tyer was a journeyman animator for Hanna-Barbera, 1967 to 1968, then worked with Ralph Bakshi and Steve Krantz on the *Fritz the Cat* animated feature until 1971. Tyer worked as a comic book artist, 1943–1955. The last years of his life were spent in seclusion trying to find work through the union.

Tyer eschewed the Disney animation style. Tyer's technique can best be described as a squash, stretch and mangle style of animation. Tyer attended Roman Catholic church regularly and gave to the Will Rogers Fund. In 1926, he married Margaret Esther Lee (two daughters, Peggy and Mary Louise; one son, James Jr.). Jim Tyer died on March 23, 1976 in Bridgeport, Connecticut.

References: *Cartoonist PROfiles* #47; Friedwald, Will. "Mighty Jim Tyer: The Animator Who Broke the Rules". *Animation Blast* 6 (Spring 2001): 29–37, 44–46, 50–51; Beck, Jerry. "Comical Tyer". *Animation Blast* 6 (Spring 2001): 38–39; Mayerson, Mark. "The Curly Howard of Cartoons: Mark Mayerson Analyzes the Art and Style of Tyer". *Animation Blast* 6 (Spring 2001): 40–43; Bakshi, Ralph. "Ralph Bakshi on Jim Tyer". *Animation Blast* 6 (Spring 2001): 50.

WEISS, William Monroe (1907–2001). William Weiss, accountant and executive producer, was born in Philadelphia, Pennsylvania on September 15, 1907, the son of Joseph and Lena (née Kaplan) Weiss. He was raised in Philadelphia, Pennsylvania. At age 12, Weiss was employed as a butcher (meat shop).

His career began with Wolf & Berger, a Philadelphia theater chain (six-year period). He was home office representative for Universal Pictures Corporation checking contracts at branches. He was educated at the University of Pennsylvania (Wharton School of Finance and Commerce) (B.S., economics (1929)).

Upon graduation, he worked as a comptroller for Audio-Cinema Inc. (Long Island City), sound engineers and consultants for companies

Fig. A1.15 – William Weiss

(Eastman Kodak, Consolidated Film) that produced industrial and medical films. Paul Terry's company, Moser & Terry, had a facilities sharing arrangement with Audio-Cinema. The studio moved to the Bronx under a rental agreement. Moser & Terry shared production facilities with Audio-Cinema. Audio-Cinema was no longer associated with the Moser & Terry product. Weiss took care of the financial affairs of both companies.

With Audio-Cinema in financial trouble due to payment of expensive sound patent royalties and poor box office returns on two features, Weiss moved to Moser & Terry in 1932 as comptroller, auditor and treasurer-secretary. Working with film exchange bookers, Weiss sold cartoons to theater chains. As their distributor Educational Pictures only distributed in the United States and Canada, Weiss sold foreign rights to the Terrytoons product to international distributors.

Fox and Educational then distributed Terry & Moser cartoons under Fox/Educational.

With Educational in financial troubles, 20th Century-Fox (Fox merged with Twentieth Century, 1935) took over distribution of Terrytoons worldwide. Weiss, business manager, negotiated contracts with 20th Century-Fox where cartoons were exhibited before features.

By the early 1950s, Weiss assumed the role of vice-president. After Paul Terry sold Terrytoons, Inc. to CBS in 1955, Weiss assumed the roles of vice-president and executive producer. Weiss hired creative talent, instituted changes in production methods, negotiated the sale of the product internationally, and attended television conventions and film festivals (Cannes and Venice). After Viacom took over Terrytoons, Weiss remained until Viacom closed Terrytoons in 1972 (retirement: September 15, 1972 (65th birthday)).

Viacom then retained Weiss as a consultant (to maintain relationships with 20th Century-Fox and other clients) for the next 25 years.

Weiss was a member of AMPAS, Motion Picture Pioneers, Motion Picture Producers and Distributors of America (Title Committee, 1941), and National Cartoonists Society (associate member). William Weiss was married (Rita Romaner, July 1935, Harrison, New York) (Son: Laddie). William Weiss died November 12, 2001 in Palm Beach, Florida.

References: 20th Century-Fox Film Corporation. "Treasurer: William Weiss". *Dynamo* (Terrytoon Section) (Chicago, Illinois). April 15, 1940, p. 4B; Ramsaye, Terry, ed. *International Motion Picture Almanac*, 1949–1950. New York: Quigley, 1949 (and 1958 edition); Weiss, William Monroe. Interview by Harvey Deneroff. New Rochelle, NY. John Canemaker Animation Collection, Fales Library, Elmer Holmes Bobst Library, NYU, New York City, June 15, 1970; Weiss, William Monroe. Interview by W. Hamonic. New Rochelle, NY, August 1996 (Paul Terry Papers).

Appendix 2

Paul Terry/Terrytoons Theatrical Shorts Filmography

Title	Release date	Series	Director	Producer	Distrib
'Sno Fun	Nov-51	HJ	ED	TT	Fox
19th Hole Club Farmer, The	24-Jan-36	FA	PT/FM	MT	E
20,000 Feats Under the Sea	23-Apr-17	PTFB	PT	PT	AK
2000 B.C.	14-Jun-31	TT	PT/FM	TMC	E
3 Game Guys	4-Aug-29	AFF	PT/JF	AVE	PE
Abominable Mountaineers, The	10-Sep-68	SC	AB	TT	Fox
Adventure by the Sea	15-Jul-64	LU	AB	TT	Fox
Adventures of Adenoid, The	10-Apr-25	AFF	PT	AVB	PE
Aesop's Fable: Foiling the Fox	Apr-50	TT	CR	TT	Fox
Aesop's Fable: Golden Egg Goosie	Aug-51	TT	ED	TT	Fox
Aesop's Fable: Happy Valley	Sep-52	SF	ED	TT	Fox
Aesop's Fable: Sparky the Firefly	Sep-53	SF	CR	TT	Fox
Aesop's Fable: The First Flying Fish	Feb-55	TT	CR	TT	Fox
Aesop's Fable: The Fox and the Duck	24-Aug-45	TT	MD	TT	Fox
Aesop's Fable: The Mosquito	29-Jun-45	GG	MD	TT	Fox
Aesop's Fable: The Tiger King	Mar-60	TT	CR	TT	Fox
Aesop's Fable: The Watch Dog	28-Sep-45	TT	ED	TT	Fox
Africa Squawks	30-Jun-39	TT	CR	TT	Fox
African Huntsman	11-Dec-24	AFF	PT	AVB	PE
African Jungle Hunt	Mar-57	PH	CR	TT	Fox
Aged in the Wood	29-Sep-23	AFF	PT	AVB	PE
Air-Cooled	17-Oct-25	AFF	PT	AVB	PE
Aladdin's Lamp	27-Dec-31	TT	PT/FM	TMC	E
Aladdin's Lamp	15-Nov-35	TT	PT/FM	MT	E
Aladdin's Lamp	22-Oct-43	TT	ED	TT	Fox
Aladdin's Lamp	28-Mar-47	GG	ED	TT	Fox
Alaska or Bust	16-Aug-28	MM	PT/FM	AVB	PE
All About Dogs	12-Jun-42	AFF	CR	TT	Fox
All Bull and a Yard Wide	16-Aug-27	TT	PT	AVB	PE
All for a Bride	4-Mar-27	AFF	PT	AVB	PE
All Out For "V"	7-Aug-42	AFF	MD	TT	Fox
All Teed Off	Jun-68	TT	AB	TT	Fox
All This and Rabbit Stew	Jul-50	SC	CR	TT	Fox

Title	Release date	Series	Director	Producer	Distrib
All's Well That Ends Well	8-Mar-40	TT	MD	TT	Fox
Alley Cat, The	17-Feb-23	AFF	PT	AVB	PE
All-Star Cast, The	20-Feb-24	AFF	PT	AVB	PE
Alpine Yodeler, The	21-Feb-36	FA	PT/FM	MT	E
Amateur Night	12-Jul-35	TT	PT/FM	MT	E
Amateur Night on the Ark	24-Apr-23	AFF	PT	AVB	PE
Amelia Comes Back	2-Aug-24	AFF	PT	AVB	PE
An Alpine Flapper	17-May-26	AFF	PT	AVB	PE
An Ideal Farm	22-Apr-24	AFF	PT	AVB	PE
An Igloo for Two	Mar-55	WW	CR	TT	Fox
Animals' Fair, The	14-Dec-23	AFF	PT	AVB	PE
Another Day, Another Doormat	Mar-59	JD	AK	TT	Fox
Ant Life as It Isn't	20-Jun-27	AFF	PT	AVB	PE
Anti-Cats	Mar-50	MM	MD	TT	Fox
Anti-Fat	4-Feb-27	AFF	PT	AVB	PE
Ants and the Grasshopper, The	10-Jul-21	AFF	PT	AVB	PE
Ants in Your Pantry	16-Feb-45	TT	MD	TT	Fox
April Showers	14-Jun-29	AFF	PT	AVB	PE
Arctic Rivals	Jun-54	WW	MD	TT	Fox
Around the World	4-Oct-31	TT	PT/FM	TMC	E
Astronut	Mar-63	DE	CR	TT	Fox
At the Circus	17-Nov-44	MM	ED	TT	Fox
At the Zoo	28-Mar-25	AFF	PT	AVB	PE
Baby Seal, The	10-Apr-41	TT	CR	TT	Fox
Baby Show, The	26-Jun-28	AFF	PT/MD	AVB	PE
Back to the Soil	12-Feb-29	AFF	PT	AVB	PE
Back to the Soil	14-Nov-41	TT	ED	TT	Fox
Bad Bandit, The	19-Jul-23	AFF	PT/MD	AVB	PE
Baffling Bunnies	Apr 56	TB	CR	TT	Fox
Ball Park, The	4-May-29	AFF	PT	AVB	PE
Balloon Snatcher	Sep-69	AN	CA/AB/CR/DT/RB	TT	PE
Banker's Daughter, The	25-Jun-33	FZ/OCH	PT/FM	MT	E
Bargain Daze	Aug-53	HJ	MD	TT	Fox

347

TERRYTOONS: The Story of Paul Terry and His Classic Cartoon Factory

Title	Release date	Series	Director	Producer	Distrib
Barnyard Actor	Jan-55	GG	CR	TT	Fox
Barnyard Amateurs	6-Mar-36	FA	PT/FM	MT	E
Barnyard Artists	8-Apr-28	AFF	PT/HS	AVB	PE
Barnyard Baseball	14-Jul-39	GG	MD	TT	Fox
Barnyard Blackout	5-Mar-43	TT	MD	TT	Fox
Barnyard Boss, The	24-Dec-37	TT	CR	TT	E
Barnyard Eggcitement	5-May-39	TT	CR	TT	Fox
Barnyard Follies	5-Sep-25	AFF	PT	AVB	PE
Barnyard Lodge Number One	2-Apr-28	AFF	PT/FM	AVB	PE
Barnyard Olympics, The	5-Sep-24	AFF	PT	AVB	PE
Barnyard Politics	26-Nov-28	AFF	PT/HS	AVB	PE
Barnyard Rodeo, A	29-Sep-23	AFF	PT	AVB	PE
Barnyard WAAC	11-Dec-42	TT	ED	TT	Fox
Baron Von Go-Go	Dec-67	JH	CA/AB	TT	PE
Barrel of Fun	Jun-72	HH	DT	TT	Fox
Bars and Stripes	31-Dec-26	AFF	PT	AVB	PE
Battle Royal, A	30-Oct-36	KK	MD/GG	TT	E
Battling Duet, A	2-Apr-28	AFF	PT/HB	AVB	PE
Beanstalk Jack	20-Oct-33	TT	PT/FM	MT	E
Beanstalk Jack	20-Dec-46	TT	ED	TT	Fox
Bear and the Bees, The	22-Jan-22	AFF	PT	AVB	PE
Beauty on the Beach	Nov-50	MM	CR	TT	Fox
Beauty Parlor, The	6-Jun-23	AFF	PT	AVB	PE
Beauty Shop, The	28-Apr-50	DD	ED	TT	Fox
Beaver Trouble	Dec-51	TT	CR	TT	Fox
Belabor thy Neighbor	Oct-70	HH	/	TT	Fox
Bell for Philadelphia, A	Jul-63	HH	DT	TT	Fox
Berry Funny	Mar-71	PO	CA	TT	Fox
Best Man Wins, The	9-Nov-23	AFF	PT	AVB	PE
Better Late Than Never	17-Mar-50	MH	RT	AVB	Fox
Big Bad Bobcat	Apr-68	SC	AB	TT	Fox
Big Build-Up, The	4-Sep-42	PP	MD/GG	TT	Fox
Big Burp, The	11-Mar-29	AFF	PT	AVB	PE
Big Chief No Treaty	Sep-62	DE	RK	TT	Fox
Big Clean-up, The	Sep-63	HH	DT	TT	Fox
Big Flood, The	27-Sep-22	AFF	PT	AVB	PE
Big Freeze, The	Dec-71	MH	RT	AVB	Fox
Big Game Fishing	Feb-68	SC	AB	TT	Fox
Big Game Hunt, The	19-Feb-37	FA	MD/GG	AVB	E
Big Game, The	2-Oct-28	AFF	PT/HB	AVB	PE
Big-Hearted Fish, The	20-Apr-26	AFF	PT	AVB	PE
Big Mo	Jul-71	PO	/	TT	Fox
Big Retreat, The	26-May-26	AFF	PT	AVB	PE

Title	Release date	Series	Director	Producer	Distrib
Big Reward, The	12-May-27	AFF	PT	AVB	PE
Big Scare, The	15-Aug-29	AFF	PT	AVB	PE
Big Shot, The	12-Apr-29	AFF	PT	AVB	PE
Big Tent, The	2-Sep-27	AFF	PT	AVB	PE
Big Top, The	12-May-38	PP	MD	TT	E
Bigger and Better Jails	19-Jan-25	AFF	PT	AVB	PE
Bigger Digger, The	Aug-74	TT	RT/RB	TT	Fox
Billy Goat Whiskers, The	10-Dec-37	TT	JF	TT	E
Billy Mouse's Akwakade	9-Aug-40	TT	ED	TT	Fox
Bird Symphony	Apr-55	TT	CR	TT	Fox
Bird Tower, The	28-Nov-41	TT	MD	TT	Fox
Birdland	23-Aug-35	TT	PT/FM	MT	E
Biting the Dust	31-Dec-24	AFF	PT	AVB	PE
Black Duck, The	1-Mar-29	AFF	PT	AVB	PE
Black Magic	18-Oct-24	AFF	PT	AVB	PE
Black Sheep, The	9-Jan-24	AFF	PT	AVB	PE
Black Sheep, The	5-Oct-34	TT	PT/FM	MT	E
Black Spider, The	1-Nov-31	TT	PT/FM	TMC	E
Blaze of Glory, A	28-Jan-28	AFF	PT/MD	AVB	PE
Blind Date	Feb-54	TT	ED	TT	Fox
Blue Plate Symphony	29-Oct-54	HJ	CR	TT	Fox
Bluebeard's Brother	29-May-32	TT	PT/FM	MT	E
Blues	28-Jun-31	TT	PT/FM	TMC	E
Boastful Cat, The	26-Aug-22	AFF	PT	AVB	PE
Body in the Bag, The	5-Jul-24	AFF	PT	AVB	PE
Bold Eagle, The	Aug-69	PO	CA/AB/CR/DT	TT	Fox
Bone of Contention, The	14-Mar-20	PM	PT	Par	Par
Bone Ranger, The	Apr-57	SN	CR	TT	Fox
Bonehead Age, The	5-Dec-25	AFF	PT	AVB	PE
Book Shop, The	5-Feb-37	PP	MD/GG	AVB	PE
Boy and His Dog, The (The Boy and the Dog)	9-Apr-22	AFF	PT	AVB	E
Boy and the Bear, The	9-Aug-22	AFF	PT	AVB	PE
Boy Friend, The	17-Nov-27	AFF	PT/HB	AVB	PE
Brave Heart, A	17-Sep-27	AFF	PT	AVB	PE
Brave Little Brave, The	Jul-56	TT	CR	TT	Fox
Break of the Day	2-Jan-29	AFF	PT/MD	AVB	PE
Brewing Trouble	22-Jun-22	AFF	PT	AVB	PE
Bringing Home the Bacon	11-Jul-41	TT	MD	TT	Fox
Bronco Buster	14-Dec-27	AFF	PT/FM	AVB	PE
Brother from Outer Space	Mar-64	AN	CR	TT	Fox
Bubbles	8-Aug-25	AFF	PT	AVB	PE
Bubbling Over	6-May-27	AFF	PT	AVB	PE
Buck Fever	26-Oct-26	AFF	PT	AVB	PE

348

Appendix 2 • Paul Terry/Terrytoons Theatrical Shorts Filmography

Title	Release date	Series	Director	Producer	Distrib
Bug Carnival	16-Apr-37	TT	MD/GG	TT	E
Bug House College Days	23-Jul-29	AFF	PT	AVB	PE
Bugged by a Bug	Jun-67	JH	CA/AB	TT	Fox
Buggy Ride, A	11-Sep-26	AFF	PT	AVB	PE
Bugs Beetle and His Orchestra	21-Jan-38	TT	JF	TT	E
Bugville Field Day	25-Jul-25	AFF	PT	AVB	PE
Bulldozing the Bull	11-Mar-51	HJ	ED	TT	Fox
Bull-ero	3-Apr-32	TT	PT/FM	MT	E
Bullfight, The	8-Feb-35	TT	PT/FM	MT	E
Bully Beef	13-Jul-30	TT	MD/GG	AC	E
Bully Frog, A	18-Sep-36	TT	PT/FM	TT	E
Bully Romance, A	16-Jun-39	GG	ED	TT	Fox
Bully, The	20-Jun-27	AFF	PT	AVB	PE
Bum Steer, A	Mar-57	BE	MD	TT	Fox
Bumper Crop, A	26-May-26	AFF	PT	AVB	PE
Burglar Alarm, The	6-Jun-23	TT	PT	AVB	PE
Burlesque	4-Sep-32	TT	PT/FM	MT	E
Busted Blossoms	10-Aug-34	TT	PT/FM	MT	E
Busy Bee, The	29-May-36	TT	MD/GG	TT	E
Butcher of Seville, The	7-Jan-44	TT	ED	TT	Fox
By Land and Air	8-Jul-29	AFF	PT/JF	AVB	PE
By the Sea	12-Jul-31	TT	PT/FM	TMC	E
Cabaret	14-Aug-29	AFF	PT/FM	AVB	PE
Camouflage	27-Aug-43	GG	ED	TT	Fox
Camp Clobber	Jul-58	CC	DT	TT	E
Canadian Capers	23-Aug-31	FA	PT/FM	TMC	E
Captain Kidder	20-Feb-24	AFF	PT	AVB	PE
Carmen's Veranda	28-Jul-44	TT	MD	TT	Fox
Carnival Week	19-Nov-27	AFF	PT/JF	AVB	PE
Cat Alarm	31-Dec-61	MM	CR	TT	E
Cat and the Canary, The	7-Aug-21	AFF	PT	AVB	PE
Cat and the Magnet, The	20-Oct-24	AFF	PT	AVB	PE
Cat and the Mice, The	1-Jan-22	AFF	PT	AVB	PE
Cat and the Monkey, The	30-Oct-21	AFF	PT	AVB	PE
Cat and the Pig, The	17-May-22	AFF	PT	AVB	PE
Cat and the Swordfish, The	26-Jan-22	AFF	PT	AVB	PE
Cat Came Back, The	16-Nov-23	AFF	PT	AVB	PE
Cat Came Back, The	18-Aug-44	TT	CR	TT	Fox
Cat Happy	Sep-50	LR	CR	TT	Fox
Cat Meets Mouse	20-Feb-42	TT	MD	AVB	PE
Cat That Failed, The	7-Aug-23	AFF	PT	AVB	PE
Cat Trouble	11-Apr-47	HJ	CR	TT	Fox
Cat's Revenge	Sep-54	LR	MD	TT	Fox

Title	Release date	Series	Director	Producer	Distrib
Cat's Revenge, The	11-Aug-23	AFF	PT	AVB	PE
Cat's Tale, A	Nov-51	TT	MD	TT	Fox
Cat's Whiskers, The	1-Sep-23	AFF	PT	AVB	PE
Catnip Capers	31-May-40	TT	MD	TT	Fox
Catnip Gang, The	Jul-49	MM	ED	TT	Fox
Cats at Law	17-Jul-21	AFF	PT	AVB	PE
Cats in a Bag	1-Dec-36	PP	MD/GG	TT	E
Caviar	23-Feb-30	TT	PT/FM	AC	E
Chain Letters	9-Aug-35	TT	PT/FM	MT	E
Champ, The	20-Sep-31	FA	PT/FM	TMC	E
Champion Chump	Apr-66	MA	AB/CR	TT	Fox
Champion of Justice, The	17-Mar-44	MM	MD	TT	Fox
Champion, The	20-Mar-24	AFF	PT	AVB	PE
Character as Revealed by the Ear	Sep-17	THIR	PT	PT	AK
Character as Revealed by the Eye	Jul-17	THIR	PT	PT	AK
Character as Revealed by the Mouth	Aug-17	THIR	PT	PT	AK
Character as Revealed by the Nose	Jun-17	THIR	PT	PT	AK
Charleston Queen, The	17-Sep-26	AFF	PT	AVB	PE
Chasing Rainbows	13-Jan-27	AFF	PT	AVB	PE
Cheating the Cheaters	14-Dec-22	AFF	PT	AVB	PE
Cherry Blossom Festival	17-Jun-63	HM	RK	TT	Fox
Chestnut Nut, The	Mar-73	PO	/	TMC	E
China	15-Nov-31	TT	MD	TT	Fox
Chipper Chipmunk, The	Mar-48	GG	PT/FM	AC	E
Chop Suey	24-Aug-30	AFF	PT	AVB	PE
Chop Suey and Noodles	6-Jul-26	AFF	PT	AVB	PE
Chris Columbo	12-May-38	TT	ED	TT	E
Christmas Cheer	12-Dec-27	AFF	PT/JF	AVB	PE
Cinderella	28-May-33	TT	PT/FM	MT	E
Circus Days	6-Sep-35	AFF	PT/FM	MT	E
Circus, The	29-Sep-23	AFF	PT	AVB	PE
City Slicker	Mar-52	LR	MD	TT	Fox
City Slickers	12-Jun-28	AFF	PT/HB	AVB	PE
Clean-Up Week	9-Feb-25	AFF	PT	AVB	PE
Clint Clobber's Cat	Jul-57	CC	CR	TT	Fox
Cloak and Stagger	Aug-56	GDD	CR	TT	Fox
Clobber's Ballet Ache	Jan-59	CC	CR	TT	Fox
Clockmaker's Dog	Jan-56	TT	CR	TT	Fox
Close Shave, A	1-Oct-37	FA/OO	MD	TT	E
Closer Than a Brother	28-Sep-25	AFF	PT	AVB	PE
Clowning	5-Apr-31	TT	PT/FM	TMC	E
Club Life in the Stone Age	23-Aug-40	TT	MD	TT	E
Club Sandwich (Dancing Mice)	25-Jan-31	FA	PT/FM	AC	E

349

TERRYTOONS: The Story of Paul Terry and His Classic Cartoon Factory

Title	Release date	Series	Director	Producer	Distrib
Coast to Coast	18-Apr-28	AFF	PT/FM	AVB	PE
Cocky Cockroach, The	10-Jul-32	TT	PT/FM	MT	E
Codfish Balls	1-Jun-30	TT	PT/FM	AC	E
Cold Romance, A	Apr-49	MM	MD	TT	Fox
Cold Steel	23-Jun-29	AFF	PT	AVB	PE
College Spirit	16-Oct-32	TT	PT/FM	MT	E
Comic Book Land	Jan-50	GG	MD	TT	Fox
Commander Great Guy	May-68	SC	AB	TT	Fox
Conceited Donkey, The	11-Dec-21	AFF	PT	AVB	PE
Concentrate	4-May-29	AFF	PT	AVB	PE
Cop's Bride, The	17-Mar-23	AFF	PT	AVB	PE
Cop's Bride, The	17-Mar-29	AFF	PT	AVB	PE
Country Mouse and City Mouse, The	31-Jul-21	AFF	PT	AVB	PE
Country Mouse and the City Cat, The	26-Jun-22	AFF	PT	AVB	PE
County Fair, The	28-Jan-28	AFF	PT/HB	AVB	PE
Covered Pushcart, The	6-Jun-23	AFF	PT	AVB	PE
Covered Pushcart, The	Sep-49	GG	MD	TT	Fox
Cowardly Watchdog, The	Aug-66	MA	DT	TT	Fox
Cracked Ice	19-Feb-27	AFF	PT	AVB	PE
Crackpot King, The	15-Nov-46	MM	ED	TT	Fox
Crawl Stroke Kid, The	12-Mar-27	AFF	PT	AVB	PE
Crime in a Big City	29-May-22	AFF	PT	AVB	PE
Cross Country Run, A	26-Jul-28	AFF	PT/HB	AVB	PE
Crossing the Delaware	Jun-61	FA	AB	TT	E
Crying Wolf	10-Jan-47	HJ	/	TT	Fox
Cuckoo Bird, The	7-Apr-39	TT	MD	TT	Fox
Cure or Kill	20-Sep-28	AFF	PT/HS	AVB	PE
Custard Pies	4-May-29	AFF	PT	AVB	PE
Cutting a Melon	9-May-29	AFF	PT	AVB	PE
Daddy's Little Darling	22-Jul-27	AFF	PT	AVB	PE
Dancing Bear, The	Apr-57	DW	CR	TT	Fox
Dancing Shoes	15-Oct-37	FA	/	TT	E
Daniel Boone Jr.	Nov-49	HJ	MD	TT	Fox
Dark Horse, A	Dec-60	HH	DT	TT	Fox
Darkest Africa	23-Nov-23	AFF	PT	AVB	PE
Darn Barn	4-May-25	AFF	PT	AVB	PE
Date For Dinner, A	Jun-65	PO	CR	TT	Fox
Day by Day in Every Way	29-Aug-47	MM	ED	TT	Fox
Day in June, A	22-Mar-23	AFF	PT	AVB	PE
Day Off, A	31-Mar-44	TT	ED	TT	Fox
Day to Live, A	24-Nov-28	AFF	PT/JF	AVB	PE
Day's Outing, A	31-May-31	TT	PT/FM	TMC	E
Dead End Cats	14-Feb-47	MM	ED	AVB	PE

Title	Release date	Series	Director	Producer	Distrib
Dear Old Switzerland	22-Dec-44	TT	ED	TT	Fox
Deep Sea Doodle	16-Sep-60	HJ	DT	TT	Fox
Deep Stuff	25-Apr-25	AFF	PT	AVB	PE
Derby Day	1-Sep-23	AFF	PT	AVB	PE
Desert Sheiks	12-Jul-24	AFF	PT	AVB	PE
Devil of the Deep	27-May-38	TT	JF	TT	E
Died in the Wool	12-May-27	AFF	PT	AVB	PE
Digging for Gold	12-May-27	AFF	PT	AVB	PE
Dingbat Land	Feb-49	GG	CR	TT	Fox
Dinky Finds a Home	7-Jun-46	DD	ED	TT	Fox
Dinner Time	17-Dec-28	AFF	PT/JF	AVB	PE
Dissatisfied Cobbler, The	8-Feb-22	AFF	PT	AVB	PE
Do Women Pay?	9-Nov-23	AFF	PT	AVB	PE
Dog and the Bone, The	15-Oct-21	AFF	PT	AVB	PE
Dog and the Bone, The	12-Nov-37	PP	GG	TT	E
Dog and the Fish, The	22-Jun-22	AFF	PT	AVB	PE
Dog and the Flea, The	31-Dec-21	AFF	PT	AVB	PE
Dog and the Mosquito	12-Aug-22	AFF	PT	AVB	PE
Dog and the Thief, The	26-Jan-22	AFF	PT	AVB	PE
Dog and the Wolves, The	27-Apr-22	AFF	PT	AVB	PE
Dog in a Mansion, A	12-Jan-40	TT	ED	TT	Fox
Dog Show, The	28-Dec-34	TT	PT/FM	MT	E
Dog Show, The	Aug-50	TT	ED	TT	Fox
Dog's Day, A	12-May-27	AFF	PT	AVB	PE
Dog's Dream, The	2-May-41	TT	ED	TT	Fox
Dog's Paradise, The	1-Dec-22	AFF	PT	AVB	PE
Dog-Gone Catfish	Aug-75	DE	/	TT	Fox
Doing Their Bit	30-Oct-42	N	CR	TT	Fox
Don't Burro Trouble	Jul-72	PO	CA/AB/CR/DT	TT	Fox
Don't Spill the Beans	Apr-65	SC	RB	AVB	PE
Donkey in the Lion's Skin, The	21-Aug-21	AFF	PT	TT	Fox
Doomsday	16-Dec-38	GG	CR	TT	Fox
Dough Boys	22-Jul-26	AFF	PT	AVB	PE
Down on the Farm	3-Dec-24	AFF	PT	AVB	PE
Down on the Levee	5-Mar-33	TT	PT/FM	MT	E
Down on the Phoney Farm	16-Oct-15	PTC	PT	PT	TFC
Down With Cats	7-Oct-43	SM/MM	CR	TT	Fox
Dr. Ha-Ha	Feb-66	JH	RB	AVB	PE
Dr. Rhinestone's Theory	Oct-67	JH	CA/AB	TT	Fox
Dream Walking	9-Jun-50	GG	CR	TT	Fox
Dreamapping	Nov-66	JH	AB/DT	AVB	PE
Dress Reversal	Jul-65	SC	RB	TT	Fox
Dribble Drabble	Jan-68	SC	AB	TT	Fox

Appendix 2 • Paul Terry/Terrytoons Theatrical Shorts Filmography

Title	Release date	Series	Director	Producer	Distrib
Drifter, The	Aug-70	MH	RB	TT	Fox
Driven to Extraction	28-Jun-63	SE	AB	TT	Fox
Drum Roll	Mar-61	HH	DT	TT	Fox
Duck Fever	Feb-55	TB	CR	TT	Fox
Dustcap Doormat	Jun-58	JD	AK	TT	Fox
Dusters, The	Aug-71	MH	RT	TT	Fox
Dutch Treat	21-Sep-30	TT	PT/FM	AC	E
Early Bird, The	26-Jun-28	AFF	PT/JF	AVB	PE
Eat Me Kitty, Eight To a Bar	27-Nov-36	TT	MD	TT	Fox
Echoes from the Alps	6-Mar-42	TT	MD	AVB	PE
Edgar Runs Again	23-May-25	AFF	PT	AVB	PE
Electronic Mouse Trap, The	26-Jan-40	TT	MD	TT	Fox
Elephant Mouse, The	6-Sep-46	MM	MD	TT	Fox
Elephant's Trunk, The	May-51	HP	MD	AVB	PE
Eliza on the Ice	4-Nov-22	AFF	PT	AVB	PE
Eliza Runs Again	6-Jun-44	MM	CR	TT	Fox
Enlarger, The	29-Jul-38	TT	CR	TT	E
Enchanted Fiddle, The	18-Nov-22	AFF	PT	AVB	PE
Enchanted Flute, The	11-Aug-29	AFF	PT/FM	AVB	PE
End of the World, The	16-Jun-25	AFF	PT	AVB	PE
English Channel Swim, The	17-Dec-25	AFF	PT	AVB	PE
Enlarger, The	Apr-71	MH	RT	TT	Fox
Eternal Triangle, The	3-Apr-22	AFF	PT	AVB	PE
Everybody's Flying	17-Jan-28	AFF	PT/JF	AVB	PE
Expert Explorer	Feb-73	HH	DT	TT	Fox
Explorer, The	22-Mar-31	FA	PT/FM	TMC	E
Exterminator, The	23-Nov-45	GG	ED	TT	Fox
Fabulous Firework Family, The	Aug-59	TT	AK	TT	Fox
Fair Exchange, A	6-May-27	AFF	PT	AVB	PE
Faithful Pup, The	12-May-29	AFF	PT/HB	AVB	PE
Famous Ride, The	Apr-60	HH	CR	TT	Fox
Fancy Plants	Jul-67	JH	CA/AB	TT	Fox
Fanny in the Lion's Den	23-Jul-33	FZ/OCH	PT/FM	MT	E
Fanny's Wedding Day	22-Sep-33	FZ/SH	PT/FM	MT	E
Farm Hands, The	20-Apr-26	AFF	PT	AVB	PE
Farmer Al Falfa and His Wayward Pup	21-Jul-17	FA	PT	TEI	TE
Farmer Al Falfa Invents a New Kite	12-Mar-16	PBC	PT	JB	Par
Farmer Al Falfa Sees New York	9-Oct-16	PBC	PT	JB	Par
Farmer Al Falfa's Ape Girl	7-Aug-32	FA	PT/FM	MT	E
Farmer Al Falfa's Bedtime Story	12-Jun-32	FA	PT/FM	MT	E
Farmer Al Falfa's Birthday Party	2-Oct-32	FA	PT/FM	MT	E
Farmer Al Falfa's Blind Pig	7-Dec-16	PBC	PT	JB	Par
Farmer Al Falfa's Bride	23-Feb-23	AFF	PT	AVB	PE
Farmer Al Falfa's Catastrophe	3-Feb-16	PBC	PT	JB	Par
Farmer Al Falfa's Egg-citement	4-Aug-16	PBC	PT	JB	Par
Farmer Al Falfa's Pet Cat	9-Nov-23	AFF	PT	AVB	PE
Farmer Al Falfa's Prize Package	31-Jul-36	FA/KK	MD/GG	TT	E
Farmer Al Falfa's Prune Plantation	3-Nov-16	PBC	PT	JB	Par
Farmer Al Falfa's Revenge	25-Aug-16	PBC	PT	JB	Par
Farmer Al Falfa's Scientific Diary	16-Apr-16	PBC	PT	JB	Par
Farmer Al Falfa's Tentless Circus	3-Jun-16	PBC	PT	JB	Par
Farmer Al Falfa's 20th Anniversary	27-Nov-36	FA	MD/GG	TT	E
Farmer Al Falfa's Watermelon Patch	29-Jun-16	PBC	PT	JB	Par
Farmer Al Falfa's Wolfhound	16-Sep-16	PBC	PT	JB	Par
Farmer and His Cat, The	17-May-22	AFF	PT	AVB	PE
Farmer and the Mice, The	26-Jan-22	AFF	PT	AVB	PE
Farmer and the Ostrich, The	26-Jan-22	AFF	PT	AVB	PE
Farmer and the Ostrich, The	1-Apr-22	AFF	PT	AVB	PE
Farmer's Goat, The	19-Jun-29	AFF	PT/JF	AVB	PE
Fashionable Fox, The	11-Sep-21	AFF	PT	AVB	PE
Fast Worker, A	16-May-25	AFF	PT	AVB	PE
Fearless Fido	20-Jul-22	AFF	PT	AVB	PE
Featherweight Champ	6-Feb-53	DD	ED	TT	Fox
Felix the Fox	Jan-48	FTF	MD	TT	Fox
Feud, The	10-Jan-36	TT	PT/FM	MT	E
Feuding Hillbillies, The	Apr-48	MM	CR	TT	Fox
Fight Game, The	26-Apr-29	AFF	PT/FM	AVB	PE
Fight to the Finish, A	14-Nov-47	MM	CR	TT	Fox
Fire Fighters, The	26-Mar-26	AFF	PT	AVB	PE
Fireman, Save My Child	22-Feb-35	TT	PT/FM	MT	E
Fireman's Bride, The	3-May-31	TT	PT/FM	TMC	E
First Fast Mail, The	May-61	HH	DT	TT	Fox
First Flight Up	Oct-62	TT	BT	MT	Fox
First Robin, The	29-Dec-39	TT	CR	TT	E
First Snow, The	11-Jan-35	TT	PT/FM	MT	E
First Telephone, The	10-Oct-47	MM	MD	TT	Fox
Fish Day	Feb-72	HH	DT	TT	Fox
Fish Story, A	26-May-29	AFF	PT	AVB	PE
Fisherman's Jinx, A	27-Apr-23	AFF	PT	AVB	PE
Fisherman's Luck	27-Jan-23	AFF	PT	AVB	PE
Fisherman's Luck	19-Jan-25	GG	ED	TT	Fox
Fishing by the Sea	30-Mar-45	HJ	CR	TT	Fox
Fishing Made Easy	19-Sep-47	GG	ED	TT	Fox
Five Fifteen, The	21-Feb-41	AFF	PT	AVB	PE
Five Orphans of the Storm	9-Nov-23	AFF	PT	AVB	PE
Five Puplets	17-May-35	TT	PT/FM	MT	E

TERRYTOONS: The Story of Paul Terry and His Classic Cartoon Factory

Title	Release date	Series	Director	Producer	Distrib
Flamboyant Arms, The	28-Apr-59	CC	CR	TT	Fox
Flat Foot Fledgling	25-Jan-52	DD	MD	TT	Fox
Flebus	Aug-57	F	EP	TT	Fox
Fleet's Out, The	Oct-62	SE	CR	TT	Fox
Flight That Failed, The	7-May-28	AFF	PT/HS	AVB	PE
Flight to the Finish, A	Dec-62	HH	DT	TT	Fox
Flipper Frolics	Jul-52	TT	CR	TT	Fox
Flop Secret	Dec-52	LR	ED	TT	Fox
Fly and the Ants, The	3-Dec-21	AFF	PT	AVB	PE
Fly Time	6-Mar-26	AFF	PT	AVB	PE
Flying Age, The	30-Apr-28	AFF	PT/JF	AVB	PE
Flying Carpet, The	28-May-24	AFF	PT	AVB	PE
Flying Cups and Saucers	Nov-49	TT	CR	TT	Fox
Flying Fever	2-Aug-24	AFF	PT	AVB	PE
Flying Fishers	26-Dec-41	GG	MD	TT	Fox
Flying Hoofs	26-Oct-27	AFF	PT	AVB	PE
Flying Oil	5-Apr-35	FA	PT/HB	MT	E
Flying South	19-Mar-37	FA	MD/GG	TT	Fox
Flying South	15-Aug-47	HJ	MD	MT	Fox
Foiled Again	14-Oct-35	FZOCHSH	PT/FM	TT	E
Footle's Picnic	Mar-60	FO	DT	TT	Fox
Footle's Train Ride	24-May-59	FO	PT	TT	Fox
Foolish Duckling	Aug-52	DD	MD	TT	Fox
Football	18-Oct-35	TT	PT/FM	MT	E
For the Love of a Gal	18-Jul-25	AFF	PT	AVB	PE
Fortune Hunters, The	11-Nov-22	AFF	PT	AVB	PE
Fortune Hunters, The	8-Feb-46	GG	CR	TT	Fox
Forty Thieves, The	13-Nov-32	TT	PT/FM	MT	E
Fox and Crow, The	14-Aug-21	AFF	PT	AVB	PE
Fox and the Goat, The	6-Nov-21	AFF	PT	AVB	PE
Fox and the Grapes, The	26-Jan-22	AFF	CR	TT	Fox
Fox Hunt	17-Feb-50	HJ	MD	TT	Fox
Fox Hunt, The	13-Oct-27	AFF	PT	AVB	PE
Foxed by a Fox	May-55	TT	CR	TT	Fox
Foxy-Fox, The	26-Jul-35	TT	PT/FM	MT	E
Frame-Up, The	30-Dec-38	GG	CR	TT	Fox
Frankenstein's Cat	27-Nov-42	SM/MM	MD	TT	Fox
Free Enterprise	23-Nov-48	HJ	MD	TT	Fox
Free Enterprise	Dec-75	HJ	MD	TT	Fox
Freight Fright	Mar-65	PO	CR	AC	E
French Fried	7-Sep-30	TT	PT/FM	TT	Fox
Friday the 13th	Jul-53	LR	MD	TT	Fox

Title	Release date	Series	Director	Producer	Distrib
Friday the Thirteenth	11-Nov-22	AFF	PT	AVB	PE
Fried Chicken	19-Oct-30	TT	PT/FM	AC	E
Friend Fox	May-75	DE	/	TT	Fox
Frog and the Catfish, The	1-Dec-22	AFF	PT	AVB	PE
Frog and the Ox, The	16-Oct-21	AFF	PT	TT	Fox
Frog and the Princess, The	7-Apr-44	GG	ED	TT	Fox
Frog, The	Oct-69	MH	RB	TT	Fox
Frogs That Wanted a King, The	27-Nov-21	AFF	PT	AVB	PE
From Rags to Riches and Back Again	20-Feb-24	AFF	PT	AVB	PE
Frozen Feet	24-Feb-39	TT	CR	TT	Fox
Frozen North, The	17-Oct-41	TT	CR	TT	Fox
Frozen Sparklers	Nov-67		RB	TT	Fox
Fruitful Farm	22-Aug-29	AFF	PT/JF	AVB	PE
Funny Bunny Business	6-Feb-42	TT	ED	TT	Fox
Gadmouse the Apprentice Good Fairy	Jan-65	SC	RB	TT	Fox
Gag Buster	Feb-57	SP	CR	AVB	PE
Gamblers, The	22-Mar-23	AFF	PT	TT	Fox
Gandy the Goose	4-Mar-38	GG	JF	TT	E
Gandy's Dream Girl	8-Dec-44	GG	MD	TT	Fox
Gaston Go Home	May-58	GC	CR	TT	Fox
Gaston is Here	May-57	GC	CR	TT	Fox
Gaston's Baby	Mar-58	GC	CR	TT	Fox
Gaston's Easel Life	Oct-58	GC	DT	TT	Fox
Gaston's Mama Lisa	Jun-59	GC	CR	TT	Fox
Gems from Gemini	Jan-66	AN	DT	TT	Fox
General's Little Helpers, The	Feb-69	PO	/	TT	Fox
Ghost Monster, The	Apr-70	MH	RB	TT	Fox
Ghost Town, The	22-Sep-44	GG	MD	TT	Fox
Git That Guitar	Sep-65	PO	AB	TT	Fox
Give Me Liberty	Aug-67		CA/AB	PT	AK
Glass Slipper, The	7-Oct-38	JH	MD	TT	Fox
Gliders, The	10-Feb-23	AFF	PT	AVB	PE
G-Man Jitters	10-Mar-39	GG	ED	TT	Fox
Go West, Big Boy	22-Feb-31	TT	PT/FM	TT	Fox
Going Ape	Jan-70	AN	CR	TMC	E
Gold Dust Bandit, The	Oct-64	LU	AB	TT	Fox
Gold Push, The	9-Jan-26	AFF	PT	TT	Fox
Golden Hen, The	24-May-46	GG	MD	AVB	PE
Golden Spoon Mary	30-Apr-17	PTFB	PT	PT	Fox
Golden West, The	25-Aug-39	TT	MD	TT	Fox
Golf Nuts	14-Dec-30	TT	PT/FM	AC	E
Good Deed Daly	Apr-55	GDD	CR	TT	Fox
Good Mousekeeping	Oct-52	LR	MD	TT	Fox

Appendix 2 • Paul Terry/Terrytoons Theatrical Shorts Filmography

Title	Release date	Series	Director	Producer	Distrib
Good Old Circus Days	22-Nov-24	AFF	PT	AVB	PE
Good Old College Days	26-Jan-24	AFF	PT	AVB	PE
Good Old Days, The	24-Dec-23	AFF	PT	AVB	PE
Good Old Irish Tunes	27-Jun-41	TT	CR	TT	Fox
Good Ship Nellie, The	6-Jan-28	AFF	PT/FM	AVE	PE
Goons from the Moon	Apr-51	MM	CR	TT	Fox
Goony Golfers	1-Dec-48	HJ	JF	TT	Fox
Goose Flies High, The	9-Sep-38	GG	PT	TT	Fox
Goose That Laid the Golden Egg, The	19-Jun-21	AFF	PT	AVE	PE
Grand Prix Winner	Mar-68	SC	AB	TT	Fox
Grand Uproar	25-Aug-33	TT	PT/FM	MT	E
Grandma's House	11-Feb-29	AFF	PT	AVB	PE
Great Explorers, The	19-Jul-23	AFF	PT	AVB	PE
Great Open Spaces, The	21-Nov-25	AFF	PT	TT	Fox
Green Line, The	7-Jul-44	MM	ED	TT	Fox
Gridiron Demons	4-Oct-28	AFF	PT/FM	AVB	PE
Growing Pains	Dec-53	TB	ED	TT	Fox
Gun Shy	22-Oct-26	AFF	PT	AVB	PE
Gypsy Fiddler, A	6-Oct-33	TT	PT/FM	MT	E
Gypsy Life	3-Aug-45	MM	CR	TT	Fox
Hair Cut-Ups	Feb-53	HJ	ED	TT	Fox
Hairless Hector	24-Jan-41	TT	VW	TT	Fox
Hansel and Gretel	5-Feb-33	TT	PT/FM	MT	E
Hansel and Gretel	Jun-52	MM	CR	TT	Fox
Happy and Lucky	18-Mar-38	PP	CR	TT	E
Happy Circus Days	23-Jan-42	TT	CR	TT	Fox
Happy Cobblers, The	May-52	TT	ED	TT	Fox
Happy Days	9-May-28	AFF	PT/JF	AVB	PE
Happy Go Luckies	9-Nov-23	AFF	PT	AVB	PE
Happy Go Lucky	28-Feb-47	HJ	CR	TT	Fox
Happy Haunting Grounds	18-Oct-40	TT	MD	TT	Fox
Happy Holland	Nov-52	MM	ED	TT	Fox
Happy Hollow Hayride	Mar-72	PO	/	TT	Fox
Happy Landing	Jun-49	HJ	MD	TT	Fox
Har Har Harpoon	Nov-74	HH	AB/MD/GD/RK/CR/MT/DT	TT	Fox
Hard Boiled Egg, The	Oct-48	TT	CR	TT	Fox
Hard Cider	12-May-27	AFF	PT	AVB	PE
Hare and Frog, The	28-Aug-21	AFF	ED	AVB	PE
Hare and the Hounds, The	23-Feb-40	TT	ED	TT	Fox
Hare and the Tortoise, The	25-Sep-21	AFF	PT	AVB	PE
Hare-Breadth Finish, A	Feb-57	TT	CR	TT	Fox
Harm Sweet Home	Nov-73	PO	/	/	Fox

Title	Release date	Series	Director	Producer	Distrib
Harvest Time	9-Feb-40	TT	CR	TT	Fox
Hashimoto-San	Oct-59	HM	RK/DT	TT	Fox
Hated Rivals, The	27-Sep-22	AFF	PT	AVB	PE
Haunted Cat, The	Dec-51	LR	ED	TT	Fox
Haunted House, The	12-Dec-25	AFF	PT	AVB	PE
Haunted Housecleaning	May-66	AN	CR	TT	Fox
Hawaiian Pineapples	4-May-30	TT	PT/FM	AC	E
Hawks of the Sea	25-Sep-24	AFF	PT	AVB	PE
Hay Ride, The	2-Apr-37	KK	MD/GG	TT	E
He Dood it Again	5-Feb-43	FA	ED	TT	Fox
Health Farm, The	4-Sep-36	SM/MM	MD/GG	TT	E
Hearts and Glowers	Jun-60	TT	MB	TT	Fox
Hearts and Showers	20-Apr-26	AFF	PT	AVB	PE
Heat's Off, The	Apr-67	JH	RB	TT	Fox
Hectormobile, The	Oct-73	TT	DT	TT	Fox
Helicopter, The	21-Jan-44	HH	ED	TT	Fox
Helpful Geni, The	Oct-51	TT	CR	TT	Fox
Helpless Hippo	Mar-54	MM	CR	TT	Fox
He-Man Seaman	Mar-62	HH	AB	TT	Fox
Henpecked Henry	28-Oct-22	AFF	PT	AVB	PE
Henry's Busted Romance	11-Nov-22	AFF	PT	AVB	PE
Hep Cat, The	6-Dec-46	MM	MD	TT	Fox
Hep Mother Hubbard	Mar-56	TT	CR	TT	Fox
Her Ben	22-Jul-26	AFF	PT	AVB	PE
Her First Egg	26-Jul-31	TT	PT/FM	TMC	E
Here's to Good Old Jail	10-Jun-38	TT	ED	TT	E
Herman the Great Mouse	20-Feb-24	AFF	PT	AVB	PE
Hermit and the Bear, The	18-Sep-21	AFF	PT	AVB	PE
Hero For a Day	Apr-53	MM	MD	TT	Fox
Hero Wins, The	10-Oct-25	AFF	PT	AVB	PE
Hey Diddle Diddle	20-Sep-35	TT	PT/FM	MT	E
Hide and Go Sidney	Jan-60	SE	AB	TT	Fox
High Flyer	Oct-72	HH	DT	TT	Fox
High Flyers, The	29-Sep-23	AFF	PT	AVB	PE
High Seas	10-Sep-28	AFF	PT/MD	AVB	PE
High Stakes [High Steaks]	27-Dec-27	AFF	PT/HS	AVB	PE
His Off Day	4-Feb-38	PP	CR	MT	E
His Trial	Jul-17	PTB	PT	PT	AK
Hitch Hikers	12-Dec-47	HJ	CR	TT	Fox
Hitchhiker, The	1-Dec-39	GG	ED	TT	Fox
Hitting the Rails	26-Oct-26	AFF	PT	AVB	PE
Hobo Hassle	Dec-74	PO	/	TT	Fox
Hokey Home Movies	Sep-72	AN	RK	TT	Fox

353

TERRYTOONS: The Story of Paul Terry and His Classic Cartoon Factory

Title	Release date	Series	Director	Producer	Distrib
Hold That Thought	26-Dec-24	AFF	PT	AVB	PE
Hold the Fort	Feb-74	HH	DT	TT	Fox
Hole in One, A	8-Jul-27	AFF	PT	AVB	PE
Holland Days	12-Jan-34	TT	PT/FM	MT	E
Hollywood Diet	11-Dec-32	TT	PT/FM	TT	E
Home Agent, The	Dec-27	AFF	PT	AVB	PE
Home Guard, The	7-Mar-41	GG	MD	TT	Fox
Home Life	Nov-62	SE	CR	TT	Fox
Home Sweet Home	26-Oct-26	AFF	PT	AVB	PE
Home Talent	28-Jun-24	AFF	PT	AVB	PE
Home Town Olympics	7-Feb-36	FA	PT/FM	MT	E
Homeless Cats	26-Apr-29	AFF	PT	AVB	PE
Homeless Pup, The	23-Jul-37	PP	GG	TT	E
Homeless Pups	22-Apr-24	AFF	PT	AVB	PE
Honor Man, The	1-Apr-27	AFF	PT	AVB	PE
Honor System, The	7-Nov-25	AFF	PT	AVB	PE
Honorable Cat Story	Nov-61	HM	CR	TT	Fox
Honorable Family Problem	30-Mar-62	HM	RK	TT	Fox
Honorable House Cat	Mar-62	HM	MD	TT	Fox
Honorable Paint in Neck	22-Aug-62	HM	RK	TT	Fox
Hook and Ladder Number One	30-Oct-32	TT	PT/FM	MT	E
Hook, Line and Sinker	22-Jul-27	FA/PP	PT	AVB	PE
Hook, Line and Sinker	28-Sep-39	AFF	ED	TT	Fox
Hopeful Donkey, The	17-Dec-43	GG	MD	TT	Fox
Horse Fly Opera	13-Jun-41	TT	ED	TT	Fox
Horse's Tale, A	Dec-27	AFF	PT	AVB	PE
Horses, Horses, Horses	10-May-27	AFF	PT	AVB	PE
Hot Rods	Jun-53	MM	ED	TT	Fox
Hot Sands	2-Nov-34	TT	PT/FM	MT	E
Hot Spell, The	10-Jul-36	FA/PP	MD/GG	TT	E
Hot Times in Iceland	4-May-25	AFF	PT	AVB	PE
Hot Turkey	4-May-30	TT	PT/FM	AC	E
Hounding the Hares	Apr-48	TT	ED	TT	Fox
House Busters	Aug-52	HJ	CR	TT	Fox
House Cleaning	2-Aug-24	AFF	PT	AVB	PE
House Cleaning Time	4-May-25	AFF	PT	AVB	PE
House of Hashimoto	23-Jul-29	AFF	PT/JF	AVB	PE
Housewife Herman	30-Nov-60	HM	CR	TT	Fox
Housing Problem, The	18-Nov-38	TT	ED	TT	Fox
Housing Shortage, The	25-Oct-46	TT	MD	TT	Fox
How to Keep Cool	4-Apr-25	AFF	PT	AVB	PE
How to Relax	Oct-53	DW	CR	TT	Fox
	Feb-54	DW	CR	TT	Fox

Title	Release date	Series	Director	Producer	Distrib
How Wet Was My Ocean	4-Oct-40	TT	ED	TT	Fox
Howling Success	Jul-54	TB	CR	TT	Fox
Hula Hula Land	Jul-49	HJ	MD	TT	Fox
Human Fly, The	16-Aug-27	AFF	PT	AC	PE
Hungarian Goulash	15-Jun-30	TT	PT/FM	AVB	E
Hungry Hounds	26-Sep-25	AFF	PT	AVB	PE
Hunter and His Dog, The	27-Apr-22	AFF	PT	AVB	PE
Hunting in 1950	23-Jan-26	AFF	PT	AVB	PE
Huntsman, The	26-Jun-28	AFF	PT/FM	AVB	PE
Hypnotic Eyes	11-Aug-33	FZ/OCH	PT/FM	MT	E
Hypnotized	Jun-52	LR	MD	TT	Fox
Ice Carnival, The	22-Aug-41	TT	ED	TT	Fox
Ice Cream for Help	Oct-71	HH	AB	TT	Fox
Ice Pond, The	15-Dec-39	TT	MD	TT	Fox
Ickle Meets Pickle	13-Nov-42	TT	CR	TT	Fox
If Cats Could Sing	Oct-50	TT	ED	TT	Fox
It Noah Lived Today	22-Apr-24	AFF	PT	AVB	PE
In Again, Out Again	16-Aug-27	AFF	PT	AVB	PE
In Dutch	13-Feb-25	AFF	PT	AVB	PE
In His Cups	30-Jun-29	AFF	PT	AVB	PE
In the Good Old Summertime	13-Sep-24	AFF	PT	AVB	PE
In the Rough	22-Jan-27	AFF	PT/HS	AVB	PE
In Vaudeville	26-Oct-26	AFF	PT	MT	E
In Venice	15-Dec-33	TT	PT/FM	AC	E
Indian Pudding	4-Apr-30	TT	PT/FM	TT	E
Injun Trouble	Jun-51	MM	ED	TT	Fox
Intruders, The	9-May-47	HJ	ED	TT	Fox
Invisibeam, The	Jan-72	AN	/	TT	Fox
Ireland or Bust	25-Dec-32	TT	PT/FM	MT	E
Irish Stew	5-Oct-30	TT	PT/FM	AC	E
Irish Sweepstakes	27-Jul-34	AFF	PT/FM	MT	E
It Must Be Love	5-Apr-40	TT	CR	TT	Fox
It's a Living	Feb-58	DD	WH	TT	Fox
It's All in the Stars	12-Apr-46	GG	CR	TT	Fox
It's for the Birds	Mar-67	JH	CA/AB	TT	Fox
Jack's Shack	30-Nov-34	TT	PT/FM	MT	E
Jail Birds	21-Sep-34	AFF	PT	MT	E
Jail Break, The	20-Sep-46	MM	ED	TT	Fox
Jail Breakers, The	6-May-29	AFF	PT	AVB	PE
Jazz Mad	9-Aug-31	TT	PT/FM	TMC	E
Jealous Fisherman, The	22-Apr-24	AFF	PT	AVB	PE
Jealous Lover	8-Jan-33	TT	PT/FM	MT	E
Jesse and James	6-Sep-31	TT	PT/FM	TMC	E

Appendix 2 • Paul Terry/Terrytoons Theatrical Shorts Filmography

Title	Release date	Series	Director	Producer	Distrib
Jingle Bells	18-Oct-31	TT	PT/FM	TMC	E
Joe's Lunch Wagon	6-Apr-34	TT	PT/FM	MT	E
Johnstown Flood, The	28-Jun-46	MM	CR	TT	Fox
Jolly Jailbird, The	12-May-24	AFF	PT	AVB	PE
Jolly Rounders, The	22-Mar-23	AFF	PT	AVE	PE
Judo Kudos	Aug-68	SC	AB	TT	Fox
Juggler of our Lady, The [The Juggler of Our Lady: A Medieval Legend]	Apr-58	TT	AK	TT	Fox
Jumping Beans	2-Nov-30	TT	PT/FM	AC	E
June Bride, A	1-Nov-35	FA	PT/FM	MT	E
June Bride, The	23-Jan-26	AFF	PT	AVB	PE
Jungle Bike Riders	14-May-25	AFF	PT	AVB	PE
Jungle Days	19-Mar-28	AFF	PT/JF	AVB	PE
Jungle Jack	May-74	LU	AB/CR/RK/DT	TT	Fox
Jungle Sports	6-Jul-26	AFF	PT	AVB	PE
Jungle Triangle, A	14-Apr-28	AFF	PT/MD	AVB	PE
Junk Man, The	28-Nov-27	AFF	PT/MD	AVB	PE
Junker, The	Jun-75	MH	RB	TT	Fox
Just a Clown	20-Apr-34	TT	PT/FM	MT	E
Just a Little Bull	19-Apr-40	TT	ED	TT	E
Just Ask Jupiter	18-Feb-38	TT	MD	TT	Fox
Kangaroo Steak	27-Jul-30	TT	PT/FM	AC	E
Keep 'Em Growing	28-Jul-43	TT	MD	TT	Fox
Keep Off the Grass	1-Apr-27	AFF	PT	AVB	PE
Kidnapped	23-Jun-29	AFF	PT	AVB	PE
Kiko and the Honey Bears	21-Aug-36	KK	MD/GG	TT	Fox
Kiko Foils a Fox	2-Oct-36	KK	MD/GG	TT	E
Kiko the Kangaroo in Red Hot Music	5-Mar-37	KK	MD/GG	TT	E
Kiko's Cleaning Day	17-Sep-37	KK	MD/GG	TT	E
King Looney XIV	14-Jun-35	TT	PT/FM	MT	E
King Rounder	Apr-64	LU	CR	TT	E
King Tut's Tomb	Aug-50	HJ	MD	TT	Fox
King Zilch	11-Jun-33	TT	PT/FM	MT	E
King's Daughter, The	4-May-34	TT	PT/FM	MT	E
Kisser Plant	Jun-64	AN	CR	TT	Fox
Kitten Sitter, The	May-49	TT	ED	TT	Fox
Klondike Strike Out	Jan-62	HH	DT	TT	Fox
Knight Out, A	28-Aug-26	AFF	PT	AVB	PE
Kooky Cucumbers	Nov-71	PO	DT	TT	Fox
L'il Whoaper	Feb-75	DE	/	TT	Fox
Lad and His Lamp, A	2-Mar-29	AFF	PT	AVB	PE
Land Boom, The	6-Jul-26	AFF	PT	AVB	PE
Land Grab	Feb-70	HH	DT	TT	Fox

Title	Release date	Series	Director	Producer	Distrib
Land o' Cotton	28-Dec-28	AFF	PT/FM	AVB	PE
Landing of the Pilgrims	1-Nov-40	TT	CR	TT	Fox
Last Ha Ha, The	26-Jul-26	AFF	PT	AVB	PE
Last Indian, The	24-Jun-38	TT	CR	TT	E
Last Mouse of Hamelin, The	Jun-55	TT	CR	TT	Fox
Last Round Up, The	14-May-43	GG	MD	TT	Fox
Last Straw, The	23-Feb-34	TT	PT/FM	MT	E
Laundry Man, The	26-Oct-28	AFF	PT	AVB	PE
Law and Order	23-Jun-50	MM	ED	TT	Fox
Lazy Little Beaver	26-Dec-47	MM	ED	TT	Fox
Leaky Faucet, The	Dec-59	TT	MT	TT	Fox
Life With Fido	21-Aug-42	DD	CR	TT	Fox
Lighter than Air	23-Jan-26	AFF	PT	AVB	PE
Lighthouse by the Sea, A	25-Sep-24	AFF	PT	AVB	PE
Lights Out	17-Apr-42	GG	ED	TT	Fox
Lindy's Cat	2-Sep-27	AFF	PT	AVB	PE
Lion and the Monkey, The	3-Oct-25	AFF	PT	AVB	PE
Lion and the Mouse	12-Nov-43	SM/MM	MD	TT	Fox
Lion and the Mouse, The	21-Feb-22	AFF	PT	AVB	PE
Lion Hunt	Mar-49	HJ	ED	TT	Fox
Lion Hunt, The	7-Jan-38	TT	MD	TT	E
Lion Hunt, The	Sep-74	HJ	ED	TT	Fox
Lion's Friend, The	18-May-34	TT	PT/FM	MT	E
Lioness and the Bugs, The	24-Jul-21	AFF	PT	AVB	PE
Liquid Dynamite	17-May-26	AFF	PT	AVB	PE
Little Anglers	Jul-52	TB	CR	TT	Fox
Little Boy Blue	30-Nov-33	TT	PT/FM	MT	E
Little Brown Jug	23-Jan-26	AFF	PT	AVB	PE
Little Game Hunter, The	5-May-29	AFF	PT	AVB	PE
Little Herman	19-Jun-15	PTC	PT	PT	TFC
Little Parade, The	26-Jul-26	AFF	PT	AVB	PE
Little Problems	Sep-51	TB	ED	TT	Fox
Little Red Hen	Jun-55	TT	CR	TT	Fox
Littlest Bully, The	9-Aug-60	SE	MB	TT	Fox
Log Rollers	Nov-53	HJ	MD	TT	Fox
Loops and Swoops	Nov-68	SC	AB	TT	Fox
Lorelei, The	29-Nov-31	TT	PT/FM	TMC	E
Lost and Foundation	Jun-70	HH	/	TT	Fox
Love at First Sight	11-Apr-22	AFF	PT	AVB	PE
Love in a Cottage	1-Sep-23	AFF	PT	PT	PE
Love in a Cottage	28-Jul-40	TT	VW	TT	Fox
Love is Blind	May-57	TT	MD	TT	Fox
Love Nest, The	7-Jun-27	AFF	PT	AVB	PE

TERRYTOONS: The Story of Paul Terry and His Classic Cartoon Factory

Title	Release date	Series	Director	Producer	Distrib
Love's Labor Won	Sep-48	MM	MD	TT	Fox
Loyal Royalty	18-May-62	HM	RK	TT	Fox
Lucky Dog	Jun-56	TT	CR	TT	Fox
Lucky Duck, The	6-Sep-40	DD	CR	TT	Fox
Lumber Jacks	22-Nov-24	AFF	PT	AVB	PE
Lyin' Lion, The	Aug-49	TT	CR	TT	Fox
Mad House, A	23-Mar-34	TT	CR	MT	E
Mad King, The	26-Jun-32	TT	PT/FM	MT	E
Magic Fish, The	19-Oct-34	TT	PT/FM	MT	E
Magic Pencil, The	15-Nov-40	GG	VW	TT	Fox
Magic Shell, The	16-May-41	TT	MD	TT	Fox
Magic Slipper	Dec-48	MM	MD	TT	Fox
Magician, The	12-Mar-27	AFF	PT	AVB	PE
Magnetic Bat, The	17-Sep-28	AFF	PT	AVB	PE
Magpie Madness	Jul-48	HJ	ED	TT	Fox
Magpie Madness	Sep-75	HJ	PT	TT	Fox
Maid and the Millionaire, The	27-Apr-22	AFF	PT	AVB	PE
Maid in China	29-Apr-38	TT	CR	TT	E
Mail Coach, The	6-Feb-26	AFF	PT	AVB	PE
Mail Man	12-Dec-28	AFF	PT/MD	AVB	PE
Mail Pilot, The	14-Feb-27	AFF	PT	AVB	PE
Man Who Laughs, The	11-Nov-22	AFF	PT	AVB	PE
Marathon Dancers, The	19-Jul-23	AFF	PT	AVB	PE
Martian Moochers	May-70	AN	RK	TT	Fox
Mayflower, The	27-Dec-35	TT	PT/FM	MT	E
McDougal's Rest Farm	31-Jan-47	HJ	MD	TT	Fox
Mechanical Bird	Feb-52	TT	ED	TT	Fox
Mechanical Cow, The	25-Jun-37	FA	JZ	TT	E
Mechanical Horse, The	9-Aug-22	GG	GB/AC	TT	PE
Medicine Man, The	1-Apr-27	AFF	PT	AVB	PE
Melvin the Magnificent	Apr-75	LU	AB/CR/KD/T	TT	Fox
Merry Blacksmith, The	12-Mar-26	AFF	PT	AVB	PE
Merry Chase, A	May-50	HJ	MD	TT	Fox
Message from the Sea, A	5-Sep-24	AFF	PT	AVB	PE
Messed Up Movie Makers	Mar-66	HJ	PT/FM	AVB	PE
Mexican Baseball	14-Mar-47	GG	PT	TT	Fox
Miami Maniacs	Feb-56	HJ	CR	TT	Fox
Mice at War	4-Sep-21	AFF	PT	AVB	PE
Mice in Council	26-Jul-21	AFF	PT	AVB	PE
Mice in Council	24-Aug-34	TT	PT/FM	MT	E
Midsummer's Day, A	28-Jul-29	AFF	PT	AVB	PE
Mighty Mouse and the Kilkenny Cats	13-Apr-45	MM	MD	TT	Fox
Mighty Mouse and the Magician	Mar-48	MM	ED	TT	Fox

Title	Release date	Series	Director	Producer	Distrib
Mighty Mouse and the Pirates	12-Jan-45	MM	CR	TT	Fox
Mighty Mouse and the Wolf	20-Jul-45	MM	ED	TT	Fox
Mighty Mouse in Krakatoa	14-Dec-45	MM	CR	TT	Fox
Mighty Mouse Meets Bad Bill Bunion	9-Nov-45	MM	MD	TT	Fox
Mighty Mouse Meets Deadeye Dick	30-May-47	MM	CR	TT	Fox
Mighty Mouse Meets Jeckyll and Hyde Cat	28-Apr-44	MM	MD	TT	Fox
Milk For Baby	8-Jul-38	TT	MD	TT	E
Miller and His Donkey, The	22-Jan-22	AFF	PT	AVB	PE
Mint Men	23-Jun-60	HJ	DT	TT	Fox
Minute and 1/2 Man, The	Jul-59	HH	DT	TT	Fox
Mischievous Cat, The	22-Jun-22	AFF	PT	AVB	PE
Missing Genie, The	Apr-63	LU	CR	TT	Fox
Mississippi Swing	7-Feb-41	TT	CR	TT	Fox
Misunderstood Giant, The	Feb-60	TT	CR	TT	Fox
Mixed Up Matador	Oct-74	LU	AB/CR/RK/DT	TT	Fox
Moans and Groans	28-Jun-35	FA	PT/FM	MT	E
Model Diary, The	11-Apr-22	AFF	PT	AVB	PE
Modern Red Riding Hood, A	3-May-35	TT	PT/FM	MT	E
Molecular Mixup	Dec-64	AN	DT	TT	Fox
Monkey Business	29-Oct-24	AFF	PT	AVB	PE
Monkey Love	24-Sep-28	AFF	PT/MD	AVB	PE
Monkey Meat	10-Aug-30	TT	PT/FM	AC	E
Monster Master, The	Jul-66	HJ	RB/CA	TT	Fox
Monsterizer, The	Oct-75	MH	RB	TT	Fox
Moose on the Loose	Nov-52	HJ	MD	TT	Fox
Moose on the Loose	Apr-74	HJ	MD	TT	Fox
Mopping Up	25-Jun-43	GG	ED	TT	Fox
More Mice Than Brains	21-Nov-25	AFF	PT	AVB	PE
Morning After, The	16-Nov-23	AFF	PT	AVB	PE
Moth and the Spider, The	8-Mar-35	TT	PT/FM	MT	E
Mother Goose Nightmare	4-May-45	GG	CR	TT	Fox
Mother Goose's Birthday Party	Dec-50	MM	CR	TT	Fox
Mount Piney	Dec-68	PO	AB	TT	Fox
Mountain Romance, A	1-Apr-38	MM	MD	TT	E
Mouse and Garden	Oct-50	LR	PT	TT	Fox
Mouse Catcher, The	27-Apr-23	AFF	PT	AVB	PE
Mouse Meets Bird	Mar-53	LR	CR	TT	Fox
Mouse Menace	Sep-53	LR	ED	TT	Fox
Mouse of Tomorrow, The	16-Oct-42	SM/MM	ED	TT	Fox
Mouse That Turned, The	20-Sep-24	AFF	PT	AVB	PE
Mouse's Bride, The	14-Jun-28	AFF	PT	AVB	PE
Movie Madness	Jan-52	HJ	CR	TT	Fox
Movie Madness	Jan-74	HJ	CR	TT	Fox

Appendix 2 • Paul Terry/Terrytoons Theatrical Shorts Filmography

Title	Release date	Series	Director	Producer	Distrib
Movie Magic	May-72	AN	AB/CR/RK/DT	TT	Fox
Mr. Winlucky	Feb-67	JH	CA/AB	TT	Fox
Mrs. Jones' Rest Farm	Aug-49	TT	ED	TT	Fox
Mrs. O'Leary's Cow	22-Jul-38	TT	ED	TT	E
Much Ado About Nothing	22-Mar-40	DD	CR	TT	Fox
Musical Madness	May-51	LR	ED	TT	Fox
Musical Parrot, The	31-Dec-26	AFF	PT	AVB	PE
My Boy Johnny	12-May-44	TT	ED	TT	Fox
My Lady's Garden	13-Jul-34	TT	PT/FM	MT	E
My Old Kentucky Home	29-Mar-46	MM	ED	TT	Fox
Mysteries of Old Chinatown	3-Dec-24	AFF	PT	AVB	PE
Mysteries of the Sea	19-Jul-23	AFF	PT	AVB	PE
Mysterious Cowboy	Sep-52	TT	MD	TT	Fox
Mysterious Hat, The	17-Feb-23	AFF	PT	AVB	PE
Mysterious Package, The	15-Dec-61	MM	MD	TT	Fox
Mysterious Stranger, The	Oct-48	MM	ED	TT	Fox
Mystery in the Moonlight	May-48	TT	MD	TT	Fox
Neck and Neck	15-May-42	AFF	MD	TT	Fox
Newcomer, The	21-Oct-38	PB	MD	TT	Fox
Nice Doggy	Oct-52	TB	ED	TT	Fox
Nick's Coffee Pot	19-May-39	TT	CR	TT	Fox
Night Life in the Army	2-Oct-42	GG	MD	TT	Fox
Night Life in Tokyo	Feb-61	HM	MD	TT	Fox
Night, The	17-Apr-42	TT	/	TT	Fox
Nine of Spades, The	2-Aug-23	AFF	PT	AVB	PE
No Sleep for Percy	Mar-55	LR	CR	TT	Fox
No Space Like Home	Sep-71	AN	AB	TT	Fox
Noah Had His Troubles	17-Dec-25	AFF	PT	AVB	PE
Noah's Athletic Club	3-Dec-24	AFF	PT	AVB	PE
Noah's Outing	25-Sep-24	AFF	PT	AVB	PE
Nobody's Ghoul	24-Jan-32	FA	PT/FM	TMC	E
Nonsense Newsreel	Apr-62	DE	DT	TT	Fox
Nuts and Squirrels	Mar-54	TT	MD	TT	E
Nutty Network, The	26-Sep-25	AFF	PT	AVB	PE
Oceans of Love	24-Mar-39	TT	MD	TT	Fox
Off to China	May-36	TT	ED	TT	E
Off to the Opera	20-Mar-36	TT	PT/FM	MT	E
Office Help	May-52	HJ	CR	TT	Fox
Oh Gentle Spring	11-Jun-25	AFF	PT	AVB	PE
Oh Susanna	3-Apr-42	TT	CR	TT	Fox
Oil Can Mystery, The	2-Apr-33	TT	PT/FM	MT	E
Oil Network	9-Jul-33	FZ/OCH	PT/FM	MT	E
Oil Thru the Day	Aug-64	DU	DT	TT	Fox

Title	Release date	Series	Director	Producer	Distrib
Old Dog Tray	21-Mar-35	FA	PT/FM	MT	E
Old Fire Horse	28-Jul-39	TT	ED	TT	Fox
Old Mother Clobber	Sep-58	CC	CR	TT	Fox
Old Oaken Bucket, The	8-Aug-41	TT	CR	TT	Fox
On the Ice	3-Dec-24	AFF	PT	AVB	PE
On the Ice	8-Feb-28	AFF	PT/FM	AVB	PE
On the Links	10-Nov-28	AFF	PT	AVB	PE
One Game Pup	11-Dec-24	AFF	PT	AVB	PE
One Good Turn Deserves Another	31-May-24	AFF	PT	AVB	PE
One Gun Gary in the Nick Of Time	27-Jan-39	OGG	ED	TT	Fox
One Hard Pull	22-Mar-23	AFF	PT	AVB	PE
One Man Dog	12-May-27	AFF	PT	AVB	PE
One Man Navy, The	5-Sep-41	GG	MD	TT	Fox
One Mouse in a Million	3-Nov-39	TT	CR	TT	Fox
One Note Tony	22-Oct-47	ONT	ED	TT	Fox
Open House	Aug-53	TB	ED	TT	Fox
Opera Night	31-May-35	TT	PT/FM	MT	E
Organ Grinder, The	29-May-24	AFF	PT	AVB	PE
Orphan Duck, The	6-Oct-39	DD	CR	TT	Fox
Orphan Egg, The	Jul-53	DD	ED	TT	Fox
Oscar's Birthday Present	Jan-71	AN	DT	TT	Fox
Oscar's Moving Day	Jan-73	AN	AB	TT	Fox
Oscar's Thinking Cap	May-71	AN	AB	TT	Fox
Our Little Nell	2-Jul-28	AFF	PT/FM	AVB	PE
Out Again In Again	1-Nov-48	HJ	CR	TT	Fox
Outer Galaxy Gazette	Sep-64	AN	DT	TT	Fox
Outer Space Visitor	Nov-59	MM	DT	TT	Fox
Outnumbered	9-Jul-28	AFF	PT/HS	AVB	PE
Outpost, The	10-Jul-42	GG	MD	TT	Fox
Over the Plate	23-Jun-25	AFF	PT	AVB	PE
Owl and the Grasshopper, The	13-Nov-21	AFF	PT	AVB	PE
Owl and the Pussycat, The	13-Jan-39	TT	ED	TT	Fox
Ozzie Ostrich Comes to Town	9-Mar-34	FA	PT/FM	MT	E
Pace that Kills, The	28-May-37	KK/OO	MD/GG	TT	E
Paint Pot Symphony	7-Jun-23	AFF	PT	AVB	PE
Paper Hangers, The	Dec-49	TT	CR	TT	Fox
Pandora	1-Jun-34	TT	PT/FM	MT	E
Pandora's Box	11-Jun-43	SM/MM	CR	TT	Fox
Papa's Day of Rest	Mar-52	TB	MD	TT	Fox
Papa's Little Helpers	Jan-52	TB	MD	TT	Fox
Paper Hangers, The	30-Jul-37	TT	MD	TT	E
Paper Monster, The	Aug-73	MH	RT/RB	TT	Fox
Park Avenue Pussycat	Jan-56	TT	CR	TT	Fox

357

TERRYTOONS: The Story of Paul Terry and His Classic Cartoon Factory

Title	Release date	Series	Director	Producer	Distrib
Pastry Panic	Oct-51	LR	MD	TT	Fox
Patriotic Pooches	9-Apr-43	TT	CR	TT	Fox
Peace Pipe	Jun-73	HH	AB	TT	Fox
Peace-Time Football	19-Jul-46	GG	MD	TT	Fox
Peanut Battle	25-Apr-62	SE	CR	TT	Fox
Pearl Crazy	May-63	HM	RK	TT	Fox
Pearl Divers, The	19-Jul-23	AFF	PT	AVB	PE
Peg Leg Pete	21-Feb-32	TT	PT/FM	MT	E
Peg Leg Pete, the Pirate	19-Apr-35	TT	PT/FM	MT	E
People's Choice	Nov-75	DE	/	TT	Fox
Perils of Pearl Pureheart	Oct-49	MM	ED	TT	Fox
Permanent Waves	10-Apr-25	AFF	PT	AVB	PE
Pests	17-Sep-26	AFF	PT	AVB	PE
Pet Problems	Apr-54	TB	ED	TT	Fox
Phantom Skyscraper, The	Dec-66	JH	AB/DT	TT	Fox
Pharaoh's Tomb	27-Apr-23	AFF	PT	AVB	PE
Phoney Express, The	22-Oct-26	AFF	PT	AVB	PE
Phony News Flashes	May-55	TT	CR	TT	Fox
Pick-Necking	8-Sep-33	FA	PT/FM	MT	E
Picnic With Papa	Dec-52	TB	MD	TT	Fox
Pie Man, The	21-Mar-25	AFF	PT	AVB	PE
Pie-Eyed Piper, The	6-May-27	AFF	PT	AVB	PE
Pigskin Capers	28-Dec-30	TT	PT/FM	AC	E
Pill Peddlers	Apr-53	TT	CR	TT	Fox
Pink Elephants	9-Jul-37	FA	DG	TT	E
Pirate Plunder Blunder	Jul-73	PO	/	TT	Fox
Pirate Ship	30-Apr-33	TT	PT/FM	MT	E
Pirate's Gold	Jan-57	HJ	ED	TT	Fox
Pirates Bold	22-Jul-26	AFF	PT	AVB	PE
Plane Goofy	29-Nov-40	TT	ED	TT	Fox
Plastic Blaster, The	Jan-75	MH	RB	TT	Fox
Play Ball	6-Mar-32	TT	PT/FM	MT	E
Play Ball	11-Jan-37	TT	MD	TT	E
Playful Puss	May-53	KK	MD	TT	Fox
Plow Boy's Revenge, The	13-Jan-27	LR	PT	TT	PE
Plumber's Helpers	May-53	TB	CR	AVB	PE
Plumber's Life, A	6-Jul-26	AFF	PT	AVB	PE
Polar Flight, A	8-Nov-28	AFF	PT	AVB	PE
Police Dogged	Jul-56	CB	CR	TT	Fox
Polo Match, The	2-Jun-29	AFF	PT	AVB	PE
Popcorn	11-Jan-31	TT	PT/FM	AC	E
Port of Missing Mice	2-Feb-45	MM	ED	TT	Fox
Post War Inventions	23-Mar-45	GG	CR	TT	Fox

Title	Release date	Series	Director	Producer	Distrib
Power of Thought	Jan-49	HJ	ED	TT	Fox
Power of Thought, The	Jun-74	HJ	ED	TT	Fox
Prehistoric Perils	Mar-52	MM	CR	TT	Fox
Prescription for Percy	Apr-54	LR	MD	TT	Fox
Presto-Chango	20-May-29	AFF	PT	AVB	PE
Pretzels	9-Mar-30	TT	PT/FM	AC	E
Pride of the Yard	Aug-54	PS	ED	TT	Fox
Prize Guest, The	2-Jun-39	TT	MD	TT	E
Prodigal Pup, The	2-Aug-24	AFF	PT	AVB	PE
Professor Offkeyski	14-Jun-40	TT	CR	TT	Fox
Proton Pulsator, The	Sep-70	AN	/	AVB	PE
Puddy the Pup and the Gypsies	24-Jul-36	FA/PP	MD/GG	TMC	E
Puddy's Coronation	14-May-37	PP	MD/GG	TT	E
Puppy Love	10-May-28	AFF	PT/MD	AVB	PE
Quack Quack	8-Mar-31	TT	PT/FM	TT	E
Queen Bee, The	30-Jan-29	AFF	PT/HS	AVB	PE
Racket Buster	Feb-49	MM	MD	TT	Fox
Radio Controlled	26-Oct-26	AFF	PT	AVB	PE
Radio Girl	17-Apr-32	TT	PT/FM	MT	E
Raiding the Raiders	9-Mar-45	MM	CR	TT	Fox
Railroaded to Fame	May-61	HH	DT	TT	Fox
Rain Drain	Sep-66	JH	AB/DT	TT	Fox
Rain Makers, The	Jun-51	HJ	CR	TT	Fox
Raisin and a Cake of Yeast, A	3-Feb-23	AFF	PT	AVB	PE
Rat's Revenge, The	26-Jan-24	AFF	PT	AVB	PE
Rats in His Garret	19-Nov-27	AFF	PT/HS	AVB	PE
Raven, The	Mar-74	MH	RT	TT	Fox
Razzberries	8-Feb-31	FA	PT/FM	AC	E
Rebel Trouble	Jun-62	DE	DT	TT	Fox
Red Headed Monkey, The	Sep-66	MH	RT/RB	TT	Fox
Red Hot Sands	7-Jul-50	AFF	PT	AVB	PE
Red Swamp Pox, The	8-Jul-27	AFF	PT	AVB	PE
Red Tractor, The	May-69	PO	/	TT	Fox
Reformed Wolf	Feb-64	DU	DT	TT	Fox
Reluctant Pup, The	Oct-54	MM	CR	TT	Fox
Return of the Monsterizer, The	Oct-53	TB	MD	TT	Fox
Rich Cat and the Poor Cat, The	Apr-73	MH	RT/RB	TT	Fox
Ride 'Em Cowboy	21-Feb-22	AFF	PT	AVB	PE
Riding High	26-Jun-28	AFF	PT/FM	AVB	PE
Rip Van Winkle	16-May-27	AFF	PT	AVB	PE
Rival Romeos	9-Feb-34	AFF	PT/FM	MT	E
River of Doubt, The	Jan-51	HJ	ED	TT	Fox
Riverboat Mission	16-Aug-27	AFF	PT	AVB	PE
	May-62	HH	DT	TT	Fox

358

Appendix 2 • Paul Terry/Terrytoons Theatrical Shorts Filmography

Title	Release date	Series	Director	Producer	Distrib
Road House, The	29-Sep-26	AFF	PT	AVB	PE
Robin Hood	22-Jan-33	TT	PT/FM	MT	E
Robin Hood in an Arrow Escape	13-Nov-36	TT	MD/GG	TT	E
Robinson Crusoe (copyrighted as Shipwrecked Brothers)	17-Nov-33	FA	PT/FM	MT	E
Robinson Crusoe's Broadcast	15-Apr-38	TT	JF	TT	E
Robots in Toyland	Aug-65	AN	CR	TT	Fox
Rac-A-Bye Sinbad	Jan-64	LU	CR	TT	Fox
Rock Hound, The	Oct-68	PO	CA/AB/CR/DT	TT	Fox
Rolling Stone, The	9-Oct-22	AFF	PT	AVB	PE
Rolling Stones	1-May-36	FA	MD/GG	TT	E
Roman Punch	20-Apr-30	TT	PT/FM	AC	E
Romance	15-May-32	TT	PT/FM	MT	E
Romantic Mouse, The	27-Sep-22	AFF	PT	AVB	PE
Romeo and Juliet	16-Apr-33	TT	PT/FM	MT	E
Rooster and the Eagle, The	3-Jun-21	AFF	PT	AVB	PE
Rough and Ready Romeo	20-Apr-26	AFF	PT	AVB	PE
Rover's Rescue	28-Jun-40	TT	VW	TT	Fox
Ruby Eye of the Monkey God, The	Jan-69		FC	TT	Fox
Runaway Balloon, The	8-May-25	AFF	PT	AVB	PE
Runaway Mouse	Jan-54	LR	MD	TT	E
Runnin' Wild	20-Mar-24	AFF	PT	AVB	PE
Runt, The	6-Jun-25	AFF	PT	AVB	PE
Runt, The	15-May-36	FA	PT	TT	E
Rupert the Runt	12-Jul-40	TT	MD	TT	Fox
Rural Romance, A	26-Jan-24	AFF	PT	AVB	PE
S.O.S.	26-Mar-25	AFF	PT	AVB	PE
Sailor's Home, The	12-Jun-36	TT	PT/FM	TT	E
Sally Sargent	1968	TT	FC	TT	Fox
Salt Water Taffy	30-Nov-30	TT	PT/FM	AC	E
Salty McGuire	8-Jan-37	TT	MD/GG	TT	E
Sappy New Year	10-Nov-61	HJ	DT	TT	Fox
Satisfied Customers	May-54	HJ	CR	TT	Fox
Saved by a Keyhole	13-Oct-27	AFF	PT	AVB	PE
Saw Mill Mystery, The	29-Oct-37	TT	CR	TT	E
Scaling the Alps	21-Mar-28	AFF	PT/MD	AVB	PE
Scarecrow, The	Aug-72	MH	RB	TT	Fox
School Birds	30-Apr-37	TT	MD/GG	TT	E
School Days	31-Dec-26	AFF	PT	AVB	PE
School Daze	18-Sep-42	N	ED	TT	Fox
Scientific Sideshow	Jun-69	AN	/	AC	E
Scotch Highball	16-Nov-30	TT	PT/FM	AC	E
Scouts to the Rescue	Apr-56	GDD	CR	TT	Fox
Scrambled Eggs	22-Aug-26	AFF	PT	AVB	PE

Title	Release date	Series	Director	Producer	Distrib
Scrap For Victory	22-Jan-43	GG	CR	TT	Fox
Scuba Duba Do	Jun-66	SC	RB	TT	Fox
See Shower, The	Feb-28	AFF	PT	AVB	PE
Search for Misery	Nov-64	PI	RK	TT	Fox
Seasick Sailors	Jul-51	LR	MD	TT	Fox
Seaside Adventure	Feb-52	TT	MD	TT	Fox
See the World	29-Jun-34	LU	PT/FM	MT	E
Seeing Ghosts	Jun-48	TT	MD	TT	Fox
Send Your Elephant to Camp	4-Jul-62	SE	AB	TT	Fox
Sham Battle Shenanigans	20-Mar-42	GG	CR	TT	Fox
Sharp Shooters	3-Dec-24	AFF	PT	AVB	PE
She Knew Her Man	29-Oct-24	AFF	PT	AVB	PE
She's In Again	3-Dec-24	AFF	PT	AVB	PE
Sheep in the Meadow	22-Sep-39	TT	MD	TT	PE
Sheik, The	17-Feb-23	AFF	PT	AVB	PE
Sherman Was Right	21-Aug-32	TT	PT	MT	E
Shipyard Symphony	19-Mar-43	TT	PT/FM	TT	Fox
Shocker, The	Dec-70	MH	ED	TT	Fox
Shootin' Fool, The	20-Apr-26	AFF	PT	AVB	PE
Short Circuit, A	17-Dec-27	AFF	PT/JF	AVB	PE
Short-Term Sheriff	May-64	DU	DT	TT	Fox
Shove Thy Neighbor	Jun-57	JD	CR	TT	Fox
Shrinker, The	Jul-69	MH	RT	TT	Fox
Sick, Sick Sidney	Aug-58	SE	AB	TT	Fox
Sidney's Family Tree	Dec-58	SE	AB	TT	Fox
Sidney's White Elephant	May-63	SE	AB	TT	Fox
Signed, Sealed and Clobbered	Nov-58	CC	CR	TT	Fox
Signs of Spring	29-Sep-27	AFF	PT	AVB	PE
Silver Streak, The	8-Jun-45	MM	ED	TT	Fox
Sing Sing Song	19-Apr-31	TT	PT/FM	TMC	E
Sink or Swim	6-Dec-26	AFF	PT	AVB	PE
Sink or Swim	Nov-52	DD	CR	TT	Fox
Skating Hounds	27-May-29	AFF	PT/MD	AVB	PE
Skunked Again	25-Dec-36	KK	MD/GG	TT	E
Sky is Falling, The	25-Apr-47	MM	MD	TT	Fox
Sky's the Limit, The	Feb-65	AN	DT	TT	Fox
Slap Happy Hunters	31-Oct-41	GG	ED	TT	Fox
Sleepless Night, A	Jun-48	HJ	CR	TT	Fox
Sleepless Night, A	Mar-75	HJ	/	MT	E
Slinky Mink	Nov-70	PO	PT/FM	TT	Fox
Slow But Sure	15-Jun-34	TT	PT	AVB	PE
Small Town Sheriff	22-Jul-27	AFF	PT	TT	Fox
Smoky Joe	25-May-45	TT	CR	TT	Fox

359

TERRYTOONS: The Story of Paul Terry and His Classic Cartoon Factory

Title	Release date	Series	Director	Producer	Distrib
Snapping the Whip	6-Jan-29	AFF	PT/HB	AVB	PE
Snappy Snapshots	Mar-53	TB	ED	TT	Fox
Snow Birds	3-Jun-29	AFF	PT	AVB	PE
Snow Man, The	11-Oct-46	TT	CR	TT	Fox
Snowman	13-Dec-40	TT	MD	TT	Fox
So Sorry, Pussycat	Mar-61	HM	AB	TT	Fox
Soap	6-Jul-25	AFF	PT	AVB	PE
Soapy Opera	Jan-53	MM	CR	TT	Fox
Some Barrier	Jul-17	PTFB	PT	PT	AK
Somewhere in Egypt	17-Sep-43	GG	MD	TT	Fox
Somewhere in the Pacific	25-Dec-42	GG	MD	TT	Fox
Son of Hashimoto	12-Apr-61	HM	CR	TT	Fox
Son Shower, The	12-Feb-28	AFF	PT/HS	AVB	PE
Songs of Erin	Mar-51	GG	CR	TT	Fox
Sour Grapes	Dec-50	DB	MD	TT	Fox
South Pole or Bust	14-Dec-34	TT	PT/FM	MT	E
Southern Horse-pitality	29-Nov-35	TT	PT/FM	AC	E
Southern Rhythm	18-Sep-32	TT	PT/FM	MT	E
Space Cowboy	May-73	AN	AB/CR/RK/DT	TT	Fox
Space Pet	Mar-69	AN	CA	TT	Fox
Spanish Love	6-Feb-26	AFF	PT	AVB	PE
Spanish Onions	23-Mar-30	TT	PT/FM	AC	E
Spare the Rod	Jan-54	MM	CR	TT	Fox
Spendthrift, The	26-Jan-22	AFF	PT	AVB	PE
Spider and the Fly, The	17-Feb-23	AFF	PT	AVB	PE
Spider's Lair, The	7-Feb-23	TT	PT/FM	TMC	PE
Spider Talks, The	24-Jan-28	AFF	PT/MD	AVB	PE
Split Level Tree House	Nov-63	SE	AB	TT	Fox
Spooks	27-Apr-23	AFF	PT	AVB	PE
Spooky-Yaki	13-Nov-63	HM	RK	TT	Fox
Sport of Kings, The	26-Jul-24	AFF	PT	AVB	PE
Spring Fever	18-Mar-51	GG	MD	TT	Fox
Spring is Here	24-Jul-32	FA	PT/FM	MT	E
Springtime	12-May-23	AFF	PT	AVB	PE
Springtime for Clobber	Jan-58	CC	CR	TT	Fox
Square Planet, The	Dec-73	LU	AB/CR/RK/DT	TT	Fox
Squirrel Crazy	Jan-51	NU	MD	TT	Fox
Stage Struck	23-Jul-29	AFF	PT	AVB	PE
Stage Struck	Feb-51	HP	MD	TT	Fox
Static	4-Aug-28	AFF	PT	AVB	PE
Steeple Jacks	Sep-51	HJ	CR	TT	Fox
Stone Age Romance, A	4-Aug-29	AFF	PT	AVB	PE
Stone Age Romeo, A	14-Dec-22	AFF	PT	AVB	PE

Title	Release date	Series	Director	Producer	Distrib
Stop, Look and Listen	Dec-49	MM	ED	TT	Fox
Stork's Mistake, The	12-May-23	AFF	PT	AVB	PE
Stork's Mistake, The	29-May-42	TT	ED	TT	Fox
Stowaways	Apr-49	HJ	CR	TT	Fox
Strange Companion	12-May-61	HM	MD	TT	Fox
Stranger Rides Again, The	4-Nov-38	TT	MD	TT	Fox
Stretcher, The	Apr-69	MH	RB	TT	Fox
String Bean Jack	26-Aug-38	TT	JF	TT	Fox
Stunt Men	23-Nov-60	HJ	MB	TT	Fox
Subway Sally	20-Jun-27	AFF	PT	AVB	PE
Sultan's Birthday	13-Oct-44	MM	BT	TT	Fox
Sultan's Cat, The	17-May-31	FA	PT/FM	TMC	E
Summertime (Summer Time)	13-Dec-31	TT	PT/FM	TMC	E
Sunday on the Farm	16-Aug-28	AFF	PT/JF	AVB	PE
Sunken Treasure	16-Oct-36	KK/PP	MD/GG	TT	E
Sunny Italy	26-Jul-28	AFF	PT/MD	AVB	PE
Sunny Italy	Mar-51	MM	CR	TT	Fox
Sunny South, The	29-Dec-33	TT	PT/FM	MT	E
Super Mouse Rides Again (Mighty Mouse Rides Again)	6-Aug-43	SM/MM	MD	TT	Fox
Super Salesman	24-Oct-47	HJ	ED	TT	Fox
Surface Surf Aces	Mar-70	PO	CA	TT	Fox
Surprisin' Exercisin'	Jul-68	PO	CA	TT	Fox
Svengali's Cat	18-Jan-46	MM	ED	TT	Fox
Swamp Snapper, The	Nov-69	PO	/	TT	Fox
Swamp Water Taffy	Jul-70	PO	/	TT	Fox
Sweet Adeline	8-Jan-29	AFF	PT/FM	AVB	PE
Swiss Cheese	18-May-30	TT	PT/FM	AC	E
Swiss Cheese Family Robinson	19-Dec-47	MM	MD	TT	Fox
Swiss Miss, A	Aug-51	MM	MD	TT	Fox
Swiss Ski Yodelers	17-May-40	TT	ED	TT	Fox
Swooning the Swooners	14-Sep-45	TT	CR	AVB	PE
Taking the Air	4-Mar-27	AFF	PT	AVB	PE
Tale of a Dog, The	Feb-59	TT	DT	TT	Fox
Tale of a Shirt	19-Feb-33	TT	PT/FM	MT	E
Talking Magpies, The	4-Jan-46	HJ	MD	TT	Fox
Tall Tale Teller	May-54	PH	CR	TT	Fox
Tall Timber Tale	Jul-51	TB	CR	TT	Fox
Taming the Cat	Jan-48	HJ	PT	AVB	PE
Taming the Cat	Jul-75	HJ	DT	TT	Fox
Tea House Mouse	Jan-63	HM	RK	TT	Fox
Tea Party	Apr-63	HH	DT	TT	Fox
Temperamental Lion	27-Dec-40	TT	CR	TT	Fox
Ten Pin Terrors	Jun-53	HJ	CR	TT	Fox

Appendix 2 • Paul Terry/Terrytoons Theatrical Shorts Filmography

Title	Release date	Series	Director	Producer	Distrib
That Old Can of Mine	14-Jun-24	AFF	PT	AVB	PE
Their Last Bean	21-Apr-39	TT	ED	TT	Fox
Third Musketeer, The	Oct-65	SC	RB	TT	Fox
Thoroughbred	29-Sep-23	AFF	PT	AVB	PE
Thousand Smile Check Up	Jan-60	HJ	MT	TT	Fox
Three Bears, The	26-Jan-34	TT	PT/FM	MT	E
Three Bears, The	10-Feb-39	TT	MD	TT	Fox
Three Blind Mice	9-Jan-26	AFF	PT	AVB	PE
Three is a Crowd	Feb-51	LR	CR	TT	Fox
Thrifty Cubs	Jan-53	TB	MD	TT	Fox
Throwing the Bull	3-May-46	MM	CR	TT	Fox
Thru Thick and Thin	26-Oct-26	AFF	PT	AVB	PE
Tiger and the Donkey, The	22-Jan-22	AFF	PT	AVB	PE
Time Eraser, The	Dec-72	MH	RT/RB	TT	Fox
Time Gallops On	Apr-52	TT	MD	TT	Fox
Timekeeper, The	Apr-72	MH	RT/RB	TT	Fox
Timid Rabbit, The	26-Nov-37	TT	MD	TT	Fox
Timid Scarecrow, The	Nov-53	DD	ED	TT	Fox
Tin Can Tourist, The	22-Jan-37	FA	MD/GG	TT	E
Tin Pan Alley Cat	Oct-60	TT	DT	TT	Fox
Tire Trouble	24-Jul-42	GG	ED	TT	Fox
Tit for Tat	22-Jan-27	AFF	PT	AVB	PE
To Be or Not To Be	Feb-63	SE	CR	TT	Fox
Tom, Tom the Piper's Son	16-Nov-34	TT	PT/FM	MT	E
Toothless Beaver, The	Dec-65	PO	CR	TT	Fox
Topsy TV	Jan-57	JD	CR	TT	Fox
Torrid Toreador, The	9-Jan-42	TT	ED	TT	Fox
Tortoise Wins Again, The	9-Aug-46	TT	CR	TT	Fox
Touchdown Demons	20-Sep-40	TT	VW	TT	Fox
Tough Egg, A	26-Jun-36	TT	MD/GG	AVB	E
Toy Man, The	Dec-69	MH	RB	TT	Fox
Toyland	27-Nov-32	TT	PT/FM	MT	E
Traffic Trouble	May-67	JH	CA/AB	TT	Fox
Trailer Life	20-Aug-37	FA	MD	TT	E
Train Terrain	Feb-71	HH	AB	TT	Fox
Transatlantic Flight, A	19-Jan-25	AFF	PT	AVB	PE
Trapeze Please	12-Jun-60	HJ	CR	TT	Fox
Traveling Salesman, The	17-Feb-23	AFF	PT	AVB	PE
Trestle Hassle	Nov-72	PO		TT	Fox
Tricky Business	1-May-42	GG	ED	TT	Fox
Trip to the Pole, A	22-Apr-24	AFF	PT	AVB	PE
Triple Trouble	Nov-48	MM	ED	TT	Fox
Trojan Horse, The	26-Jul-46	MM	MD	TT	Fox

Title	Release date	Series	Director	Producer	Distrib
Tropical Fish	14-May-33	FA	PT/FM	MT	E
Trouble in Baghdad	13-Sep-63	LU	CR	TT	Fox
Troubles on the Ark	17-Feb-23	AFF	PT	AVB	PE
Truckload of Trouble, A	25-Oct-49	TT	CR	TT	Fox
Tusk, Tusk	3-Apr-60	SE	MT	TT	Fox
Twelve O'Clock and All Ain't Well	25-Jul-41	TT	ED	TT	Fox
Twinkle, Twinkle Little Telstar	Nov-65	AN	AB	TT	Fox
Two Barbers, The	1-Sep-44	MM	ED	TT	Fox
Two Explorers, The	12-Aug-22	AFF	PT	AVB	PE
Two Headed Giant, The	11-Aug-39	TT	CR	TT	Fox
Two of a Trade	27-Sep-22	AFF	PT	AVB	PE
Two Slick Traders, The	12-Aug-22	AFF	PT	AVB	PE
Two Ton Baby Sitter	4-Sep-60	SE	DT	TT	Fox
Two Trappers, The	1-Dec-22	AFF	PT	AVB	PE
Ugly Duckling, The	19-Sep-25	AFF	PT	AVB	PE
Uncle Joey	18-Apr-41	TT	MD	TT	Fox
Uncle Joey Comes to Town	19-Sep-41	TT	MD	TT	Fox
Underdog	13-Mar-29	AFF	PT	AVB	PE
Uninvited Pests, The	29-Nov-46	HJ	CR	TT	Fox
Unsung Hero	Jul-61	HH	AB	TT	Fox
Up in the Air	6-Mar-26	AFF	PT	AVB	PE
Uranium Blues	Mar-56	TT	CR	TT	Fox
Valley Forge Hero	Jul-74	HH	DT	AVB	PE
Venus and the Cat	9-Oct-21	AFF	PT	AVB	PE
Venus of Venice	22-Jul-26	AFF	PT	AVB	PE
Village Blacksmith	2-Dec-38	TT	MD	TT	Fox
Village Blacksmith, The	3-Nov-33	FA	PT/FM	MT	E
Villain in Disguise, The	2-Jan-22	AFF	PT	AVB	PE
Villain Still Pursued Her, The	3-Sep-37	FZ/OCH	PT	TT	E
Villain's Curse, The	10-Jan-32	TT	CR	TMC	E
Voodoo Spell, A	Jan-67	JH	CA/AB	TT	Fox
Walrus Hunters, The	11-Aug-23	AFF	PT	AVB	PE
Wandering Minstrel, The	4-Jan-28	TT	PT/HB	AVB	PE
War Bride, The	20-Apr-28	AFF	PT/HB	AVB	PE
Wash Day	29-Jul-29	AFF	PT/MD	AVB	PE
Watch the Butterfly	Oct-66	PO	DT	TT	Fox
Watchdog, The	20-Oct-39	TT	ED	TT	Fox
Water Cure, The	16-Apr-29	AFF	PT	AVB	PE
Watered Stock	17-Sep-26	AFF	PT	AVB	PE
Wayward Dog, The	25-Dec-21	AFF	PT	AVB	PE
Wayward Hat, The	Jul-60	FO	DT	TT	Fox
Weather Magic	May-65	AN	CA	TT	Fox
Welcome Little Stranger	3-Oct-41	DD	CR	TT	Fox

361

TERRYTOONS: The Story of Paul Terry and His Classic Cartoon Factory

Title	Release date	Series	Director	Producer	Distrib
Western Trail, The	3-Apr-36	FA	MD/GG	TT	E
What a Little Sneeze Will Do	10-Jan-41	TT	ED	TT	Fox
What a Night	25-Jan-35	FA	PT/FM	MT	E
What Happens at Night	30-May-41	TT	CR	TT	Fox
When Knights Were Bold	21-Mar-41	TT	VW	TT	Fox
When Men Were Men	18-Jul-25	AFF	PT	AVB	PE
When Mousehood Was in Flower	Jul-53	MM	CR	TT	Fox
When Snow Flies	6-May-27	AFF	PT	AVB	PE
When Winter Comes	22-Apr-24	AFF	PT	AVB	PE
Where Friendship Ceases	31-Dec-26	AFF	PT	AVB	PE
Where There's Smoke	Feb-62	DE	RK	TT	Fox
Which is Witch	Sep-67	JH	RB	TT	Fox
White Elephant, A	27-Dec-28	AFF	PT/HS	AVB	PE
Who Killed Cock Robin?	19-Mar-33	TT	PT/FM	MT	E
Who's Dragon	Sep-73	LU	AB	TT	Fox
Who's Who in the Jungle	19-Oct-45	GG	ED	TT	Fox
Why Argue	17-Sep-26	AFF	PT	AVB	PE
Why Mice Leave Home	20-Feb-24	AFF	PT	AVB	PE
Why Mules Leave Home	7-Sep-34	FA	PT/FM	MT	E
Wicked Cat, The	4-Mar-22	AFF	PT	AVB	PE
Wicked City, The	23-Jan-26	AFF	PT	AVB	PE
Wicked Wolf, The	8-Mar-46	MM	MD	TT	Fox
Wicky Wacky Romance, A	17-Nov-39	TT	ED	TT	Fox
Wide Open Spaces	Nov-50	GG	ED	TT	Fox
Wild Cats of Paris	31-Oct-25	AFF	PT	AVB	PE
Wild Life	Sep-59	HJ	MT	TT	Fox
Wilful Willie	26-Jun-42	TT	CR	TT	Fox
Wind Bag	Jun-71	HH	AB	TT	Fox
Wind Jammers, The	23-Jan-26	AFF	PT	AVB	PE

Title	Release date	Series	Director	Producer	Distrib
Window Washers, The	20-Jul-25	AFF	PT	AVB	PE
Wine, Women and Song	4-Jul-25	AFF	PT	AVB	PE
Winning the West	16-Aug-46	MM	ED	TT	Fox
Wise Quacks	Feb-53	DD	MD	TT	Fox
Witch's Cat, The	Jul-48	MM	MD	TT	Fox
Wolf and the Crane, The	2-Oct-21	AFF	PT	AVB	PE
Wolf and the Kid, The	6-Dec-21	AFF	PT	AVB	PE
Wolf in Cheap Clothing, A	17-Apr-36	TT	MD/GG	TT	E
Wolf in Sheep's Clothing, The	4-Mar-22	AFF	PT	AVB	PE
Wolf! Wolf!	22-Jun-44	MM	MD	TT	Fox
Wolf's Pardon, The	5-Dec-47	AFF	ED	TT	Fox
Wolf's Side of the Story	23-Sep-38	TT	CR	TT	Fox
Wolf's Tale, A	27-Oct-44	TT	CR	TT	Fox
Woman and the Hen, The	20-Nov-21	AFF	PT	AVB	PE
Woman's Honor, A	19-Jul-24	AFF	PT	AVB	PE
Wood Choppers, The	9-May-29	AFF	PT	AVB	PE
Wooden Indian, The	Jan-49	TT	CR	TT	Fox
Wooden Money	6-Jan-29	AFF	PT/JF	AVB	PE
Woodland	1-May-32	FA	PT/FM	MT	E
Woodman Spare That Tree	Feb-51	TT	ED	TT	Fox
Worm That Turned, The	22-Jun-22	AFF	PT	AVB	PE
Wot's All Th' Shootin' Fer	3-May-40	TT	VW	TT	Fox
Wreck of the Hesperus	11-Feb-44	MM	MD	TT	Fox
Yarn About a Yarn, A	1-Aug-25	AFF	PT	AVB	PE
Yarn About Yarn, A	12-Dec-41	TT	CR	TT	Fox
Ye Olde Songs	20-Mar-32	FA	PT/FM	MT	E
Ye Olde Toy Shop	13-Dec-35	TT	PT/FM	MT	E
Yokel Duck Makes Good	26-Nov-43	TT	ED	TT	Fox
Yokohama Yankee, A	Jan-55	TT	CR	TT	Fox

Series: {AFF – Aesop's Film Fables | AN – Astronut | BE – Beefy | CB – Clancy the Bull | CC – Clint Clobber | DB – Dingbat | DD – Dinky Duck | DE – Deputy Dawg | DU – Duckwood | DW – Dimwit | F – Flebus | FA – Farmer Al Falfa | FO – Foofle | FTF – Felix the Fox | FZ – Fanny Zilch | GC – Gaston Le Crayon | GDD – Good Deed Daly | GG – Gandy Goose | HH – Hector Heathcote | HJ – Heckle and Jeckle | HM – Hashimoto Mouse | HP – Half Pint | JD – John Doormat | JH – James Hound | KK – Kiko the Kangaroo | LR – Little Roquefort | LU – Luno | MA – Martian Moochers | MH – Mighty Heroes | MM – Mighty Mouse | N – Nancy | NU – Nutsy | OCH – Oil Can Harry | OGG – One Gun Gary | ONT – One Note Tony | OO – Ozzie Ostrich | PB – Panda Bear | PBC – Paramount-Bray Cartoons | PH – Phony Baloney | PI – Pitiful Penelope | PM – Paramount Magazine | PO – Possible Possum | PP – Puddy the Pup | PS – Percival Sleuthhound | PTC – Paul Terry Cartoons | PTFB – Paul Terry Feature Burlesques | SC – Sad Cat | SE – Sidney the Elephant | SF – Sparky the Firefly | SH – Stronghearf | SM – Super Mouse | SN – Sniffer | SP – Spoofy | TB – Terry Bears | THIR – Terry Human Interest Reels | TT – Terrytoons | VV – Victor the Volunteer | WW – Willie Walrus}

Director: {AB – Arthur Bartsch | AC – Al Chianto | AK – Al Kouzel | BT – Bill Tytla | CA – Cosmo Anziotti | CR – Connie Rasinski | DT – Dave Tendlar | ED – Eddie Donnelly | EP – Ernest Pintoff | FC – Fred Calvert | FM – Frank Moser | GB – George Bakes | GG – George Gordon | HB – Harry Bailey | HS – Hugh Shields | JF – John Foster | JZ – Jack Zander | MD – Mannie Davis | MT – Marty B. Taras | PT – Paul Terry | RB – Ralph Bakshi | RK – Robert Kuwahara | RT – Robert Taylor | VW – Volney White | WH – Win Hoskins}

Producer: {AC – Audio-Cinema | AVB – Amedee J. Van Beuren | JB – John R. Bray | MT – Moser & Terry | Par – Paramount | PT – Paul Terry | TEI – Thomas Edison Inc. | TT – Terrytoons (Terry-Toon) | TMC – Terry, Moser & Coffman}

Distributor: {AK – A. Kay Company | E – Educational Pictures | Fox – 20th Century-Fox Film Corporation | Par – Paramount | PE – Pathé Exchange | TE – Thomas A. Edison, Inc. | TFC – Thanhouser Film Corp.

(Note: By 1933, Educational Pictures began working with Fox Film Exchanges to distribute the animated cartoons. By the spring of 1935, Fox Film Corporation had merged with 20th Century Pictures to form 20th Century-Fox Film Corporation which continued to work with Educational Pictures to distribute the films until 1936 when 20th Century-Fox became sole distributor.)

Appendix 3

Paul Terry/Terrytoons: Television Cartoon Series

THE ADVENTURES OF LARIAT SAM

Lariat Sam was a friendly, naive and honest cowboy who rode a poetry-reading derby-hatted horse named Tippytoes (also known as "Wonder Horse"). The stories were set in the Old West and usually centered on Lariat Sam's constant battles with arch-rival and nemesis, Badlands Meeney. The cartoon series was created by Robert Keeshan's company, Robert Keeshan and Associates, and written for *The Captain Kangaroo Show*. In respect to the concerns of Robert Keeshan that the cartoons avoid excessive violence, the creators of the program decided that the hero's weapon of choice should be his lariat rather than a six-shooter. The cartoons were presented in three parts during the program. Later, the cartoons were packaged for syndication.

CBS Television Productions. Black-and-White. Color.
Five minute episodes. Thirty minute program.
Premiered on CBS September 10, 1962 and ran until August 27, 1965.
Produced by Bill Weiss. Directed by Arthur Bartsch, Robert Kuwahara, Connie Rasinski and Dave Tendlar.
[All televised shorts. Shorts not released theatrically]

Voices: Lariat Sam: Dayton Allen; **Tippytoes**, his horse: Dayton Allen

Episodes:

Horse Opera Hoax
Rock-A-Bye Badlands
Great Race for Office Space
Arts and Craftiness
Ding-A-Ling Circus Saga

Weatherman Mish Mosh
Cowhide 'N Seek
Bushwack in Toyland
People Catcher
Mark of Zero

Below the Water Lion
Badlands Cannonball
Water Color Witchcraft

THE ASTRONUT SHOW

Astronut was a small friendly alien who was the loyal companion of Oscar Mild, a mild mannered bachelor who was constantly being harangued by his boss, Mr. Bellow. Astronut first appeared in the Terrytoons short *Astronut* (Rasinski, 1963), a Deputy Dawg cartoon, and later in several theatrical cartoons from 1964 to 1965. With the success of the theatrical run of cartoons, in August 1965, Astronut was featured in his own half-hour series for syndication and several Astronut cartoons were produced for the television program.

In the late 1960s, Terrytoons stars Hashimoto Mouse, Sidney the Elephant, and Luno the Flying Horse, each stars of their own theatrical film series, were made a part of the show. In the early 1970s, Viacom, the program's distributor, reprogrammed the series with supporting episodes from other Terrytoons favorites Possible Possum, Sad Cat, and James Hound.

A Terrytoons Production. Color. A 26-week 30-minute schedule.
Premiered: August 23, 1965. Syndicated.
Produced by Bill Weiss. Directed by Connie Rasinski, Dave Tendlar, Arthur Bartsch, Robert Kuwahara and Cosmo Anzilotti.

ASTRONUT (One per show)

Voices: Astronut: Dayton Allen, Lionel Wilson, Bob McFadden; **Oscar Mild**, his friend: Bob McFadden; (Other voice artists: John Myhers)
[*released theatrically]

Episodes:

Brother from Outer Space*
The Sky's the Limit*
Scientific Sideshow*
Oscar's Moving Day*
Gems from Gemini*
No Space Like Home*
The Kisser Plant*
Robots in Toyland*
Haunted Housecleaning*

Oscar's Birthday Present*
Martian Moochers*
Movie Magic*
Outer Galaxy Gazette*
Oscar's Thinking Cap*
Balloon Snatcher*
Molecular Mixup*
Going Ape*
Space Cowboy*

Hokey Home Movies*
The Invisibeam*
Martian Recipe
Twinkle, Twinkle, Little Telstar*
Proton Pulsator*
Jolly Jupiter
Weather Magic*
Space Pet*

HASHIMOTO (One per show)

Voices: Hashimoto: John Myhers, **Hanako**, his wife: John Myhers, **Yuriko**, his daughter: John Myhers, **Saburo**, his son: John Myhers
[*released theatrically]

Episodes:

Hashimoto-San*
Strange Companion*
Tea House Mouse*
House of Hashimoto*
Honorable House Cat*
Cherry Blossom Festival*

So Sorry, Pussycat*
Honorable Family Problem*
Spooky-Yaki*
Night Life in Tokyo*
Loyal Royalty*
The Potter's Wheel Heel

Honorable Cat Story*
Honorable Paint In Neck*
Doll Festival
Son of Hashimoto*
Pearl Crazy*

SIDNEY (One per show)

Voices: Sidney the Elephant: Dayton Allen, Lionel Wilson, **Stanley the Lion**: Dayton Allen, **Cleo the Giraffe**: Dayton Allen
[*released theatrically]

Episodes:

Sick, Sick Sidney*
Home Life*
Banana Binge
Sidney's Family Tree*
Sidney's White Elephant*
Clown Jewels
Hide and Go Sidney*

Driven to Extraction*
Tree Spree
Tusk, Tusk*
Send Your Elephant to Camp*
Really Big Act
The Littlest Bully*
Peanut Battle*

Meat, Drink, and Be Merry
Two-Ton Baby Sitter*
Fleet's Out*
Split-Level Tree House*
To Be or Not To Be*

LUNO (One per show)

Voices: Luno, the white stallion: Bob McFadden; **Tim**, his child companion: Bob McFadden
[*released theatrically]

Episodes:

The Missing Genie*
Melvin the Magnificent*
The Gold Dust Bandit*
The Poor Pirate
Trouble in Baghdad*
Adventure by the Sea*

Island of the Giants
The Flying Chariot
Roc-A-Bye Sinbad*
Mixed Up Matador*
King Neptune's Castle
King Rounder*

The Square Planet*
The Prehystoric Inventor
Who's Dragon*
Jungle Jack*
1772

Appendix 3 • Paul Terry/Terrytoons: Television Cartoon Series

SAD CAT (One per show)
Voices: Sad Cat: Bob McFadden, **Gadmouse**: Bob McFadden, **Impresario**: Bob McFadden, **Latimore**: Bob McFadden, **Fenimore**: Bob McFadden
[All shorts released theatrically]

Episodes:

The Apprentice Good Fairy
Dribble Drabble
Commander Great Guy
Don't Spill the Beans
Judo Kudos

The Abominable Mountaineers
The Third Musketeer
Grand Prix Winner
Loops and Swoops
Dress Reversal

All Teed Off
Scuba Duba Do
Big Game Fishing

POSSIBLE POSSUM (One per show)
Voices: Possible Possum: Lionel Wilson, **Billy Bear**: Lionel Wilson, **Owlawishus Owl**: Lionel Wilson, **Macon Mouse**: Lionel Wilson
[*released theatrically]

Episodes:

Freight Fright*
Surface Surf Aces*
Pirate Plunder Blunder*
Trestle Hassle*
Berry Funny*
Slinky Mink*
Big Mo*
Darn Barn*
Happy Hollow Turkey Shoot
Harm Sweet Home*
The Chestnut Nut*
Friendship
Kooky Cucumbers*

Swamp Water Taffy*
The Steel Stealer
Hobo Hassle*
The Red Swamp Pox*
The Pickle Pirate
The Rock Hound*
The General's Little Helpers*
Showboat Showoff
Don't Burro Trouble*
Mount Piney*
Popcorn Poachers
Happy Hollow Hay Ride*
Git That Guitar*

Black and Blue Jay
Surprisin' Exercisin'*
Watch Me Butterfly*
Findin' the Phantom
The Toothless Beaver*
Swamp Snapper*
Rootin' Tootin' Pumpkin Lootin'
The Bold Eagle*
Big Bad Bobcat*
Southern Super Market
Sleep Slip Up

JAMES HOUND (One per show)
Voices: James Hound: Dayton Allen
[All shorts released theatrically]

Episodes:

Give Me Liberty
The Monster Master
Baron Von Go-Go
Dr. Ha-Ha
The Phantom Skyscraper
Which is Witch

Dream Napping
A Voodoo Spell
Frozen Sparklers
Rain Drain
The Heat's Off
It's for the Birds

Fancy Plants
Bugged by a Bug
Traffic Trouble
Mr. Winlucky
Dr. Rhinestone's Theory

BARKER BILL'S CARTOON SHOW

Barker Bill's Cartoon Show was television's first weekly cartoon series and featured strictly the vintage black-and-white films from the Terrytoons library. The 15-minute cartoon show was sponsored by Post Sugar Jets and was seen twice a week. Only a picture of the program's host was seen on camera with a wacky announcer providing the introductions to the animated cartoons. Terrytoons cartoons featured on the show included Kiko the Kangaroo, Farmer Al Falfa, Puddy the Pup, and others. In 1956, *Barker Bill's Cartoon Show* ended and was replaced by a syndicated program, *Terry Toons Club* (later re-titled *Terry Toons Circus*), hosted by Claude Kirchner on WWOR-TV New York.

A Terrytoons Production. Black-and-White. Fifteen minutes.
Premiered on CBS November 18, 1953 and ran to November 25, 1956.

CBS CARTOON THEATER

Comedian Dick Van Dyke hosted this 30-minute collection of Terrytoons cartoons, which originated from WCBS, New York. Four cartoons were shown on each program including the adventures of Heckle and Jeckle, Little Roquefort, and Dinky Duck. The program was quickly put together as a replacement for the failed western series *Brave Eagle* starring Keith Larson. Since Dick Van Dyke was already under contract by CBS as a utility performer suitable for daytime programs, quiz shows, and summer replacements, he was asked to host the program.

In between the cartoon shorts, Van Dyke conversed with such Terrytoons animated characters as Gandy Goose and Heckle and Jeckle. Van Dyke stood in a standard "den" set speaking to the cartoon characters on a wall-sized screen with no realistic interaction between the host and the cartoon characters. *CBS Cartoon Theater* was scheduled directly opposite ABC's lavishly produced Wednesday evening weekly, *Disneyland*. Of note is that *CBS Cartoon Theater* was the first network prime-time series featuring animation (and not *The Flintstones* as is sometimes cited).

A CBS Terrytoons Production. Black-and-White. Thirty minutes.
Premiered on CBS June 13, 1956 and ran to September 5, 1956.

Voices: Heckle: Dayton Allen, Roy Halee; **Jeckle**: Dayton Allen, Roy Halee; **Gandy Goose/Sourpuss**: Arthur Kay; **Little Roquefort**: Tommy Morrison; **Percy the Cat**: Tommy Morrison

COMMONWEALTH CARTOON PACKAGE

Cartoon classics such as Ub Iwerks' Flip The Frog and Willie Whopper, Paul Terry's Aesop's Fables, and even some Walt Disney vintage shorts along with other cartoon favorites comprised this series of vintage cartoons offered for local programming.

Black-and-White. Thirty minutes.
Premiered: 1951. Syndicated.

DEPUTY DAWG SHOW

Deputy Dawg was a slow witted southern lawman who struggled to maintain law and order in Mississippi while being pestered by pranksters Vincent "Vince" Van Gopher, Ty Coon The Racoon, Muskie The Muskrat, and Pig Newton. While trying to track down these mischief makers, Deputy Dawg was constantly trying to ingratiate himself to the Sheriff while at the same time being the constant object of hero worship from Elmer, his lookalike little nephew.

Deputy Dawg was created by Terrytoons writer/animator Larz Bourne. Deputy Dawg debuted in October 1960 in over 47 television markets, mostly in the South and Midwest, primarily in the 6 p.m. to 7 p.m. time slot. The rest of the country settled for the 104 Deputy Dawg cartoons as solo "fillers", minus the rest of the Terrytoons package. The program was sponsored by the W. H. Lay Potato Chips company. A number of Lay potato chip commercials featuring the southern lawman were produced to accompany the program.

The rigors of maintaining a heavy television production schedule, heavier than the studio had ever previously experienced, forced Terrytoons to go outside of the studio for directing and writing talent. The result was inconsistent stories and varying production values. Although the cartoons were produced using cost-effective limited animation, the productions were nicely stylized and the backgrounds well-rendered.

Thanks to the vocal talent genius of Dayton Allen, Hal Erickson in *Television Cartoon Shows: An Illustrated Encyclopedia, 1949 through 1993* rightly notes that Deputy Dawg sounded like Frank Fontaine's "Crazy Guggenheim" character (whom Fontaine was calling "John L. C. Sivoney" in 1960). Vincent Van Gopher possessed the vocal sounds of character actor Percy Helton (1894–1971) (a voice that sounded like the cross between a squeak toy and a raspy gasp). The supporting character actors ranged from Groucho Marx (whom Allen would use quite effectively in the Heckle and Jeckle cartoons) to Hugh Herbert (1887–1952).

Appendix 3 • Paul Terry/Terrytoons: Television Cartoon Series

As a result of the success of the television series and from requests from theater managers across the country, most notably in Texas, CBS released some of the made-for-television cartoons theatrically in 1962. Unfortunately, the cartoons looked unfinished and cheap on the wider screen. Seven years later, Deputy Dawg premiered on NBC in a new series *The Deputy Dawg Show*. This new vehicle repeated episodes from the original series and featured two additional segments comprised of previously released Gandy Goose cartoons and Terrytoons Classics.

A Terrytoons Production. Color. Thirty minutes.
Syndicated: October 1960 ("Deputy Dawg").
Premiered on NBC: September 11, 1971 and ran to September 2, 1972 (*The Deputy Dawg Show*).
Produced by Bill Weiss. 104 Six minute cartoons.
Created and written by Larz Bourne. Directed by Dave Tendlar, Bob Kuwahara, Connie Rasinski, Bill Tytla, George Gordon, and Ralph Bakshi.
Additional screenplays by Jack Mercer, Cal Howard, Chris Jenkyns, T. Hee, Dick Kinney, and Al Bertino.

Voices: Deputy Dawg: Dayton Allen, **Vincent Van Gopher**: Dayton Allen; **Ty Coon the Racoon**: Dayton Allen, **Muskie the Muskrat**: Dayton Allen; **The Sheriff**: Dayton Allen
[*released theatrically]

Episodes:

Li'l Whooper*
Mama Magnolia's Pecan Pies
Duped Deputy
Astronut*
Tennessee Walkin' Horse
Lawman to the Rescue
Friend Fox*
Peanut Pilferer
Peach Pluckin' Kangaroo
People's Choice*
Mr. Moose
The Never Glades
Dog-Gone Catfish*
National Lazy Day
Feud for Thought
Big Chief No Treaty*
Little Red Fool House
The Poster Caper
Where There's Smoke*
The Yoke's on You
Diamonds in the Rough
Rebel Trouble*
Echo Park
Double-Barreled Boom Boom
Nobody's Ghoul*
Physical Fatness
Spare That Tree
Welcome Mischa Mouse
Corn Cribber
The Pig Rustler
Rabid Rebel
Herman the Hermit
Chicken Bull
Space Varmit
Heat Wave

Hex Marks the Spot
Deputy Dawg's Nephew
Long Island Duckling
Something to Crow About
Seize You Later, Alligator
Tents Moments
Catfish Crisis
National Spoof Day
Dagnabit Rabbit
Show Biz Whiz
Aig Plant
Tourist Tirade
Save Ol' Piney
Penguin Panic
Orbit a Little Bit
Pinch Hittin' for a Pigeon
Shotgun Shambles
Dry Spell
Home Cookin'
Kin Folk
Terrific Traffic
Protestin' Pilot
Lynx Th' Jinx
Safe An' Insane 4th
Mule-Itary Maneuvers
The Bird Burglar
Low Man Lawman
Millionaire Deputy
Watermelon Watcher
Open Wide
All Tuckered Out
Dragon My Foot
Th' Catfish Poachin' Pelican
The Hungry Astronaut
Star for a Day

The Milkweed from Space
Museum of th' South
Th' Two Inch Inchworm
Bad Luck Day
Scare Cure
Law and Disorder
Royal Southern Dismounted Police
The Great Grain Robbery
Honey Tree
Stuck Duck
Corn Pone Limited
Henhouse Hassle
Go Go Go-rilla
Space Invitation
Oil Tycoons
Grandpa Law
You're Fired an' I'm Fired
Cotton-Pickin' Picnic
Champion Whopper Teller
The Pink Flamingo
Noise Annoys
Daddy Frog Legs
Imperfect Crime
Beaver Battle
Science Friction
Obnoxious Obie
Ship Aha Ha
On the Lam With Ham
Elusive Louie
The Fragrant Vagrant
Just Ghost to Show You
The Governor's Guide
Creek Mud Monster
Mountain Melvin Meets Hairy Harry

FARMER ALFALFA

Farmer Al Falfa, along with his barnyard of animal friends, was the main star of this series comprised of old Terrytoon cartoons along with brand new segments.

A Terrytoons Production. Black-and-White. Color. Thirty minutes. Syndicated.
Premiered 1956.

THE HECKLE AND JECKLE CARTOON SHOW

The two mischievous magpies of theatrical cartoon fame hosted a collection of other theatrically released Terrytoon cartoons along with their own pesky misadventures. Other cartoon segments included Little Roquefort, Gandy Goose, and Dinky Duck, plus an assortment of miscellaneous Terrytoons cartoons under the title of *Terrytoon Classics*, several of which starred the Terry Bears.

A CBS Terrytoons Production. Color. Thirty minutes.
Premiered on CBS October 14, 1956 and ran to September 1957.
Rebroadcast on CBS September 1965 and ran to September 3, 1966.
Rebroadcast on NBC September 6, 1969 and ran to September 7, 1971. Syndicated.

HECKLE AND JECKLE (One per show)
Voices: Heckle: Dayton Allen, Roy Halee; **Jeckle**: Dayton Allen, Roy Halee;
[All shorts released theatrically]

Episodes:

The Talking Magpies	Flying South	Magpie Madness
The Stowaways	King Tut's Tomb	Movie Madness
Ten Pin Terrors	Pirate's Gold	Deep Sea Doodle
The Uninvited Pests	Fishing by the Sea	Free Enterprise
Happy Landing	The Rival Romeos	Off to the Opera
Bargain Daze	Miami Maniacs	Stunt Men
McDougal's Rest Farm	The Super Salesman	Out Again In Again
Hula Hula Land	Bulldozing the Bull	Housebusters
Log Rollers	Wild Life	Sappy New Year
Happy Go Lucky	The Hitch Hikers	Goony Golfers
Dancing Shoes	The Rainmaker	Moose on the Loose
Blind Date	Thousand Smile Check Up	Messed Up Movie Makers
Cat Trouble	Taming the Cat	The Power of Thought
The Fox Hunt	Steeple Jacks	Hair Cut-Ups
Satisfied Customers	Mint Men	The Lion Hunt
The Intruders	A Sleepless Night	Pill Peddlers
A Merry Chase	Sno' Fun	
Blue Plate Symphony	Trapeze Please	

DINKY DUCK (One per show)
Voices: Dinky Duck: (no voice)
[All shorts released theatrically]

Episodes:

The Orphan Duck	Featherweight Champ	The Foolish Duckling
Dinky Finds a Home	The Lucky Duck	The Timid Scarecrow
Wise Quacks	Flat Foot Fledgling	Life With Fido
Much Ado About Nothing	The Orphan Egg	Sink or Swim
The Beauty Shop	Welcome Little Stranger	It's a Living

LITTLE ROQUEFORT (One per show)
Voices: Little Roquefort: Tommy Morrison; **Percy the Cat**: Tommy Morrison
[All shorts released theatrically]

Episodes:

Cat Happy
City Slicker
Mouse Menace
Mouse and Garden
Hypnotized
Runaway Mouse
Three is a Crowd

Good Mousekeeping
Prescription for Percy
Musical Madness
Flop Secret
The Cat's Revenge
Seasick Sailors
Mouse Meets Bird

No Sleep for Percy
Pastry Panic
Playful Puss
The Haunted Cat
Friday the 13th

GANDY GOOSE (One per show)
Voices: Gandy Goose/Sourpuss: Arthur Kay, Tommy Morrison
[All shorts released theatrically]

Episodes:

Gandy the Goose
Night Life in the Army
It's All in the Stars
The Goose Flies High
Camouflage
The Golden Hen
Doomsday
Somewhere in Egypt
Peace-Time Football
G-Man Jitters
Aladdin's Lamp
Mexican Baseball
Hook, Line and Sinker
The Frog and the Princess
The Chipper Chipmunk

The Home Guard
The Ghost Town
Dingbat Land
The One-Man Navy
Gandy's Dream Girl
The Covered Pushcart
Slap Happy Hunters
Post-War Inventions
Comic Book Land
Sham Battle Shenanigans
Fisherman's Luck
Dream Walking
The Night
Mother Goose Nightmare
Wide Open Spaces

Lights Out
The Mosquito
Songs of Erin
Tricky Business
Who's Who in the Jungle
Spring Fever
The Outpost
The Exterminator
Barnyard Actor
Tire Trouble
Fortune Hunters
The Last Round-Up*
Mopping Up*
Somewhere in the Pacific*

TERRYTOON CLASSICS
Voices: Terry Bears: Doug Moye, Roy Halee, Phil Scheib

Episodes: *(not available)*

THE HECTOR HEATHCOTE SHOW

Hector Heathcote was a Revolutionary War minuteman who had a habit of playing a key role in the major events of the country's history. Hector Heathcote was created by Eli Bauer and first introduced in the CBS-Terrytoons cartoon *Minute and ½ Man* (Tendlar, 1959). As the series progressed, the creators decided to have him reshape history at different time periods though the creators never divulged how Hector was able to travel through time to appear at these key happenings in history. Wherever he went in history, whether he was helping to build a railroad in the 1860s or delivering the mail as a member of the Pony Express, Hector would be wearing an 18th Century tricorner hat. Some episodes featured Winston, Heathcote's bulldog, who spoke in a Churchillian manner and provided wise advice to the befuddled Hector. Despite Hector's major accomplishments, he rarely received the credit he deserved, partly because he always seemed to stumble into these historical events and never achieved what he originally intended to accomplish (such as inventing the harvester when trying to invent the airplane).

The *Hector Heathcote Show* was comprised of recycled theatrical cartoons. The program's other cartoon components included Hashimoto and Sidney the Elephant. The theatrical cartoons shown on the program were bestowed with a number of awards, prizes, and honors. *The Minute and ½ Man* (Tendlar, 1959) won first prize at the Venice Film Festival. *Sidney's Family Tree* (Bartsch, 1958) was nominated for an Academy Award. *Hashimoto San* (Kuwahara, 1959) was selected for showing at Cannes. Of the 71 cartoons broadcast during the program's two-year run on NBC Television, only 39 had previously been seen in the theaters. The result was a difference in quality of animation in the two packages.

A CBS Terrytoons Production. Color. Thirty minutes. Premiered on NBC October 5, 1963 and ran to September 25, 1965.
Produced by Bill Weiss. Directed by Arthur Bartsch, Martin B. Taras, Dave Tendlar, Connie Rasinski, Bill Tytla, Bob Kuwahara, and Mannie Davis.
Music by Philip Scheib and Jim Timmens.

HECTOR HEATHCOTE (One per show)
Voices: Hector Heathcote: John Myhers
[*released theatrically]

Episodes:

*The Minute and ½ Man**
*Tea Party**
*Lost and Foundation**
*The Famous Ride**
*A Bell for Philadelphia**
*Wind Bag**
*Daniel Boone, Jr.**
*The Big Cleanup**
*Barrel of Fun**
*The Unsung Hero**
*Flight to the Finish**
*Ice Cream for Help**

*The First Fast Mail**
*Peace Pipe**
*Expert Explorer**
*Crossing the Delaware**
*The Hectormobile**
*Klondike Strike Out**
*Drum Roll**
*Belabour thy Neighbor**
*High Flyer**
*Railroaded to Fame**
*Har Har Harpoon**
Pig in a Poke

*Land Grab**
*The First Telephone**
Search for a Symbol
*First Flight Up**
*Train Terrain**
Messy Messenger
*Riverboat Mission**
*Hold the Fort**
Hats off to Hector
*He-Man Seaman**
*Valley Forge Hero**

HASHIMOTO (One per show)
Voices: Hashimoto: John Myhers, **Hanako his wife:** John Myhers, **Yuriko**, his daughter: John Myhers, **Saburo** his son: John Myhers
[*released theatrically]

Episodes:

*Hashimoto-San**
*Strange Companion**
*Tea House Mouse**
*House of Hashimoto**
*Honorable House Cat**
*Cherry Blossom Festival**

*So Sorry, Pussycat**
*Honorable Family Problem**
*Spooky-Yaki**
*Night Life in Tokyo**
*Loyal Royalty**
The Potter's Wheel Heel

*Honorable Cat Story**
*Honorable Paint In Neck**
Doll Festival
*Son of Hashimoto**
*Pearl Crazy**

SIDNEY THE ELEPHANT (One per show)
Voices: Sidney the Elephant: Dayton Allen, Lionel Wilson, **Stanley the Lion:** Dayton Allen, **Cleo the Giraffe:** Dayton Allen
[*released theatrically]

Episodes:

*Sick, Sick Sidney**
*Home Life**
Banana Binge
*Sidney's Family Tree**
*Sidney's White Elephant**
Clown Jewels
*Hide and Go Sidney**

*Driven to Extraction**
Tree Spree
*Tusk, Tusk**
*Send Your Elephant to Camp**
Really Big Act
*The Littlest Bully**
*Peanut Battle**

Meat, Drink, and Be Merry
*Two-Ton Baby Sitter**
*Fleet's Out**
*Split-Level Tree House**
*To Be or Not To Be**

Appendix 3 • Paul Terry/Terrytoons: Television Cartoon Series

THE MIGHTY HEROES

In 1966, Ralph Bakshi was named supervising director for Terrytoons. He soon approached CBS executives with several non-superhero concepts, but his ideas were soundly rejected. With the rise in superhero television programs in the late 1960s, most notably the live-action *Batman* series that premiered on ABC television in 1966, Bakshi decided to create the Mighty Heroes. The Mighty Heroes were a team of bumbling superheroes designed not to imitate the traditional superhero model but were created to parody the campy *Batman* series and the superhero craze that was sweeping the nation.

Episodes featured five defenders of justice: Diaper Man, Tornado Man, Rope Man, Strong Man and Cuckoo Man. Diaper Man was a quick witted "Diaper Infant" who lived in a crib and used his baby bottle as a weapon. Tornado Man was a television weatherman who turned himself into a spinning tornado. Rope Man was a sailor who transformed himself into a human lasso. Strong Man, a moving-man by occupation, was a brawny and not so bright character who actually looked like a superhero. Finally, there was Cuckoo Man who had Chaplinesque features, lived in a cuckoo clock, and had problems flying and therefore was always trying to keep up with the rest of the team.

The Mighty Heroes battled such dastardly villains as the Shocker, the Stretcher and the Toy Man. Director Bakshi next went on to supervise the original *Spiderman* cartoon series in September of 1967. From there Bakshi moved into producing ground-breaking, and often controversial, animated features like *Fritz The Cat*, *Heavy Traffic*, *Coonskin*, *American Pop*, *Wizards*, and *Lord of the Rings*.

A total of 20 episodes were created for television. The show lasted only one season with all 20 episodes being broadcast. The demise of the program is all that more surprising considering the fine quality of the cartoons and the fact that the program was competing against NBC's very forgettable look-a-like competition, *The Super Six*. Afterwards, the programs segments were re-run as part of the syndicated *Mighty Mouse Playhouse* half-hour. Between 1969 and 1971, about half of the episodes were released as theatrical cartoons. During the 1970s and 1980s, they were syndicated separately, and appeared alongside Bugs Bunny and Popeye in local kid programs all over America.

A Terrytoons Production. Color. Thirty minutes.
Premiered on CBS October 29, 1966 and ran to September 2, 1967.
Created by Ralph Bakshi. Directed by Ralph Bakshi and Bob Taylor.

Voices: The Mighty Heroes: Herschel Bernardi, Lionel Wilson
[All shorts released theatrically]

Episodes:

The Plastic Blaster	*The Enlarger*	*The Raven*
The Drifter	*The Return of the Monsterizer*	*The Stretcher*
The Scarecrow	*The Shrinker*	*The Big Freeze*
The Frog	*The Toy Man*	*The Bigger Digger*
The Shocker	*The Paper Monster*	*The Monsterizer*
The Time Eraser	*The Ghost Monster*	*The Timekeeper*
The Junker	*The Dusters*	

THE MIGHTY MOUSE PLAYHOUSE

After CBS purchased the Terrytoons film library from Paul Terry in late 1955, the network used the collection to create *The Mighty Mouse Playhouse*. Beginning in December 1955, the cartoon show was shown regularly on Saturday mornings. Each half-hour program opened with the Mighty Mouse theme song.

Mister Trouble never hangs around,
When he hears this Mighty sound:

"*Here I come to save the day!*"

That means that Mighty Mouse is on the way!

TERRYTOONS: The Story of Paul Terry and His Classic Cartoon Factory

Yes sir, when there is a wrong to right,
Mighty Mouse will join the fight!
On the sea or on the land,
He's got the situation well in hand!

Marshal Barer, a writer/producer for "Golden Records", the famous U. S. children's record label of the 1940s and 1950s, wrote the lyrics, while Terrytoons long-time studio musician, Philip Scheib, composed the music.

The *Mighty Mouse Playhouse* was a phenomenal success and despite challenges from other cartoon programs such as Hanna-Barbera's *Ruff and Reddy* series which first aired in December 1957, the program remained a staple of network television through 1966. Throughout the program's 12-year run on CBS, *The Mighty Mouse Playhouse* relied solely on the theatrical Terry cartoons as the producers were reluctant to tamper with the program's popularity by adding the made-for-television shorts. *The Mighty Mouse Playhouse* was so popular that the program maintained an average 11.6 rating with a 45.8 percent audience share throughout its 12-year CBS run.

The series strongly impacted the cartoon industry as cartoon studios began to follow the success of the show with their own fully animated series. The series also revived the career of the super mouse and earned CBS a fortune through character toys, books and other merchandise. The series featured one or two Mighty Mouse adventures plus an assortment of Paul Terry cartoons.

In 1967, Viacom purchased the Terrytoons library from CBS and packaged *The Mighty Mouse Show*. Under the syndicated version, two series joined the package Luno, the flying white stallion and his time traveling friend Tim, and *The Mighty Heroes*, featuring Diaper man, Tornado Man, Rope Man, Strong Man and Cuckoo Man, a group of half-witted clumsy superheroes who battled such dastardly villains as the Shocker, the Stretcher and the Toy Man. Episodes from both series received theatrical distribution as well.

The demise of *Mighty Mouse Playhouse* can be largely attributed to the animated competition produced by Hanna-Barbera (*The Flintstones*) and Jay Ward Productions (*The Bullwinkle Show*) in the mid-1960s.

A CBS Terrytoons Production. Color. Thirty minutes. All theatrical cartoons.
Premiered on CBS: December 10, 1955 and ran to October 2, 1966.
Syndicated: 1967.

MIGHTY MOUSE
Voices: Mighty Mouse: Tom Morrison, Roy Halee (singing voice); **Narrator:** Tom Morrison
[All shorts released theatrically]

Episodes:

The Mouse of Tomorrow	Lion and the Mouse	A Swiss Miss
My Old Kentucky Home	The Jail Break	The Green Line
Cold Romance	Beauty on the Beach	The Sky is Falling
Frankenstein's Cat	Wreck of the Hesperus	A Cat's Tale
Throwing the Bull	The Crackpot King	Mighty Mouse Meets Deadeye Dick
The Catnip Gang	Down With Cats	The Two Barbers
He Dood it Again	The Champion of Justice	Prehistoric Perils
The Johnstown Flood	The Hepcat	Sultan's Birthday
Perils of Pearl Pureheart	Sunny Italy	A Date for Dinner
Pandora's Box	Mighty Mouse Meets Jeckyll and Hyde Cat	Hansel and Gretel
The Trojan Horse		At the Circus
Stop, Look and Listen	Crying Wolf	The First Snow
Super Mouse Rides Again	Goons from the Moon	Happy Holland
Winning the West	Eliza on the Ice	Mighty Mouse and the Pirates
Anti-Cats	Dead End Cats	A Fight to the Finish
Mother Goose's Birthday Party	Injun Trouble	Soapy Opera
The Electronic Mouse Trap	Wolf! Wolf!	Port of Missing Mice
Law and Order	Aladdin's Lamp	Swiss Cheese Family Robinson

Appendix 3 • Paul Terry/Terrytoons: Television Cartoon Series

Hero for a Day	Racket Buster	Reformed Wolf
Raiding the Raiders	Mighty Mouse and the Wolf	Mighty Mouse in Krakatoa
Lazy Little Beaver	The Witch's Cat	Triple Trouble
Hot Rods	Spare the Rod	Outer Space Visitor
Mighty Mouse and the Kilkenny Cats	Gypsy Life	Svengali's Cat
Mighty Mouse and The Magician	Love's Labor Won	Magic Slipper
Cat Alarm	Helpless Hippo	The Mysterious Package
The Silver Streak	Mighty Mouse Meets Bad Bill Bunion	The Wicked Wolf
The Feuding Hillbillies	The Mysterious Stranger	When Mousehood Was in Flower

THE MIGHTY HEROES

Voices: The Mighty Heroes: Herschel Bernardi, Lionel Wilson
[All shorts released theatrically]

Episodes:

The Plastic Blaster	The Enlarger	The Raven
The Drifter	The Return of the Monsterizer	The Stretcher
The Scarecrow	The Shrinker	The Big Freeze
The Frog	The Toy Man	The Bigger Digger
The Shocker	The Paper Monster	The Monsterizer
The Time Eraser	The Ghost Monster	The Timekeeper
The Junker	The Dusters	

LUNO

Voices: Luno, the white stallion: Bob McFadden; **Tim**, his child companion: Bob McFadden
[*released theatrically]

Episodes:

The Missing Genie*	Island of the Giants	The Square Planet*
Melvin the Magnificent*	The Flying Chariot	The Prehysteric Inventor
The Gold Dust Bandit*	Roc-A-Bye Sinbad*	Who's Dragon*
The Poor Pirate	Mixed Up Matador*	Jungle Jack*
Trouble in Baghdad*	King Neptune's Castle	1772
Adventure by the Sea*	King Rounder*	

TOM TERRIFIC

Tom Terrific was a curly haired boy who derived his super powers from his funnel shaped hat. According to the opening theme song, the hat had the ability to transform Tom into any shape or object he desired including a "plane on high", a "diesel train roaring by", or a "bumble bee, or a tree". Along with help from his pet dog, Mighty Manfred the Wonder Dog, who was more interested in a long nap then helping Tom save the world, the two would track down criminals, the main nemesis being Crabby Appleton who was "rotten to the core".

Each Tom Terrific story lasted five episodes and was initially presented in a daily cliff-hanger format on *The Captain Kangaroo Show*. Tom Terrific was the brainchild of Terrytoons creative director Gene Deitch who created Tom in late 1956 about one year after the studio was sold to CBS. Unfortunately, the budget to produce the cartoons was virtually non-existent. As a result, the background music consisted solely of a banjo and harmonica. The characters were simple transparent line drawings. The backgrounds were extremely crude and were many times simply a horizon line to add depth to the cartoon. Nevertheless, the concept of a cartoon character transforming himself into any object or shape he desired was a clever and innovative device that ran against the static unappealing cartoon stars of the day.

Whatever the cartoons lacked visually, they made up for with clever dialogue and engaging personalities. Much of the creative storylines can be attributed to cartoonist, children's book writer, and playwright Jules Feiffer. The result was one of the best cartoon programs to be created during the 1950s. At its peak, *The Captain Kangaroo*

TERRYTOONS: The Story of Paul Terry and His Classic Cartoon Factory

Show had an audience of 3.5 million. While children loved the cartoons for engaging stories involving the bold adventures of Tom, the adults enjoyed the witty banter between characters, the innovative uses of the animated form, and the cliffhanger formats that took them back to the days of serial movies and radio.

Following the serialization on CBS Television's daily live-action *Captain Kangaroo Show*, the episodes were edited into 26 half-hour adventures and syndicated nationwide. Despite the official 1961 termination date listed below, the cartoons remained on the *Captain Kangaroo Show* until at least 1965.

A Terrytoons Production in association with CBS Films.
Black-and-white. Thirty minutes.
Premiered on CBS June 10, 1957 and ran to September 21, 1961. Syndicated.
Produced by Gene Deitch.

Voices: Tom Terrific/Mighty Manfred: Lionel Wilson

Episodes: [All televised shorts]
1957–1958

Nasty Knight
Captain Kidney Bean
Track Meet Well Done
The Pill of Smartness
The Gravity Maker

Great Calendar Mystery
Sweet Tooth Sam
Scrambled Dinosaur Eggs
Elephants Stew
Snowy Picture

Who Stole the North Pole
Crabby Appleton Dragon
Instant Tantrums

1958–1959

Missing Mail Mystery
Crabby Park
Robin's Nest Crusoe
The Prince Frog
The Million Manfred Mystery

The Everlasting Birthday Party
Isotope Feeney's Foolish Fog
The Flying Sorcerer
Go West, Young Manfred
Moon Over Manfred

Big Dog Show-Off
The Silly Sandman
The End of Rainbows

Image credits

Source	Figure No.
Author	1.1, 1.2, 2.3, 2.5, 6.1, 6.2, 7.2, 7.3, 8.2, 11.9, 13.8, 14.4, 15.1, 15.2, 15.3, 15.4, 15.5, 15.6, 18.3, 21.6, 23.3, 23.7, 24.4, 24.5, 25.5, 27.2, 27.4, A1.2
Gene Deitch	23.2
George Washington University Archives	10.1
Heritage Auctions	1.3, 1.4, 1.5, 1.6, 2.4, 2.6, 4.3, 4.4, 4.5, 7.4, 8.4, 8.5, 13.2, 20.3, 21.7, 27.1, AC.1, F.1
Jerry Beck	22.2, 22.3
Library of Congress, Prints and Photographs Division, Washington, DC	2.7, 2.8, 5.4, 5.5, 7.1, 10.8
Patricia Ann Terry Leahy, Câron Terry Caswell Lazar, and Paul Terry Layton	2.1, 2.2, 3.1, 3.2, 3.3, 3.4, 3.5, 3.6, 5.2, 5.3, 6.3, 6.4, 8.1, 8.3, 9.1, 9.2, 9.3, 9.4, 10.2, 10.3, 10.4, 10.5, 10.6, 10.7, 11.1, 11.2, 11.3, 11.4, 11.5, 11.6, 11.7, 11.8, 12.1, 12.2, 12.3, 12.4, 12.5, 12.6, 13.1, 13.3, 13.4, 13.5, 13.6, 13.7, 14.1, 14.2, 14.3, 16.1, 16.2, 16.4, 16.5, 16.6, 16.7, 16.8, 17.1, 17.2, 17.3, 17.4, 17.5, 17.6, 17.7, 17.8, 17.9, 17.10, 17.11, 17.12, 18.5, 18.7, 19.1, 19.3, 19.4, 19.5, 19.6, 20.1, 20.2, 20.4, 20.5, 20.7, 20.8, 20.9, 20.10, 21.1, 21.2, 21.3, 21.4, 21.5, 22.1, 22.4, 22.5, 22.6, 22.7, 23.1, 23.4, 23.5, 24.3, 25.8, 26.1, 26.2, 26.3, 26.4, 26.5, 26.6, 26.7, 26.8, 27.3, 27.5, 27.6, A1.1, A1.3, A1.4, A1.5, A1.6, A1.7, A1.8, A1.9, A1.10, A1.11, A1.12, A1.13, A1.14, A1.15
San Francisco History Center, San Francisco Public Library	4.1, 4.2, 5.1
Terrytoons, CBS Corporation	16.3, 18.1, 18.2, 18.4, 18.6, 19.2, 20.6, 23.6, 24.1, 24.6, 24.7, 24.8, 25.1, 25.2, 25.3, 25.4, 25.6, 25.7

Index of Personalities

This index is a complete alphabetical list of all individuals, other than Paul Terry, referenced in the Acknowledgements, Foreword, Chapters, and Appendix 1. Page references to Paul Terry are indexed in the Main Index. Image references are in *italics*.

A

Addison, Walter Nichols	*183*, *188*, 198-199
Adel, JJ.	184
Adelaide (Adelaide and Hughes)	344
Aesop	98-99
Ainsworth, Sidney	82
Alaric I	8 (n. 7)
Albee, Edward Franklin, II	99-100, 110, 121
Alberti, Nick	vii, *298*, 319-320, 329, 331
Alden, John	1, 8 (n. 4)
Alden, Priscilla	1
Alden, Susanna	1
Aldrich, Raymond Elbert	173-174, 182-183
Algar, James	29
Allen, Dayton	vii, 213, 225-226, 297, 301-302, 304, 306, 331-334, *333*
Allen, Elvi (née Daniels)	333
Allen, Fred	226, 333
Allen, Heck	276
Allen, Steve	333
Alvord, Dean	125
Anderson, Alexander	vii, *68*, 236-237, 255, 335
Anderson, Alexander Hume	17 (n. 45), 25
Anderson, Carl Thomas	77-79
Anderson, Jesse Sylvester "Vet"	53, 101-102, 104, 112 (n. 26), *115*, 119
Anderson, Maxwell	32
Anderson, Mignon	71
Andriot, Lucien	91
Anzilotti, Cosmo	vii, *298*, 308, 316
Arbuckle, Fatty	85
Augustson, Clifford	vii, *188*, 199, 331
Avery, Tex	ix

B

Babbitt, Art	ix, 114, 126-128, 132, *137*, 231-232, 282, 325
Badgley, Helen	71
Bailey, Adrian	168
Bailey, Henry (Harry) D.	85, 95, 101-102, 104, *115*, 119, 203
Bairnsfeather, Bruce	124
Bajus, Don	327 (n. 23)
Bakshi, Eddie	334
Bakshi, Elaine	308
Bakshi, Elizabeth	334
Bakshi, Mark	316, 334
Bakshi, Preston	334
Bakshi, Ralph	ix, vii, 281, *298*, *299*, 308-314, 316-317, 329, 331, 334, *334*, 345
Bakshi, Victoria	334
Baldwin, Gerald	327 (n. 23)
Ball, Lucille	131
Barbera, Joseph	ix, 140 (n. 40), 168-169, 204, 273-275, 301, 340
Barer, Marshall	265
Barnstyn, J. C.	135
Barré, Raoul	69, 74, 79, 102, 107-108, 114, 148, 268-269, 338, 342
Barrett, Henry R.	174-175, 184
Barrier, Michael	vii, 270
Barsky, Bud	117
Bartlett, Leland	30
Bartsch, Arthur Daniel	335
Bartsch, Arthur E.	*188*, *191*, *227*, 236, 250, 255, *256*, 271, *298*, 301, 310, 312, 335, *335*
Bartsch, Margarethe (née Woll [Wall])	335
Bartsch, Marguerite Catherine (née Collins)	335
Bartsch, Robert E.	335
Basinger, Kim	334
Bass, Saul	325
Batchelor, Joy	325
Bathgate, Joe	*188*
Bauer, Dianne	328
Bauer, Eli	vii, 281-282, 284-285, *291*, 301-302, 328, 331
Bazelon, Irwin	292
Beck, Jerry	ix-x, viii, 270-272, 276, 290
Beck, Martin	100
Becker, Stephen	268
Beckerman, Howard	vii, 329, 331
Belafonte, Harry	306
Bell, Carl	327 (n. 23)
Bell, Vinnie	vii, *298*
Benchley, Robert	33
Bendazzi, Giannalberto	269
Berger (Wolf & Berger)	345
Berke, Ben	143
Berle, Milton	283
Berlin, Irving	60
Berliner, Emile	18
Bernardi, Herschel	316
Bigge, Maria	3
Bill, Buffalo	228
Billings, Warren	31
Bishop, Mildred	*188*
Blackton, James Stuart	60-61, 63, 67
Blanchard, Jean-Pierre	302
Blanchard, Robert	252
Blaney, Charles E.	70
Blechman, R. O.	viii, 281, 287-288
Bogart, Humphrey	228
Bogert, Stephen G.	10
Boito, Arrigo	18
Bolke, Bradley	333
Bolke, Helen (née Freedman)	333
Bolke, Solomon	333

377

TERRYTOONS: The Story of Paul Terry and His Classic Cartoon Factory

Bonaparte, Napoleon 83
Bonfiglio (née Goodson), Thomas 126, 129, 140 (n. 39)
Boone, Daniel 228, 302
Borden, William Cline 89
Borough, Randal William 28-29, 35-36 (n. 13)
Boss, Yale 71
Bosustow, Steve 278, 325
Bourne, Larz 281, *283*, *298*, *299*, 302, 313
Bourne, Polly (Mrs. Polly Donnelly) vii, 237, 338
Bower, Morris L. 88
Bowers, Charles 107-108
Bozzetto, Bruno 325
Bradley, Scott 272
Brady, William A. 70
Branscombe, Charles 55 (n. 29)
Bray, John Randolph 67-69, 74, 77-80, 85, 85 (n. 2, 3), 94, 107-108, 115-116, 129, 146-147, 213, 258, 268, 325
Bray, Margaret Till 77, 85 (n. 1), 126
Breer, Robert 327 (n. 23)
Brencic, Makovec 221
Brennan, Arthur D. 175, 177, 184
Brennan, Mark *188*
Breughel, Pieter 126
Brinstey 55 (n. 28)
Bromfield, John Davenport 53
Bronstrup, Gustavo A. 29
Brooks, Mel 317
Brown, "Bunny" 203
Bryant, Gamaliel 6
Bryant, John 3
Bryant, Mary (née Potter) 6
Bryant, Phebe Hussey 5-6
Bubb, Benjamin Clarence 45, 54 (n. 3)
Budd, Roy Leighton 74, 77, 79-80, 101
Budney, Charles vii
Budney, George vii
Budney, Teofil 342-343
Buell, Marjorie Henderson 201
Burbank, Luther 105
Burgstaller, Alois 38
Burness, Pete 325
Burr, C. C. 198
Burton, John W. 290-291
Bushell, Bob vii
Bushmiller, Ernie 200-201
Byrne, Thomas 126, 129, 140 (n. 40)
Byrnes, Gene 308

C

Caldwell, Jordan vii, 292
Callahan 55 (n. 28)
Calonius, Lars 282
Calvert, Fred 318
Campanari, Giuseppe 38
Canemaker, John 332
Cannata, George *174*
Cannon, Bobe 278
Carey, Sarah 8 (n. 6), 9 (n. 17)
Carino, Frank *188*
Carleton, Lloyd B. 71
Carlson, Gregory I., Rev. viii
Carnegie, Dale 323
Carpenter, A. (Dr.) 129
Carpenter, Col. 8 (n. 6)
Carreon, Jose *137, 174*
Carroll, James 89
Carswell, JJ. 184
Caruso, Enrico 38
Casey, James P. 29
Casey, Pat 110
Castleton, Barbara 82
Caswell, Lucy Shelton vii
Catlin, Edwin B. 48
Caulfield, Don *298*
Cavanaugh, Walter 52
Ceplair, Larry 269
Chambers, Robert 107-108
Chaplin, Charlie 84-85, 106, 261
Chapman, W. W. 49
Chase, Charley *106*
Chiarito, Al *298*
Chiovetta, Nicholas (Mrs.) vii
Christ, Jesus 212
Clampett, Bob 325, *326*
Clark, Bert 95
Clark, John D. 155, 161-162
Clark, Les 290
Clark, William Andrews 46-47
Clemshaw 34
Cleveland, Grover 22-23
Close, JJ. 184
Cobb, Irvin S. 33
Coburn, Charles 124
Cochrane, Martha *188*
Coffman, Joseph Wilfred 124-125, 134-136, 138, 342
Coffroth, Jimmy 42
Coghlan, John 32
Cohen (King), Ed *137*
Cohen, Milton 246
Cohl, Emile 60-61, 63, 146
Colby, Vincent 79

Coleman, William Tell 12-13
Collier, Barron Gift 58, 65 (n. 5), 84
Collier, Nathan Leo 101-104
Collier, Theron *188*, 237
Collier, Thurlo *188*, 240
Collins, Ashton B. 204
Columbus, Christopher 25
Connery, Sean 317
Constant, Benjamin 48
Corbett, Henry W. 49-50
Corelli, Bob *298, 299*
Craig, Adele McLain [Kennedy] 336
Craig, Anderson *188, 190*, 236, 250-252, *257*, 265, 271, 294, 335-336, *336*, 339
Craig, Anderson, Jr. 336
Craig, Arthur Still 335
Craig, Catherine (née Cahill) 336
Craig, Melle Rosimin (née Campbell) 335
Crane, Doug vii, 328, 332
Crocker, Charles 12
Crothers, Robert 30
Cruickshank, Sally 271
Cruze, James 71
Cuccinata, Carlo *188*
Culhane, Shamus 256, 317, 325, 345
Cummings, Hope vii, 312
Cummings, William H. 13-14
Cunningham (Cunningham & Walsh) 293
Cunningham, Ricki (Joan) vii, *297*
Custer, General 228

D

D'Angelo, Armand *174*
D'Arcy, Roy 134
d'Avino, Carmen 325
Da Vinci, Leonardo 285
Dadone, Diana vii
Daly, Marcus 46-48
Danglo, Dan vii
Daniels, Les 268
Darby, Thomas (Rev.) 237
Darling, Jay N. 64
Darwin, Charles 110
Date, Hideo 340
Davey, Randall Vernon 251, 335
David, Tissa 325
Davidovich, Basil 275
Davidowitz [Davidovitz], Samuel 336
Davidowitz [Davidovitz], Sarah Rosa (née Berkowitz) 336

378

Index of Personalities

Davis, Art 336
Davis, George vii, *259, 298*
Davis, Emanuel "Mannie"
  104, 107-108, 114, *115,*
  119, 121, 126, 133,
  152, 167-168, *174,*
  178, 188, 194, 199,
  203, 208, 210, 225,
  232, 236, 246, 264-265,
  271, 308, 321, *323,*
  336-337, *336*
Davis, Florence J. (née Goodstein) 337
Davis, James 337
Davis, Jean vii
Davis, JJ. 184
Davis, Owen 70
Davis, Phil 336
Davis, Sid 336
Davis, Susan 337
Day, Harvey B. 155,
  161-162, 164, 167,
  180-181, *188,* 222
de Young, Charles 34
de Young, Meichel Harry 34, 40,
  44 (n. 17)
Dean, Julie *174*
DeForest, Lee 120
Deitch, Eugene "Gene"
  Merril vii, 278-293, *281,*
  294-295, 301-302,
  309, 321, 345
DelBello, Alfred Benedict 326
Deneroff, Harvey vii
Dennin, Hannah C. 80
Dewey, Frederick Hastings 53
Diefenbaker, John 108
Dirks, Rudolph 102
Disney, Walt ix, 29, 106, 120-121,
  127, 144-148,
  153, 159, 168,
  170, 190-191, 194,
  197, 199, 203-205,
  210-211, 214-216,
  217, 222-223,
  231-234, 242,
  244-245, 248, 251,
  255, 260-262,
  264, 267-272,
  275-276, 278, 282,
  286, 292, 313,
  322, 324-325,
  332, 343, 345
Dixon, James E. 13
Dockstader, Tod 281
Donnelly, Ann (Sheridan) 337
Donnelly, Daniel Webster 25

Donnelly, Edwin *115, 174, 188,* 208,
  211, 214-215, 225,
  228, 236-237, 249,
  264-265, 271,
  337-338, *337*
Donnelly, Edwin E. 338
Donnelly, Ellen (née Sommers) 338
Donnelly, Mary (née Bourne) 338
Donnelly, Patricia Ann 338
Donnelly, Raymond 338
Donnelly, Virginia M. 338
Donnelly, William J. 337
Donzetti, Gaetano 229
Dorgan, Thomas Aloysius 32,
  54, 60, 98
Douglas, James 339
Doyle, Sir Arthur Conan 18
Dreiser, Theodore 336
Dryer, Thomas J. 49-50
Duchamp, Marcel 323
Dugan, Catherine 6
Durante, Jimmy 189, 227, 243
Durston, John Hurst 46-48, 55 (n. 13)
Dwiggins, Marge *188*

E

Edel, Harold 83
Edison, Thomas A. 69, 74,
  89, 94, 102, 107,
  130, 132-134,
  337-338, 342, 344
Edouarde, Carl 121
Eggleston, Charles Hayden 48
Einstein, Albert 110
Eisenberg, Harvey 153,
  157 (n. 93), *174*
Eldridge, Mary 4
Eletto, Carmen *188,* 199, 237
Eletto, Rocco *167, 174, 188,* 237
Eletto, Vincent *174, 188,* 237
Eline, Marie 71
Eliot, George 73
Ellis, Charles, P. 8
Elton, Leslie 79, 98
Ely, Van Horn 70
Englund, Steven 260
Epstein, Lewis 80
Ernst (Ernst & Co.) 323
Eshbaugh, Ted 130, 204
Estabrook, Howard 98-101, 110
Evans, Thomas L. W. 88-89
Ezekiels, Mark 14

F

Fairbanks, Madeline 71

Fairbanks, Marion 71
Falk, Nat 199, 268
Favata, Ray vii, 281, 292
Fawcett, Sara A. 130
Feiffer, Jules 281-282, *291,* 292
Fennell, Paul 116
Ferber, Edna 98
Ferguson, Colleen M. vii-viii
Ferguson, Norman 115-116, *115,*
  119-120, 127, 264
Fernandes, Esmeralda *167, 174, 188*
Ferri, Roger 169
Fields, Gracie 64
Figlozzi, Donald *188*
Finnegan (Sauter-Finnegan
  Orchestra) 309
Fisher, Bud 34, 42, 54, 74,
  79, 107, 206, 337
Fitch, George K. (Deacon) 30
Fitzsimmons, John A. 63
Fleischer (brothers) 108,
  112 (n. 26), 120, 126,
  199, 245, 322
Fleischer, Dave 231, 325
Fleischer, Max ix,
  86 (n. 21), 110, 118,
  120, 126-129, 148,
  161, 197, 231, 302
Flohri, Emil 79
Flora, James 283
Focht, Bill vii, 251,
  295-296, 317, 340
Foldes, Peter 325
Fontaine, Frank 304
Foray, June 325
Fortune, Larry 220
Foster, Doris A. 339
Foster, Grace (née Ashton) 339
Foster, John 101-102, 104,
  115, *115,* 119, 122,
  164, *174, 179,* 188,
  188, 191, 203-208,
  220, 232, 236,
  337-339, *338,* 341
Foster, John, Sr. 338
Foster, John J. 339
Foster, Louise (née Daab) 338
Foster, Warren 276
Fowler, Jessie Allen *82,* 83-84
Fox, Bill 259
Fox, Gill 204
Fox, William 63
France, Anatole 288
Franklin, Chester 91
Franklin, Sidney 91

379

Freedman, Herman	110	Gray, Joe	vii	Hays, Will H.	136
Frees, Paul	325	Greco, Sal	*298*	Healy, T.	84
Freleng, Friz	290	Greeley, Horace	46	Hearst, George	51
Freud, Sigmund	127	Green, Bert	115	Hearst, William Randolph	42, 50-52, 57 (n. 66), 60, 74, 94, 102-103, 107-108, 110, 115, 130, 147, 342
Friedman, Lillian	197	Green, Frank M.	18		
Friedwald, Will Timbes	215	Greening, Harry Cornell	77-78		
Frohman, Charles	98	Gregory, Carl Louis	191-192		
Fuller, Ving	115	Grey, Romer	189		
Funston, Frederick	40-42, *40*, 44 (n. 32)	Griffin, Merv	333	Heck, Will S.	61
		Griffith, David W.	132, 136, 211, 344	Heimlich, Freda [Bertha] (née Nussbaum)	110
		Gros, Raymond	53	Heimlich, Gerson	110
G		Gross (Schwartz & Gross)	154	Heimlich, Irma (Mrs. Paul Terry)	110-111, 117, *120*, 139 (n. 19), 222, 326
Gallo, Fortune	136	Guadagno, Terry	296		
Gardner, T. E. J.	84	Guggenheim	326		
Gattoni, Steve	*188*, 240	Gunnison, Stanley E.	250, 335		
Gentilella, John	vii, *188*, 265, *287*, 308, 331	Gurney, Eric	275	Heimlich, Milton	222
		Gushue, Muriel	vii, 238	Heinze, Fritz Augustus	47
Gentilella, Matthew	*188*			Helton, Percy	304
Gerberding, C.O.	29-30	**H**		Henderson, Skitch	226
Geronimi, Clyde	275	Haas, Edward K.	174	Henry, Buck	317
Gershwin, George	336	Hagarty, JJ.	184	Heraldson, Donald	269
Giannini, Amadeo Pietro	190-191	Halas, John	324-325	Herbert, Hugh	228, 304
Giannini, Attilio Henry	190-191	Halee, Roy, Jr.	viii	Herman, John	168
Gilbert (Gilbert & Sullivan)	215	Halee, Royal Walter	viii, 213, 225, *263*, 297	Herriman, George	79
Gilbert, Charles Allan	77-78			Herrman, Alexander	69
Gilbridge, Mary	80	Hall, Robert	282	Hershfield, Harry	54, 57 (n. 65)
Gillett, Burton	107-108, 113 (n. 60), 115, 128, 204, 244, 337	Halper, David	238	Hewitt (Kelly, Hewitt & Harte)	181
		Hammerstein, Oscar	121	Hickey, Michael	46
		Hammons, Earle Wooldridge	125, 138, 143, 145, 152, 154, 162-167, 173-175, 177-184	Hickie, Mike	vii
Gillette, King Camp	24			Hicks, Bill	105, 115, *115*, 120
Gitchell, Albert	91			Hicks, Wilson	153
Giuliani, Leo	308			Higgins, David William	53, 56 (n. 54)
Glackens, Louis M.	77-79	Hampft, Burt	317	Hilberman, David	292, 325
Glackens, William	78	Hand, David	129	Hill, William Lair	50
Gleason, Walter	*174, 188, 259, 298*	Handy, Jam	244, 278, 344	Hilliker, Daisy (née Douglas)	339
Gleichman, Philip	70	Hanlon, Dan	81	Hilliker, Douglas "Bill"	236, 252-253, 265, 271, 294-296, 325, 336, 339-340, *339*
Godwin, Frank	91	Harburg, Yip	261		
Goetz, Ben	138	Hard, Anna Augusta Margareta (née Nilsson)	186 (n. 101), 342		
Goldberg, Reuben Lucius	33, 42, 60, 64, 107, 168				
		Harding, La Verne	197	Hilliker, Mary	340
Golden, Thomas	282	Hardy, Oliver	106	Hilliker, Mary D.	340
Golden, William	279	Harkins, "Uncle Jim"	226	Hilliker, Nelson H.	339
Goldman, Frank Lyle	124, 128, 134, 139 (n. 3), 203, 338	Harrington, Pat, Jr.	226	Hirliman, Charles J.	110, 116, 117
		Harrison, Benjamin	34	Hirliman, George	117
Goldman, Les	327 (n. 23)	Harte (Kelly, Hewitt & Harte)	181	Hitchcock, Alfred	285
Goodman, Benny	228	Hathcock, Jerry	318	Hite, Charles J.	73
Goodman, Edwin	323	Hatton, Frank	59	Hitler, Adolf	153, 214, 222
Gordon, Dan	128, 168, 273-275	Hauptmann, Bruno Richard	186 (n. 103)	Hogan, Rich	276
Gordon, George	126, 128, 146, 167-168, *174*, 264, 275, 337, 341			Holladay, Ben	50
		Hauptmann, Manfried	186 (n. 103)	Hollander, Bernard	84, 86 (n. 44)
		Havenner, Franck	32	Hollingworth, Joseph Archie	50
Granata, Gloria	*297*	Hawkins, Emery	275	Holloway, Margaret	3
Grant, John	256	Hawkinson, Warren	vii, *188*	Hope, Bob	131, 283
Gray, Harold	334	Hawxhurst, Henry Ivens	29	Hopkins, Mark	12, 29, 54, 252, 339

Index of Personalities

Hornick, Charles W.	53	
Horvath, Ferdinand Huszti	107, 112 (n. 55), *115*, 120, 126, 133, 264	
Houlton	19	
Howard, William K.	152	
Hubley, Faith	267	
Hubley, John	267, 278-279	
Huemer, Dick	102	
Hughes (Adelaide and Hughes)	344	
Humphries, Mark	91	
Huntington, Collis P.	12	
Hurd, Earl	67-69, 74, 75 (n. 11, 16), 77, 80, 95, 116, 147, 268	
Hurter, Albert	115	
Hurtz, Bill	278, 325	
Huston, John	251	
Hutchins, Robert Maynard	194	
Hutchinson, Walter J.	191	

I

Igoe, Herbert	60
Image, Jean	325
Ireland, Merritte Weber	89
Irving, Jay	334
Ising, Rudy	244, 344
Ivanoff, Alexander N.	134, *174*, *175*, 199
Ivanov-Vano, Ivan	325
Iwerks, Ub	168, 325

J

Jacobson, Louis	125
Jackson, Charles Samuel	51
Jackson, Stonewall	228
James, Earl	*188*
Janocha, Bill	viii
Jenney, Caroline Coleman	1, 5-6, 8 (n. 6)
Jenney, James Nathaniel	9 (n. 17)
Jenney, John	8 (n. 6), 9 (n. 17)
Jenney, Levi	1, 8 (n. 6)
Jenney, William Le Baron	9 (n. 17)
Jenney, William Proctor	1
Joffre, Joseph Jacques Césaire	83
Johnston, JJ.	184
Johnston, Ollie	29
Johnston, W. Ray	117
Jones, Chuck	114, 150, 199, 325
Joplin, Scott	292
Josephson, Marvin	289, 293
Jury, Richard H.	19-20

K

Kahn, William	245
Kalfus, Albert ("Arthur Kay")	*179*, 187-188, 341
Kalloch, Isaac C.	34
Kalloch, Isaac C. (son of)	34
Kanfer, Stefan	269-270
Karloff, Boris	288
Katsushika, Hokusai	299, 340
Katz, Raymond	214, 216
Kaufman, George S.	154
Keane, Francis Marion	50
Keeshan, Bob	226, 289, 301
Keith, Benjamin Franklin	99-100, 110, 121-122
Keller, Father James	323-324, *326*
Keller, Helen	18
Kelley, Ray	viii, 168, *174*, 275
Kelly, Al	226
Kelly, D. Theodore	154-155, 165-166, 179, 181
Kempton, Captain Manasseh	8 (n. 6)
Kessler, Saul	*188*
Keystone Cops	107
Khitruk, Feodor	325
Kimball, Ward	325
King, A. F. A.	89, 96 (n. 20)
King, Dr.	89
King, Ernest Frothingham	96 (n. 20)
King, Jack	115, 126
King, Peggy Roberts	*188*
King, Thomas	29
King, Thomas Starr	32
King (of William), James	29
Kinney, Jack	200
Kirchner, Claude	263
Kirkbride, Charles N.	19-20
Klein, Isidore	114, 126, 130, 203-209, 223, 275, 325, 339, 343
Klein, J. Alan	*174*
Kleine, George B.	63, 98
Kneitel, Ruth	325
Knox, Charles	48
Koffler, Helice	vii
Komar, Helen	vii
Kouzel, Al	281-283, 288, 331
Krantz, Steve	130, 334, 345
Kresse, Bill	vii
Kubert, Joe	260
Kupper, William J.	161
Kuwahara, Denis J.	340
Kuwahara, Julia (née Susuki [Suzuki])	340
Kuwahara, Michel F.	vii, 340
Kuwahara, Robert	271, *285*, 298-301, 340-341, *340*
Kuwahara, Rokuro	340
Kuwahara, Yushu	340

L

La Badie, Florence	71
La Cava, Gregory	102, 125
Laemmle, Carl	70
Lafitte, John	302
Laguionie, Jean Francois	332
Lah, Mike	327 (n. 23)
Lahr, Bert	228
Lampert, Harry	281
Lander, E. J.	100
Lane, Rose Wilder	32
Lantz, Michael	343
Lantz, Walter	94, 102, 115, 129, 144, 148-149, 159, 168, 200, 203, 214, 216, 231, 242, 267-268, 271, 276, 276 (n. 2), 325, 333
Lauder, E. J.	110
Laurel, Stan	106
Laurens, Jean-Paul	48
Laurie, Joe, Jr.	206
Lawrence, Elliot	310
Lawrence, Robert	279, 286, 295
Lawson, Huron Willis	89-90
Lay, W. H.	303
Lazansky, P. J.	184
Leonard, Harry	90, 95
Leppert, Rudolph	48
Leventhal, Jack (Jacob)	79-80, 90
Levitow, Abe	325
Levy, Arnie	vii, *298*
Lewis, Grace	24
Lewis, Jerry	132
Lewis, Sinclair	32
Lincoln, Abraham	32, 51, 83
Lindbergh, Charles	153, 186 (n. 103), 281
Little, Frank Patrick	126, 129, 140 (n. 41), *188*
Littlejohn, Fini	327 (n. 23)
Littlejohn, William	231, 239, 327 (n. 23)
Livingston, Crawford	76 (n. 51)
Lodge, Ralph	*188*
Logan, Jim	vii, 232
Lokey, Hicks	102, 115-116, *115*
London, Jack	44 (n. 12), 51
Lonergan, Lloyd	73

381

Longfellow, Henry Wadsworth	210	
Longhurst, C. D.	84	
Loomis, William H.	48	
Loth, Dottie	*167, 188*	
Lovey, Alan L.	53	
Lowrie, Donald	31	
Lungard	90	
Luria, Emanuel	174, 184	
Lye, Len	325	

M

MacConnell, John "Jack" S.	237, *298*
MacMillan, Norma	306
McAllister, Mary	82
McAtee, Sylvester	32
McAvoy, George	*188*, 236, *262*
McCabe, Thomas J.	110
McCarthy, Joseph	292
McCausland, A. H.	168
McCay, Winsor	61-65, 67-68, 74, 75 (n. 10), 114, 146, 271
McClellan, George B.	46
McCrory, John Robert	107, 113 (n. 56), 128, 147-148
McFadden, Bob	306, 310
McGuire Sisters	306
McKee, Donald	53, 57 (n. 58), 101, 104, 164, *188*, 203-205, 207-208, 339
McKee, Robinson	153, *174*, *188*
McKinley, William	24, 32
McLaren, Norman	326
McLaughlin, Renee	*137*
McManus, John	*115*
McNamara, Thomas	54
McPherson, Mary	vii
Maltese, Michael	150, 157 (n. 74), 276
Maltin, Leonard	168, 269-270
Mandelbaum, E.	70
Manne, Max	146, *193*
Mansfield, Jayne	132
Marcus, Lou	*174*
Martin, Andre	327 (n. 23)
Martin, Dean	132
Martini, Tina	vii
Marx Brothers	107, 131
Marx, Groucho	228, 304
Marx, Harpo	228
Mary, Virgin	288
Mathews, Bill	325

Maurer, Leonard	260
Maurer, Norman	260
May, George	*188*
Mayer, Nicholas	246
Melvin, Mya	296
Mergenthaler, Ottmar	48, 50
Messmer, Otto	107, 325
Meyer, Carl "Mike"	168, *174*, 274
Meyerfeld, Morris, Jr.	100
Milburn, Richard	225
Miner, Loring	91
Mintz, Charles B.	128, 204
Missinne, Jeff	106
Mooney, Tom	31
Moran, Joe	*188*
Morris, W. C.	79
Morrison, Barbara	341
Morrison, Christina Frances (née Heinzer)	150, 237, 341
Morrison, Elizabeth (née DuBois)	341
Morrison, Lynn	341
Morrison, Mildred E.	150
Morrison, Thomas	341
Morrison, Thomas James	149-150, 165-166, 168, *174*, *178*, 188, *188*, *196*, 203-204, 207-208, 210, 213, 236-237, 240, 246, *247*, 264, 280-281, *285*, 287, 289, 298, *299*, 301-302, 310, 321, 339, 341, *341*
Morrison, Thomas John	150, 341
Morschauser (Judge)	174
Morschauser, Joseph, Jr.	174
Moser, Alvina (née Krause)	342
Moser, Frank	64, 74, 77, 95, 101, *103*, 104, *104*, 107, 115, *115*, 119, 121, 124-135, *131*, *133*, 137, *137*, 138, 143-146, 148-149, 151-155, 159, 162-169, 173-184, 204, 320, 341-342, *342*, 343-345
Moser, Isabel Fairclough	184, 186 (n. 101), 342
Moser, John Frank	186 (n. 101), 342
Moser, John Jacob	342
Moser, Marjorie	186 (n. 101), 342
Moye, Doug	249-250, *259*, 283, *298*, *299*, *319*

Mozart, Wolfgang Amadeus	38
Muffati, Steve	204
Mullins, Priscilla	1, 8 (n. 4)
Mundstock, David	83
Munsey, Frank Andrew	58-60
Murdoch, Rosa	28, 32-33
Murdock, J. J.	110
Murakami, Jimmy	327 (n. 23)
Murphy, Harry Daniels	50
Murphy, James Edward, Jr.	51
Muse, Kenneth	275
Mussolini, Benito	214, 251
Myhers, Johnny	300

N

Nash, James A.	221
Natwick, Grim	325
Navoni, Jim	54
Neal-Lunsford, Jeffrey	271, 277 (n. 34)
Neilsen, A. Rutgers	198
Nelson, Barrie	327 (n. 23)
Nesbitt, James	30
Newland, Marv	271
Nicholas, George	275
Nicholson, Norman C.	174, 179
Nickerson, William Emery	24
Nishiura, Shingo	340
Noah	104, 110
Nolan, Bill	69, 109, 115, 128, 148
Noonan, Dan	153, 157 (n. 92)
Noring, Kamma	*188*
Norling, John A.	90
Normand, Mabel	85

O

O'Connor, Kendall	276
O'Farrell, P. A.	47
O'Neil, Barry	71
Okubo, Benji	340
Older, Fremont	30-32
Oriolo, Joe	251
Otero, Manuel	327 (n. 23)
Outcault, Richard F.	60, 77
Owens, Bob	296
Owens, Gary	319
Ozene, D.	251

P

Paduano, Leonard C.	332
Pal, George	199-200, 214, 216, 267, 276 (n. 2)
Palmer, Tom	128
Paratore, John	*298*, *299*
Parmenter, George Edward	29

Index of Personalities

Patigian, Haig 32, 36 (n. 36)
Patin, Ray 130, 282
Pearlman, Julius M. 14
Pearson, Ralph 126, *137*, 153, *174*
Peel, Spence 325
Pendleton, Edna 81
Perrin, Charles F. *188*, 193-195, 237
Perrin, Maurice 15
Pershing, John 32, 83
Peters, Dave *188*
Peterson, Ken 325
Peyser, Abraham 28
Phelps, John *188*
Pickering, Loring 30
Pickering, Loring, Jr. 30
Pickering, Rose Crothers 30
Pickford, Mary 54, 82
Pintoff, Ernest 276 (n. 2), 281, 285-286, 333
Pitt, Brad 334
Pittock, Henry 50
Platt, Kin (née Milton Platkin) 153, 157 (n. 94), 210
Plotnick, Gene 327 (n. 23)
Plympton, Bill 282
Pojar, Bretislav 325
Polansky, Norm *167*, *188*
Polhemus, C. B. 19
Pope, Joanna 4
Popesco-Gopo, Ian 325
Porter, Edwin S. 67
Porter, Robert P. 59
Powers, Patrick Anthony 89, 94, 101
Pratt, W. A. 70
Prendergast, Michael *174*, *188*, *200*
Prestwich, John Alfred 69
Proctor, Susanna 1
Prosek, Joseph Anton 20-21
Puehl, Barbara *297*
Pulitzer, Joseph 60

Q
Questel, Mae 226
Quigley, Bill vii
Quimby, Fred 127, 148, 200, 214, 216
Quirk, Constance *188*, 240

R
Rabbit, Byron 197
Rackham, Arthur 334
Randall, Mike 54
Ranlett, E. L. 125
Rasinski, Alma K. 312, 343
Rasinski, Conrad vii, 258

Rasinski, John Conrad "Connie" 126-127, 130-131, *137*, 153, *174*, *188*, 195, 197, 211, 215, 217, 225, 228, 232, 236-237, 241 (n. 10), 246, *247*, 248-249, *256*, 258, 264-265, 271, *275*, 280, 283, 301, 308-309, 312-313, 321, 342-343, *343*
Rasinski, Joseph vii, 130, 153, *174*, *188*, *233*, 237, 240, 258, *259*, *298*, *299*, 312, 331, 343
Rasinski, Marie Agnes Byrne (née Gleason) 343
Rasinski, Michalina (née Plaga) 342
Rasinski, Walter 342
Rauh, Dick 327 (n. 23)
Raymond, Sid vii, 225, 229
Reagan, Ronald 261
Reddy, George J. 118
Reed, A. D. 77
Reed, Walter (Maj.) 89, *95*
Reeve, Roy M. 88
Regal, Edna May *188*
Rehberg, Eddie 240
Reid, Albert T. 64, 342
Reiner, Carl 297
Reisenweber, John Nicholas 63-64
Reisenweber, John, Jr. 63-65
Renza, C. *188*
Revere, Paul 154, 302
Rigby, Clarence 77, 79
Ripley, Robert LeRoy 54, 57 (n. 66), 60, 63
Risto, Vivie 174
Roberts, Cliff 292
Roberts, George I. 197
Roberts, Margaret (Peggy) 197, 207
Robeson, Paul 261-262, 322
Robinson, Edward G. 228-229, *328*
Robinson, Watson D. 85
Rock, Mary 6
Rock, Robert *188*
Rockefeller, John D. 6, 8
Rockwell, Norman 130, 251, 343
Rogalli, Paul 134
Rogers, Anna [Hannah] 3
Rogers, Henry Huddleston 6, 8
Rogers, Will 103
Rollinson 13
Roosevelt, Eleanor 261

Roosevelt, Franklin 232
Roosevelt, Theodore 53, 67, 77, 83
Rosenbaum, Robert 331
Ross, Robert 88
Rossburg, Ralph *298*, *299*
Rossini, Giachino Antonio 136
Roth, Herb 33, 60, 169
Roth, Tom 327 (n. 23)
Rubens, Peter Paul 83
Ruiz, Jose Maria "Pepe" 236-238, 240
Russell, Frederick 89
Russell, William 71

S
Sacks, Carl O. *174*
Sancier, Ralph 220, 331
Sangretti, S. J. 85
Santry, Philip 153, *174*
Sarka, Charles 126, *137*
Sauter (Sauter-Finnegan Orchestra) 309
Sawin, Ezekiel R. 4, 9 (n. 14)
Scagnelli, Irene vii
Scheib, Adelaide L. (née Grahlfs) 344
Scheib, Augusta (née Lichtenberger) 343
Scheib, Barbara Anna 344
Scheib, Philip, Sr. 343
Scheib, Philip A. *131*, 132, *133*, 138, 143-144, 146, 155, 160, 164, 167, 169, *174*, 181, *188*, *195*, *197*, 199, 232, *250*, 253, 262, 265, 269, 272-273, *274*, 276, 288, 294, 309, 343-344, *343*
Schenck, Joe 150
Schickel, Richard 256
Schiff, Harry 154
Schlaifer, L. J. 81
Schlesinger, Leon 127, 131, 144, 148-150, 159, 168, 189, 200, 231
Schmitz, Eugene 41, 44 (n. 32)
Schudde, Frank *174*, *188*, 194, 236-237, 245, *253*, 308
Schudde, Lester *182*, *188*, 237
Schwalberg, A. W. 262
Schwartz (Schwartz & Gross) 154
Schwartz, Zack 292
Schwarz, William T. 88

383

TERRYTOONS: The Story of Paul Terry and His Classic Cartoon Factory

Schwin, Newt	278-280	
Scott, Harvey Winfield	50	
Scott, Mabel Julienne	82	
Scott, Rev. Dr.	14	
Scott, W. W.	103	
Sculia	126	
Searl, Leon	115	
Seeger, Hal	333, 345	
Selzer, Edward	214, 216	
Selznick, David	75 (n. 34)	
Selznick, Lewis J.	70-71, 75 (n. 34), 268	
Selznick, Myron	75 (n. 34)	
Seuss (Dr.)	129	
Shacter, Samuel A.	174-176, 178-181, 184	
Shakespeare, William	18, 22	
Shallenberger, Wilbert	76 (n. 51)	
Shapiro, Alan	296	
Shaw, Artie	228	
Sheehan (Dr.)	129	
Sherman, Frank	115, *115*, 119-120, 122 (n. 7), 126	
Shields, Hugh M. "Jerry"	74, 84-85, 95, 101, 104, *115*, *117*, 118-119, 126, *137*, *174*	
Shoham, Aviv	221	
Shortridge, Samuel	14	
Shute, Bessie	15	
Sickles, Noel Douglas	153-154	
Siegel, A. E.	105	
Siegelstein, Fred	197	
Silver, Charles	vii	
Silverman, Fred	314, 319	
Silverman, Larry	109, 126, 128, *188*, 193-194, 308	
Simonton, James W.	29-30	
Simpson, Ernest S.	40-41, 53	
Simpson, Russell	82	
Skelton, Red	131	
Skinner, George A.	125	
Skirball, Jack H.	162, 178, 181	
Skouras, Spyros P.	286	
Slovick, Lyle	vii	
Smith, Alice	31	
Smith, Buffalo Bob	226	
Smith, Dave	vii	
Smith, Ed	327 (n. 23)	
Smith, Fletcher	256	
Smith, Lewis E.	108	
Smith, Orilla	71	
Smith, Theobald	89	
Snow, Marguerite	71	
Soccodato, Paul	vii	
Soglow, Otto	244	
Solomon, Barbara	vii	
Sommer, Paul	126, 129-130, *174*	
Sorrell, Herbert	231, 234	
Sparks, Ned	225	
Spreckels, John D.	53, 57 (n. 55)	
Stahl, Al	vii, *188*, 203-205, 207-208, 217-220, 339	
Stalin, Joseph	261	
Stalling, Carl	272	
Stallings, George Vernon	102, 107-108, 113 (n. 58), 203, 244	
Stanfield, Bob	108	
Stanford, Jane Lathorp	35	
Stanford, Leland	12, 35	
Stein, Milton	*167*, *188*	
Stephenson, Ralph	269	
Stevens, Elizabeth	4	
Stevens, Thomas	18	
Stevens, W. M.	252	
Stockton (Mr.)	143	
Stoddard, Francis H.	5	
Storer, Doug	57 (n. 66)	
Strudler, Marty	296	
Stuart, Edward P.	336	
Sullivan (Gilbert & Sullivan)	215	
Sullivan, Anne	18	
Sullivan, Pat	95, 107, 116, 129, 271, 337	
Sunday, Billy	83	
Sussman, William	161-162, 164	
Sutro (Brothers & Company)	150, 341	
Swift, Allen	283-284	
T		
Taft, William H.	83	
Takamoto, Iwao	318	
Taracka, Mary	vii	
Taras, Marty	*188*, 331	
Tarricone, Terry (Angelo)	vii, *298*	
Tashlin, Frank	131-132	
Taylor, Frederick Winslow	67	
Taylor, Robert W.	14	
Teasdale (Dr.)	129	
Temeg, Anna	105	
Tendlar, Dave	*298*, *299*, 301	
Terry, Atkin Adams	6, 9 (n. 18)	
Terry, Benjamin	3-4	
Terry, Benjamin (II)	3-4	
Terry, Benjamin (III)	4	
Terry, Bernard Jenney	9 (n. 18)	
Terry, Bessie Spratt	17 (n. 42)	
Terry, Caroline Dell	14-15, 20, *21*, *25*, 48
Terry, Dinah	4
Terry, Elisa (Elisha) P.	4
Terry, Franklin	9 (n. 18)
Terry, Horatio Proctor	9 (n. 18), 15
Terry, Horatio Proctor (II)	14
Terry, Isaiah Franklin	4-6, 9 (n. 13)
Terry, John	3
Terry, John Coleman (I)	9 (n. 18), 15
Terry, John Coleman (II)	15, 19-20, *21*, *25*, 25, 28-29, 33, 43, 44 (n. 40, 41), 45-49, *49*, 53-54, 65, 74, 79, 84-85, 94-95, 99, 101, 108-110, 114, 115, 122 (n. 2), 125-126, 128, 153-154, 157 (n. 96)
Terry, Joseph Tripp	6, 8, 9 (n. 18), *10*, 10-15, 17 (n. 23), *20*, *21*, 19-22, 24-25, *25*, 38-39, 48, 51-52, *68*, 87, 110
Terry, Joseph Tripp, Jr.	14-15, 19-20, *21*, 25
Terry, Loretta Hitchcock	6, 9 (n. 18)
Terry, Lt. Thomas	3
Terry, Minnie (née Perrin)	*11*, 14-15, 19-22
Terry, Olga Bernice	15, *21*, *25*, 25, 39-40, 48, 52, *68*
Terry, Patricia Ann	vii, 117, *149*, 222, *235*, 259, 264, 324, 327-330
Terry, Phenius	4
Terry, Robert	4
Terry, Sarah	4
Terry, Seth	4
Terry, Sir Thomas	3, 9 (n. 11)
Terry, Susan Burt	9 (n. 18)
Terry, Thomas	3
Thanhouser, Edwin	71, 73-74, 76 (n. 51, 57)
Theodemir (Dietrich von Bern)	8 (n. 7)
Theodoric I	8 (n. 7)
Theodoric the Great	8 (n. 7)
Thomas, Frank	29
Thomas, Olive	75 (n. 34)
Thompson, Major	110
Thompson, Thomas F.	181
Thorndike, Willis H.	48
Thornton, Pamela	vii
Thorson, Charles	199
Three Stooges	107

Index of Personalities

Tiller, Ralph 126
Timmens, Jim 309-310, 344
Tinée, Mae 105, 112 (n. 49)
Trevor, Claire viii, 149, 210
Trowbridge, John William 48, 55 (n. 24)
Trudeau, Pierre 108
Truesdale, Philemon Edwards 89-90
Truex, Ernest 100
Tucker, Sophie 64
Tuthill, F. 30
Tyer, James ix, *115*, 204, 240, 244-245, *252*, 264, 271, 286, 290, 292, 296, 308, *314*, 344-345, *344*
Tyer, James, Jr. 345
Tyer, John Francis 344
Tyer, Mary E. (née Navin) 344
Tyer, Mary Esther (née Lee) 345
Tyer, Mary Louise 345
Tyer, Peggy 345
Tytla, Vladimir "Bill" ix, viii, *70*, 109, 114-115, *115*, 119, 126, 131, 133, *137*, 144, 204, *205*, *209*, 210-211, 215, 217, 223, 232, 264-265, 271, 292, 343
Twain, Mark 22, 51, 53

U

Ubinas, Dave vii, 296, 331

V

Van Beuren, Amede 100-102, 106, 110, 115, *118*, 120-122, 124, 126, 127, 130-131, 148-149, 153, 159, 167-169, 198, 204, 214, 244, 335, 337, 338, 342
Van Brunt, Oscar *115*, 116
Van der Beek, Stan 327 (n. 23)
Van Vleck, Maria 28, 32-33
Vanderbilt, Cornelius 10
Veiller, Bayard 32
Verdi, Giuseppe 18
Verne, Jules 81
Vernick, Edith 327 (n. 23)
Victoria, Queen 18
Vincent, Frank 110
Vinciguerra, Carlo 168, *188*, 217, 232,
240, 242, 265, 271, *275*, 296
Vita, John *176*, *188*, 229, 250-252, 265, 271, 294, 296, 331, 336
von Richthofen, Baron 169
Von Tucher, Marianne *297*
Vogel, Nathan 176-177, 181
Vogel, Sandy vii
Vukotic, Dusan 325

W

Wagner, Richard 38
Waldeyer, Ted *115*, 116, *137*
Wallach, Charles W. 88
Wallis, James Frank 88
Wallsworth, Warren W. 48
Walsh (Cunningham & Walsh) 293
Walsh, Frank 234-235
Walters, Henry (Sen.) 110
Walters, J. Henry 100
Ward, Dan *174*, *188*, 264-265
Wardman, Ervin 60
Waring, Fred 213
Warner, Charles Dudley 22
Washington, George 302
Wayburn, Ned 64
Webster, H.T. 33
Weichsel, Florence 324
Weinstein, Irving 322
Weiss brothers 117
Weiss, Joseph 345
Weiss, Laddie 346
Weiss, Lena (née Kaplan) 345
Weiss, Rita (née Romaner) 346
Weiss, William vii, 136-138, 146, 152, 155, 164-167, 173-177, *174*, 179-184, *188*, 191, 205, 222, 235, *246*, 263-264, 279-280, 285-286, 288, 290-292, 294-295, 301, 309, 312, 314, 318-319, 329, 345-346, *345*
Welles, Orson 261
Werschkul, Milton Waters 50-51
Westover, Russell Channing 32-33, 36 (n. 38), 84
Whipp, James V. *188*
White, Gordon Stowe 198, 202 (n. 60)
White, Joseph L. 199
White, Lloyd *188*
White, Volney *188*, 189-190
Whitney, John 286, 327 (n. 23)
Whittier, Gordon *188*, 238
Williams, George *115*
Williams, Henry B. 13
Williams, Irma 161
Williams, Richard 148
Williamson (Williamson Submarine Film Corporation) 81
Williamson, Hugh S. 175-178, 181, 184
Wilson, Al 134
Wilson, Lionel 290, 297-298, 316
Wilson, Woodrow 83, 87
Winchell, Walter 228
Winkler, George 128
Winner, Septimus 225
Winters, Jonathan 297
Wobber, Herman 161
Wolpe, Stefan 309
Wolf (Wolf & Berger) 345
Wolf, Fred 325
Wood, Benjamin 28
Wood, Gene 296, 301
Wood, Meyer 28
Wood, Samuel N. 28
Woolworth, Frank W. ix, 168
Worcester, Retta Scott 197
Wormser, I. Maurice 184
Wyeth, N. C. 334
Wynn, Ed 187, 290

Y

Yardley, Ralph Oswald 32-33, 36 (n. 37), 53-54
Yates, Herbert 117
Young, Clara Kimball 75 (n. 34), 76 (n. 51)
Young, Cyrus 126, 128-129, 244
Young, John Philip 35
Young, Whitney M., Jr. 332
Yung, Tom Kim 194

Z

Zaffo, George *188*, 193, 250-252, 265, 271, 294, 336
Zaffo, Mary vii, *188*, 193
Zaffo, Tom vii
Zago, John vii, 251, 295-296, 301, 316, 340
Zander, Jack vii, 168, 273-275, 282
Zeman, Karel 325
Zuro, Josiah 121

385

Index of Animated Film Production Titles and Characters

This index is a complete alphabetical list of all animated features, shorts and series, along with character names, referenced in the Acknowledgements, Foreword, Chapters, and Appendix 1. Production titles are in *italics*. The series associated with the productions are in square brackets. Further descriptors are in round brackets. Live-action features are included in the index and are referenced in round brackets. Page references to images are in *italics*.

A

Abominable Mountaineers (1968) [Sad Cat]	312
Adventure by the Sea (1964) [Luno]	306
Adventures of Lariat Sam, The (TV series)	290, 296, 300-301, 333, 340
Adventures of Oky Doky (TV series)	226, 333
Aesop's Fable: Foiling the Fox (1950) [Terry-Toon]	339
Aesop's Film Fables (theatrical cartoon series)	ix, 4, 98-111, *99*, 114-122, *119*, 124, 130, 214-215, 263, 325, 337-339
Aesop's Sound Fables (theatrical cartoon series)	102, 120-121, 337, 338
African Jungle Hunt (1957) [Phony Baloney]	258
Aladdin's Lamp (1943) [Gandy. Goose]	189
Aladdin's Lamp (1947) [Mighty Mouse]	229
Ali Baba Bunny (1957) [Merrie Melodies]	290
All Out For "V" (1942) [Terry-Toon]	199, 337
All Teed Off (1968) [Sad Cat]	312
All This and Rabbit Stew (1950) [Dingbat]	248
Amateur Night on the Ark (1923) [Aesop's Film Fables]	104, 110
American Pop (1981)	334
And to Think That I Saw It on Mulberry Street (1944) [Puppetoon]	214
Andy Panda	216
Animal Farm (1954)	325
Animated Grouch Chaser (theatrical cartoon series)	342
Another Day, Another Doormat (1959) [John Doormat]	283
Another Fallen Idol (1915) [Pathé News]	78
Aquarium (1956)	286
Arctic Rivals (1954) [Willie the Walrus]	258
Artist's Dream, The (aka *The Dachshund and the Sausage*) (1913)	67
Astronut	226, 297, 300, 304-306, 317, 333, 335, 340
Astronut (series of TV and theatrical cartoons)	304-306, 317
Astronut (1962) [Deputy Dawg]	304
At the Circus (1944) [Mighty Mouse]	*12*, 211
Audioscopics (series)	90

B

Babes in the Woods (1932) [Silly Symphonies]	338
Baby Huey	250
Baby Weems	255
Bad Bandit, The (1923) [Aesop's Film Fables]	105
Bad Bill Bunion	217, 228
Bad Luck Blackie (1949)	276
Baffling Bunnies (1956) [The Terry Bears]	249
Ball Park, The (aka *Socking the Apple*, 1929) [Aesop's Film Fables]	104-105, 115
Bambi (1941)	157 (n. 92), 222, 272
Banana Binge (1961) [Sidney the Elephant]	291
Banker's Daughter, The (1933) [Fanny Zilch/Oil Can Harry]	151
Barker Bill	257, *261*, 263, 340-341
Barker Bill's Cartoon Show (TV series)	257, 263
Barney Google	204
Barnyard Actor (1955) [Gandy Goose]	190
Barnyard Blackout (1943) [Gandy Goose]	214
Barnyard WAAC (1942) [Terry-Toon]	206, 214
Barrier, The (1917) (live-action)	82
Batfink (TV series)	345
Battle of San Pietro, The (1945) (live-action)	251
Battling Duet, A (1928) [Aesop's Film Fables]	105
Beanstalk Jack (1946) [Terry-Toon]	206
Beany and Cecil (TV series)	*326*
Beat the Clock (TV series)	338
Beauty on the Beach (1950) [Mighty Mouse]	253
Beauty Shop, The (1950) [Dinky Duck]	196, 341
Becky Sharp (1935) (live-action)	160
Beefy	291-292
Better Late Than Never (1950) [Victor the Volunteer]	248
Betty Boop	107, 203, 269, 302, 337
Big Build-Up, The (1942) [Puddy the Pup]	170
Big Freeze	316
Big Game Fishing (1968) [Sad Cat]	312
Big Reward, The (1927) [Aesop's Film Fables]	104, 114
Big Top, The (1938) [Puddy the Pup]	170
Big-Hearted Fish, The (1926) [Aesop's Film Fables]	104

Index of Animated Film Production Titles and Characters

Billy Bear	297, 313
Billy Bounce	345
Billy Goat's Whiskers, The (1937) [Terry-Toon]	204, 338
Billy Mouse's Akwakade (1940) [Terry-Toon]	198
Blind Date (1954) [Heckle and Jeckle]	228
Blitz Wolf (1942)	200
Blonde Captive, The (1931) (live-action)	121
Blue Plate Symphony (1954) [Heckle and Jeckle]	227, 258
Blues (1931) [Terry-Toon]	131, 133-134
Blues Pattern (1956)	286
Bo Peep	210, 215
Bobby Bumps	77, 80, 95
Bobby Bumps (theatrical cartoon series)	77, 80, 95
Bone of Contention (1919) [Paramount Magazine [Paramount Picture Magazine]]	95
Bone Ranger, The (1957) [Sniffer]	291-292
Boob Weekly, The (theatrical cartoon series)	107
Boomtown (1985)	282
Brave Little Tailor (1938) [Mickey Mouse]	270
Bringing Up Father (theatrical cartoon series)	342
Brother from Outer Space (1964) [Astronut]	304
Brownie Bear	337
Buck Fever (1926) [Aesop's Film Fables]	114
Bud and Susie (theatrical cartoon series)	95, 342
Bugs Beetle and His Orchestra (1938) [Terry-Toon]	204
Bugs Bunny	199, 203, 225, 290
Building Friends for Business (1949)	278
Bulldozing the Bull (1951) [Heckle and Jeckle]	226, 254
Bullfight, The (1935) [Terry-Toon]	170
Bully for Bugs (1953) [Looney Tunes]	150
Bum Steer, A (1957) [Beefy]	291, 297
By the Sea (1931) [Terry-Toon]	131, 343

C

Camp Clobber (1958) [Clint Clobber]	284
Candlebert	288
Captain and the Kids	199, 340
Captain and the Kids (theatrical cartoon series)	199, 340
Captain Kangaroo (TV series)	289-290, 296, 301, 340
Captain Kidney Bean	289, 297
Casper	196, 250, 302
Cat Alarm (1961) [Mighty Mouse]	294, 302
Cat Concerto, The (1947) [Tom and Jerry]	217
Cat Happy (1950) [Little Roquefort]	247
Cat Trouble (1947) [Heckle and Jeckle]	226, 229
Cat's Revenge (1954) [Little Roquefort]	247
Cat's Tale, The (1951)	253
Catnip Gang	243, 253
Catnip Gang, The (1949) [Mighty Mouse]	243
Caviar (1930) [Terry-Toon]	133
Champion Chump (1966) [Martian Moochers]	317
Champion of Justice, The (1944) [Mighty Mouse]	210
Character as Revealed by the Ear (1917) [Terry Human Interest Reels]	84
Character as Revealed by the Eye (1917) [Terry Human Interest Reels]	83
Character as Revealed by the Mouth (1917) [Terry Human Interest Reels]	84
Character as Revealed by the Nose (1917) [Terry Human Interest Reels]	83
Charlie Cartoons (theatrical cartoon series)	85, 101
Charlie in Carmen (aka *Charlie: A Moving Cartoon*) (1916) [Charlie Cartoons]	85
Charlie the Tuna	316
Charlton	318
Chef Donald (1941) [Donald Duck]	216
Chesty	227
Chicken Man	316
Chico Pico	258
Chip 'n' Dale	248
Cinderella (1950)	254
Cinderfella (1960)	132
Cinema Luke (theatrical cartoon series)	98
City Slicker (1952) [Little Roquefort]	247
Clair de lune espagnol [*Spanish Moonlight*, aka *The Man in the Moon* (US), aka *The Moon-Struck Matador* (UK)] (1909)	61
Clancy (bulldog)	229, 258
Clancy (Chief of the Mouse Protection Bureau)	253
Clint Clobber	282-284, 297, *328*
Clint Clobber's Cat (1957) [Clint Clobber]	284
Cloak and Stagger (1956) [Good Deed Daly]	258-259
Clobber's Ballet Ache (1959) [Clint Clobber]	284
Clowning (1931) [Terry-Toon]	131
Coal Black and de Sebben Dwarfs (1943) [Merrie Melodies]	276
Cold Romance, A (1949) [Mighty Mouse]	242
Colonel Heeza Liar	68, 77, 79-80, 108, 258
Colonel Heeza Liar (theatrical cartoon series)	68, 77, 79-80, 108
Colonel Heeza Liar's African Hunt [Colonel Heeza Liar] (1914)	68
Colonel Pureheart	242-243
Color Classics (theatrical cartoon series)	336
Color Rhapsody (theatrical cartoon series)	112 (n. 55), 159, 203-204, 216
Cool and the Crazy (1994) (live-action)	334
Cool World (1992) (live-action and animated)	334
Come Take a Trip on My Airship (1924) [Song Car-Tune]	120
Comic Book Land (1949) [Gandy Goose]	189, 253, 339
Commonwealth Cartoon Package (TV series)	266 (n. 15)
Confessions of a Stardreamer (1978)	332
Conrad	318
Coonskin (1975)	334
Cotton Club, The (1984) (live-action)	333
Cotton Pickin' Picnic (1962) [Deputy Dawg]	303
Country Cousin, The (1936) [Silly Symphonies]	199
Courtship of Miss Vote, The (1916) [Pathé News]	79

387

Covered Wagon, The (1923) (live-action)	121
Cowardly Watchdog, The (1966) [Martian Moochers]	317
Crabby Appleton	289, 297
Crackpot King, The (1946) [Mighty Mouse]	228
Critic, The (1963)	286
Crossing the Delaware (1961) [Hector Heathcote]	302
Crusader Rabbit	190, 255, 335
Crusader Rabbit (television cartoon series)	190, 255, 335
Crying Wolf, The (1947) [Mighty Mouse]	212, 229
Cubby Bear	102, 214, 337-338
Cubby Bear (theatrical cartoon series)	102, 214, 337-338
Cuckoo Man	297, *310*, 314-316
Cutting a Melon (1927) [Aesop's Film Fables]	104

D

Daffy Duck	187, 203
Dancing Mice (aka *Club Sandwich*) [Terry-Toon] (1931)	130-131
Daniel Boone, Jr. (1960) [Hector Heathcote]	302
Darn Barn (1965) [Possible Possum]	313
Day to Live, A (1931) [Terry-Toon]	131
Dayton Allen Show (TV series)	333
Dead End Cats (1947) [Mighty Mouse]	229
Demon Cat	*205*
Dennis the Dogfish	258
Depth Study (1957)	292, 295
Deputy Dawg	226, *296*, 297, 300, 302-304, 306, 309, 313, 319-320, 332-334, 340
Deputy Dawg Show, The (TV series)	*296*, 297, 303-304, 313
Der Fuehrer's Face (1943) [Donald Duck]	200, 216
Desperate Dumkopf	258
Diamond Jill	318
Diaper Man	*310*, 314-316
Died in the Wool (1927) [Aesop's Film Fables]	104
Dimwit	*3*, *32*, *73*, 225, 227, 229, 253-254, 258
Dingbat	*2*, 248
Dingbat Land (1949) [Gandy Goose]	248
Dinky Duck	2, 195-198, 203, 259-260, 287-288, 291, 302, *328*, *330*
Dinner Time (1928) [Aesop's Film Fables]	120-121
Disorderly Orderly, The (1964) (live-action)	132
Doc Owl	215
Doctor Soakem (1919) [Joys and Glooms]	94
Dog and the Bone, The (1937) [Puddy the Pup]	170, 187, 203, 341
Dog, Cat and Canary (1945) [Color Rhapsody]	214
Doing Their Bit (1942) [Nancy]	200
Doll Festival (1961) [Hashimoto Mouse]	299-300
Donald Duck	200, 203-204, 216
Donald's Crime (1945) [Donald Duck]	216
Donkey Otie	307
Don't Spill the Beans (1965) [Sad Cat]	311
Doomsday (1938) [Gandy Goose]	188
Down on the Phoney Farm (1915) [Paul Terry Cartoons] [Farmer Al Falfa]	74, 76 (n. 64), 80
Down With Cats (1943) [Super Mouse]	209
Dr. Ha-Ha	*309*, 318
Dr. Ha-Ha (1966) [James Hound]	318
Dr. No (1962) (live-action)	317
Dress Reversal (1965) [Sad Cat]	311
Drifter	316
Driven to Extraction (1963) [Sidney the Elephant]	291
Drum Roll (1961) [Hector Heathcote]	302
Duck Amuck (1953) [Merrie Melodies]	276
Duck Dodgers in the 24 1/2th Century (1953) [Merrie Melodies]	276
Duckwood	307
Dumbo (1941)	157 (n. 92); 210, 248, 272, 324
Dustcap Doormat (1958) [John Doormat]	283

E

Easy Winners, The (TV series)	292
Edward G. Robinson Cat	229, *329*
Einstein Theory of Relativity, The (1923)	110
El Toro Pantso	254
Electronic Mousetrap, The (1946) [Mighty Mouse]	228
Elephant Mouse, The (1951) [Half Pint]	248
Eliza on the Ice (1944) [Mighty Mouse]	210
Elmer Elephant (1936) [Silly Symphonies]	338
Enchanted Drawing, The (1900)	60
English Channel Swim, The (1925) [Aesop's Film Fables]	105
Enlarger	316
Explorer, The (1931) [Terry-Toon]	130

F

Famous Ride, The (1959) [Hector Heathcote]	302
Fancy Plants (1967) [James Hound]	318
Fanny in the Lion's Den (1933) [Fanny Zilch/Oil Can Harry]	151
Fanny's Wedding Day (1933) [Fanny Zilch/Strongheart]	151
Fanny Zilch	150-151
Fantasia (1940)	128, 191, 210, 222
Fantasmagorie (1908)	61
Farm Hands, The (1926) [Aesop's Film Fables]	114
Farmer Al Falfa	5, 23, 53, 74, 77, 79-80, 82, 95, 99, *101*, 102, 115, *127*, 131, 169-170, 206, 213-214, 225, 229, 256-257, 263, 338, 342
Farmer Al Falfa and His Terrytoon Pals (1956) (TV series)	263
Farmer Al Falfa's Blind Pig (1916) [Paramount-Bray Cartoons]	80

Index of Animated Film Production Titles and Characters

Farmer Al Falfa's Catastrophe (1916) [Paramount-Bray Cartoons] — 80
Farmer Al Falfa's Prize Package (1936) [Farmer Al Falfa/Kiko the Kangaroo] — 169
Farmer Al Falfa's 20th Anniversary (1936) [Farmer Al Falfa] — 206
Farmer Gray — 257
Featherweight Champ (1953) [Dinky Duck] — 196
Felix the Cat — 95, 107, 129, 251, 296, 337, 345
Fenimore — 310-312, *311*
Fight on for Old (1956) — 286
Fight to the Finish, A (1947) [Mighty Mouse] — 61, 230, *245*
Fire and Ice (1983) — 334
Fireman's Bride, The (1931) [Terry-Toon] — 131
First Fast Mail, The (1961) [Hector Heathcote] — 302
First Flight Up (1962) [Hector Heathcote] — 302
Fish Fry (1944) [Andy Panda] — 214
Fishing by the Sea (1947) [Heckle and Jeckle] — 229
Flamboyant Arms (1959) [Clint Clobber] — 284
Flat Foot Fledgling (1952) [Dinky Duck] — 196
Flebus — 269, 286, 290, *328*
Flebus (1957) — 269, 286
Flint Locke — 297
Flintstones, The (TV series) — 296
Flip the Frog — 89
Flop Secret (1952) [Little Roquefort] — 247
Flowers and Trees (1932) [Silly Symphonies] — 159
Flying South (1947) [Heckle and Jeckle] — 229
Foiled Again (1935) [Fanny Zilch/Oil Can Harry/Strongheart] — 151
Foofle — 282, 284
Foofle's Picnic (1959) [Foofle] — 284
Foofle's Train Ride (1959) [Foofle] — 284
For Scent-imental Reasons (1949) [Looney Tunes] — 150
Fox and Crow — 203, 278
Fox and Crow (theatrical cartoon series) — 278
Fox and the Crow (1921) [Aesop's Film Fables] — 99
Fox and the Grapes, The (1941) [Fox and Crow] — 203
Fox Hunt, The (1927) [Aesop's Film Fables] — 115
Frame-Up, The (1938) [Gandy Goose] — 188
Frankenstein's Cat (1942) [Super Mouse] — 208
Free Enterprise (1948) [Heckle and Jeckle] — 225, 228, 243
Freight Fright (1965) [Possible Possum] — 313
Friday the 13th (1953) [Little Roquefort] — 247
Fried Chicken (1930) [Terry-Toon] — 133
Fritz the Cat (1972) — 334, 345
Frog — 316
Frog and the Princess, The (1944) [Gandy Goose] — 189
From Russia With Love (1963) (live-action) — 317
Fun and Fancy Free (1947) — 272
Fun from the Press (theatrical cartoon series) — 108

G

G. I. Joe — 299, 305
G Man Jitters (1939) [Gandy Goose] — 7
Gadmouse — 310-312, *311*
Gadmouse, the Apprentice Good Fairy (1965) [Sad Cat] — 310-311, 334
Gag Buster (1957) [Spoofy] — 291-292
Gandy Goose — ix, *2, 7, 14, 31*, 187-190, 198, 203-204, 214, 229, 242, 248, 253, 256, 259-260, 304, 335, 338-339, 341
Gandy Goose in the Outpost (1942) [Gandy Goose] — 190
Gandy the Goose (aka *The Gandy Goose*, 1938) [Gandy Goose] — 187, 204, 339
Gaston Go Home (1958) [Gaston Le Crayon] — 285
Gaston is Here (1957) [Gaston Le Crayon] — 285
Gaston Le Crayon — 282, 284-285, 297, *328*
Gaston's Baby (1957) [Gaston Le Crayon] — 285
Gaston's Easel Life (1958) [Gaston Le Crayon] — 285
Gaston's Mama Lisa (1959) [Gaston Le Crayon] — 285
Gay Purr-ee (1962) — 190
Geisha Boy, The (1958) (live-action) — 132
Gentleman's Gentleman, A (1941) — 275
Gerald McBoing Boing Show, The (TV series) — 286
Gertie the Dinosaur — 63-65, 67, 74, 114, 271
Gertie the Dinosaur (1914) — 63-65, 67, 74, 114, 271
Get Smart (TV series) — 317
Ghost Monster — 316
Girl Can't Help It, The (1956) (live-action) — 131-132
Git That Guitar (1965) [Possible Possum] — 313
Glass Slipper, The (1938) [Terry-Toon] — 206
Go West Big Boy (1931) [Terry-Toon] — 131
Goggle the Zok Man — 284
Going Ape (c. 1965) [Astronut] — 306
Gold Dust Bandit, The (1964) [Luno] — 306
Golden Hen, The (1946) [Gandy Goose] — 190
Golden Spoon Mary (1917) [Terry Feature Burlesques] — 82
Goldfinger (1964) (live-action) — 317
Goldwyn-Bray Comic (theatrical cartoon series) — 102, 108, 338
Goldwyn-Bray Pictographs (theatrical cartoon series) — 107-108
Golf Nuts (1930) [Terry-Toon] — 128
Good Deed Daly — 258-259
Good Deed Daly (theatrical cartoon series) — 258-259
Good Deed Daly (1955) [Good Deed Daly] — 258
Good Mousekeeping (1952) [Little Roquefort] — 247
Goodbye, My Lady Love (1924) [Song Car-Tune] — 120
Goofy — 128, 203-204
Goony Golfers (1948) [Heckle and Jeckle] — 244
Goose Flies High, The (1938) [Gandy Goose] — 188, 204, 339
Goose That Laid the Golden Egg, The (1921) [Aesop's Film Fables] — 101, 105

389

TERRYTOONS: The Story of Paul Terry and His Classic Cartoon Factory

Grand Prix Winner (1968) [Sad Cat]	312
Grandma's House (1929) [Aesop's Film Fables]	118
Great Mouse Detective (1986)	148
Great Piggy Bank Robbery, The (1946) [Looney Tunes]	276
Green Line, The (1944) [Mighty Mouse]	205, 211, *265*
Greenland's Icy Mountains (1916) [Paramount-Bray Cartoons]	78
Gulliver's Travels (1939)	189, 199, 302
Gypsy Code, The (1930) (live-action)	134
Gypsy Fiddler (1933) [Terry-Toon]	151, 216

H

Half Pint	248
Hair Cut-Ups (1953) [Heckle and Jeckle]	228
Hanako	299, *305*
Hank the Rooster	214
Hansel and Gretel (1952) [Mighty Mouse]	245
Happy Go Lucky (1947) [Heckle and Jeckle]	229
Happy Holland (1952) [Mighty Mouse]	257
Happy Hooligan	102, 114, 125, 130, 338, 342
Happy Hooligan (theatrical cartoon series)	102, 114, 125, 130, 338, 342
Hashimoto	298-300, 302, *305*, 306, 335, 340
Hashimoto-San (1959) [Hashimoto Mouse]	298-299
Haunted Cat, The (1951) [Little Roquefort]	246
Haunted Hotel, The (1907) (live-action animated)	60-61
Hawaiian Pineapples (1930) [Terry-Toon]	128, 133
He Dood It Again (1943) [Super Mouse]	208-209
Heat's Off, The (1967) [James Hound]	318
Heavy Traffic (1973)	334
Heckle and Jeckle	ix, *2, 3, 32, 72, 73*, 206, 213, 225-229, *230*, 242-244, 253-254, 256-260, 264, 272-273, 276, 292, 294, 296-297, 304, *315, 328, 330*, 332-333
Hector Heathcote	297, 300-302, *300*, 335, 340
Hector Heathcote Show, The (TV series)	297, *300*, 302
Hectormobile, The (1973) [Hector Heathcote]	302
He-Man Seaman (1962) [Hector Heathcote]	302
Henry the Rooster	214
Hep Cat, The (1946) [Mighty Mouse]	228
Here's to Good Old Jail (1938) [Terry-Toon]	338
Hero Wins, The (1925) [Aesop's Film Fables]	114
Hey Good Lookin' (1982)	334
Hide and Go Sidney (1960) [Sidney the Elephant]	291
High Stakes (1927) [Aesop's Film Fables]	105
Hiroshi	299
His Trial (1917) [Terry Feature Burlesques]	82
Hitch Hikers, The (1947) [Heckle and Jeckle]	228-229
Hobo Hassle (1974) [Possible Possum]	313
Hodge Podge (theatrical cartoon series)	109
Hokey Home Movies (1972) [Astronut]	305-306
Holiday Land (1934) [Color Rhapsody]	159
Holland Days (1933) [Terry-Toon]	151-152
Hollywood or Bust (1956) (live-action)	132
Home Guard, The (1941) [Gandy Goose]	190, 214
Honeymoon Hotel (1934) [Merrie Melodies]	159
Honorable Cat Story (1961) [Hashimoto Mouse]	299
Horses, Horses, Horses (1927) [Aesop's Film Fables]	120
Hot Turkey (1930) [Terry-Toon]	128
House Busters (1952) [Heckle and Jeckle]	227
House of Hashimoto (1960) [Hashimoto Mouse]	299
Housewife Herman (1938) [Terry-Toon]	339
How A Mosquito Operates (aka *The Story of a Mosquito*) (1912)	63
How to Keep Cool (1953) [Dimwit]	258
How to Play Football (1944) [Goofy]	214
How to Relax (1954) [Dimwit]	258
Howdy Doody and His Magic Hat (1952)	278
Howdy Doody Show, The (live-action TV series)	226, 284, 333
Hula Hula Land (1949) [Heckle and Jeckle]	225
Humorous Phases of Funny Faces (1906)	60-61
Hunchback of Notre Dame, The (1923)	121
Hungarian Goulash (1930) [Terry-Toon]	128, 133-134
Hyde Cat	13, *70*, 210
Hypnotic Eyes (1933) [Fanny Zilch/Oil Can Harry]	151
Hypnotized (1952) [Little Roquefort]	247

I

I Pagliacci (1931) (live-action)	136
Ichiro	299
If We Lived on the Moon (1920) [Goldwyn-Bray Pictographs]	107
Igloo for Two, An (1955) [Willie the Walrus]	258
Igor	*309*, 318
Impressario	*311*
In Dutch (1925) [Aesop's Film Fables]	4
In the Rough (1927) [Aesop's Film Fables]	117-118
In Lunyland (1916) [Paramont-Bray Cartoons]	79
Incredible Mr. Limpet, The (1964) (live-action and animated)	128
Indian Pudding (1930) [Terry-Toon]	128
Inki, the Lion Hunter	199
Intruders, The (1947) [Heckle and Jeckle]	206, 229
Invisibeam, The (1965) [Astronut]	306
Irish Stew (1930) [Terry-Toon]	128
Isotope Feeney, the Meany	289, 297
Itchy Brother	284
It's A Living (1957) [Dinky Duck]	196-197, 287-288, 302
It's For the Birds (1967) [James Hound]	318
It's Only Money (1962) (live-action)	132

J

J. Leffingwell Strongheart	150-151, 230

Index of Animated Film Production Titles and Characters

Jack's Shack (1934) [Terry-Toon]   204, 338
Jail Break, The (1946) [Mighty Mouse]   228
James Hound   306, *309*, 317-318, 334
Jasper   216
Jasper and the Beanstalk (1945) [Puppetoon]   216
Jazz Singer (1927) (live-action)   120
Jealous Lover (1933) [Terry-Toon]   151
Jerry on the Job (theatrical cartoon series)   338, 342
John Doormat   282-283, 297, *328*
Johnstown Flood (1946) [Mighty Mouse]   206, 209, 212, 228
Jolly Green Giant   316
Jolly Jupiter (c. 1965) [Astronut]   306
Jolly Little Elves (1934) [Cartune]   159
Jonny Quest (TV series)   318-319
Joys and Glooms (theatrical cartoon series)   94, 107, 114, 342
Judge Rummy   102, 108, 114, 130, 338, 342
Judge Rummy (theatrical cartoon series)   102, 108, 114, 130, 338, 342
Judge's Crossword Puzzles (theatrical cartoon series)   109, 125
Juggler of Our Lady: A Medieval Legend, The (1958)   viii, 269, 272, 287-288
Juke Box Jamboree (1942) [Swing Symphony]   200
Jumping Beans (1930) [Terry-Toon]   128
June Bride, The (1926) [Aesop's Film Fables]   104
Jungle Book (1967)   272
Junker   *310*, 316
Junker, The (1967) [Mighty Heroes]   *310*, 316

K

Katzenjammer Kids   53, 102, 107-108, 130, 338
Katzenjammer Kids (theatrical cartoon series)   102, 107-108, 130, 338
Keep 'Em Growing (1943) [Terry-Toon]   214, 344
Kid Kelly (theatrical cartoon series)   342
Kids in a Shoe [Color Classics]   336
Kiko and the Honey Bears (1936) [Kiko the Kangaroo]   169
Kiko Foils the Fox (1936) [Kiko the Kangaroo]   169
Kiko the Kangaroo   5, *147*, 169-170, 187, 256
Kiko the Kangaroo in Red Hot Music (1937) [Kiko the Kangaroo]   169
Kiko's Cleaning Day (1937) [Kiko the Kangaroo]   169
Kilkenny Cats, The (1945) [Mighty Mouse]   215
King Leonardo and His Short Subjects (TV series)   284
King Neptune (1932) [Silly Symphonies]   338
King of Kings (1927) (live-action)   121
King Rounder   306
King Rounder (1964) [Luno]   306
King-Size Canary (1947)   276
Kismet (1920) (live-action)   121
Knighty Knight Bugs (1958) [Looney Tunes]   290
Koko the Clown   86 (n. 21), 107, 337

Kooky Cucumbers (1971) [Possible Possum]   313
Korn Plastered in Africa [Trader Korn's Laffalong]   113 (n. 56)
Krakatoa Katy   217
Krazy Kat   109, 128, 130, 204, 342
Krazy Kat (theatrical cartoon series)   109, 112 (n. 55), 128, 130, 204, 342

L

L. B. Cornwell Productions (theatrical cartoon series)   125
La Cucaracha (1934) (live-action)   160
La traversee de l'Atlantique a la rame (1978)   332
Lampoons (theatrical cartoon series)   108
Lariat Sam   290, 296, 300-301, 333, 335, 340
Last Indian, The (1938) [Terry-Toon]   192
Last Round Up, The (1943) [Gandy Goose]   214
Latimore   310-312, *311*
Law and Disorder (1962) [Deputy Dawg]   303
Law and Order (1950) [Mighty Mouse]   253
Le Peintre néo-impressionniste [The Neo-Impressionistic Painter] (1910)   61
Le Tout Petit Faust [The Little Faust, aka The Beautiful Margaret (US)] (1910)   61
Lemon Drop Kid, The (1951) (live-action)   131
Les Joyeaux Microbes [The Joyous Microbes, aka The Merry Microbes (UK)] (1909)   61
Let's Take a Trip (live-action TV series)   279
Life Cartoon Comedies (theatrical cartoon series)   125
Life With Feathers (1945) [Merrie Melodies]   216
Life With Fido (1942) [Dinky Duck]   195-196
Limehouse Harry   258
Lindy's Cat (1927) [Aesop's Film Fables]   115
Lion and the Mouse (1943) [Super Mouse]   209
Lion Hunt (1955)   286
Lion Hunt, The (1949) [Heckle and Jeckle]   244
Little Brown Jug (1926) [Aesop's Film Fables]   104, 114
Little Herman   69-70, 73-74, 77
Little Herman (1915) [Paul Terry Cartoons]   1, 8 (n. 1, 2), 69-71, 73-74, 75 (n. 28, 30), 77
Little Hiawatha (1937) [Silly Symphonies]   199
Little Jimmy (theatrical cartoon series)   342
Little King, The (theatrical cartoon series)   244, 344
Little Lulu (theatrical cartoon series)   201, 302
Little Mermaid (1989)   148
Little Nell   228, 230, 242
Little Nemo   62, 63, 67
Little Nemo in Slumberland (aka Little Nemo) (1911)   63, 67
Little Problems (1951) [The Terry Bears]   249
Little Red Riding Hood (1922) [Laugh-O-Grams]   1
Little Red Riding Rabbit (1944) [Merrie Melodies]   290
Little Roquefort   2, 246-248, 259-260, 291, *328*, *330*, 335, 341

391

Little Rural Riding Hood (1949)	276	Mighty Mouse and the Wolf (1945) [Mighty Mouse]	215
Looney Tunes (theatrical cartoon series)	248	Mighty Mouse in Gypsy Life (1945) [Mighty Mouse]	215-216
Loops and Swoops (1968) [Sad Cat]	312		
Lord of the Rings (1978)	334	Mighty Mouse in Krakatoa (1945) [Mighty Mouse]	212, 217
Love in a Cottage [Aesop's Film Fables]	110		
Loves Labor Won (1948) [Mighty Mouse]	viii, 242	Mighty Mouse Meets Bad Bill Bunion (1945) [Mighty Mouse]	217
Lucky Duck	195-196		
Lucky Duck, The (1940) [Dinky Duck]	195-196	Mighty Mouse Meets Deadeye Dick (1947) [Mighty Mouse]	229-230
Luno	226, 306, 333, 335		
Lunyland Pictures (1914)	79	Mighty Mouse Meets Jeckyll and Hyde Cat (1944) [Mighty Mouse]	13, 70, 210

M

		Mighty Mouse Playhouse (TV series)	213, 265, 314, 341
Macon Mouse	297, 313	Mighty Mouse: The New Adventures (TV series)	334
Mad House, A (1934) [Terry-Toon]	152		
Magic Pencil, The (1940) [Gandy Goose]	189-190	Milton the Monster	306, 345
Magic Slipper (1948) [Mighty Mouse]	242	Milton the Monster (TV series)	306, 345
Mail Pilot, The (1927) [Aesop's Film Fables]	105	Minute and 1/2 Man, The (1959) [Hector Heathcote]	301-302
Mail Pilot, The (1933) [Mickey Mouse]	140 (n. 39)	Miss Nanny Goat	79
Martian Moochers	297, 300, 317, 340	Miss Nanny Goat (theatrical cartoon series)	79
Mayflower, The (1935) [Terry-Toon]	163	Missing Genie, The (1963) [Luno]	306
McDougal's Rest Farm (1947) [Heckle and Jeckle]	229	Mister Magoo (TV series)	278
Mechanical Cow, The (1937) [Farmer Al Falfa]	5	Mitzi Mouse	62
Merrie Melodies (theatrical cartoon series)	159	Molecular Mixup (1964) [Astronut]	304
Merry Blacksmith, The (1926) [Aesop's Film Fables]	105	Moley Mole	303
Merry Chase, A (1950) [Heckle and Jeckle]	228, 253-254	Molly Moo Cow	167, 204
Merv Griffin Show, The (live-action TV series)	333	Monkey Meat (1930) [Terry-Toon]	133
Messed Up Movie Makers (1966) [Heckle and Jeckle]	297, 315	Monster Master, The (1966) [James Hound]	318
		Monsterizer	316
Mexican Baseball (1947) [Gandy Goose]	229	Moose on the Loose (1952) [Heckle and Jeckle]	225
Mexican Border, The (1916) [Pathé News]	79	Mopping Up (1943) [Gandy Goose]	14
Mice in Council (1934) [Terry-Toon]	154	Mother Goose's Birthday Party (1950) [Mighty Mouse]	206
Mice in Council, The (1921) [Aesop's Film Fables]	99, 105-106, 109	Mother, Pin a Rose on Me (1924) [Song Car-Tune]	120
Mickey Mouse	89, 121, 190, 203-204, 275, 298, 340	Mouse Meets Bird (1953) [Little Roquefort]	246
		Mouse of Tomorrow, The (1942) [Super Mouse]	208, 210-211, 213, 343
Mickey's Circus (1936) [Mickey Mouse]	276		
Mickey's Mechanical Man (1933 [Mickey Mouse]	140 (n. 39)	Mouse Trouble (1944) [Tom and Jerry]	214
		Movie Madness (1952) [Heckle and Jeckle]	257
Mighty Hercules (TV series)	296, 345	Mr. and Mrs. Plushbottom	210
Mighty Heroes	297, 310, 314-317, 334	Mr. and Mrs. Rabbit	215
Mighty Heroes, The (TV series)	297, 310, 314-317, 334	Mr. Bellow	304, 306
Mighty Manfred the Wonder Dog	289, 297	Mr. Bug Goes to Town (aka Hoppity Goes to Town) (1942)	191
Mighty Mouse	viii, ix, 1, 2, 12, 13, 62, 64, 70, 106, 189, 197, 205, 209, 206-217, 216, 219, 222-223, 228-230, 239, 242-243, 245-246, 245, 253, 256-257, 259-260, 263, 264-265, 268-269, 271, 272-273, 273, 275-276, 288, 292, 294-295, 297, 302, 303, 312, 314, 319-320, 328, 329, 330, 332, 334-345, 341, 343	Mr. Flamboyant	284
		Mr. General	313
		Mr. Instant, the Instant Thing King	289
		Mr. Nicely	304
		Mr. Winlucky (1967) [James Hound]	318
		Ms. Q	317
		Much Ado About Nothing (1940) [Dinky Duck]	195
		Munro (1960)	282
		Musical Parrot, The (1926) [Aesop's Film Fables]	105
Mighty Mouse and the Mighty Heroes (TV series)	314	Muskie the Muskrat	226, 303, 333
Mighty Mouse and the Pirates (1945) [Mighty Mouse]	215	Mutt and Jeff	34, 74, 78-79,

Index of Animated Film Production Titles and Characters

102-103, 107-108, 110, 114-115, 128, 130, 337-338
Mutt and Jeff (theatrical cartoon series) 74, 78-79, 102-103, 107-108, 110, 114-115, 128, 130, 337-338
My Boy Johnny (1944) [Terry-Toon] 214, 338
My Old Kentucky Home (1946) [Mighty Mouse] 228
Mynah Bird 199
Mysterious Package, The (1948) [Mighty Mouse] 294
Mysterious Stranger, The (1948) [Mighty Mouse] 242

N
Nancy 200-201
National Spoof Day (1962) [Deputy Dawg] 303
'Neath the Bababa Tree [Dr. Seuss Cartoon] (1931) 129
Nice Doggy (1952) [The Terry Bears] 249
Night Life in the Army (1942) [Gandy Goose] 214
Night Life in Tokyo (1961) [Hashimoto Mouse] 299
"No Chin" Charlie 243, 253
No Sleep for Percy (1955) [Little Roquefort] 206, 247
Noah's Outing (1932) [Farmer Al Falfa] 206
Nudnik 282, 284
Nudnik Show, The (1991) (TV series) 282
Nutsy the Squirrel 248

O
Odie Colognie 284
Off to China (1936) [Terry-Toon] 342
Off to the Opera (1952) [Heckle and Jeckle] 257-258
Officer Piffles 78
Oh, Mabel (1924) [Song Car-Tune] 120
Oil Can Harry 2, *61*, 150-151, 213, 230, 242-243, 246, 253, 257, 272, 294, 341
Oil Can Mystery, The (1933) [Fanny Zilch/Oil Can Harry] 151
Oil Thru the Day (1964) [Duckwood and Donkey Otie] 307
Old Man and the Flower (1962) 333
Old Mill, The (1937) [Silly Symphonies] 199
Old Mother Clobber (1958) [Clint Clobber] 284
Old San Francisco (1927) (live-action) 121
On the Ice (1924) [Aesop's Film Fables] 105
One Froggy Evening (1955) [Merrie Melodies] 276
One Good Turn Deserves Another (1924) [Aesop's Film Fables] 106
One Man Dog, The (1927) [Aesop's Film Fables] 105
One Man Navy, The (1941) [Gandy Goose] 214
One Mouse in a Million (1939) [Terry-Toon] 208
One Note Tony 229
One Note Tony (1947) [One Note Tony] 229
Orphan Duck, The (1939) [Dinky Duck] 195
Oscar Mild 304-306
Oscar's Birthday Present (1971) [Astronut] 304
Out Again In Again (1948) [Heckle and Jeckle] 228, 243-244

Out of the Inkwell (theatrical cartoon series) 86 (n. 21), 90, 107-108, 337
Out of the Inkwell (TV series) 345
Outer Galaxy Gazette (1964) [Astronut] 304-305
Outer Space Visitor (1959) [Mighty Mouse] 294
Outlaw, The (1943) (live-action) 202 (n. 60)
Owl and the Pussycat (1939) [Terry-Toon] 189
Owlawishus 297, 313
Ozzie Ostrich 169-170
Ozzie Ostrich Comes to Town (1937) [Ozzie Ostrich] 170

P
Pandora's Box (1943) [Super Mouse] x, 209
Papa Bear 249
Paramount Cartoons (theatrical cartoon series) 101
Paramount Magazine (theatrical cartoon series) 95, 101
Parrotville Parrots 167
Pastry Panic (1951) [Little Roquefort] 247
Pastry Town Wedding (1934) [Rainbow Parade] 159
Paul Bunyan (1958) 290
Peace Pipe (1973) [Hector Heathcote] 302
Peace-Time Football (1946) [Gandy Goose] 190
Pearl Crazy (1963) [Hashimoto Mouse] 299
Pearl Pureheart 2, *61*, 213, 230, 242-243, 253, 257, 294, *329*, 341
Pen and Ink Vaudeville (theatrical cartoon series) 125
Percival Sleuthhound 258
Percy (mechanical man) 78
Percy – Brains He Has Nix (1916) [Paramount-Bray Cartoons] 78
Percy Puss 206, 246-247, *330*, 341
Performing Painter (1956) 286
Perils of Pearl Pureheart, The (1949) [Mighty Mouse] 242-243
Phantom Skyscraper, The (1966) [James Hound] 318
Phony Baloney 258
Pickle Pirate, The (c. 1965) [Possible Possum] 313
Picnic With Papa (1952) [The Terry Bears] 249
Pig Newton 226, 303, 333
Pigs in a Polka (1943) [Merrie Melodies] 200
Pigskin Capers (1930) [Terry-Toon] 128, 131, 343
Pill Peddlers (1953) [Heckle and Jeckle] 227
"Pinhead" Schlabotka 243, 253, 258, 294
Pinkerton Pup 78
Pinocchio (1940) 191, 210, 334
Pirate Ship (1933) [Terry-Toon] 152
Pitiful Penelope 307
Plastic Blaster 316
Plastigrams (series) 90
Plumber's Helpers (1953) [The Terry Bears] 249
Pluto 127, 170, 275
Poet and Peasant, The (1946) [Andy Panda] 216
Police Dog, The (theatrical cartoon series) 78, 102
Police Dogged (1956) [Clancy the Bulldog] 258

393

Poor Cinderella (1934) [Betty Boop]	159	Reluctant Dragon, The (1941) (live-action and animated)	232, 255
Pop the Cop	306	Riff-Raff	284
Popcorn (1931) [Terry-Toon]	128, 131	Rippling Romance (1945) [Color Rhapsody]	216
Popeye	161, 203-204, 262, 284, 302, 316	Rival Romeos (1950) [Heckle and Jeckle]	226-227
Popeye (TV series)	161, 203-204, 262, 284, 302, 316	River of Doubt, The (1927) [Aesop's Film Fables]	120
Porky Pig	203	Riverboat Mission (1962) [Hector Heathcote]	302
Porky's Duck Hunt (1937) [Looney Tunes]	187	Robin Hood	151
Port of Missing Mice, The (1945) [Mighty Mouse]	215	Robin Hood (1933) [Terry-Toon]	151
Possible Possum	226, 297, 306, 312, 313, 333, 335	Robinson Crusoe's Broadcast (1938) [Terry-Toon]	191
		Robots in Toyland (1965) [Astronut]	304
Possible Possum (TV cartoon series)	226, 297, 306, 313, 333, 335	Roc-A-Bye Sinbad (1964) [Luno]	306
		Rock-A-Bye Baby (1958) (live-action)	132
Post War Inventions (1945) [Gandy Goose]	189	Rocket Robin Hood (TV series)	334
Power and the Glory (1933) (live-action)	152	Roman Punch (1930) [Terry-Toon]	128, 133
Power of Thought, The (1948) [Heckle and Jeckle]	225, 228, 244	Rooster and the Eagle, The (1921) [Aesop's Film Fables]	99
Power Puss	253	Rope Man	297, *310*, 314-316
Prehistoric Perils (1952) [Mighty Mouse]	245, 257	Rover	215
Prescription for Percy (1954) [Little Roquefort]	206	"Roving Thomas" (series)	99
Pride of the Yard (1954) [Percival Sleuthhound]	258	Ruby Eye of the Monkey God, The (1969)	318-319
Private Life of Helen Troy, The (1927) (live-action)	121	Rudolph	286
Professor Mad	318	Ruff and Reddy	265
Puddy the Pup	5, *149*, 169-170, 187, 256, 341	Ruff and Reddy (TV series)	265
		Rugrats, The (TV series)	292
Puddy the Pup and the Gypsies (1936) [Puddy the Pup]	170	Runaway Mouse (1954) [Little Roquefort]	247
Puddy the Pup in Cats in a Bag (1936) [Puddy the Pup]	170	**S**	
		Saburo	299, *305*
Puddy the Pup in Sunken Treasure (1936) [Puddy the Pup]	170	Sad Cat	306, 310-312, *311*, 334-335
		Sailor's Home, The (1936) [Terry-Toon]	342
Puddy the Pup in the Bookshop (1937) [Puddy the Pup]	170	Sally Sargent	319
		Sally Sargent (1968)	318-319
Puddy's Coronation (1937) [Puddy the Pup]	170	Salt Water Taffy (1930) [Terry-Toon]	128
Pump Trouble (1952)	278	Sappy New Year (1961) [Heckle and Jeckle]	227, 297
Puss Gets the Boot (1940) [Tom and Jerry]	298, 340	Saw Mill Mystery, The (1937) [Oil Can Harry]	151
		School Days (1926) [Aesop's Film Fables]	119-120
Q		School Daze (1942) [Nancy]	200
Quack Quack (1931) [Terry-Toon]	131	Scotch Highball (1930) [Terry-Toon]	133
Quiet Please! (1945) [Tom and Jerry]	216-217	Scouts to the Rescue (1956) [Good Deed Daly]	258
		Scrap for Victory (1943) [Gandy Goose]	214
R		Scrappy	204
Rabbit of Seville (1950) [Looney Tunes]	150, 276, 290	Scuba Duba Do (1966) [Sad Cat]	311
Rabbit Seasoning (1952) [Merrie Melodies]	290	Search for Misery (1964) [Pitiful Penelope]	307
Racket Buster, The (1949) [Mighty Mouse]	*329*	Seasick Sailors (1951) [Little Roquefort]	247
Raiding the Raiders (1945) [Mighty Mouse]	215	Send Your Elephant to Camp (1962) [Sidney the Elephant]	291
Rainbow Parade (theatrical cartoon series)	159, 167, 204, 250, 335	Sham Battle Shenanigans (1942) [Gandy Goose]	214
Raven	316	Shenanigan Kids	102, 108, 338
Razzberries (1931) [Terry-Toon]	131	Shenanigan Kids, The (theatrical cartoon series)	102, 108, 338
Really Big Act (1961) [Sidney the Elephant]	291		
Red Hot Riding Hood (1943)	276	Shocker	316
Red Riding Hood	215	Short-Term Sheriff (1964) [Duckwood and Donkey Otie]	307
Red Tractor, The (1964) [Duckwood and Donkey Otie]	307		

Index of Animated Film Production Titles and Characters

Shorty the Runt	243, 253
Shrinker	316
Sick, Sick Sidney (1958) [Sidney the Elephant]	290
Sidney the Elephant	282, 290-291, 297, 302, 306, *317*, 333, 335,
Sidney's Family Tree (1958) [Sidney the Elephant]	290
Signed, Sealed and Clobbered (1958) [Clint Clobber]	284
Silhouette Fantasies (theatrical cartoon series)	78
Silk Hat Harry	125, 130
Silly Hoots (theatrical cartoon series)	95
Silly Sandman	297
Silly Symphonies (theatrical cartoon series)	89, 112 (n. 55), 140 (n. 40), 204, 215, 298, 338, 340, 344
Silver Streak, The (1945) [Mighty Mouse]	215
Simon Bar-Sinister	284
Sing Sing Song (1931) [Terry-Toon]	131
Sketchografs (theatrical cartoon series)	125
Sky's the Limit, The (1965) [Astronut]	306
Small Town Sheriff, The (1927) [Aesop's Film Fables]	115
Snappy Snapshots (1953) [The Terry Bears]	249
Sniffer	291-292
Sniffles the Mouse	199
'Sno Fun (1951) [Heckle and Jeckle]	228
Snow White and the Seven Dwarfs (1937)	128, 148, 157 (n. 92), 190-191, 199, 210, 222, 231, 276, 298, 340
Snuffy Smith (TV series)	345
So Sorry, Pussycat (1961) [Hashimoto Mouse]	299
Some Barrier (1917) [Terry Feature Burlesques]	82
Song Car-Tunes (theatrical cartoon series)	108, 110, 120
Soapy Opera, A (1953) [Mighty Mouse]	257
Sour Grapes (1950) [Dingbat]	248
Sourpuss	2, *31*, 189-190, 214, 229, 242
Southern Supermarket (c. 1967) [Possible Possum]	313
Space Pet (c. 1965) [Astronut]	306
Spanish Love (1926) [Aesop's Film Fables]	114
Spanish Onions (1930) [Terry-Toon]	133
Special Delivery (1978)	332
Spicy City (1997)	334
Spider-Man (TV series)	334
Spoofy	291-292
Squirrel Crazy (1951) [Nutsy]	248
Stage Struck (1951) [Half Pint]	248
Steamboat Willie (1928) [Mickey Mouse]	120-121
Steeple Jacks (1951) [Heckle and Jeckle]	253
Steve Allen Show, The (live-action TV series)	333
Stone Age, The (theatrical cartoon series)	199
Stone Age Adventure, A (1915) [Bray Cartoons]	78
Stop, Look and Listen (1949) [Mighty Mouse]	243
Stowaways, The (1949) [Heckle and Jeckle]	244
Strange Companion (1961) [Hashimoto Mouse]	299
Stretcher	316
String Bean Jack (1938) [Terry-Toon]	191, 204, 272, 338-339
Strong Man	297, *310*, 314-316
Struggle, The (1931) (live-action)	132, 136, 344
Stunt Men (1960) [Heckle and Jeckle]	226, 297
Subway Sally (1927) [Aesop's Film Fables]	114
Sultan's Birthday, The (1944) [Mighty Mouse]	*209*, 211, 253
Sunny Italy (1951) [Mighty Mouse]	253
Super Mouse	*x*, 208-210, 212, *213*, 217, 275, 312, 343
Super Mouse Rides Again (1943) [Super Mouse]	209
Super Salesmen, The (1947) [Heckle and Jeckle]	227, 229
Superego	312
Superman	106, 207-210, 262-263, 315-316
Suzy the Seal	258
Svengali's Cat (1946) [Mighty Mouse]	228
Sweet Tooth Sam	289
Swiss Miss, A (1951) [Mighty Mouse]	253
Swooner Crooner (1944) [Looney Tunes]	214
Sword in the Stone (1963)	272
Sylvester the Cat	216, 248
Sylvester the Fox	*2*, 248

T

2000 B.C. (1931) [Terry-Toon]	*127*, 131
20,000 Feats Under the Sea (1917) [Terry Feature Burlesques]	81-82
Tachibara	299
Tad's Cat (theatrical cartoon series)	98
Taking the Air (1927) [Aesop's Film Fables]	105
Talking Magpies, The (1946) [Heckle and Jeckle]	225
Tall Tale Teller, The (1954) [Phony Baloney]	258
Tall Timber Tale (1951) [The Terry Bears]	249
Taming the Cat (1948) [Heckle and Jeckle]	227, 243
Taro	299
Teddy Bears, The (1907) (live-action animated)	67
Tee-Witt	316
Ten Pin Terrors (1953) [Heckle and Jeckle]	258
Tennessee Tuxedo and His Tales (TV series)	284
Terry Bears, The	*2*, *248*, 248-250, 259-260, 304, *330*
Terry Feature Burlesques (theatrical cartoon series)	80-83
Terry Human Interest Reels (theatrical cartoon series)	81-84, *82*
Terry Toons Circus (TV series)	263
Terry Toons Club (TV series)	263
Terrytoons Classics (TV series)	304
Third Musketeer, The (1965) [Sad Cat]	311
Thomas (cat)	*101*
Thousand Smile Check Up (1960) [Heckle and Jeckle]	296-297
Three Bears, The (1934) [Terry-Toon]	152

395

TERRYTOONS: The Story of Paul Terry and His Classic Cartoon Factory

Three Little Pigs	128, 215
Three Little Pigs, The (1933) [Silly Symphonies]	128
Throwing the Bull (1946) [Mighty Mouse]	206, 228-229
Thunderball (1965) (live-action)	317
Tim	306
Time Eraser	316
Timekeeper	316
Tippytoes	301
Toby Tortoise Returns (1936) [Silly Symphonies]	199
Toddle Tales (theatrical cartoon series)	204, 244, 344
Tom and Jerry (MGM)	203, 207, 214, 216-217, 246, 284, 298, 340
Tom and Jerry (Van Beuren)	102
Tom and Jerry (TV series)	284
Tom Terrific	279, *281*, 281-282, 289-290, *289*, 295, *295*, 295-297, 301, 332, 345
Tom Terrific (TV series)	279, *281*, 282, 289-290, *289*, 295-297, *295*, 301, 332, 345
Tony Sarg's Almanac (theatrical cartoon series)	125
Toonerville Trolley (gang)	167, 204
Toonerville Trolley (theatrical cartoon series)	167, 204
Tooter the Turtle	284
Topsy TV (1957) [John Doormat]	282-283
Tornado Man	297, *310*, 314-316
Toy Man	316
Tree Spree (1961) [Sidney the Elephant]	291
Triple Trouble (1948) [Mighty Mouse]	242
Trojan Horse, The (1946) [Mighty Mouse]	228
Trouble in Baghdad (1963) [Luno]	306
Tulips Shall Grow (1942) [Puppetoons]	200
Tusk, Tusk (1960) [Sidney the Elephant]	291
Tweetie Pie	248
Two Barbers, The (1944) [Mighty Mouse]	211
Two Headed Giant (1939) [Terry-Toon]	270
Two Ton Babysitter (1960) [Sidney the Elephant]	291
Tycoon the Racoon	226, 303, 333

U

Ugly Duckling, The [Aesop's Film Fables]	105
Uncle Sam's Christmas (1916) [Pathé News]	79
Underdog (TV series)	284
Uninvited Pests, The (1946) [Heckle and Jeckle]	225
Unsung Hero (1961) [Hector Heathcote]	302

V

Victor the Volunteer	248
Villain Still Pursued Her, The (1937) [Oil Can Harry]	151
Vincent "Vince" Van Gopher	226, 303-304, 313, 333
Violinist, The (1959)	286

W

Walrus Hunters, The (1923) [Aesop's Film Fables]	105
Walter the Walrus	258
War Bride, The (1928) [Aesop's Film Fables]	118, 206
Watch the Butterfly (1966) [Possible Possum]	313
Wayward Hat, The (1960) [Foofle]	284
Weather Magic (1965) [Astronut]	305
Welcome Little Stranger (1941) [Dinky Duck]	196
What's Opera, Doc? (1957) [Merrie Melodies]	150, 276, 290
When Knights Were Bold (1915) [Bray Cartoons]	78
When Mousehood was in Flower (1953) [Mighty Mouse]	257
When Noah's Ark Embarked (1917) [Powers Cartoons]	94
Who's Minding the Store (1963)(live-action)	132
Whozit Weekly (theatrical cartoon series)	98
Why Me? (1978)	332
Wicked Wolf, The (1946) [Mighty Mouse]	228
Wicky Wacky Romance, A (1939) [Terry-Toon]	197, 208
Will Success Spoil Rock Hunter? (1957) (live-action)	132
Willie the Spendthrift	210
Willie the Walrus	258
Willie Whopper	89
Wind Jammers, The (1926) [Aesop's Film Fables]	119
Window Washers, The (1925) [Aesop's Film Fables]	110
Wine, Women and Song (1925) [Aesop's Film Fables]	105
Winky Dink	226, 335
Winky Dink and You (TV series)	226, 333
Winning the West (1946) [Mighty Mouse]	228
Winston	302
Witch's Cat, The (1948) [Mighty Mouse]	*34*
Wizards (1977)	334
Wolf! Wolf! (1944) [Mighty Mouse]	210
Wolf's Pardon, The (1947) [Terry-Toon]	229
Woodland Café (1937) [Silly Symphonies]	140 (n. 40)
Woody Woodpecker	203, 335
Wreck of the Hesperus, The (1944) [Mighty Mouse]	210
Wynken, Blynken and Nod (1938) [Silly Symphonies]	199

Y

Yankee Doodle Mouse, The (1943) [Tom and Jerry]	217
Yoke's On You, The (1962) [Deputy Dawg]	303
Your Flag and My Flag (1917)	94
Yuriko	299, *305*

General Index

This index is an alphabetical list providing access to all subjects found in Chapters 1 to 27. The index excludes references to personalities and animated film production titles which are indexed separately.

A

A. Kay Company	80-84
Abie the Agent	54
Académie Julian	48
Academy Award	95, 98, 159, 286
Academy Awards (ceremony)	200, 214, 216-217, 267, 271, 276 (n. 2), 290-291
Academy of Motion Picture Arts and Sciences	198, 267-268, 271, 282
Academy Pictures	292
Acadia University	108
Action Comics	209
Adelphi Theater	132
Adventures of a Pair of Jacks	79
Adventures of Mighty Mouse, The	260
Aesop's Fables	98-99
Aesop's Fables (animated cartoons)	
Aesthetics and design	106, 109-110, 118-119
Animation production processes	103-105, 116, 119
Animators, directors and other production staff	101-103, 107-109, 114-116, *115*, *117*, 119-120
Audience screening of	105
Cats and mice as central characters	105-106
Critical reviews	105, 110, 117-118, 120-121
Film editing of	*116*
First all-talking cartoon with synchronized dialogue	120
Length of	103
Morals, use of	104-105
Musicians	121
Production concerns	109-110
Production schedule and timelines	101
Production staff requirements	104
Reorganization of production processes	119
Sound and music department	121
Sound processes	120-121
Story creation	103-104
Studio reorganization after Terry departure	122
Success and popularity, reasons for	106-107
Technological innovations, lack of	118
Terry, Paul, dismissal and settlement of contract	121-122
AIDS	92
Albany (N.Y.) Law School	174
Albert T. Reid Art School	64
Alcazar (San Francisco theater)	34
Aldrich Family, The	297
Alexander the Cat	79
Alice Mine	46
All Is Vanity	78
Alonzo	53-54, 65 (n. 20)
Alta California	30
Amalgamated Copper Company	47
American	282
American Broadcasting Corporation	313
American Fotofone Company	89
American Heart Association	278
American Institute of Phrenology	83
American Magazine	282
American Party of Labor	237
American Press Association	107
American School of Design	116
American Tobacco Company	129
American Union of Telephone Workers, Local No. 1	237
Anaconda (MT)	
Anaconda Mine	46
Founding and early history	46
Name origin	46
Population (1906)	47
Anaconda Company	47
Anaconda Standard, The	29, 43, 45-49, 50, 53
Anderson Craig Studios	252
Animated Film, The (1973)	269
Animated films	
Animated cartoons, little drawing power for exhibitors	262
Animation production, expensive	67, 159-160
Color cartoons, expensive to produce	159-160
Methods used to reduce production costs	67-69, 146-148
Patents	68-69, 191
Peg system of registration, development of	69
Production costs	146, 262-263
Story man, value of	276
Animation industry	
African-Americans	249
Animators, short supply	126-127
Bankruptcies and economic problems in	146-147
Early disinterest in working with television	255
Independent studios producing television animation	256
Labor strikes and union activities, history (pre-Terrytoons strike)	230-232
Propaganda work during World War Two	213-214
Story artists and gag artists, quality talent in short supply	275-276
Television, effect on	262-263
Working conditions	146-149
World War Two, effect on	213
Annapolis Naval Academy	129
Antoine's (restaurant, New Orleans, LA)	*218*
Appellate Division for the Second Judicial Department (N.Y.)	175
Archambault Restaurant	150
Argosy	58
Around the World on a Bicycle	18
Art Directors Club (NYC)	295

397

TERRYTOONS: The Story of Paul Terry and His Classic Cartoon Factory

Art Students League 64, 107-108, 115, 128-130, 211, 214, 281-282
Artemas Ward, Inc. 58
ASIFA (Association Internationale du Film D'Animation) 271
Associated Animators 204
Associated Artists Productions 262
Associated Press 30, 34
Associated Press Feature Service 153
Atchison, Topeka & Santa Fe Railroad 23
Atlas Sound Studios 143
Audience response to animated cartoons, surveys of 105, 146, 155 (n. 17), 206, 255, 273
Audio-Cinema 124-126, 128-130, 132-138
Audio Productions, Inc. 203-204
AyVeeBee Corporation 100

B

B.F. Keith Vaudeville Circuit 110
Bakery & Confectionery Workers' Int'l Union Local No. 1 237
Bakshi-Krantz 130
Ballet Russe 134
Baltimore Sun 48
Ban deodorant 306
Bank of America 190-191
Bank of America National Association 134
Bank of Missouri 30
Banshees' Silver Lady Award 33
Baptist Church 22
Barré-Bowers studio 102, 107-108, 115, 130
Bay State Film Productions 252
Beeton's Christmas Annual 18
Bell & Howell (camera) 69
Bell Publishing Company 130
Bell Telephone Labs 136
Bell Telephone System 136
Beloved Herring Maven (Vita) 284
Beltmakers Union Local 40 237
Bicyclist (Penny-farthing), trek around the world 18
Big Book, The (series) 252
Billboard, The 105
Bimetallism or Monometallism (1896) 35
Black Death 92
Blackie's Steakhouse 148
Blacklisting in Hollywood 260
Bluebook 157 (n. 92)
Bob Hope Show, The 283
Bonefoot and Fudge 309
Boob McNutt 33

Box Office Attractions 63
Boy Scouts of America 149-150, 324
Brain and Skull (1909) 83
Brain Roofs and Porticoes (1898) 83
Bray-Gilbert Studios 78
Bray-Hurd Process Company 69, 116
Bray Pictures Corporation 107
Bray Productions 77-78, 80, 85, 101, 108
Bray studio 77, 80, 94, 101-102, 126
Bray Studios Incorporated 68
Breaks 103
Bridge 33
Bridgeport Central High 251
British Academy of Film and Television Arts 288
British Airways 226
Bronx Zoo 134, 199
Brooklyn Bridge 242
Brooklyn Daily Eagle 67, 140 (n. 41), 153
Brooklyn Eagle, The 48, 79
Bruno and Pietro 79
Brushmakers Union Local 16303 237
Brussels World's Fair 286
Bud Fisher Film Corp. 79
Bugle Calls (1901) 28
Bulletin (Portland) 50
Bulletin (San Francisco) 29-34, 42, 53-54
Butte Miner 47
Bystander 102

C

C. C. Burr Enterprises 198
California Gold Rush 10-11
California Journalism Hall of Fame 29
California Line Clipper Ships 13
California Mid-Winter International Exposition of 1894 34
Call (San Francisco) 29-30, 40, 42, 50-51, 53, 84
Call Building *30*, 41
Cameo Theatre 69, 105
Camp Devens (Mass.) 92
Camp Dix (N.J.) 92
Camp Funston (Fort Riley, Kansas) 91
Campbell's Soup 306
Canada Dry 252
Cannes (Film Festival) 299
Capitol (records) 213
Captured! 107
Carpenter-Goldman Labs 124, 128
Carthay Circle Theatre 190
Cartoon Film Service, Inc. 85, 94, 101
Cartoon Films, Inc. 116

Cartoons: One Hundred Years of Cinema Animation (1994) 269
Casey, Crime Photographer 283
Catholic University of America 18
CBS Animation 304
CBS Films Inc. 263, 320
CBS Radio 278-279
CBS Television Films Sales Inc. 278
CBS-Terrytoons
 Animated series and shorts 283-292, 294, 296-307, 310-319
 Animators 296, *298-299*, 308-309, 312-313, *334*
 Background department 294-296
 CinemaScope format 286-288
 Deitch, Gene, creative contributions 278-293
 Demise and closure 319-320
 Disgruntled employees 280
 Heckle and Jeckle shorts 294, 296-297
 Layout artists and character designers *191*, *227*, 281-286, 298-299, *335*
 Mighty Mouse shorts 294
 Music department 288, 309-310
 Opaquers *279*, *297*
 Story department 281-283, 287-288, *291*, 292, 298-299, 302, 306, 310
 Studio remodelling 281
 Voice actors 226, 283-284, 297-298, 300, 304, 306, 316, *319*
CBS-TV 292
Cel Aesthetics: A Method for the Analysis of Animated Cartoons (1994) 272
Celebrity Productions 89
Central Pacific Railroad 12
Central Park Theatre 136
Chapman Advertising Company 50
Chicago Art Institute 54
Chicago Daily News 54, 198
Chicago Herald 198
Chicago Journal 68-69
Chicago Professional School of Cartooning 302
Chicago Tribune 105
Children's (Art) Studio *323*, 324
Chinatown (San Francisco) *43*
Chronicle Building (San Francisco) *30*, 34, 40-42
Chronicle-Herald (Halifax) 108
Chronochrome 160
Cincinnati Commercial Tribune 61

General Index

Cincinnati Enquirer, The 61
Cinecolor 159
Cineffects 140 (n. 41)
CinemaScope 196, 255, 280, 286-288
Cinerama 255
Clarion Pictures 117
Clifford 282
Cocoanut Grove (Ambassador Hotel) 200
Colemanite 12
College Humor 130
College of New Rochelle 237
Collier's 45, 130, 153, 157 (n. 92), 252, 282
Colonial Theater 63
Colony Club 331
Columbia Broadcasting System (CBS) 250, 257, 263, 265, 269, 273, 278-281, 286-287, 292, 295, 300-301, 304, 313-315, 317-320, 321, 324, 329
Columbia Pictures 112 (n. 55), 129, 144, 159, 199, 203-204, 214, 216, 267, 276, 278
Columbia University 110, 175
Columbian University 89
Comic Art in America (1959) 268
Comic operettas 150-152
Comix: A History of Comic Books in America (1971) 268-269
Commercial Artists and Designers Union (CADU) 231
Commercial School 28
Communist Party USA 261
Complete Guide to Cartooning 308
Comstock Lode 12
Comstock Mine 46
Coney Island 253
Conference of Studio Unions (CSU) 231, 234
Consolidated Film Industries 136, 138, 142 (n. 104)
Consolidated Film Laboratories 117
Consolidated Sewing Machine Company of New York 110
Contemporary Music School 309
Continental Building and Loan Association of San Francisco 25
Coo Coo Comics 210
Cooper Medical College (San Francisco, CA) 21
Cooper Union Art School 107, 129
Copperopolis 46
Coronet 157 (n. 92)
Cosmopolitan Studios 102
Country Gentleman, The 102
Country Playhouse (Westport, CT) 324

Court of Appeals (New York State) 184
Craftsman 142 (n. 104)
Creators of Life (1975) 269
Crossword Film Company 109
Cumming School of Art 64

D

Dachau concentration camp 251
Daily Courier, The (Connellsville) 108
Daily Evening Bulletin 29
Daily Examiner 51
Daily Graphic 115
Daily Item, The 319
Daily Union (San Diego) 35
Dale Carnegie Institute 323
Damrosch Conservatory of Music 150
Demael Greeting Cards 281
Dauntless Durham of the U.S.A. 54
DC Comics 106, 282
DePatie-Freleng Enterprises 130
Dell (Publisher) 259-260
Dell Comics 260
Democratic Party 46, 330
Democratic Press 51
Democratic Women 330
Desperate Desmond 54
Detective Comics, Inc. 209
Dispatch (St. Paul) 84
Distributors
  Change in 152
  Complaints about Moser-Terry cartoons 143, 145, 162, 164, 175, 177, 181 182
  Demands of 145
  Importance to animated cartoon producers 144
  Producers' contractual difficulties with 144
Doc Syke 115
Dodsworth 297
Don Patrol 282
Doug Moye and his Glee Club Orchestra 249
Doug Moye and his Rhythm Ramblers 249
Dougie Moye's Club Sky Vue Orchestra 249
Dramatic Chronicle 34
Drano 284
Dream of the Rarebit Fiend 62-63
Dum Dum and Dee Dee 309

E

East Coast Animation Studios, Inc. 197
Eastern Color Printing 236
Eastern Front 105
Eastern Services Studio, Inc. 138

Eastman Kodak Co. 129, 136
Eastman School of Music 309
École des Beaux-Arts 69
Edison Hotel 198
Edison Phonograph Company 89
Edison Studios 69, 102, 107
Educational Pictures [Educational Films Corporation of America] 109, 125, 133, 135, 137-138, 143-145, 149, 152, 155, 162, 164-167, 173, 175, 178-184, 213, 268, 273
1887, Historical events during the year 18
Electrical Research Products Inc. 136
Elza Poppin 115
Embassy (hotel) 154
Empire State Building 242
Episcopalian Church 22
Erbograph 142 (n. 104)
Essanay Film Manufacturing Company 82
Etaples (camp) 91
European Line 10
Evening Journal (New York) 54, 59-60
Evening Journal (Portland) 51
Evening News (Detroit) 67
Evening Sun (New York) 59, 115
Evening Telegram (New York) 62
Evening Telegram (Portland) 50
Evening World (New York) 59
Eveready 284
Every Move a Picture, Yours Truly the Tumblebee Brothers 79
Examiner (San Francisco) 29, 33, 42, 51-52, 84
Examiner Building *30*, 41
Exhibitors, indifference to exhibition of animated shorts 161-162, 262
Exhibitors' Herald 105
Experimental Center of Cinematography 300
Experimental School of Art 251

F

Fables Pictures (studio) 53, 79, 100-110, *102-104*, 114-116, *116-117*, 118-122, 124, 126, 128, 130, 133, 152, 203-204, 215, 244, 273
Fables Pictures, Inc. (company) 100-101, 110, 122
Fairhaven (Mass.), early economy, history and culture 6
Fairhaven Branch Railroad Company 5-6
Fairhaven National Bank 5
Fairhaven Savings Bank 5

399

TERRYTOONS: The Story of Paul Terry and His Classic Cartoon Factory

Falley Seminary (Fulton, NY) 48
Famous Funnies 236
Famous Players-Lasky Corporation 95
Famous Studios 140 (n. 41), 196, 201, 217, 234, 244-245, 250, 262-263, 267, 275, 302
Fawcett Publications 282
Fawcett School of Industrial Arts 130
Fayetteville Museum of Art 331
Federal Bureau of Investigation 262
Federal Communications Commission 320
Federation of Screen Cartoonists 231
Felix the Cat Productions 107, 296
50 Greatest Cartoons: As Selected by 1,000 Animation Professionals, The 270-271, 276, 290
Film Daily 163, 167, 169, 173, 187, 190, 195, 197-199, 225, 228
Film Graphics 256
Filmation Associates 130, 157 (n. 92), 313, 319
First Transcontinental Railroad 10
Fleischer Studios 107-108, 116, 126-129, 140 (n. 40), 144, 148, 150, 153, 159, 161, 168, 189, 191, 197, 199, 203-204, 220, 230-231, 236, 245, 251, 267-268, 270, 272-273, 302, 322,
Fletcher-Smith 140 (n. 41), 256
Florida Federation of Women's Clubs 324
Foolish Questions 33
Ford (Motor Co.) 306
Fowler & Wells Co. 83
Fox Film Corporation 144, 152, 161-162, 164-165
Fox-Metropolitan 160
Frank Holmes School of Illustration 54
Frankenberry cereal 306
Fred Waring's Pennsylvanians 213
Free Press (Detroit) 102
French Riviera, earthquake 18
Fritz von Blitz 78
Frugality, definition of 221

G
Gandy Goose
 Creation of 204
 Propaganda tool 214
Gangbusters 283
Gaumont 61, 63
Gene Deitch Associates, Inc. 293
General Foods 257

General Grant National Memorial 139 (n. 19)
General Motors Exhibition Hall 199
George Kleine Productions 98
George Pal (studio) 199-200, 267
George Washington Medical School and Hospital 88, 89
George Washington University 89-90, 93, 116
George Washington University Hospital 88, 93
Geritol 306
German American Fire Insurance Company 25
Gilbert and Sullivan Revisited 309
Gilded Age 22-23
Gilded Age: A Tale of Today, The (1873) 22
Glaziers' Local Union 1087 237
Globe (New York) 59-60, 64, 102
Golden Age of American Animation 103, 126, 155 (n. 17), 182, 259, 267, 270, 321
Golden Argosy 58
Golden Gate Park 34, 102
Golden Records 213, 265, 310
Goldilocks and the Three Bears 67
Good Housekeeping 282
Gov. Clinton Hotel 199
Gramophone, patent for 18
Grand Central Art School 250
Grand Central Station 179
Grand Opera House (San Francisco) 38, 42
Graphic Films Corporation 124
Grauman's Chinese Theatre 214, 216
Grauman's Institute 35
Great Colonial Hurricane of 1635 193
Great Depression 126-127, 135-136, 144, 149, 152-153, 160, 204, 276, 298, 322
Great Wave of Kanagawa, The 299
Guggenheim Museum 326

H
Halifax Chronicle 108
Hand Book on Mental Science (1896) 83
Hanna-Barbera Productions 116, 130, 148, 157 (n. 92-94), 265, 273, 296, 313, 318-319
Happy Trailings 204
Harman-Ising Productions 140 (n. 40), 144, 199, 244, 268
Harmony Borax Works 12
Harper's 18, 67, 78

Harvard University 60, 90
Harvest of Stars, The 213
Harvey Comics 263
Have You Seen Alonzo? 54
Hawes Academy 4
Healing of Sam Leake, The 31
Hearst International Features Service 102, 115
Heart Mountain Relocation Camp 298
Heck and Avery's Family Theater 61
Heckle and Jeckle
 Creation of 225
 Difference between the magpies 225, 227-228
 Paul Terry's opinion of 228
 Personalities 227
 Revival of 292
 Theme song of 225
 Voice work 226
Heckle and Jeckle (comic book) 260
Hedwig Film Laboratories 142 (n. 104)
Hendey Machine Company 130
Henry 161
Herald (Boston) 79
Herald (Halifax) 108
Herald (Salt Lake City) 53
Hirlagraph Laboratories 117, 124
Hirlagraph Motion Picture Company 117
Hogan's Alley 60
Hollywood Cartoons: American Animation in its Golden Age (1999) 270
Hollywood Reporter 260
Holy Family Grammar School 197
Homeless Hector 54
Honolulu Advertiser 33
Hook and Ladder No. 1, the Larchmont Fire Department 324
Hostess Ho Hos 284
Hostess Twinkies 284
Hotel Marcus Daly 46
Hotel Monterey 154
Hotel Shelton 166, 179
House Committee on Un-American Activities 232, 260-262
House of Representatives (U.S.) 260
How and Why Wonder Book, The (series) 252
How To Make Animated Cartoon: The History and Technique (1941) 199, 268
Howdy Doody Show, The 284
Hudson Valley Art Association 184
Hurricane of 1938 (New England Hurricane of 1938) 192-193

General Index

I
Illiterate Digest 103
Imperial Conservatory of Music 134
In Our School 64
Independent Electrical Supply Co. 70
Indoor Sports 32
Industrial Arts School (New York) 324
Industrial Insurance Employees
 Union Local 30 237
Inquisitive Clarence 79
Inter Mountain (Butte) 53
Interborough Rapid Transit 58
International Alliance of
 Theatrical Stage Employees
 (I.A.T.S.E.) 231, 240
International Brotherhood of Painters,
 Decorators and Paperhangers
 of America 231, 234, 240
International Film Service 94, 99,
 102, 107-108, 110, 130
International Harvester 40
International League of Press Clubs 34
International Stalin Prize 261
Irving Trust Company 168

J
J. Amedee Van Beuren 198
Jam Handy studio 139 (n. 3), 244, 278
Japanese Tea Garden (S.F.) 34
Jim Timmens and his Jazz
 All-Stars 309
Jim Timmens Orchestra 310
John McCrory studio 128, 147-148
Johnny Wise 32
Journal-American (New York) 197
Journalism in California (1915) 35
Judge 67, 78, 102, 130
Junktown 309

K
K.C. Motion Picture Company 107
Kalfus-Mond Inc. 187
Kansas City Art Institute and
 School of Design 250-251
Kaufman Specials 83
Kaufman Studios 154
Keith-Albee theater circuit 99-100
 110, 121
Kermit the Hermit 282
KESE (Kline, Edison, Selig &
 Essanay) 94
Kinemacolor 160
King Features Syndicate 33, 115, 306
Kiss Me Kate 300
Kiwanis Club (Rye, NY) 324
Klondike Gold Rush 24
Knights of Columbus 245-246
Kohl & Middleton Dime Museum 61

Korean War 295

L
L'Enfant Terrible, definition 308
Ladies' Home Journal 102
Lafayette College 174
Lafayette Society 330
Laffs in News Dispatches 115
"Lala Palooza" 33
Lambs Club (N.Y.) 324
Larchmont Public Library 324
"Last Spike" 10
Laugh-O-Grams studio 251
Leader, The (San Mateo, CA) 19-20
Lee Enterprises 47
Leon Schlesinger Productions
 131, 144, 148-150,
 159, 168, 189, 200, 231
Les Arts Incohérents 61
Liberty Loan Committee 149
Licensing deal with CBS 257
Life 54, 67, 78, 102, 130
Life of Francois J. Gall (1896) 83
Life's Darkest Moments 33
Lincoln Records 140 (n. 41), 213
Listen to the Mockingbird (1855) 225
Literary Digest, The 48, 105, 108
Little Ah Sid, The Chinese Kid 79
Little Johnny and His Teddy Bears 67
Little King, The 244
Little Nemo in Slumberland 62, 67
Little Roquefort Comics 260
Little Sammy Sneeze 62
Lohengrin 38
London Guarantee and
 Accident Company 25
London Humorist 102
London Opinion 102
Los Angeles High School 278
Los Angeles Polytechnic High
 School 298
Loucks & Norling 140 (n. 41)
Lumber Mutual Casualty Company 181

M
M. H. de Young Memorial Museum
 (Palace of Fine Arts) 34
MacPhail School of Music
 and Drama 300
MAD 316
Mail (New York) 59
Major Ozone's Fresh Air Crusade 79
Mamaroneck Public Library 324
Manhattan Opera House 121
Manual of Obstetrics 89
Marcus Loew (theater chain) 83

Mark Hopkins Art
 Institute 29, 54, 252
Mark Strand (theater) 120
Marriage of Figaro 38
Marvel Comics 196, 259
Mayflower 1
Mayor's Conference on the
 Aging (New Rochelle, N.Y.) 324
McClure Newspaper Syndicate 67
McGill University 30
Medical College of the Pacific 21
Mefistofele 18
Mein Kampf 222
Memorial Hospital for Cancer
 and Allied Diseases (N.Y.) 327
Metro 90
Metro-Goldwyn-Mayer 57 (n. 65),
 94, 127, 129, 140 (n. 40),
 148-149, 153, 157 (n. 93-94),
 199-200, 203, 207,
 214, 216, 231, 246, 267,
 270, 275-276, 298, 301
Metropolitan Art School 250
Metropolitan Motion Picture Club 161
Michigan State University 285
Mighty Mouse
 Character antecedents 106
 Christ-like figure 212
 Creation of 205-208
 Domicile of 212
 First cartoon as resident
  of stars 210-211
 First cartoon disguised as
  "mysterious stranger" 230
 First cartoon with redesign 211
 First official cartoon 210
 Girlfriend of 230
 Key to studio success and
  prosperity 222-223
 Most popular cartoon themes 212
 Name change from Super
  Mouse 209-210
 Origin of 209
 Origins in Super Mouse 208-209
 Popularity, reasons for 211-212
 Redesign by Connie Rasinski 211
 Theme antecedent 197
 Voice of 213, 341
Mighty Mouse (comic book) 259
Mighty Mouse Square 329
Mike and Ike (They Look Alike) 33
Mill and the Floss, The 73
Miller Rubber Co. 169
Minoco 213
Miracle, The 262
Mr. O. U. Absentmind 67
Mitchell (camera) 69
Models, Use of for art instruction 144

401

TERRYTOONS: The Story of Paul Terry and His Classic Cartoon Factory

Modern Trusts (1902) 35
Montana Ore Purchasing Company 47
Moorish Gardens 100
Morals, Use of at Fables Pictures 104-105, *108*
Morgan Iron Works 10
Morning Call (San Francisco) 19, 30, 53
Morning Chronicle (San Francisco) 34
Morse Dry Dock Company 214
Moser, Frank
  Animation abilities 132
  Biography of 64, 184
  Fear of not obtaining contract with distributor 144
  Frugalness of 144
  Physical picture *131*, *133*, *137*, *342*
  Refusal to yield corporate interest 143
  Response to complaints about cartoons 143-144
  Studio management responsibilities 132, 145
  Trust in Bill Weiss with respect to his personal finances 166
Moser & Terry
  Animated cartoons, critical reviews 133-134, 151-152, 162-163
  Animated cartoons, suggestions by Moser to improve quality 159, 162-164
  Animators, duties of 132, 163
  Animosity between partners 143-144
  Artists on staff 126-132, *137*
  Audio-Cinema agreement 124-125
  Complaints about entertainment quality and lack of color in cartoons 143, 145, 160-164, 173, 182
  Contractual negotiations with Audio-Cinema 134-135
  Contractual negotiations with distributor 138, 145, 149, 152, 155
  Difficulties in retaining talent 126, 274-275
  Dissolution of 1932 corporation 143
  Distributor refuses to renew contract 164-165
  Establishment of studio 124-126
  Film processing *129*
  Formation of partnership 124
  Incorporation in 1932 143
  Incorporation in 1934 154-155
  Original music, use of 132
  Partnership agreement, first entered 134
  Production costs 137-138
  Production staff size 132
  Purchase of Moser's stake in the company by Paul Terry 166
  Revenues and finances 136-138
  Royalties, payment of 132
  Staff, salary increases 153
  Studio departments 132
  Studio organization 132
  Working conditions at 127
Moser-Terry legal proceedings
  Aldrich, Judge Raymond E. ,
    Biography of 173-174
    Personality and temperament 174
  Answers (pleadings), filed by defendants 173
  Appeal of Supreme Court, Appellate Division 184
  Appeal of Supreme Court decision by Frank Moser 183-184
  Attorneys for plaintiff Moser and defendants, biographies of 174-175
  Court of Appeals (N.Y.), appeal to denied 184
  Damages and remedies sought by Moser 173
  Day, Harvey B. (examinations of) 180-181
  Decision of Supreme Court, Appellate Division, Second Department 184
  Decision of Supreme Court, 9th Judicial District 182-183
  Hammons, Earle (examinations of) 177-179
  Kelly, D. Theodore (examinations of) 181
  Lessons learned from trial 182
  Moser, Frank (examinations of) 175-176
  Moser, Frank, Complaint (pleading) of 173
  Moser, Frank, pleadings - allegations of fraud and misrepresentation 173
  Nicholson, Norman (examinations of) 179
  Scheib, Philip (examinations of) 181
  Skirball, Jack (examinations of) 181
  Terry, Paul (examinations of) 180
  Thompson, Thomas F. (examinations of) 181
  Trial dates 173
  Vogel, Nathan (examinations of) 176-177
  Weiss, William (examinations of) 179-180
Motion Picture Association of America 261
Motion Picture Daily, The 179
Motion Picture Industry, Great Depression effect on 149, 152-153, 160
Motion Picture News 84
Motion Picture Screen Cartoonist's Guild, Local 841 (Hollywood Screen Cartoonists) 231, 236, 242
Mountain Dew 306
Movca Film Company 84-85, 101
Moving Picture World 74, 95
Moviola 146, 148, 163-164, 181, 232, 284
Mrs. Avery 98
Munsey's Magazine 58
Munsey's Weekly 58
Museum of Arts and Industrial Crafts (Larchmont and Mamaroneck) 324
Museum of Modern Art (N.Y.) 257, 278, 320
Music in Terrytoons cartoons 146
Musical "mellerdrammers" 150-151
Mutt and Jeff (*Augustus Mutt*) 34, 74
Mutt and Jeff Films, Inc. 78-79, 110
My Life in Prison 31
My Own Story 32
Mystery Writers of America Edgar Award 153

N

Nancy 200
National Academy of Design 64, 130, 198, 217
National Art Academy 128
National Broadcasting Company 263, 278, 281, 302, 304, 313, 317
National Cartoonists Society 33, 324
National Comics 263
National Film Board of Canada 270-271
National Film Features [National Film Booking Service] 81-82
National Labor Relations Board 233, 235, 239-240
National Lampoon 282
National Periodicals 209
National Printing and Engraving Company 61
National Statuary Hall Collection 32
Never Let Satan's Foot Get in the Door 262
New Bedford (Mass.), early economy, history and culture 6
New Bedford & Fairhaven Street Railway Company 5
New England Surgical Society 90
New Era, The 214

General Index

New Masses	130	
New Rochelle		
Effect of studio on economy	264	
History and demographics	154	
Honors to Paul Terry	263	
New Rochelle Council on the Arts	328, 331	
New Rochelle High School	332	
New Rochelle Public Library	331	
New Rochelle Senior High School	197	
New Standard Dictionary	48	
New Terrytoons	259	
New York American	51, 54, 59, 103	
New York Art Directors Gold Medal	279	
New York Athletic Club	110	
New York Evening School of Industrial Design	114	
New York Graphic	54	
New York Herald	48, 59, 62, 69, 78-79	
New York Herald Tribune	54, 102, 252	
New York Journal	32, 54, 60, 128	
New York Law School	181	
New York Post	59	
New York School of Design	116	
New York State Supreme Court	173, 175, 184	
New York Sun	59-60, 128	
New York Times	18, 30, 59, 71, 173, 268	
New York University	47, 83, 150, 160, 174, 297	
New York World	33, 48, 53, 59-60, 79, 102, 214	
New York World's Fair (1964)	199	
New Yorker	130, 204	
Newburgh Daily News	108	
Newspaper Guild of New York	237	
Nob Hill	*39*, 39-40	
Norman	282	
Norman Pierce Company	33	
North Pole	242	
Northern Pacific Railway	23	
Notlek Tennis Courts	100	
Nude Descending a Staircase, No. 2 (1912)	323	
NY Dramatic Mirror	85	

O

Oakland Tribune	42, 84
Ocean Queen	10-11
Of Mice and Magic: A History of American Animated Cartoons (1979)	168, 269-270
Off the Cuff	310
Official Gazette	95
Omni	282

On the Line	237
1,000 Jokes	282
1,000th animated cartoon produced by Paul Terry, honors for	257
Oregon Journal	51
Oregonian (Portland)	45, 49-51
Original Dixieland Jazz Band	64
Orizaba	11
Orpheum (chain of theaters)	100
Orpheum (theater (S.F.))	53
Otello	18
Otis Art Institute	298
Our Gang	54
Our Own Movies	103
Overland Route	10
Oxford English Dictionary	221

P

Pacific Gas and Electric Company	32
Pacific Mail Steamship Company	23
Pacific Railroad	10
Panama Canal Railroad	11
Panama-Pacific Exposition (1915)	53
Panic of 1893	22-24
Pantages Theatre (Hollywood, CA)	290
Pantomime Productions	130
Paramount-Bray Cartoons	79
Paramount Cartoon Studios	263
Paramount Pictures	77, 94-95, 98-101, 114, 144, 149, 160, 200, 203, 214, 216, 231, 245, 262-263, 267-268, 284, 292, 302, 317-318
Paramount-Publix	149
Pardon My Glove	60
Park East	282
Park Row	59, *59*
Parsons School of Design	295
Passing Show	102
Pat Sullivan Studio	129
Pathé	67-68, 77-79, 85, 100, 106-107, 109, 121-122, 160, 198
Pathé Exchange, Inc.	79, 106-107
Pathé News	78
Pathé studio	121
Paul Terry Scholarship Award	324
Paul Terry's Comics	250, 260
Paul Terry's Mighty Mouse Comics	260
Paul Terry's Terry-Toons Comics	260
Penthouse	282
Pepto-Bismol	306
Percy – Brains He Has Nix	78
Peter Pauper Press	33
Petrograd Institute of Technology	134

Philadelphia and Reading Railroad	22
Philadelphia Motion Picture Council	161
Phoenix Art Institute (N.Y.C.)	130, 250
Phoenix Fire Insurance Company (of Hartford)	25
Phrenological Dictionary (1895)	83
Phrenological Institute	83
Phrenological Magazine	83
Phrenology	81, *82*, 83-84
Piazza Venezia (Rome)	251
Picart Studios, Inc.	125, 134-135
Pines (Publisher)	260
Pintoff Productions	286
Placer Times	30
Playboy	282
Plaza Hotel (N.Y.)	289
Polytechnic High School	28-29, 32-33, 60
Popular Mechanics	95
Popular Science	192
Porgy and Bess Revisited	309
Port Chester High School	251
Post Sugar Jets	257
Poughkeepsie Business College	58
Powers Cinephone	89
Powers Company	89
Powers Film Products Company	89
Pratt Institute	250-251, 282
Preparedness Day Bombing (1916)	31
Presbyterian Church	22
Press (New York)	58-60, 64-65, 70
Press, The (Binghamton, NY)	48
Prestwich Manufacturing Company	69
Prince Errant	78
Prizmacolor	160
Professor Blackart	79
Progressive Republican	59
Prom (records)	213
Promontory Summit	10
Protection and Progress (1900)	35
Puck	78-79, 102
Pulitzer Prize	33
Punch	282

Q

Queen of the Pacific	10-11
Queen Victoria's Golden Jubilee	18

R

R.M.S. *Lusitania*	87
Radio Keith Orpheum	122, 123 (n. 49), 129, 144, 149, 160, 167-168, 182, 198, 203, 214, 216
Railroad Magazine	253
Raoul Barré studio	148

403

Rarus Mine	47	Aftershock	40	*Scribner's*	78
Ray Patin Productions	130, 282	Casualties	41	*Seattle Post-Intelligencer*	50
Register (Des Moines)	64	Damage caused to Chronicle		Selective Service Act of 1917	87
Reisenweber's Restaurant	63-65	building	40	Sepia	187
Rembrandt Films	282	Damage caused to Terry		*Serious Business: The Art*	
Reporter	157 (n. 92)	residence	38-40	*and Commerce of Animation*	
Republic Film Laboratories	142 (n. 104)	Date and time	38	*in America from Betty Boop*	
Republic Pictures	142 (n. 104)	Devastation caused by		*to Toy Story* (1997)	269-270
Republican national conventions		quake	38-40, *42*	Shamus Culhane Productions	256
(1888, 1892)	34	Duration	38	Sherman Silver Purchase Act	23
Retrospective Mondiale du		Economic costs	41	Shrewd, definition of	222
Cinema Animation (1967)	324-325	Effect on Enrico Caruso	38	Shubert Film Corporation	70
Reuben Award	33	Effect on Paul Terry's career	43	Shubert Theatrical Company	70
Reveille (Butte)	47	Epicenter of quake	38	*Si Swapper*	78
Revolutionary War (U.S.)	301-302	Financial costs to Paul Terry	42	*Sick, Sick, Sick: A Guide to*	
Richard Williams studio	148	Fire	*39*, 39-41	*Non-Confident Munro* [Feiffer]	282
Ripley's Believe It or Not!	54	Fire damage to Newspaper		Sign-Pictorial & Display Union	237
Riverside Theatre	105	Row buildings	41-42	Signal Corps Photographic	
Rivoli Theater	105, 150	Firefighting and firebreaks	41	Center	140 (n. 41)
RKO-Radio Pictures	198, 200	Looting during	40-41	Skyport Restaurant	167
Robert Lawrence Productions	279, 295	Magnitude of quake	38-39	Smell-O-Vision	256
Robert Q. Lewis TV Show	284	Military and police law		*Smoothies, The*	132
Rocky Mountain News (Denver, CO)	50	enforcement	40	*Social Security in America* (1967)	324
Rome Playhouse	300	Paul Terry's journey through		Song Ads	130
Rome Theatre Guild	300	quake ravaged city	39-40	Sound effects in Terrytoons	
Romer Grey Pictures Limited	189	Paul Terry's location during		cartoons	146, *193*
Rondaliers Quartet	213	earthquake, alternate		*Sound of Music, The*	300
Rosario	53	version	44 (n. 41)	South Carolina Lunatic Asylum	18
Roxy Theatre	238	Paul Terry's photographic		*South Shore Press*	214
Royal Conservatory (Leipzig)	121	work	40-41	Southern Music Company	132
Rube Goldberg Machine Contests	33	Paul Terry's travel to		Southern Pacific Railroad	18, 23
Rusty Riley	91	Oakland to escape fire	42-43	Spanish Influenza (1918-1919)	91-94
Rye Presbyterian Church		San Francisco Film Festival	286	Speakers' Forum	324
(Rye, N.Y.)	327	*San Francisco News*	45	St. John Publications	250, 259-260
		San Francisco Presidio	80	*St. Louis Democrat*	198
S		San Francisco-San Jose Railroad	19	*St. Louis Globe*	198
Saffir-Simpson Hurricane Scale	192	San Francisco Vigilance Committee	29	Standard Comics (Nedor	
Salvation Army	45	San Mateo (CA), early history		Publishing, Inc.)	210
San Carlo Grand Opera Company	136	to 1894	19-20	Standard Oil	6, 8, 47
San Carlo Symphony	136	Sanrio	157 (n. 92)	*Standard-Star, The* (New	
San Francisco		Sara A. Fawcett Drawing School	130	Rochelle, NY)	268
Anti-Chinese riots of 1877	12	*Saturday Evening Post*	32, 102,	*Stanford Chaparral, The*	29, 35
Barbary Coast	11		130, 252, 282	Stanford University	29, 35, 45
Chinatown	12	*Saturday Review*	282	*Star-Journal, The* (Sandusky, OH)	103
Chinese laborers	12	School of Industrial Art	281, 308	State Board of Equalization (CA)	85
Exclusionary policies	12	School of Visual Arts	329	States' Rights	83, 85, 117
Fires, 1848-1851	11-12	Scoop Scandals Ltd.	128	Stern Conservatory of Music	132
History, 1848-1864	11-12	*Scorchy Smith*	153-154	Stock market crashes (1929)	126, 150
Population and demo-		Screen Actors Guild	261	Story creation at Fables	
graphics, 1860s	11	Screen Cartoonist's Guild,		Studios	103-104
Vigilance committees	12-13	Local 852	231, 239	*Story of the Wooden Babes in*	
San Francisco Art Institute	48	Screen Cartoonists Local 1461		*the Wonder Woods, The*	79
San Francisco Chronicle	29, 32-35,	(Brotherhood of Painters,		Storyboard Films (John and	
	42, 44 (n. 17), 48, 51,	Decorators and Paperhangers –		Faith Hubley)	267, 279
	53-54, 60, 84, 252	A.F.L.)	231-234, 236-240	Strand (Detroit)	83
San Francisco earthquake and		Screen Gems	112 (n. 55), 144,	Strand (N.Y.)	83, 121, 132
fire (1906)			199, 204, 214, 216,	Street Railways Advertising	
			231, 268, 277 (n. 20)	Company	58

General Index

Students' Army Training Corps 90
Study in Scarlet, A 18
Successful Man of Business, The (1900) 28
Sunday Oregonian 50
Superman 207-209
Super Mouse (*Coo Coo Comics*) 210
Swift-Chaplin 129
Sydney Ducks 11-12
Syracuse Standard 47-48
Syracuse University 48, 175, 285

T

T.R. in Cartoon (1910) 53
Technicolor 159-160, 187, 197-198, 215
Techniscope 255
Telegram (New York) 59
Telephone Hour, The 213
Television
  Hollywood studios' response to growth 255-256
  Household purchases of sets, 1946-1954 255
  Terrytoons cartoon series (1950s) 263, 266 (n. 16)
Tempo Productions 292
Terr'ble Thompson! 279, 289
Terry (surname), origin of 1-2
Terry Bears Comics 260
Terry, Paul
  Academy Award nominations, response to 200
  Achievements 276, 332
  Advertising car cards artist 58
  Aesthetics of Terrytoons cartoons, opinion of 264
  Afro-Americans, hiring of 322
  Anaconda (MT), experiences 47-49, *52*
  Anaconda Standard (MT), employment with 48-49
  Animals, use of as central cartoon charters (reasons for) 80
  Animated cartoon short production, comparison to restaurant business 159
  Animated cartoon quality of Moser-Terry shorts, comfortable with 145, 164
  Animated cartoons, opinion on value to exhibitors 262
  Animation, early interest in 24
  Animation festivals, appearance at 324-326
  Animation industry, inspiration to enter 64-65
  Animation industry, interest in returning to 326
  Animation technology, experiments in 191-192
  Animation work of 132, 146
  Artwork and artistic activities *322*, 322-323, *325*
  Attire and clothing 206-207, 221
  Auction work, assisting father 21
  Automobiles, use of 220, 281
  Awards and honors 198, 257, 263-264, 324-326
  Barksy, Bud, financing of 117
  Benefactor of scholarship 324
  Benevolence towards staff 150, 264
  Birth of 18-19
  Bray Productions, employment with 77-80
  Bulletin (San Francisco), employment with 29-30, 53
  Business investment in Terryscopes 264, *270*
  Business philosophy on cartoon production 168
  Business practices, childhood 24
  Butte, Montana, travels from Portland to 45-46
  Call (San Francisco), employment with 53
  Career accomplishments 264-265
  Caricaturist, employment as 52
  Cartoon characters, appealing (opinion of) 208
  Cartoon characters, decision to create main characters appearing consistently 167, 169
  Cartoon mice, use of 207
  Cel animation, opinion on development of *84*
  Celluloid system, claims to inventing 74
  Charitable and philanthropic work 324, *325*
  Childhood of 20-25
  Chronicle (San Francisco), employment with 54
  Cigar, direction of in mouth as barometer for his mood 194
  Cigars, fondness for 194
  Color cartoons, decides to produce 187
  Color cartoons, resistance to produce 159, 162, 187
  Comic strip artist (*Alonzo*) 53-54
  Commercial sponsors, contracts with 257
  Communist dictatorship in Dominican Republic (U.S. intervention in), opinion on 323
  Competition with other studios, opinion on 264
  Contractual benefits from sale of the studio 321
  Creation of first animated cartoon, *Little Herman* (1915) 1, 69-70
  Creativity of 212
  Creator of Heckle and Jeckle concept of two identical magpies 225
  Critical opinions on body of work 268-271
  Daughter of 117, *149*, 222, *235*, 259, 264, 324, 327-330
  Death of 327
  Descendant of *Mayflower* passengers 1
  Demands to Moser after incorporation 143
  Dietary practices and eating habits 327
  Difficulties in retaining talent 127, 275
  Disney, Walt, dislike for 168
  Distributor, fear of losing 255
  Distributors, response to demands of 145, 169
  Draft board registration and conscription, World War I 87
  Drawing, early interest in 24
  8th Avenue Studio, animation work at 94
  Education, home school 22
  Education, public school 24
  Efforts to hire Vladimir Tytla 210
  Employment, childhood 23-24
  Employment practices of 193-195, 197-198, 264, 321-322
  Estabrook, Howard, contracts to produce animated cartoons for 98-100
  Evening-Journal (Portland), employment with 51
  Examiner (San Francisco), employment with 51-52
  Exemption claimed on WWI draft registration card 87
  Eyesight, poor (myopia) 25, 88
  Fables Pictures, Inc., departure and release from 121-122
  Fables Pictures, Inc., founding and ownership interest in 100
  Fables Pictures, Inc., sale of shares and interest in 122
  Fables Pictures Studio, producer, director and story

405

work at 100-110, 114, 116, 118-121
Family residence
  (1885-1890) 19-20
  (1895-1896) 22
  (1897-1905) 24, 26 (n. 42), 38
  (1906) 38
  Domestic servant, use of 21
  Interior of
    (1887-1890) 20
    (1890-1896) 21
Farmer Al Falfa, design of 80
Farmer Al Falfa, inspiration for 80
Father (Joseph Tripp Terry) 6, 8, 9 (n. 18), *10*, 10-15, 17 (n. 23), *20*, *21*, 19-22, 24-25, *25*, 38-39, 48, 51-52, *68*, 87, 110
  Appearance and dress *20*, 21, *21*
  Auctioneer, talents of 21
  Biography and early life in Massachusetts 6-8
  Business advice to Paul Terry to avoid partnerships 166
  Career as an auction and commission merchant 13-15, 21, 24
  Career in insurance industry 24-25
  Child-rearing views 24
  Death of 110
  Educator 22
  Employment as a fruit importer 14
  Employment as a furniture dealer 15, 20
  Employment as a real estate agent and broker 14-15
  Employment as a shipping clerk and tea merchant 13
  Employment with William T. Coleman & Co. 13
  Honesty of 21
  Incubation of germs, belief in 22
  Lawsuit against 24
  Marriage to Minnie Bernice Perrin 14
  Reaction to Paul's birth 19
  Religious values and faith 21-22
  Residence with 51
  Residential addresses in San Francisco, 1864-1885 13-15
  Residential move to San Mateo 15
  Travel from Massachusetts to San Francisco 10-11

Fear of losing distributor, lack of 144-145
Freemasonry, involvement in *81*, 94
Frugality of 220-222, 264, 275, 321
Funeral and cremation of 327
Funerals, attendance at 323-324
Gags, borrowing of from other cartoons 220, 273
Gags, collector of 206, 273
Genealogy of 1, 3-6, 8
Generosity of 220, 322, 324, 326
Golf, love of 197
Grandchildren, relations with 324
Hammons, Earle
  Business relationship and friendship with 125, 145, 178-179
  Convinces to renew contract after purchase of studio 166, 178
Hays office, election to 191
Health habits, childhood 22
Heckle and Jeckle, considers best cartoons 228
Heimlich, Irma (spouse), honeymoon with 110, *120*
Heimlich, Irma (spouse), love and courtship of 110
Heimlich, Irma (spouse), values opinion of 110
High school studies 28
Hiring practices 194, 197, 236-237
Hirlagraph Motion Picture Company, loans to 116-117
Hollywood blacklisting, opinions on 260
Humor and jokes, opinions and beliefs on 80, 220, 273, 281
Idolizes brother John C. Terry 29
Illustrator (commercial), employment as 28-29
Illustrator (humor magazine), employment as 29
Injuries suffered from San Francisco earthquake 38, 43 (n. 5)
Inventions of 191-192
Investments in animation technology, lack of 272
Jews, efforts to assist in emigration from Nazi Germany 222, 322
Jokes, opinion on creation of 206
Keith-Albee Circuit, contractual negotiations with 100, 110
Laguna Beach, CA, plans to establish cartoon studio in 199
Latin, studies in 35
Laurels of 332

Licensing and merchandising efforts 250, 259-260
Lifespan, eager to live a long life 326
Lifestyle of 220
Lightning sketch artist, performs act with brother John C. Terry 53-54
Lindbergh, Charles, admiration for 281
Little Herman (1915)
  Production of 69-70
  Reviews of 74
  Running time 70
  Sale of to Thanhouser Film Corporation 73-74, 76 (n. 57)
  Synopsis of 69-70
Loans to staff and relatives 322
Loyalty to staff 264-265
Marriage to Irma Heimlich 110
Memberships of 324
Mojave Desert 242
Money management practices 221
Mother (Minnie Bernice Perrin) *11*, 14-15, 19-22
  Appearance *11*, 14
  Artistic abilities and artwork 14, 20
  Birth date and place 14
  Death of 20-21
  Last Will and Testament 21
  No memories of 21
Mouse characters, first to use in animated cartoons 106
Music and sound effects in cartoons, opinion of 146, 288
Musical lyrics, contributions to 262, *274*
Napping habits 194, 236
Naval architect, ambitions to become 28
Newspaper cartoonist, employment as 58-60
Newspaper photographer, employment as 33-35
Non-discriminatory practices towards staff 197, 249-250, 261
Objectives in incorporating 143
Oregonian, The, employment with 50-51
Original music, preference for 132
Palmistry, interest in 83
Panic of 1893 and depression, effect on family 22-24
Paramount Pictures, work as producer and director 94-95, 98-99
Patents on animation process, legal proceedings with Bray 116

General Index

Patents on invention 191
Paul Terry Co., photography business 52
Personal name, sources for 19
Photographs of earthquake published in *Anaconda Standard* 46
Photography, lessons in 33
Phrenology, fascination with and cartoons *82*, 83-84
Physical description 87
Portland, Oregon, journey to (1906) 45
Portland, Oregon, sells earthquake photographs (1906) 45
Practices to devise story ideas 212
Preparedness, belief in 221
Printing, engraving and designing firm, employment for 33
Promises made to staff after retirement 264, 321
Promises to Moser upon incorporation 154
Public speaking, industry and community 160-161
Public speaking classes, involvement in 324
Publicist, hires 198
Radio-Keith-Orpheum, disputes with 121-122
Recreational activities of 197, 219, 221, 324
Regrets in licensing characters 259
Religious upbringing 22
Residential addresses (1927-1971) 110-111, *177*
Response to complaints about cartoons 143-144
Retirement 321-327
Right to free speech without recrimination, opinion on 261-262, 322
Roman Catholic clergy, friendship with 323-324, *326*
Sale of studio and assets to CBS 263-265, 321, 324
Screen credits, policy and practice 274, 280
Selznick, Lewis (attempt to sell first cartoon to) 70-71, 268
Shrewdness of 221-222
Siblings
    Caroline Dell Terry 14, 15, 20, *21*, *25*
    Horatio Proctor Terry 14
    John Coleman Terry, Jr. 15, 19-20, *21*, *25*, 25, 28-29, 33, 43, 44 (n. 40, 41), 45-49, *49*, 53-54,
65, 74, 79, 84-85, 94-95, 99, 101, 108-110, 114, 115, 122 (n. 2), 125-126, 128, 153-154, 157 (n. 96)
    Joseph Tripp Terry Jr. 14-15, 19-20, *21*, 25
    Olga Bernice Terry 15, *21*, 25, *25*, 39-40, 48, 52, *68*
Singing abilities 28
Sound cartoons, opposition to 120
Soundtrack practices 132
Spanish Influenza, suffers from 93-94
Speech disorder of 24-25, 160
Spouse, love of and relationship with 326
Staff retention, policy on 153, 322
Staff, treatment of 114, 167, 193-194, 207, 217-220, 232, 264, 275, 321-322
Stahl, Al (personality conflict with) 217-220
Stanford University, attempts to be admitted 35
States' Rights producers, financing of through Terry Trading Corporation 117
Stock market crash (1929), effect on Terry's finances 126
Stories, understanding of importance 145-146, 273
Stories and plots, opinion on 99, 103
Story work 132, 145-146, 150, 206, 219-220, 273
Talent, Incorporated, involvement in 74
Television, appearance on 324
Television, decision to work with 256
Television, opinion on value of shorts to networks 256
Television cartoons, contractual arrangement with distributor 256-257
Television cartoons, early lack of interest in producing 215, 255
Terry family lineage 3-6, 8
Terry, John Coleman, grief over loss 154
Theatrical feature (animated), no interest in producing 190-191, 215
Theatrical feature (live-action), interest in producing 191
Theatrical features (animated), public attraction to, opinion on 191

30th Anniversary celebration in animation 222, *244*
Threats to Moser 154
Trademark of "Alfalfa" granted *79*, 95
25th Anniversary in animated cartoons, celebrates 197-198
Two-reeler, plans to produce 198
Tytla, Vladimir, respect and admiration for artistic talents 114
Unions and unionization, opinion of 232
United States Army, discharge from 94, *93-94*
United States Army, enlistment into 89
United States Army, honors and medals 94
United States Army, promotion in rank 90, *92*
United States Army, work for the Instruction Laboratory on training filmstrips 88-91, 94
Universal Film Manufacturing Company, declines contract 98
Usher, employment as 28
Vacations of 117, 211, 220, 224 (n. 62), 324-325
Van Beuren, Amedee, conflicts and disputes with 121
Van Beuren, Amedee, contractual negotiations with 121-122
Vietnam War (U.S. participation in), opinion on 260, 323
Vision restrictions 220
Visual training field cartoons, lack of interest in producing 215
Walt Disney animation, respect and admiration for 168
War and armed aggression, opinion on 87-88
Weather, birth date 19
Winsor McCay, influenced by 64-65
Woolworth's, comparison of his studio to 168
World's Columbian Exposition (Chicago World's Fair), dreams of attending 25
Terry-Moser-Coffman (partnership)
    Benefits of adding Joseph Coffman as a Partner 135
    Formation of partnership 135
Terry-Toons Comics 199, 259-260
Terry Trading Corporation 117, 124
Terryscopes 264
Terrytoons studio
    Achievements 276, 332
    Animation, production methods 146

407

Animation art, destruction
  and donation of   320, 329
Animation art, marketing
  efforts   259
Animators
  Artistic talent   *194, 252,
    256,* 271, *275, 287,
    336-337, 343-344*
  Footage quota   145, 194-195
  Production requirements
      145, 194-195
Archives   320
Artistic staff and key
  artists   129-130, 140 (n. 41),
    174, 188-189, 265,
    335-341, 343-344
Background department,
  artistic talent   *190, 257,*
    271-272, *336, 339*
Background department,
  history   250
Background department,
  key artists   250-253, 271
Camera and photography
  department   150, *233, 259,* 272
Cartoon Product
  Aesthetics of   133
  Budgets for   222
  Cartoon characters, decision
    to focus on characters
    appearing consistently 167, 169
  Cartoon characters,
    problems with appeal of
      170, 196, 200-201
  Cartoon superstars, lack of   203
  Color cartoon, first   191, 204
  Colorization of cartoons 159-162,
      164, 167, 187,
      191, 197-198, 215
  Comparison to other Golden
    Age studios   161, 164,
      267-268, 276
  Complaints about
    Audiences, from   188
    Distributor and exhibitors,
      from   143, 145,
        160-164, 273
  Critical reviews of   133-134,
      187, 190, 199
      200, 225, 269-273
  Director credits, studio
    policy regarding   203
  Foreign distribution   191
  Gags, reuse of   206, 219
  Lack of originality and
    humor   133, 273
  Lack of success at Academy
    Awards, reasons for   267-268
  Length of cartoon shorts,
    comparison to other studios 272

Length of cartoon shorts,
  method to determine   280-281
One-shot cartoons and
  new cartoon characters
  of 1950s   246-249,
    258-259, 291-292
Oscar®-nominated cartoons 200,
    214, 216, 265, 290
Photographs of   198
Plots, humorless   273
Poor sound quality   133-134
Problems with   133-134
Recycled animation in   272
Robeson, Paul
  (involvement in)   261-262
Sound and editing problems   134
Sound effects,
  deficiencies in   146, 272
Soundtracks (dialect and
  dubbing)   191
Stereotypes in   187-188
Technical and artistic
  merit   267-268
Television series   263
Time to produce one short   132
Comic books   259-260
Distributor demands   170
Documentary one-reeler on
  animated cartoon production   229
Family operation   264, 322
Film drying and processing
    125, 129, 200
Film footage requirements
  for staff   194-195
Foreign markets   135
Hours of operation   236
Inking and Painting
  department   150, *167, 192, 212*
Investments into improving
  quality of cartoons   167-169,
      191, 198
Labor strike (1947)
  Cost to Terry   242
  Employee recruitment
    by Terry during   236-237
  Employees who participated
    in and avoided labor
    strike   236-237
  Family affair   237
  Harassment of Terry by
    picketers   237
  Instigator, organizer and
    leader of   236
  Length of   230, 240
  Local 1461 certified as
    bargaining agent   232-233
  Local 1461 decertified
    as bargaining agent   239-240

Local 1461 looks for
  outside union support   237
Party by picketers   238
Picketing of theaters   238
Publications during   237
Reasons for failure of strike   240
Strategy of Terry during
  strike   236
Strike begins   236
Strike ends   240
Strikers cross picket
  lines   238-240
Work schedule of Terry
  during strike   236-237
Labor union unrest (pre-Strike)
  (1943-1947)
  Delay tactics of Terry to
    avoid strike (1943-
    1947)   233-236
  I.A.T.S.E. Local 841 (New
    York) - The Animation Guild,
    forced to sign with   242
  Local 1461 certified as
    collective bargaining unit
    by National Labor Relations
    Board   232-233
  Terry signs contract with
    union without shop clause
    (1944-1945)   233
Logo redesign   281
Marketing efforts   169
Model makers   183,198-199
Music and sound effects   *193,
    195, 197, 250,*
    272, 276, *343*
Musical production methods   146
Paint room   *215*
Production schedule demands   169
Retrospective and Animation
  Arts Festival   328-332, *329*
  Animation artwork at   329
  Attendees   331
  Dates of   331
  Dinner and scheduled events 331
  Planning and organizing
    the event   328-331
  Success of   332
Sound editing   *175*
Sound effect production
  methods   146
Staff
  Angry at Terry for broken
    promises   264, 280, 321
  Artistic talent of
    production staff   271-273
  Bonuses and gifts to   232
  Family members
    employed   264, 322
  Gags of   300

408

General Index

Increase in artists and
   staff   168-169
Loyal and industrious   321
Salaries, wages and
   remuneration of   167, 226,
   232, 236, 275
Size and growth   167-169,
   198, 264, 331
World War Two
   involvement   199, 213
Story department   150,
   164, 167-168,
   178-179, 180, 190, *196*,
   203-208, 219-220,
   273-275, *338, 340-341*
Studio equipment,
   condition of   221, 232
Studio, Edison (Bronx) (1932-1934)
   Artistic staff   *137*
   Cramped quarters at   134
   Move to   134
   Production accident at   134
   Production at   134-138, 143-154
   Studio renovations and
      remodeling   134
   Studio location   134
Studio (Harlem) (1931-1932)
   Contract to produce at
      location   138
   Employee fears of studio
      neighbors   152
   Move to   143
   Production at   143-154
   Studio location   152
Studio (Long Island)
   (1930-1931)   124-130
Studio, Pershing Square
   Building (1934-1949)
   Construction, design
      and history   *151*, 154
   Deficiencies with   246
   Doubles studio space   167
   Hurricane, effects of   192-193
   Studio location in   154, 217
   Studio relocation to   154
Studio, 38 Centre Avenue
   (1949-1967)
   Benefits to Terry   246
   Design, appearance
      and size   *243*, 245-246
   History of building   245-246
   Move to   245
   Remodelled   281
   Voice actors at   225-226,
      229, *247, 263, 333*
Surveillance of staff   193-194
Westchester County economy,
   effect on   264

World War Two, effect on
   production and supplies   213
Terrytoons Studio Days   332
Terrytoons, The Terry Bears   260
Texaco Star Theater   283
Thanhouser Film Corporation   1, 71, 73
Thirty-six Views of Mount Fuji   299
This Week   157 (n. 92)
Thomas A. Edison Company   94, 132
Three Dimension Comics   260
Three Little Fishes (1939)   132
Tiffany & Co. Foundation   217
Tiffany's   168
Tillie the Toiler   33, 84
Time (magazine)   268
Timely Comics   259
Timely Films   100, 104
Timely Topics   199
Times (Sacramento)   30
Times-Transcript (Sacramento)   30
Times-Union (Albany, N.Y.)   105
Timid Soul, The   33
To You My Beloved Comrade   261
Toots and Casper   51
Topics of the Day Film
   Company   104-105
Torrington High School   130
Toyland   79
Trans-Lux Productions   161, 251
Trans-Lux Television   296
Transcript (Sacramento)   30
Transfilm Inc.   256, 282
Treasure Records   140 (n. 41)
Tribune (New York)   59-60
Truesdale Hospital   90
Tuberculosis Society of America   129
TV Arts Productions   190
TV Guide   290
TV Spots   129-130
20th Century-Fox   144, 150,
   152-153, 155, 161-162,
   164-165, 168-169, 175,
   181-182, 190-191,
   198-199, 203, 222-223,
   234, 236, 253-254,
   255- 257, 268, 280,
   286-287, 319-320, 332

U

U.M. & M. TV Corp.   262-263
U.S. Conciliation Service   234, 239
Ub Iwerks studio   168
Ukiyo-e   299
Uncle George Washington Bings   78
Union Pacific Railroad   23
United Artists   144, 317
United Booking Office   100

United Copper   47
United Features Syndicate   279
United Hospital (Port Chester,
   New York)   326
United Productions of America
   190, 267, 270, 278-279,
   286-287, 289, 292, 294
United Public Workers of America,
   C.I.O.   237
United Scenic Artists   237
United States Air Force   278
United States Army   88-91, 94,
   102, 211, 292
United States Army Instruction
   Laboratory, description   88-89
United States Army Medical
   Museum and Library   89, 94
United States Army Sanitary Corps   90
United States Army Signal
   Corps   251, 282
United States Civil War   10-11, 23, 30
United States Congress   46, 87
United States Constitution   260
United States Department of Labor   234
United States Marines   211
United States Navy   128, 211,
   302, 306
United States Patent Office   95
United States Public Health Service   91
United States Senate   46
Universal Film Corp.   70, 79
Universal Film Manufacturing
   Company   98
Universal-Joker (releasing company)   77
Universal Pictures
   Corporation   89, 94, 136
Universal Studios   144, 148-149,
   157 (n. 94), 168, 200,
   208, 214, 216, 268
University of California Berkeley   252
University of California Los Angeles   282
University of Chicago   194
University of Heidelberg   47
University of Pennsylvania   146
University of Rochester   309
University of Rome   300
University of Southern California   286
Ursuline School for Girls   197
Us Boys   54
USA Network   320

V

V.B.K Corporation   100
Vacuum Oil Company   98
Valencia Hotel   40
Van Beuren Billposting Company   100
Van Beuren Corporation   106, 122
Van Beuren Studios   101-102,

409

TERRYTOONS: The Story of Paul Terry and His Classic Cartoon Factory

116, 122, 126, 130-131, 140 (n. 41), 144, 148-149, 152-153, 159, 167-169, 182, 204, 214, 217, 244, 250, 270
Van Kelton Stadium Airdomes 100
Vanderbilt University 116
Variety 117, 260
Variety Club (N.Y.) 324
Venice (California) Junior High School 278
Venice Children's Film Festival (12th International Exhibition of Film for Children, Venice, 1960) 302
Viacom International, Inc. 306, 320
Victor (records) 213
Victor Talking Machine Company 89
Vietnam War 260, 323
Viking 310
Village Voice 282
VistaVision 255
Vitagraph 63
Vitaphone 129
Voice actors 225-226, 229, *247, 263,* 283-284, 297-298, 300, 304, 316, *319, 333*
Voice from the Underworld 31
Voice of Firestone, The 213

W

W. H. Lay Potato Chips 303
WINS (radio station) 226
Walt Disney
  Acrimony with former staff 292
  Aesthetical views 222
  Artists, efforts to recruit 127, 211
  Cartoon budgets and production, approach to 222
  Communist infiltration in Hollywood, efforts to oppose 260-261
  Dinner Time (1927), opinion of 120-121
  Financing of films through public stock 191
  First animated cartoon 1
  Exhibitors, approach to 222
  Investment in animation technology 272
  Loan to finance production of features 191
  Money management practices 147
  Payments for gags 276
  Shorts production output, comparisons 332
  Struggles to find quality gags 276
Walt Disney Studio

Academy Awards, success at 159, 200, 222, 267
Animated characters, shorts and features 121, 159, 161, 170, 190-191, 199-200, 231-232, 248, 254-255, 270, 275-276
Animated features, early history 222
Animation stylistics 245, 313
Artistic staff 29, 89, 116, 121, 128, 140 (n. 39-40), 157 (n. 92) (n.94), 197, 199, 204-205, 215, 244, 251, 298
Cartoon characters, popular 170, 190, 203
Critical opinion of animated shorts 270
Distributor of 144, 168
Employment practices 322
Film footage requirements and quota at 148, 194
I.A.T.S.E. Local 839 (Los Angeles) - The Animation Guild, joined 242
Inclusion in *How To Make Animated Cartoons* 268
Labor strike and union activities at 210, 231-232
Oscar®-nominated shorts 159, 200, 214, 216, 290
Oscar®-winning shorts during Golden Age, total 267
Production methods 146, 148
Recycled animation in features 272
Story department 205, 275
Weak storylines in animated shorts 275
Walt Disney Productions, trademark suit 106
Walt Disney's World of Fantasy 168
Walter Lantz Productions 129, 140 (n. 40), 144, 148-149, 159, 168, 200, 203, 214, 216, 231, 242, 267-268, 271, 276
Warner Bros. 129, 131, 144, 149-150, 159, 168, 187, 199-200, 203, 214, 216, 231, 236, 242, 267-268, 270, 276, 290, 309, 318
Washington (DC) Fire Department 90
Washington (DC) Police Department 90
Washington Post 92-93
We're Working For Defense 199
Weber's Theatre 98
Weekly Meeting of the Tuesday Women's Club, The 33
Weekly Oregonian, The 50
Weekly Sunday Times 29

Westchester Country Club 110, 221, 322, 324
Westchester County Court 175
Westchester Federal Savings Bank 220
Western Electric 124, 136-138
Western Front 88-89, 91
Western Publishing 157 (n. 92), 259-260
Westervelt & Co. Shipyard 10
Whaling industry, New England (19th century) 6, 8
Wharton School of Finance and Commerce 136
Whig Party 50
White Plains Publishing Co. 174
Wid's Daily 105, 109
Widow Wise 48
Will S. Heck's Wonder World and Theater 61
Willada Records 140 (n. 41)
William T. Coleman and Co. Wholesale Grocery and Ship Outfitters 12
William Tell 136
Williamson Submarine Film Corporation 81
Window Cleaners Union Local 2 (New York, N.Y.) 237
Woo Woo Bird, The 78
Woolworth's 168
Workers Party (New York Local) 237
World Film Corporation 70
World Special Films Corporation 70
World War One 87-94, 102, 105, 107, 110, 132, 149, 252, 265
World War Two 199, 211, 213-214, 222, 231-232, 251, 269, 279, 283, 292, 298, 306, 322
World Wide (production company) 152
World's Columbian Exposition (Chicago World's Fair, 1893) 25, 27 (n. 68), 34
World's Fair (San Francisco) 121

Y

Yale Law School 194
Yale Mobile Hospital Unit 90
Yale University 18, 47
Yellow Journalism 51, 60
Yellow Kid, The 48
Yellow River flood (1887) 18
Yonkers Art Association 184

Z

Zac-David (Tempo) 256
Zimmerman Telegram 87
Zuro Opera Company 121